Business Mathematics

Eighth Edition

Charles D. Miller

Stanley A. Salzman
American River College

Gary Clendenen
University of Texas—Tyler

 ADDISON-WESLEY

An imprint of Addison Wesley Longman, Inc.

Reading, Massachusetts • Menlo Park, California • New York • Harlow, England
Don Mills, Ontario • Sydney • Mexico City • Madrid • Amsterdam

Publisher: Jason A. Jordan

Acquisitions Editor: Jennifer Crum

Assistant Editor: Adam Hamel

Editorial Project Managers: Kari Heen, Ruth Berry

Managing Editor: Ron Hampton

Cover and Text Designer: Susan Carsten

Production Coordinator: Jane DePasquale

Prepress Services Buyer: Caroline Fell

Marketing Manager: Craig Bleyer

Marketing Coordinator: Laura Rogers

Manufacturing Coordinator: Evelyn Beaton

Composition: UG/GGS Information Services, Inc.

Library of Congress Cataloging-in-Publication Data

Miller, Charles D., 1942–
    Business mathematics/Charles D. Miller, Stanley A. Salzman, Gary
Clendenen.—8th ed.
        p.   cm.
    Includes index.
    ISBN 0-321-04503-3   (Annotated Instructor's Edition: 0-321-05664-7)
    1. Business mathematics.   2. Business mathematics—Programmed
instruction.   I. Salzman, Stanley A.   II. Clendenen, Gary.
III. Title.
HF5691.M465   1999
650′.01′513—dc21   98-48200
                                                    CIP

1 2 3 4 5 6 7 8 9 10   VH   03 02 01 00 99

CONTENTS

PREFACE

The eighth edition of *Business Mathematics* has been extensively revised to ensure maximum student interest in each chapter of the text. More than ever, real-life examples from today's business world have been incorporated; new examples from actual companies and the people who run them are woven throughout the book to serve as applications of the concepts presented. Many new photographs, news clippings, and graphs have been added to increase the relevance of chapter content to the world students know. The globalization of our society is emphasized through examples and exercises that highlight foreign countries and international topics.

The new edition reflects the extensive business and teaching experience of the authors, as well as the suggestions of many reviewers nationwide. Providing solid, practical, and up-to-date coverage of business mathematics topics, the text begins with a brief review of basic mathematics and goes on to introduce key business topics, such as bank services, payroll, business discounts and markups, stocks and bonds, consumer loans, taxes and insurance, depreciation, financial statements, and business statistics. The text is accompanied by a greatly enhanced supplements package that provides many avenues—both print and media—for students to further practice and explore the concepts discussed in the chapters. (Please see pages x-xii of this Preface for full descriptions of the student and instructor supplements available.)

New Content Highlights

The material in Chapter 4, Bank Services, has been updated in keeping with the latest banking trends and practices. Banking charges and credit card deposit slips reflect the latest available materials. The reconciliation form has been simplified once again to reflect current industry changes.

In Chapter 5, Payroll, all wages and salaries have been updated along with FICA, Medicare, and tax-withholding rates. State withholding tax has been modified to more accurately represent state income taxes throughout the nation.

Chapter 8, Simple Interest, has been updated to reflect current interest rates. Substantial new material on inflation and the consumer price index has been added to Chapter 9, Compound Interest. New examples show that a raise may not be of much help to an employee, depending on the increase in the cost of living that the employee experiences. Numerous drill and application exercises have been changed in Chapter 9, and the chapter's theme company is now Bank of America, whose recent merger with NationsBank created one of the largest banks in the world.

The sections on stocks and bonds in Chapter 10, Annuities, Stocks, and Bonds, have been updated to reflect more current price information. Emphasis is placed on using annuities to save for retirement and other long term purposes, including education of children. New coverage of Roth IRAs and mutual funds has been added to Sections 10.1 and 10.4 respectively.

Chapter 11, Business and Consumer Loans, has been updated to reflect current interest rates, and the last section of the chapter has been modified to emphasize mortgages and real estate loans. Many students will be able to relate easily to this section since they may be planning to buy a home or may have bought one recently. Additional examples of the cost of home ownership are provided in the Financial and Estate Planning foldout—a new feature of the eighth edition (described in full on page viii of this Preface).

In Chapter 12, Taxes and Insurance, the latest available tax forms and tables have been included in Section 12.2, Personal Income Tax. Insurance rates for motor vehicles and life insurance have been updated to more accurately reflect today's insurance costs.

Data from recent McDonald's Corporation financial statements are included in Chapter 14, Financial Statements and Ratios, so students learn about financial statements using actual data from a company they know. Many of the problems in Chapter 15, Business Statistics, have been changed, and a number of graphs showing data from the business world have been added to increase the chapter's sense of realism.

Appendix A, Equations and Formulas, includes additional business application examples that better demonstrate the value of the subject matter. Appendix B, Scientific Calculators, contains greatly expanded coverage of scientific calculators for professors who allow students to use calculators. Appendix C, Financial Calculators, reviews the basic functions of financial calculators.

New Features

Chapter Openers   Many chapters introduce a new or popular business—such as Starbucks Coffee, The Home Depot, or McDonald's—to capture students' interest. Chapter openers present the owner, manager, or employee of the business, and that person is discussed throughout the chapter in the context of the company he or she represents.

Enhanced Treatment of Real-World Applications   The eighth edition places greater emphasis on real-world applications. Application problems have been updated throughout to be as relevant as possible to today's students, and they reference well-known companies such as Home Depot, McDonald's, Bank of America, Starbucks, Borders, and Levi's. Applications are now preceded by headings that highlight coverage of subjects like sports, vacations, and the cost of weddings. New to the eighth edition is an applications index that allows students to locate problems that are applicable to a specific career field or area of interest.

New Art Program   The art program of the eighth edition includes not only new color photographs, but also graphs and charts that utilize actual data from a variety of recognized sources. Rendered to draw student attention while emphasizing the data itself, the graphs and charts help students see that the mathematics of business is inherent to the world around them.

Internet Integration   Recognizing the increasing relevance of the World Wide Web to today's business world, we have thoroughly integrated the Internet with chapter content. Throughout each chapter, a Web icon and keywords are placed next to selected examples, referring students to the *Business Mathematics* Web site (www.mathbusiness.com) for on-line exploration of the concepts covered in the examples. On the Web site, students will find several Web Applications for each chapter listed by keyword; these applications provide links to corporate Web sites and ask students to answer questions that will help them understand how real companies use mathematical concepts in their daily operations.

'Net Assets   In each chapter, a one-page feature emphasizes the growing importance of the World Wide Web in business by showing an example of a company's Internet home page and providing questions that relate that company's on-line activities to the chapter concepts. Some of the corporations highlighted operate solely over the Internet. This feature, suitable even for students without access to the Web, is ideal for self-contained assignments that will illustrate the relevance of business math to actual corporate situations. For a more in-depth exploration of each 'Net Assets page in the text, students may visit the *Business Mathematics* Web site (www.mathbusiness.com), where an extended 'Net Assets On-line activity is provided for each chapter.

Financial and Estate Planning Foldout   This innovative, six-page foldout focuses on key subject areas involved in personal finance and estate planning. Divided into nine sections, the foldout includes several guided activities to help students become actively involved in understanding their personal finances and investing wisely. Students are encouraged to look at maximizing lifetime earnings through career and education, and they are advised on how to save money, secure adequate insurance, build up a cash reserve, and avoid accumulating short-term debt. They are also asked to think about long-range planning related to home ownership, retirement, and wills. Finally, students can assess their current financial situation by completing a budget worksheet. The material in the foldout relates closely to the content in Chapters 3, 9, 10, 11, 12, 14, and 15 of the text.

Reality Check   Many of the newspaper clippings, magazine articles, and other media items in the text are flagged with a reality check icon in the margin. By drawing students' eyes to these real media sources, the reality check icon helps emphasize the practical, everyday relevance of business mathematics.

Investigative Questions   The Investigate feature, marked by the icon, now appears at the end of every chapter's Summary Exercise. The Investigate questions require higher-level thinking skills and encourage students to apply the chapter material in a practical way, or go outside the classroom to seek additional knowledge. Many of these questions are ideal for collaborative assignments.

Scientific Calculator Appendix   This edition includes a new appendix (Appendix B) containing extensive coverage of scientific calculators. A number of exercises are provided to help students develop their calculator skills.

Quick Review with Chapter Terms   The revised end-of-chapter Quick Review feature now begins with a list of key terms from the chapter and the pages on which they first appear. The Quick Review now uses a two-column format (Concepts and Examples) to help the student review all the main points presented in the chapter.

Additional Features

Numerous Exercises   Mastering business mathematics requires working through many exercises, so we have included more than 2600 in the eighth edition. They range from simple drill problems to application exercises that require several steps to solve. All problems have been independently checked to ensure accuracy.

Graded Application Exercises   All application exercises are arranged in pairs and increase progressively in difficulty. This arrangement prepares students to work the more difficult exercises as they proceed through the exercise set. Each even-numbered application exercise is the same type of problem as the previous odd-numbered exercise. This allows students to solve an odd-numbered exercise, check the answer in the answer section, and then solve the following even-numbered exercise.

Supplementary Exercises   Sets of supplementary exercises occur throughout the book to help students review and synthesize difficult concepts. For example, two sets in Chapter 3 require students to distinguish among the different elements of a percent problem and decide upon the correct method of solution. A set in Chapter 8 gives practice in distinguishing simple interest from simple discount; another set in Chapter 13 combines methods of calculating depreciation.

Problem Solving in Business   Found throughout each chapter, the Problem Solving in Business application is tied to the business introduced in the chapter opener. This approach demonstrates to the student how specific topics are used by those operating the business.

Newspaper and Magazine Articles   A wide selection of current newspaper and magazine articles from various news media sources appears within each chapter. These current, eye-catching items are tied to examples within the chapter sections and are a constant reminder to students of the relevance of the chapter content to current business trends and topics.

Calculator Solutions   Calculator solutions, identified with the calculator symbol , appear after selected examples. These solutions show students the keystrokes needed to obtain the example solution.

Cumulative Reviews   Three Cumulative Reviews, found at the end of Chapters 3, 7, and 10, help students review groups of related chapter topics and reinforce understanding.

Financial Calculators   Financial calculators are presented in Appendix C, along with exercises that may be solved by students using the financial calculator of their choice.

Cautionary Remarks   Common student difficulties and misunderstandings appear as Notes and Problem-Solving Hints. These features are given a special graphic treatment to help students locate them.

Quick Start Solutions to Exercises   Selected exercises in the exercise sets—usually the first of each type of exercise—are denoted by a Quick Start head and include answers with solutions to help students get started. This on-the-spot reinforcement gives students both the confidence to continue working practice problems and the knowledge of which topics may require additional review.

Writing Exercises   Designed to help students better understand and relate the concepts within a section, these exercises require a written answer of a few sentences. They are flagged in the Annotated Instructor's Edition by the ✎ icon and often include references to a specific learning objective to help students formulate an answer.

Summary Exercises   Every chapter ends with a Summary Exercise that has been designed to help students apply what they have learned in the chapter. These problems require students to synthesize most or all of the topics they have covered in the chapter in order to solve one cumulative exercise. Ending with a feature labeled Investigate, these exercises offer the student an opportunity to further develop problem-solving skills beyond the classroom. The Investigate questions may be worked out as a group or individual activity, depending on the instructor's preference.

Example Titles   Each example has a title to help students understand the purpose of the example. The titles can also help students work the exercises and study for quizzes and exams.

Flexibility   After basic prerequisites have been met, the chapters in this text can be taught in any order to give instructors maximum freedom in designing courses. Chapter prerequisites are as follows.

Chapter	Prerequisite	Chapter	Prerequisite
1	None	9	Simple interest
2	None	10	Simple interest
3	Arithmetic	11	Simple interest
4	Percent	12	Percent
5	Percent	13	Percent
6	Percent	14	Percent
7	Percent	15	Percent
8	Percent		

Pretest   A business mathematics pretest is included in the introduction of the book. This pretest can help students and instructors identify individual and class strengths and weaknesses.

Chapter Tests   Each chapter ends with a chapter test that reviews all of the topics in the chapter and helps evaluate student mastery.

Equations and Formulas   A review of equations, business applications of equations, and ratios and proportions is included in Appendix A. Instructors may find it appropriate to introduce this material to lay the groundwork for an alternative approach to the mathematics of buying and selling (Chapters 6 and 7), interest (Chapters 8 and 9), annuities (Chapter 10), and consumer loans (Chapter 11).

Glossary   A glossary of key words, located at the back of the book, provides a quick reference for the main ideas of the course.

Summary of Formulas   The inside covers of *Business Mathematics* provide a handy summary of commonly used information and business formulas from the book.

Supplements

Annotated Instructor's Edition
ISBN 0-321-05664-7

The Annotated Instructor's Edition provides immediate access directly on the page to the worked-out answers to all exercises. In addition, an answer section at the back of both the Student and Instructor's Editions gives answers to odd-numbered section exercises and answers to all chapter test exercises. Writing exercises are marked with the ✎ icon exclusively in the AIE so that instructors may use discretion in assigning these problems.

Printed Test Bank/Instructor's Resource Manual/Transparency Masters
ISBN 0–321–06694–4

This extensive supplement contains teaching suggestions; two pretests—one in basic mathematics and one in business mathematics; six different test forms for each chapter (four short-answer and two multiple-choice); two final examinations; numerous application exercises (test items) for each chapter; answers to all test materials; suggested answers to the writing questions in the text; and a selection of transparency masters.

TestGen-EQ/QuizMaster-EQ CD-ROM
ISBN 0–321–06282–5

This powerful test-generation software is provided on a dual-platform Windows/Macintosh CD-ROM. TestGen-EQ's friendly graphical interface enables instructors to easily view, edit, and add questions, transfer questions to tests, and print tests in a variety of fonts and forms. Search and sort features help the instructor locate questions quickly and arrange them in a preferred order. Several question formats are available, including short-answer, true/false, multiple-choice, essay, and matching. A built-in question editor allows the instructor to create graphs, import graphics, and insert variable numbers, text, and mathematical symbols and templates. Computerized test banks include algorithmically defined problems organized according to the textbook. Instructors can create and export practice tests into HTML for use on the World Wide Web. Using **QuizMaster-EQ**, instructors can post tests and quizzes created in Test-Gen to a computer network so that students can take them on-line. Instructors can set preferences for how and when tests are administered. QuizMaster automatically grades the exams and allows the instructor to view or print a variety of reports for individual students, classes, or courses.

PowerPoint Presentations and Adobe Acrobat Tables and Forms

PowerPoint presentations for each chapter include forms, tables, schedules and sample documents appearing in the eighth edition of *Business Mathematics*. These presentations can be downloaded from the Instructor's Resources section of the book's Web site, www.mathbusiness.com. Instructors can customize chapter presentations using Microsoft PowerPoint; presentations can also be run with Power-Point Viewer, which is free, downloadable software available from Microsoft's Web site (www.microsoft.com). Selected tables and forms from the book are available in Adobe Acrobat format, which means they can be printed easily to paper or transparencies. The Adobe Acrobat Reader is also freely available to download from the Internet (www.adobe.com).

Web Site (www.mathbusiness.com)

New to the eighth edition of *Business Mathematics*, this comprehensive on-line supplement is thoroughly integrated with the text and provides a number of resources for both students and instructors.

For related Web
activities, go to
www.mathbusiness.com

Keyword: coffee

Web Applications   For each chapter, the Web site contains several Web Applications, which are flagged by an icon and keyword in the text. By going to the site and entering the keyword for a given application, students can access questions that direct them to real company URLs to find specific information. The Web Applications are ideal for out-of-class individual or group assignments.

'Net Assets On-line   The 'Net Assets On-line activity for each chapter expands on the corresponding 'Net Assets page in the text. Each activity is tied to a particular industry or company and provides open-ended questions that require students to combine Web-based research with writing and critical thinking skills. Research guidance, tips for getting started, and hints on how to check the validity of Internet sources are provided.

Career Page   The Web site includes a Career Page featuring links to other Web sites that provide assistance with interviewing, resume-building, job searches, and other career-building topics.

InterAct Math Tutorial Exercises   Through the Web site, students can download a plug-in that allows them to access Addison Wesley Longman's InterAct Math Tutorial exercises (described in full on page xii) for free. InterAct Math exercises are correlated to section-level objectives and give students the freedom to practice skills at their own pace.

Instructor's Resources Page   This portion of the site provides the following instructor-support material:

- Downloadable PowerPoint presentations and Adobe Acrobat tables and forms (described on page xi)
- Password-protected solutions to the Web site's student activity features (Web Applications and 'Net Assets On-line)
- Password-protected Adobe Acrobat PDF files of the Chapter Tests from the text (available both with and without answers)
- Password-protected Adobe Acrobat PDF files of the Cumulative Reviews from the text (available both with and without answers)

InterAct Math Tutorial Software

ISBN 0-321-06917-X

The InterAct Math Tutorial Software, provided on a dual-platform Windows/Macintosh CD-ROM, has been developed by professional software engineers working closely with a team of experienced math instructors. The software provides exercises that correspond to each section-level objective in the text; these exercises require the same computational and problem-solving skills as the section exercises in the book. Each InterAct Math exercise is accompanied by an example and an interactive guided solution designed to involve students in the solution process and help them identify precisely where they are having trouble. For each section of the text, the software tracks student activity and scores, which can be printed out in summary form.

InterAct Math Plus Instructor Software

ISBN 0-201-63555-0 (Windows)/ISBN 0-201-64805-9 (Macintosh)

Used in conjunction with the InterAct Math Tutorial Software (0-321-06917-X), this networkable software provides instructors with full course management capabilities for tracking and reporting student use of the tutorial software. Instructors can create and administer on-line tests, summarize student results, and monitor student progress in the software.

MathXL

ISBN 0-201-68141-2 (text bundled with MathXL coupon package)

MathXL is a Web-based testing and tutorial system that allows students to take practice tests similar to the chapter tests in their book. MathXL generates a personalized study plan that indicates students' strengths and pinpoints topics where they need more practice. The program then provides the practice and instruction students need to improve their skills. The user's test scores and practice sessions are tracked by the program so that students can monitor their progress throughout the semester. The mathxl.com Web site requires each student to purchase a user ID and log-in password, which can be bundled with the eighth edition of *Business Mathematics* upon request. Students who already have the text may purchase the MathXL coupon package by having their bookstore order ISBN 0-201-61665-3.

Math Tutor Center

ISBN 0-201-66334-1 (Text bundled with Math Tutor Center registration)

The Addison Wesley Longman Math Tutor Center will provide FREE tutoring to students using the eighth edition of *Business Mathematics*. Assisted by qualified mathematics instructors via toll-free telephone number, fax, or e-mail, students can receive tutoring on examples, exercises, and problems contained in the text. Each new book can be bundled with a registration number that provides the student with a free six-month subscription to the service. Students who already have the text may purchase a subscription to the Math Tutor Center by having their bookstore order ISBN 0-201-44461-5. The Math Tutor Center is open Sunday through Thursday from 3 PM to 10 PM Eastern Standard Time.

Videotape Series and Telecourse

The Southern California Community College Consortium has produced a videotape series based on *Business Mathematics* called *By the Numbers*, which has been aired over the Public Broadcasting System (PBS). Your school can offer a telecourse using the videotapes along with *Business Mathematics* and the teleguide for the *By the Numbers* series. The videotapes can also be purchased for use in a traditional lecture course. Contact Intelecom at 626-796-7300 or your Addison Wesley Longman sales consultant for further information.

Acknowledgments

We would like to thank the many users of the seventh edition for their insightful observations and suggestions for improving this book. We also wish to express our appreciation and thanks to the following reviewers for their contributions.

Viola Bean, Boise State University; Joan Bookbinder, Elgin Community College; Donald F. Boyer, Jefferson College; Betty Carden, Northwestern Michigan College; Mary Emily Cooke, Surry Community College; Bobbie D. Corbett, Northern Virginia Community College; Kathleen Crall, Des Moines Area Community College; Ky L. Davis, Muskingum Area Technical College; Frank A. Di Ferdinando, Hudson County Community College; Richard N. Dodge, Jackson Community College; John M. Doran, Des Moines Area Community College, Boone Campus; Acie B. Earl, Black Hawk College; Brad A. Fittro, Kentucky College of Business, Lexington Campus; Robert W. Hampton, CPA; Howard R. Hunnius, John Tyler Community College; JoEllen Hunt, South Hills School of Business and Technology; George F. Manicone, Raritan Valley Community College; Gary Martin, DeVry Institute of Technology, Decatur Campus; John F. Mastriani, El Paso Community College; A. Ally Mishal, Stark State College of Technology; Gary Murray, Rose State College; Gordon Niemi, Northwestern Michigan College; Lawrence Petersen, County College of Morris; F. Warren Pitcher, Des Moines Area Community College; Anthony M. Ponder, Sinclair Community College; Professor Donald A. Ryktarsyk, Schoolcraft College; Lynn E. Shuster, Central Pennsylvania Business School; Del Spencer, Trinity Valley Community College; Jimmie A. Van Alphen, Ozarks Technical Community College; Anne V. Wallace, Fox Valley Technical College.

Our appreciation goes to Anne Wallace of Fox Valley Technical College and to Deana Richmond, who checked all of the exercises and examples in the book for accuracy. We would also like to express our gratitude to our colleagues at American River College and the University of Texas at Tyler who have helped us immeasurably with their support and encouragement: Robert Garrett, Bill Monroe, Barbara Weeks, James Bralley, and Richard Gonsalves.

Also, special thanks and appreciation go to Larry and Cyndi Clendenen, who spent a great deal of time working with us to make the manuscript as accurate as possible.

The following individuals at Addison Welsey Longman had a large impact on this eighth edition of *Business Mathematics*, and we are grateful for their many efforts:

Jason Jordan, publisher; Jenny Crum, acquisitions editor; Adam Hamel, assistant editor; Kari Heen, senior editorial project manager; Ruth Berry, editorial project manager; Ron Hampton, managing editor; Susan Carsten, senior designer; Jane DePasquale, production coordinator; Lorie Reilly, media producer; Stephanie Baldock, assistant media producer; Craig Bleyer, senior marketing manager; Laura Rogers, marketing coordinator; and Evelyn Beaton, manufacturing coordinator.

Stanley A. Salzman
Gary Clendenen

Introduction for Students

Success in Business Mathematics

With a growing need for record keeping, establishing budgets, and understanding finance, taxation, and investment opportunities, mathematics has become a greater part of our daily lives. This text applies mathematics to daily business experiences. Your success in future business courses and pursuits will be enhanced by the knowledge and skills you will gain in this course.

Studying business mathematics is different from studying subjects like English or history. The key to success is regular practice. This should not be surprising. After all, can you learn to ski or play a musical instrument without a lot of regular practice? The same is true for learning mathematics. Working problems nearly every day is the key to becoming successful. Here are some suggestions to help you succeed in business mathematics.

1. **Pay attention in class to what your instructor says and does, and make careful notes.** Note the problems the instructor works on the board and copy the complete solutions. Keep these notes separate from your homework to avoid confusion.

2. **Don't hesitate to ask questions in class.** Asking questions is not a sign of weakness, but of strength. There are almost always other students with the same question who are too shy to ask.

3. **Determine whether tutoring is available and know how to get help when needed.** Use the instructor's office hours and contact the instructor for suggestions and direction.

4. **Before you start on your homework assignment, rework the problems the instructor worked in class.** This will reinforce what you have learned. Many students say, "I understand it perfectly when you do it, but I get stuck when I try to work the problem."

5. **Read your text carefully.** Many students read only enough to get by, usually only the examples. Reading the complete section will help you to be successful with the homework problems. As you read the text, work the example problems and check the answers. This will test your understanding of what you have read. Pay special attention to highlighted statements and those labeled "Note" and "Problem Solving Hint."

6. **Do your homework assignment only after reading the text and reviewing your notes from class.** Estimate the answer before you begin working the problem in the worktext. Check your work before looking at the answers in the back of the book. If you get a problem wrong and are unable to see why, mark that problem and ask your instructor for help.

7. **Work as neatly as you can using a *pencil*, and organize your work carefully.** Write your symbols clearly, and make sure the problems are clearly separated from each other.

8. **After you have completed a homework assignment, look over the text again.** Try to decide what the main ideas are in the lesson. Often they are clearly highlighted or boxed in the text.

9. **Keep any quizzes and tests that are returned to you for studying for future tests and the final exam.** These quizzes and tests indicate what your instructor considers most important. Be sure to correct any test problems that you missed. Write all quiz and test scores on the front page of your notebook.

10. **Don't worry if you do not understand a new topic right away.** As you read more about it and work through the problems, you will gain understanding. No one understands each topic completely right from the start.

Kathi L. Cap   1-11-2000

Name   Date   Class

PRETEST IN BUSINESS MATHEMATICS

This pretest will help you determine your areas of strength and weakness in the business mathematics presented in this book.

1. Round 9.86 to the nearest tenth.

2. Round $.054 to the nearest cent.

3. Round $549.49 to the nearest dollar.

4. Multiply: 6718
                  $\times 2392$

5. Divide: $35\overline{)11{,}032}$

6. Change $6\frac{3}{8}$ to an improper fraction.

7. Change $\frac{43}{32}$ to a mixed number.

8. Write $\frac{30}{42}$ in lowest terms. $\frac{15}{21}$ $\frac{5}{7}$

9. Add: $\frac{5}{8}$ $\frac{5}{8}$
              $\frac{3}{4}$ $\frac{6}{8}$
             $+\frac{1}{2}$ $\frac{4}{8}$ $\frac{15}{8}$

10. Add: $7\frac{1}{2}$ $\frac{15}{2}$ $\frac{90}{12}$
               $2\frac{1}{4}$ $\frac{9}{4}$ $\frac{27}{12}$
             $+10\frac{2}{3}$ $\frac{32}{3}$ $\frac{128}{12}$
                                         $\frac{245}{12}$

11. Subtract: $\frac{5}{8} - \frac{5}{24}$ $\frac{10}{24}$ $\frac{5}{12}$
          $\frac{15}{24}$

12. Subtract: $83\frac{3}{4}$ $\frac{335}{4}$ $\frac{1675}{20}$
                  $-21\frac{2}{5}$ $\frac{107}{5}$ $\frac{428}{20}$
                                          $210\frac{3}{20}$

13. Multiply: $\frac{3}{8} \times \frac{3}{5}$ $\frac{9}{40} =$

14. Divide: $15\frac{1}{4} \div 5\frac{1}{8}$ $\frac{175}{200}$ $\frac{7}{8}$ $\frac{61}{4} \div \frac{41}{8}$ $\frac{122}{8} \div \frac{41}{8}$

15. Express .875 as a common fraction. $\frac{.875}{1000}$ $\frac{87.5}{100}$

16. Express $\frac{3}{4}$ as a decimal.

17. Subtract: 598.316
                  $- 79.839$

18. Multiply: 20.72
                  $\times 6.46$

19. Divide: $1.2\overline{)309.6}$ $\frac{175}{875}$ 5

20. Express $\frac{3}{8}$ as a percent.

1. _____9.9_____

2. _____.05_____

3. ___549⁰⁰___

4. __16,069,456__

5. ___315.20___

6. ___$\frac{51}{8}$___

7. ___$1\frac{11}{32}$___

8. ___5/7___

9. ___$1\frac{7}{8}$___

10. ___$20\frac{5}{12}$___

11. ___5/12___

12. ___$105\frac{3}{20}$___

13. ___9/40___

14. _____

15. ___7/8___

16. ___.75___

17. _____

18. _____

19. _____

20. _____

21. Net World spent 1.7% of its sales on insurance premiums. If sales amounted to $292,560, what amount was spent on insurance premiums?

21. _____

22. What annual rate of return is needed to receive $1920 in one year on an investment of $48,000?

22. _____

23. Auto Electric offers an oxygen sensor at a list price of $289, less trade discounts of 20/30. What is the net cost?

23. _____

24. A warehouse employee at a computer manufacturer is paid $11.50 per hour with time and a half for all hours over 40 in a week. Find the employee's gross pay if she worked 46 hours in one week.

24. _____

25. How long will it take an investment of $12,500 to earn $125 in interest at 4% per year?

25. _____

26. An invoice from Collier Windows amounting to $20,250 is dated October 6 and offers terms of 3/10, n/30. If the invoice is paid on October 14, what amount is due?

26. _____

27. Find the percent of markup based on selling price if an electric oven costing $336 is sold for $480.

27. _____

28. Find the single discount equivalent to a series discount of 20/10.

28. _____

29. Using the straight-line method of depreciation, find the annual depreciation on a lawn tractor that has a cost of $9375, an estimated life of six years, and a scrap value of $375.

29. _____

30. A retailer sells an oak desk for $828.20 after deducting 18% from the original price. Find the original price.

30. _____

CHAPTER 1

Whole Numbers and Decimals

Starbucks Coffee Company was formed by three college students. The company's name comes from Captain Starbuck, the first mate in Herman Melville's novel, *Moby Dick*. Starbucks prides itself on being a good citizen both in and around its store locations and in the various coffee-producing countries where it does business. The company makes significant contributions to charities that focus on children, the environment, the arts, and AIDS research. In the year 2000, Starbucks had reached the goal of having stores in Canada, in each state of the U.S. and having its products sold around the world.

Paul Crockett is the manager of a Starbucks Coffee location. Paul began working part time for Starbucks when he was a student at a community college and was promoted to store manager within six months of graduation. He has between 20 and 25 employees at his store and he must continually recruit and train new people to replace the employees who go on to college or other careers. Each day, Paul works with scheduling and payroll, computes sales and sales taxes, and orders and pays for inventory. All of these activities involve working with whole numbers and decimals.

Businesses use mathematics every day—to prepare a payroll, find the interest on a loan, take an inventory, check a firm's income statement, or calculate the markup on an item to be sold at a profit. Even with calculators, a businessperson must understand the fundamentals of arithmetic. The most difficult part of solving a problem is often knowing how to set the problem up and then deciding on the procedure that will best solve the particular problem. The first two chapters of this book review arithmetic, and the rest of the chapters then apply these mathematical ideas to actual business situations.

1.1 | Whole Numbers

Objectives

1. Define whole numbers.
2. Round whole numbers.
3. Add whole numbers.
4. Round numbers to estimate an answer.
5. Subtract whole numbers.
6. Multiply whole numbers.
7. Multiply by omitting zeros.
8. Divide whole numbers.

PROBLEM SOLVING IN BUSINESS

The employees at Starbucks Coffee Company must be cross-trained so that they can perform several tasks. Food preparation, cash-register operation, and all beverage-preparation positions require basic mathematical skills.

Paul Crockett, the manager, knows the importance of basic mathematics skills and he recently began giving a short math test to all employee applicants. All employees are expected to know how to read numbers, round whole numbers, add, subtract, multiply, and divide. With this knowledge, Paul and his employees can work more accurately and better serve the customers.

OBJECTIVE 1 Define whole numbers. The standard system of numbering, the **decimal system**, uses the ten one-place **digits** 0, 1, 2, 3, 4, 5, 6, 7, 8, and 9. Combinations of these digits represent any number needed. The starting point of this system is the **decimal point** (.). This section considers only the numbers made up of digits to the left of the decimal point—the **whole numbers**. The following diagram names the first ten places held by the digits to the left of the decimal point. The number 8,321,456,795 is used as an example. To help in reading the number, a **comma** is used at every third place, starting at the decimal point and moving left. An exception to this is that commas are frequently omitted in four-digit numbers, such as 5892 or 2318.

Whole Numbers

Trillions			Billions			Millions			Thousands			Ones			
Hundred trillions	Ten trillions	Trillions	Hundred billions	Ten billions	Billions	Hundred millions	Ten millions	Millions	Hundred thousands	Ten thousands	Thousands	Hundreds	Tens	Ones (units)	Decimal point
					8	3	2	1	4	5	6	7	9	5	.

> **NOTE** Commas are not shown on most calculators.

The number 8,321,456,795 is read "eight billion, three hundred twenty-one million, four hundred fifty-six thousand, seven hundred ninety-five." Notice that the word *and* is not used with whole numbers. The word *and* represents the decimal point and is discussed in Section 1.4.

EXAMPLE 1
Expressing Whole Numbers in Words

Express the following numbers in words.
(a) 7835   **(b)** 111,356,075   **(c)** 17,000,017,000

Solution

(a) seven thousand, eight hundred thirty-five
(b) one hundred eleven million, three hundred fifty-six thousand, seventy-five
(c) seventeen billion, seventeen thousand

OBJECTIVE 2 Round whole numbers. Business applications often require **rounding** numbers. For example, money amounts are commonly rounded to the nearest cent. However, money amounts can also be rounded to the nearest dollar, hundred dollars, thousand dollars, or even hundreds of thousands of dollars and beyond.

Use the following steps for **rounding whole numbers.**

Rounding Whole Numbers

Step 1   Locate the **place** to which the number is to be rounded. Draw a line under that place.

Step 2A   If the first digit to the right of the underlined place is **5 or more, increase** the digit in the place to which you are rounding by one.

Step 2B   If the first digit to the right of the underlined place is **4 or less, do not change** the digit in the place to which you are rounding.

Step 3   **Change** all digits to the right of the underlined digit to zeros.

EXAMPLE 2

Rounding Whole Numbers

Round each number.
(a) 368 to the nearest ten
(b) 67,433 to the nearest thousand
(c) 1,498,985 to the nearest million

Solution

(a) *Step 1* Locate the place to which the number is being rounded. Draw a line under that place.

$$3\underline{6}8$$

— place to which number is rounded

Step 2 The digit to the right of that place is 8, which is 5 or more, so increase the tens digit by 1.

Step 3 Change all digits to the right of the tens place to zero: 368 rounded to the nearest ten is 370.

(b) *Step 1* Find the place to which the number is being rounded. Draw a line under that place.

$$6\underline{7},433$$

— place to which number is rounded

Step 2 The digit after the underlined place is 4, which is 4 or less, so do not change the thousands digit.

Step 3 Change all digits to the right of the thousands place to zero. 67,433 rounded to the nearest thousand is 67,000.

(c) 1,498,985 rounded to the nearest million is 1,000,000.

> **NOTE** When rounding a number, look at the digit just to the right of the digit being rounded. Do not look beyond this digit.

The four basic **operations** that may be performed on whole numbers—**addition**, **subtraction**, **multiplication**, and **division**—are reviewed in this section.

Objective 3 Add whole numbers. In **addition**, the numbers being added are **addends**, and the answer is the **sum** or **total** or **amount**, as follows.

$$\begin{array}{rl} 8 & \text{addend} \\ +\ 9 & \text{addend} \\ \hline 17 & \text{sum (answer)} \end{array}$$

Add numbers by arranging them in a column with units above units, tens above tens, hundreds above hundreds, thousands above thousands, and so on. Use the decimal point as a reference for arranging the numbers. If a number does not include a decimal point, the decimal point is assumed to be at the far right.

85   no decimal point indicated

85.   decimal point assumed to be at far right

— decimal point

> **NOTE** **Checking answers** is important in problem solving. The most common method of checking answers in addition is to re-add the numbers from bottom to top.

EXAMPLE 3

Adding with
Checking

To find the one-day total amount of purchases at the Starbucks that he manages, Paul Crockett needed to add the following amounts and check the answer.

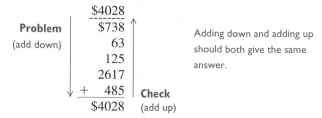

	$4028
Problem	$738
(add down)	63
	125
	2617
	+ 485	**Check**
	$4028	(add up)

Adding down and adding up should both give the same answer.

Adding from the top down results in an answer of $4028. Check for accuracy by adding again—this time from the bottom up. If the answers are the same, the sum is most likely correct. If the answers are different, there is an error in either adding down or adding up, and the problem should be reworked. Both answers agree in this example, so the sum is correct.

OBJECTIVE 4 Round numbers to estimate an answer. Front-end rounding is used to estimate an answer. With front-end rounding, each number is rounded so that all the digits are changed to zero, except the first digit, which is rounded. Only one nonzero digit remains.

EXAMPLE 4

Using Front-End
Rounding to
Estimate an
Answer

With the information in the following graphic, use front-end rounding to estimate the total circulation of the five sports publications.

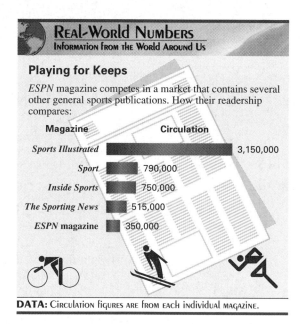

Real-World Numbers
INFORMATION FROM THE WORLD AROUND US

Playing for Keeps

ESPN magazine competes in a market that contains several other general sports publications. How their readership compares:

Magazine	Circulation
Sports Illustrated	3,150,000
Sport	790,000
Inside Sports	750,000
The Sporting News	515,000
ESPN magazine	350,000

DATA: CIRCULATION FIGURES ARE FROM EACH INDIVIDUAL MAGAZINE.

Solution

3,150,000	→	3,000,000
790,000	→	800,000
750,000	→	800,000
515,000	→	500,000
+ 350,000	→	+ 400,000
		5,500,000

all digits changed to zero except first digit, which is rounded

estimated answer

The total circulation of the five sports publications is 5,500,000 (estimated).

> **NOTE** When using front-end rounding, only one nonzero digit (first digit) remains. All digits to the right are zeros.

OBJECTIVE **5** **Subtract whole numbers.** A **subtraction** problem is set up much like an addition problem. The top number is the **minuend**, the number being subtracted is the **subtrahend**, and the answer is the **difference**, as follows.

$$
\begin{array}{rl}
23 & \text{minuend} \\
-7 & \text{subtrahend} \\
\hline
16 & \text{difference}
\end{array}
$$

Subtract one number from another by placing the subtrahend directly under the minuend. Be certain that units are above units, tens above tens, and so on. Then begin at the right column and subtract the subtrahend from the minuend.

When a digit in the subtrahend is larger than the corresponding digit in the minuend, use **borrowing**, as shown in the next example.

EXAMPLE 5
Subtracting with Borrowing

Subtract 2894 hot cups from 3783 hot cups in inventory. First, write the problem as follows.

$$
\begin{array}{r}
3783 \\
-2894
\end{array}
$$

In the units column, subtract 4 from 3 by borrowing a 1 from the tens column in the minuend, to get 1 ten + 3, or 13, in the units column with 7 now in the tens column. Then subtract **4 from 13** for a result of 9. Complete the subtraction as follows.

$$
\begin{array}{cccc}
2 & 16 & 17 & 13 \\
\cancel{3} & \cancel{7} & \cancel{8} & \cancel{3} \\
-2 & 8 & 9 & 4 \\
\hline
& 8 & 8 & 9 \quad \text{hot cups}
\end{array}
$$

In this example, the tens are borrowed from the hundreds column, and the hundreds are borrowed from the thousands column.

Check an answer to a subtraction problem by adding the answer (difference) to the subtrahend. The result should equal the minuend.

EXAMPLE 6
Subtraction with Checking

Subtract 1635 from 5383. Check the answer.

Problem   **Check**

$$
\text{Problem} \downarrow
\begin{array}{r}
5383 \quad \text{minuend} \\
-1635 \quad \text{subtrahend} \\
\hline
3748 \quad \text{difference}
\end{array}
\qquad
\begin{array}{r}
5383 \\
+1635 \\
\hline
374
\end{array}
$$

(subtract down) This result should equal the minuend. Check (add up)

Multiplication is a quick method of addition. For example, 3×4 can be found by adding 3 a total of 4 times, since 3×4 means $3 + 3 + 3 + 3 = 12$. However, it is not practical to use the addition method for large numbers. For example, 103×92 would be found by adding 103 a total of 92 times; instead, find this result with multiplication.

> **NOTE** The symbols used for multiplication are "$\times$" and a "•" between two numbers. Also, two or more numbers within parentheses that are next to each other "( )( )" means to multiply. With a computer, the ∗ means to multiply.

OBJECTIVE **6** **Multiply whole numbers.** The number being multiplied is the **multiplicand**, the number doing the multiplying is the **multiplier**, and the answer is the **product**. For example:

$$
\begin{array}{rl}
3 & \text{multiplicand} \\
\times4 & \text{multiplier} \\
\hline
12 & \text{product}
\end{array}
$$

When the multiplier contains more than one digit, **partial products** must be used, as in the following example which shows the product of 57 and 23.

EXAMPLE 7

Multiplying Whole Numbers

A motorcycle that gets 57 miles per gallon used 23 gallons of gasoline on a recent trip. To find the total number of miles traveled, multiply the miles traveled per gallon of gasoline, 57, by the number of gallons of gasoline used, 23.

$$
\begin{array}{r}
57 \quad \text{multiplicand} \\
\times \ 23 \quad \text{multiplier} \\
\hline
171 \quad \text{partial product } (3 \times 57) \\
114 \quad \text{partial product } (2 \times 57, \text{ one position to the left}) \\
\hline
1311 \quad \text{product}
\end{array}
$$

Find the product of 57 and 23 by first multiplying 57 by 3 (the 3 is taken from the units column of the multiplier). The product of 57 and 3 is 171, which is a partial product. Next multiply 57 by 2 (from the tens column of the multiplier), and get 114 as a partial product. Since the 2 in the multiplier is from the tens column, write the partial product 114 one position to the left so that 4 is under the tens column. Finally, add the partial products, and get the product 1311.

> **NOTE** If the multiplier had more digits, each partial product would be placed one additional position to the *left*.

OBJECTIVE **7** **Multiply by omitting zeros.** If the multiplier or multiplicand or both end in zero, save time by first omitting any zeros at the right of the numbers and then replacing omitted zeros at the right of the final answer. This shortcut is useful even with calculators. For example, find the product of 240 and 13 as follows.

$$
\begin{array}{r}
240 \quad \text{Omit the zero in the calculation.} \\
\times \ 13 \quad \text{Replace the omitted zero at the right of} \\
\hline
72 \quad \text{312 for a final answer (product) of 3120.} \\
24 \\
\hline
3120
\end{array}
$$

EXAMPLE 8

Multiplying Omitting Zeros

In the following multiplication problems, omit zeros in the calculation and then replace omitted zeros to obtain the product.

(a)
$$
\begin{array}{cc}
150 & 15 \\
\times \ 70 & \times \ 7 \\
\hline
& 105 \ + \textbf{3 zeros} \\
& 10{,}500 \ \text{answer}
\end{array}
$$

(b)
$$
\begin{array}{cc}
300 & 3 \\
\times \ 70 & \times \ 7 \\
\hline
& 21 \ + \textbf{2 zeros} \\
& 21{,}000 \ \text{answer}
\end{array}
$$

> **NOTE** A shortcut for multiplying by 10, 100, 1000, and so on is to just add the number of zeros to the number being multiplied. For example,
>
> $$33 \times 10 \ = \ 33 \text{ and } \textbf{1} \text{ zero } = 330$$
> $$56 \times 100 \ = \ 56 \text{ and } \textbf{2} \text{ zeros} = 5600$$
> $$732 \times 1000 = 732 \text{ and } \textbf{3} \text{ zeros} = 732{,}000$$

OBJECTIVE **8** **Divide whole numbers.** Various symbols are used to show **division**. For example, $\div$ and $\overline{)}\,$ both mean "divide." Also, a — with a number above and a number below, as in a fraction, means division. In printing, or when seen on computer screen, the bar is often written /, so that, for example, 24/6 means to divide 24 by 6.

The **dividend** is the number being divided, the **divisor** is the number doing the dividing, and the **quotient** is the answer.

Write "15 divided by 5 equals 3" in any of the following ways.

$$15 \div 5 = 3$$

dividend   divisor   quotient
(answer)

$$\text{divisor } \quad 5\overline{)15} \quad \begin{array}{l} \text{quotient (answer)} \\ 3 \\ \text{dividend} \end{array}$$

$$\begin{array}{l} \text{dividend} \\ \text{divisor} \end{array} \quad \frac{15}{5} = 3 \quad \text{quotient (answer)}$$

EXAMPLE 9

Dividing Whole Numbers

To divide 1095 baseball cards evenly among 73 collectors, you must divide 1095 by 73. Write the problem as follows.

$$73\overline{)1095}$$

Since 73 is larger than 1 or 10 but smaller than 109, begin by dividing 73 into 109. There is 1 of the 73s in 109, so place 1 over the digit 9 in the dividend, as shown. Then multiply 1 and 73.

$$\begin{array}{r} 1 \\ 73\overline{)1095} \\ 73 \\ \hline 36 \end{array} \qquad 1 \times 73 = 73$$

Then subtract 73 from 109, getting 36. The next step is to bring down the 5 from the dividend, placing it next to the remainder 36. This gives the number 365. The divisor, 73, is then divided into 365 with a result of 5, which is placed to the right of the 1 in the quotient. Since 73 divides exactly 5 times into 365, the final answer (quotient) is exactly 15, as shown.

$$\begin{array}{r} 15 \\ 73\overline{)1095} \\ 73 \\ \hline 365 \\ 365 \\ \hline 0 \end{array}$$

    Often part of the quotient must be expressed as a remainder, or as a **fraction part** or **decimal part**, of the quotient. The fraction part of the quotient is discussed in the next chapter. The decimal part of the quotient, most commonly used, is discussed later in this chapter.

EXAMPLE 10

Dividing with a Remainder in the Answer

Divide 126 by 24. Express the remainder in each of the three forms.

Remainder	Fraction	Decimal

$$\begin{array}{r} 5\,\text{R}6 \\ 24\overline{)126} \\ 120 \\ \hline 6 \end{array} \qquad \begin{array}{r} 5\frac{6}{24} \\ 24\overline{)126} \\ 120 \\ \hline 6 \end{array} \qquad \begin{array}{r} 5.25 \\ 24\overline{)126.00} \\ 120 \\ \hline 6\,0 \\ 4\,8 \\ \hline 1\,20 \\ 1\,20 \\ \hline 0 \end{array}$$

In the first form, the answer 5 R6 is usually difficult to work with. The second form, $5\frac{6}{24}$, is precise and defines the remainder as $\frac{6}{24}$. The third form, 5.25, is also precise in its meaning. For the time being, write remainders as fractions, using the remainder as the top number (numerator) and the divisor as the bottom number (denominator). After studying decimals, express the quotient in the manner most useful in the problem being solved. (After studying fractions, write fractional remainders in lowest terms, $\frac{6}{24} = \frac{1}{4}$.)

If a divisor contains zeros at the far right, as in 30 or 300 or 8000, drop the zeros in the divisor and move the decimal point in the dividend the same number of positions to the left as there were zeros dropped from the divisor. For example, divide 108,000 by 900 by letting

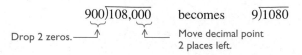

$$900\overline{)108{,}000} \quad \text{becomes} \quad 9\overline{)1080}$$

Drop 2 zeros. ──────┘   └────── Move decimal point 2 places left.

Divide 7320 by 30 by letting

$$30\overline{)7320} \quad \text{become} \quad 3\overline{)732}$$

> **NOTE**   The shortcut of dropping zeros from the divisor and moving the decimal point the same number of places to the left in the dividend saves time and eliminates errors that may result from using larger numbers.

EXAMPLE 11

Dropping Zeros to Divide

Divide, dropping zeros from the divisor.

(a) $40\overline{)11{,}000}$ **(b)** $3500\overline{)31{,}500}$ **(c)** $200\overline{)18{,}800}$

Solution

(a)
$$\begin{array}{r} 275 \\ 4\overline{)1100} \\ \underline{8} \\ 30 \\ \underline{28} \\ 20 \\ \underline{20} \\ 0 \end{array}$$

(b)
$$\begin{array}{r} 9 \\ 35\overline{)315} \\ \underline{315} \\ 0 \end{array}$$

(c)
$$\begin{array}{r} 94 \\ 2\overline{)188} \\ \underline{18} \\ 8 \\ \underline{8} \\ 0 \end{array}$$

EXAMPLE 12

Checking Division Problems

In a division problem, check the answer by multiplying the quotient (answer) and the divisor. Then add any remainder. The result should be the dividend. If the result is not the same as the dividend, an error exists and the problem should be reworked.

Check the following division problems.

(a)
$$\begin{array}{r} 22 \\ 19\overline{)418} \\ \underline{38} \\ 38 \\ \underline{38} \\ 0 \end{array}$$

(b)
$$\begin{array}{r} 37 \\ 716\overline{)26{,}492} \\ \underline{21\ 48} \\ 5\ 012 \\ \underline{5\ 012} \\ 0 \end{array}$$

(c)
$$\begin{array}{r} 85\ \text{R6} \\ 418\overline{)35{,}536} \\ \underline{33\ 44} \\ 2\ 096 \\ \underline{2\ 090} \\ 6 \quad \text{remainder} \end{array}$$

Solution   Match

(a)
$$\begin{array}{r} 19 \\ \times\ 22 \\ \hline 38 \\ 38 \\ \hline 418 \end{array}$$
correct

(b)
$$\begin{array}{r} 716 \\ \times\ 37 \\ \hline 5012 \\ 2148 \\ \hline 26{,}492 \end{array}$$
correct

(c)
$$\begin{array}{r} 418 \\ \times\ 85 \\ \hline 2090 \\ 3344 \\ \hline 35{,}530 \\ +\ \ 6 \quad \text{remainder} \\ \hline 35{,}536 \quad \text{correct} \end{array}$$

> **PROBLEM-SOLVING HINT**   When checking a division problem that has a remainder, be sure to add the remainder to get the check answer. Also, when an answer is rounded, be alert to the fact that the check answer will not be perfect. The rounded answer does not allow a perfect check.

Name   Date   Class

Multiply. (See Example 7.)

Quick Start

33.   218
          × 43
         ─────
          654
          872
         ─────
          9374

34.   672
          × 56

35.   1896
          × 62

36.   7318
          × 38

37.   6452
          × 263

38.   7143
          × 295

39.   1109
          × 7311

40.   9503
          × 3411

Estimate the following answers by using front-end rounding. Then find the exact answers. (See Example 4.)

Quick Start

41. Estimate   **Exact**
                rounds
       8000 ←── to ──   8215
         60 ←───   56
        700 ←───   729
     + 4000   + 3605
     ────────   ────────
       12,760   12,605

42. Estimate   **Exact**
                          2685
                            73
                           592
       +   + 7183
                        ────────

43. Estimate   **Exact**
                           783
       −   − 238

44. Estimate   **Exact**
                           942
       −   − 286

45. Estimate   **Exact**
                           638
       ×   × 47

46. Estimate   **Exact**
                           864
       ×   × 74

Multiply, omitting zeros in the calculation and then replacing them at the right of the product to obtain the final answer. (See Example 8.)

Quick Start

47.   370
          × 180
         ─────
           37
          × 18
         ─────
          666   2 zeros
                  ↙
         66,600

48.   520
          × 400

49.   3760
          × 6000

50.   7200
          × 1300

Divide. Use fractions to express any remainders. (See Examples 9 and 10.)

Quick Start

           1241 ¼
51. 4)4965
          4
         ───
          09
           8
         ───
          16
          16
         ───
          05
           4
         ───
           1

52. 7)13,214

53. 43)19,715

54. 93)81,452

55. Explain why checking the answer is an important step in solving math problems.

56. In your personal and business life, which math calculations are most important to check? Why?

Divide each of the following, dropping zeros from the divisor. Express any remainder as a fraction. (See Examples 10 and 11.)

57. $180\overline{)429{,}350}$

$$\begin{array}{r} 2\,385\tfrac{5}{18} \\ 18\overline{)42{,}935} \\ \underline{36\phantom{{,}000}} \\ 6\,9 \\ \underline{5\,4} \\ 1\,53 \\ \underline{1\,44} \\ 95 \\ \underline{90} \\ 5 \end{array}$$

58. $320\overline{)360{,}990}$

59. $1300\overline{)75{,}800}$

60. $1600\overline{)253{,}100}$

Express each of the following numbers in words. (See Example 1.)

61. U.S. MAIL VOLUME   The United States Postal Service set a record of 280,489,000 postmarked pieces of mail on a single day.

62. YOSEMITE PARK VISITORS   Yosemite National Park had 3,485,000 visitors last year.

63. AID TO FAMILIES WITH DEPENDENT CHILDREN   The total Aid to Families with Dependent Children (AFDC) in the United States last year was $18,630,604,733.

64. GROSS NATIONAL PRODUCT   The gross national product for the United States (the sum of all goods and services sold) was $7,637,685,362,159

Solve each of the following application problems.

RECREATION EQUIPMENT RENTAL   *American River Raft Rentals lists the following daily raft rental fees. Notice that there is an additional $2 launch fee payable to the park system for each raft rented. Use this information to solve Exercises 65 and 66.*

American River Raft Rentals

Size	Rental Fee	Launch Fee
4-person	$28	$2
6-person	$38	$2
10-person	$70	$2
12-person	$75	$2
16-person	$85	$2

65. On a recent Tuesday the following rafts were rented: 6 4-person; 15 6-person; 10 10-person; 3 - 12-person; and 2 16-person. Find the total receipts including the $2-per-raft launch fee.

65. _____

66. On the 4th of July the following rafts were rented: 38 4-person; 73 6-person; 58 10-person; 34 12-person; and 18 16-person. Find the total receipts including the $2-per-raft launch fee.

66. _____

1.2 | Application Problems

Objectives

1. Find indicator words in application problems.
2. Learn the four steps for solving application problems.
3. Learn to estimate answers.

Problem Solving in Business

When Paul Crockett became a manager at a Starbucks Coffee store, he had to brush up on his math skills. He remembered that certain words indicate addition, subtraction, multiplication, and division. He and his employees got together and listed some of these words.

For related Web activities, go to www.mathbusiness.com

Keyword: coffee

Many business-application problems require mathematics. You must read the words carefully to decide how to solve the problem.

Objective 1 **Find indicator words in application problems.** Look for **indicators** in the application problem—words that indicate the necessary operations—either addition, subtraction, multiplication, or division. Some of these words appear below.

Addition	Subtraction	Multiplication	Division	Equals
plus	less	product	divided by	is
more	subtract	double	divided into	the same as
more than	subtracted from	triple	quotient	equals
added to	difference	times	goes into	equal to
increased by	less than	of	divide	yields
sum	fewer	twice	divided equally	results in
total	decreased by	twice as much	per	are
sum of	loss of			
increase of	minus			
gain of	take away			

Objective 2 **Learn the four steps for solving application problems.**

Steps for Solving Application Problems

Step 1 Read the problem carefully, and be certain that you understand what the problem is asking. It may be necessary to read the problem several times.

Step 2 Before doing any calculations, work out a plan and try to visualize the problem. Know which facts are given and which must be found. Use word *indicators* to help determine your plan.

Step 3 Estimate a *reasonable answer* using rounding.

Step 4 *Solve* the problem by using the facts given and your plan. Does the answer make sense? If the answer is reasonable, *check* your work. If the answer is not reasonable, begin again by rereading the problem.

NOTE Be careful not to make the mistake that some students do—they begin to solve a problem before they understand what the problem is asking. Be certain that you know what the problem is asking before you try to solve it.

OBJECTIVE **3** **Learn to estimate answers.** A plan gives a systematic approach to a problem, resulting in more successful solutions. Each of the steps is important, but special emphasis should be placed on step 3, estimating a reasonable answer. Many times an answer just *does not fit* the problem.

What is a *reasonable answer*? Read the problem and estimate the approximate size of the answer. Should the answer be part of a dollar, a few dollars, hundreds, thousands, or even millions of dollars? For example, if a problem asks for the retail price of a shirt, would an answer of $20 be reasonable? $1000? $.65? $65?

Always make an estimate of a reasonable answer. Always look at the answer and decide if it is reasonable. These steps will give greater success in problem solving.

EXAMPLE 1

Using Word Indicators to Help Solve a Problem

At a recent garage sale, the total sales were $584. If the money was divided equally among Tom, Rosetta, Maryann, and José, how much did each receive?

SOLUTION

After reading the problem and understanding that the four members in the group divided $584, work out a plan. The word indicators, *divided equally*, suggest that $584 should be divided by 4. A reasonable answer would be slightly less than $150 each ($600 ÷ 4 = $150). Find the actual answer by dividing $584 by 4.

$$\begin{array}{r} 146 \\ 4\overline{)584} \end{array}$$ Each person should get $146.

The answer is reasonable, so check the work.

$$\begin{array}{r} 146 \\ \times \quad 4 \\ \hline \$584 \end{array}$$ The answer is correct.

EXAMPLE 2

Solving an Application Problem

One week, Paul Crockett decided to total his sales at Starbucks. The daily sales figures were $2358 on Monday, $3056 on Tuesday, $2515 on Wednesday, $1875 on Thursday, $3978 on Friday, $3219 on Saturday, and $3008 on Sunday. Find his total sales for the week.

SOLUTION

The sales for each day are given and the total sales are needed. The word indicators, *total sales*, tell you to add the daily sales to arrive at the weekly total. Since the sales are about $3000 each day for a week of 7 days, a reasonable estimate would be around $21,000 (7 × $3000 = $21,000). Find the actual answer by adding the sales for each of the 7 days.

$$\begin{array}{r} \$20,009 \quad \text{Check} \\ \$2358 \\ \$3056 \\ \$2515 \\ \$1875 \\ \$3978 \\ \$3219 \\ + \quad \$3008 \\ \hline \$20,009 \end{array}$$ $20,009 sales for the week

The answer $20,009 is reasonable.

EXAMPLE 3

Solving an Application Problem

Use the information in the following graphic to find each of the following.

(a) Find the difference in annual earnings between a high school graduate and a person with an Associate of Arts degree.

(b) In one year, a person with a bachelor's degree will earn how much less than a person with a professional degree?

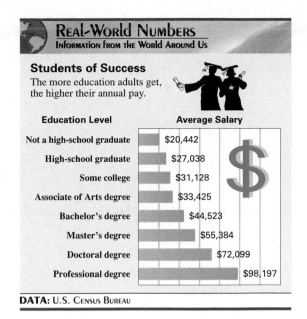

Solution

The word indicator in **(a)** is *difference* and the word indicator in **(b)** is *less than*. Both of these words indicate that we must subtract.

(a) $33,425
  − 27,038
  $6387   difference in earnings

(b) $98,197
  − 44,523
  $53,674   less than a person with a professional degree

Example 4
Solving a Two-Step Problem

In May, the landlord of an apartment building received $720 from each of eight tenants. After paying $2180 in expenses, how much money did the landlord have left?

Solution

Step 1 The amount of rent is given along with the number of tenants. Multiply the amount of rent by the number of tenants to arrive at the monthly income. Since the rent is about $700 and there are 8 tenants, a *reasonable estimate* would be around $5600 ($700 × 8 = $5600).

  $720
  × 8
  $5760   monthly income (this is reasonable)

Step 2 Finally, subtract the expenses from the monthly income.

  $5760
  − 2180
  $3580   amount remaining

Name _____ Date _____ Class _____

1.2 | EXERCISES

Solve the following application problems.

1. **COMPETITIVE CYCLIST TRAINING** During a week of training, Rob Andrews rode his bike 80 miles on Monday, 75 miles on Tuesday, 135 miles on Wednesday, 40 miles on Thursday, and 52 miles on Friday. What is the total number of miles he rode in the five-day period?

1. _____

2. During a recent week, Starbucks Coffee sold 325 pounds of Estate Java coffee, 75 pounds of Encanta Blend coffee, 137 pounds of Ethiopia Sidamo coffee, 495 pounds of Starbucks House-Blend Decaf coffee, and 105 pounds of New Guinea Peaberry coffee. Find the total number of pounds of these coffees sold.

2. _____

3. **ATM CRIME** According to *ATM Crime and Security* newsletter, in one region there were 70 ATM burglaries and attempted burglaries in 1992 and 200 in 1997. How many more of these crimes were there in 1997 than in 1992?

3. _____

4. **ATM FACTS** The amount of cash in an ATM ranges from $15,000 in small machines to $250,000 in large bank machines. How much more money is there in the large machines than in the small machines?

4. _____

5. **VIETNAM VETERANS** A group of American soldiers and nurses, veterans of the Vietnam War, rode bicycles from Hanoi to Saigon (Ho Chi Minh City). If they rode 75 miles each day and the trip took 16 days, find the distance between these two cities in Vietnam.

5. _____

6. **WORLD POPULATION GROWTH** The world population grows by 10,000 people each hour. Find the increase in world population in one year of 365 days.

6. _____

7. **AUTOMOBILE WEIGHT** A car weighs 2425 pounds. If its 582-pound engine is removed and replaced with a 634-pound engine, find the weight of the car after the engine change.

7. _____

8. **PRESCHOOL MANAGER** Tiffany Connolly has $2324 in her preschool operating account. After spending $734 from this account, the class parents raise $568 in a rummage sale. Find the balance in the account after depositing the money from the rummage sale.

8. _____

9. **BUSINESS ENTERPRISES** There are 24 million business enterprises in the United States. If only 7000 of these businesses are large businesses having 500 or more employees, while the rest are small and midsize businesses, find the number of small and midsize businesses.

9. _____

10. **WEIGHING FREIGHT** A truck weighs 9250 pounds when empty. After being loaded with firewood, the truck weighs 21,375 pounds. What is the weight of the firewood?

10. _____

11. **EMPLOYER BUYOUTS** Last year 15,293 federal workers applied for buyouts (a bonus to retire early) which was the chance to get a $25,000 going-away present from Uncle Sam. If all of these employees received the bonus, find the total cost of the buyouts.

11. _____

12. EARLY RETIREMENT   This year the government will offer a $25,000 early retirement bonus to 60,000 federal workers. If all of these employees receive this bonus, find the total cost to the government.

12. _____

13. HOTEL-ROOM COSTS   In a recent survey of high-priced hotels the least expensive was Harrah's at a cost of $65 per night while several of the hotels in the group were $90 per night. Find the amount saved on a five-night stay at the least expensive hotel instead of staying at one of the more expensive hotels.

13. _____

14. LUXURY HOTELS   The most expensive hotel room in a recent study was the Ritz-Carlton at $375 per night, while the least expensive was Motel 6 at $32 per night. Find the amount saved in a four-night stay at Motel 6 instead of staying at the Ritz-Carlton.

14. _____

15. PHYSICALLY IMPAIRED   The Enabling Supply House purchases 6 wheelchairs at $1256 each and 15 speech compression recorder-players at $895 each. Find the total cost.

15. _____

16. COLLEGE BOOKSTORE   Find the total cost if a college bookstore buys 17 computers at $506 each and 13 printers at $482 each.

16. _____

17. THEATER RENOVATION   A theater owner is remodeling and wants to provide enough seating for 1250 people. The main floor has 30 rows of 25 seats in each row. If the balcony has 25 rows, how many seats must be in each row of the balcony to satisfy the owner's seating requirements?

17. _____

18. PACKING AND SHIPPING   Nancy Hart makes 24 grapevine wreaths per week to sell to gift shops. She works 30 weeks a year and packages six wreaths per box. If she ships equal quantities to each of five shops, find the number of boxes each shop will receive.

18. _____

1.3 | Basics of Decimals

Objectives

1. **Read and write decimals.**
2. **Round decimals.**

Objective 1 Read and write decimals. A **decimal** is any number written with a decimal point, such as 6.8, 5.375, or .000982. Decimals, like fractions, can be used to represent parts of a whole. These parts are "less than 1." Section 1.1 discussed how to read the digits to the *left* of the decimal point (whole numbers). Read the digits to the *right* of the decimal point as shown here.

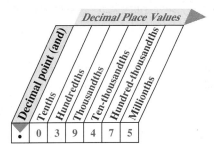

The decimal 9.7 is read as "nine and seven tenths." The word *and* represents the decimal point. Also, 11.59 is read "eleven and fifty-nine hundredths," and 72.087 is read as "seventy-two and eighty-seven thousandths."

> **NOTE** The word *and* is used only to separate a whole number and a fraction or a whole number and a decimal. Also, notice that all decimals *end* in *th*'s.

EXAMPLE 1
Reading Decimal Numbers

Read the following decimals.
(a) 19.08   **(b)** .097   **(c)** 7648.9713

Solution

(a) nineteen and eight hundredths
(b) ninety-seven thousandths
(c) seven thousand, six hundred forty-eight and nine thousand, seven hundred thirteen ten-thousandths.

Objective 2 Round decimals. It is important to be able to round decimals. For example, the 7-Eleven is selling two candy mints for \$.75 but you want to buy only one mint. The price of one mint is \$.75 ÷ 2, which is \$.375, but you cannot pay part of a cent. So the store rounds the price up to \$.38 for one mint.
  Use the following steps for rounding decimals.

Rounding Decimals

Step 1 Find the place to which the rounding is being done. Draw a line **after** that place to show that you are cutting off the rest of the digits.

Step 2A Look **only** at the **first** digit you are cutting off. If the first digit is **5 or more**, increase by one the digit in the place to which you are rounding.

Step 2B If the first digit to the right of the line is **4 or less**, do not change the digit in the place to which you are rounding.

Step 3 **Drop** all digits to the right of the place to which you have rounded.

> **NOTE** Do not move the decimal point when rounding.

EXAMPLE 2

Rounding Decimal Numbers

Round 98.5892 to the nearest tenth.

Solution

Step 1 Locate the tenths digit and draw a line.

$$98.5|892$$
└── tenths digit

The tenths digit here is 5.

Step 2 Locate the digit just to the right of the line.

$$98.5|892$$
└── just to the right of the line

The digit just to the right of the line is 8.

Step 3 If the digit found in step 2 is 4 or less, leave the digit of step 1 alone. If the digit found in step 2 is 5 or more, increase the digit of step 1 by 1. The digit found in step 2 here is 8, so 98.5892 rounded to the nearest tenth is

$$98.6$$
└── increase 5 by 1

EXAMPLE 3

Rounding to the Nearest Thousandth

Round .008572 to the nearest thousandth.

Solution

Locate the thousandths digit and draw a line.

$$.008|572$$
└── thousandths digit

Since the digit to the right of the line is 5, increase the thousandths digit by 1; .008572 rounded to the nearest thousandth is .009.

EXAMPLE 4

Rounding the Same Decimal to Different Places

Round 24.6483 to the nearest

(a) thousandth.   **(b)** hundredth.   **(c)** tenth.

Solution

Use the method just described.

(a) 24.6483 to the nearest thousandth is 24.648.
(b) 24.6483 to the nearest hundredth is 24.65.
(c) 24.6483 to the nearest tenth is 24.6.

> **PROBLEM-SOLVING HINT**   The answer to part (c) may be surprising because of the answer in (b). However, **always round a number by going back to the *original number*, and not to some number that was rounded from the original number.**

EXAMPLE 5

Rounding to the Nearest Dollar

Round to the nearest dollar.

(a) $48.69   **(b)** $594.36   **(c)** $2689.50   **(d)** $.61

Solution

(a) Locate the digit representing the dollar and draw a line.

$$\$48.|69$$
└── dollar digit

Since the digit to the right of the line is 6, increase the dollar digit by 1; $48.69 rounded to the nearest dollar is $49.

(b) $594.36 rounded to the nearest dollar is $594.
(c) $2689.50 rounded to the nearest dollar is $2690.
(d) $.61 rounded to the nearest dollar is $1.

1.4 | Addition and Subtraction of Decimals

Objectives

1. Add decimals.
2. Estimate answers.
3. Subtract decimals.

Problem Solving in Business

As manager of Starbucks, Paul Crockett is responsible for making bank deposits to the company checking account. These banking activities require the ability to accurately add and subtract decimal numbers.

Objective 1 Add decimals. Decimals are added in much the same way as whole numbers are added. The main difference with decimals is that the decimal points must be kept in a column.

Example 1

Adding Decimals and Checking with Estimation

Add 9.83, 6.4, 17.592, and 3.087, or

$$
\begin{array}{r}
9.83 \\
6.4 \\
17.592 \\
3.087 \\
\end{array}
$$

by first lining up decimal points.

$$
\begin{array}{r}
9.83 \\
6.4 \qquad \text{Line up decimal points.}\\
17.592 \\
3.087 \\
\hline
36.909 \\
\end{array}
$$

Add by columns, just as with whole numbers. One way to keep the digits in their correct columns is to place zeros to the right of each decimal, so that each number has the same number of digits following the decimal point. Attaching zeros to this example gives the following.

$$
\begin{array}{r}
9.830 \qquad \text{All numbers now have three}\\
6.400 \qquad \text{places after the decimal point.}\\
17.592 \\
3.087 \\
\hline
36.909 \\
\end{array}
$$

> **NOTE** Placing zeros to the right of the decimal point does not change the value of a number. For example, 4.21 = 4.210 = 4.2100, and so on.

Objective 2 Estimate answers. Check that digits were not added in the wrong columns by estimating the answer. For the numbers just added, estimate by using front-end rounding.

Problem	Estimate
9.830	10
6.400	6
17.592	20
+ 3.087	+ 3
36.909	39

> **NOTE** The estimate shows the answer is reasonable and that the decimal points were lined up properly.

EXAMPLE 2
Adding Dollars and Cents

During a recent week, Paul Crockett made the following bank deposits to the Starbucks business account: $783.38, $2341.15, $1175.94, $338.71, and $1562.53. Use front-end rounding to estimate the total deposits and then find the total deposits.

Solution

Estimate	Problem
$800	$783.38
2000	2341.15
1000	1175.94
300	338.71
+ 2000	+ 1562.53
$6100	$6201.71

The total deposits for the week were $6201.71.

Objective **3** **Subtract decimals.** Subtraction is done in much the same way as addition. Line up the decimal points and place as many zeros after each decimal as needed. For example, subtract 17.432 from 21.76 as follows.

$$\begin{array}{r} 21.760 \\ -17.432 \\ \hline 4.328 \end{array}$$ Place one zero after the top decimal.

EXAMPLE 3
Estimating and then Subtracting Decimals

First estimate using front-end rounding and then subtract.

(a)   11.7
    − 4.923

(b)   39.428
    − 27.98

Solution

Attach zeros as needed, and then subtract.

(a) Estimate	Problem	(b) Estimate	Problem
10	11.700	40	39.428
− 5	− 4.923	− 30	− 27.980
5	6.777	10	11.448

Name   Date   Class

1.4 | EXERCISES

The Quick Start exercises in each section contain solutions to help you get started.

First use front-end rounding to estimate and then add the following decimals. (See Examples 1 and 2.)

Quick Start

1. Estimate		Problem	2. Estimate		Problem	3. Estimate		Problem
40	←	37.25	600	←	623.15			6.23
20	←	18.9	700	←	734.29			3.6
+ 8	←	+ 7.5	+ 700	←	+ 686.26			5.1
68		63.65	2000		2043.7			7.2
							+	+ 1.69

4. Estimate	Problem	5. Estimate		Problem	6. Estimate		Problem
5	4.61			2156.38			1889.76
7	7.28			5.26			21.42
3	2.79			2.791			19.35
12	12.15		+	+ 6.983		+	+ 8.1
+ 16	+ 16.39						
43	43.22						

7. Estimate		Problem	8. Estimate		Problem	9. Estimate		Problem
		6133.78			743.1			1798.419
		506.124			3817.65			68.32
		18.63			2.908			512.807
+		+ 7.527			4123.76			643.9
				+	+ 21.98		+	+ 428.

Place each of the following numbers in a column and then add. (See Example 1.)

Quick Start

10. $58.546 + 19.2 + 8.735 + 14.58 =$ __101.061__

11. $12.15 + 6.83 + 61.75 + 19.218 + 73.325 =$ __173.273__

12. $197.4 + 83.72 + 17.43 + 25.63 + 1.4 =$ _____

13. $27.653 + 18.7142 + 9.7496 + 3.21 =$ _____

14. $73.618 + 19.18 + 371.82 + 355.125 =$ _____

15. It is a good idea to estimate an answer before actually solving a problem. Why is this true? (See Objective 2.)

16. In your own words, explain why placing zeros to the right of the decimal point does not change the value of a number. (See Objective 1.)

Solve each of the following application problems.

17. BUSINESS-MEETING COST   As refreshments for a staff meeting, Dan Evans bought $14.82 worth of muffins, $20.75 worth of croissants, and $15.79 worth of cookies. How much money did he spend altogether?

17. _____

18. EMPLOYEE COMPENSATION   Ellen Shrain, a sales representative, earned $759.27 in commission, $235.75 as a premium, and received $87.04 for mileage. Find the total amount that she received.

18. _____

19. TOTAL SALES RECEIPTS   The daily receipts for one week at Andy's Yard and Garden were $1768.12, $1412.46, $1089.73, $1586.63, $1986.40, $1821.43, and $1470.38. Find the total receipts for the week.

19. _____

First use front-end rounding to estimate the answer, and then subtract. (See Example 3.)

Quick Start

20. Estimate	Problem	21. Estimate	Problem	22. Estimate	Problem
20 − 7 13	19.74 − 6.58 13.16	40 − 8 32	35.86 − 7.91 27.95	−	51.215 − 19.708

23. Estimate	Problem	24. Estimate	Problem	25. Estimate	Problem
−	27.613 − 18.942	−	325.053 − 85.019	−	3974.61 − 892.59

26. Estimate	Problem	27. Estimate	Problem	28. Estimate	Problem
−	7.8 − 2.952	−	27.8 − 13.582	−	5 − 1.9802

CHECKING-ACCOUNT RECORDS   *Paul Crockett's Starbucks outlet had a bank balance of $5382.12 on March 1. During March, Paul deposited $60,375.82 received from sales, $3280.18 received as credits from suppliers, and $75.53 as a county tax refund. He paid out $27,282.75 to suppliers, $4280.83 for rent and utilities, and $12,252.23 for salaries. Find each of the following.*

Quick Start

29. How much did Crockett deposit in March?

$60,375.82 (sales) + $3280.18 (credits) + $75.53 (refund) = $63,731.53

29. $63,731.53

30. How much did he pay out?

$27,282.75 (suppliers) + $4280.83 (rent) + $12,252.23 (salaries) = $43,815.81

30. $43,815.81

31. What was his final balance at the end of March?

31. _____

32. In April, Crockett deposited $48,620.15 and paid out $51,728.18. Find the balance in the account at the end of April.

32. _____

1.5 | Multiplication and Division of Decimals

Objectives

1. Multiply decimals.
2. Divide decimals.
3. Divide a decimal by a decimal.

PROBLEM SOLVING IN BUSINESS	Managing a business requires the ability to multiply and divide decimal numbers. Paul Crockett, the manager at Starbucks, applies these skills in many ways; some examples include payroll, purchasing, and sales.

Objective ☐ **Multiply decimals.** Decimals are multiplied as if they were whole numbers. (It is not necessary to line up the decimal points.) The decimal point in the answer is then found as follows.

Positioning the Decimal Point

Step 1 Count the number of digits to the right of the decimal point in each of the numbers being multiplied.

Step 2 In the answer, count from right to left the number of places found in step 1. It may be necessary to attach zeros to the left of the answer in order to correctly place the decimal point.

Example 1

Multiplying Decimals

Multiply

(a) 8.34 × 4.2   **(b)** .032 × .07

Solution

(a) First multiply the given numbers as if they were whole numbers.

$$
\begin{array}{r}
8.34 \quad \longleftarrow \text{ 2 decimal places} \\
\times \quad 4.2 \quad \longleftarrow \text{ 1 decimal place} \\
\hline
1668 \\
3336 \\
\hline
35.028 \quad \longleftarrow \text{ 3 decimal places in answer}
\end{array}
$$

There are two decimal places in 8.34, and one in 4.2. This means there are $2 + 1 = 3$ decimal places in the final answer. Find the final answer by starting at the right and counting three places to the left.

$$35.028 \qquad \text{3 places to the left}$$

(b) Here, it is necessary to attach zeros at the left in the answer.

$$
\begin{array}{r}
.032 \quad \longleftarrow \text{ 3 decimal places} \\
\times \quad .07 \quad \longleftarrow \text{ 2 decimal places} \\
\hline
.00224 \quad \longleftarrow \text{ 5 decimal places in answer}
\end{array}
$$

Attach 2 zeros.

The next example uses the formula for the gross pay (the pay before deductions) of a worker paid by the hour.

Gross pay = Number of hours worked × Pay per hour

| **Example 2** | Find the gross pay of a Starbucks employee working 28.5 hours at a rate of $7.15 per hour. |

Multiplying Two
Decimal Numbers

Solution

Find gross pay by multiplying the number of hours worked by the pay per hour.

$$
\begin{array}{r}
28.5 \quad \longleftarrow \text{ I place} \\
\times \quad 7.15 \quad \longleftarrow \text{ 2 places} \\
\hline
1425 \\
285 \\
1995 \\
\hline
203.775 \quad \longleftarrow \text{ 3 places in answer}
\end{array}
$$

This worker's gross pay, rounded to the nearest cent, is $203.78.

The following graphic shows the average daily customer visits (in millions) to McDonald's around the world.

For related Web
activities, go to
www.mathbusiness.com

Keyword:
hoops

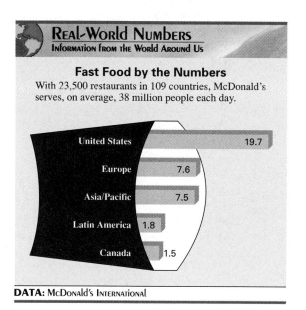

| **Example 3** | If McDonald's is open 364 days a year (closed Christmas), find the total number of customer visits in one year in the United States. |

Applying Decimal
Multiplication

Solution

Find the total number of customer visits in one year by multiplying the number of days in the year by the number of customer visits each day.

$$
\begin{array}{r}
19.7 \quad \longleftarrow \text{ I place} \\
\times \ 364 \quad \longleftarrow \text{ 0 places} \\
\hline
788 \\
1182 \\
591 \\
\hline
7170.8 \quad \longleftarrow \text{ I place}
\end{array}
$$

The total number of customer visits in one year in the United States is 7170.8 million (7,170,800,000 customer visits).

Objective **2** **Divide decimals.** Divide the decimal 21.93 by the whole number 3 by first writing the division problem as usual.

$$3\overline{)21.93}$$

Place the decimal point in the quotient directly above the decimal point in the dividend and perform the division.

Decimal point
moves straight up.

$$\begin{array}{r} 7.31 \\ 3\overline{)21.93} \end{array}$$

Check by multiplying the divisor and the quotient. The answer should equal the dividend.

$$\begin{array}{r} 7.31 \\ \times \quad 3 \\ \hline 21.93 \end{array} \leftarrow \text{matches dividend}$$

Sometimes it is necessary to place zeros after the decimal point in the dividend. Do this if a remainder of 0 is not obtained. Adding zeros *does not change* the value of the dividend. For example, divide 1.5 by 8 by dividing and placing zeros as needed.

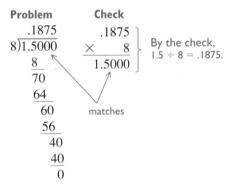

A remainder of 0 might not be obtained even though extra zeros are placed after the dividend. For example, when 4.7 is divided by 3, a remainder of 0 is never obtained. The digit 6 repeats indefinitely. In such a case, round to the nearest thousandth, although different problems might require rounding to a different number of decimal places. Rounding to the nearest thousandth gives 4.7 ÷ 3 = 1.567. Round to the nearest thousandth by carrying out the division to four places and then rounding to three places. Check by multiplying 1.567 by 3. The answer will be only approximately equal to the dividend, because of the rounding.

$$\begin{array}{r} 1.5666 \\ 3\overline{)4.7000} \\ \underline{3} \\ 1\,7 \\ \underline{1\,5} \\ 20 \\ \underline{18} \\ 20 \\ \underline{18} \\ 20 \\ \underline{18} \\ 2 \end{array}$$

> **NOTE** When rounding an answer, be certain to carry the answer one place further than the position to which you are rounding.

EXAMPLE 4

Dividing a Decimal by a Whole Number

Divide and check the following.

(a) $27.52 \div 32$ (b) $153.4 \div 8$

Solution

	Problem	Check		Problem	Check
	.86	.86		19.175	19.175
(a)	32)27.52	× 32	(b)	8)153.400	× 8
	25 6	172		8	153.400
	1 92	258		73	
	1 92	27.52		72	
	0			1 4	
				8	
				60	
				56	
				40	
				40	
				0	

Objective ③ Divide a decimal by a decimal. Divide by a decimal by first converting the divisor to a whole number. For example, to divide 27.69 by .3, convert .3 to a whole number by moving the decimal one place to the right. Then, move the decimal in the dividend, 27.69, one place to the right so the value of the problem does not change.

.3.)27.6.9

First, convert decimal to a whole number.

Then, move the decimal in the dividend the same number of places to keep the value of the problem.

After moving the decimal point, write the original problem as $276.9 \div 3$, and then divide as shown.

$$
\begin{array}{r}
92.3 \\
3)\overline{276.9} \\
27 \\
\hline
6 \\
6 \\
\hline
09 \\
9 \\
\hline
0
\end{array}
$$

> **NOTE** Sometimes it is necessary to place zeros after the dividend. As before, attach zeros and divide until the quotient has one more digit than the desired precision, and then round.

EXAMPLE 5

Dividing a Decimal by a Decimal

Divide and check the following.

(a) $17.6 \div .25$ (b) $5 \div .42$

Solution

	Check
70.4	70.4
(a) .25.)17.60.0	× .25
17 5	3520
10 0	1408
10 0	17.600

Zeros were placed after 17.6.

	Check
11.9047	11.905
(b) .42.)5.00.0000	× .42
4 2	23810
80	47620
42	5.00010
38 0	
37 8	
2 00	
1 68	
320	
294	
26	

(The check is off a little due to rounding.)

Rounding the answer to the nearest thousandth gives 11.905.

> **NOTE** When checking an answer that has been rounded, the check will be off a little.

Name _____   Date   Class

1.5 | EXERCISES

The Quick Start exercises in each section contain solutions to help you get started.

First estimate using front-end rounding and then multiply. (See Example 1.)

Quick Start

1. Estimate		Problem	2. Estimate		Problem	3. Estimate	Problem
50	←	48.7	20	←	16.6		34.1
× 4	←	× 3.8	× 4	←	× 4.2	×	× 6.8
200		185.06	80		69.72		

4. Estimate	Problem	5. Estimate	Problem	6. Estimate	Problem
	40.55		43.8		69.3
×	× 6.04	×	× 2.04	×	× 2.81

Multiply each of the following decimals.

Quick Start

7.	.532		8.	.259		9.	21.7
	× 3.6			× 6.2			× .431
	.532	← 3 decimals		.259	← 3 decimals		
	3.6	← 1 decimal		× 6.2	← 1 decimal		
	1.9152	← 4 decimals		1.6058	← 4 decimals		

10.	76.9	11.	.0408	12.	2481.9
	× .903		× .06		× .003

CALCULATING GROSS EARNINGS *Find the gross pay for each worker at the rates given below. Round to the nearest cent. (See Examples 2 and 3.)*

Quick Start

13. 28.6 hours at $7.25 per hour

   28.6 × $7.25 = $207.35

13. **$207.35** _____

14. 33.4 hours at $8.35 per hour

14. _____

15. 27.9 hours at $11.42 per hour, and 5.9 hours at $9.06 per hour

15. _____

16. 11.4 hours at $8.59 per hour, and 23.9 hours at $10.06 per hour

16. _____

Divide each of the following, and round your answer to nearest thousandth. (See Examples 4 and 5.)

17. $8\overline{)52.34}$

18. $4\overline{)20.84}$

19. $411.63 \div 15$

20. $2.43\overline{)9.6153}$

21. $.65\overline{)37.6852}$

22. $15.62 \div .28$

23. In your own words, write the rule for placing the decimal point in the answer of a decimal multiplication problem. (See Objective 1.)

24. Describe what must be done with the decimal point in a decimal division problem. Include the divisor, dividend, and quotient in your description. (See Objectives 2 and 3.)

Solve each of the following application problems.

Quick Start

25. VENDING-MACHINE COST The Generic Cold-Drink Vendor (Model CD-777G) is priced at $2299.99 at Price Costco. Find the cost of 14 of these machines.

   $14 \times \$2299.99 = \$32,199.86$

25. $\underline{\$32,199.86}$

26. MALL-SHOPPING FACTS A recent study showed that the average trip to the mall lasts 4.4 hours, which is longer than a football game. How many hours would be needed for 8 of these trips to the mall?

26. _____

27. STOCKHOLDER LOSSES British Imports announced a $38 million loss, or $.58 a share. Find the number of shares of stock in the company. Round to the nearest tenth of a million.

27. _____

28. Money Store officials said that they expect to post a loss of $42 million, or $.65 a share. Find the number of shares of stock in the company. Round to the nearest tenth of a million.

28. _____

29. OLYMPIC GOLD COINS If a five-dollar Olympic gold coin weighs 8.359 grams, find the number of coins that can be produced from 221 grams of gold. Round to the nearest whole number.

29. _____

30. MEDICINE DOSAGE Each dosage of a medication contains 1.62 units of a certain ingredient. Find the number of dosages that can be made from 57.13 units of the ingredient. Round to the nearest whole number.

30. _____

31. STAMP COLLECTORS The Elvis Presley stamp is the most popular commemorative stamp to be saved in collections. If 124 million of these 29¢ stamps were saved, find the amount paid for these stamps.

31. _____

32. There were 76.2 million commemorative wildflower stamps saved in collections making it the second most-popular stamp to the Elvis Presley stamp. Find the total amount paid for these 29¢ stamps.

32. _____

OLYMPIC LONG JUMPERS *Use the table of Olympic long-jump records to solve Exercises 36 and 37. To find an average, add up the values you are interested in and then divide the sum by the number of values. Round your answer to the nearest tenth.*

Country	Length
U.S.	8.50 meters
Jamaica	8.29 meters
U.S.	8.24 meters
France	8.19 meters
U.S.	8.17 meters
Slovenia	8.11 meters
Belarus	8.07 meters

33. Find the average length of the long jumps made by U.S. athletes.

36. _____

34. Find the average length of all the long jumps listed in the table.

37. _____

35. GERMAN MANAGEMENT EARNINGS A department manager at Karstadt, Germany's largest department store, earns $2365 each month for working a 37-hour week. Find **(a)** the number of hours worked each month and **(b)** the manager's hourly earnings. (1 month = 4.3 weeks) Round to the nearest cent.

(a) _____
(b) _____

36. WAL-MART MANAGER EARNINGS A department manager at Wal-Mart in the U.S. earns $2528 each month for working a 48-hour week. Find **(a)** the number of hours worked each month and **(b)** the manager's hourly earnings. (1 month = 4.3 weeks) Round to the nearest cent.

(a) _____
(b) _____

For related Web activities, go to www.mathbusiness.com

'Net Assets

Starbucks

STATISTICS

• 1971: First store opens in Seattle, Washington

• 1995: Starbucks Coffee Japan, Ltd.

• 1998: Named in 100 Best Companies to Work For by *Fortune* magazine

• 2000: Stores total 2000

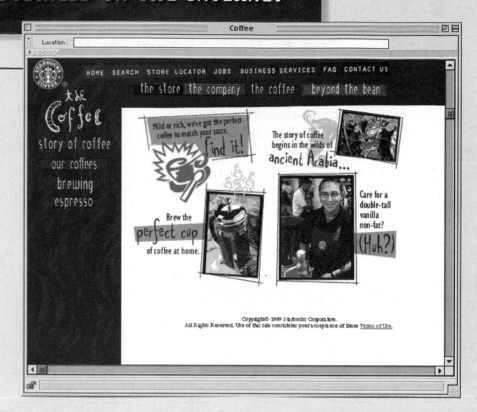

Starbucks purchases, roasts, and sells high-quality whole-bean coffee along with brewed coffees and a variety of pastries and confections and coffee-related accessories. With over 2000 stores by the year 2000, the company's retail goal is to become the leading retailer and brand of coffee in each of its target markets. To accomplish this they will continue to provide the finest-quality products and superior customer service. Through the company's continuing efforts to develop new products and find new markets, the company is becoming a truly global brand.

Of particular interest to Starbucks is its involvement in charitable and cultural organizations such as AIDS/HIV research and education, children's welfare and education, arts and culture, and environmental awareness and clean water.

1. If an employee removes 32.6 pounds of Guatemalan coffee beans from a bag weighing 50 pounds, find the number of pounds of beans remaining.

2. A coffee-measuring scoop will hold .0225 pounds of coffee beans. How many measuring scoops are contained in 1 pound of coffee beans. Round to the nearest whole number.

3. Based on your knowledge of the Starbucks Coffee Company, the products that they sell, and the company business philosophy, what kind of a statement do you think the company is trying to make about itself?

4. In addition to using decimals in measuring coffee, name six additional applications of decimals in a Starbucks store.

CHAPTER 1 | Quick Review

CHAPTER TERMS

Review the following terms to test your understanding of the chapter. For each term you do not know, refer to the page number found next to that term.

addends [**p. 3**]
addition [**p. 3**]
amount [**p. 3**]
borrowing [**p. 5**]
checking answers [**p. 3**]
comma [**p. 2**]
decimal [**p. 21**]
decimal part [**p. 7**]
decimal point [**p. 2**]

decimal system [**p. 2**]
difference [**p. 5**]
digits [**p. 2**]
dividend [**p. 6**]
dividing decimals [**p. 31**]
division [**p. 6**]
divisor [**p. 6**]
fraction part [**p. 7**]
front-end rounding [**p. 4**]

indicator words [**p. 15**]
minuend [**p. 5**]
multiplicand [**p. 5**]
multiplication [**p. 5**]
multiplier [**p. 5**]
multiplying decimals [**p. 29**]
operations [**p. 3**]
product [**p. 5**]
quotient [**p. 6**]

rounding [**p. 23**]
rounding decimals [**p. 21**]
subtraction [**p. 5**]
subtrahend [**p. 5**]
sum [**p. 3**]
total [**p. 3**]
whole numbers [**p. 2**]

CONCEPTS	EXAMPLES
1.1 Reading and writing whole numbers The word *and* is not used. Commas help divide thousands, millions, and billions. A comma is not needed with a four-digit number.	795 is written "seven hundred ninety-five." 9,768,002 is written "nine million, seven hundred sixty-eight thousand, two."
1.1 Rounding whole numbers Rules for rounding: 1. Identify position to be rounded. Draw a line under that place. 2. If digit to the right of the underlined place is 5 or more, increase by 1; if 4 or less, do not change. 3. Change all digits to the right of the underlined digit to zero.	Round: 72_6 to the nearest ten — 5 or more, so add 1 to tens position; tens position So, 726 rounds to 730 1_, 498,586 to the nearest million — 4 or less, do not change; millions position So, 1,498,586 rounds to 1,000,000
1.1 Front-end rounding Front-end rounding leaves only the first digit as a nonzero digit. All other digits are changed to zero.	Round each of the following using front-end rounding. 76 rounds to 80 348 rounds to 300 6512 rounds to 7000 23,751 rounds to 20,000 652,179 rounds to 700,000
1.1 Addition of whole numbers Add from top to bottom, starting with units and working left. To check, add from bottom to top.	1140 687 **Problem** (add down) 26 **Check** (add up) 9 + 418 1140
1.1 Subtraction of whole numbers Subtract subtrahend from minuend to get difference, borrowing when necessary. To check, add the difference to the subtrahend to get the minuend.	**Problem** **Check** 621 4738 4089 − 649 + 649 4089 4738

CONCEPTS	EXAMPLES

1.1 Multiplication of whole numbers

The multiplicand is multiplied by the multiplier, giving the product. When the multiplier has more than one digit, partial products must be used.

$$
\begin{array}{r}
78 \quad \text{multiplicand} \\
\times\ 24 \quad \text{multiplier} \\
\hline
312 \quad \text{partial product} \\
156 \quad \text{partial product (one position left)} \\
\hline
1872 \quad \text{product}
\end{array}
$$

1.1 Divison of whole numbers

÷ and $\overline{)}$ mean divide.

A — as in $\frac{25}{5}$ means divide 25 by 5.

Also, the / as in 25/5 means to divide 25 by 5.

Remainders are usually expressed as decimals.

Problem

$$
\begin{array}{r}
44 \quad \text{quotient} \\
\text{divisor}\ \ 2\overline{)88} \quad \text{dividend} \\
\underline{88} \\
0
\end{array}
$$

If answer is rounded, check will not be perfect.

1.2 Application problems

Follow the steps.

1. Read the problem carefully.
2. Work out a plan using *indicator words* before starting.
3. Estimate a reasonable answer.
4. Solve the problem. If the answer is reasonable, check; if not, start over.

Manuel earns $118 on Sunday, $87 on Monday, and $63 on Tuesday. Find his total earnings for the three days.

Total means to add.

$$
\begin{array}{r}
\$268 \quad \text{Check} \\
\overline{} \\
118 \\
\$87 \\
+\ \$63 \\
\hline
\$268 \quad \text{total earnings}
\end{array}
$$

1.3 Reading and rounding decimals

Decimal Place Values

Decimal point (and) · Tenths · Hundredths · Thousandths · Ten-thousandths · Hundred-thousandths · Millionths

. 0 7 3 2 6 5

1.3 is read "one and three tenths"

Round .073265 to the nearest ten-thousandth

.0732|65

ten-thousandth position

Since the digit to the right is 6, increase the ten-thousandths digit by 1 and drop all digits to the right. .073265 rounds to .0733.

1.4 Addition and subtraction of decimals

Decimal points must be in a column. Attach zeros to keep digits in their correct columns.

Add: 5.68 + 785.3 + .007 + 10.1062.

Line up decimal points

$$
\begin{array}{r}
5.6800 \leftarrow \\
785.3000 \leftarrow \text{Attach zeros.} \\
.0070 \leftarrow \\
+\ 10.1062 \\
\hline
801.0932
\end{array}
$$

1.5 Multiplication of decimals

Multiply as if decimals are whole numbers. Place decimal point as follows.

1. Count digits to the right of decimal points.
2. Count from right to left the same number of places as step 1. Zeros may be attached if necessary.

Multiply $.169 \times .21$

$$
\begin{array}{r}
.169 \quad \text{3 decimal places} \\
\times\ .21 \quad \text{2 decimal places} \\
\hline
169 \\
338 \\
\hline
.03549 \quad \text{5 decimal places in answer}
\end{array}
$$

Attach one zero.

CONCEPTS	EXAMPLES

1.5 Division of decimals

Divide 52.8 by .75

1. Move the decimal point in the divisor all the way to the right.

2. Move the decimal point the same number of places to the right in the dividend.

3. Place a decimal point in the answer position directly above the dividend decimal point.

4. Divide as with whole numbers.

```
                70.4            Check
        .75.)52.80.0            70.4
             52 5             ×  .75
             ────            ──────
                30            3520
                00            4928
             ────           ──────
                30 0        52.800
                30 0
             ────
                   0
```

CHAPTER 1 | SUMMARY EXERCISE
The Cost of Wedding Bells

Weddings can be very simple or very extravagant. Likewise, the cost of a wedding can be relatively low or extremely expensive. The following graph gives some of the costs involved in a wedding. Use this information to answer the questions that follow.

'Til Debt Do You Part

With 188 guests, the average wedding costs from $15,000 to $20,000. Most of the money is spent on the following:

Reception	$7000
Engagement ring	$3000
Photography	$1088
Flowers	$863
Wedding gown	$852

Source: Interep Radio Store

(a) What is the total of the costs shown in the graph?

(a) _____

(b) The total in **(a)** is how much less than the "average wedding cost," both the low and high average?

(b) _____

(c) If you decide to spend $7000 for your wedding reception, and the cost per guest is $32, how many guests can you invite? How much of your budgeted amount will be left over?

(c) _____

(d) If 150 guests are invited to the wedding and $7000 is budgeted for the reception, find the amount that can be spent per person. Round to the nearest cent.

(d) _____

(e) If you budget $4000 for the wedding reception and the cost per person is $27, how many guests can you invite and how much of your budgeted amount will be left over?

(e) _____

(f) If you budget $1000 for the wedding reception and the cost per person is $15, how many guests can you invite and how much of your budgeted amount will be left over?

(f) _____

(g) The bridal party will need five bouquets that cost $36.25 each and five boutonnieres each costing $7.50. If a total of $863 is budgeted for flowers, find the amount that remains to be spent for other floral arrangements.

(g)

Investigate

List six expenses associated with a wedding that are not included above. List six things that could be changed to bring the cost of the wedding down. What are some costs associated with a wedding where you live? You may have to ask some friends or relatives who have been recently involved in wedding planning.

Name   Date   Class

CHAPTER 1 | TEST

To help you review, the numbers in brackets show the section in which the topic was discussed.

Round as indicated. **[1.1]**

1. 847 to the nearest ten

2. 18,952 to the nearest hundred

3. 263,568 to the nearest thousand

1. _____850_____

2. _____19000_____

3. _____264000_____

Round each of the following using front-end rounding. **[1.1]**

4. 41,544

5. 650,996

6. One week April Wilson earned the following commissions: Monday, $124; Tuesday, $88; Wednesday, $62; Thursday, $137; Friday, $195. Find her total amount of commissions for the week. **[1.2]**

4. _____40,000_____

5. _____700,000_____

6. _____600_____

7. A rental business buys three airless sprayers at $1540 each, five rototillers at $695 each, and eight 25-foot ladders at $38 each. Find the total cost of the equipment purchased. **[1.2]**

7. _____8000_____

Round as indicated. **[1.3]**

8. $5.0384 to the nearest cent

9. $715.255 to the nearest cent

10. $3528.48 to the nearest dollar

8. _____5.04_____

9. _____715.26_____

10. _____3528_____

Solve each problem. **[1.4 AND 1.5]**

11. $9.6 + 8.42 + 3.715 + 159.8 =$ _____

12.
```
   2.715
  32.78
 426.3
+ 37
```

13.
```
  341.4
- 207.8
 133.6
```

14. $3.8 - .0053$ 3.8053

15.
```
 21.98
×  .72
```
15.8256

16.
```
 218.6
× .037
```
8.0882

17. $21.8\overline{)252.008}$ 11.56

18. $57.358 \div 2.41 =$ _____   **19.** $79.135 \div 18.62 =$ _____

20. Find the total cost of 32.6 gallons of solvent at $13.48 per gallon and 18.5 gallons of acid at $3.56 per gallon.   **[1.4 AND 1.5]**

20. _____

21. Roofing material costs $54.52 per square (10 ft × 10 ft). The roofer charges $35.75 per square for labor, plus $3.65 per square for supplies. Find the total cost for 26.3 squares of installed roof.   **[1.4 AND 1.5]**

21. _____

22. A Federal law requires that all residential toilets sold in the U.S. must use no more than 1.6 gallons of water per flush. Prior to this legislation, conventional toilets used 3.4 gallons of water per flush. Find the amount of water saved in one year by a family flushing the toilet 22 times each day. (1 year = 365 days)   **[1.4 AND 1.5]**

22. _____

23. Barry bought 16.5 meters of rope at $.48 per meter and three meters of wire at $1.05 per meter. How much change did he get from three $5 bills?   **[1.4 AND 1.5]**

23. _____ $3.93 _____

24. The earnings of Sierra West Bancorp last year were $1.4 million, or $.39 per share of stock. Find the number of shares of stock in the company. Round to the nearest tenth of a million.   **[1.5]**

24. _____

25. A concentrated fertilizer must be applied at the rate of .058 ounce per seedling. Find the number of seedlings that can be fertilized with 14.674 ounces of fertilizer.   **[1.5]**

25. _____

CHAPTER 2

FRACTIONS

Kate Morgan has been employed at The Home Depot for several years. During this time she has worked in the hardware and plumbing departments and is now in the cabinetry department. She has been in this department for a year and a half and enjoys helping contractors and homeowners plan and design new and replacement cabinets for their kitchens and bathrooms. Knowing and using fractions is a key part of Kate's job everyday as she helps determine the exact space available for new cabinets.

The previous chapter discussed whole numbers and decimals. This chapter looks at *fractions*—numbers, like decimals, that can be used to represent parts of a whole. Fractions and decimals are two ways of representing the same quantity. Fractions are used in business and our personal lives. For example, the following newspaper clipping gives the size of the sleeping compartments for women on the U.S. Navy's *USS Sullivans*.

Reality Check

Destroyer Fits Women, Too

ABOARD THE *USS SULLIVANS*—The *Sullivans* is equipped with the Navy's most advanced missiles and submarine-spotting sonar. But it wasn't only designed to have the latest in high-tech military equipment. It also was built with the idea that women would be among its crew. So what is it like for women on board?

Sleeping areas for enlisted personnel have doors. Visitors of the opposite gender must announce "Man on deck" or "Woman on deck" before entering.

Each of two berthing compartments for women holds 18 bunks, or racks, stacked three high. Each rack has a blue privacy curtain and is $26\frac{1}{2}$ inches wide by $6\frac{1}{2}$ feet long. There is $17\frac{3}{4}$ inches of space between the 3-inch-thick mattress and the bottom of the rack above.

Male racks are identical, except many are in much larger berthing areas. The largest of the male compartments holds 105 racks, another holds 70, a third 40. The other two compartments for men hold 24 and 18 racks.

Source: USA Today, 1/12/98. Reprinted by permission

43

2.1 | BASICS OF FRACTIONS

Objectives

1. Recognize types of fractions.
2. Convert mixed numbers to improper fractions.
3. Convert improper fractions to mixed numbers.
4. Write a fraction in lowest terms.
5. Use the rules for divisibility.

$\frac{2}{3}$ means 2 parts
out of 3 equal parts

A **fraction** represents part of a whole. Fractions are written in the form of one number over another, with a line between the two numbers, as in the following.

$$\frac{5}{8} \quad \frac{1}{4} \quad \frac{9}{7} \quad \frac{13}{10}$$

The number above the line is the **numerator**, and the number below the line is the **denominator**. In the fraction $\frac{2}{3}$, the numerator is 2 and the denominator is 3. The denominator is the number of equal parts into which something is divided. The numerator tells how many of these parts are needed. For example, $\frac{2}{3}$ is "2 parts out of 3 equal parts," as shown in the figure to the left.

Objective 1 **Recognize types of fractions.** If the numerator of a fraction is smaller than the denominator, the fraction is a **proper fraction**. Examples of proper fractions are $\frac{2}{3}$, $\frac{3}{4}$, $\frac{15}{16}$, and $\frac{1}{8}$. A fraction with a numerator greater than or equal to the denominator is an **improper fraction**. Examples of improper fractions are $\frac{17}{13}$, $\frac{19}{12}$, and $\frac{5}{5}$. A proper fraction has a value less than 1, while an improper fraction has a value greater than or equal to 1.

To write a whole number as a fraction, place the whole number over 1; for example, $7 = \frac{7}{1}$ and $12 = \frac{12}{1}$. The sum of a fraction and a whole number is a **mixed number**. Examples of mixed numbers include $5\frac{2}{3}$ (a short way of writing $5 + \frac{2}{3}$), $3\frac{5}{8}$, and $9\frac{5}{6}$. A mixed number can be converted to an improper fraction as follows.

Objective 2 **Convert mixed numbers to improper fractions.** To convert the mixed number $4\frac{5}{8}$ to an improper fraction, first multiply the denominator of the fraction part (in this case, 8) and the whole number part (in this case, 4). This gives $4 \times 8 = 32$. Then add the product (32) to the numerator (in this case, 5). This gives $32 + 5 = 37$. This sum is the numerator of the new improper fraction. The denominator stays the same.

$$4\frac{5}{8} = \frac{37}{8} \overset{\longleftarrow}{} (4 \times 8) + 5$$

Notice in the newspaper clipping below that The Home Depot stock jumped $1\frac{5}{8}$ to $68\frac{1}{2}$. These are both mixed numbers. The Home Base stock was up $\frac{3}{8}$, which is a proper fraction.

Reality Check

Market View

Daily Stock Report—Shares of The Home Depot jumped $1\frac{5}{8}$ to close at $68\frac{1}{2}$. The home-improvement center reported increased quarterly earnings. Shares of Home Base, on a report of increased earnings, were up $\frac{3}{8}$ to close at $8\frac{3}{16}$.

Source: *USA Today,* 3/98. Reprinted by permission.

EXAMPLE 1

Converting Mixed
Numbers to
Improper Fractions

The increase in value and the closing price of The Home Depot stock are both expressed as mixed numbers. Convert these mixed numbers to improper fractions.

(a) $1\frac{5}{8}$ **(b)** $68\frac{1}{2}$

Solution

(a) First multiply 8 (the denominator) and 1 (the whole number), and then add 5 (the numerator). This gives $(8 \times 1) + 5 = 8 + 5 = 13$. (The parentheses are used to show that 8 and 1 are multiplied first.)

$$1\frac{5}{8} = \frac{13}{8} \leftarrow (8 \times 1) + 5$$

(b) $68\frac{1}{2} = \frac{(2 \times 68) + 1}{2} = \frac{137}{2}$

OBJECTIVE **3** **Convert improper fractions to mixed numbers.** To convert an improper fraction to a mixed number, divide the numerator of the improper fraction by the denominator. The quotient is the whole-number part of the mixed number and the remainder is used as the numerator of the fraction part. The denominator stays the same. For example, convert $\frac{17}{5}$ to a mixed number by dividing 17 by 5.

$$\begin{array}{r} 3 \\ 5\overline{)17} \\ \underline{15} \\ 2 \end{array}$$

The whole-number part is the quotient 3. The remainder 2 is used as the numerator of the fraction part. Keep 5 as the denominator.

$$\frac{17}{5} = 3\frac{2}{5}$$

EXAMPLE 2

Converting
Improper Fractions
to Mixed Numbers

Convert the following improper fractions to mixed numbers.

(a) $\frac{27}{4}$ **(b)** $\frac{29}{8}$ **(c)** $\frac{71}{9}$ **(d)** $\frac{42}{7}$

Solution

(a) Convert $\frac{27}{4}$ to a mixed number by dividing 27 by 4.

$$\begin{array}{r} 6 \\ 4\overline{)27} \\ \underline{24} \\ 3 \end{array}$$

The whole-number part of the mixed number is 6. The remainder 3 is used as the numerator of the fraction. Keep 4 as the denominator.

$$\frac{27}{4} = 6\frac{3}{4}$$

(b) Divide 29 by 8 to convert $\frac{29}{8}$ to a mixed number.

$$\begin{array}{r} 3 \\ 8\overline{)29} \\ \underline{24} \\ 5 \end{array} \qquad \frac{29}{8} = 3\frac{5}{8}$$

(c) Divide 71 by 9.

$$\begin{array}{r} 7 \\ 9\overline{)71} \\ \underline{63} \\ 8 \end{array} \qquad \frac{71}{9} = 7\frac{8}{9}$$

(d) Divide 42 by 7.

$$7)\overline{42} \qquad \frac{42}{7} = 6$$
$$\underline{42}$$
$$0$$

> **NOTE**   A proper fraction has a value that is smaller than 1, while an improper fraction has a value that is 1, or greater.

Objective 4️⃣ **Write a fraction in lowest terms.**   If both the numerator and denominator of a fraction cannot be divided without remainder by any number other than 1, then the fraction is in **lowest terms**. For example, 2 and 3 cannot be divided without remainder by any number other than 1, so the fraction $\frac{2}{3}$ is in lowest terms. In the same way, $\frac{1}{9}, \frac{4}{11}, \frac{12}{17},$ and $\frac{13}{15}$ are in lowest terms.

When both numerator and denominator *can* be divided without remainder by a number other than 1, the fraction is *not* in lowest terms. For example, both 15 and 25 may be divided by 5, so the fraction $\frac{15}{25}$ is not in lowest terms. Write $\frac{15}{25}$ in lowest terms by dividing both numerator and denominator by 5, as follows.

$$\frac{15}{25} = \frac{15 \div 5}{25 \div 5} = \frac{3}{5}$$

Divide by 5.

EXAMPLE 3

Writing Fractions in Lowest Terms

Write the following fractions in lowest terms.

(a) $\frac{15}{40}$ **(b)** $\frac{33}{39}$

Solution

Look for a number that can be divided into both the numerator and denominator.

(a) Both 15 and 40 can be divided by 5.

$$\frac{15}{40} = \frac{15 \div 5}{40 \div 5} = \frac{3}{8}$$

(b) Divide by 3.

$$\frac{33}{39} = \frac{33 \div 3}{39 \div 3} = \frac{11}{13}$$

Objective 5️⃣ **Use the rules for divisibility.**   It is sometimes difficult to tell which numbers will divide evenly into another number. The following rules can sometimes help.

Rules for Divisibility

A number can be divided by:

2   if the last digit is 0, 2, 4, 6, or 8
3   if the sum of the digits is divisible by 3
4   if the last two digits are divisible by 4
5   if the last digit is 0 or 5
6   if the number is even and the sum of the digits is divisible by 3
8   if the last three digits are divisible by 8
9   if the sum of all the digits is divisible by 9
10 if the last digit is 0

Example 4

Using the
Divisibility Rules

Determine whether the following statements are true.

(a) 3,746,892 is divisible by 4.
(b) 15,974,802 is divisible by 9.

Solution

(a) The number 3,746,892 is divisible by 4, since the last two digits form a number divisible by 4.

$$3, 746, 8\underline{92}$$

—— 92 is divisible by 4.

(b) See if 15,974,802 is divisible by 9 by adding the digits of the number.

$$1 + 5 + 9 + 7 + 4 + 8 + 0 + 2 = \underbrace{36}$$

—— 36 is divisible by 9.

Since 36 is divisible by 9, the given number is divisible by 9.

PROBLEM-SOLVING HINT   Testing for divisibility by adding the digits works only for 3 and 9.

2.2 | Addition and Subtraction of Fractions

Objectives

 1 Add and subtract like fractions.
2 Find the least common denominator.
3 Add and subtract unlike fractions.
4 Rewrite fractions with a common denominator.

Problem Solving in Business

Kate Morgan must use fractions on a daily basis as she works with contractors and homeowners at The Home Depot. The measurements of cabinets, trim pieces, and room sizes never seem to come out even—they always have fractions of an inch.

Objective **1** **Add and subtract like fractions.** Fractions with the same denominator are called **like fractions**. Such fractions have a **common denominator**. For example, $\frac{3}{4}$ and $\frac{5}{4}$ are *like* fractions with a common denominator of 4, while $\frac{4}{7}$ and $\frac{4}{9}$ are not *like* fractions. Add or subtract like fractions by adding or subtracting the numerators, and then place the result over the common denominator.

Example 1

Adding and Subtracting Like Fractions

Add or subtract.

(a) $\frac{3}{4} + \frac{1}{4} + \frac{5}{4}$ (b) $\frac{13}{25} - \frac{7}{25}$

Solution

The fractions in both parts of this example are like fractions. Add or subtract the numerators and place the result over the common denominator.

(a) $\frac{3}{4} + \frac{1}{4} + \frac{5}{4} = \frac{3 + 1 + 5}{4}$ ⟵ Add the numerators.
   ⟵ Write the common denominator.

$= \frac{9}{4} = 2\frac{1}{4}$ ⟵ Write the answer as a mixed number.

(b) $\frac{13}{25} - \frac{7}{25} = \frac{13 - 7}{25} = \frac{6}{25}$

For related Web activities, go to www.mathbusiness.com

Keyword: do-it-yourself

Objective **2** **Find the least common denominator.** Fractions with different denominators, such as $\frac{3}{4}$ and $\frac{2}{3}$, are **unlike fractions**. Add or subtract unlike fractions by first writing the fractions with a common denominator. The **least common denominator (LCD)** for two or more fractions is the smallest whole number that can be divided, without remainder, by all the denominators of the fractions. For example, the least common denominator of the fractions $\frac{3}{4}$, $\frac{5}{6}$, and $\frac{1}{2}$ is 12, since 12 is the smallest number that can be divided by 4, 6, and 2.

Notice that in the cabinet specifications from American Landmark Cabinetry, the fractions shown in the following shelf-end base drawing are *like fractions* $23\frac{3}{16}$, $10\frac{9}{16}$, and $11\frac{3}{16}$. However, in the drawing of the shelf-end peninsula base, the fractions are unlike fractions, $22\frac{7}{16}$, $11\frac{3}{32}$, and $11\frac{5}{8}$.

Shelf-End Base: Cross Section

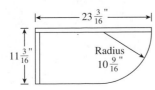

Shelf-End Peninsula Base: Cross Section

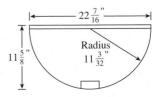

There are two methods of finding the least common denominator.

Inspection. With small denominators, it may be possible to find the least common denominator by inspection. For example, the least common denominator for $\frac{1}{3}$ and $\frac{1}{5}$ is 15, the smallest number that can be divided by both 3 and 5.

Method of prime numbers. If the least common denominator cannot be found by inspection, use the method of prime numbers, as explained in the next example.

> A **prime number** is a number that can be divided without remainder only by itself and by 1. Prime numbers are 2, 3, 5, 7, 11, 13, 17, and so on.

> **NOTE** All prime numbers other than 2 are odd numbers. All odd numbers, however, are not prime numbers. For example, 27 is the product of 3 and 9.

EXAMPLE 2

Finding the Least Common Denominator

Use the method of prime numbers to find the least common denominator for $\frac{5}{12}$, $\frac{7}{18}$, and $\frac{11}{20}$.

Solution

First write the three denominators: 12   18   20

Begin by trying to divide the three denominators by the first prime number, 2. Write each quotient directly above the given denominator. (This way of writing the division is just a handy way of writing the separate problems $2\overline{)12}$, $2\overline{)18}$, and $2\overline{)20}$.)

$$\begin{array}{r} 6\quad 9\ 10 \\ \hline 2)\overline{12\ 18\ 20} \end{array}$$

Two of the new quotients, 6 and 10, can still be divided by 2, so perform the division again. Since 9 cannot be divided evenly by 2, just bring up the 9.

$$\begin{array}{r} 3\quad 9\quad 5 \qquad \text{Just bring 9 up.}\\ \hline 2)\ 6\quad 9\ 10 \\ \hline 2)\overline{12\ 18\ 20} \end{array}$$

None of the new quotients in the top row can be divided by 2, so try the next prime number, 3. The numbers 3 and 9 can be divided by 3, and one of the new quotients can still be divided by 3, so the division is performed again.

$$\begin{array}{r} 1\quad 1\quad 5 \\ \hline 3)\ 1\quad 3\quad 5 \\ \hline 3)\ 3\quad 9\quad 5 \\ \hline 2)\ 6\quad 9\ 10 \\ \hline 2)\overline{12\ 18\ 20} \end{array}$$

Since none of the new quotients in the top row can be divided by 3, try the next prime number, 5. The number 5 can be used only once, as shown.

$$\begin{array}{r} 1\quad 1\quad 1 \\ \hline 5)\ 1\quad 1\quad 5 \\ \hline 3)\ 1\quad 3\quad 5 \\ \hline 3)\ 3\quad 9\ 10 \\ \hline 2)\ 6\quad 9\ 10 \\ \hline 2)\overline{12\ 18\ 20} \end{array}$$

Now that the top row contains only 1's, find the least common denominator by multiplying the prime numbers in the left column.

The least common denominator is $2 \times 2 \times 3 \times 3 \times 5 = 180$.

> **NOTE**   It is not necessary to start with the smallest prime number as shown in Example 2. In fact, no matter which prime number we start with, we will still get the same least common denominator.

EXAMPLE 3

Finding the Least Common Denominator

Find the least common denominator for $\frac{3}{8}$, $\frac{5}{12}$, and $\frac{9}{10}$.

Solution

Write the denominators in a row and use the method of prime numbers.

$$
\begin{array}{r}
1\;\;1\;\;\;1 \\
5)\overline{1\;\;\;1\;\;\;5} \\
3)\overline{1\;\;\;3\;\;\;5} \\
2)\overline{2\;\;\;3\;\;\;5} \\
2)\overline{4\;\;\;6\;\;\;5} \\
\text{Start here} \rightarrow \quad 2)\overline{8\;\;12\;\;10}
\end{array}
$$

The least common denominator is $2 \times 2 \times 2 \times 3 \times 5 = 120$.

> **PROBLEM-SOLVING HINT**   Sometimes it is tempting to use a number that is not prime when solving for the least common denominator. This should be avoided because the result is often something different from the least common denominator.

Unlike fractions may be added or subtracted using the following steps.

Adding or Subtracting Unlike Fractions

Step 1   Find the least common denominator.

Step 2   Rewrite the unlike fractions as like fractions having the least common denominator.

Step 3   Add or subtract numerators, placing answers over the least common denominator and reducing to lowest terms.

Objective **3**   **Add and subtract unlike fractions.**   To add or subtract unlike fractions, rewrite the fractions with a common denominator. Since Example 2 shows that 180 is the least common denominator for $\frac{5}{12}$, $\frac{7}{18}$, and $\frac{11}{20}$, these three fractions can be added if each fraction is first written with a denominator of 180.

Step 1
$$\frac{5}{12} = \frac{}{180} \qquad \frac{7}{18} = \frac{}{180} \qquad \frac{11}{20} = \frac{}{180}$$

Objective **4**   **Rewrite fractions with a common denominator.**   To rewrite the preceding fractions with a common denominator, first divide each denominator from the original fractions into the common denominator.

$$
12)\overline{180}^{\;15} \qquad 18)\overline{180}^{\;10} \qquad 20)\overline{180}^{\;9}
$$

Next multiply each quotient by the original numerator.

$$15 \times 5 = 75 \qquad 10 \times 7 = 70 \qquad 9 \times 11 = 99$$

Finally:

Step 2

$$\frac{5}{12} = \frac{75}{180} \qquad \frac{7}{18} = \frac{70}{180} \qquad \frac{11}{20} = \frac{99}{180}$$

Now add the fractions.

Step 3

$$\frac{5}{12} + \frac{7}{18} + \frac{11}{20} = \frac{75}{180} + \frac{70}{180} + \frac{99}{180} = \frac{75 + 70 + 99}{180}$$

$$= \frac{244}{180} = 1\frac{64}{180} = 1\frac{16}{45}$$

EXAMPLE 4

Adding and Subtracting Unlike Fractions

Add or subtract.

(a) $\frac{3}{4} + \frac{1}{2} + \frac{5}{8}$ **(b)** $\frac{9}{10} - \frac{3}{8}$

SOLUTION

(a) Inspection shows that the least common denominator is 8. Rewrite the fractions so they each have a denominator of 8. Then add.

$$\frac{3}{4} + \frac{1}{2} + \frac{5}{8} = \frac{6}{8} + \frac{4}{8} + \frac{5}{8} = \frac{6 + 4 + 5}{8} = \frac{15}{8} = 1\frac{7}{8}$$

(b) The least common denominator is 40. Rewrite the fractions so they each have a denominator of 40. Then subtract.

$$\frac{9}{10} - \frac{3}{8} = \frac{36}{40} - \frac{15}{40} = \frac{36 - 15}{40} = \frac{21}{40}$$

Fractions can also be added or subtracted vertically, as in the next example.

EXAMPLE 5

Adding and Subtracting Unlike Fractions

Add or subtract.

(a) $\frac{2}{9} + \frac{3}{4}$ **(b)** $\frac{11}{16} + \frac{7}{12}$ **(c)** $\frac{7}{8} - \frac{5}{12}$

SOLUTION

First rewrite the fractions with a least common denominator.

(a)

$$\begin{aligned} \frac{2}{9} &= \frac{8}{36} \\ + \frac{3}{4} &= \frac{27}{36} \\ \hline &\frac{35}{36} \end{aligned}$$

(b)

$$\begin{aligned} \frac{11}{16} &= \frac{33}{48} \\ + \frac{7}{12} &= \frac{28}{48} \\ \hline &\frac{61}{48} = 1\frac{13}{48} \end{aligned}$$

(c)

$$\begin{aligned} \frac{7}{8} &= \frac{21}{24} \\ - \frac{5}{12} &= \frac{10}{24} \\ \hline &\frac{11}{24} \end{aligned}$$

All calculator solutions are shown using a scientific calculator. The calculator solution to Example 5(b) uses the fraction key on the scientific calculator.

11 [a%] 16 [+] 7 [a%] 12 [=] $1\frac{13}{48}$

Note: All calculator solutions use a scientific calculator. Refer to Appendix B for scientific calculator basics.

2.3 | Addition and Subtraction of Mixed Numbers

Objectives

1. Add mixed numbers.
2. Add with carrying.
3. Subtract mixed numbers.
4. Subtract with borrowing.

<table>
<tr><td>

Problem Solving in Business

</td><td>

Total customer satisfaction is important to Kate Morgan and The Home Depot. Complete accuracy is just as important in the small jobs in hardware and trim as it is in the large jobs in cabinets and installation. To achieve this accuracy, Morgan knows that mixed numbers must be added and subtracted carefully and that all calculations must then be checked to make sure they are correct.

</td></tr>
</table>

Objective 1 **Add mixed numbers.** To add mixed numbers, first add the fractions. Then add the whole numbers and combine the two answers. For example, add $16\frac{1}{8}$ and $5\frac{5}{8}$ as shown.

$$\overbrace{+=}^{\text{sum of fractions}}$$
$$16\frac{1}{8} + 5\frac{5}{8} = 21\frac{6}{8}$$
$$\underbrace{+=}_{\text{sum of whole numbers}}$$

Write $\frac{6}{8}$ in lowest terms as $\frac{3}{4}$, so that $16\frac{1}{8} + 5\frac{5}{8} = 21\frac{3}{4}$.

Example 1

Adding Mixed Numbers

Add $9\frac{2}{3}$ and $6\frac{1}{4}$.

Solution

Inspection shows that 12 is the least common denominator. Write $9\frac{2}{3}$ as $9\frac{8}{12}$, and $6\frac{1}{4}$ as $6\frac{3}{12}$. Then add. The work can be organized as shown here.

$$9\frac{2}{3} = 9\frac{8}{12}$$
$$+ 6\frac{1}{4} = 6\frac{3}{12}$$
$$\overline{\qquad\quad 15\frac{11}{12}}$$

Objective 2 **Add with carrying.** If the sum of the fraction parts of mixed numbers is greater than 1, carry the excess from the fraction part to the whole number part.

Example 2

Adding with Carrying

A rubber gasket must extend around all four edges (perimeter) of the dishwasher door panel shown below before it is installed. Find the length of gasket material needed. Add $34\frac{1}{2}$ inches and $23\frac{3}{4}$ inches and $34\frac{1}{2}$ inches and $23\frac{3}{4}$ inches.

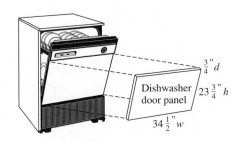

Dishwasher door panel $23\frac{3}{4}$" h

$\frac{3}{4}$" d

$34\frac{1}{2}$" w

Solution

$$34\frac{1}{2} = 34\frac{2}{4}$$

$$23\frac{3}{4} = 23\frac{3}{4}$$

$$34\frac{1}{2} = 34\frac{2}{4}$$

$$+\ 23\frac{3}{4} = 23\frac{3}{4}$$

$$\frac{10}{4} = 2\frac{2}{4}$$

$$114\frac{10}{4} = 114 + \frac{10}{4} = 114 + 2\frac{2}{4} = 116\frac{2}{4} = 116\frac{1}{2}\ \text{inches}$$

> **NOTE** When adding mixed numbers, first add the fraction parts, then add the whole number parts. Then combine the two answers.

Objective 3 Subtract mixed numbers. To subtract two mixed numbers, change the mixed numbers, if necessary, so that the fraction parts have a common denominator. Then subtract the fraction parts and the whole number parts separately. For example, subtract $3\frac{1}{12}$ from $8\frac{5}{8}$ by first finding that the least common denominator is 24. Then rewrite the problem as shown.

$$8\frac{5}{8} - 3\frac{1}{12}$$

↑ use ↑
24
as a common
denominator

$$8\frac{15}{24} - 3\frac{2}{24}$$

Now subtract the
fraction parts
and subtract the
whole-number parts.

$$8\frac{15}{24}$$
$$-\ 3\frac{2}{24}$$
$$5\frac{13}{24}$$

Subtract fractions.
Subtract whole numbers.

Objective 4 Subtract with borrowing. The following example shows how to subtract when borrowing is needed.

EXAMPLE 3

Subtracting with Borrowing

(a) Subtract $6\frac{3}{4}$ from $10\frac{1}{8}$.   **(b)** Subtract $15\frac{7}{12}$ from 41.

Solution

Start by rewriting each problem with a common denominator.

(a)

$$10\frac{1}{8} = 10\frac{1}{8}$$
$$-\ 6\frac{3}{4} = \ 6\frac{6}{8}$$

Subtracting $\frac{6}{8}$ from $\frac{1}{8}$ requires borrowing from the whole number 10.

$$10\frac{1}{8} = 9 + 1 + \frac{1}{8}$$
$$= 9 + \frac{8}{8} + \frac{1}{8} = 9\frac{9}{8}\quad 1 = \frac{8}{8}$$

Rewrite the problem as shown.
Check by adding $3\frac{3}{8}$ and $6\frac{3}{4}$.
The answer should be $10\frac{1}{8}$.

$$10\frac{1}{8} = 9\frac{9}{8}$$
$$-\ 6\frac{6}{8} = 6\frac{6}{8}$$
$$3\frac{3}{8}$$

(b)

$$41$$
$$-\ 15\frac{7}{12}$$

To subtract the fraction $\frac{7}{12}$ requires borrowing from 41.

$$41 = 40 + 1 = 40 + \frac{12}{12} = 40\frac{12}{12}\quad 1 = \frac{12}{12}$$

Rewrite the problem as shown.
Check by adding $25\frac{5}{12}$ and $15\frac{7}{12}$.
The answer should be 41.

$$41 = 40\frac{12}{12}$$
$$-\ 15\frac{7}{12} = 15\frac{7}{12}$$
$$25\frac{5}{12}$$

The calculator solution to Example 3(a) uses the fraction key.

$$10\ \boxed{\text{a\%}}\ 1\ \boxed{\text{a\%}}\ 8\ \boxed{-}\ 6\ \boxed{\text{a\%}}\ 3\ \boxed{\text{a\%}}\ 4\ \boxed{=}\ 3\frac{3}{8}$$

Note: All calculator solutions use a scientific calculator. Refer to Appendix B for scientific calculator basics.

2.4 | Multiplication and Division of Fractions

Objectives

1. Multiply proper fractions.
2. Use cancellation.
3. Multiply mixed numbers.
4. Divide fractions.
5. Divide mixed numbers.
6. Multiply or divide by whole numbers.

PROBLEM SOLVING IN BUSINESS

Most of the cabinets sold by The Home Depot are standard size units and modules that can be combined to satisfy varied applications and room sizes. However, all too often, Kate Morgan finds that various components and trim pieces must be custom sized. In order to do this, she must multiply and divide fractions.

Objective 1 Multiply proper fractions. To multiply two fractions, first multiply the numerators to form a new numerator and then multiply the denominators to form a new denominator. Write the answer in lowest terms if necessary. For example, multiply $\frac{2}{3}$ and $\frac{5}{8}$ by first multiplying the numerators and then the denominators. This gives:

$$\frac{2}{3} \times \frac{5}{8} = \frac{\overbrace{2 \times 5}}{\underbrace{3 \times 8}} = \frac{10}{24} = \frac{5}{12} \quad \text{(in lowest terms)}$$

Multiply numerators.
Multiply denominators.

Objective 2 Use cancellation. This problem can be simplified by **cancellation**, a modification of the method of writing fractions in lowest terms. For example, find the product of $\frac{2}{3}$ and $\frac{5}{8}$ by cancelling as follows.

$$\frac{\overset{1}{\cancel{2}}}{3} \times \frac{5}{\underset{4}{\cancel{8}}} = \frac{1 \times 5}{3 \times 4} = \frac{5}{12}$$

Divide 2 into both 2 and 8.

EXAMPLE 1

Multiplying Common Fractions

Multiply.

(a) $\frac{6}{11} \times \frac{7}{8}$ (b) $\frac{35}{12} \times \frac{32}{25}$

Solution

Use cancellation in both of these problems.

(a) $\frac{\overset{3}{\cancel{6}}}{11} \times \frac{7}{\underset{4}{\cancel{8}}} = \frac{3 \times 7}{11 \times 4} = \frac{21}{44}$

2 was divided into both 6 and 8.

(b) $\frac{\overset{7}{\cancel{35}}}{\underset{3}{\cancel{12}}} \times \frac{\overset{8}{\cancel{32}}}{\underset{5}{\cancel{25}}} = \frac{7 \times 8}{3 \times 5} = \frac{56}{15} = 3\frac{11}{15}$

4 was divided into both 12 and 32, while 5 was divided into both 35 and 25.

NOTE When cancelling, be certain that a numerator and a denominator are both divided by the same number.

OBJECTIVE **3 Multiply mixed numbers.** To multiply mixed numbers, change the mixed numbers to improper fractions and then multiply them. For example, multiply $6\frac{1}{4}$ and $2\frac{2}{3}$ as follows.

$$6\frac{1}{4} \times 2\frac{2}{3} = \underbrace{\frac{25}{4} \times \frac{8}{3}}_{} = \frac{25}{\cancel{4}} \times \frac{\overset{2}{\cancel{8}}}{3} = \frac{25 \times 2}{1 \times 3} = \frac{50}{3} = 16\frac{2}{3}$$

↑ Change to improper fractions.

EXAMPLE 2

Multiplying Mixed Numbers

Multiply.

(a) $5\frac{5}{8} \times 4\frac{1}{6}$ (b) $1\frac{3}{5} \times 3\frac{1}{3} \times 1\frac{3}{4}$

Solution

(a) $\dfrac{\overset{15}{\cancel{45}}}{8} \times \dfrac{25}{\underset{2}{\cancel{6}}} = \dfrac{15 \times 25}{8 \times 2} = \dfrac{375}{16} = 23\frac{7}{16}$

(b) $\dfrac{\overset{2}{\cancel{8}}}{\underset{1}{\cancel{5}}} \times \dfrac{\overset{2}{\cancel{10}}}{3} \times \dfrac{7}{\underset{1}{\cancel{4}}} = \dfrac{2 \times 2 \times 7}{1 \times 3 \times 1} = \dfrac{28}{3} = 9\frac{1}{3}$

The calculator solution to Example 2(b) uses the fraction key.

1 $\boxed{\text{a\%}}$ 3 $\boxed{\text{a\%}}$ 5 $\boxed{\times}$ 3 $\boxed{\text{a\%}}$ 1 $\boxed{\text{a\%}}$ 3 $\boxed{\times}$ 1 $\boxed{\text{a\%}}$ 3 $\boxed{\text{a\%}}$ 4 $\boxed{=}$ $9\frac{1}{3}$

Note: All calculator solutions use a scientific calculator. Refer to Appendix B for scientific calculator basics.

The following recipe is easy to follow using the proper measuring cups and spoons. Sometimes you may want to double or triple a recipe or perhaps, cooking for a small group, you need to cut the recipe in half. To double the recipe, multiply each ingredient by 2; to triple the recipe, multiply by 3; and to halve the recipe you'll need to divide by 2.

For related Web activities, go to www.mathbusiness.com

Keyword: recipe

Quaker Choc Oat-Chip Cookies

1 cup (2 sticks) margarine or butter, softened
1 $\frac{1}{4}$ cups firmly packed brown sugar
$\frac{1}{2}$ cup granulated sugar
2 eggs
2 tablespoons milk
2 teaspoons vanilla
1 $\frac{3}{4}$ cups all-purpose flour
1 teaspoon baking soda

$\frac{1}{2}$ teaspoon salt (optional)
2 $\frac{1}{2}$ cups Quaker® Oats
     (quick or old fashioned, uncooked)
One 12-ounce package (2 cups)
     Nestlé® Toll House® semi-sweet
     chocolate morsels
1 cup coarsely chopped nuts
     (optional)

Heat oven to 375°F. **Beat** margarine and sugars until creamy.
Add eggs, milk and vanilla; beat well.
Add combined flour, baking soda and salt; mix well. **Stir** in oats, chocolate morsels and nuts; mix well.
Drop by rounded measuring tablespoonfuls onto ungreased cookie sheet.
Bake 9 to 10 minutes for a chewy cookie or 12 to 13 minutes for a crisp cookie.
Cool 1 minute on cookie sheet; remove to wire rack. Cool completely. **ABOUT 5 DOZEN**

Reprinted by permission of the Quaker Oats Company.

EXAMPLE 3

Multiplying Mixed Numbers by a Whole Number

(a) Find the amount of Quaker Oats needed if the preceding recipe for Quaker Choc Oat-Chip Cookies is doubled (multiply by 2).

(b) How many cups of all-purpose flour are needed when the recipe is tripled (multiply by 3)?

Solution

(a) $2\dfrac{1}{2} \times 2 = \dfrac{5}{\overset{}{\underset{1}{\cancel{2}}}} \times \dfrac{\overset{1}{\cancel{2}}}{1} = \dfrac{5 \times 1}{1 \times 1} = \dfrac{5}{1} = 5$ cups

(b) $1\dfrac{3}{4} \times 3 = \dfrac{7}{4} \times \dfrac{3}{1} = \dfrac{7 \times 3}{4} = \dfrac{21}{4} = 5\dfrac{1}{4}$ cups

Objective $\boxed{4}$ **Divide fractions.** To divide two fractions, invert the second fraction and then multiply the first fraction by the inverted second fraction. (Invert a fraction by exchanging the numerator and the denominator.)

For example, divide $\frac{3}{8}$ by $\frac{7}{12}$ by inverting the second fraction and then multiplying by $\frac{12}{7}$, the inverted form.

$$\frac{3}{8} \div \frac{7}{12} = \frac{3}{8} \times \frac{12}{7} = \frac{3}{\cancel{8}} \times \frac{\overset{3}{\cancel{12}}}{7} = \frac{3 \times 3}{2 \times 7} = \frac{9}{14}$$

— invert second fraction
— multiply

> **NOTE** The second fraction (divisor) is inverted when dividing by a fraction. Cancellation is done *only after inverting*.

EXAMPLE 4

Dividing Common Fractions

Divide.

(a) $\dfrac{25}{36} \div \dfrac{15}{18}$ **(b)** $\dfrac{21}{8} \div \dfrac{14}{16}$

$\dfrac{25}{36} \times \dfrac{18}{15}$ $\dfrac{5}{2} \times \dfrac{1}{3} = \dfrac{5}{6}$

Solution

Invert the second fraction and then multiply.

(a) $\dfrac{25}{36} \div \dfrac{15}{18} = \dfrac{\overset{5}{\cancel{25}}}{\underset{2}{\cancel{36}}} \times \dfrac{\overset{1}{\cancel{18}}}{\underset{3}{\cancel{15}}} = \dfrac{5 \times 1}{2 \times 3} = \dfrac{5}{6}$

(b) $\dfrac{21}{8} \div \dfrac{14}{16} = \dfrac{\overset{3}{\cancel{21}}}{\underset{1}{\cancel{8}}} \times \dfrac{\overset{1}{\cancel{16}}}{\underset{\underset{1}{2}}{\cancel{14}}} = \dfrac{3 \times 1}{1 \times 1} = 3$

Objective $\boxed{5}$ **Divide mixed numbers.** To divide mixed numbers, first change all mixed numbers to improper fractions, as in the following example.

$$3\frac{5}{9} \div 2\frac{2}{5} = \frac{32}{9} \div \frac{12}{5} = \frac{\overset{8}{\cancel{32}}}{9} \times \frac{5}{\underset{3}{\cancel{12}}} = \frac{8 \times 5}{9 \times 3} = \frac{40}{27} = 1\frac{13}{27}$$

Objective $\boxed{6}$ **Multiply or divide by whole numbers.** To multiply or divide by a whole number, write the whole number as a fraction over 1. For example:

$$3\frac{3}{4} \times 16 = 3\frac{3}{4} \times \frac{16}{1} = \frac{15}{4} \times \frac{16}{1} = \frac{15}{\cancel{4}} \times \frac{\overset{4}{\cancel{16}}}{1} = 15 \times 4 = 60$$

— whole number over 1

Also:

$$2\frac{2}{5} \div 3 = \frac{12}{5} \div \frac{3}{1} = \frac{\overset{4}{\cancel{12}}}{5} \times \frac{1}{\underset{1}{\cancel{3}}} = \frac{4 \times 1}{5 \times 1} = \frac{4}{5}$$

The following newspaper article reports that the prices of computer stocks have fallen. The stock of Gateway 2000 fell $1\frac{3}{8}$ ($$1\frac{3}{8}$) to close at $$37\frac{5}{8}$. Stock values are shown as mixed numbers representing the dollar value for one share. An investor must multiply the number of shares being purchased or sold by this mixed number to determine the total value of the stock.

Reality Check

Tech Stocks Take Hit

NEW YORK—Technology stocks suffered their worst one-day drop in eight weeks Thursday after **Intel** warned that earnings will fall short of expectations. After the close, **Motorola** said that it, too, will report disappointing earnings, suggesting that the sell-off may be far from over.

Highlights: Intel plunged $10\frac{13}{16}$, or 13%, to $$75\frac{5}{8}$ on volume of more than 92 million shares, sparking a widespread decline in other tech stocks. Falling: **Dell Computer**, $7\frac{3}{16}$ to $$131\frac{7}{8}$; **Microsoft**, $2\frac{1}{4}$ to $$80\frac{1}{16}$; **Gateway 2000**, $1\frac{3}{8}$ to $$37\frac{5}{8}$; and **Cisco Systems**, $3\frac{3}{8}$ to $$61\frac{7}{8}$.

Source: USA Today. Reprinted by permission.

Example 5

Multiplying a Whole Number by a Mixed Number

Chia Ling purchased 80 shares of Gateway 2000 stock at a price of $$37\frac{5}{8}$. Find her total cost for the stock.

Solution

Multiply the number of shares purchased by the price per share, $37\frac{5}{8}$, or $\frac{301}{8}$.

$$80 \times \frac{301}{8} = \frac{\overset{10}{\cancel{80}}}{1} \times \frac{301}{\underset{1}{\cancel{8}}} = \frac{10 \times 301}{1 \times 1} = \frac{3010}{1} = \$3010$$

The total cost of the stock purchased by Ling is $3010.

> **PROBLEM-SOLVING HINT**   It is often best to change a fraction or mixed number to a decimal number. This procedure is discussed in Section 2.5.

Example 6

Dividing a Whole Number by a Mixed Number

To complete a custom-designed cabinet, oak trim pieces must be cut exactly $2\frac{1}{4}''$ long so that they can be used as dividers in a spice rack. Find the number of pieces that can be cut from a piece of oak that is 54 inches in length.

Solution

To divide the length of the piece of oak by $2\frac{1}{4}$, or $\frac{9}{4}$, invert and then multiply.

$$54 \div 2\frac{1}{4} = 54 \div \frac{9}{4} = \frac{\overset{6}{\cancel{54}}}{1} \times \frac{4}{\underset{1}{\cancel{9}}} = \frac{6 \times 4}{1 \times 1} = \frac{24}{1} = 24$$

The number of trim pieces that can be cut from the oak stock is 24.

Name   Date   Class

50. PARTY PLANNING   Each guest at a party will eat $\frac{5}{16}$ pound of peanuts. How many guests will 10 pounds   **50.** _____
of peanuts serve?

51. FIREWOOD SALE   Amy Folsom had a small pickup truck that would carry $\frac{2}{3}$ cord of firewood. Find the   **51.** _____
number of trips needed to deliver 40 cords of wood.

52. WEATHER STRIPPING   Bill Rhodes has a 200-yard roll of weather stripping material. Find the number of   **52.** _____
pieces of weather stripping $\frac{5}{8}$ yard in length that may be cut from the roll.

For related Web activities, go to www.mathbusiness.com

'Net Assets

THE HOME DEPOT

STATISTICS

- 1978: Established

- 1998: $30.2 billion annual sales

- 1999: 170,000 employees

- 2002: 1600 stores (estimated)

The Home Depot is the country's largest home improvement center. Today, Home Depot services exporters and importers worldwide. According to Arthur M. Blank, president and CEO, "The Home Depot is thriving in an industry that offers many opportunities for continued growth, and we are excited about our prospects for the future."

The company's progressive corporate culture includes a philanthropic budget that is directed back to the communities Home Depot serves and the interests of its employees through a matching- gift program. The major focuses are affordable housing, at-risk youth, and the environment. Team Depot, an organized volunteer force, was developed in 1992 to promote volunteer activities with the local communities the stores serve. For five consecutive years, the company has been ranked by *Fortune* magazine as America's Most-Admired Retailer.

1. A gutter downspout is 10 feet long. If a piece of gutter downspout 8 feet 8 3/8 inches is needed for a job, find the length of the piece remaining. (*Hint:* one foot equals 12 inches)

2. Home Depot stock is selling for $63 3/8 per share. Find the number of shares that can be purchased for $17,238.

3. Give five specific situations in which fractions and mixed numbers would be used in a home-improvement store.

4. From your own experiences and those of family members and classmates, list eight specific activities where the ability to work with fractions would be needed.

2.5 | CONVERTING DECIMALS TO FRACTIONS AND FRACTIONS TO DECIMALS

Objectives

1. Convert decimals to fractions.
2. Convert fractions to decimals.
3. Know common decimal equivalents.

Objective **1** **Convert decimals to fractions.** A common method of converting a decimal to a fraction is by thinking of the decimal as being written in words, as in the preceding chapter. For example, think of .47 as **"forty-seven hundredths."** Then write this in fraction form as

$$.47 = \frac{47}{100}$$

In the same way, .3, read as **"three tenths,"** is written in fraction form as

$$.3 = \frac{3}{10}$$

Also, .963, read **"nine hundred sixty-three thousandths,"** is written in fraction form as

$$.963 = \frac{963}{1000}$$

Another method of converting a decimal to a fraction is by first removing the decimal point. The remaining number is the numerator of the fraction. The denominator of the fraction is 1 followed by as many zeros as there were digits to the right of the decimal point in the original number.

EXAMPLE 1
Converting
Decimals to
Fractions

Convert the following decimals to fractions.

(a) .3   **(b)** .98   **(c)** .654

Solution

(a) There is one digit following the decimal point in .3. Make a fraction with 3 as the numerator. For the denominator, put 10, which is 1 followed by one zero, to obtain

$$.3 = \frac{3}{10}$$

1 followed by 1 zero

This fraction is in lowest terms.

(b) There are two digits following the decimal point in .98. Make a fraction with 98 as the numerator and 100 as the denominator.

$$.98 = \frac{98}{100} = \frac{49}{50} \text{ (lowest terms)}$$

1 followed by 2 zeros

(c) There are three digits following the decimal point in .654.

$$.654 = \frac{654}{1000} = \frac{327}{500} \text{ (lowest terms)}$$

1 followed by 3 zeros

Objective **2** **Convert fractions to decimals.** Convert a fraction to a decimal by dividing the numerator of the fraction by the denominator. Place a decimal point after the numerator and attach one zero at a time to the right of the decimal point as the division is performed. Keep going until the division produces a remainder of zero or until the desired degree of accuracy is reached.

EXAMPLE 2

Converting Fractions to Decimals

Convert the following fractions to decimals.

(a) $\frac{1}{8}$ (b) $\frac{2}{3}$

SOLUTION

(a) Convert $\frac{1}{8}$ to a decimal by dividing 1 by 8.

$$8\overline{)1.}$$

Since 8 will not divide into 1, place a 0 to the right of the decimal point. Now 8 goes into 10 once, with a remainder of 2.

$$\begin{array}{r} .1 \\ 8\overline{)1.0} \\ \underline{8} \\ 2 \end{array}$$ Be sure to move the decimal point up.

Continue placing zeros to the right of the decimal point and continue dividing. The division now gives a remainder of 0.

$$\begin{array}{r} .125 \\ 8\overline{)1.000} \\ \underline{8} \\ 20 \\ \underline{16} \\ 40 \\ \underline{40} \\ 0 \end{array}$$ Keep attaching zeros.

remainder of 0

Therefore, $\frac{1}{8} = .125$.

(b) Divide 2 by 3.

$$\begin{array}{r} 0.6666 \\ 3\overline{)2.0000} \\ \underline{1\ 8} \\ 20 \\ \underline{18} \\ 20 \\ \underline{18} \\ 20 \\ \underline{18} \\ 2 \end{array}$$ Keep attaching zeros.

This division results in a repeating decimal and is often written as $.\overline{6}$ or $.6\overline{6}$ or $.66\overline{6}$. Rounded to the nearest thousandth $\frac{2}{3} = .667$.

The calculator solution to this example is

2 ÷ 3 = 0.666666667

Note: All calculator solutions use a scientific calculator. Refer to Appendix B for scientific calculator basics.

OBJECTIVE 3 Know common decimal equivalents. Some of the more common decimal equivalents of fractions are listed in the margin. These decimals appear from least to greatest value and are rounded to the nearest ten-thousandth. Sometimes decimals must be carried out further to give greater accuracy, while at other times they are not carried out as far and are rounded sooner.

DECIMAL EQUIVALENTS

$\frac{1}{16} = .0625$

$\frac{1}{9} = .1111$

$\frac{1}{8} = .125$

$\frac{1}{7} = .1429$

$\frac{1}{6} = .1667$

$\frac{3}{16} = .1875$

$\frac{1}{5} = .2$

$\frac{1}{4} = .25$

$\frac{5}{16} = .3125$

$\frac{1}{3} = .3333$

$\frac{3}{8} = .375$

$\frac{7}{16} = .4375$

$\frac{1}{2} = .5$

$\frac{9}{16} = .5625$

$\frac{5}{8} = .625$

$\frac{2}{3} = .6667$

$\frac{11}{16} = .6875$

$\frac{3}{4} = .75$

$\frac{13}{16} = .8125$

$\frac{5}{6} = .8333$

$\frac{7}{8} = .875$

CHAPTER 2 | Quick Review

CHAPTER TERMS

Review the following terms to test your understanding of the chapter. For each term you do not know, refer to the page number found next to that term.

cancellation [p. 63]	improper fraction [p. 44]	lowest terms [p. 46]	prime number [p. 52]
common denominator [p. 51]	inspection [p. 52]	method of prime numbers	proper fraction [p. 44]
decimal equivalent [p. 74]	least common denominator	[p. 52]	unlike fractions [p. 51]
denominator [p. 44]	(LCD) [p. 51]	mixed number [p. 44]	
fraction [p. 44]	like fractions [p. 51]	numerator [p. 44]	

CONCEPTS	EXAMPLES
2.1 Types of fractions Proper: Numerator smaller than denominator. Improper: Numerator equal to or greater than denominator. Mixed: Whole number and proper fraction.	proper fractions $\dfrac{2}{3}, \dfrac{3}{4}, \dfrac{15}{16}, \dfrac{1}{8}$ improper fractions $\dfrac{17}{8}, \dfrac{19}{12}, \dfrac{11}{2}, \dfrac{5}{3}, \dfrac{7}{7}$ mixed fractions $2\dfrac{2}{3}, 3\dfrac{5}{8}, 9\dfrac{5}{6}$
2.1 Converting fractions Mixed to improper: Multiply denominator by whole number and add numerator. Improper to mixed: Divide numerator by denominator and place remainder over denominator.	$7\dfrac{2}{3} = \dfrac{23}{3}$ $\dfrac{17}{5} = 3\dfrac{2}{5}$
2.1 Writing fractions in lowest terms Divide the numerator and denominator by the same number.	$\dfrac{30}{42} = \dfrac{30 \div 6}{42 \div 6} = \dfrac{5}{7}$
2.2 Adding like fractions Add numerators and reduce to lowest terms.	$\dfrac{3}{4} + \dfrac{1}{4} + \dfrac{5}{4} = \dfrac{3+1+5}{4} = \dfrac{9}{4} = 2\dfrac{1}{4}$
2.2 Finding a least common denominator Inspection method: Look to see if the least common denominator can be found. Method of prime numbers: Use prime numbers to find the least common denominator.	$\dfrac{1}{3} + \dfrac{1}{4} + \dfrac{1}{10}$ $\begin{array}{r} 1 \quad 1 \quad 1 \\ 5)\overline{1 \quad 1 \quad 5} \\ 3)\overline{3 \quad 1 \quad 5} \\ 2)\overline{3 \quad 2 \quad 5} \\ 2)\overline{3 \quad 4 \quad 10} \end{array}$ Multiply the prime numbers. $2 \times 2 \times 3 \times 5 = 60 \text{ LCD}$
2.2 Adding unlike fractions 1. Find the least common denominator. 2. Rewrite fractions with the least common denominator. 3. Add numerators, placing answers over LCD and reduce to lowest terms.	$\dfrac{1}{3} + \dfrac{1}{4} + \dfrac{1}{10}$ LCD = 60 $\dfrac{1}{3} = \dfrac{20}{60}, \dfrac{1}{4} = \dfrac{15}{60}, \dfrac{1}{10} = \dfrac{6}{60}$ $\dfrac{20+15+6}{60} = \dfrac{41}{60}$

CONCEPTS	EXAMPLES
2.2 Subtracting fractions 1. Find the least common denominator. 2. Subtract numerator of subtrahend, borrowing if necessary. 3. Write difference over LCD and reduce to lowest terms.	$$\frac{5}{8} - \frac{1}{3} = \frac{15}{24} - \frac{8}{24} = \frac{7}{24}$$
2.3 Adding mixed numbers 1. Add fractions. 2. Add whole numbers. 3. Combine the sums of whole numbers and fractions. Write answer in simplest terms.	$$9\frac{2}{3} = 9\frac{8}{12}$$ $$+\,6\frac{3}{4} = 6\frac{9}{12}$$ $$15\frac{17}{12} = 16\frac{5}{12}$$
2.3 Subtracting mixed numbers 1. Subtract fractions, borrowing if necessary. 2. Subtract whole numbers. 3. Combine the differences of whole numbers and fractions.	$$8\frac{5}{8} = 8\frac{15}{24}$$ $$-\,3\frac{1}{12} = 3\frac{2}{24}$$ $$5\frac{13}{24}$$
2.4 Multiplying proper fractions 1. Multiply numerators and denominators. 2. Reduce answer to lowest terms if cancelling was not done.	$$\frac{6}{11} \times \frac{7}{8} = \frac{\overset{3}{\cancel{6}}}{11} \times \frac{7}{\underset{4}{\cancel{8}}} = \frac{21}{44}$$
2.4 Multiplying mixed numbers 1. Change mixed numbers to improper fractions. 2. Cancel if possible. 3. Multiply as proper fractions.	$$1\frac{3}{5} \times 3\frac{1}{3} = \frac{8}{\underset{1}{\cancel{5}}} \times \frac{\overset{2}{\cancel{10}}}{3} = \frac{8}{1} \times \frac{2}{3}$$ $$= \frac{16}{3} = 5\frac{1}{3}$$ Always reduce to lowest terms.
2.4 Dividing proper fractions Invert the divisor and multiply as fractions.	$$\frac{25}{36} \div \frac{15}{18} = \frac{\overset{5}{\cancel{25}}}{\underset{2}{\cancel{36}}} \times \frac{\overset{1}{\cancel{18}}}{\underset{3}{\cancel{15}}} = \frac{5}{2} \times \frac{1}{3} = \frac{5}{6}$$
2.4 Dividing mixed numbers Change mixed numbers to improper fractions. Invert the divisor, cancel if possible, and multiply as proper fractions.	$$3\frac{5}{9} \div 2\frac{2}{5} = \frac{32}{9} \div \frac{12}{5} = \frac{\overset{8}{\cancel{32}}}{9} \times \frac{5}{\underset{3}{\cancel{12}}}$$ $$= \frac{40}{27} = 1\frac{13}{27}$$
2.5 Converting decimals to fractions Think of the decimal as being written in words, then write in fraction form. Reduce to lowest terms.	Convert .47 to a fraction. Think of .47 as "**forty-seven hundredths**," then write as $\frac{47}{100}$.
2.5 Converting fractions to decimals Divide the numerator by the denominator. Round if necessary.	Convert $\frac{1}{8}$ to a decimal. $$\frac{1}{8} = .125$$ $$\begin{array}{r} .125 \\ 8\overline{)1.000} \\ \underline{8} \\ 20 \\ \underline{16} \\ 40 \\ \underline{40} \\ 0 \end{array}$$

CHAPTER 2 | SUMMARY EXERCISE

FRACTIONS IN YOUR FINANCIAL FUTURE

Although retirement is many years off, David Perry has been investing his savings by buying stock in several companies. The daily changes in stock prices are shown in most major newspapers and while there are hundreds of stocks, the list here shows just eight companies.

Stock Market News

52 Week High	Low		Close	Net Change
$68\frac{1}{2}$	33	AT&T	$56\frac{7}{16}$	$-\frac{1}{8}$
$81\frac{3}{8}$	$51\frac{5}{16}$	CocaCola	$78\frac{1}{16}$	$+\frac{11}{16}$
$38\frac{3}{16}$	$22\frac{9}{16}$	FruitLoom	$35\frac{7}{16}$	$-\frac{3}{8}$
$89\frac{7}{16}$	59	GenElec	$87\frac{7}{8}$	$+\frac{3}{8}$
$79\frac{3}{4}$	$54\frac{3}{8}$	ReynMetl	$60\frac{13}{16}$	$-1\frac{1}{8}$
$32\frac{3}{4}$	23	Rubbermaid	$32\frac{3}{8}$	$+\frac{1}{2}$
$37\frac{7}{8}$	$25\frac{3}{16}$	SherwinWill	$33\frac{1}{2}$	-1
$54\frac{3}{4}$	$29\frac{1}{2}$	WalMart	$54\frac{5}{16}$	$-\frac{1}{16}$

(a) Stock prices use fractions to show parts of a dollar. For example, $\frac{1}{4}$ = \$.25; $\frac{1}{2}$ = \$.50 and $\frac{3}{4}$ = \$.75. Find the amounts represented by $\frac{3}{8}, \frac{3}{16}, \frac{7}{8}$ and $\frac{13}{16}$. Do not round.

(a) _____

The left-hand columns of the preceding table show the highest and lowest price for the stock over the last 52 weeks (one year). Then comes the company name followed by the current price (close). The right-hand column shows how much the price has changed from the previous day (net change). Use this information to answer the following. Write all final answers in dollars and cents rounded to the nearest cent.

(b) Find the difference between the highest price and the lowest price for Sherwin Williams in the last year.

(b) _____

(c) Find the difference between the highest and the lowest price for Fruit of the Loom during the last year.

(c) _____

(d) Which company had the greatest difference between the highest price and the lowest price for the year?

(d) _____

(e) David Perry bought 80 shares of General Electric stock at the closing price. Find his cost.

(e) _____

(f) David Perry bought 100 shares of Wal-Mart stock at closing price. Find his cost.

(f) _____

(g) With a $2000 investment, how many whole shares of Rubbermaid stock could be purchased at the closing price?

(g) _____

(h) During the past year David Perry has bought 50 shares of Coca-Cola at $63\frac{1}{2}$ and 30 shares of Reynolds Metals at $76\frac{3}{4}$. Using the closing price, find the gain or loss on each of these stocks and the gain on their combined investment. Be sure to express a loss with a minus sign ("−") before the number.

(h) _____

Investigate

Find the New York Stock Exchange (NYSE) listing in a newspaper. Select one or more stocks that had closing prices that ended in halves, quarters, eighths, sixteenths, thirty-seconds, and sixth-fourths of a dollar. Write the name of the stock, the closing price, and the closing price rounded to the nearest cent for each stock that you selected.

Name   Date   Class

CHAPTER 2 | TEST

To help you review, the numbers in brackets show the section in which the topic was discussed.

Write each of the following fractions in lowest terms.   [2.1]

1. $\dfrac{24}{40} = $ _3/5_

2. $\dfrac{375}{1000} = $ _3/8_

3. $\dfrac{84}{132} = $ _____

Convert each of the following improper fractions to a mixed number, and write it in lowest terms.   [2.1]

4. $\dfrac{65}{8} = $ _8 1/8_

5. $\dfrac{56}{12} = $ _4 2/3_

6. $\dfrac{120}{45} = $ _2 2/3_

Convert each of the following mixed numbers to an improper fraction.   [2.1]

7. $7\dfrac{3}{4} = $ _____

8. $18\dfrac{4}{5} = $ _____

9. $18\dfrac{3}{8} = $ _____

Find the least common denominator of each of the following groups of denominators.   [2.2]

10. $2, 6, 5 = $ _30_

11. $6, 8, 15 = $ _120_

12. $6, 9, 12, 24 = $ _72_

Solve each of the following problems.   [2.2–2.4]

13.
$$\begin{array}{r} \frac{1}{5} \\ \frac{3}{10} \\ + \frac{3}{8} \end{array}$$

14.
$$\begin{array}{r} 32\frac{3}{16} \\ -17\frac{1}{4} \end{array}$$

15.
$$\begin{array}{r} 126\frac{3}{16} \\ -89\frac{7}{8} \end{array}$$

16. $67\dfrac{1}{2} \times \dfrac{8}{15} = $

17. $33\dfrac{1}{3} \div \dfrac{200}{9} = $

Solve each of the following application problems.

18. Jennifer Fleming, pastry chef, used $23\frac{1}{2}$ pounds of powdered sugar for one recipe, $34\frac{3}{4}$ pounds of powdered sugar for another recipe, and $17\frac{5}{8}$ pounds of powdered sugar for a third recipe. If Fleming started with two 50-pound sacks of powdered sugar, find the amount of powdered sugar remaining.   **[2.3]**

18. _____

19. Ellen Burke bought 25 shares of Korea Equity stock for $\$8\frac{3}{8}$ per share and 16 shares of Snyder Oil stock for $\$12\frac{1}{4}$ per share. How much did she pay altogether?   **[2.4]**

19. _____

20. A painting contractor arrived at a 6-unit apartment complex with $147\frac{1}{2}$ gallons of exterior paint. If his crew sprayed $68\frac{1}{2}$ gallons on the wood siding, rolled $37\frac{3}{8}$ gallons on the masonry exterior, and brushed $5\frac{3}{4}$ gallons on the trim, find the number of gallons of paint remaining.   **[2.3]**

20. _____

21. Find the number of window-blind pull cords that can be made from $157\frac{1}{2}$ yards of cord if $4\frac{3}{8}$ yards of cord are needed for each blind.

21. _____

Convert the following decimals to fractions.   **[2.5]**

22. $.625 =$

23. $.77 =$

Convert the following fractions to decimals. Round to the nearest thousandth.   **[2.5]**

24. $\frac{3}{4} =$ _____

25. $\frac{8}{9} =$ _____

CHAPTER 3

PERCENT

Thomas Dugally is a real estate broker with Century 21 Realty. He is a college graduate who was employed in the shipping industry for several years before going into real estate. He says that the real estate field offers him many challenges, a great deal of flexibility in planning his work schedule, and he loves not having to work indoors all of the time.

Mathematics, especially percentages, is something that he must use every day. He is constantly calculating loan charges, determining buyer loan qualifications, figuring real estate commissions, and determining and explaining property tax amounts and property insurance premiums to his clients.

Percents are widely used in business and everyday life. For example, interest rates on automobile loans, home loans, and other installment loans are almost always given as percents. Advertisers often claim that their products perform a certain percent better than other products or cost a certain percent less. Stores often advertise sale prices as being a certain percent off the regular price. In business, marketing costs, damage, and theft may be expressed as a percent of sales; profit as a percent of investment; and labor as a percent of cost of production. Current government figures about inflation, recession, and unemployment are also reported as percents. The package of Hungry Jack pancake mix, shown at the left, reminds us of the powerful use of percents in advertising and in the selling of products as well.

This chapter discusses the various types of percent problems that will be used throughout the text.

3.1 | WRITING DECIMALS AND FRACTIONS AS PERCENTS

For related Web activities, go to www.mathbusiness.com

Keyword: cookbook

Objectives

1. Write a decimal as a percent.
2. Write a fraction as a percent.
3. Write a percent as a decimal.
4. Write a percent as a fraction.
5. Write a fractional percent as a decimal.

Percents represent parts of a whole, just as fractions or decimals do. **Percents** are **hundredths**, or parts of a hundred. "One percent" means 1 of 100 equal parts. Percents are written with a percent sign (%). For example, 25% refers to 25 out of 100 equal parts ($\frac{25}{100}$), 50% refers to 50 out of 100 equal parts ($\frac{50}{100}$), and 100% refers to all 100 of the 100 equal parts ($\frac{100}{100}$). Therefore, 100% is equal to the whole item. If a percent is larger than 100% (for example, 150%), more than one item has been divided into 100 equal parts, and 150 of the parts are being considered ($\frac{150}{100}$).

Objective **1** **Write a decimal as a percent.** To write a decimal as a percent, **move the decimal point two places to the right and attach a percent sign (%).**

For example, write .75 as a percent by moving the decimal point two places to the right and attaching a percent sign, for the result of 75%.

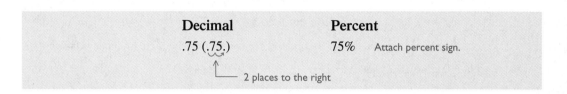

Decimal	Percent	
.75 (.75.)	75%	Attach percent sign.

2 places to the right

Example 1

Changing Decimals to Percents

Change the following decimals to percents.

(a) .25   **(b)** .38   **(c)** .65

Solution

Move the decimal point two places to the right and attach a percent sign.

(a) 25%   **(b)** 38%   **(c)** 65%

If there is nothing in the hundredths position, place zeros to the right of the number to hold the hundredths position. For example, the decimal .5 is expressed as 50% and the whole number 1.2 is expressed as 120%.

$$.5 = .50.\% = 50\%$$

attach zero

$$1.2 = 1.20.\% = 120\%$$

attach zero

Example 2

Writing Decimals as Percents

Write the following decimals as percents.

(a) .7   **(b)** 1.3   **(c)** .1   **(d)** 3

Solution

It is necessary to attach zeros here.

(a) 70%   **(b)** 130%   **(c)** 10%   **(d)** 300%

If the decimal extends past the hundredths position the resulting percent includes decimal parts of whole percents.

Example 3

Writing Decimals as Percents

When reading a real estate newsletter, Thomas Dugally sees the following decimals. Write these decimals as percents.

(a) .857   **(b)** .0057   **(c)** .0025

Solution

(a) 85.7%   **(b)** .57%   **(c)** .25%

NOTE   In Example 3 both (b) and (c) are less than 1%. They are decimal parts of one percent.

Objective **2** **Write a fraction as a percent.** There are two ways to write a fraction as a percent. One way is to write the fraction first as a decimal. For example, one way to express the fraction $\frac{2}{5}$ as a percent is to write $\frac{2}{5}$ as a decimal by dividing 2 by 5. Then write the decimal as a percent.

Fraction	Decimal	Percent
$\frac{2}{5}$	.4	40%

EXAMPLE 4
Writing Fractions as Percents

An advertising account representative is given the following data in fraction form and must change the data to percent.

(a) $\frac{1}{4}$ (b) $\frac{3}{5}$ (c) $\frac{7}{8}$

Solution
First write each fraction as a decimal, and then write the decimal as a percent.

(a) $\frac{1}{4} = .25 = 25\%$ (b) $\frac{3}{5} = .6 = 60\%$ (c) $\frac{7}{8} = .875 = 87.5\%$

A second way to write a fraction as a percent is by multiplying the fraction by 100%. For example, write the fraction $\frac{2}{5}$ as a percent by multiplying $\frac{2}{5}$ by 100%, as follows:

$$\frac{2}{5} = \frac{2}{5} \times 100\% = \frac{200\%}{5} = 40\%$$

Objective **3** **Write a percent as a decimal.** To write a percent as a decimal, **move the decimal point two places to the left and drop the percent sign.** For example, 50% becomes .50 or .5, 100% becomes 1, and 352% becomes 3.52.

EXAMPLE 5
Writing Percents as Decimals

To calculate some insurance claims, an insurance agent must change the following percents to decimals.

(a) 25%   (b) 50%   (c) 142%   (d) $37\frac{1}{2}\%$ (*Hint:* $37\frac{1}{2}\% = 37.5\%$)

Solution
Move the decimal point two places to the left, and drop the percent sign.

(a) .25   (b) .5   (c) 1.42   (d) .375

PROBLEM-SOLVING HINT   In Example 5(d) change $37\frac{1}{2}\%$ to 37.5%. It is usually best to change fractional percents to the decimal form and then change the percent to a decimal.

Objective **4** **Write a percent as a fraction.** To write a percent as a fraction, first change the percent to a decimal.

EXAMPLE 6

Writing Percents as Fractions

The data in the following bar graph is from the National Association of Realtors and shows the technology tools used by star salespeople and the percent who use these tools. Write the following percents, seen in the bar graph, as fractions.

(a) 72%   **(b)** 63%   **(c)** 36%

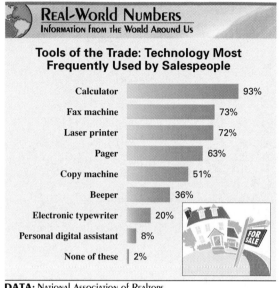

ReaL-World Numbers
INFORMATION FROM THE WORLD AROUND US

Tools of the Trade: Technology Most Frequently Used by Salespeople

Calculator	93%
Fax machine	73%
Laser printer	72%
Pager	63%
Copy machine	51%
Beeper	36%
Electronic typewriter	20%
Personal digital assistant	8%
None of these	2%

DATA: NATIONAL ASSOCIATION OF REALTORS

Solution

First write each percent as a decimal and then write the decimal as a fraction in lowest terms.

(a) $72\% = .72 = \dfrac{72}{100} = \dfrac{18}{25}$ **(b)** $63\% = .63 = \dfrac{63}{100}$ **(c)** $36\% = .36 = \dfrac{36}{100} = \dfrac{9}{25}$

Objective **5** **Write a fractional percent as a decimal.** A fractional percent such as $\frac{1}{4}\%$ has a value less than 1%. In fact, $\frac{1}{2}\%$ is equal to $\frac{1}{2}$ of 1%. Write a fractional percent as a decimal by first changing the fraction to a decimal, leaving the percent sign. For example, first write $\frac{1}{2}\%$ as .5%. Then write .5% as a decimal by moving the decimal point two places to the left and dropping the percent sign.

$$\frac{1}{2}\% = .5\% = .005$$

Written as a decimal with percent sign remaining.

EXAMPLE 7

Writing Fractional Percents as Decimals

The following percents appear in a newspaper article and you wonder what they would look like as decimals. Write each of the following fractional percents as decimals.

(a) $\dfrac{1}{5}\%$ **(b)** $\dfrac{3}{4}\%$ **(c)** $\dfrac{1}{8}\%$

Solution

Begin by writing the fraction as a decimal.

(a) $\dfrac{1}{5}\% = .2\% = .002$ **(b)** $\dfrac{3}{4}\% = .75\% = .0075$ **(c)** $\dfrac{1}{8}\% = .125\% = .00125$

The following chart shows many fractions and their percent equivalents. It is helpful to memorize the more commonly used ones.

Fraction and Percent Equivalents

$\frac{1}{100} = 1\%$	$\frac{1}{9} = 11\frac{1}{9}\%$	$\frac{1}{3} = 33\frac{1}{3}\%$	$\frac{4}{5} = 80\%$
$\frac{1}{50} = 2\%$	$\frac{1}{8} = 12\frac{1}{2}\%$	$\frac{3}{8} = 37\frac{1}{2}\%$	$\frac{5}{6} = 83\frac{1}{3}\%$
$\frac{1}{25} = 4\%$	$\frac{1}{7} = 14\frac{2}{7}\%$	$\frac{2}{5} = 40\%$	$\frac{7}{8} = 87\frac{1}{2}\%$
$\frac{1}{20} = 5\%$	$\frac{1}{6} = 16\frac{2}{3}\%$	$\frac{1}{2} = 50\%$	$1 = 100\%$
$\frac{1}{16} = 6\frac{1}{4}\%$	$\frac{3}{16} = 18\frac{3}{4}\%$	$\frac{3}{5} = 60\%$	$1\frac{1}{4} = 125\%$
$\frac{1}{12} = 8\frac{1}{3}\%$	$\frac{1}{5} = 20\%$	$\frac{5}{8} = 62\frac{1}{2}\%$	$1\frac{1}{2} = 150\%$
$\frac{1}{10} = 10\%$	$\frac{1}{4} = 25\%$	$\frac{2}{3} = 66\frac{2}{3}\%$	$1\frac{3}{4} = 175\%$
		$\frac{3}{4} = 75\%$	$2 = 200\%$

3.2 | Finding Part

> 1. Know the three quantities of a percent problem.
> 2. Learn the basic percent formula.
> 3. Solve for part.
> 4. Recognize the terms associated with base, rate, and part.
> 5. Calculate sales tax.
> 6. Learn to standardize the format of percent problems.

Problem Solving in Business

As a real estate agent with Century 21 Realty, Thomas Dugally is paid on a commission plan. When he produces income for the company as a result of a sale, a sale of his listing by someone else, or a rental agreement that is completed, he is paid a portion of this income. Currently, Dugally is looking for a home in the $120,000 price range for Stephen and Heather Hall, a couple he met at an open house.

For related Web activities, go to www.mathbusiness.com

Keyword:
discounts

Objective 1 Know the three quantities of a percent problem. Problems in percent contain three main quantities. Usually two of these quantities are given and the third quantity must be found. The three key quantities in a percent problem are as follows.

1. **Base:** The whole or total, starting point, or that to which something is being compared.
2. **Rate:** A number followed by % or *percent.*
3. **Part:** The result of multiplying the base and the rate. The part is a *part* of the base, as sales tax is a part of the total sales, or as the number of sports cars is part of the total number of cars.

> **NOTE** Percent and part are different quantities. The stated percent in a given problem is always the rate. The part is the product of the base and the rate. Thus, the part is a quantity and never appears with *percent* or % following it.

Objective 2 Learn the basic percent formula. The base, rate, and part are related by the basic **percent formula.**

$$P = B \times R \qquad P = R \times B$$
$$\text{Part} = \text{Base} \times \text{Rate} \quad \text{or} \quad \text{Part} = \text{Rate} \times \text{Base}$$

Four bedrooms, 2 baths, huge backyard, new roof and carpet, centrally located near town within easy walk of shopping and schools. Neat as a pin throughout. $120,000.

Objective 3 Solve for part. If Thomas Dugally finds a $120,000 home for the Halls and is paid a 6% commission, use the formula $P = B \times R$ to find 6% of $120,000. Multiply the base, $120,000, by the rate, (6%). The rate must be changed to a decimal before it is multiplied.

$$P = B \times R$$
$$P = \$120{,}000 \times 6\%$$
$$P = \$120{,}000 \times .06 \quad \text{or} \quad \begin{array}{r} \$120{,}000 \\ \times \quad .06 \\ \hline \$7200 \end{array}$$

Finally, 6% of $120,000 is $7200.

EXAMPLE 1
Solving for Part

Solve for part, using $P = B \times R$.

(a) 4% of 50   (b) 1.2% of 180   (c) 140% of 225   (d) $\frac{1}{4}$% of 560
(*Hint:* $\frac{1}{4}$% = .25%)

SOLUTION

(a)   50   (b)   180   (c)   225   (d)   560
    $\times$ .04 $\times$ .012 $\times$ 1.4 $\times$ .0025
      2.00   2.160   315.0   1.4000

EXAMPLE 2
Finding Part

The following bar graph shows that 27% of the office workers would like more storage space. If there are 14 million office workers, how many would want more storage space.

SOLUTION

The number of office workers, 14 million, is the base. The rate, 27%, is the portion of the total number of office workers who want more storage space. Since the number of office workers who want more storage space is part of the total number of office workers, find the number of office workers who want more storage space by using the formula to find part.

$$P = B \times R$$
$$P = 14 \text{ million} \times 27\%$$
$$P = 14 \text{ million} \times .27$$
$$P = 3.78 \text{ million}$$

The number of office workers who want more storage space is 3.78 million or 3,780,000.

The calculator solution to this example is

14 $\boxed{\times}$ 27 $\boxed{\%}$ $\boxed{=}$ 3.78   or   14 $\boxed{\times}$ .27 $\boxed{=}$ 3.78

Note: All calculator solutions use a scientific calculator. Refer to Appendix B for scientific calculator basics.

OBJECTIVE **4** **Recognize the terms associated with base, rate, and part.** Percent problems have certain similarities. For example, some phrases are associated with the base in the problem. Other phrases lead to the part, while % or *percent* following a number identifies the rate. The following chart helps distinguish between the base and the part.

Words and Phrases Associated with Base and Part

Usually indicates the base	Usually indicates the part
Sales ⟶	Sales tax
Investment ⟶	Return
Savings ⟶	Interest
Value of bonds ⟶	Dividends
Retail price ⟶	Discount
Last year's anything ⟶	Increase or decrease
Value of real estate ⟶	Rent
Old salary ⟶	Raise
Total sales ⟶	Commission
Value of stocks ⟶	Dividends
Earnings ⟶	Expenditures
Original ⟶	Change

Objective 5 **Calculate sales tax.** Calculating sales tax is a good example of finding part. States, counties, and cities often collect taxes on sales to the consumer (called retail sales). The sales tax is a percent of the sale. This percent varies from as low as 3% in some states to 8% or more in other states. The formula used for finding sales tax is as follows.

$$P = B \times R$$
$$\text{Sales tax} = \text{Sales} \times \text{Sales tax rate}$$

EXAMPLE 3
Calculating Sales Tax

Racy Feed and Pet Supply sold $284.50 worth of merchandise. If the sales tax rate was 5%, how much tax was paid? Find the total cost including the tax.

Solution

The amount of sales, $284.50, is the starting point or base, and 5% is the rate. Since the tax is a *part* of total sales, use the formula $P = B \times R$ to find it.

$$P = B \times R$$
$$P = \$284.50 \times 5\%$$
$$P = \$284.50 \times .05 = 14.225 = \$14.23$$

The tax, or part, is $14.23.

To find the total amount of sales and tax, the amount of sales ($284.50), is added to the sales tax, $14.23. The total sales and tax is $298.73 ($284.50 + $14.23).

Identify the rate, base, and part with the following.

Base: tends to be preceded by the word *of* or *on*; tends to be the *whole*.
Rate: is followed by a percent sign or the word *percent*.
Part: is in the same units as the base and is usually a portion of the base.

Objective 6 **Learn to standardize the format of percent problems.** Percent problems often take the following form.

% of something is something

For example:

5% of the automobiles sold

4.2% of the workers are unemployed

20% of the income is tax

70% of the students are done

When expressed in this standard form, the elements in the percent problem appear in the order

$$R \quad \times \quad B \quad = \quad P$$

Rate ×   Base   =   Part

%   of   something   is   something

> **NOTE**   Rate is identified by % (the percent sign); the word *of* means × (multiplication); the multiplicand, or number being multiplied, is the base; the word *is* means = (equals); and the product, or answer, is part of the base.

The following survey results show that 91% of the 2008 teens in a survey rated going to the movies as "in."

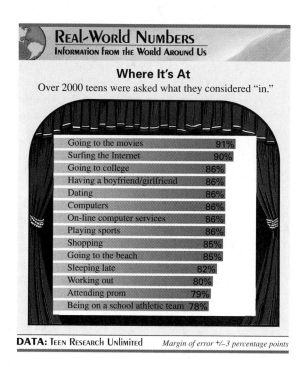

Where It's At

Over 2000 teens were asked what they considered "in."

Going to the movies	91%
Surfing the Internet	90%
Going to college	86%
Having a boyfriend/girlfriend	86%
Dating	86%
Computers	86%
On-line computer services	86%
Playing sports	86%
Shopping	85%
Going to the beach	85%
Sleeping late	82%
Working out	80%
Attending prom	79%
Being on a school athletic team	78%

DATA: TEEN RESEARCH UNLIMITED   *Margin of error +/–3 percentage points*

The rate, which is the percent selecting going to the movies as "in" is 91%; the base, or number of teens in the survey, is 2008; and the number of teens rating going to the movies as "in," is the part. Find part, the number of teens who rated going to the movies as "in." Round to the nearest whole number.

$$R \quad \times \quad B \quad = \quad P$$
$$91\% \times 2008 = 1827.28 = 1827 \text{ teens (rounded)}$$

EXAMPLE 4

Identifying the Elements in Percent Problems

Identify the elements given in the following percent problems and determine which element must be found.

(a) During a recent sale, Stockdale Marine offered a 15% discount on all new recreation equipment. Find the discount on a jet ski originally priced at $2895. First arrange this problem in standard form.

%	of	something	is	something
%	of	price	is	discount
15%	of	$2895	=	discount
R	×	B	=	P

At this point, check that rate is given, base is given, and part must be found. Find the discount by multiplying 15%, or .15, by $2895.

$$.15 \times \$2895 = \$434.25$$

The amount of the discount is $434.25.

(b) Round Table Pizza spends an amount equal to 5.8% of its sales on advertising. If sales for the month were $12,500, find the amount spent on advertising. First arrange this problem in standard form.

%	of	something	is	something
%	of	sales	is	advertising
5.8%	of	$12,500	=	advertising
R	×	*B*	=	*P*

Rate is given as 5.8%, base (sales) is $12,500, and part (advertising) must be found. Find the amount spent on advertising by multiplying .058 and $12,500.

$$.058 \times \$12,500 = \$725$$

The amount spent on advertising is $725.

3.3 | Finding Base

Objectives

1. Use the basic percent formula to solve for base.
2. Find the amount of sales when tax amount and tax rate are both known.
3. Find the amount of investment when expense and rate of expense are known.

Problem Solving in Business

REALTY

Thomas Dugally of Century 21 Realty must help buyers select properties that they can afford. Real estate lenders have strict guidelines that determine the maximum loan that they will give a buyer. Usually, the lender will limit the borrowers' monthly house payment to no more than 28% to 36% of their monthly income.

Objective 1 **Use the basic percent formula to solve for base.** In some problems, the rate and part are given, but the base, or starting point, must be found. The formula $P = B \times R$ can be used to get the **formula for base.** The following diagram illustrates the formula $P = B \times R$. To find the formula for base, cover B. Now the letter P is left over the letter R. Think of this as meaning $\frac{P}{R}$, or part ÷ rate.

$$\text{Base} = \frac{\text{Part}}{\text{Rate}} \quad \text{or} \quad B = \frac{P}{R}$$

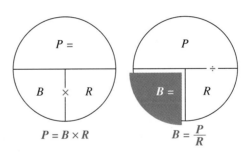

$$P = B \times R \qquad B = \frac{P}{R}$$

NOTE When using this formula, P (part) is always on top.

Suppose that Stephen and Heather Hall told Thomas Dugally that they are able to make a monthly payment of $770. If this is 28% of their monthly income, how can Dugally find the amount of their monthly income? The key word here, indicating that the amount of monthly income is the base is the word *of*. To find the amount of their monthly income, insert the rate (28%) and the part ($770) into the formula.

$$B = \frac{P}{R} \quad \text{Replace } P \text{ with 770 and } R \text{ with .28 to get}$$

$$B = \frac{770}{.28} = 2750. \text{ The amount of their monthly income is } \$2750.$$

Example 1

Solving for Base

Solve for base, using the formula $B = \frac{P}{R}$.

(a) 8 is 4% of _____.   (b) 135 is 15% of _____.
(c) 1.25 is 25% of _____.

Solution

(a) $\frac{8}{.04} = 200$ (b) $\frac{135}{.15} = 900$ (c) $\frac{1.25}{.25} = 5$

Objective **2**   **Find the amount of sales when tax amount and tax rate are both known.**   In business problems involving sales tax, the amount of sales is always the base.

EXAMPLE 2

Finding Sales when Sales Tax Is Given

For related Web activities, go to www.mathbusiness.com

Keyword: shoes

The 5% sales tax collected by Famous Footwear was $780. What was the amount of total sales?

SOLUTION

Here the rate of tax collection is 5%, and taxes collected are a part of total sales. The rate in this problem is 5%, the part is $780, and the base, or total sales, must be found. Arrange the problem in standard form.

$$R \quad \times \quad B \quad = \quad P$$

%   of   something   is   something

5%   of   total sales   is $780 (tax)

Using the formula $B = \frac{P}{R}$:

$$B = \frac{780}{.05} = \$15{,}600 \text{ total sales}$$

REALITY CHECK

The calculator solution to this example is

780 ÷ .05 = 15600.

Note: All calculator solutions use a scientific calculator. Refer to Appendix B for scientific calculator basics.

PROBLEM-SOLVING HINT   It is important to consider whether an answer is reasonable. A common error in a base problem is to confuse the base and the part. In Example 2, if the taxes, $780, had been mistakenly used as the base, the resulting answer would have been $39 ($780 × 5%). Obviously, $39 is not a reasonable amount for total sales, given $780 as sales tax.

The newspaper clipping to the left states that the number of income-tax refunds and the average amount of a refund have both risen since last year and that this should help to strengthen the economy. In these calculations, the tax-refund numbers from last year are the base, or starting point, the amounts to which this year is being compared.

Objective **3**   **Find the amount of investment when expense and rate of expense are known.** When solving problems involving investments, the amount of the investment is the base.

EXAMPLE 3

Finding the Amount of an Investment

The yearly maintenance cost of an apartment complex is $3\frac{1}{2}\%$ of its value. If maintenance cost is $73,500 per year, find the value of the apartment complex.

SOLUTION

First set up the problem: $R \quad \times \quad B \quad = \quad P$

$3\frac{1}{2}\%$ of   value   is   maintenance cost

$3\frac{1}{2}\%$ of   value   is $73,500

Find the value of the apartment complex, the base, with the formula $B = \frac{P}{R}$.

$$B = \frac{73{,}500}{.035} = \$2{,}100{,}000 \text{ value of complex.}$$

NOTE   When working with a fraction of a percent it is best to change the fraction to a decimal. In Example 3, $3\frac{1}{2}\%$ was changed to 3.5%, which equals .035.

3.3 | Finding Base

Objectives

1. Use the basic percent formula to solve for base.
2. Find the amount of sales when tax amount and tax rate are both known.
3. Find the amount of investment when expense and rate of expense are known.

Problem Solving in Business

REALTY

Thomas Dugally of Century 21 Realty must help buyers select properties that they can afford. Real estate lenders have strict guidelines that determine the maximum loan that they will give a buyer. Usually, the lender will limit the borrowers' monthly house payment to no more than 28% to 36% of their monthly income.

Objective 1 Use the basic percent formula to solve for base. In some problems, the rate and part are given, but the base, or starting point, must be found. The formula $P = B \times R$ can be used to get the **formula for base.** The following diagram illustrates the formula $P = B \times R$. To find the formula for base, cover B. Now the letter P is left over the letter R. Think of this as meaning $\frac{P}{R}$, or part ÷ rate.

$$\text{Base} = \frac{\text{Part}}{\text{Rate}} \quad \text{or} \quad B = \frac{P}{R}$$

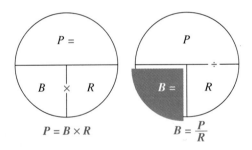

$$P = B \times R \qquad\qquad B = \frac{P}{R}$$

> **NOTE** When using this formula, P (part) is always on top.

Suppose that Stephen and Heather Hall told Thomas Dugally that they are able to make a monthly payment of $770. If this is 28% of their monthly income, how can Dugally find the amount of their monthly income? The key word here, indicating that the amount of monthly income is the base is the word *of*. To find the amount of their monthly income, insert the rate (28%) and the part ($770) into the formula.

$$B = \frac{P}{R} \quad \text{Replace } P \text{ with 770 and } R \text{ with .28 to get}$$

$$B = \frac{770}{.28} = 2750. \text{ The amount of their monthly income is \$2750.}$$

EXAMPLE 1
Solving for Base

Solve for base, using the formula $B = \frac{P}{R}$.

(a) 8 is 4% of _____.   (b) 135 is 15% of _____.
(c) 1.25 is 25% of _____.

Solution

(a) $\dfrac{8}{.04} = 200$ (b) $\dfrac{135}{.15} = 900$ (c) $\dfrac{1.25}{.25} = 5$

Objective ② Find the amount of sales when tax amount and tax rate are both known. In business problems involving sales tax, the amount of sales is always the base.

EXAMPLE 2

Finding Sales when Sales Tax Is Given

For related Web activities, go to www.mathbusiness.com

Keyword: shoes

The 5% sales tax collected by Famous Footwear was $780. What was the amount of total sales?

Solution

Here the rate of tax collection is 5%, and taxes collected are a part of total sales. The rate in this problem is 5%, the part is $780, and the base, or total sales, must be found. Arrange the problem in standard form.

$$R \times B = P$$

% of something is something

5% of total sales is $780 (tax)

Using the formula $B = \frac{P}{R}$:

$$B = \frac{780}{.05} = \$15,600 \text{ total sales}$$

The calculator solution to this example is

780 ÷ .05 = 15600.

Note: All calculator solutions use a scientific calculator. Refer to Appendix B for scientific calculator basics.

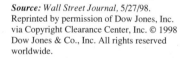

REALITY CHECK

PROBLEM-SOLVING HINT It is important to consider whether an answer is reasonable. A common error in a base problem is to confuse the base and the part. In Example 2, if the taxes, $780, had been mistakenly used as the base, the resulting answer would have been $39 ($780 × 5%). Obviously, $39 is not a reasonable amount for total sales, given $780 as sales tax.

The newspaper clipping to the left states that the number of income-tax refunds and the average amount of a refund have both risen since last year and that this should help to strengthen the economy. In these calculations, the tax-refund numbers from last year are the base, or starting point, the amounts to which this year is being compared.

Objective ③ Find the amount of investment when expense and rate of expense are known. When solving problems involving investments, the amount of the investment is the base.

EXAMPLE 3

Finding the Amount of an Investment

The yearly maintenance cost of an apartment complex is $3\frac{1}{2}$% of its value. If maintenance cost is $73,500 per year, find the value of the apartment complex.

Solution

First set up the problem:

$$R \times B = P$$

$3\frac{1}{2}$% of value is maintenance cost

$3\frac{1}{2}$% of value is $73,500

Find the value of the apartment complex, the base, with the formula $B = \frac{P}{R}$.

$$B = \frac{73,500}{.035} = \$2,100,000 \text{ value of complex.}$$

NOTE When working with a fraction of a percent it is best to change the fraction to a decimal. In Example 3, $3\frac{1}{2}$% was changed to 3.5%, which equals .035.

3.4 | Finding Rate

Objectives

1. Use the basic percent formula to solve for rate.
2. Find the rate of return when the amount of the return and the investment are known.
3. Solve for the percent remaining when the total amount and amount used are given.
4. Find the percent of change.

Problem Solving in Business

REALTY

At Century 21 Realty, where Thomas Dugally is a real estate broker, all of the expenses of running the real-estate office are compared to the income generated from sales and leasing activities. The most meaningful way of making these comparisons is by calculating all expense items as a percent of income. Dugally often calculates the rate as he makes decisions on how to run his business.

Objective 1 Use the basic percent formula to solve for rate. In the third type of percent problem, the part and base are given, and the rate must be found. The **formula for rate** is found from the formula $P = B \times R$. The diagram shows that to find the formula for rate, cover R to get $\frac{P}{B}$, or part ÷ base.

$$\text{Rate} = \frac{\text{Part}}{\text{Base}} \quad \text{or} \quad R = \frac{P}{B}$$

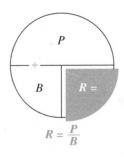

$$R = \frac{P}{B}$$

NOTE   When using this formula, P (part) is always on top.

The formula $P = B \times R$ can be used to find either P, B, or R as long as the values of two of the elements are known. When either B or R must be found, the known value must be divided into P, on the other side of the equal sign.

Find B:	Find R:
$P = B \times R$	$P = B \times R$
$B = \dfrac{P}{R}$	$R = \dfrac{P}{B}$

See why this works by using numbers.

$10 = ? \times 2$	$10 = 5 \times ?$
$? = \dfrac{10}{2}$	$? = \dfrac{10}{5}$
$? = 5$	$? = 2$

After the division, the known numbers are on one side of the equal sign, and the unknown number is on the other side of the equal sign.

The rate is identified by % or **percent**. For example, what percent of 32 is 8? Using the formula $R = \frac{P}{B}$ gives

$$R = \frac{8}{32} = .25 = 25\%.$$

Thus, 8 is 25% of 32, or 25% of 32 is 8.

Example 1

Solving for Rate

Solve for rate.

(a) 13 is _____% of 52.   **(b)** _____% of 500 is 100.

(c) 54 is _____% of 12.

Solution

(a) $\frac{13}{52} = .25 = 25\%$ **(b)** $\frac{100}{500} = .2 = 20\%$ **(c)** $\frac{54}{12} = 4.5 = 450\%$

NOTE   When finding rate, be sure to change your answer to percent.

Objective **2** **Find the rate of return when the amount of the return and the investment are known.** The rate of return in an investment problem may be found using the basic percent formula.

Example 2

Finding the Rate of Return

Thomas Dugally invested $1710 in a new computer. As a result of having this equipment, he had additional income of $1440. Find the rate of return.

Solution

First set up the problem.

$$\begin{array}{ccccc} R & \times & B & = & P \\ \% & \text{of} & \text{something} & \text{is} & \text{something} \\ \text{What \% of} & & \text{investment} & \text{is} & \text{income?} \\ \text{What \% of} & & \$1710 & \text{is} & \$1440? \end{array}$$

The amount of investment, $1710, is the base, and the return, $1440, is the part. The return is part of the total investment. Using the formula $R = \frac{P}{B}$, let $P = 1440$ and $B = 1710$.

$$R = \frac{1440}{1710} = \frac{144}{171} = .8421 \text{ or } 84.2\% \qquad \text{rounded to the nearest tenth of a percent}$$

Objective **3** **Solve for the percent remaining when the total amount and amount used are given.** In some problems, the total amount of something and the amount used are given and the percent remaining must be found.

Example 3

Solving for the Percent Remaining

A roof is expected to last 12 years (its total "life") before it needs replacement. If the roof is 10 years old, what percent of the roof's life remains?

Solution

The total life of the roof (12 years) is the base. Subtract the amount of life already used, 10 years, from the total life, 12 years, to find the number of years remaining: 12 years (total life) − 10 years (life used) = 2 years (life remaining). The life remaining is part of the entire life. By the formula $R = \frac{P}{B}$:

$$R = \frac{2}{12} = \frac{1}{6} = .166\ldots \text{ or } 16.7\% \qquad \text{rounded to the nearest tenth of a percent}$$

If the age of the roof (10 years) had been used as part, the resulting answer, 83.3% (rounded), would be the percent of life used. Find the percent of remaining life by subtracting 83.3% from 100%. The result, 16.7%, would be the percent of life remaining, the same answer.

NOTE   Remember that base is always 100%.

OBJECTIVE **4** **Find the percent of change.** The basic percent formula is used to find the **percent of increase** and the **percent of decrease**.

EXAMPLE 4
Finding the Percent of Increase

Sales of digital cameras at Circuit City climbed from $36,600 last month to $113,460 this month. Find the percent of increase.

Solution

The sales last month, $36,600, is the base. Subtract the sales last month, $36,600, from the sales this month, $113,460, to find the increase in sales volume.

$$\$113,460 - \$36,600 = \$76,860 \text{ increase in sales volume (part)}$$

For related Web activities, go to www.mathbusiness.com

Keyword: pager

Since the increase in sales volume is the part, solve for rate. Use the formula $R = \frac{P}{B}$.

$$R = \frac{\$76,860}{\$36,600} = 2.1 \text{ or } 210\%$$

The percent of increase in sales volume is 210%.

The calculator solution to this example is

$$\boxed{(}\ 113460\ \boxed{-}\ 36600\ \boxed{)}\ \boxed{\div}\ 36600\ \boxed{=}\ 2.1.$$

Note: All calculator solutions use a scientific calculator. Refer to Appendix B for scientific calculator basics.

> **PROBLEM-SOLVING HINT** Remember, to find the percent of increase, the first step is to determine the *amount of increase*. The base is *always* the original amount, last year's or last month's amount, and the amount of increase is the part.

Both of the following newspaper articles show that the sales of single-family homes declined in the month of April. The decline in sales was measured from the home sales in March and determined to be 2.5%. The two articles each give a different reason for the decline.

Reality Check

Sales of Existing Homes Declined 2.5% in April

Sales of existing single-family homes declined 2.5% in April but continued at a brisk pace, underlining both the health and stability of the nation's residential real estate market.

The National Association of Realtors said existing homes changed hands at a seasonally adjusted annual rate of 4.77 million units, compared with a rate of 4.89 million units in March and a rate of 4.04 million units in April 1997. March's rate was the highest since the Realtors' association began tracking the sales rate in 1968, so April's drop was expected by most economists.

The nation's housing market continues to benefit from a strong economy. Record low unemployment levels and high consumer confidence have encouraged Americans to buy homes. Mortgage rates have been helpful as well. After a slight drop below 7% on the typical 30-year fixed-rate mortgage in January, mortgage rates drifted between 7.1% and 7.2% in February and March, according to mortgage buyer Freddie Mac. One year ago at that time, the rate on a 30-year fixed-rate mortgage exceeded 8%.

Because closing the sale of a home can take four to eight weeks, the sales rate is affected by interest rates in the months before.

At the same time, home prices have risen steadily but not alarmingly. The Realtors' association said the median home price in April rose 6.2% to $128,200, compared with $120,700 in April 1997, but much of that rise came from increased activity at the high-price end of the housing market. Half of all houses sell for more than the median price, while half sell for less.

HOME SALES: The National Association of Realtors said sales of single-family homes fell 2.5% in April to 4.77 million units on an annualized basis from 4.89 million in March. Analysts blamed the dip on foul weather.

Source: Money magazine

Source: Wall Street Journal, 5/27/98. Reprinted by permission of Dow Jones, Inc. via Copyright Clearance Center, Inc. © 1998 Dow Jones & Co., Inc. All rights reserved worldwide.

EXAMPLE 5

Finding the
Percent of
Decrease

Sales of existing single-family homes fell to a seasonally adjusted annual number of 4.77 million units this month from 4.89 million units last month. Find the percent of decrease.

Solution

The base is always the previous period, in this example, last month, which is 4.89 million units. Subtract the number of units sold this month, 4.77 million units, from the number of units sold last month, 4.89 million units, to find the decrease in the number of units sold.

$$4.89 \text{ million} - 4.77 \text{ million} = .12 \text{ million decrease in sales (part)}$$

By the formula $R = \dfrac{P}{R}$:

$$R = \frac{.12}{4.89} = .0245 = 2.5\% \text{ (rounded)}$$

The percent of decrease is 2.5%.

The calculator solution to this example is to subtract to find the difference and then divide.

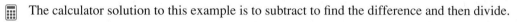

4.89 $\boxed{-}$ 4.77 $\boxed{=}$ .12 $\boxed{\div}$ 4.89 $\boxed{=}$ 0.0245 = .025 (rounded)

Note: All calculator solutions use a scientific calculator. Refer to Appendix B for scientific calculator basics.

> **PROBLEM-SOLVING HINT**   To find the percent of decrease, the first step is to determine the *amount of decrease*. The amount of decrease is the part in the problem and the base is *always* the original amount or last year's, last month's, or last week's amount.

Name   Date   Class

NATIONWIDE HOME SALES *The number of existing single-family homes sold in four regions of the country in the same month of two separate years are shown in the table below.*

Existing Home Sales

Region	Last Year	This Year
Northeast	32,000	36,000
Midwest	65,000	66,300
South	82,000	77,500
West	54,000	49,600

Use the table above to answer Exercises 17–20.

17. Find the percent of increase in sales in the northeastern region.

17. _____

18. Find the percent of increase in sales in the midwestern region.

18. _____

19. What is the percent of decrease in sales in the southern region?

19. _____

20. What is the percent of decrease in sales in the western region?

20. _____

21. VENDING-MACHINE SALES Of the total candy bars contained in a vending machine, 240 bars have been sold. If 25% of the bars have been sold, find the total number of candy bars that were in the machine.

21. _____

22. TOTAL SALES If the sales tax rate is $7\frac{1}{2}\%$ and the sales tax collected is $942.30, find the total sales.

22. _____

23. FAMILY BUDGETING Stephen and Heather Hall established a budget allowing 25 percent of their total income for rent, 30 percent for food, 8 percent for clothing, 20 percent for travel and recreation, and the remainder for savings. Stephen takes home $1950 per month and Heather takes home $28,500 per year. How much will the couple save in a year?

23. _____

24. CHICKEN-NOODLE SOUP In one year there were 350 million cans of chicken noodle soup sold (all brands). If 60% of this soup is sold in the cold-and-flu season (October through March), find the number of cans sold in the cold-and-flu season.

24. _____

25. FLOOD INSURANCE According to the Federal Emergency Management Agency (FEMA) there are 11 million buildings at risk of flooding. The agency finds that only 2.6 million of these are currently insured for flooding. Find the percent that are insured.

25. _____

26. REFRIGERATOR CAPACITY A Hotpoint refrigerator has a capacity of 11.5 cubic feet in the refrigerator and 5.5 cubic feet in the freezer. What percent of the total capacity is the capacity of the freezer?

26. _____

27. SIDE-IMPACT COLLISIONS Automobile accidents involving side-impact collision resulted in 9000 deaths last year. If automobiles were manufactured to meet a side-impact standard it is estimated that 63.8% of these deaths would have been prevented. How many deaths would have been prevented?

27. _____

28. NEW-HOME PRICES The average price of a new home rose 4.2%. If the average price of a new home was $131,500, find the average price after the increase.

28. _____

29. U.S. PATENT RECIPIENTS Among the 50 companies receiving the greatest number of U.S. patents last year, 18 were Japanese companies. What percent of the top 50 companies were Japanese companies?

29. _____

30. LAYOFF ALTERNATIVE Instead of laying off workers, a company cut all employee hours from 40 hours a week to 30 hours a week. What percent were employee hours cut?

30. _____

3.5 | INCREASE AND DECREASE PROBLEMS

Objectives

1. Learn to identify an increase or a decrease problem.
2. Apply the basic diagram for increase word problems.
3. Use the basic percent formula to solve increase problems.
4. Apply the basic diagram for decrease word problems.
5. Use the basic percent formula to solve decrease problems.

PROBLEM SOLVING IN BUSINESS

The real estate market is in constant change. Thomas Dugally of Century 21 Realty knows that real estate values are always changing, usually going up, occasionally going down, but never staying the same. Dugally needs to keep track of the market and must calculate increases and decreases in value on a regular basis.

Objective 1 **Learn to identify an increase or decrease problem.** Businesses commonly look at how amounts change, either up or down. For example, a manager might need to know the percent by which sales have increased or costs have decreased, while a consumer might need to know the percent by which the price of an item has changed. Identify these **increase** and **decrease** problems as follows.

Identifying Increase and Decrease Problems

Increase problem. The base (100%) *plus* some portion of the base, gives a new value which is the part. Phrases such as *after an increase of*, *more than*, or *greater than* often indicate an increase problem. The basic formula for an increase problem is

$$\text{Original} + \text{Increase} = \text{New value.}$$
$$\text{(base)} \qquad\qquad \text{(part)}$$

Decrease problem. The part equals the base (100%) *minus* some portion of the base, giving a new value. Phrases such as *after a decrease of*, *less than*, or *after a reduction of* often indicate a decrease problem. The basic formula for a decrease problem is

$$\text{Original} - \text{Decrease} = \text{New value.}$$
$$\text{(base)} \qquad\qquad \text{(part)}$$

> **NOTE** Base is always the original amount and both increase and decrease problems are *base* problems. Base is always 100%.

EXAMPLE 1
Using a Diagram to Understand an Increase Problem

The value of a home sold by Thomas Dugally this year is $121,000, which is 10% more than last year's value. Find the value of the home last year.

Solution

Use a diagram to help solve this problem. Remember that base is the starting point, or that to which something is compared. In this case the base is last year's value. Call base 100%, and remember that

$$\text{Original} + \text{Increase} = \text{New value.}$$

Objective **2** Apply the basic diagram for increase word problems.

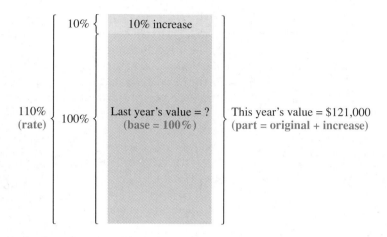

This diagram shows that the 10% increase is based on last year's value (which is unknown) and not on this year's value of $121,000. To get this year's value, add 10% of last year's value to the amount of last year's value.

Objective **3** Use the basic percent formula to solve increase problems.

	Original	+	Increase	=	New value
	100%	+	**10%**	=	**110%**

This year's value is all of last year's value (100%) plus 10% of last year's value (or 100% + 10% = 110%). Since this year's value is 110% of last year's value, find last year's value, or the base. The formula $B = \frac{P}{R}$ gives

$$B = \frac{\$121{,}000}{\mathbf{110\%}}$$ ⟵ An amount that is all of base plus 10% of base.
⟵ 100% + 10%

$$B = \frac{\$121{,}000}{\mathbf{1.1}}$$ ⟵ 110% changed to 1.1 (change % to decimal)

$$B = \$110{,}000$$ ⟵ last year's value

Now check the answer.

$$
\begin{array}{ll}
\$110{,}000 & \longleftarrow \text{ last year's value} \\
+\quad 11{,}000 & \longleftarrow \text{ 10\% of \$110,000} \\
\hline
\$121{,}000 & \longleftarrow \text{ this year's value}
\end{array}
$$

PROBLEM-SOLVING HINT The common error in solving an increase problem is thinking that the base is given and that the solution can be found by solving for part. Remember that the number given in Example 1 above, $121,000, is the result of having added 10% of the base to the base (100% + 10% = 110%). In fact, $121,000 is the part, and base must be found.

The following graphic shows the rate of world population growth over many decades and the length of time that it takes for the population to double at various rates of growth. Population growth rates are an example of increase problems because each year's rate of growth (increase) is based on the previous year. Similarly, last year's rate of growth was based on the year prior to that.

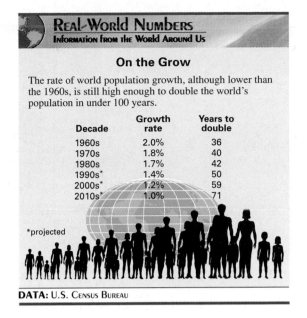

The next example shows how to handle *two* increases.

EXAMPLE 2

Finding Base after
Two Increases

At Builders Doors, production last year was 20% more than the year before. This year's production is 93,600 doors, which is 20% more than last year's. Find the number of doors produced two years ago.

SOLUTION

The two 20% increases cannot be added together because the increases are from two different years, or two separate bases. The problem must be solved in two steps. First, use a diagram to find last year's production.

The diagram shows that last year's production plus 20% of last year's production equals this year's production. If $P = 93,600$ and $R = 100\% + 20\% = 120\%$, the formula $B = \frac{P}{R}$ gives

$$B = \frac{93,600}{120\%} = \frac{93,600}{1.2} = 78,000 \text{ last year's production}$$

Production last year was 78,000 doors. Production for the preceding year (two years ago) must now be found. Use another diagram.

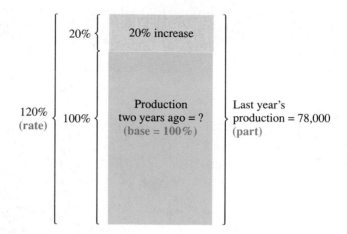

Thus, production two years ago added to 20% of production two years ago equals last year's production.

Using the formula $B = \frac{P}{R}$ with P equal to 78,000 and R equal to 120%:

$$B = \frac{78,000}{120\%} = \frac{78,000}{1.2} = 65,000 \text{ production 2 years ago}$$

Check the answer.

65,000	production two years ago
+ 13,000	20% increase
78,000	production last year
+ 15,600	20% increase
93,600	production this year

The calculator solution to this example divides in a series.

93600 $\div$ 1.2 $\div$ 1.2 $=$ 65000

Note: All calculator solutions use a scientific calculator. Refer to Appendix B for scientific calculator basics.

PROBLEM-SOLVING HINT   It is important to realize that the two 20% increases cannot be added together to equal one increase of 40%. Each 20% increase is calculated on a different base.

EXAMPLE 3

Using a Diagram to Understand a Decrease Problem

After Sport About deducted 10% from the price of a pair of skis, Brandon Bleyer paid $135. What was the original price of the skis?

SOLUTION

Use a diagram again, and remember that base is the starting point, in this case the original price. As always, the base is 100%. Use the decrease formula.

Original	−	Decrease	=	New value
100%	−	10%	=	90%

OBJECTIVE **4** Apply the basic diagram for decrease word problems.

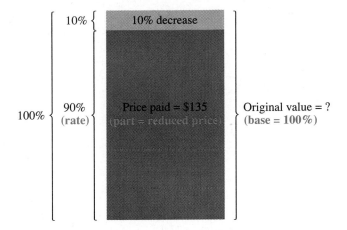

OBJECTIVE **5** Use the basic percent formula to solve decrease problems. The diagram shows that 10% was deducted from the original price. The result equals the price paid, which is 90% of the original price. Since the original price is needed, and the diagram shows that the original price here is the base, use the formula $B = \frac{P}{R}$.

But what should be used as the rate? The rate 10% cannot be used because the original price is unknown (the price to which 10% was applied). The rate 90% (the difference, 100% − 10% = 90%) must be used since 90% of the original price is the $135 price paid. Now find the base.

$$B = \frac{P}{R}$$

$$B = \frac{135}{90\%} = \frac{135}{.9} = \$150 \text{ original price}$$

Check the answer.

$$\begin{array}{rl} \$150 & \text{original price} \\ - \quad 15 & \text{10\% discount} \\ \hline \$135 & \text{price paid} \end{array}$$

> **PROBLEM-SOLVING HINT**   The common mistake made in Example 3 is thinking that the reduced price, $135, is the base. The original price is the base while the reduced price, $135, is a result after subtracting 10% from the base. The reduced price is the part or 90% *of the base* (100% − 10% = 90%).

Name _____ Date _____ Class _____

21. **NURSING-HOME CARE** The cost of nursing-home care in the United States will jump nearly 12% to $66 billion next year. Find the cost of nursing home care this year. (Round to the nearest tenth of a billion.)

21. _____

22. **EXPENSIVE RESTAURANTS** Among New York City's 20 most expensive restaurants, the average per-meal cost increased 6.5% to $69.33 in the last year. Find the price of this meal before the increase.

22. _____

23. **SURPLUS-EQUIPMENT SALES** In a three-day public sale of Jackson County surplus equipment, the first day brought $5750 in sales and the second day brought $4186 in sales, with 28% of the original equipment left to be sold on the third day. Find the value of equipment left to sell.

23. _____

24. **COLLEGE EXPENSES** After spending $3450 for tuition and $4350 for dormitory fees, Donald Cole finds that 35% of his original savings remains. Find the amount of his savings that remains.

24. _____

25. **ROLL WITH IT** This year's sales of Charmin toilet tissue are $1.052 billion. If this is a decrease in sales of 2.4% from last year, find last year's sales. (Round to the nearest thousandth of a billion.)

25. _____

26. **CONDOMINIUM SALES** If an owner quickly sold her condominium for $86,330, which was a loss of 11% of the original purchase price, how much had the owner paid originally?

26. _____

27. **WINTER-WHEAT PLANTING** Even though wheat prices rose during the planting season, farmers planted only 50.2 million acres of winter wheat varieties. If this is 2% fewer acres than last year, find the number of acres planted last year. (Round to the nearest tenth of a million.)

27. _____

28. **LEATHER-CLOTHING SALES** Department stores and specialty chains sold 4.1 million leather jackets and coats this year. If this is a 38% drop in sales from last year, find last year's sales. (Round to the nearest tenth of a million.)

28. _____

29. **COMMUNITY-COLLEGE ENROLLMENT** In 1999, the student enrollment at American River College was 8% more than it was in 1998. If the enrollment was 23,328 students in 2000, which was 8% more than it was in 1999, find the student enrollment in 1998.

29. _____

30. **UNIVERSITY FEES** Students at the state universities are outraged. The annual university fees were 30% more last year than they were the year before. If the fees are $2704 per year this year, which is 30% more than they were last year, find the annual student fees two years ago.

30. _____

31. **PERSONAL COMPUTERS** Worldwide personal-computer shipments rose 15% this year to 79.81 million units. Find the number of personal computers shipped last year.

31. _____

32. **MINORITY LOANS** A large mortgage lender made 52% more loans to minorities this year than last year. If the number of loans to minorities this year is 2660, find the number of loans made to minorities last year.

32. _____

33. **NEW-HOME SALES** New-home sales this year in the Sacramento, California area were 14% fewer than last year. If the number of new homes sold this year was 5645, find the number of new homes sold last year. (Round to the nearest whole number.)

33. _____

34. **NEW-HOME PRICES** The median price for a new home in the Sacramento, California area is $148,950—down 2.5% from last year. Find the median price for a new home last year. (Round to the nearest dollar.)

34. _____

CHAPTER **3** | Quick Review

CHAPTER TERMS

Review the following terms to test your understanding of the chapter. For each term you do not know, refer to the page number found next to that term.

CONCEPTS	EXAMPLES
3.1 Writing a decimal as a percent Move the decimal point two places to the right and attach a percent sign (%).	$.75(.75.) = 75\%$
3.1 Writing a fraction as a percent First change the fraction to a decimal. Then move the decimal point two places to the right and attach a percent sign (%).	$\dfrac{2}{5} = .4$ $.4 \,(.40.) = 40\%$
3.1 Writing a percent as a decimal Move the decimal point two places to the left and drop the percent sign (%).	$50\% \,(.50.\%) = .5$
3.1 Writing a percent as a fraction First change the percent to a decimal. Then write the decimal as a fraction in lowest terms.	$15\% \,(.15.\%) = .15 = \dfrac{15}{100} = \dfrac{3}{20}$
3.1 Writing a fractional percent as a decimal First change the fraction to a decimal, leaving the percent sign. Then move the decimal point two places to the left and drop the percent sign (%).	$\dfrac{1}{2}\% = .5\%$ $.5\% = .005$
3.2 Solving for part, using the percent formula $$\text{Part} = \text{Base} \times \text{Rate}$$ $$P = B \times R$$ $$P = BR$$ _____ % of _____ is _____	A company offered a 15% discount on all sales. Find the discount on sales of $1850. $$P = B \times R$$ $$P = \$1850 \times 15\%$$ $$P = \$1850 \times .15 = \$277.50 \text{ discount}$$
3.2 Using the standard format to solve percent problems Express the problem in the format $$R \times B = P$$ where % of something is something. Notice that *of* means $\times$ and *is* means $=$.	A shop gives a 10% discount on all repairs. Find the discount on a $175 repair. $$R \times B = P$$ % of something is something 10% of repair is discount $.1 \times \$175 = \$17.50$ discount
3.3 Using the percent formula to solve for base Use $P = B \times R$. $$B = \dfrac{P}{R}$$	If the sales tax rate is 4%, find amount of sales if the sales tax is $18. $$R \times B = P$$ % of something is something 4% of sales is $18 (tax) $$B = \dfrac{18}{.04} = \$450 \text{ sales}$$

CONCEPTS	EXAMPLES
3.4 Using the percent formula to solve for rate Use $P = B \times R$. 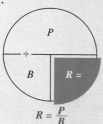 $R = \dfrac{P}{B}$	The return is $307.80 on an investment of $3420. Find the rate of return. $$R \times B = P$$ % of something is something What % of investment is return? What % of $3420 is $307.80? $$R = \dfrac{307.8}{3420} = .09 = 9\%$$
3.4 Finding the percent of change Calculate the change (increase or decrease) that is the part. Base is amount before the change. Use $R = \dfrac{P}{B}$.	Production rose from 3820 units to 5157 units. Find the percent of increase. $$5157 - 3820 = 1337 \text{ change (increase)}$$ $$R = \dfrac{1337}{3820} = .35 = 35\%$$
3.5 Drawing a diagram and using the percent formula to solve increase problems Solve for base given rate (110%) and part (after increase). 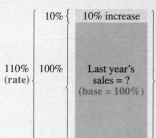	This year's sales are $121,000, which is 10% more than last year's sales. Find last year's sales. Original + Increase = New Value $$100\% + 10\% = 110\%$$ Using $B = \dfrac{P}{R}$ $$B = \dfrac{\$121{,}000}{110\%} = \dfrac{\$121{,}000}{1.1}$$ $$= \$110{,}000 \text{ last year's sales}$$ Check: $\begin{array}{lr} \$110{,}000 & \text{last year's sales} \\ +\quad 11{,}000 & \text{(10\% of \$110,000)} \\ \hline \$121{,}000 & \text{this year's sales} \end{array}$
3.5 Drawing a diagram and using an equation to solve a decrease problem Solve for base given rate (90%) and part (after decrease). 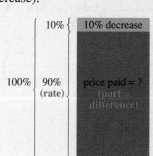	After a deduction of 10% from the price, a customer paid $135. Find the original price. Original − Decrease = New value $$100\% - 10\% = 90\%$$ Using $B = \dfrac{P}{R}$ $$B = \dfrac{135}{.9} = \$150 \text{ original price}$$ Check: $\begin{array}{lr} \$150 & \text{original price} \\ -\quad 15 & \text{(10\% discount)} \\ \hline \$135 & \text{price paid} \end{array}$

CHAPTER 3 | SUMMARY EXERCISE

MATHEMATICS for the COLLECTOR

Collecting baseball cards is an activity enjoyed by many that can also be very profitable. For instance, a 1952 Jackie Robinson rookie baseball card is currently valued at $1000. Listed below are some popular rookie cards along with price information for this year and last year. Find the card price last year, the percent of change from last year, or the card price this year as necessary. Round dollar amounts to the nearest dollar, and percents to the nearest percent.

The Ups and Downs of Last Year

Rookie Card	Card Price Last Year	Card Price This Year	% Change From Last Year
Chipper Jones	$40	_____	0%
Cal Ripken, Jr.	$75	$70	_____
Nomar Garciaparra	_____	$30	650%
Nolan Ryan	$1000	_____	−10%
Ken Griffey, Jr.	_____	$100	33%
Frank Thomas	$90	$80	_____
Will Clark	$6	_____	−17%
Mark McGwire	_____	$150	650%
Sammy Sosa	$3	$150	_____
Alex Rodriguez	$40	$30	_____

For related Web activities, go to www.mathbusiness.com

Keyword:
batter up

Investigate

List five things that people collect. From your own experience as a collector or after talking with a collector, do you feel that collecting is a good way to invest money? Find some price guides for collectables. Use the price guide to determine which variables can determine the value of a collectable. How would numbers be used by a collector? Name three types of investments that you feel are as good as, or better than, collectables.

For related Web activities, go to www.mathbusiness.com

'Net Assets

CENTURY 21

STATISTICS

- 1999: Headquarters in Parsippany, New Jersey

- 110,000 brokers and agents

- 6300 offices in 25 countries

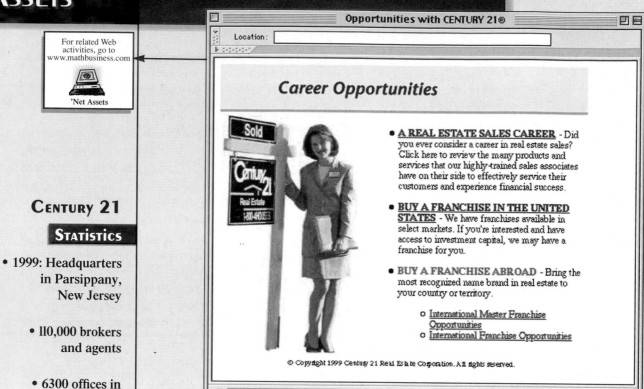

Century 21 is franchiser of the world's largest residential real estate sales organization. It provides comprehensive training, management, administrative, and marketing support for more than 6300 independently owned and operated offices with over 110,000 brokers and agents in more than 25 countries worldwide.

Century 21 is the number-one consumer brand in the real estate industry and has the largest network and greatest global coverage of any competing brand. It is dedicated to continually providing buyers and sellers of real estate with the highest level of services possible.

1. A report by Century 21 says that home values in a certain area have increased by 8.2% since last year. Find the value of a home today that was valued at $125,000 last year.

2. Total property sales in a Century 21 office this month were $4.76 million. If total sales last month were $4.25 million, find the percent of increase.

Phone or visit a Century 21 office in your community and introduce yourself as a student before asking the following questions.

3. In what kinds of applications does the real estate industry use percent? Describe a minimum of six.

4. What are the advantages of working at Century 21? Ask for five positive characteristics of a career in real estate. Do you think that a career in real estate is for you? Why or why not?

Name _____   Date _____   Class _____

CHAPTER **3** | TEST

To help you review, the numbers in brackets show the section in which the topic was discussed.

Solve each of the following.   [3.1 THROUGH 3.4]

1. 18 members is 12% of what number of members?

1. _____ 150 _____

2. What is 5% of 480 vans?

2. _____ 24 _____

3. 33 shippers is 3% of what number of shippers?

3. _____ 1100 _____

4. 36 accounts is what percent of 1440 accounts?

4. _____ $2\frac{1}{2}$% _____

5. What is $\frac{1}{4}$% of $1500?

5. _____ 3.75 _____

6. Find the fractional equivalent of 24%.

6. _____

7. 24 loads is $2\frac{1}{2}$% of how many loads?

7. _____

8. Change 87.5% to its fractional equivalent.

$$\frac{875}{1000} \quad \frac{35}{40} \quad \frac{7}{8}$$

8. _____ $\frac{7}{8}$ _____

9. $70.55 is what percent of $830?

9. _____ $8\frac{1}{2}$% _____

10. What is the fractional equivalent of $\frac{1}{2}$%?

$$\frac{.50\%}{\frac{50}{100}\,00} \quad \frac{1}{200}$$

10. _____ $\frac{1}{200}$ _____

11. One share of stock in Telefono de Mexico sells for $45.50 and pays a 2% dividend. Find the dividend per share.   **[3.2]**

11. _____ 91¢ _____

12. A supervisor at Barrett Manufacturing finds that rejects amount to 1120 units per month. If this amounts to .5% of total monthly production, find the total monthly production.   **[3.3]**

12. _____

13. Auto sales in eight Asian countries are expected to drop 29.2% this year from last year's sales of 3.83 million vehicles. Find the number of vehicles expected to be sold this year (after the drop). Round to the nearest hundredth of a million.   **[3.2]**

13. _____

14. It is estimated that 3 million people in the U.S. who are between the ages 55 and 64 have no health insurance. If this is 14% of the people in this age bracket, find the number of Americans in this age bracket. Round to the nearest hundredth of a million.   **[3.3]**

14. _____

15. A retail store with a monthly advertising budget of $3400 decides to set up a media budget. They plan to spend 22% for television, 38% for newspaper, 14% for outdoor signs, 15% for radio, and the remainder for bumper stickers. **(a)** What percent of the total budget do they plan to spend on bumper stickers? **(b)** How much do they plan to spend on bumper stickers for the entire year?   **[3.2]**

(a) _____

(b) _____

16. The government is offering a $25,000 bonus to federal employees for retiring early. After taxes and other deductions the employee will receive only $17,000. What percent of the bonus will the employee actually receive?   **[3.4]**

16. _____

17. A digital camera is marked "reduced 25%, now only $637.50." Find the original price of the digital camera.   **[3.5]**

17. _____

18. Last year's backpack sales were 10% more than they were the year before. This year's sales are 1452 units, which is 10% more than last year. Find the number of backpacks sold two years ago.   **[3.5]**

18. _____

19. One day on the London Stock Exchange, Unilever's stock shares increased 12.3 pence to 449.5 pence. Find the percent of increase.   **[3.4]**

19. _____

20. The number of residential housing permits issued in the U.S. this year is predicted to be 1.38 million. If this is an increase of 15% over last year, find the number of permits issued last year.   **[3.5]**

20. _____

Name   Date   Class

Cumulative Review | Chapters 1–3

To help you review, the numbers in brackets show the section in which the topic was introduced.

Round each of the following numbers as indicated.   **[1.1 and 1.3]**

1. 78,572 to the nearest hundred

2. 4,732,489 to the nearest thousand

3. 62.65 to the nearest tenth

4. 215.6749 to the nearest hundredth

1. _____

2. _____

3. _____

4. _____

Solve each of the following problems.   **[1.1 through 1.5]**

5.
```
   351
   763
  2478
+   17
```

6.
```
  45,867
− 37,985
```

7.
```
   634
×   38
```

8.
```
  2450
×  320
```

9. 6290 ÷ 74 = _____

10. 22,850 ÷ 102 = _____
(*Hint:* Write the answer as a mixed number.)

11. .46 + 9.2 + 8 + 17.514 = _____

12.
```
  45.36
− 23.7
```

13.
```
  29.8
× .41
```

14. $21.8\overline{)396.76}$

Solve the following application problems.

15. Bryan Gripka decides to establish a budget. He will spend $450 for rent, $325 for food, $320 for child care, $182 for transportation, $150 for other expenses, and he will put the remainder in savings. If his take-home pay is $1620, find his savings.   **[1.1]**

15. _____

16. The Enabling Supply House purchases 6 wheelchairs at $1256 each and 15 speech compression recorder-players at $895 each. Find the total cost.   **[1.1–1.2]**

16. _____

17. Software Supply had a bank balance of $29,742.18 at the beginning of April. During the month, the firm made deposits of $14,096.18 and $6529.42. A total of $18,709.51 in checks was paid by the bank during the month. Find the firm's checking account balance at the end of April.   **[1.4]**

17. _____

18. Christine Grexa pays $53.19 each month to the Bank of Bolivia. How many months will it take her to pay off $1436.13?   **[1.5]**

18. _____

Solve each of the following problems.   **[2.1 through 2.4]**

19. Write $\dfrac{48}{54}$ in lowest terms. _____

20. Write $8\dfrac{1}{8}$ as an improper fraction. _____

21. Write $\dfrac{107}{15}$ as a mixed number. _____

22. $1\dfrac{2}{3} + 2\dfrac{3}{4} = $ _____

23. $5\dfrac{7}{8} + 7\dfrac{2}{3} = $ _____

24. $6\dfrac{1}{3} - 4\dfrac{7}{12} = $ _____

25. $8\dfrac{1}{2} \times \dfrac{9}{17} \times \dfrac{2}{3} = $ _____

26. $3\dfrac{3}{4} \div \dfrac{27}{16} = $ _____

Solve each of the following application problems.

27. The area of a piece of land is $63\dfrac{3}{4}$ acres. One-third of the land is sold. What is the area of the land that is left?   **[2.4]**

27. _____

28. To prepare for the state real estate exam, Bonnie Maddison studied $5\dfrac{1}{2}$ hours on the first day, $6\dfrac{1}{4}$ hours on the second day, $3\dfrac{3}{4}$ hours on the third day, and 7 hours on the fourth day. How many hours did she study altogether?   **[2.3]**

28. _____

29. The storage yard at American River Raft Rental has four sides and is enclosed with $527\dfrac{1}{24}$ feet of security fencing around it. If three sides of the yard measure $107\dfrac{2}{3}$ feet, $150\dfrac{3}{4}$ feet, and $138\dfrac{5}{8}$ feet, find the length of the fourth side.   **[2.3]**

29. _____

30. Play-It-Now Sports Center has decided to divide $\dfrac{2}{3}$ of the company's profit sharing funds evenly among the eight store managers. What fraction of the total amount will each receive?   **[2.4]**

30. _____

Solve each of the following problems.   **[2.5]**

31. Change .35 to a fraction.

31. _____

32. Change $\dfrac{2}{3}$ to a decimal. Round to the nearest thousandth.

32. _____

Name   Date   Class

Solve each of the following problems.   **[3.1 through 3.4]**

33. Change $\frac{5}{8}$ to a percent _____

34. Change .25% to a decimal. _____

35. Find 18% of 2500 prospects. _____

36. Find 134% of $80. _____

37. 275 sales is what percent of 1100 sales? _____

38. 375 patients is what percent of 250 patients? _____

Solve each of the following application problems.

39. The U.S. Patent Office received 230,000 patent applications last year and issued 112,091 patents. What percent of the patent applications resulted in patents? Round to the nearest tenth of a percent.   **[3.4]**

39. _____

40. The world population last year was 5.75 billion people. If 32% of the world population was under the age of 15, find the number of people in the world who were under the age of 15.   **[3.2]**

40. _____

41. Bookstore sales of the *Physicians' Desk Reference*, which contains prescription drug information, rose 13.7% this year. If sales this year were 111,150 copies, find last year's sales. (Round to the nearest whole number.)   **[3.5]**

41. _____

42. After deducting 11.8% of total sales as her commission, George-Ann Hornor, a salesperson for Marx Toy Company, deposited $35,138.88 to the company account. Find the total amount of her sales.   **[3.5]**

42. _____

CHAPTER 4

BANK SERVICES

Books On Line did not begin as a business on the Internet. Long before the Web became a viable business forum, Jill Owens owned and operated a small specialty bookstore dealing in antique, rare, and out-of-print books. The books that she buys and sells are highly collectable and usually quite expensive. Her customers are a very selective group of people who in the past have been difficult to find. In short, she just was not able to increase the size of her market during the several years she owned her store.

Judging that most people who have access to the Internet will search it for their hobbies and interests, Jill decided to try a new approach in selling her specialty product. In less than one month, business was booming and Jill's business became known as Books On Line.

As her business has grown, one of the most important decisions made by Jill Owens was selecting a bank that would offer her the services to help her operate her business profitably and with the greatest efficiency. Knowing about each service that a bank offers can help anyone, regardless of whether they own or operate a business.

Modern banks and savings institutions offer many services; they are more than just places to deposit savings and take out loans. Today, many types of savings accounts are offered, as well as several varieties of checking accounts. Additional services such as home and business banking with the use of computers, automated teller machines (ATMs), credit cards, debit cards, investment securities services, collection of notes (covered in Chapter 8), and even payroll services to the business owner are also available.

This chapter examines checking accounts and check registers and how to use them. It also discusses business checking-account services, the depositing of credit-card transactions, and, finally, bank reconciliation (balancing a checking account).

4.1 | CHECKING ACCOUNTS AND CHECK REGISTERS

Objectives

1. Identify the parts of a check.
2. Know the types of checking accounts.
3. Find the monthly service charges.
4. Identify the parts of a deposit slip.
5. Identify the parts of a check stub.
6. Complete the parts of a check register.

One of the first bank services that Books On Line needed was a business checking account. Jill Owens knew that she would be receiving checks from customers and that she would be using checks to pay her suppliers and all of the other expenses of operating her business. Example 1 shows how the monthly service charge for her checking account is determined.

For related Web activities, go to www.mathbusiness.com

Keyword: checks

OBJECTIVE ☐1 Identify the parts of a check. Even with the growth in **electronic commerce (EC)**, where goods are purchased and sold electronically, the majority of business transactions today still involve checks.

A small business may write several hundred checks each month and take in several thousand, while large businesses can take in several million checks in a month. This heavy reliance on checks makes it important for all people in business to have a good understanding of checks and checking accounts. The various parts of a check are explained in the following diagram.

Reality Check

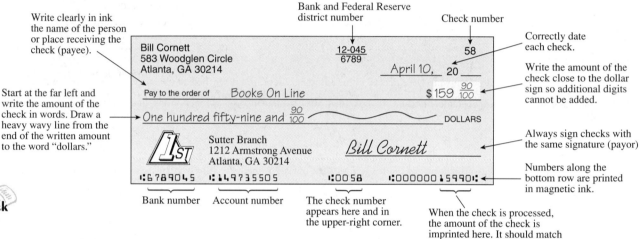

Write clearly in ink the name of the person or place receiving the check (payee).

Bank and Federal Reserve district number

Check number

Correctly date each check.

Write the amount of the check close to the dollar sign so additional digits cannot be added.

Start at the far left and write the amount of the check in words. Draw a heavy wavy line from the end of the written amount to the word "dollars."

Always sign checks with the same signature (payor)

Numbers along the bottom row are printed in magnetic ink.

Bank number   Account number

The check number appears here and in the upper-right corner.

When the check is processed, the amount of the check is imprinted here. It should match the check amount ($159.90).

OBJECTIVE ☐2 Know the types of checking accounts. Two main types of checking accounts are available.

Personal checking accounts are used by individuals. The bank supplies printed checks (normally charging a check-printing fee) for the customer to use. Some banks offer the checking account at no charge to the customer, but most require that a minimum monthly balance remain in the checking account. If the minimum balance is not maintained during any month, a service charge is applied to the account. Today, the **flat-fee checking account** is common. For a fixed charge per month, the bank supplies the checking account, a supply of printed checks, a bank charge card, an ATM card, a debit card, and a host of other services. **Interest paid** on checking account balances is common with personal checking accounts. These accounts are offered by savings-and-loan associations, credit unions, and banks and are available to individuals as well as a few business customers. These accounts often require much higher minimum balances than regular accounts.

Business checking accounts often receive more services and have greater activity than do personal accounts. For example, banks often arrange to receive payments on debts due to business firms. The bank automatically credits the amount to the business account.

Today, the **automated teller machine (ATM)**, offered by many banks, savings and loans, and credit unions, allows the customer to perform a great number of transactions. The ATM card and **electronic banking** allow cash withdrawals and deposits, transfer of funds from one account to another, including the paying of credit-card accounts or other loans, and account-balance inquiries. In addition, through several networking arrangements, the customer may make purchases and receive cash advances from hundreds, and in some cases thousands, of participating businesses nationally, and often worldwide.

For example, through one computer networking system, the use of the customer ATM card and a personal code will give the customer access to their account at over 100,000 Star System®,

Cirrus, or Plus ATM locations. Unless they are making a withdrawal from their own bank's ATM, the customer will usually pay a fee ranging from less than $1.00 to about $3.00 for each transaction.

> **NOTE**   Students traveling on exchange trips in foreign countries can often get cash in the local currency using their ATM cards.

These ATM cards are **debit cards**, not credit cards. When you use your debit card at a **point-of-sale terminal,** the amount of your purchase is instantly subtracted from your bank account and credit is given to the seller's bank account. When you use a credit card, you usually sign a receipt, however, when using a debit card you enter your **personal identification number (PIN)**, your special code that authorizes the transaction. Cash can also be obtained from many ATM machines using credit cards such as Visa and MasterCard.

> **NOTE**   When using the ATM card, remember to keep receipts so that the transaction can be subtracted from your bank balance. Be certain to subtract any fees that are charged for using the ATM card.

The use of **electronic funds transfer (EFT)** is a popular alternative to paper checks because EFT saves money. The following bar graph shows the growth in the use of paperless checks and indicates that *each* electronic transfer saves business or the government 40 cents.

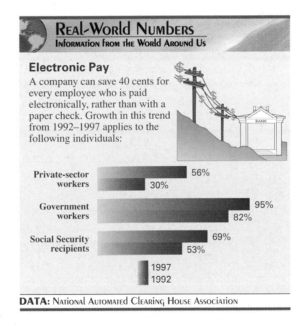

DATA: National Automated Clearing House Association

Objective **3**   **Find the monthly service charges.**   Service charges for business checking accounts are based on the average balance for the period covered by the statement. This average balance determines the **maintenance charge per month**, to which a **per-debit charge** (per-check charge) is added. The charges generally apply without regard to the amount of account activity. The following table shows some typical bank charges for a business checking account.

Average Balance	Maintenance Charge Per Month	Per-Check Charge
Less than $500	$12.00	$.20
$500–$1999	$7.50	$.20
$2000–$4999	$5.00	$.10
$5000 or more	0	0

EXAMPLE 1

Finding the Checking Account Service Charge

Find the monthly service charge for the following business accounts.

(a) Pittsburgh Glass, 38 checks written, average balance $883

According to the preceding table, an account with an average balance between $500 and $1999 has a $7.50 maintenance charge for the month. In addition, there is a per debit (check) charge of $.20. Since 38 checks were written, find the service charge as follows:

$$\$7.50 + \mathbf{38(\$.20)} = \$7.50 + \mathbf{\$7.60} = \$15.10$$

(b) Fargo Western Auto, 87 checks written, average balance $2367

Since the average balance is between $2000 and $4999, the maintenance charge for the month is $5.00 plus $.10 per debit (check). The monthly service charge is

$$\$5.00 + \mathbf{87(\$.10)} = \$5.00 + \$8.70 = \$13.70.$$

The calculator solutions to this example use chain calculations with the calculator observing the order of operations.

(a) 7.5 $\boxed{+}$ 38 $\boxed{\times}$ .2 $\boxed{=}$ 15.1

(b) 5 $\boxed{+}$ 87 $\boxed{\times}$ .1 $\boxed{=}$ 13.7

Note: All calculator solutions use a scientific calculator. Refer to Appendix B for scientific calculator basics.

OBJECTIVE $\boxed{4}$ **Identify the parts of a deposit slip.** Money, either cash or checks, is placed in a checking account with a **deposit slip** or **deposit ticket** (see the following sample). The account number is printed at the bottom in magnetic ink. The slip contains blanks for entering any currency (bills) or coin (change), as well as any checks that are to be deposited.

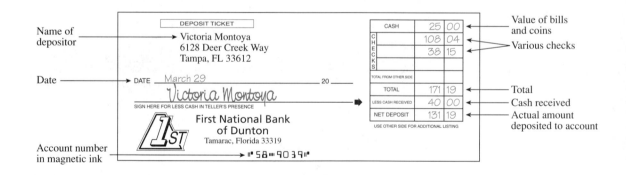

When a check is deposited, it should have "for deposit only" and either the depositor's signature or the company stamp placed on the back within 1.5 inches of the trailing edge (as seen in the following figure). In this way, if a check is lost or stolen before it is deposited, it will be worthless to anyone finding it. Such an endorsement, which limits the ability to cash a check, is called a **restricted endorsement**. An example of a restricted endorsement is shown on the following page along with two other types of endorsements. The most common endorsement by individuals is the **blank endorsement**, where only the name of the person being paid is signed. This endorsement should be used only at the moment of cashing the check. The **special endorsement**, used to pass on the check to someone else, might be used to pay a bill on another account.

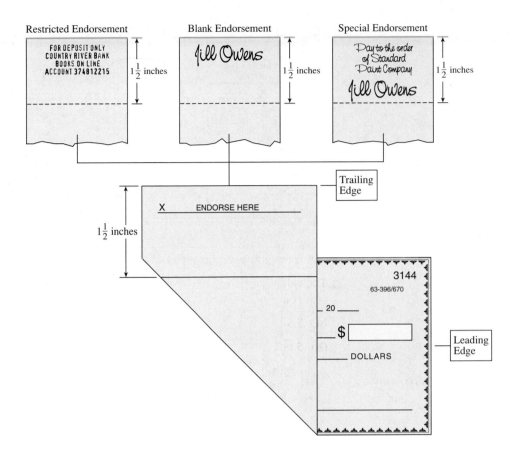

After the check is endorsed, it is normally cashed or deposited at a bank. The payee is either given cash or receives a credit in his or her account for the amount of the check. The check is then routed to a Federal Reserve Bank, which forwards the check to the payer's bank. After going through this procedure, known as **processing**, the check is then **canceled** and returned to the payer. The check will now have additional processing information on its back as shown below.

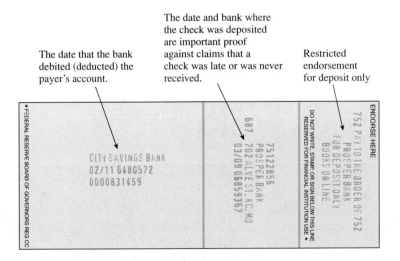

A two-sided commercial deposit slip is shown in the figure on the following page. Notice that much more space is given for an itemized list of customers' checks that are being deposited to the business account. Many financial institutions require that the bank and Federal Reserve district numbers be shown in the description column of the deposit slip. These numbers appear in the upper right-hand corner of the check and are identified in the sample check in this section.

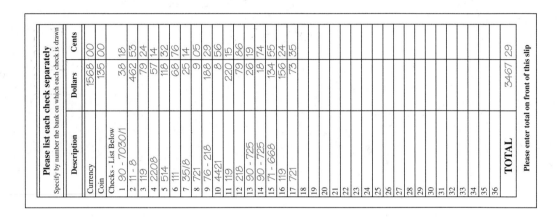

Objective 5 Identify the parts of a check stub. A record must be kept of all deposits made and all checks written. Business firms normally do this with a **check stub** for *each* check. These check stubs provide room to list the date, the person or firm to whom the check is paid, and the purpose of the check. Also, the check stub provides space to record the balance in the account after the last check was written (called the **balance brought forward**, abbreviated "Bal. Bro't. For'd." on the stub), and any sums deposited since the last check was written. The balance brought forward and amount deposited are added to provide the current balance in the checking account. The amount of the current check is then subtracted and a new balance is found. This **balance forward** from the bottom of the check stub should be written on the next check stub. A typical check stub is shown in the following figure.

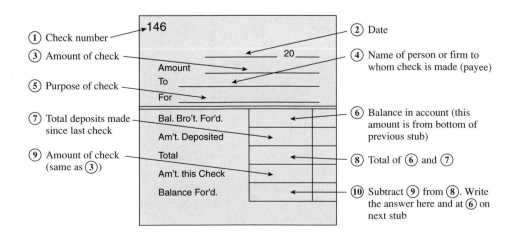

EXAMPLE 2

Completing a
Check Stub

Check number 2724 was made out on June 8 to Lillburn Utilities as payment for water and power. Assume that the check was for $182.15, that the balance brought forward is $4245.36, and that deposits of $337.71 and $193.17 have been made since the last check was written. Complete the check stub.

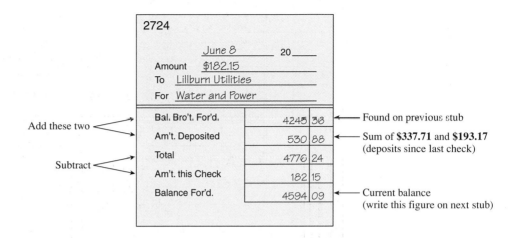

2724		
June 8 20 ___		
Amount $182.15		
To Lillburn Utilities		
For Water and Power		
Bal. Bro't. For'd.	4245	36
Am't. Deposited	530	88
Total	4776	24
Am't. this Check	182	15
Balance For'd.	4594	09

Add these two →

Subtract →

← Found on previous stub

← Sum of **$337.71** and **$193.17** (deposits since last check)

← Current balance (write this figure on next stub)

Solution

Banks offer many styles of checkbooks. Notice that the following two styles shown offer two stubs and may be used for payroll. The stub next to the check can be used as the employee's record of earnings and deductions. The second style provides space on the check itself for listing a group of invoices or bills that are being paid with that same check.

Check stub   Check

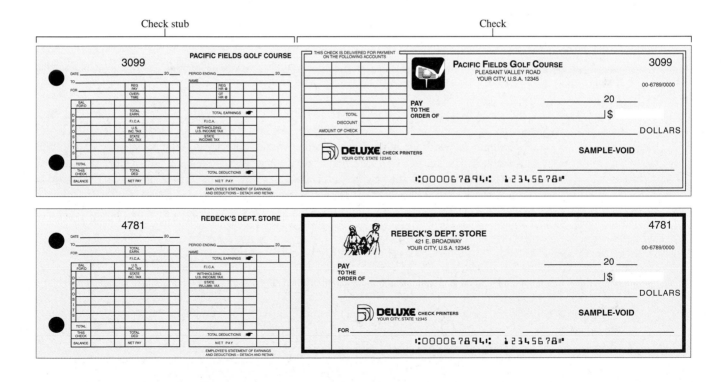

OBJECTIVE 6 Complete the parts of a check register. Some depositors prefer a **check register** to check stubs, while others use both. A check register, such as the following one, shows the checks written and deposits made at a glance. The column headed with a check mark is used to record each check after it has cleared or when it is received back from the bank.

CHECK NO.	DATE	CHECK ISSUED TO	AMOUNT OF CHECK		✓	DATE OF DEP.	AMOUNT OF DEPOSIT		BALANCE	
		BALANCE BROUGHT FORWARD →							3518	72
1435	5/8	Swan Brothers	378	93					3139	79
1436	5/8	Class Acts	25	14					3114	65
1437	5/9	Mirror Lighting	519	65					2595	00
		Deposit				5/10	3821	17	6416	17
1438	5/10	Woodlake Auditorium	750	00					5666	17
		Deposit				5/12	500	00	6166	17
1439	5/12	Rick's Clowns	170	80					5995	37
1440	5/14	Y.M.C.A.	219	17					5776	20
	5/14	ATM	120	00					5656	20
		Deposit				5/15	326	15	5982	35
1441	5/16	Stage Door Playhouse	825	00					5157	35
1442	5/17	Gilbert Eckern	1785	00					3372	35
		Deposit				5/19	1580	25	4952	60

NOTE   ATM transactions for cash withdrawals and purchases must be entered on check stubs or in the check register. The transaction amount and the charge for each transaction must then be subtracted to maintain an accurate balance.

4.2 | Checking Services and Credit-Card Transactions

Objectives

1. Recall available bank services.
2. Understand interest-paying checking plans.
3. Determine deposits with credit-card transactions.
4. Calculate the discount fee on credit-card deposits.

For related Web
activities, go to
www.mathbusiness.com

Keyword:
charge

Card Craze

- Total bank credit cards in circulation in the U.S.: 460 million.

- Number of bank card issuers: 9000.

- Top 10 issuers' share of the market: 55%.

- Average balance: $1828 per card, $3019 per family.

- Accounts 30 or more days past due: 4.33%.

- Average interest rate: 17.98%; fewer than one card in five has a rate under 16.5%.

Source: *Consumer Reports,* 1/96. Reprinted by permission.

Objective 1 Recall available bank services. Most business checking-account charges are determined by either the average balance or minimum balance in the account, together with specific charges for each service performed by the bank. Some of the services provided by banks, along with the *typical charges*, are listed here.

ATM cards are used as debit cards when making point-of-sale purchases. The fee for purchases varies from $.10 per transaction to $1.00 per month for unlimited transactions. When used at the ATM machine there is usually no fee at any branch of your bank, a fee as high as $2.00 at other banks, and an international fee as high as $5.00.

An **overdraft** occurs when checks are written for which there are **nonsufficient funds (NSF)** in the checking account and the customer has no overdraft protection. (This may also be referred to as *bouncing a check*.) A typical charge to the writer of the check is $10 to $30 per check. The same charges occur when a check is returned because it was improperly completed.

Overdraft protection is given when an account balance is insufficient to cover the amount of a check and an overdraft occurs. Charges for this vary among banks.

A **returned-deposit item** is a check that was deposited and then returned to the bank, usually because of lack of funds in the account of the person or firm writing the check. A common charge to the depositor of the check is $5.00.

A **stop-payment order** is a request to the bank from a depositor that the bank not honor a check the depositor has written ($15.00 per request).

A **cashier's check** is a check written by the financial institution itself. It therefore has the full faith and backing of the institution ($5.00 per check).

A **money order** is a purchased instrument that is often used in place of cash and is sometimes required instead of a personal or business check ($4.00 each).

A **notary service** (official certification of a signature on a document) is a service that is required on certain business documents. Occasionally this service is free to customers but there is usually a charge ($10.00).

Objective 2 Understand interest-paying checking plans. Federal banking regulations allow both personal and business interest-paying checking plans. Some of the plans combine two accounts, a savings account and a checking account, while others are simply checking accounts that collect interest on the average daily balance.

Objective 3 Determine deposits with credit-card transactions. The clipping at the side gives some facts and figures regarding **credit cards** and their popularity. With the continuing growth in electronic commerce, more and more credit-card transactions are being completed electronically by the retailer. However, a great number of retailers continue to process their credit-card sales mechanically. These credit-card sales are deposited into a business checking account with a **merchant batch header ticket** such as the one in Example 1. This form is used with Visa or MasterCard credit-card deposits. Notice that the form lists both sales slips and credit slips (refunds). Entries in each of these categories are totaled and the total credits are subtracted from the total sales to give the net amount of deposit.

The merchant batch header ticket is a triplicate form. The *bank copy* along with the charge slips, credit slips, and a printed calculator tape showing the itemized deposits and credits are deposited in the business checking account.

EXAMPLE 1

Calculating Deposits with Credit-Card Transactions

Books On Line had the following credit-card sales and refunds. Complete a merchant batch header ticket.

Sales		Refunds (Credit)
$82.31	$146.50	$13.83
$38.18	$78.80	$25.19
$65.29	$63.14	$78.56
$178.22	$208.67	

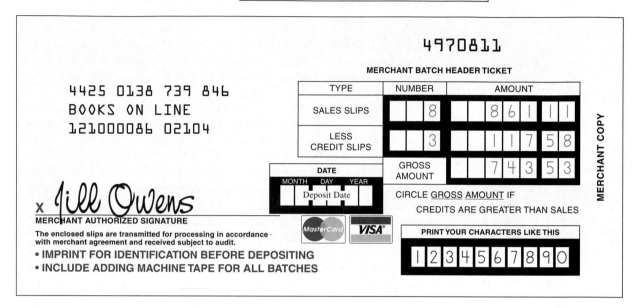

For related Web activities, go to www.mathbusiness.com

Keyword: books

Solution

All credit slips and sales slips must be totaled. The number of each of these and the totals are written at the right on the form. The total sales slips are $861.11 and the credit slips total $117.58. The difference is the gross amount; here $743.53 is the gross amount.

Objective **4** **Calculate the discount fee on credit-card deposits.** The bank collects a fee (a percent of sales) from the merchant and also an interest charge from the card user on all accounts not paid in full at the first billing. Although credit-card transactions are deposited frequently by a business, the bank calculates the discount fee on the net amount of the credit-card deposits since the last bank statement date. The fee paid by the merchant varies from 2% to 5% of the sales slip amount and is determined by the type of processing used (electronic or manual), the dollar volume of credit-card usage by the merchant, and the average amount of the sale at the merchant's store. All credit-card deposits for the month are added and the fee is subtracted from the total at the statement date.

EXAMPLE 2

Finding the Discount and the Credit Given on a Credit-Card Deposit

If the deposit in Example 1 represented total credit-card deposits for the month, find the fee charged and the credit given to the merchant at the statement date if Books On Line pays a 3% fee.

Solution

Since the total credit-card deposit for Books On Line is $743.53 and the fee is 3%, the discount charged is

$$\$743.53 \times .03 \ (3\%) = \text{\$22.31 discount charge (rounded)}$$

Out of a deposit of $743.53, the merchant will receive a credit of $743.53 − **$22.31** = **$721.22**.

The calculator solution to this example is

$$\$743.53 \ \boxed{-} \ 3 \ \boxed{\%} \ \boxed{=} \ 721.2241.$$

Note: All calculator solutions use a scientific calculator. Refer to Appendix B for scientific calculator basics.

Name _____ Date _____ Class _____

4.2 | EXERCISES

The Quick Start *exercises in each section contain solutions to help you get started.*

CREDIT-CARD DEPOSITS *Fry's Electronics does most of its business on a cash basis or through its own credit department, although it does honor major bank charge cards. In a recent period, the business had the following credit-card charges and credits. (See Examples 1 and 2.)*

Sales		Credits
$78.56	$38.15	$29.76
$875.29	$18.46	$102.15
$330.82	$22.13	$71.95
$55.24	$707.37	
$47.83	$245.91	

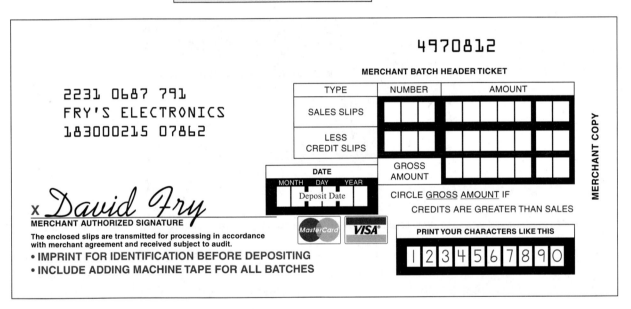

Quick Start

1. What is the total amount of sales slips?

1. $2419.76

$78.56 + $875.29 + $330.82 + $55.24 + $47.83 + $38.15 + $18.46 +
$22.13 + $707.37 + $245.91 = $2419.76

2. Find the total of the credit slips.

2. $203.86

$29.76 + $102.15 + $71.95 = $203.86

3. If these sales and credits are deposited, what is the gross amount of the deposit?

3. _____

4. If the bank charges Fry's Electronics a 3% fee, find the amount of the charge at the statement date.

4. _____

5. Find the amount of the credit given to Fry's Electronics after the fee is subtracted.

5. _____

CREDIT-CARD DEPOSITS   *Chris Campbell, owner of Bayside Jeepers, had the following credit-card transactions during a recent period. Complete a merchant batch header ticket.*

Sales		Credits
$25.18	$77.51	$38.15
$15.73	$357.18	$106.86
$338.97	$472.73	$44.38
$56.73	$129.68	
$255.18	$12.76	

4970813

MERCHANT BATCH HEADER TICKET

3218 4566 719 433
BAYSIDE JEEPERS
421000621 06205

TYPE	NUMBER	AMOUNT
SALES SLIPS		
LESS CREDIT SLIPS		
GROSS AMOUNT		

DATE

MONTH   DAY   YEAR

Deposit Date

x *Chris Campbell*
MERCHANT AUTHORIZED SIGNATURE

The enclosed slips are transmitted for processing in accordance with merchant agreement and received subject to audit.
• **IMPRINT FOR IDENTIFICATION BEFORE DEPOSITING**
• **INCLUDE ADDING MACHINE TAPE FOR ALL BATCHES**

CIRCLE <u>GROSS</u> <u>AMOUNT</u> IF
CREDITS ARE GREATER THAN SALES

MERCHANT COPY

MasterCard   **VISA**

PRINT YOUR CHARACTERS LIKE THIS

1 2 3 4 5 6 7 8 9 0

6. What is the total amount of the sales slips?   6. _____

7. Find the total of the credit slips.   7. _____

8. Find the gross deposit when the sales and credits are deposited.   8. _____

9. If the fee paid by the business is $4\frac{1}{2}\%$, find the amount of the charge at the statement date.   9. _____

10. Find the amount of the credit given to Bayside Jeepers after the fee is subtracted.   10. _____

CREDIT-CARD DEPOSITS *Maureen Tomlin Studios had the following credit-card transactions during a recent period. Complete a merchant batch header ticket.*

Sales		Credits
$7.84	$98.56	$13.86
$33.18	$318.72	$58.97
$50.76	$116.35	
$12.72	$23.78	
$9.36	$38.95	
$118.68	$235.82	

4970814

MERCHANT BATCH HEADER TICKET

TYPE	NUMBER	AMOUNT
SALES SLIPS		
LESS CREDIT SLIPS		
	GROSS AMOUNT	

4425 3857 328 811
MAUREEN TOMLIN STUDIOS
215200081 10395

DATE
MONTH   DAY   YEAR
Deposit Date

x *Maureen Tomlin*
MERCHANT AUTHORIZED SIGNATURE

The enclosed slips are transmitted for processing in accordance with merchant agreement and received subject to audit.
• **IMPRINT FOR IDENTIFICATION BEFORE DEPOSITING**
• **INCLUDE ADDING MACHINE TAPE FOR ALL BATCHES**

CIRCLE GROSS AMOUNT IF
CREDITS ARE GREATER THAN SALES

MasterCard   VISA®

PRINT YOUR CHARACTERS LIKE THIS
1234567890

MERCHANT COPY

11. What is the total amount of the sales slips?   11. _____

12. Find the total of the credit slips.   12. _____

13. Find the gross amount of deposit when the sales and credits are deposited.   13. _____

14. If the fee paid by the business is 3%, find the amount of the charge at the statement date.   14. _____

15. Find the amount of the credit given to Maureen Tomlin Studios after the fee is subtracted.   15. _____

CREDIT-CARD DEPOSITS   *Dara DeLong owns The Cellular Center, a shop that sells new and used cellular phones and accessories and does a major portion of its business in adjustments and repairs. The following credit-card sales and credits took place during a recent period. Complete a merchant batch header ticket.*

Sales		Credits
$14.86	$76.15	$43.15
$49.70	$226.17	$17.06
$183.60	$63.95	
$238.75	$111.10	
$18.36	$77.86	
$52.08	$32.62	

4970815

MERCHANT BATCH HEADER TICKET

3856 7384 221 685
THE CELLULAR CENTER
113060008 03629

TYPE	NUMBER	AMOUNT
SALES SLIPS		
LESS CREDIT SLIPS		
	GROSS AMOUNT	

DATE
MONTH   DAY   YEAR
Deposit Date

X *Dara DeLong*
MERCHANT AUTHORIZED SIGNATURE

CIRCLE GROSS AMOUNT IF
CREDITS ARE GREATER THAN SALES

The enclosed slips are transmitted for processing in accordance with merchant agreement and received subject to audit.
• IMPRINT FOR IDENTIFICATION BEFORE DEPOSITING
• INCLUDE ADDING MACHINE TAPE FOR ALL BATCHES

MasterCard   VISA

PRINT YOUR CHARACTERS LIKE THIS
1234567890

MERCHANT COPY

16. Find the amount of the sales slips for the period.

16. _____

17. Find the total of the credit slips.

17. _____

18. Find the gross deposit when the sales and credits are deposited.

18. _____

19. If the fee paid by the shop is 5%, find the amount of the charge at the statement date.

19. _____

20. Find the amount of the credit given to The Cellular Center after the fee is subtracted.

20. _____

21. List and describe in your own words four services offered to business checking-account customers. (See Objective 1.)

22. The merchant accepting a credit card from a customer must pay a fee of 2% to 5% of the transaction amount. Why is the merchant willing to do this? Who really pays this fee? (See Objective 3.)

4.3 | RECONCILIATION

Objectives

1. Know the importance of reconciling a checking account.
2. Reconcile a bank statement with a checkbook.
3. Understand the term *check outstanding*.
4. Understand the term *adjusted bank balance* or *current balance*.

PROBLEM SOLVING
IN BUSINESS

Jill Owens, owner of Books On Line, knows the importance of keeping accurate checking-account records. She has received checks from customers drawn on accounts with nonsufficient funds (NSF), but with great pride she says "I have never bounced a business check." Example 1 shows how Jill Owens recently balanced her business checking account.

For related Web
activities, go to
www.mathbusiness.com

Keyword:
bookworm

Objective **1** **Know the importance of reconciling a checking account.** Once a month, banks send their checking-account customers a **bank statement**. This bank statement shows all deposits made during the period covered by the statement, as well as all the checks paid by the bank and any automated teller machine (ATM) debit-card transactions. Bank charges for the month covered by the statement are also listed. This is especially important with a business checking account because the bank charge normally varies from month to month. On occasion, a customer's check that was deposited has to be returned due to nonsufficient funds (NSF) in the account. This is identified as a **returned check** and the amount of the check must be subtracted from the checkbook balance along with any other charges. The business must then resolve this matter with the writer of the bad check.

Objective **2** **Reconcile a bank statement with a checkbook.** Many businesses have automatic deposits made to their accounts from customers and other sources. These amounts must be added to the checkbook balance. When the bank statement is received, it is very important that its accuracy be verified. In addition, it is a good time to check the accuracy of the check register, being certain that all checks written have been listed and subtracted, and that all deposits have been added to the checking-account balance. The process of checking the bank statement and the check register is called **reconciliation**. The following bank statement is for Books On Line.

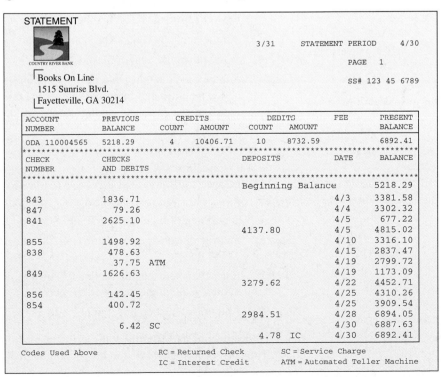

STATEMENT

COUNTRY RIVER BANK

3/31 STATEMENT PERIOD 4/30

PAGE 1

Books On Line
1515 Sunrise Blvd.
Fayetteville, GA 30214

SS# 123 45 6789

ACCOUNT NUMBER	PREVIOUS BALANCE	CREDITS COUNT	AMOUNT	DEBITS COUNT	AMOUNT	FEE	PRESENT BALANCE
ODA 110004565	5218.29	4	10406.71	10	8732.59		6892.41

CHECK NUMBER	CHECKS AND DEBITS		DEPOSITS	DATE	BALANCE
			Beginning Balance		5218.29
843	1836.71			4/3	3381.58
847	79.26			4/4	3302.32
841	2625.10			4/5	677.22
			4137.80	4/5	4815.02
855	1498.92			4/10	3316.10
838	478.63			4/15	2837.47
	37.75	ATM		4/19	2799.72
849	1626.63			4/19	1173.09
			3279.62	4/22	4452.71
856	142.45			4/25	4310.26
854	400.72			4/25	3909.54
			2984.51	4/28	6894.05
	6.42	SC		4/30	6887.63
			4.78 IC	4/30	6892.41

Codes Used Above	RC = Returned Check	SC = Service Charge
	IC = Interest Credit	ATM = Automated Teller Machine

Reconciliation is best done on the forms usually printed on the back of the bank statement. An example of the reconciliation process follows. The codes on the bank statement indicate the following: RC means Returned Check; SC means Service Charge; IC means Interest Credit; and ATM means Automated Teller Machine.

EXAMPLE 1
Reconciling a
Checking Account

Books On Line received its bank statement. The statement shows a balance of $6892.41, after a bank service charge of $6.42 and an interest credit of $4.78. Books On Line's checkbook now shows a balance of $7576.38. Reconcile the account using the form that follows.

OBJECTIVE 3 Understand the term *check outstanding*. Compare the list of checks on the bank statement with the list of checks written by the firm. Checks that have been written by the firm but do not yet appear on the bank statement have not been paid by the bank as of the date of the statement. These unpaid checks are called **checks outstanding**. The following table shows those checks written by the firm that are outstanding.

Number	Amount	Number	Amount
846	$42.73	857	$79.80
852	$598.71	858	$160.30
853	$68.12		

After listing the outstanding checks in the space provided on the form, total them. The total is $949.66.

OBJECTIVE 4 Understand the term *adjusted bank balance* or *current balance*. The following steps are used to reconcile the checking account of Books On Line.

Step 1   Enter the new balance from the front of the bank statement. The new balance is $6892.41. Write this number in the space provided on the reconcilement form.

Step 2   List any deposits made that have not yet been recorded by the bank (deposits in transit). Suppose that Books On Line has deposits of $892.41 and $739.58 that are not yet recorded. These numbers are written at step 2 on the form.

Step 3   All the numbers from steps 1 and 2 are added. At this point, the total is $8524.40.

Step 4   Write down the total of outstanding checks. The total is now $949.66.

Step 5   Subtract the total in step 4 from the number in step 3. The result here is $7574.74, called the **adjusted bank balance** or the **current balance**. This number should represent the current checking-account balance.

Now look at the firm's own records.

Step 6   List the firm's checkbook balance. As mentioned in the problem, the checkbook balance for Books On Line is $7576.38. This number is entered on line 6.

Step 7   Enter any charges not yet deducted. The check charge here is $6.42. Since there are no other fees or charges, enter $6.42 on line 7.

Step 8   Subtract the charges on line 7 from the checkbook balance on line 6 to get $7569.96.

Step 9   Enter the interest credit on line 9. The interest credit here is $4.78. (This amount is interest paid on the money in the account.)

Step 10   Add the interest on line 9 to line 8 to get $7574.74, the same result as in step 5.

Since the result from step 10 is the same as the result from step 5, the account is **balanced** (reconciled). The correct current balance in the account is $7574.74.

Checks Outstanding		
Number	\$	Amount
846	\$	42	73
852		598	71
853		68	12
857		79	80
858		160	30
Total	\$	949	66

Compare the list of checks paid by the bank with your records. List and total the checks not yet paid.

(1) Enter new balance from bank statement: \$ 6892.41

(2) List any deposits made by you and not yet recorded by the bank: + 892.41
   + 739.58
   +
   +

(3) Add all numbers from lines above.
Total: 8524.40

(4) Write total of checks outstanding: − 949.66

(5) Subtract (4) from (3).
This is adjusted bank balance: \$ 7574.74

To reconcile your records:

(6) List your checkbook balance: \$ 7576.38

(7) Write the total of any fees or charges deducted by the bank and not yet subtracted by you from your checkbook: − 6.42

(8) Subtract line (7) from line (6).   7569.96

(9) Enter interest credit: (Add to your checkbook)   + 4.78

(10) Add line (9) to line (8).
Adjusted checkbook balance.   \$ 7574.74

New balance of your account; this number should be same as (5).

If the account does not balance, either the bank or the customer has made an error. Typical errors include forgetting to enter a deposit or check in the check register, transposing figures (writing 961 as 916, for example), or making an addition or subtraction error. Often customers forget to subtract one of the bank service fees from the account balance. Occasionally, the bank may charge the customer an amount different from the check amount. Check for this error by comparing the number printed by the bank in magnetic ink in the lower right-hand corner of the check to the amount for which the check was written.

The following graphic and accompanying newspaper article say that "big banks charge bigger ATM fees." The business person as well as the consumer must look for the best value and convenience when selecting a banking-services provider.

NOTE Reconciling the bank statement is an important step in maintaining accurate checking-account records and in helping to avoid writing checks for which there are nonsufficient funds. In addition to nonsufficient funds charges, which can be costly, many businesses view a person or business who writes bad checks as irresponsible.

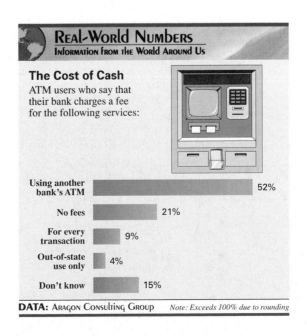

Real-World Numbers
Information from the World Around Us

The Cost of Cash
ATM users who say that their bank charges a fee for the following services:

Using another bank's ATM	52%
No fees	21%
For every transaction	9%
Out-of-state use only	4%
Don't know	15%

DATA: Aragon Consulting Group   *Note: Exceeds 100% due to rounding*

Reality Check

Big Banks Charge Bigger ATM Fees

The number of banks charging noncustomers to use their automated teller machines jumped 58% the past year, according to a report Wednesday.

The second annual survey of 470 banks in 28 states by the U.S. Public Interest Research Group (PIRG) says big banks charge ATM access fees more often than small banks and their fees are higher.

On average, they charge $1.35, vs. $1.16 for small banks.

Two years ago, the biggest ATM networks began allowing ATM owners to charge noncustomers an access fee, also called a surcharge. These fees often come on top of fees banks charge their own customers who use another bank's ATM.

The access fees are controversial. At least 25 state legislatures are considering banning or capping them, U.S. PIRG says. Federal legislation has also been introduced to ban them.

"Consumers should not be charged twice to use the ATM only once," says Ed Mierzwinski, consumer program director at U.S. PIRG.

Many small banks oppose access fees. Years ago, big banks urged small banks to join the ATM networks instead of investing in their own machines, says Donald Glass, president of the Community Bank League of New England. Now small banks are at a disadvantage because they have few ATMs to offer customers who want to avoid access fees.

The American Bankers Association (ABA) defends the fees. "Access fees have led to tremendous ATM growth," says Donald Ogilvie of the ABA, giving consumers greater access to their money.

An ATM in a convenience store couldn't break even without access fees, says Donald Davis of *Bank Network News*.

For related Web activities, go to www.mathbusiness.com

Keyword:
bounced

Source: USA Today, 4/2/98. Reprinted by permission.

Example 2

Reconciling a Checking Account

Using the information on the following check register and the bank statement, reconcile the following checking account. Compare the items appearing on the check register to the bank statement. A ✓ indicates that the check appeared on the previous month's bank statement. (Codes indicate the following: RC means Returned Check; SC means Service Charge; IC means Interest Credit; ATM means Automated Teller Machine.)

CHECK NO.	DATE	CHECK ISSUED TO	AMOUNT OF CHECK	✓	DATE OF DEP.	AMOUNT OF DEPOSIT	BALANCE
		BALANCE BROUGHT FORWARD →					2782 95
721	7/11	Miller's Outpost	138 50	✓			2644 45
722	7/12	Barber Advertising	73 08				2571 37
723	7/18	Wayside Lumber	318 62	✓			2252 75
		Deposit			7/20	980 37	3233 12
724	7/25	I.R.S.	836 15				2396 97
725	7/26	John Lessor	450 00				1946 97
726	7/28	Sacramento Bee	67 80				1879 17
727	8/2	T.V.A.	59 25				1819 92
728	8/3	Carmichael Office	97 37				1722 55
		Deposit			8/6	875 45	2598 00
ATM	8/5	ATM Cash	80 00				2518 00

Bank Statement

```
**************************************************************
CHECK      CHECKS                 DEPOSITS      DATE    BALANCE
NUMBER     AND DEBITS
**************************************************************
                                                7/20    2325.83
722        73.08                                7/22    2252.75
                                  980.37        7/24    3233.12
724        836.15                               7/28    2396.97
725        450.00    49.07 RC                   7/30    1897.90
727        59.25     80.00 ATM    3.22 IC       8/4     1761.87
                     7.60  SC                   8/5     1754.27
```

Checks Outstanding		
Number	Amount	
726	$ 67	80
728	97	37
Total	$ 165	17

Compare the list of checks paid by the bank with your records. List and total the checks not yet paid.

(1) Enter new balance from bank statement: $ 1754.27

(2) List any deposits made by you and not yet recorded by the bank:
+ 875.45
+ _____
+ _____
+ _____

(3) Add all numbers from lines above.
Total: 2629.72

(4) Write total of checks outstanding: − 165.17

(5) Subtract (4) from (3).
This is adjusted bank balance: $ 2464.55

To reconcile your records:

(6) List your checkbook balance: $ 2518.00

(7) Write the total of any fees or charges deducted by the bank and not yet subtracted by you from your checkbook: − 56.67   (Returned check and service charge)

(8) Subtract line (7) from line (6).   2461.33

(9) Enter interest credit: (Add to your checkbook) + 3.22

(10) Add line (9) to line (8).
Adjusted checkbook balance. $ 2464.55

New balance of your account; this number should be same as (5).

Since the adjusted bank balance from step 5 is the same as the new balance from step 10, the account is reconciled (balanced). The correct current balance in the account is $2464.55.

For related Web
activities, go to
www.mathbusiness.com

'Net Assets

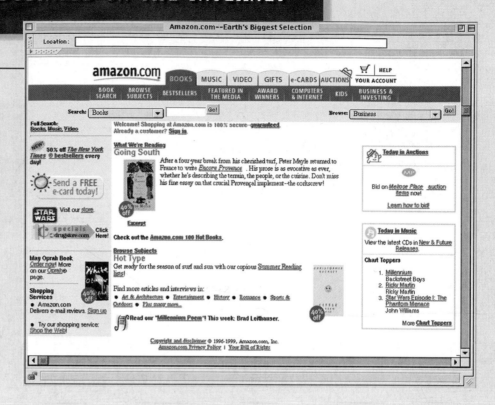

AMAZON.COM

STATISTICS

- 1995: Established

- 1995: 3 million World
Wide Web buyers

- 1999: 4.7 million
titles of books, videos,
music CDs, and
computer games

- 2002: 125 million Web
buyers (estimated)

Amazon.com was started in 1995 by Jeff Bezos, who realized the potential for doing business on-line when he read of the 2300% annual growth in Web use. Using the business skills he acquired working on Wall Street, Bezos launched Amazon.com, the world's biggest bookstore. At first, he was selling books to a handful of customers. Today, Amazon.com is the world's e-commerce leader offering millions of book, CD, and DVD titles to millions of customers.

As the fastest-growing retailer in history, the Amazon.com corporate philosophy is simple: "If it's good for our customers, it's worth doing." The company mission is to leverage technology and expertise to provide the best buying experience on the Internet.

1. If Amazon.com pays a monthly checking-account fee of $5.00 plus $.10 per check. Find the total checking account charge for a month when 836 checks were written.

2. The total credit-card sales for Amazon.com during a certain period were $837,422, while credit-card returns for the same period were $28,225. Find **(a)** the gross amount of the credit-card deposit and **(b)** the amount of credit given to Amazon.com after a fee of 2% is subtracted.

3. List and explain three advantages of buying your textbooks on the Internet. List and explain three disadvantages of buying your textbooks on the Internet.

4. By asking your classmates, coworkers, and friends, find someone who has purchased a book on the Internet. What was their experience like? Did they save money? Did they get quick delivery? Would they recommend this method of purchase to others?

CHAPTER 4 | Quick Review

CHAPTER TERMS

*Review the following terms to test your understanding of the chapter. For
each term you do not know, refer to the page number found next to that term.*

ATM cards [**p. 49**]
automated teller machine
    (ATM) [**p. 138**]
balance brought forward
    [**p. 142**]
balance forward [**p. 142**]
bank statement [**p. 155**]
blank endorsement [**p. 140**]
business checking account
    [**p. 138**]
canceled (check) [**p. 141**]

cashier's check [**p. 149**]
check register [**p. 143**]
check stub [**p. 142**]
checks outstanding [**p. 156**]
debit cards [**p. 139**]
deposit slip [**p. 140**]
deposit ticket [**p. 140**]
electronic banking [**p. 138**]
electronic commerce [**p. 138**]
electronic funds transfer (EFT)
    [**p. 139**]

flat-fee checking account
    [**p. 138**]
interest-paid (accounts) [**p. 138**]
maintenance charge per month
    [**p. 139**]
merchant batch header ticket
    [**p. 149**]
money order [**p. 149**]
nonsufficient funds (NSF)
    [**p. 149**]
notary service [**p. 149**]

overdraft [**p. 149**]
overdraft protection [**p. 149**]
per-debit charge [**p. 139**]
personal checking account
    [**p. 138**]
processing (check) [**p. 141**]
reconciliation [**p. 155**]
restricted endorsement [**p. 140**]
returned check [**p. 155**]
returned-deposit item [**p. 149**]
special endorsement [**p. 140**]
stop-payment order [**p. 149**]

CONCEPTS	EXAMPLES
4.1 Checking-account service charges There is usually a checking-account maintenance charge and often a per-check charge.	Find the monthly checking-account service charge for a business with 36 checks and transactions, given a monthly maintenance charge of $7.50 and a $.20 per check charge. $\$7.50 + 36(\$.20) = \$7.50 + \$7.20 =$ $\$14.70$ monthly service charge

4.2 Bank services offered
 	
 The checking account customer must be aware of various banking services that are offered.
	Overdraft protection:
	    Offered to protect the customer from bouncing a check (NSF).
	 ATM card:
	    Used at automated teller machine to get cash or used as a debit card to make purchases.
	 Stop-payment order:
	    Stops payment on a check written in error.
	 Cashier's check:
	    A check written by the financial institution itself.
	 Money order:
	    An instrument used in place of cash.
	 Notary service:
	    An official certification of a signature or document.

4.2 Deposits with credit-card transactions All credit-card refunds must be subtracted from total credit-card sales to find the net deposit. The discount charge is then subtracted from this total.	The following are credit-card charges and credits. 		**Charges**		**Credits**	 |---|---|---|---| 	$28.15	$78.59	$21.86	 	$36.92	$63.82	$19.62	 **(a)** Find total charges. **$28.15 + $36.92 + $78.59 + $63.82 = $207.48** **(b)** Find total credits. **$21.86 + $19.62 = $41.48** **(c)** Find gross deposit. $207.48 − **$41.48 = $166** **(d)** Given a 3% fee, find the amount of the charge. $166 × **.03 = $4.98** **(e)** Find the amount of credit given to the business. $166 − **$4.98 = $161.02**
4.3 Reconciliation of a checking account A checking-account customer must periodically verify checking-account records with those of the bank or financial institution. The bank statement is used for this.	The accuracy of all checks written, deposits made, service charges incurred, and interest paid is checked and verified. The customer's checkbook balance and bank balance must be the same for the account to reconcile, or balance.

CHAPTER 4 | SUMMARY EXERCISE
The Banking Activities of a Retailer

Shafali Patel owns a retail store specializing in women's imported clothing. She sells authentic traditional fabrics and women's accessories from various parts of Europe, India, and other countries. Many of her customers use credit cards for their purchases and her credit-card sales in a recent month amounted to $6438.50. During the same period she had $336.81 in credit slips and Ms. Patel pays a credit-card fee of $3\frac{1}{2}\%$.

    When she received her bank statement, the balance was $4228.34. The checks outstanding were found to be $758.14, $38.37, $1671.88, $120.13, $2264.75, $78.11, $3662.73, $816.25, and $400. Ms. Patel had both her credit-card deposit and bank deposits of $458.23, $771.18, $235.71, $1278.55, $663.52, and $1475.39 that were not recorded.

(a) Find the gross deposit when the credit-card sales and credits are deposited.   (a) _____

(b) Find the amount of the credit given to Ms. Patel after the fee is subtracted.   (b) _____

(c) What is the total of the checks outstanding?   (c) _____

(d) Find the total of the deposits that were not recorded.   (d) _____

(e) Find the current balance in Ms. Patel's checking account.   (e) _____

Investigate

Contact three banks or credit unions, other than your own, and ask about their charges for a personal checking account. Compare these fees to what you or your family members or friends pay for their checking accounts. Is there a way for you to get free checking? Name three considerations, besides cost, that are important to you when selecting a bank. Based on what you have learned, would it be a good idea for you to change banks?

Name   Date   Class

CHAPTER 4 | TEST

To help you review, the numbers in brackets show the section in which the topic was discussed.

Use the table on page 139 to find the monthly checking-account service charge for the following accounts.   **[4.1]**

1. The Sub Shop, 42 checks, average balance $1478   1. _____

2. Sangi Market, 35 checks, average balance $485   2. _____

3. Old English Chimney Sweep, 52 checks, average balance $3017   3. _____

Complete the following three check stubs for the Jack Armstrong International Trucking Company. Find the balance forward at the bottom of each stub.   **[4.1]**

Checks Written

Number	Date	To	For	Amount
1561	Aug. 6	Fuel Depot	Fuel	$6892.12
1562	Aug. 8	First Bank	Payment	$1258.36
1563	Aug. 14	Security Service	Guard dogs	$416.14

Deposits made: $1572 on Aug. 7, $10,000 on Aug. 10.

4.

1561
_____ 20____
Amount _____
To _____
For _____

Bal. Bro't. For'd.	$16,409	82
Am't. Deposited		
Total		
Am't. this Check		
Balance For'd.		

5.

1562
_____ 20____
Amount _____
To _____
For _____

Bal. Bro't. For'd.		
Am't. Deposited		
Total		
Am't. this Check		
Balance For'd.		

6.

1563
_____ 20____
Amount _____
To _____
For _____

Bal. Bro't. For'd.		
Am't. Deposited		
Total		
Am't. this Check		
Balance For'd.		

Chuck Hickman owns Campus Bicycle Shop near campus. The shop sells new and used bicycles and does repairs as well. The following credit-card transactions occurred during a recent period.   **[4.2]**

Sales		Credits
$118.68	$235.82	$15.36
$7.84	$98.56	$57.47
$33.18	$318.72	
$50.76	$116.35	
$12.72	$23.78	
$9.36	$38.95	

7. Find the total amount of sales slips for the store.

7. _____

8. What is the total amount of the credit slips?

8. _____

9. Find the gross amount of the deposit.

9. _____

10. Assuming that the bank charges the retailer a 4% discount charge, find the amount of the discount charge at the statement date.

10. _____

11. Find the amount of the credit given to Campus Bicycle Shop after the fee is subtracted.

11. _____

12. Tracey Pittrof Antiques is a regular customer of Books On Line. Use the information in the following table to reconcile her checking account on the form that follows.   **[4.3]**

12. _____

Balance from bank statement		$4721.30
Checks outstanding	3221	$82.74
(check number is given first)	3229	$69.08
	3230	$124.73
	3232	$51.20
Deposits not yet recorded		$758.06
		$32.51
		$298.06
Bank charge		$2.00
Interest credit		$9.58
Checkbook balance		$5474.60
Current balance		

Checks Outstanding	
Number	Amount
Total	

Compare the list of checks paid by the bank with your records. List and total the checks not yet paid.

(1) Enter new balance from bank statement: _____

(2) List any deposits made by you and not yet recorded by the bank: + _____
+ _____
+ _____
+ _____

(3) Add all numbers from lines above. Total: _____

(4) Write total of checks outstanding: − _____

(5) Subtract (4) from (3). This is adjusted bank balance: _____

To reconcile your records:

(6) List your checkbook balance: _____

(7) Write the total of any fees or charges deducted by the bank and not yet subtracted by you from your checkbook: − _____

(8) Subtract line (7) from line (6). _____

(9) Enter interest credit: (Add to your checkbook) + _____

(10) Add line (9) to line (8). Adjusted checkbook balance. _____

New balance of your account; this number should be same as (5).

CHAPTER 5

Payroll

Paige Dunbar worked part-time for Blockbuster Video while in college and became a full-time employee after graduation. She was recently promoted to manager of her own Blockbuster Video store. As a store manager with over forty-five employees, she has many responsibilities. One of the most important of these responsibilities is overseeing the weekly payroll for her full-time and part-time employees. This chapter provides the essential information on calculating and working with payroll.

Preparing the payroll is one of the most important jobs in any office. Payroll records must be accurate and the payroll must be prepared on time so that the necessary checks can be written. The first step in preparing the payroll is to determine the **gross earnings** (the total amount earned). There are many methods used to find gross earnings and several of these are discussed in this chapter. A number of **deductions** may be subtracted from gross earnings to arrive at the **net pay**, the amount actually received by the employee. These various deductions also will be discussed in this chapter. Finally, the employer must keep records to maintain an efficient business and to satisfy legal requirements.

5.1 | GROSS EARNINGS: WAGES AND SALARIES

Objectives

1. Understand the methods of calculating gross earnings for salaries and wages.
2. Find overtime earnings for over 40 hours of work per week.
3. Use the overtime premium method of calculating gross earnings.
4. Find overtime earnings for over 8 hours of work per day.
5. Understand double time, shift differentials, and split-shift premiums.
6. Find equivalent earnings for different pay periods.
7. Find overtime for salaried employees.

PROBLEM SOLVING IN BUSINESS

Blockbuster Video hires most of its employees as part-time workers and pays them on an hourly basis. Paige Dunbar, the manager, will occasionally ask part-time and full-time employees to work overtime (over 8 hours in one day). When employees work more than 8 hours in one day they are paid time and a half. Having a thorough understanding of payroll helps a manager operate a business more efficiently and results in improved employee relations.

For related Web activities, go to www.mathbusiness.com

Keyword: wages

Objective **1** **Understand the methods of calculating gross earnings for salaries and wages.** Several methods are used for finding an employee's pay. Two of these methods (salaries and wages) are discussed in this section; two additional methods (piecework and commission) will be discussed in the next section. Many employees live from paycheck to paycheck. Understanding how your total pay is calculated can eliminate the unwanted surprises that come with living from one paycheck to the next. The following bar graph shows how unprepared many workers are to cope with a period of unemployment.

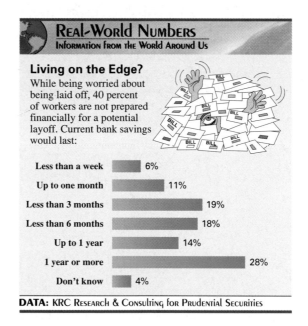

In many businesses, the first step in preparing the payroll is to look at the **time card** maintained for each employee. The following time card shows the dates of the pay period; the employee's name and other personal information; the days, times, and hours worked; the total number of hours worked; and the signature of the employee as verification of the accuracy of the card. While the card shown is filled in by hand, many companies use a time clock that automatically stamps days, dates, and times on the card. The information on these cards is then transferred to a **payroll ledger** (a chart showing all payroll information) such as the one shown in Example 1.

Eboni Perkins, whose payroll card is shown, is a department manager at Blockbuster Video and is paid an **hourly wage** of $9.80. Her gross earnings can be calculated with the following formula.

Gross earnings = Number of hours worked × Rate per hour

For example, if Perkins works 7 hours at $9.80 per hour, her gross earnings would be

Gross earnings = 7 × **$9.80** = $68.60.

EMPL. NO. <u>1375</u>   **PAYROLL CARD**   CARD NO. _____
NO TIME CLOCK REQUIRED

FULL
NAME Eboni Perkins   AGE (IF UNDER 18)

ADDRESS 1900 East Lake   SOCIAL
                                 SECURITY NO. 545–06–3189

DATE
EMPLOYED   POSITION Department MGR   RATE $9.80

PAY PERIOD
STARTING 7/23   ENDING 7/27

| DATE | REGULAR TIME | | | | | OVER TIME | | |
	IN	OUT	IN	OUT	DAILY TOTALS	IN	OUT	DAILY TOTALS
7/23	8:00	11:50	12:20	4:30	8	4:30	6:30	2
7/24	7:58	12:00	12:30	4:30	8	5:00	7:30	2.5
7/25	8:00	12:00	12:30	4:32	8			
7/26	7:58	12:05	12:35	4:30	8	4:30	5:00	.5
7/27	8:01	12:00	1:00	5:00	8			

APPROVED BY PD   TOTAL REGULAR TIME 40   5

| REGULAR DAYS WORKED | 5 @ | 8 HRS. @ | EARNINGS 9.80 | $ | 392.00 |

ADDITIONAL COMPENSATION:
VALUE OF MEALS, LODGING, GIFTS, ETC.   AMOUNT $ _____

COMMISSIONS, FEES,
BONUSES, GOODS, ETC. OT 5 @ 14.⁷⁰   AMOUNT $ 73.50

OTHER REMUNERATIONS (KIND) _____ $ _____

DEDUCTIONS: TOTAL EARNINGS $ 465.50

I CERTIFY THE FOREGOING TO BE A CORRECT ACCOUNT OF THE TIME WORKED
AND WAGES RECEIVED:

SIGNATURE _____   DATE PAID _____

EXAMPLE 1

Completing a
Payroll Ledger

Paige Dunbar is doing the payroll for two employees, Abruzzo and Williams. The first thing she must do is complete a payroll ledger.

| | Hours Worked | | | | | | | Total Hours | Rate | Gross Earnings |
Employee	S	M	T	W	Th	F	S			
Abruzzo, S.	—	2	4	8	6	3	—		$8.40	
Williams, N.	—	3.5	3	7	6.75	7	—		$7.12	

Solution

First, find the total number of hours worked by each person.

Abruzzo: $2 + 4 + 8 + 6 + 3 = $ **23 hours**

Williams: $3.5 + 3 + 7 + 6.75 + 7 = $ **27.25 hours**

Multiply the number of hours worked and the rate per hour to find the gross earnings.

Abruzzo: Williams:
23   27.25
$\times$ $8.40 $\times$ $7.12
$193.20   **$194.02**

The payroll ledger can now be completed.

Employee	Hours Worked							Total Hours	Rate	Gross Earnings
	S	M	T	W	Th	F	S			
Abruzzo, S.	—	2	4	8	6	3	—	23	$8.40	$193.20
Williams, N.	—	3.5	3	7	6.75	7	—	27.25	$7.12	$194.02

The following newspaper clipping discusses the number of workers who work overtime hours and are not paid properly for these additional hours worked.

More Workers Putting in Free Overtime Hours

Employees who put in long hours don't always take home fatter paychecks. Many work free.

The practice, called "pay jacking" by labor unions, occurs when workers eligible for overtime pay don't get the cash they're due. Some say the trend is mounting as job insecurity grows.

"There's coercion out there," says Jeffrey Chamberlain, an Albany, N.Y., lawyer with expertise in labor law. "There's the wink that says, 'You work extra and I'll promote you.'"

Those workers covered by the Fair Labor Standards Act must be paid 1.5 times their wage for each hour over 40 worked in a week. Employers can't swap the cash with extra time off.

But the rules don't apply to everyone. Those who are exempt may include employees who get a fixed salary or work in professional, administrative or executive ranks.

"Some are not familiar with the regulations," says Michael Karpeles, a Chicago employment lawyer. "There's a lot of stuff going on under the radar because of ignorance."

Source: USA Today, 1/14/98. Reprinted by permission.

OBJECTIVE **2** **Find overtime earnings for over 40 hours of work per week.** The **Fair Labor Standards Act**, which covers the majority of full-time employees in the United States, establishes a workweek of 40 hours and sets the minimum hourly wage. The law states that an **overtime** wage (a higher-than-normal wage) must be paid for all hours worked over 40 hours per workweek. Also, many companies not covered by the Fair Labor Standards Act have voluntarily followed the practice of paying a **time-and-a-half rate** ($1\frac{1}{2}$ times the normal rate) for any work over 40 hours per week. With the time-and-a-half rate, gross earnings are found with the following formula.

Gross earnings = Earnings at regular rate + Earnings at time-and-a-half rate

EXAMPLE 2	Complete the following payroll ledger.
Completing a Payroll Ledger with Overtime	

Employee	S	M	T	W	Th	F	S	Reg.	O.T.	Reg. Rate	Reg.	O.T.	Total
				Hours Worked				**Total Hours**			**Gross Earnings**		
Clark, J.	6	9	8.25	8	9	4.5	—			$7.90			
Jenders, P.	—	10	6.75	9	6.25	10	4.25			$9.48			

Solution

First, find the total number of hours worked.

$$\text{Clark: } 6 + 9 + 8.25 + 8 + 9 + 4.5 = \textbf{44.75 hours}$$

$$\text{Jenders: } 10 + 6.75 + 9 + 6.25 + 10 + 4.25 = \textbf{46.25 hours}$$

Both employees worked more than 40 hours. Gross earnings at the regular rate can now be found as discussed previously. Clark earned $40 \times \$7.90 = \$316$ at the regular rate, and Jenders earned $40 \times \$9.48 = \$379.20$ at the regular rate. To find overtime earnings, first find the number of overtime hours worked by each employee.

$$\text{Clark: } 44.75 - 40 = \textbf{4.75 overtime hours}$$

$$\text{Jenders: } 46.25 - 40 = \textbf{6.25 overtime hours}$$

The regular rate given for each employee can be used to find the time-and-a-half rate.

$$\text{Clark: } 1\frac{1}{2} \times \$7.90 = \$11.85$$

$$\text{Jenders: } 1\frac{1}{2} \times \$9.48 = \$14.22$$

Now find the overtime earnings.

$$\text{Clark: } 4.75 \text{ hours} \times \textbf{\$11.85} \text{ per hour} = \$56.29 \quad \text{(rounded to the nearest cent)}$$
$$\text{Jenders: } 6.25 \text{ hours} \times \textbf{\$14.22} \text{ per hour} = \$88.88 \quad \text{(rounded)}$$

The ledger can now be completed.

Employee	S	M	T	W	Th	F	S	Reg.	O.T.	Reg. Rate	Reg.	O.T.	Total
				Hours Worked				**Total Hours**			**Gross Earnings**		
Clark, J.	6	9	8.25	8	9	4.5	—	40	4.75	$7.90	$316	$56.29	$372.29
Jenders, P.	—	10	6.75	9	6.25	10	4.25	40	6.25	$9.48	$379.20	$88.88	$468.08

Employees say that they are working harder and longer. In addition to overtime earnings, many of these workers give other reasons for putting in extra hours. The following bar graph shows the reasons they are doing this.

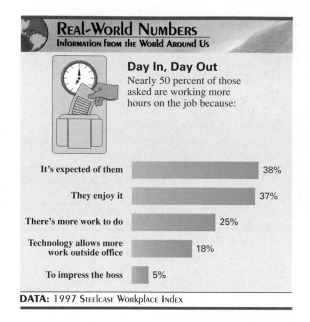

Real-World Numbers
Information from the World Around Us

Day In, Day Out
Nearly 50 percent of those asked are working more hours on the job because:

It's expected of them	38%
They enjoy it	37%
There's more work to do	25%
Technology allows more work outside office	18%
To impress the boss	5%

DATA: 1997 Steelcase Workplace Index

Objective **3** Use the overtime premium method of calculating gross earnings. Gross earnings with overtime is sometimes calculated with the **overtime premium method**. With this method, which produces the same result as the method used in Example 2, add the total hours at the regular rate to the overtime hours at one-half the regular rate to arrive at gross earnings.

Overtime Premium Method

$$
\begin{array}{ll}
\text{Straight-time earnings} & \leftarrow \text{ total hours worked} \times \text{regular rate} \\
\underline{+ \text{ Overtime premium}} & \leftarrow \text{ overtime hours worked} \times \tfrac{1}{2} \text{ regular rate} \\
\text{Gross earnings} &
\end{array}
$$

Example 3

Using the Overtime Premium Method

This week, Marcy Pleu worked 40 regular hours and 12 overtime hours. Her regular rate of pay is $12.38 per hour. Find her total gross pay, using the overtime premium method.

Solution

Pleu's total hours are 52(40 + 12), and her overtime premium rate is $6.19($\tfrac{1}{2} \times$ $12.38).

$$
\begin{array}{lll}
52 \text{ hours} \times \textbf{\$12.38} = \$643.76 & \text{regular-rate earnings} \\
\underline{12 \text{ overtime hours} \times \ \ \textbf{\$6.19} = \ \ \$74.28} & \text{overtime premium} \\
\phantom{12 \text{ overtime hours} \times \ \ \$6.19 = \ \ } \$718.04 & \text{gross earnings}
\end{array}
$$

The calculator solution uses the order of operations to first find the regular earnings, then the overtime earnings, and finally adds these together.

52 ⊠ 12.38 ⊞ 12 ⊠ 12.38 ⊠ .5 ⊟ 718.04

Note: All calculator solutions use a scientific calculator. Refer to Appendix B for scientific calculator basics.

> **NOTE** Many companies prefer the overtime premium method since it readily identifies the extra cost of overtime labor. Quite often, excessive use of overtime indicates inefficiencies in management.

Objective **4** Find overtime earnings for over 8 hours of work per day. Some companies pay the time-and-a-half rate for all time worked over 8 hours in any one day no matter how many hours are worked in a week. This **daily overtime** is shown in the next example.

EXAMPLE 4

Finding Overtime Each Day

Peter Harris worked 10 hours on Monday, 5 hours on Tuesday, 7 hours on Wednesday, and 12 hours on Thursday. His regular rate of pay is $10.10. Find his gross earnings for the week.

	S	M	T	W	Th	F	S	Total Hours
Reg.	—	8	5	7	8	—	—	28
O.T.	—	2	—	—	4	—	—	6

Solution

Harris worked more than 8 hours on Monday and Thursday. On Monday, he had $10 - 8 = 2$ hours of overtime, with $12 - 8 = 4$ hours of overtime on Thursday. In total, he earns $2 + 4 = 6$ hours of overtime. His regular hours are 8 on Monday, 5 on Tuesday, 7 on Wednesday, and 8 on Thursday, for a total of

$$8 + 5 + 7 + 8 = 28$$

hours at the regular rate. His hourly earnings are $10.10. At the regular rate he earns

$$28 \times \$10.10 = \$282.80.$$

If the regular rate is $10.10, the time-and-a-half rate is

$$\$10.10 \times 1\frac{1}{2} = \$15.15$$

He earned time and a half for 6 hours.

$$6 \times \$15.15 = \$90.90$$

His gross earnings are

$$\underbrace{\$282.80}_{\substack{\text{total} \\ \text{regular pay}}} + \underbrace{\$90.90}_{\substack{\text{total} \\ \text{overtime}}} = \underbrace{\mathbf{\$373.70}}_{\substack{\text{gross} \\ \text{earnings}}}$$

NOTE There are many careers that require unusual work schedules and do not pay overtime for over 40 hours worked in one week or over 8 hours worked in one day. An obvious example is the work schedule of a firefighter where the employee may work 24 hours and then get 48 hours off.

Objective 5 **Understand double time, shift differentials, and split-shift premiums.** In addition to premiums paid for overtime, other **premium payment plans** include **double time** for holidays and, in some industries, Saturdays and Sundays. A **shift differential** is often given to compensate employees for working less-desirable hours. For example, an additional amount per hour or per shift might be paid to swing shift (4 P.M. to midnight) and graveyard shift (midnight to 8:00 A.M.) employees.

Restaurant employees and telephone operators often receive a **split-shift premium**. Hours are staggered so that the employees are on the job during only the busiest times. For example, an employee may work 4 hours, be off 4 hours, and then work another 4 hours. The employee is paid a premium because of this less-desirable schedule.

Some employers offer **compensatory time**, or **comp time**, for overtime hours worked. Instead of additional money, an employee is given time off from the regular work schedule as compensation for overtime hours already worked. Quite often the compensating time is calculated at $1\frac{1}{2}$ times the overtime hours worked. For example, 12 hours might be given as compensation for 8 hours of previously worked overtime. Occasionally, an employee is given a choice of overtime pay or comp time. Many companies reserve the use of compensatory time for their supervisory or managerial employees. Also, compensatory time is very common in government agencies.

Objective ⑥ **Find equivalent earnings for different pay periods.** The second common method of finding gross earnings uses a **salary**, a fixed amount given as so much per **pay period** (time between paychecks). Common pay periods are weekly, biweekly, semimonthly, and monthly.

COMMON PAY PERIODS

Monthly	12 paychecks each year
Semimonthly	Twice each month; 24 paychecks each year
Biweekly	Every 2 weeks; 26 paychecks each year
Weekly	52 paychecks each year

NOTE   One person's salary might be a certain amount per month, while another person might earn a certain amount every 2 weeks. Many people receive an annual salary, divided among shorter pay periods.

EXAMPLE 5
Determining Equivalent Earnings

You are a career counselor and want to compare the earnings of four clients that you have helped to find jobs. Michael Hirsch receives a weekly salary of $273, Melanie Goulet receives a biweekly salary of $1686, Carla Lampsa receives a semimonthly salary of $736, and Tom Shaffer receives a monthly salary of $1818. For each worker, find the following: **(a)** earnings per year, **(b)** earnings per month, and **(c)** earnings per week.

Solution

Michael Hirsch

(a) $273 × 52 = $14,196 per year
(b) $14,196 ÷ 12 = $1183 per month
(c) $273 per week

Melanie Goulet

(a) $1686 × 26 = $43,836 per year
(b) $43,836 ÷ 12 = $3653 per month
(c) $1686 ÷ 2 = $843 per week

Carla Lampsa

(a) $736 × 24 = $17,664 per year
(b) $736 × 2 = $1472 per month
(c) $17,664 ÷ 52 = $339.69 per week

Tom Shaffer

(a) $1818 × 12 = $21,816 per year
(b) $1818 per month
(c) $21,816 ÷ 52 = $419.54 per week

The average annual starting salaries for college graduates in various majors are shown below. While these figures are an average, they show the range of pay among several professions.

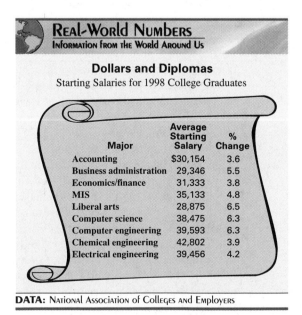

REAL-WORLD NUMBERS
INFORMATION FROM THE WORLD AROUND US

Dollars and Diplomas
Starting Salaries for 1998 College Graduates

Major	Average Starting Salary	% Change
Accounting	$30,154	3.6
Business administration	29,346	5.5
Economics/finance	31,333	3.8
MIS	35,133	4.8
Liberal arts	28,875	6.5
Computer science	38,475	6.3
Computer engineering	39,593	6.3
Chemical engineering	42,802	3.9
Electrical engineering	39,456	4.2

DATA: NATIONAL ASSOCIATION OF COLLEGES AND EMPLOYERS

ObjECTIVE **7** **Find overtime for salaried employees.** A salary is ordinarily paid for the performance of a certain job, regardless of the number of hours worked. However, the Fair Labor Standards Act requires that employees in certain salaried positions receive additional compensation for overtime. Like a wage earner, such salaried positions are paid time and a half for all hours worked over 40 hours per week.

EXAMPLE 6

Finding Overtime for Salaried Employees

Caralee Woods is paid $872 a week as an executive assistant. If her normal workweek is 40 hours, find her gross earnings for a week in which she works 45 hours.

Solution

The executive assistant's salary has an hourly equivalent of

$$\frac{\$872}{40 \text{ hours}} = \$21.80 \text{ per hour}$$

Since she must be paid overtime at the rate of $1\frac{1}{2}$ times her regular pay, she will get $1\frac{1}{2} \times \$21.80$, or $32.70 per hour for overtime. Her gross earnings for the week are

$872.00	salary for 40 hours
+ $163.50	overtime for 5 hours (5 × $32.70)
$1035.50	weekly gross earnings

The calculator solution to this example is

872 [+] 872 [÷] 40 [×] 1.5 [×] 5 [=] 1035.5

Note: All calculator solutions use a scientific calculator. Refer to Appendix B for scientific calculator basics.

5.2 | GROSS EARNINGS: PIECEWORK AND COMMISSIONS

Objectives

1. Find the gross earnings for piecework.
2. Determine the gross earnings for differential piecework.
3. Find the gross pay for piecework with a guaranteed hourly wage.
4. Calculate the overtime earnings for piecework.
5. Find the gross earnings using commission rate times sales.
6. Determine a commission using the variable commission rate.
7. Find the gross earnings with a salary plus commission.

OBJECTIVE 1 Find the gross earnings for piecework. The salaries and wages of the previous section are **time rates**, because they depend only on the actual time an employee is on the job. The two methods described in this section are **incentive rates**, because they are based on production and pay an employee for actual performance on the job. The five help-wanted ads from the classified section of the newspaper are for jobs offering incentive rates of pay. The ad for truck drivers lists piece rates of $.46975 and $.48475 per mile, while the automotive, insurance, loan officer, and industrial-sales positions pay on a commission plan.

HELP WANTED

Over-The-Road Sleeper Team Drivers

Earn $.46975/Mi Doubles $.48475/Mi Triples $18.40/Hour

Outstanding Full-time Benefits: Family Medical Insurance, Pension, paid Holidays, up to 5 wks paid vacation, 401K, Part-time leading to Full-time position.

Requirements include: Class A CDL with Airbrakes, Doubles and HazMat endorsement, DOT Physical and D/A Test Safe Driving Record 2 years' verifiable
Doubles Experience

MUST PASS PRE-EMPLOYMENT DRUG SCREENING

HELP WANTED

Automotive

UP TO
30%
COMMISSION

- No Exp Nec/Will Train
- Buick, Olds, Pont, GMC
- VW, Mazda, Isuzu
- Great Bonus Plan
- 401K
- Paid Vacations
- Medical & Dental Plan
  Apply in person

Crossroads Auburn Auto Ctr 2725 Grass Valley Highway

INSURANCE SALES & MANAGEMENT
Positions available for licensed life agents. Top commission, renewals, bonuses & bnfts.

LOAN OFFICERS
Locally owned mtg broker seeking exper. top producing loan officers for our Cameron Park ofc. All aspects of mtg loans including govt, conv & constr. Excel support staff provided. Top comm. pd with benefits.

SALES
Industrial Sales Rep. Japanese co. seeking people who just finished school or other for entry level industrial sales rep to travel US & Canada No exp nec, will train. Base sal $18K + commission, health ins & 401K. Traveling expenses prov for airline tickets, hotel, food expense, car rental etc. Oppty for quick advancement.

Source: Sacramento Bee, 6/7/98. Reprinted by permisssion.

A **piecework rate** pays an employee so much per item produced. Gross earnings are found with the following formula.

$$\text{Gross earnings} = \text{Pay per item} \times \text{Number of items}$$

For example, a cabinet finisher who finishes 23 cabinets and is paid a piecework rate of $4 per cabinet would have total gross earnings of

$$\text{Gross earnings} = \$4 \times 23 = \$92.$$

EXAMPLE 1

Finding Gross Earnings for Piecework

Dona Kenly is paid $.73 for sewing a jacket collar, $.86 for a sleeve with cuffs, and $.94 for a lapel. One week she sewed 318 jacket collars, 112 sleeves with cuffs, and 37 lapels. Find her gross earnings.

Solution

Multiply the rate per item by the number of that type of item.

Item	Rate		Number		Total
Jacket collars	$.73	×	318	=	$232.14
Sleeves with cuffs	$.86	×	112	=	$96.32
Lapels	$.94	×	37	=	$34.78

Find the gross earnings by adding the three totals from the table.

$$\$232.14 + \$96.32 + \$34.78 = \$363.24$$

OBJECTIVE **2** **Determine the gross earnings for differential piecework.** There are many variations to the straight piecework rate just described. For example, some rates have **quotas** that must be met, with a premium for each item produced beyond the quota. These plans offer an added incentive within an incentive. Typical is the **differential piece rate** plan, by which the rate paid per item depends on the number of items produced.

EXAMPLE 2

Using Differential Piecework

Suppose Metro Electric pays assemblers as follows:

1–100 units	$2.10 each
101–150 units	$2.25 each
151 or more units	$2.40 each

Find the gross earnings of a worker producing **214 units.**

Solution

```
  214      ← (total units)
- 100      ← (first 100 units) ——→    100 units at $2.10 each = $210.00
  114
-  50      ← (next 50 units) ——→       50 units at $2.25 each = $112.50
   64      ← (number over 150) →       64 units at $2.40 each = $153.60
                                      214 total units         = $476.10
```

The gross earnings are $476.10.

> **NOTE** With differential piecework, the highest amount paid applies to only the last units produced. In Example 2, $2.10 is paid for units 1–100, $2.25 is paid for units 101–150, and $2.40 is paid on only those units beyond unit 150, which in this case is 64 units.

OBJECTIVE **3** **Find the gross pay for piecework with a guaranteed hourly wage.** The piecework, and differential piecework rates are frequently modified to include a guaranteed hourly pay rate. This is often necessary to satisfy federal and state laws concerning minimum wages. With this method, the employer may pay either the minimum wage or the piecework earnings, whichever is higher.

EXAMPLE 3

Finding Earnings with a Guaranteed Hourly Wage

A tire installer at the Tire Center is paid $8.40 per hour for an 8-hour day, or $.95 per tire installed—whichever is higher. Find the weekly earnings for an employee having the following rate of production.

Monday	85 tires
Tuesday	70 tires
Wednesday	88 tires
Thursday	68 tires
Friday	82 tires

Solution

The hourly earnings for an 8-hour day are **$67.20** (8 × **$8.40**). If the piecework earnings for the day are less than this amount, the hourly earnings will be paid.

Monday	85 × $.95 =	$80.75 piece rate
Tuesday	~~70 × $.95~~ =	**$67.20 hourly (piece rate is $66.50)**
Wednesday	88 × $.95 =	$83.60 piece rate
Thursday	~~68 × $.95~~ =	**$67.20 hourly (piece rate is $64.60)**
Friday	82 = $.95 =	$77.90 piece rate
		$376.65 weekly earnings

> **NOTE**   Since the piecework earnings on Tuesday and Thursday in Example 3 are below the hourly minimum, the hourly rate is paid on those days.

Objective **4** **Calculate the overtime earnings for piecework.** Piecework employees, like other workers, are paid time and a half for overtime. It is most common for the overtime rate to be $1\frac{1}{2}$ times the regular rate per piece.

EXAMPLE 4

Calculating Earnings with Overtime Piecework

Tracy Light is paid $.84 per circuit board soldered. During one week she solders 480 circuit boards on regular time and 104 circuit boards during overtime hours. Find her gross earnings for the week if time and a half per panel is paid for overtime.

Solution

$$\text{Gross earnings} = \text{Earnings at regular piece rate} + \text{Earnings at overtime piece rate}$$
$$= 480 \times \$.84 + 104 \times (1\tfrac{1}{2} \times \$.84)$$
$$= \$403.20 + \$131.04$$
$$= \$534.24$$

A **commission rate** pays a salesperson either a fixed percent of sales or a fixed amount per item sold. Commissions are designed to produce maximum output from the salesperson, since pay is directly dependent on sales. There are three main types of commission arrangements.

Objective **5** **Find the gross earnings using commission rate times sales.** With **straight commission**, the salesperson is paid a fixed percent of sales. Gross earnings are found with the following formula.

> Gross earnings = Commission rate × Sales

EXAMPLE 5

Determining Earnings Using Commission

A real estate broker is paid a 6% commission. Find the commission on a house selling for $118,500.

Solution

The broker would receive 6% × $118,500 = .06 × $118,500 = $7110 for selling the house. The number 6% is called the commission rate, or the **rate of commission**.

Before commission is calculated, any **returns** from customers, or any **allowances**, such as discounts, must be subtracted from sales.

EXAMPLE 6
Subtracting
Returns when
Using Commission

Janet Drumm had sales of $8295, with returns and allowances of $950. If her commission rate is 14%, find her gross earnings.

SOLUTION

The returns and allowances must first be subtracted from gross sales, and the difference, net sales, then multiplied by the commission rate.

$$\text{Gross earnings} = (\$8295 - \$950) \times 14\%$$
$$= \$7345 \times .14$$
$$= \$1028.30$$

> **PROBLEM-SOLVING HINT**   Before calculating the commission, all items returned are first subtracted from the amount of sales. The company will not pay a commission on sales that are not completed.

OBJECTIVE **6** **Determine a commission using the variable commission rate.** The **sliding scale**, or **variable commission**, is a method of pay designed to retain top-producing salespeople. Under such a plan, a higher rate of commission is paid as sales get larger and larger.

EXAMPLE 7
Finding Earnings
Using Variable
Commission

Marika Colgan sells videotapes to video-rental stores, such as Blockbuster Video, and is paid as follows.

Sales	Rate
Up to $10,000	6%
$10,001–$20,000	8%
$20,001 and up	9%

Find Colgan's earnings if she has video sales of $32,768.

SOLUTION

$32,768	← (total sales)				
− 10,000	← (first $10,000) →	$10,000 at 6%	=	$600.00
$22,768					
− 10,000	← (next $10,000) →	$10,000 at 8%	=	$800.00
$12,768	← (over $20,000) →	$12,768 at 9%	=	$1149.12
		$32,768 total sales	=	$2549.12 total commissions

OBJECTIVE **7** **Find the gross earnings with a salary plus commission.** With a **salary plus commission**, the salesperson is paid a fixed sum per pay period, plus a commission on all sales. This method of payment is commonly used by large retail stores. Gross earnings with salary plus commission are found with the following formula.

> Gross earnings = Fixed amount per pay period + Amount earned on commission

Many salespeople like this method. It is especially attractive to beginning salespeople who lack selling experience. While providing an incentive, it offers the security of a guaranteed income to cover basic living costs. Occasionally, this income is an earnings advance or a **draw**, which is a loan against future commissions. This loan is paid back when future commissions are earned.

EXAMPLE 8

Adding Commission to a Salary

Pat Quinlin is paid $225 per week by the Potters Exchange, plus 3% on all sales over $500. During a certain week, her total sales were $972. Find her gross earnings.

SOLUTION

She is paid a 3% commission on all sales over $500 (there is no commission earned on the first $500). During the given week, she is paid a commission on $972 − $500 = $472. The commission is .03 × $472 = $14.16. Her gross earnings are thus $225 (fixed amount per week) + $14.16 (earned commissions) = $239.16.

EXAMPLE 9

Subtracting a Draw to Find Earnings

Elizabeth Owens has sales of $28,560 for the month and is paid a 7% commission on all sales. She has had draws of $750 for the month. Find her gross earnings after repaying the drawing account.

SOLUTION

$$
\begin{aligned}
\text{Gross earnings} &= \text{Commissions} - \text{Draw} \\
&= (.07 \times \$28{,}560) - \$750 \\
&= \$1999.20 - \$750 \\
&= \$1249.20
\end{aligned}
$$

> **NOTE** Commission earning plans are a strong deterrent to attracting new salespeople. It is for this reason that many companies offer the salary plus commission and the draw plans to help fill sales positions.

For related Web activities, go to www.mathbusiness.com

'Net Assets

SOCIAL SECURITY ADMINISTRATION

STATISTICS

• 1935: Social Security Act passed

• 1937: First Social Security taxes collected

• 1965: Medicare bill signed into law

• 1998: 6 million families received $49 billion in disability payments.

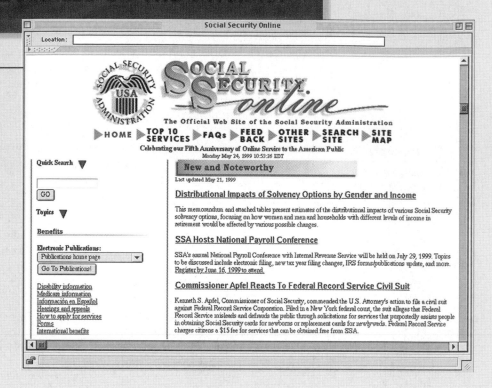

In the 1930s, during the Great Depression, the United States economy continued to move away from one based primarily on agriculture to one based on industrial production. The uncertainties associated with disability and old age, which in the past were the responsibility of family and local community, were becoming a much greater concern to many Americans. This concern resulted in the Social Security Act of 1935. Both the employee and employer were to contribute to a fund that would then provide benefits to retiring workers.

On January 1, 1940, the first monthly retirement check was issued to Ida May Fuller of Ludlow, Vermont in the amount of $22.54. Miss Fuller received retirement checks for 35 years until her death in 1975 at the age of 100. Today, on the Internet, we can get electronic publications from the Social Security Administration in addition to information on benefits and many more on-line direct services.

1. If a store manager is paid an annual salary of $31,200, find her equivalent earnings for monthly, semi-monthly, and biweekly pay periods.

2. Last month, the employees at a Blockbuster Video outlet paid a total of $792 in FICA, $237 in Medicare tax, and $2217 in federal withholding tax. Find the total amount that the employer must send to the Internal Revenue Service.

3. Speak with a family member, a friend, or someone else that you know who receives Social Security benefits. List three or more things that they like about Social Security. List three or more suggestions that they would have to improve Social Security.

4. Do you think that participation in the Social Security system should be voluntary or mandatory? List the possible advantages of each choice.

5.3 | Social Security, Medicare, and Other Taxes

Objectives

- **1** Understand FICA.
- **2** Find the maximum FICA tax paid by an employee in one year.
- **3** Understand Medicare tax.
- **4** Find FICA tax and Medicare tax.
- **5** Determine the FICA tax and the Medicare tax paid by a self-employed person.
- **6** Find state disability insurance deductions.

Problem Solving in Business

After finding the gross earnings of each employee at Blockbuster Video, all deductions for each employee must be subtracted. Two deductions taken from all employees, no matter what they earn, are FICA (Social Security) and Medicare. As Paige Dunbar does the payroll, she must be certain that she has deducted the correct amounts from each employee's gross earnings.

Finding gross earnings is only the first step in preparing a payroll. The employer must then subtract all required deductions from gross earnings. For most employees, these deductions include Social Security tax, Medicare tax, federal income tax withholding, and state tax withholding. Other deductions may include state disability insurance, union dues, retirement, vacation pay, credit union savings or loan payments, purchase of bonds, uniform expenses, group insurance plans, and charitable contributions. Subtracting these deductions from gross earnings results in **net pay**, the amount the employee receives.

For related Web activities, go to www.mathbusiness.com

Keyword: contributions

Objective 1 Understand FICA. The **Federal Insurance Contributions Act (FICA)** was passed into law in the 1930s in the middle of the Great Depression. This plan, now called **Social Security**, was originally designed to give monthly benefits to retired workers and their survivors. As the number of people receiving benefits has increased along with the individual benefit amounts, people paying into Social Security have had to pay a larger amount of earnings into this fund each year. From 1937 through 1950 an employee paid 1% of income into Social Security, up to a maximum of $30 per year. This amount has increased over the years until an employee in 1999 paid 6.2% of income to FICA and 1.45% to **Medicare**, which together can total $5553.90 and more per year.

For many years both the Social Security tax rate and the Medicare tax rate were combined, however since 1991 these tax rates have been expressed individually. The following table shows the tax rates and the maximum earnings on which Social Security and Medicare taxes are paid by the employee. The employer pays the same rate as the employee *matching dollar for dollar* all employee contributions. Self-employed people pay double the rate paid by those who are employees (they are paying for both employee and employer).

	Social Security Tax		Medicare Tax	
Year	**Social Security Tax Rate**	**Employee Earnings Subject to the Tax**	**Medicare Tax Rate**	**Employee Earnings Subject to the Tax**
1991	6.2%	$53,400	1.45%	$125,000
1992	6.2%	$55,500	1.45%	$130,200
1993	6.2%	$57,600	1.45%	$135,000
1994	6.2%	$59,600	1.45%	all
1995	6.2%	$61,200	1.45%	all
1996	6.2%	$62,700	1.45%	all
1997	6.2%	$65,400	1.45%	all
1998	6.2%	$68,400	1.45%	all
1999	6.2%	$72,600	1.45%	all

FOR MORE INFORMATION

If you want an estimate of what your Social Security benefits will be, call the Social Security Administration, (800) 772-1213, and follow the voice prompts to request a free Personal Earnings and Benefit Estimate Statement.

Reach the Social Security Administration on-line at *http://www.ssa.gov*. The site offers an abundance of information, including how to apply for new or lost Social Security cards, facts about benefits, and answers to frequently asked questions.

Source: Today's Realtor, 10/96.

> **NOTE** Congress sets the tax rates and the maximum employee earnings subject to both Social Security tax and Medicare tax each year. Because these tax rates change, we will use 6.2% of the first $70,000 that the employee earns in a year for Social Security tax. For Medicare tax, we will use 1.45% of everything that the employee earns in a year. These figures are used in all examples and exercises in this chapter.

Each employee must have a Social Security card. Most post offices have application forms for the cards. All money set aside for an individual is credited to his or her account according to the Social Security number. Mistakes are rare, but they do occur. For this reason, every employee should submit a **Request for Earnings and Benefit Estimate Statement** every 2 years or so, by filling out a form like the one shown below. There is a limit of about 3 years, after which errors may not be corrected. The magazine clipping at the left tells how to get one of these forms by phoning a toll-free number. Additional information may be obtained using the World Wide Web.

Request for Earnings and Benefit Estimate Statement

☐ Please check this box if you want to get your statement in Spanish instead of English.

Please print or type your answers. When you have completed the form, fold it and mail it to us. (If you prefer to send your request using the internet, contact us at http://www.ssa.gov)

1. Name shown on your Social Security card:

    First Name   Middle Initial

    Last Name Only

2. Your Social Security number as shown on your card:
    ☐☐☐-☐☐-☐☐☐☐

3. Your date of birth (Mo.-Day-Yr.)
    ☐☐-☐☐-☐☐☐☐

4. Other Social Security numbers you have used:
    ☐☐☐-☐☐-☐☐☐☐
    ☐☐☐-☐☐-☐☐☐☐

5. Your Sex: ☐ Male ☐ Female

For items 6 and 8 show only earnings covered by Social Security. Do NOT include wages from state, local, or federal government employment that are NOT covered for Social Security or that are covered ONLY by Medicare.

6. Show your actual earnings (wages and/or net self-employment income) for last year and your estimated earnings for this year.

    A. Last year's actual earnings: *(Dollars Only)*
    $☐☐☐,☐☐☐.**0 0**

    B. This year's estimated earnings: *(Dollars Only)*
    $☐☐☐,☐☐☐.**0 0**

7. Show the age at which you plan to stop working.
    ☐☐ *(Show only one age)*

8. Below, show the average yearly amount (not your total future lifetime earnings) that you think you will earn between now and when you plan to stop working. Include performance or scheduled pay increases or bonuses, but not cost-of-living increases.

    If you expect to earn significantly more or less in the future due to promotions, job changes, part-time work, or an absence from the work force, enter the amount that most closely reflects your future average yearly earnings.

    If you don't expect any significant changes, show the same amount you are earning now (the amount in 6B).

    Future average yearly earnings: *(Dollars Only)*
    $☐☐☐,☐☐☐.**0 0**

9. Do you want us to send the statement:
    • To you? Enter your name and mailing address.
    • To someone else (your accountant, pension plan, etc.)? Enter your name with "c/o" and the name and address of that person or organization.

    Name

    Street Address (Include Apt. No., P.O. Box, or Rural Route)

    City   State   Zip Code

    NOTICE:
    I am asking for information about my own Social Security record or the record of a person I am authorized to represent. I understand that if I deliberately request information under false pretenses, I may be guilty of a federal crime and could be fined and/or imprisoned. I authorize you to use a contractor to send the statement of earnings and benefit estimates to the person named in item 9.

    ▶

    Please sign your name (Do Not Print)

    Date   (Area Code) Daytime Telephone No.

Form **SSA-7004-SM**

OBJECTIVE **2** **Find the maximum FICA tax paid by an employee in one year.** Remember that Social Security tax is paid on only the first $70,000 of gross earnings in our examples. An employee earning $70,000 during the first 10 months of a year would pay no more Social Security tax on additional earnings that year. The maximum Social Security tax to be paid by an employee is $70,000 × 6.2% = $70,000 × .062 = $4340.

OBJECTIVE **3** **Understand Medicare tax.** Medicare tax is paid on all earnings in our examples. The total earnings are multiplied by 1.45%.

> **NOTE** Only 7% of all income earners are affected by the Social Security maximum.

OBJECTIVE **4** **Find FICA tax and Medicare tax.** When finding the amounts to be withheld for Social Security tax and Medicare tax, the employer must use the current rates and the maximum earnings amount.

EXAMPLE 1

Finding FICA Tax and Medicare Tax

Imagine you are Paige Dunbar, the manager of a Blockbuster Video outlet. Find the Social Security tax and Medicare tax for Abruzzo and Williams.

(a) Abruzzo; $193.20 **(b)** Williams; $194.02

SOLUTION

(a) The Social Security tax is found by multiplying gross earnings by 6.2%.

$$\$193.20 \times 6.2\% = \$193.20 \times .062 = \$11.98 \text{ (rounded)}$$

Medicare tax is found by multiplying gross earnings by 1.45%.

$$\$193.20 \times 1.45\% = \$193.20 \times .0145 = \$2.80 \text{ (rounded)}$$

(b) The Social Security tax is

$$\$194.02 \times 6.2\% = \$194.02 \times .062 = \$12.03 \text{ (rounded)}.$$

The Medicare tax is

$$\$194.02 \times 1.45\% = \$194.02 \times .0145 = \$2.81 \text{ (rounded)}.$$

EXAMPLE 2

Finding FICA Tax

Megan Galvin has earned $66,791.08 so far this year. Her gross earnings for the current pay period are $4842.08. Find her Social Security tax.

SOLUTION

Social Security tax is paid on only the first $70,000 earned in a year. Galvin has already earned $66,791.08. Subtract $66,791.08 from $70,000, to find that she has to pay Social Security tax on only $3208.92 of her earnings for the current pay period.

$70,000.00	maximum earnings subject to Social Security tax
− 66,791.08	earnings to date
$3,208.92	earnings on which tax is due

The Social Security tax on $3208.92 is $198.95 ($3208.92 × 6.2%). Therefore, Galvin pays $198.95 for the current pay period and no additional Social Security tax for the rest of the year.

The following graphic shows what people of different age brackets expect from Social Security retirement income. Do you see a difference in the retirement expectations of those in the older age brackets versus those in the younger age brackets?

REAL-WORLD NUMBERS
INFORMATION FROM THE WORLD AROUND US

There's Always Social Security...
Amount of retirement income respondents expect from Social Security

Age	Most	Fair amount	Very little	None
18–29	4%	23%	50%	20%
30–49	6%	20%	51%	20%
50–59	13%	32%	40%	7%
Now retired	28%	37%	20%	12%

DATA: PUTNAM INVESTMENTS SURVEY

Objective **5** Determine the FICA tax and the Medicare tax paid by a self-employed person. People who are self-employed pay higher Social Security tax and higher Medicare tax than people who work for others. There is no employer to match the employee contribution so the self-employed person pays a rate that is double that of the employee. In our examples the self-employed person pays 12.4% of gross earnings for Social Security tax and 2.9% of gross earnings for Medicare tax.

EXAMPLE 3

Finding FICA and Medicare Tax for the Self-Employed

Find the Social Security tax and the Medicare tax paid by Sashaya Davis a self-employed Web-page designer who earned $44,480 this year.

Solution

$$\text{Social Security tax} = \$44{,}480 \times 12.4\% = \$44{,}480 \times .124 = \$5515.52$$
$$\text{Medicare tax} = \$44{,}480 \times 2.9\% = \$44{,}480 \times .029 = \$1289.92$$

> **NOTE** All employers and those who are self-employed should have the current tax rates for both Social Security and Medicare. These can always be found in **Circular E, Employer's Tax Guide**, which is available from the Internal Revenue Service.

Objective **6** **Find state disability insurance deductions.** Many states have a state disability program. Qualifying employees must pay a portion of their earnings to the program. If an employee is injured and unable to work, the program pays the employee during the period of disability. A typical program requires an **SDI deduction** of 1% of gross earnings on the first $31,800 earned each year, with no payment on earnings above this amount.

EXAMPLE 4

Finding State Disability Insurance Deductions

Find the state disability deduction for an employee at Comet Auto Parts with gross earnings of $418 this pay period. The SDI rate is 1%, and the employee has not earned $31,800 this year.

Solution

The state disability deduction is $4.18 ($418 × 1%).

EXAMPLE 5

Knowing SDI Maximum Deductions

Milo Lacy has earned $30,620 so far this year. Find the SDI deduction if gross earnings this pay period are $3096. Use an SDI rate of 1% on the first $31,800.

Solution

The SDI deduction will be taken on $1180 of the current gross earnings.

$31,800	maximum earnings subject to SDI
− 30,620	earnings this year
$1180	earnings subject to SDI

The SDI deduction is $11.80 ($1180 × 1%).

> **NOTE** Always be aware of the current rates and the maximum annual earning amounts against which FICA, Medicare, and SDI payroll deductions may be taken. Those involved in payroll work must always be up to date on federal and state laws and practices.

5.4 | INCOME TAX WITHHOLDING

Objectives

1. Understand the Employee's Withholding Allowance Certificate.
2. Find the federal withholding tax using the wage bracket method.
3. Find the federal withholding tax using the percentage method.
4. Find the state withholding tax using the state income tax rate.
5. Find net pay when given gross wages, taxes, and other deductions.
6. Find the quarterly amount owed to the Internal Revenue Service.

PROBLEM SOLVING IN BUSINESS

After completing the payroll at Blockbuster Video, Paige Dunbar must be certain that all FICA taxes, Medicare taxes, and federal withholding taxes withheld from employees are sent to the Internal Revenue Service. Additionally, it's essential that Paige keeps current with all of the changes in the tax codes that affect withholding.

The **personal income tax** is the largest single source of money for the federal government. The law requires that the bulk of the tax owed by an individual be paid periodically, as the income is earned. For this reason, employers must deduct money from the gross earnings of almost every employee. These deductions, called **income tax withholdings**, are sent periodically to the Internal Revenue Service. The amount of money withheld depends on several factors.

Marital status. Generally, the withholding tax for a married person is less than the withholding tax for a single person making the same income.

OBJECTIVE **1** **Understand the Employee's Withholding Allowance Certificate.** Each employee must file with their employer a W-4 form, as shown. On this form, the employee states the number of **withholding allowances** being claimed along with additional information so that the employer can withhold the proper amount for income tax.

Form **W-4** Department of the Treasury Internal Revenue Service	**Employee's Withholding Allowance Certificate** ► **For Privacy Act and Paperwork Reduction Act Notice, see page 2.**	OMB No. 1545-0010 200_

1 Type or print your first name and middle initial	Last name	**2** Your social security number

Home address (number and street or rural route)	**3** ☐ Single ☐ Married ☐ Married, but withhold at higher Single rate. Note: *If married, but legally separated, or spouse is a nonresident alien, check the Single box.*
City or town, state, and ZIP code	**4** If your last name differs from that on your social security card, check here. **You** must call 1-800-772-1213 for a new card . . . ► ☐

5 Total number of allowances you are claiming (from line H above or from the worksheets on page 2 if they apply) .	**5**
6 Additional amount, if any, you want withheld from each paycheck	**6** $
7 I claim exemption from withholding for 200_, and I certify that I meet **BOTH** of the following conditions for exemption: • Last year I had a right to a refund of **ALL** Federal income tax withheld because I had **NO** tax liability **AND** • This year I expect a refund of **ALL** Federal income tax withheld because I expect to have **NO** tax liability. If you meet both conditions, write "EXEMPT" here . . . . ►	**7**

Under penalties of perjury, I certify that I am entitled to the number of withholding allowances claimed on this certificate, or I am entitled to claim exempt status.

Employee's signature
(Form is not valid
unless you sign it) ► _____   **Date** ► _____

8 Employer's name and address (Employer: Complete 8 and 10 only if sending to the IRS)	**9** Office code (optional)	**10** Employer identification number

Cat. No. 10220Q

Tables for Wage Bracket Method of Withholding

SINGLE Persons—WEEKLY Payroll Period
(For Wages Paid in   )

If the wages are —		And the number of withholding allowances claimed is —										
At least	But less than	0	1	2	3	4	5	6	7	8	9	10
		The amount of income tax to be withheld is —										
125	130	11	4	0	0	0	0	0	0	0	0	0
130	135	12	4	0	0	0	0	0	0	0	0	0
135	140	13	5	0	0	0	0	0	0	0	0	0
140	145	14	6	0	0	0	0	0	0	0	0	0
145	150	14	7	0	0	0	0	0	0	0	0	0
150	155	15	7	0	0	0	0	0	0	0	0	0
155	160	16	8	0	0	0	0	0	0	0	0	0
160	165	17	9	1	0	0	0	0	0	0	0	0
165	170	17	10	2	0	0	0	0	0	0	0	0
170	175	18	10	3	0	0	0	0	0	0	0	0
175	180	19	11	3	0	0	0	0	0	0	0	0
180	185	20	12	4	0	0	0	0	0	0	0	0
185	190	20	13	5	0	0	0	0	0	0	0	0
190	195	21	13	6	0	0	0	0	0	0	0	0
195	200	22	14	6	0	0	0	0	0	0	0	0
200	210	23	15	8	0	0	0	0	0	0	0	0
210	220	25	17	9	1	0	0	0	0	0	0	0
220	230	26	18	11	3	0	0	0	0	0	0	0
230	240	28	20	12	4	0	0	0	0	0	0	0
240	250	29	21	14	6	0	0	0	0	0	0	0
250	260	31	23	15	7	0	0	0	0	0	0	0
260	270	32	24	17	9	1	0	0	0	0	0	0
270	280	34	26	18	10	2	0	0	0	0	0	0
280	290	35	27	20	12	4	0	0	0	0	0	0
290	300	37	29	21	13	5	0	0	0	0	0	0
300	310	38	30	23	15	7	0	0	0	0	0	0
310	320	40	32	24	16	8	1	0	0	0	0	0
320	330	41	33	26	18	10	2	0	0	0	0	0
330	340	43	35	27	19	11	4	0	0	0	0	0
340	350	44	36	29	21	13	5	0	0	0	0	0

MARRIED Persons—WEEKLY Payroll Period
(For Wages Paid in   )

If the wages are —		And the number of withholding allowances claimed is —										
At least	But less than	0	1	2	3	4	5	6	7	8	9	10
		The amount of income tax to be withheld is —										
440	450	48	40	33	25	17	9	1	0	0	0	0
450	460	50	42	34	26	18	11	3	0	0	0	0
460	470	51	43	36	28	20	12	4	0	0	0	0
470	480	53	45	37	29	21	14	6	0	0	0	0
480	490	54	46	39	31	23	15	7	0	0	0	0
490	500	56	48	40	32	24	17	9	1	0	0	0
500	510	57	49	42	34	26	18	10	3	0	0	0
510	520	59	51	43	35	27	20	12	4	0	0	0
520	530	60	52	45	37	29	21	13	6	0	0	0
530	540	62	54	46	38	30	23	15	7	0	0	0
540	550	63	55	48	40	32	24	16	9	1	0	0
550	560	65	57	49	41	33	26	18	10	2	0	0
560	570	66	58	51	43	35	27	19	12	4	0	0
570	580	68	60	52	44	36	29	21	13	5	0	0
580	590	69	61	54	46	38	30	22	15	7	0	0
590	600	71	63	55	47	39	32	24	16	8	1	0
600	610	72	64	57	49	41	33	25	18	10	2	0
610	620	74	66	58	50	42	35	27	19	11	4	0
620	630	75	67	60	52	44	36	28	21	13	5	0
630	640	77	69	61	53	45	38	30	22	14	7	0
640	650	78	70	63	55	47	39	31	24	16	8	0
650	660	80	72	64	56	48	41	33	25	17	10	2
660	670	81	73	66	58	50	42	34	27	19	11	3
670	680	83	75	67	59	51	44	36	28	20	13	5
680	690	84	76	69	61	53	45	37	30	22	14	6
690	700	86	78	70	62	54	47	39	31	23	16	8
700	710	87	79	72	64	56	48	40	33	25	17	9
710	720	89	81	73	65	57	50	42	34	26	19	11
720	730	90	82	75	67	59	51	43	36	28	20	12
730	740	92	84	76	68	60	53	45	37	29	22	14

Tables for Wage Bracket Method of Withholding, continued

SINGLE Persons—MONTHLY Payroll Period
(For Wages Paid in   )

If the wages are—		And the number of withholding allowances claimed is—										
At least	But less than	0	1	2	3	4	5	6	7	8	9	10
		The amount of income tax to be withheld is—										
840	880	96	62	28	0	0	0	0	0	0	0	0
880	920	102	68	34	1	0	0	0	0	0	0	0
920	960	108	74	40	7	0	0	0	0	0	0	0
960	1,000	114	80	46	13	0	0	0	0	0	0	0
1,000	1,040	120	86	52	19	0	0	0	0	0	0	0
1,040	1,080	126	92	58	25	0	0	0	0	0	0	0
1,080	1,120	132	98	64	31	0	0	0	0	0	0	0
1,120	1,160	138	104	70	37	3	0	0	0	0	0	0
1,160	1,200	144	110	76	43	9	0	0	0	0	0	0
1,200	1,240	150	116	82	49	15	0	0	0	0	0	0
1,240	1,280	156	122	88	55	21	0	0	0	0	0	0
1,280	1,320	162	128	94	61	27	0	0	0	0	0	0
1,320	1,360	168	134	100	67	33	0	0	0	0	0	0
1,360	1,400	174	140	106	73	39	5	0	0	0	0	0
1,400	1,440	180	146	112	79	45	11	0	0	0	0	0
1,440	1,480	186	152	118	85	51	17	0	0	0	0	0
1,480	1,520	192	158	124	91	57	23	0	0	0	0	0
1,520	1,560	198	164	130	97	63	29	0	0	0	0	0
1,560	1,600	204	170	136	103	69	35	1	0	0	0	0
1,600	1,640	210	176	142	109	75	41	7	0	0	0	0
1,640	1,680	216	182	148	115	81	47	13	0	0	0	0
1,680	1,720	222	188	154	121	87	53	19	0	0	0	0
1,720	1,760	228	194	160	127	93	59	25	0	0	0	0
1,760	1,800	234	200	166	133	99	65	31	0	0	0	0
1,800	1,840	240	206	172	139	105	71	37	4	0	0	0
1,840	1,880	246	212	178	145	111	77	43	10	0	0	0
1,880	1,920	252	218	184	151	117	83	49	16	0	0	0
1,920	1,960	258	224	190	157	123	89	55	22	0	0	0
1,960	2,000	264	230	196	163	129	95	61	28	0	0	0
2,000	2,040	270	236	202	169	135	101	67	34	0	0	0

MARRIED Persons—MONTHLY Payroll Period
(For Wages Paid in   )

If the wages are—		And the number of withholding allowances claimed is—										
At least	But less than	0	1	2	3	4	5	6	7	8	9	10
		The amount of income tax to be withheld is—										
2,040	2,080	228	195	161	127	93	60	26	0	0	0	0
2,080	2,120	234	201	167	133	99	66	32	0	0	0	0
2,120	2,160	240	207	173	139	105	72	38	4	0	0	0
2,160	2,200	246	213	179	145	111	78	44	10	0	0	0
2,200	2,240	252	219	185	151	117	84	50	16	0	0	0
2,240	2,280	258	225	191	157	123	90	56	22	0	0	0
2,280	2,320	264	231	197	163	129	96	62	28	0	0	0
2,320	2,360	270	237	203	169	135	102	68	34	0	0	0
2,360	2,400	276	243	209	175	141	108	74	40	6	0	0
2,400	2,440	282	249	215	181	147	114	80	46	12	0	0
2,440	2,480	288	255	221	187	153	120	86	52	18	0	0
2,480	2,520	294	261	227	193	159	126	92	58	24	0	0
2,520	2,560	300	267	233	199	165	132	98	64	30	0	0
2,560	2,600	306	273	239	205	171	138	104	70	36	3	0
2,600	2,640	312	279	245	211	177	144	110	76	42	9	0
2,640	2,680	318	285	251	217	183	150	116	82	48	15	0
2,680	2,720	324	291	257	223	189	156	122	88	54	21	0
2,720	2,760	330	297	263	229	195	162	128	94	60	27	0
2,760	2,800	336	303	269	235	201	168	134	100	66	33	0
2,800	2,840	342	309	275	241	207	174	140	106	72	39	5
2,840	2,880	348	315	281	247	213	180	146	112	78	45	11
2,880	2,920	354	321	287	253	219	186	152	118	84	51	17
2,920	2,960	360	327	293	259	225	192	158	124	90	57	23
2,960	3,000	366	333	299	265	231	198	164	130	96	63	29
3,000	3,040	372	339	305	271	237	204	170	136	102	69	35
3,040	3,080	378	345	311	277	243	210	176	142	108	75	41
3,080	3,120	384	351	317	283	249	216	182	148	114	81	47
3,120	3,160	390	357	323	289	255	222	188	154	120	87	53
3,160	3,200	396	363	329	295	261	228	194	160	126	93	59
3,200	3,240	402	369	335	301	267	234	200	166	132	99	65

For related Web
activities, go to
www.mathbusiness.com

Keyword:
withholdings

A W-4 form is usually completed when a person starts a new job. A married person with three children normally claims five allowances (one each for the employee and spouse and one for each child). However, if both spouses are employed, each may claim himself or herself. The number of allowances may be raised if an employee has been receiving a refund of income taxes or the number may be lowered if the employee has had a balance due in previous tax years. The W-4 form has instructions to help determine the proper number of allowances. Some people enjoy receiving a tax refund when filing their income tax return, so they claim fewer allowances, having more withheld from each check. Other individuals would rather receive more of their income each pay period, so they claim the maximum number of allowances to which they are entitled. The exact number of allowances *must* be claimed when income tax is filed.

Amount of gross earnings. The withholding tax is found on the basis of the gross earnings per pay period. Income tax withholding is applied to all earnings—not just earnings up to a certain amount as with Social Security. Generally, the higher a person's gross earnings, the more withholding tax paid.

There are two methods that employers use to determine the amount of federal withholding tax to deduct from paychecks: the **wage bracket method** and the **percentage method**.

Objective **2** **Find the federal withholding tax using the wage bracket method.** The Internal Revenue Service supplies withholding tax tables to be used with the wage bracket method. These tables are very extensive, covering weekly, biweekly, monthly, and daily pay periods. The preceding pages show samples of the withholding tables. Two of the tables are for people who are paid weekly, both single and married. The other two tables are for both single and married people who are paid monthly.

EXAMPLE 1

Finding Federal
Withholding Using
the Wage Bracket
Method

Lisa Revies is single and claims no withholding allowances. (Some employees do this to receive a refund from the government or to avoid owing taxes at the end of the year. The proper number will be used when filing her income tax return.) Use the wage bracket method (tax tables) to find her withholding tax if her weekly gross earnings are $328.75.

Solution

Use the table for single persons—weekly payroll period. The given earnings are found in the row "at least $320 but less than $330." Go across this row to the column headed "0" (for no withholding allowances). From the table, the withholding is $41.

EXAMPLE 2

Using the Wage
Bracket Method
for Federal
Withholding

Larry Sifford is married, claims three withholding allowances, and has monthly gross earnings of $2947.35. Find his withholding tax using the wage bracket method.

Solution

Use the table for married persons—monthly payroll period. Look down the two left columns, and find the range that includes Sifford's gross earnings: "at least $2920 but less than $2960." Read across the table to the column headed "3" (for the three withholding allowances). The withholding tax is $259. Had Sifford claimed six withholding allowances, his withholding tax would have been only $158.

Objective **3** **Find the federal withholding tax using the percentage method.** Many companies today prefer to use the *percentage method* to determine federal withholding tax. The percentage method does not require the several pages of tables needed with the wage bracket method and is more easily adapted to computer applications in the processing of payrolls.

Percentage Method Income Tax Withholding Table

Payroll Period	One Withholding Allowance
Weekly	$ 51.92
Biweekly	103.85
Semimonthly	112.50
Monthly	225.00
Quarterly	675.00
Semiannually	1,350.00
Annually	2,700.00
Daily or miscellaneous (each day of the payroll period)	10.38

Tables for Percentage Method of Withholding

TABLE 1—WEEKLY Payroll Period

(a) SINGLE person (including head of household)—

If the amount of wages after subtracting withholding allowances is: The amount of income tax to withhold is:

Not over $51 . . . . . $0

Over—	But not over—		of excess over—
$51	—$517	. 15%	—$51
$517	—$1,105	. $69.90 plus 28%	—$517
$1,105	—$2,493	. $234.54 plus 31%	—$1,105
$2,493	—$5,385	. $664.82 plus 36%	—$2,493
$5,385	. . . . .	. $1,705.94 plus 39.6%	—$5,385

(b) MARRIED person—

If the amount of wages after subtracting withholding allowances is: The amount of income tax to withhold is:

Not over $124 . . . . $0

Over—	But not over—		of excess over—
$124	—$899	. 15%	—$124
$899	—$1,855	. . $116.25 plus 28%	—$899
$1,855	—$3,084	. $383.93 plus 31%	—$1,855
$3,084	—$5,439	. $764.92 plus 36%	—$3,084
$5,439	. . . . .	. $1,612.72 plus 39.6%	—$5,439

TABLE 2—BIWEEKLY Payroll Period

(a) SINGLE person (including head of household)—

If the amount of wages after subtracting withholding allowances is: The amount of income tax to withhold is:

Not over $102 . . . . $0

Over—	But not over—		of excess over—
$102	—$1,035	. 15%	—$102
$1,035	—$2,210	. $139.95 plus 28%	—$1,035
$2,210	—$4,987	. $468.95 plus 31%	—$2,210
$4,987	—$10,769	. $1,329.82 plus 36%	—$4,987
$10,769	. . . . .	. $3,411.34 plus 39.6%	—$10,769

(b) MARRIED person—

If the amount of wages after subtracting withholding allowances is: The amount of income tax to withhold is:

Not over $248 . . . . $0

Over—	But not over—		of excess over—
$248	—$1,798	. 15%	—$248
$1,798	—$3,710	. $232.50 plus 28%	—$1,798
$3,710	—$6,167	. $767.86 plus 31%	—$3,710
$6,167	—$10,879	. $1,529.53 plus 36%	—$6,167
$10,879	. . . . .	. $3,225.85 plus 39.6%	—$10,879

TABLE 3—SEMIMONTHLY Payroll Period

(a) SINGLE person (including head of household)—

If the amount of wages after subtracting withholding allowances is: The amount of income tax to withhold is:

Not over $110 . . . . $0

Over—	But not over—		of excess over—
$110	—$1,121	. 15%	—$110
$1,121	—$2,394	. $151.65 plus 28%	—$1,121
$2,394	—$5,402	. $508.09 plus 31%	—$2,394
$5,402	—$11,667	. $1,440.57 plus 36%	—$5,402
$11,667	. . . . .	. $3,695.97 plus 39.6%	—$11,667

(b) MARRIED person—

If the amount of wages after subtracting withholding allowances is: The amount of income tax to withhold is:

Not over $269 . . . . $0

Over—	But not over—		of excess over—
$269	—$1,948	. 15%	—$269
$1,948	—$4,019	. $251.85 plus 28%	—$1,948
$4,019	—$6,681	. $831.73 plus 31%	—$4,019
$6,681	—$11,785	. $1,656.95 plus 36%	—$6,681
$11,785	. . . . .	. $3,494.39 plus 39.6%	—$11,785

TABLE 4—MONTHLY Payroll Period

(a) SINGLE person (including head of household)—

If the amount of wages after subtracting withholding allowances is: The amount of income tax to withhold is:

Not over $221 . . . . $0

Over—	But not over—		of excess over—
$221	—$2,242	. 15%	—$221
$2,242	—$4,788	. $303.15 plus 28%	—$2,242
$4,788	—$10,804	. $1,016.03 plus 31%	—$4,788
$10,804	—$23,333	. $2,880.99 plus 36%	—$10,804
$23,333	. . . . .	. $7,391.43 plus 39.6%	—$23,333

(b) MARRIED person—

If the amount of wages after subtracting withholding allowances is: The amount of income tax to withhold is:

Not over $538 . . . . $0

Over—	But not over—		of excess over—
$538	—$3,896	. 15%	—$538
$3,896	—$8,038	. $503.70 plus 28%	—$3,896
$8,038	—$13,363	. $1,663.46 plus 31%	—$8,038
$13,363	—$23,571	. $3,314.21 plus 36%	—$13,363
$23,571	. . . . .	. $6,989.09 plus 39.6%	—$23,571

EXAMPLE 3

Finding Federal Withholding Using the Percentage Method

Steve Tomlin is married, claims four withholding allowances, and has weekly gross earnings of $1150. Use the percentage method to find his withholding tax.

Solution

Step 1 Find the withholding allowance for *one* on the weekly payroll period in the percentage method income tax withholding table. The amount is $51.92. Since Tomlin claims four allowances, multiply the one withholding allowance ($51.92), by his number of withholding allowances (4).

$$\$51.92 \times 4 = \$207.68$$

Step 2 Subtract the amount in step 1 from gross earnings.

$$\$1150 - \$207.68 = \$942.32$$

Step 3 Find the "married person weekly" section of the percentage method withholding table. Since $942.32 is over $899 but not over $1855, an amount of $116.25 is added to 28% of the excess over $899 as shown in the highlighted line in Table 1.

$$\$942.32 - \$899 = \$43.32 \quad \text{excess over \$899}$$
$$\$43.32 \times 28\% = \$43.32 \times .28 = \$12.13$$
$$\$116.25 + \$12.13 = \$128.38 \quad \text{withholding tax}$$

The calculator solution to this example is

1150 [−] 4 [×] 51.92 [−] 899 [=] [×] .28 [+] 116.25 [=] 128.3796

Note: All calculator solutions use a scientific calculator. Refer to Appendix B for scientific calculator basics.

> **NOTE** The amount of withholding tax found using the wage bracket method can vary slightly from the amount of withholding tax found using the percentage method. Any differences would be eliminated when the income tax return is filed.

Objective [4] **Find the state withholding tax using the state income tax rate.** Many states and cities also have an income tax collected by withholding. Income taxes vary from state to state with no income tax in the states of Alaska, Florida, Nevada, South Dakota, Texas, Washington, and Wyoming. A few states have a flat tax rate (percent of income) as a **state income tax** while the majority of the states issue tax tables with taxes going as high as 9% and 10%. A few of the states income tax rates are shown in the following figure.

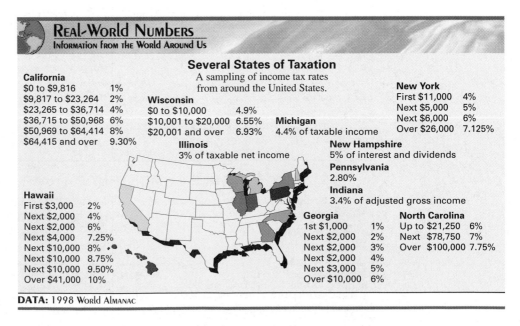

REAL-WORLD NUMBERS
Information from the World Around Us

Several States of Taxation
A sampling of income tax rates from around the United States.

California
$0 to $9,816	1%
$9,817 to $23,264	2%
$23,265 to $36,714	4%
$36,715 to $50,968	6%
$50,969 to $64,414	8%
$64,415 and over	9.30%

Wisconsin
$0 to $10,000	4.9%
$10,001 to $20,000	6.55%
$20,001 and over	6.93%

Michigan
4.4% of taxable income

Illinois
3% of taxable net income

New Hampshire
5% of interest and dividends

Pennsylvania
2.80%

Indiana
3.4% of adjusted gross income

New York
First $11,000	4%
Next $5,000	5%
Next $6,000	6%
Over $26,000	7.125%

Hawaii
First $3,000	2%
Next $2,000	4%
Next $2,000	6%
Next $4,000	7.25%
Next $10,000	8%
Next $10,000	8.75%
Next $10,000	9.50%
Over $41,000	10%

Georgia
1st $1,000	1%
Next $2,000	2%
Next $2,000	3%
Next $2,000	4%
Next $3,000	5%
Over $10,000	6%

North Carolina
Up to $21,250	6%
Next $78,750	7%
Over $100,000	7.75%

DATA: 1998 World Almanac

EXAMPLE 4

Finding State Withholding Tax

Andrea Novak has gross earnings for the month of $3642. If her state has a 4.4% income tax rate, find the state withholding tax.

SOLUTION

State withholding tax can be found by multiplying 4.4% by the amount of earnings.

$$4.4\% \times \$3642 = .044 \times \$3642 = \$160.25 \text{ (rounded)}$$

The amount of state withholding tax is $160.25.

OBJECTIVE **5** **Find net pay when given gross wages, taxes, and other deductions.** It is common for employees to request additional deductions, such as union dues and credit union payments. The final amount of pay received by the employee, called the net pay, is given by the following formula.

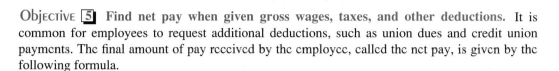

Net pay = Gross earnings − FICA tax (Social Security)
− Medicare tax − Federal withholding tax
− State withholding tax − Other deductions

EXAMPLE 5

Determining Net Pay after Deductions

Ann Stypuloski is married and claims three withholding allowances. Her weekly gross earnings are $538.25. Her state withholding is 2.5% and her union dues are $20. Find her net pay using the percentage method of withholding.

SOLUTION

First find FICA (Social Security) tax, which is $33.37, then Medicare, which is $7.80. Federal withholding tax is $38.77 and state withholding is $13.46. Total deductions are

$33.37	FICA tax (6.2%)
7.80	Medicare tax (1.45%)
38.77	federal withholding
13.46	state withholding (2.5%)
+ 20.00	union dues
$113.40	total deductions

Find net pay by subtracting total deductions from gross earnings.

$538.25	gross earnings
− 113.40	total deductions
$424.85	net pay

Stypuloski will receive a check for $424.85.

OBJECTIVE **6** **Find the quarterly amount owed to the Internal Revenue Service.** An employee's contribution to Social Security and Medicare must be matched by the employer.

EXAMPLE 6

Finding the Amount of FICA and Medicare Tax Due

If the employees at Fair Oaks Automotive Repair pay a total of $789.10 in Social Security tax and $182.10 in Medicare tax, how much must the employer send to the Internal Revenue Service?

SOLUTION

The employer must match this and send a total of $971.20 ($789.10 + $182.10 from employees) + $971.20 (from employer) = $1942.40 to the government.

> **NOTE**   In addition to the employee's Social Security tax and a matching amount paid by the employer, the employer must also send the amount withheld for income tax to the Internal Revenue Service on a quarterly basis.

Example 7

Finding the Employer's Amount Due the IRS

Suppose that during a certain quarter Blockbuster Video has collected $2765.42 from its employees for FICA tax, $638.17 for medicare tax, and $3572.86 in federal withholding tax. Compute the total amount due to the government from Blockbuster Video.

Solution

$2765.42	collected from employees for FICA tax
2765.42	equal amount paid by employer
638.17	collected from employees for Medicare tax
638.17	equal amount paid by employer
3572.86	federal withholding tax
$10,380.04	total due to government

The firm must send $10,380.04 to the Internal Revenue Service.

Each quarter employers must file **Form 941, the Employer's Quarterly Federal Tax Return**. The form itemizes total employee wages and earnings, the income taxes withheld from employees, the FICA taxes withheld from employees, and the FICA taxes paid by the employer. In addition, Form 941 divides the quarter into its three months and the amounts of the tax liability (employee and employer) are entered on the line of the proper month in that quarter.

The **Federal Unemployment Tax Act (FUTA)** requires employers to pay an additional tax. This **unemployment insurance tax**, paid entirely by employers, is used to pay unemployment benefits to an individual who has become unemployed and is unable to find work. In general, all employers who paid wages of $1000 or more in a calendar quarter, or had one or more employees for some part of a day in 20 different weeks, must file an Employer's Annual Federal Unemployment (FUTA) Tax Return.

The employer must pay 6.2% of the first $7000 in earnings for that year for each employee. Since most states have unemployment taxes, the employer is given credit for these when filing the FUTA return. As soon as the employee reaches earnings of $7000, no additional unemployment tax must be paid.

The **fringe benefits** offered today are very important to employees. These are the extras being offered by the employer that go beyond the paycheck. The following graphic lists several fringe benefits and shows what percent of the business owners, both male and female, offer these fringe benefits.

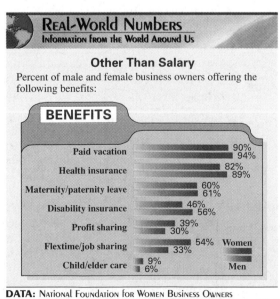

Real-World Numbers
Information from the World Around Us

Other Than Salary
Percent of male and female business owners offering the following benefits:

BENEFITS

Benefit		
Paid vacation	90%	94%
Health insurance	82%	89%
Maternity/paternity leave	60%	61%
Disability insurance	46%	56%
Profit sharing	39%	30%
Flextime/job sharing	54% (Women)	33%
Child/elder care	9%	6% (Men)

DATA: National Foundation for Women Business Owners

CHAPTER 5 | Quick Review

CHAPTER TERMS

Review the following terms to test your understanding of the chapter. For each term you do not know, refer to the page number found next to that term.

allowances [p. 186]
commission rate [p. 185]
compensatory (comp) time [p. 175]
daily overtime [p. 174]
deductions [p. 169]
differential piece rate [p. 184]
double time [p. 175]
draw [p. 186]
Fair Labor Standards Act [p. 172]
Federal Insurance Contributions Act (FICA) [p. 191]

Federal Unemployment Tax Act (FUTA) [p. 204]
fringe benefits [p. 204]
gross earnings [pp. 169, 200]
hourly wage [p. 170]
incentive rates [p. 183]
income tax withholdings [p. 197]
marital status [p. 197]
Medicare [p. 191]
net pay [pp. 169, 191]
overtime [p. 172]
overtime premium method [p. 174]

pay period [p. 176]
payroll ledger [p. 170]
percentage method [p. 200]
personal income tax [p. 197]
piecework rate [p. 183]
premium payment plans [p. 175]
quotas [p. 184]
rate of commission [p. 185]
Request for Earnings and Benefit Estimate Statement [p. 192]
returns [p. 186]

salary [p. 176]
salary plus commission [p. 186]
shift differential [p. 175]
sliding scale [p. 186]
Social Security [p. 191]
split-shift premium [p. 175]
state income tax [p. 202]
straight commission [p. 185]
time card [p. 170]
time rates [p. 183]
time-and-a-half rate [p. 172]
variable commission [p. 186]
wage bracket method [p. 200]
withholding allowances [p. 197]

CONCEPTS	EXAMPLES
5.1 Gross earnings Gross earnings = Hours worked × Rate per hour	40 hours worked at $7.10 per hour. Gross earnings = **40 × $7.10 = $284**
5.1 Gross earnings with overtime First, find the regular earnings. Then, determine overtime pay at overtime rate. Finally, add regular and overtime earnings.	40 regular hours at $7.10 per hour. 10 overtime hours at time and a half. Gross earnings = $$(40 \times 7.10) + \left(10 \times 7.10 \times 1\frac{1}{2}\right)$$ $$= \$284 + \$106.50 = \$390.50$$
5.1 Common pay periods | Pay Period	Paychecks Per Year
Monthly	12
Semimonthly	24
Biweekly	26
Weekly	52		Find the earnings equivalent of $1400 per month for other pay periods. $$\text{Semimonthly} = \frac{1400}{2} = \$700$$ $$\text{Biweekly} = \frac{1400 \times 12}{26} = \$646.15$$ $$\text{Weekly} = \frac{1400 \times 12}{52} = \$323.08$$
5.1 Overtime for salaried employees First, find the hourly equivalent. Next, multiply the hourly equivalent rate by the overtime hours by $1\frac{1}{2}$. Finally add overtime earnings to the salary.	Salary is $324 per week for 40 hours. Find earnings for 46 hours. $$\$324 \div 40 = \$8.10 \text{ per hour}$$ $$\$8.10 \times 6 \times 1\frac{1}{2} = \$72.90 \text{ overtime}$$ $$\$324 + \$72.90 = \$396.90$$
5.2 Gross earnings for piecework Gross earnings = Number of items × Pay per item	Items produced, 175; pay per item, $.65; find gross earnings. $$175 \times \$.65 = \$113.75$$

CONCEPTS	EXAMPLES
5.2 Gross earnings for differential piecework The rate paid per item produced varies with level of production.	1–100 items $.75 each 101–150 items $.90 each 151 or more items $1.04 each Find gross earnings for producing 214 items. $100 \times \$.75 = \$75.00$ (first 100 units) $\ \ 50 \times \$.90 = \$45.00$ (next 50 units) $\ \ \underline{64 \times \$1.04 = \$66.56}$ (number over 150) 214 total items $186.56
5.2 Overtime earnings on piecework Gross earnings = Earnings at regular rate + Earnings at overtime rate	Items produced on regular time, 530; items produced on overtime, 110; piece rate $.34; find gross earnings. Gross earnings = $$(530 \times \$.34) + 110\left(1\tfrac{1}{2} \times \$.34\right) = \$180.20 + \$56.10$$ $$= \$236.30$$
5.2 Straight commission Gross earnings = Commission rate × Amount of sales	Sales of $25,800; commission rate is 5%. $$.05 \times \$25,800 = \$1290$$
5.2 Variable commission Commission rate varies at different sales levels.	Up to $10,000, 6%; $10,001–$20,000, 8%; $20,001 and up, 9% Find the commission on sales of $32,768. $.06 \times \$10,000 = \ \ \$600.00$ (first $10,000) $.08 \times \$10,000 = \ \ \$800.00$ (next $10,000) $.09 \times \underline{\$12,768} = \underline{\$1149.12}$ (amount over $20,000) $\ \ \ \ \ \ \ \ \ \$32,768 \ \ \ \ \$2549.12$ $\ \$Total $\ $commission
5.2 Salary and commission Gross earnings = Fixed earnings + Commission	Salary, $250 per week; commission rate, 3%; find gross earnings on sales of $6848. Gross earnings = $\$250 + (.03 \times \$6848) = \$250 + \$205.44$ $= \$455.44$
5.2 Commission with a drawing account Gross earnings = Commission − Draw	Sales for month, $28,560; commission rate, 7%; draw is $750 for month; find gross earnings. Gross earnings = $(.07 \times \$28,560) - \$750 = \$1999.20 - \$750$ $= \$1249.20$
5.3 FICA; Social Security tax The gross earnings are multiplied by the tax rate. When the maximum earnings are reached, no additional FICA is withheld that year.	Gross earnings, $458; Social Security tax rate, 6.2%; find Social Security tax. $$\$458 \times .062 = \$28.40$$
5.3 Medicare tax The gross earnings are multiplied by the Medicare tax rate. When the maximum earnings are reached, no additional Medicare tax is withheld that year.	Gross earnings, $458; Medicare tax rate, 1.45%; find Medicare tax. $$\$458 \times .0145 = \$6.64$$

CONCEPTS	EXAMPLES
5.3 State disability insurance deductions Multiply the gross earnings by the SDI tax rate. When the maximum earnings are reached, no additional taxes are paid in that year.	Gross earnings, $2880; SDI tax rate, 1%; find SDI tax. $$\$2880 \times .01 = \$28.80$$
5.4 Federal withholding tax Tax is paid on total earnings. No maximum as with FICA.	Single employee with 3 allowances; weekly earnings of $326; find the federal withholding tax. Using wage bracket amount "at least $320, but less than $330," withholding is $18. With the percentage method withholding is $$\$326 - (\$51.92 \times 3) = \$170.24$$ $$\$170.24 - \$51 = \$119.24$$ $$\$119.24 \times .15 = \$17.89$$
5.4 State withholding tax Tax is paid on total earnings. No maximum as with FICA.	Married employee with weekly earnings of $392; find the state withholding tax given a state withholding tax rate of 4.5%. $$4.5\% \times \$392 = .045 \times \$392 = \$17.64$$
5.4 Quarterly report, Form 941 Filed each quarter; FICA and federal withholding are sent to the IRS (FICA + Medicare) × 2 (employer matches) + federal withholding tax	If quarterly FICA withheld from employees is $5269, Medicare tax is $1581, and federal withholding tax is $14,780, find the total owed to the IRS. $$(\$5269 + \$1581) \times (2) + \$14,780$$ $$= \$28,480$$

CHAPTER 5 | SUMMARY EXERCISE
Payroll: Finding Your Take-Home Pay

Paige Dunbar, the manager of a Blockbuster Video, receives an annual salary of $32,240, which is paid weekly. Her normal workweek is 40 hours and she is paid time and a half for all overtime. She is single and claims one withholding allowance. Her deductions include FICA, Medicare, federal withholding, state disability insurance, state withholding, credit union payments of $125, retirement deductions of $75, association dues of $12, and a Diabetes Association contribution of $15. Find each of the following for a week in which she works 52 hours.

(a) Regular weekly earnings   (a) _____

(b) Overtime earnings   (b) _____

(c) Total gross earnings   (c) _____

(d) FICA   (d) _____

(e) Medicare   (e) _____

(f) Federal withholding   (f) _____

(g) State disability   (g) _____

(h) State withholding (Assume the state income tax rate is 4.4%)   (h) _____

(i) Net pay   (i) _____

Investigate

Look at the statement that you received with your last paycheck. Be certain that your gross earnings are correct. Understand and check all of the deductions made by your employer. Subtract all deductions from your gross earnings to be certain that your net pay is accurate.

Name   Date   Class

CHAPTER 5 | TEST

To help you review, the numbers in brackets show the section in which the topic was discussed.

Complete the following payroll ledger. Find the total gross earnings for each employee. Time and a half is paid on all hours over 40 in one week. **[5.1]**

Employee	Hours Worked	Reg. Hrs.	O.T. Hrs.	Reg. Rate	Gross Earnings
1. Darasz	48.5			$9.14	
2. Davidson	38.25			$7.40	

Solve the following application problems.

3. Judy Martinez is paid $34,060 annually. Find the equivalent earnings if this amount is paid (**a**) weekly, (**b**) biweekly, (**c**) semimonthly, and (**d**) monthly. **[5.1]**

(**a**) _____
(**b**) _____
(**c**) _____
(**d**) _____

4. At Jalisco Electronics in Mexicali, Mexico, assemblers are paid according to the following differential piece rate scale: 1–20 units in a week, $4.50 each; 21–30 units, $5.50 each; and $7 each for every unit over 30. Adrian Ortega assembled 28 units in one week. Find his gross pay. **[5.2]**

4. _____

5. Samantha Walker receives a commission of 6% for selling a $115,000 house. Half the commission goes to the broker, and half the remainder to another salesperson. Walker gets the rest. Find the amount she receives. **[5.2]**

5. _____

*An employee is paid a salary of $6015 per month. If the current FICA rate is 6.2% on the first $70,000 of earnings, and the Medicare tax rate is 1.45% of earnings, how much should be withheld for (**a**) FICA tax and (**b**) Medicare tax during the following months?* **[5.3]**

6. March (**a**) _____   (**b**) _____   **7.** December (**a**) _____   (**b**) _____

Find the federal withholding tax using the wage bracket method for each of the following employees.
[5.4]

8. Flahive: 2 withholding allowances, single, $278.65 weekly earnings.

8. _____

9. Hoffa: 2 withholding allowances, married, $705.91 weekly earnings

9. _____

10. Howard: 3 withholding allowances, married, $2208.79 monthly earnings

10. _____

11. Kluesner: 4 withholding allowances, single, $1757.23 monthly earnings

11. _____

12. Lawrence: 6 withholding allowances, married, $2580.76 monthly earnings

12. _____

Find the net pay for each of the following employees after FICA, Medicare, federal withholding tax, state disability, and other deductions have been made. Assume that none has earned over $70,000 so far this year. Assume a FICA rate of 6.2%, Medicare rate of 1.45%, and a state disability rate of 1%. Use the percentage method of withholding.   **[5.3 AND 5.4]**

13. Precilo: $1852.75 monthly earnings, 1 withholding allowance, single, $37.80 in other deductions

13. _____

14. Colley: $522.11 weekly earnings, 4 withholding allowances, married, state withholding of $15.34, credit union savings of $20, educational television contribution of $7.50

14. _____

15. Harper: $677.92 weekly earnings, 6 withholding allowances, married, state withholding of $22.18, union dues of $14, charitable contribution of $15

15. _____

Solve the following application problems.

16. A salesperson is paid $452 per week plus a commission of 2% on all sales. The salesperson sold $712 worth of goods on Monday, $523 on Tuesday, $1002 on Wednesday, $391 on Thursday, and $609 on Friday. Returns and allowances for the week were $114. Find the employee's **(a)** Social Security tax (6.2%), **(b)** Medicare tax (1.45%), and **(c)** state disability insurance (1%) for the week   **[5.3 AND 5.4]**

(a) _____
(b) _____
(c) _____

17. Susan Hessney earned $68,809.85 so far this year. This week she earned $1852.82. Find her **(a)** FICA tax and **(b)** Medicare tax for this week's earnings.   **[5.3]**

(a) _____
(b) _____

For Exercises 18 and 19, find **(a)** *the Social Secuirity tax and* **(b)** *the Medicare tax for each of the following self-employed people. Use a FICA tax rate of 12.4% and a Medicare tax rate of 2.9%.*   **[5.3]**

18. Kyle: $23,417.21

(a) _____
(b) _____

19. Biondi: $34,539.04

(a) _____
(b) _____

20. The employees of Quick-Lube paid a total of $418.12 in Social Security tax last month, $96.48 in Medicare tax, and $1217.34 in federal withholding tax. Find the total amount that the employer must send to the Internal Revenue Service.

20. _____

CHAPTER 6

MATHEMATICS OF BUYING

Dick and Jeanne Hill own Oaks Hardware, a traditional hardware store in Fair Oaks Village. It is an ace Hardware franchise and carries the usual hardware merchandise and a unique selection of household and gift items.

The store purchases inventory items at a retailer's discounted price (trade discount) and then receives an invoice from the supplier. When the invoice is paid, it is most common for another discount (cash discount) to be taken. The owners of the store realize how important these discounts are in contributing to the profitability of their business.

Retail businesses make a profit by purchasing items and then selling them for more than they cost. There are several steps in this process: Manufacturers buy raw materials and component parts and assemble them into products that can be sold to other manufacturers or **wholesalers**. The wholesaler buys from manufacturers or other wholesalers and sells to the **retailer**, who sells directly to the ultimate user, the **consumer**.

Documents called **invoices** help businesses keep track of sales, while various types of discounts help them buy products at lower costs to increase profits. Recent technology has enabled businesses to replace much of their paper-based business processes with electronic solutions, known collectively as *electronic commerce* (EC). Expect to see further changes in how business is conducted in the future. This chapter covers the mathematics needed for working with invoices and discounts—the mathematics of buying.

6.1 | INVOICES AND TRADE DISCOUNTS

Objectives

1. Complete an invoice.
2. Understand common shipping terms.
3. Identify invoice abbreviations.
4. Calculate trade discounts and understand why they are given.
5. Differentiate between a single discount and a series, or chain, discount.
6. Calculate series discounts.
7. Use complements to solve series discounts.
8. Use a table to find the net cost equivalent of series discounts.

PROBLEM SOLVING IN BUSINESS

Dick and Jeanne Hill, owners of Oaks Hardware, must have a thorough understanding of invoices, trade discounts, and cash discounts. As a small, independent hardware store they must carry first-quality items, buy at the best price, and take all earned discounts.

An invoice is a printed record of a purchase and sale. For the seller it is a **sales invoice** and records a sale; for the buyer it is a **purchase invoice** and records a purchase. The invoice identifies the seller and the buyer; describes the items purchased; states the quantity purchased, the unit price of each item, and the **extension total** (the number of items purchased times the price per unit); applies any discounts and shipping and insurance charges; and provides the **invoice total** (the sum of the extension totals).

OBJECTIVE ☐1 **Complete an invoice.** The following document serves as a sales invoice for J. B. Sherr Company and as a purchase invoice for Oaks Hardware. The numbers in the **units shipped** (or "SHIPPED" as seen in the invoice below) column multiplied by the **unit price** give the **amount**, or extension total, for each item. The **total invoice amount** is the sum of the extension totals.

J. B. SHERR Co.

SHOWROOM AND WAREHOUSE
1704 ROLLINS ROAD
BURLINGAME, CA 94010
TELEPHONE: (650) 697-3430
TO ORDER 1-800-660-1422

INVOICE

SOLD TO:
OAKS HARDWARE   OAK007
10136 FAIR OAKS BLVD.
FAIR OAKS   CA 95628

PAGE NO. 1 OF

SHIP TO:
OAKS HARDWARE
10136 FAIR OAKS BLVD.
FAIR OAKS   CA 95628

INVOICE DATE	INVOICE NO.
03/17	0002271-IN

TERMS: 1% 15 DAYS, NET 30

SALESMAN	ENTRY NUMBER	ENTRY DATE	SHIPPING DATE	SHIPPED VIA	CUSTOMER ORDER NO./DEPT.
0008	0002280	03/17		UPS	3-13

TAG #	QTY. ORD.	SHIPPED	UNIT	STOCK NUMBER	DESCRIPTION	SUGG. RETAIL	UNIT PRICE	AMOUNT
1	12	12	EACH	736-080	IMPT NATURAL SEA SPONGE	.00	2.400	28.80
2	1	0	EA	267-6682	ACRYLIC BUTTER DISH	6.39	3.760	.00
3	1	1	EA	267-6683	ACRYLIC CREAM & SUGAR S	6.39	3.760	3.76
4	1	1	EA	267-6684	ACRYLIC NAPKIN HOLDER	5.29	3.140	3.14
5	6	6	EACH	694-322	IMPT WENOL METAL POLISH	7.79	4.650	27.90
6	6	6	EACH	694-353	IMPTRED BEAR POLISH	7.39	4.370	26.22
7	1	1	EA	274-10012	FRIENDSHIP MIXING BOWL	31.50	18.750	18.75
8	1	0	EACH	274-10014	FRIENDSHIP MIXING BOWL	44.90	26.500	.00
9	2	2	EA	589-31008	FLEXIBLE CHOPPING MATS	3.93	2.360	4.72
10	1	1	EA	589-22153	CORNER SINK SHELF W/SUC	2.79	1.600	1.60
11	6	0	EACH	281-7950	GEMCO JUICER W/GLASS JA	4.59	2.730	.00
12	2	2	EACH	54-611	ARDEN WAFFLE TOWEL—BLUE	3.19	1.900	3.80
13	2	2	EACH	54-612	ARDEN WAFFLE TOWEL—GREE	3.19	1.900	3.80
14	2	2	EACH	60-6	ASHLAND TIRE MAT 18.5 X	18.75	11.250	22.50
15	2	2	EACH	998-713	3 HALF/RD DRAGON 18 X 30	.00	5.200	10.40
16	2	2	EACH	998-143	3 WELCOME MAT 18 X 30	.00	6.910	13.82
17	3	3	EACH	998-303	3 MB PLAIN MAT 18 X 30	.00	8.640	25.92
18	2	2	EACH	998-504	4 HALF/RD MB PLAIN 20 X 3	.00	10.550	21.10
19								
20								

NON-TAX TOTAL	TAXABLE TOTAL	SALES TAX	FREIGHT	MISC.	INVOICE TOTAL
216.23	.00	.00	19.45		235.68

ALL ITEMS NOT SHIPPED ARE CANCELLED. PLEASE REORDER

PLEASE PAY FROM THIS INVOICE

ALL ORDERS SUBJECT TO CREDIT ACCEPTANCE. PRICES SUBJECT TO CHANGE WITHOUT NOTICE. SHORTAGES MUST BE REPORTED WITHIN 10 DAYS. NO RETURNS ACCEPTED WITHOUT PRIOR AUTHORIZATION. PAST DUE ACCOUNTS SUBJECT TO INTEREST (1½% PER MO.) PLUS COLLECTION CHARGES.

CUSTOMER'S COPY

Trade and cash discounts, discussed later in this chapter, *are never applied to shipping and insurance charges.* For this reason, shipping and insurance charges are often not included in the invoice total, so the purchaser must add them to the invoice total to find the total amount due. In the J. B. Sherr Company invoice the freight (shipping) charges are included in the INVOICE TOTAL space.

OBJECTIVE **2** **Understand common shipping terms.** The shipping term **FOB (free on board)**, followed by the words **shipping point** or **destination**, commonly appears on invoices. The term *FOB shipping point* means that the *buyer* pays for shipping and that ownership of the merchandise passes to the purchaser prior to shipment. The term *FOB destination* means that the *seller* pays the shipping charges and retains ownership until the goods reach the destination. This distinction is important in the event that the merchandise is lost or damaged during shipment.

The shipping term **COD** means **cash on delivery.** When goods are sent COD, the shipper delivers to the purchaser on receipt of enough cash to pay for the goods. When goods are moved over water, the shipping term **FAS,** which means **free alongside ship,** is common. Goods shipped this way are delivered to the dock with all freight charges paid to that point by the shipper.

OBJECTIVE **3** **Identify invoice abbreviations.** A number of abbreviations are used on invoices to identify measurements, quantities of merchandise, shipping terms, and additional discounts. The most common ones are found in the following box.

Invoice Abbreviations

ea.	each	drm.	drum
doz.	dozen	cs.	case
gro.	gross (144 items)	bx.	box
gr gro.	great gross (12 gross)	sk.	sack
qt.	quart	pr.	pair
gal.	gallon (4 quarts)	C	Roman numeral for 100
bbl.	barrel	M	Roman numeral for 1000
ml	milliliter	cwt.	per hundredweight
cl	centiliter	cpm.	cost per thousand
l	liter	@	at
in.	inch	lb.	pound
ft.	foot	oz.	ounce
yd.	yard	g	gram
mm	millimeter	kg	kilogram
cm	centimeter	ROG	receipt of goods
m	meter	ex. or x	extra dating
km	kilometer	FOB	free on board
ct.	crate	EOM	end of month
cart	carton	COD	cash on delivery
ctn.	carton	FAS	free alongside ship

OBJECTIVE **4** **Calculate trade discounts and understand why they are given.** **Trade discounts** are often given to businesses or individuals who buy an item for resale or produce an item that will then be sold. The seller usually gives the price of an item as its **list price** (the suggested price at which the item can be sold to the public). Then the seller gives a trade discount that is subtracted from the list price. The result is **the net cost** or **net price** (the amount paid by the buyer). Find the net cost with the following formula.

$$\text{Net cost} = \text{List price} - \text{Trade discount} \qquad \text{or} \qquad \begin{array}{r} \text{List price} \\ - \ \underline{\text{Trade discount}} \\ \text{Net cost} \end{array}$$

> **NOTE** The terms *net cost* and *net price* both refer to the amount paid by the buyer. However, net cost is the preferred term since this is the cost of an item to the business.

EXAMPLE 1
Calculating a
Single Trade
Discount

The list price of a Shredmaster Home/Office Shredder is $99.80, and the trade discount is 25%. Find the net cost.

Solution

First find the amount of the trade discount by finding 25% of $99.80.

$$R \times B = P$$
$$25\% \times \$99.80 = .25 \times \$99.80 = \$24.95$$

Subtract $24.95 from the list price of $99.80.

$99.80	list price
− 24.95	**trade discount**
$74.85	net cost

The net cost of the shredder is $74.85.

OBJECTIVE **5** **Differentiate between a single discount and a series, or chain, discount.** In Example 1, a **single discount** of 25% was offered. Sometimes two or more discounts are combined into a **series** or **chain discount**. A series discount is written, for example, as 20/10, which means that a 20% discount is subtracted from the list price, and *from this difference* another 10% discount is subtracted. Another discount of 15% could be attached to the series discount of 20/10, giving a new series discount of 20/10/15.

REASONS WHY TRADE DISCOUNTS CHANGE

Price changes may cause trade discounts to be raised or lowered.

As the *quantity purchased* increases, the discount offered may increase.

The buyer's position in *marketing channels* may determine the amount of discount offered. (A wholesaler would receive a larger discount than a succeeding retailer.)

Geographic location may influence the trade discount. An additional discount may be offered to increase sales in a particular area.

Seasonal fluctuations in sales may influence the trade discounts offered.

Competition from other companies may cause the raising or lowering of trade discounts.

The following advertisement indicates that the retail store received some very large trade discounts so that they are able to offer customers as much as 50%–70% off the list price. These high discounts may have resulted from very large quantities of merchandise purchased or perhaps it was the end of the season or the last of a production cycle for the manufacturer.

For related Web activities, go to www.mathbusiness.com

Keyword: tools

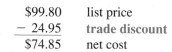

save **50-70%** off original prices when you take an extra **33% off**

Here's an example of how you save:
20.00 reg. price
14.99 Sale price
−5.00 33% off
9.99 Final price

OBJECTIVE **6** **Calculate series discounts.** Three methods can be used to calculate a series discount and net cost. The first of these is by **calculating discounts separately.**

EXAMPLE 2
Calculating Series
Trade Discounts

Oaks Hardware is offered a series discount of 20/10 on a Porter-Cable cordless drill with a list price of $150. Find the net cost after the series discount.

Solution

First, multiply the decimal equivalent of 20% (.2) by $150. Then subtract the product ($30) from $150, getting $120. Then multiply the decimal equivalent of the second discount, 10% (.1), by $120. Subtract the product ($12) from $120, getting $108, the net cost. Write this calculation as follows.

$$\begin{array}{ll} \$150 & \text{list price} \qquad \text{Discount: 20/10} \\ \underline{-\ \ 30} & (.2 \times \$150) \\ \$120 & \\ \underline{-\ \ 12} & (.1 \times \$120) \\ \$108 & \text{net cost} \end{array}$$

After the first discount, each discount is applied to the balance remaining after the preceding discount or discounts have been subtracted. This method demonstrates how trade discounts are applied, but this is usually *not* the preferred method for finding invoice amount.

> **NOTE** **Single discounts in a series are *never* added together**; for example, a series discount of 20/10 is *not the same* as a discount of 30%.

OBJECTIVE **7** **Use complements to solve series discounts.** By this second method of finding the net cost, first find the **complement** (with respect to 1, or 100%) of each single discount. The complement is the number that must be added to a given discount to get 1. For example, the complement (with respect to 1) of 20%, or .2, is .8 since .2 + .8 = 1. The complement (with respect to 1) of 40%, or .4, is .6. Other typical complements (with respect to 1) are as follows.

Discount	Complement with Respect to 100%	Decimal Equivalent of Discount	Complement with Respect to 1
10%	90%	.1	.9
15%	85%	.15	.85
25%	75%	.25	.75
30%	70%	.3	.7
35%	65%	.35	.65
50%	50%	.5	.5

The complement of the discount is the portion actually paid. For example, 10% discount means 90% is paid, 25% discount means 75% is paid, and 50% discount means 50% is paid.

Multiply each of the complements of the single discounts to get the **net cost equivalent**, or percent paid. Then multiply the net cost equivalent (percent paid) by the list price to obtain the net cost.

EXAMPLE 3
Using
Complements to
Find the Net Cost

Oaks Hardware is offered a series discount of 20/10 on a Porter-Cable cordless drill with a list price of $150. Find the net cost after the series discount.

Solution

For a series discount of 20/10, the complements (with respect to 1) of 20% and 10% are .8 and .9. Multiplying the complements gives .8 × .9 = .72, the net cost equivalent. (In other words, receiving a series discount of 20/10 is the same as paying 72% of the list price.) Find the net cost by multiplying .72 by the list price of $150, to get $108 as the net cost. Write this calculation as

Step 1.   Series discount   20 / 10
                                                       ↓   ↓
Step 2.   Find complements with respect to 1   .8   .9
                                                       ↓   ↓
Step 3.   Multiply complements   .8 × .9 = .72   net cost equivalent

$$
\begin{array}{rl}
\$150 & \text{list price} \\
\times\ .72 & \text{net cost equivalent} \\
\hline
300 & \\
1050 & \\
\hline
\$108.00 & \text{net cost}
\end{array}
$$

Find the amount of the discount by subtracting the net cost from the list price.

$$
\begin{array}{rl}
\$150 & \text{list price} \\
-\ 108 & \text{net cost} \\
\hline
\$\ 42 & \text{amount of discount}
\end{array}
$$

On many calculators you can subtract the discount percents from the list price in a series calculation.

150 − 20 % − 10 % = 108

Note: All calculator solutions use a scientific calculator. Refer to Appendix B for scientific calculator basics.

EXAMPLE 4

Using Complements to Solve Series Discounts

The list price of an outdoor patio furniture set is $210. Find the net cost after a series discount of 20/10/10.

SolutioN

Start by finding the complements with respect to 1 of each discount.

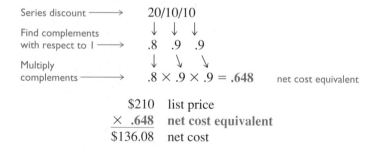

Series discount ⟶   20/10/10
                          ↓   ↓   ↓
Find complements
with respect to 1 ⟶   .8   .9   .9
                          ↓   ↘   ↘
Multiply
complements ⟶   .8 × .9 × .9 = .648   net cost equivalent

$$
\begin{array}{rl}
\$210 & \text{list price} \\
\times\ .648 & \text{net cost equivalent} \\
\hline
\$136.08 & \text{net cost}
\end{array}
$$

> **PROBLEM-SOLVING HINT**   **Never round the net cost equivalent.** Doing so will often result in a net cost that is incorrect. If the net cost equivalent in Example 4 had been rounded to .65 the resulting net cost would have been $136.50 (.65 × $210). This error of $.42 demonstrates the importance of not rounding the net cost equivalent.

Objective **8**   **Use a table to find the net cost equivalent of series discounts.**   People working with series discounts every day often use a table to find the net cost equivalents for various series discounts. For example, the following table shows that the net cost equivalent for a series discount of 20/10/10 is .648, the number located both to the right of 10/10 and below 20%.

Because changing the order in which numbers are multiplied does not change the answer, the order of the discounts in a series does not change the net cost equivalent. A 10/20 series is the same as a 20/10 series, and a 15/10/20 is identical to a 20/15/10.

Net Cost Equivalents of Series Discounts

	5%	10%	15%	20%	25%	30%	35%	40%
5	.9025	.855	.8075	.76	.7125	.665	.6175	.57
10	.855	.81	.765	.72	.675	.63	.585	.54
10/5	.81225	.7695	.72675	.684	.64125	.5985	.55575	.513
10/10	.7695	.729	.6885	.648	.6075	.567	.5265	.486
15	.8075	.765	.7225	.68	.6375	.595	.5525	.51
15/10	.72675	.6885	.65025	.612	.57375	.5355	.49725	.459
20	.76	.72	.68	.64	.6	.56	.52	.48
20/15	.646	.612	.578	.544	.51	.476	.442	.408
25	.7125	.675	.6375	.6	.5625	.525	.4875	.45
25/20	.57	.54	.51	.48	.45	.42	.39	.36
25/25	.534375	.50625	.478125	.45	.421875	.39375	.365625	.3375
30	.665	.63	.595	.56	.525	.49	.455	.42
40	.57	.54	.51	.48	.45	.42	.39	.36

> **NOTE** Do not round net cost equivalents. Doing so can cause an error in the net cost.

EXAMPLE 5
Using a Table of Net Cost Equivalents

Using the table of net cost equivalents, find the net cost equivalent of the following series discounts.

(a) 10/20 **(b)** 20/30 **(c)** 25/20/10 **(d)** 35/20/15

Solution

(a) .72 **(b)** .56 **(c)** .54 **(d)** .442

Product manufacturers must adjust the trade discounts offered to retailers so that the retailer can sell products at a competitive price while earning a reasonable profit. There is a great amount of competition in most industries that makes advertising and promotion extremely necessary in attracting customers to the store. The following graphic shows the ad-spending growth in four countries around the world. Notice the tremendous growth in advertising expenditures in the three developing countries.

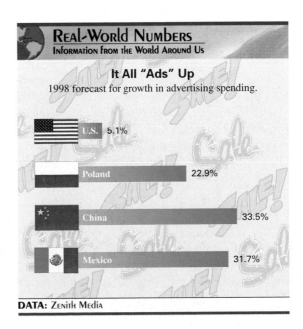

REAL-WORLD NUMBERS
Information from the World Around Us

It All "Ads" Up
1998 forecast for growth in advertising spending.

U.S. 5.1%
Poland 22.9%
China 33.5%
Mexico 31.7%

DATA: Zenith Media

| Name | Date | Class |

59. Explain the difference between a single trade discount and a series or chain trade discount.

60. Identify and explain four reasons that might cause series trade discounts to change. (See Objective 5.)

61. Explain what a complement (with respect to 1 or 100%) is. Give an example. (See Objective 7.)

62. Using complements, explain how to find the net cost equivalent of a 25/20 series discount. Explain why a 25/10/10 series discount is not the same as a 25/20 discount. (See Objective 7.)

Solve each of the following application problems in trade discount. Round to the nearest cent.

Quick Start

63. PURCHASING GOLF CLUBS The list price of a Pro Select Tour Classic 11-piece golf set is $399.99. If the series discount offered is 10/10/25, what is the net cost after trade discounts?

$.9 \times .9 \times .75 = .6075$
$\$399.99 \times .6075 = 242.993 = \$242.99$ (rounded)

63. $242.99

64. NURSING-CARE PURCHASES Roger Wheatley, a restorative nursing assistant (RNA), finds that the list price of one dozen adjustable walkers is $1680. Find the cost per walker if a series discount of 40/25 is offered.

64. _____

65. HARDWARE DISCOUNT Oaks Hardware purchases an extension ladder list priced at $120. It is available at either a 10/15/10 discount or a 20/15 discount. **(a)** Which discount gives the lower price? **(b)** Find the difference in net cost.

(a) _____
(b) _____

66. BULK CHEMICALS Brazilian Chemical Supply offers a series discount of 20/20/10 on all bulk purchases. If a 35,000-gallon tank (bulk) of industrial solvent is list priced at $28,500, what is the net cost after trade discounts?

66. _____

67. DANCE SHOES   How much will Giselle Papalewis, a dance instructor, pay for three-dozen pairs of dance shoes if the list price is $144 per dozen and a series discount of 10/25/30 is offered?

67. _____

68. COMMERCIAL TOOL PURCHASE   Kaci Salmon, an automotive mechanics student, is offered mechanic's net prices on all purchases at Gilbert Tool Supply. If mechanic's net prices mean a 20/10 discount, how much will Salmon spend on a Porter-Cable belt sander that is list priced at $245?

68. _____

69. TRADE-DISCOUNT COMPARISON   The Office Depot offers a series trade discount of 30/20 to its regular customers. Patrick Cleary, a new employee in the billing department, understood the 30/20 terms to mean 50% and computed this trade discount on a list price of $5440. How much difference did this error make in the amount of the invoice?

69. _____

70. Tamara Johnson-Draper has a choice of two supplies of fiber optics for her business. Tyler Suppliers offers a 20/10/25 discount on a list price of $5.70 per unit. Irving Optics offers a 30/20 discount on a list price of $5.40 per unit. **(a)** Which supplier gives her the lower price? **(b)** Find the amount saved if she buys 12,500 units from the lower-priced supplier. (*Hint:* Do not round.)

(a) _____
(b) _____

6.2 | Single Discount Equivalents

Objectives

1 Express a series discount as an equivalent single discount.
2 Find the net cost by multiplying the list price by the complements of the single discounts in a series.
3 Find the list price given the series discount and the net cost.

Objective **1** **Express a series discount as an equivalent single discount.** Series or chain discounts must often be expressed as a single discount rate. Find a **single discount equivalent to a series discount** by multiplying the complements (with respect to 1 or 100%) of the individual discounts. As in the previous section, the result is the net cost equivalent. Then subtract the net cost equivalent from 1. The result is the single discount that is the equivalent to the series discount. *The single discount equivalent is expressed as a percent.*

Finding the Single Discount Equivalent

Single discount equivalent = 1 − Net cost equivalent

Example 1

Finding a Single Discount Equivalent

If Air Clean Manufacturing offered a 20/10 discount to wholesale accounts on all heater filters, what would the single discount equivalent be?

Solution

Series discount $\longrightarrow$ 20 / 10

Find complements with respect to 1 $\longrightarrow$ .8   .9

Multiply complements $\longrightarrow$ .8 × .9 = .72   net cost equivalent

$$
\begin{array}{rl}
1.00 & \text{base} \\
- \ .72 & \text{net cost equivalent (remains)} \\
\hline
.28 & \text{or 28\% was discounted}
\end{array}
$$

The single discount equivalent of a 20/10 series discount is 28%.

Objective **2** **Find the net cost by multiplying the list price by the complements of the single discounts in a series.** Net cost can be found by multiplying the list price by the complements of each of the single discounts in a series as shown in the next example.

Example 2

Finding the Net Cost Using Complements

The list price of an oak entertainment center is $970. Find the net cost if trade discounts of 20/15/5 are offered.

Solution

Multiply as follows.

Net cost = List price × Complements of individual discounts
Net cost = $970 × .8 × .85 × .95

20 / 15 / 5

Net cost = $626.62

The net cost of the oak entertainment center is $626.62.

The calculator solution to this example is

$$970 \boxed{\times} .8 \boxed{\times} .85 \boxed{\times} .95 \boxed{=} 626.62.$$

Note: All calculator solutions use a scientific calculator. Refer to Appendix B for scientific calculator basics.

OBJECTIVE **3** **Find the list price given the series discount and the net cost.** Sometimes the net cost after trade discounts is given, along with the series discount, and the list price must be found.

EXAMPLE 3
Solving for List Price

Find the list price of a handmade rug that has a net cost of $544 after trade discounts of 20/20.

SOLUTION

Use a net cost equivalent. Start by finding the percent paid, using complements.

Series discount → 20 / 20
                          ↓   ↓
Complements   .8 × .8 = **.64** remains (net cost equivalent)
with respect to 1 ___↑_____↑___

As the work shows, **.64, or 64%**, of the list price was paid. Find the list price with the standard percent formula.

% of something is something   Check the answer.

64% of   list price is $544

R	×	B	= P

or

$$B = \frac{P}{R} = \frac{544}{.64} = \$850 \text{ list price}$$

$850	list price
− 170	(.2 × $850)
$680	
− 136	(.2 × $680)
$544	net cost

The list price of the rug is $850.

EXAMPLE 4
Solving for List Price

Find the list price of a 6-foot fiberglass stepladder having a series discount of 10/30/20 and a net cost of $45.36.

SOLUTION

Use complements to find the percent paid.

Series discount ⟶ 10 / 30 / 20
                          ↓   ↓   ↓
                       .9 × .7 × .8 = **.504** remains (percent paid)
Complements
with respect to 1 ___↑____↑____↑___

Therefore, **.504** of the list price is $45.36. Use the formula for base.

$$B = \frac{P}{R} = \frac{\$45.36}{.504} = \$90 \text{ list price}$$

The list price of the stepladder is $90. Check this answer as in the previous example.

PROBLEM-SOLVING HINT   Notice that Examples 3 and 4 are decrease problems similar to those shown in Chapter 3, Section 5. They are still base problems but may look different because the discount is now shown as a series of two or more discounts rather than a single percent decrease as in Chapter 3. If you need help refer to Section 3.5.

6.3 | CASH DISCOUNTS: ORDINARY DATING METHOD

Objectives

1. Calculate cash discounts and know why they are offered.
2. Use the ordinary dating method.
3. Determine whether cash discounts are earned.
4. Use postdating when calculating cash discounts.

PROBLEM SOLVING IN BUSINESS

At Oaks Hardware, Jeanne Hill pays close attention to all invoices received from suppliers. Besides the fact that invoices can frequently have errors in them, she wants to be certain that all of these invoices are paid early enough to receive any additional cash discounts that are offered. She prides herself that she has never missed a final due date and has said, "I'm never overdue on an account."

Objective 1 **Calculate cash discounts and know why they are offered.** **Cash discounts** are offered by sellers to encourage prompt payment by customers. In effect, the seller is saying, "Pay me quickly, and receive a discount." Businesses often borrow money for their day-to-day operation. Immediate cash payments from customers decrease the need for borrowed money.

To find the net cost when a cash discount is offered, begin with the list price and subtract any trade discounts. From the result, subtract the cash discount. Use the following formula.

> **FINDING THE NET COST**
>
> Net cost = (List price − Trade discount) − Cash discount

> **NOTE** If an invoice amount includes shipping and insurance charges, subtract these charges first, before a cash discount is taken; then add them back to find net cost after the cash discount is subtracted.

The type of cash discount appears on the invoice, under TERMS, which can be found in the bottom right-hand corner of the Hershey invoice on the next page. Many companies using automated billing systems state the exact amount of the cash discount on the invoice. This eliminates all calculations on the part of the buyer. The Hershey invoice is an example of an invoice stating the exact amount of the cash discount. This exact amount is found at the bottom of the invoice. Not all businesses do this, however, so it is important to know how to determine cash discounts.

For related Web activities, go to www.mathbusiness.com

Keyword: dating

Objective 2 **Use the ordinary dating method.** There are many methods for finding cash discounts, but nearly all of these are based on the **ordinary dating method**. The methods discussed here and in the next section are the most common in use today. The ordinary dating method of cash discount, for example, is expressed on an invoice as

2/10, n/30 or **2/10, net 30**

and is read "two ten, net thirty." The first digit is the rate of discount (2%), the second digit is the number of days allowed to take the discount (10 days), and n/30 (net 30) is the total number of days given to pay the invoice in full, if the buyer does not use the cash discount. If this invoice is paid within 10 days from the date of the invoice, a 2% discount is subtracted from the amount owed; or, if payment is made between the 11th and 30th days from the invoice date, the entire amount of the invoice is due. After 30 days from the date of the invoice, the invoice is considered overdue and may be subject to a late charge.

To find the due date of an invoice, use the number of days in each month, given in the following chart.

The Number of Days in Each Month

30-Day Months	31-Day Months		Exception
April	January	August	February
June	March	October	(28 days normally;
September	May	December	29 days in leap year)
November	July		

For related Web activities, go to www.mathbusiness.com

Keyword: chocolate

NOTE   Leap years occur every 4 years. They are the same as Summer Olympic years and presidential-election years in the United States. If a year is evenly divisible by the number 4, it is a leap year. The years 2004 and 2008 are both leap years because they are evenly divisible by 4.

Objective [3] **Determine whether cash discounts are earned.**   Find the date that an invoice is due by counting from the next day after the date of the invoice. The date of the invoice is never counted. Another way to determine due dates is to add the given number of days to the starting date. For example, to determine 10 days from April 7, add the number of days to the date $(7 + 10 = 17)$. The due date, or 10 days from April 7, is April 17.

When the discount date or net payment date falls in the next month, find the number of days remaining in the current month by subtracting the invoice date from the number of days in the month. Then find the number of days in the next month needed to equal the discount period or net payment period. For example, find 15 days from October 20 as follows.

$$
\begin{array}{rl}
31 & \text{days in October} \\
-\,20 & \text{the beginning date, October 20} \\
\hline
11 & \text{days remaining in October} \\
\\
15 & \text{total number of days} \\
-\,11 & \text{days remaining in October} \\
\hline
4 & \text{November (future date)}
\end{array}
$$

Therefore, November 4 is 15 days from October 20.

EXAMPLE 1

Finding Cash
Discount Dates

A Hershey Chocolate invoice is dated January 2 and offers terms of 2/10, net 30. Find **(a)** the last date on which the 2% discount may be taken, and **(b)** the net payment date.

Solution

(a) Beginning with the invoice date, January 2, the last date for taking the discount is January 12 $(2 + 10)$.

(b) The net payment date is February 1 $(31 - 2 = 29$ days remaining in January plus 1 day in February.)

EXAMPLE 2

Finding the
Amount Due on
an Invoice

An invoice received by Oaks Hardware for $840 is dated July 1 and offers terms of 2/10, n/30. If the invoice is paid on July 8 and the shipping and insurance charges, which were FOB shipping point, are $18.70, find the total amount due.

Solution

1. The invoice was paid 7 days after its date $(8 - 1 = 7)$; therefore, the 2% cash discount is taken.

2. The **2%** cash discount is found on $840. The discount to be taken is $840 \times .02 = \$16.80$.

3. The cash discount is subtracted from the invoice amount to determine the amount due.

$840 invoice amount − **$16.80 cash discount (2%)** = $823.20 amount due

4. The shipping and insurance charges are added to find the total amount due.

$823.20 amount due + **$18.70 shipping insurance** = $841.90 total amount due.

NOTE When the terms of an invoice are 2/10, only **98%** (100% − 2%) of the invoice must be paid during the first 10 days. In Example 2, the amount due may be found as follows.

$$\underbrace{\$840}_{\substack{\uparrow \\ \text{invoice} \\ \text{amount}}} \times \underbrace{.98}_{\substack{\uparrow \\ \text{complement} \\ \text{of 2\%}}} = \underbrace{\$823.20}_{\substack{\uparrow \\ \text{amount} \\ \text{due}}}$$

PROBLEM-SOLVING HINT A cash discount is never taken on shipping and insurance charges. Be certain that shipping and insurance charges are excluded from the invoice amount before calculating the cash discount. Shipping and insurance charges must then be added back in to find the total amount due.

Objective **4** **Use postdating when calculating cash discounts.** In the ordinary dating method, the cash discount date and net payment date are both counted from the date of the invoice. Occasionally, an invoice is **postdated**: The seller places a date that is after the actual invoice date, sometimes labeling it **AS OF**. For example, the following Levi Strauss invoice is dated 07/25 AS OF 08/01. Both the cash discount period and the net payment date are counted from 08/01 (August 1). This results in giving additional time for the purchaser to pay the invoice and receive the discount.

For related Web
activities, go to
www.mathbusiness.com

Keyword:
501

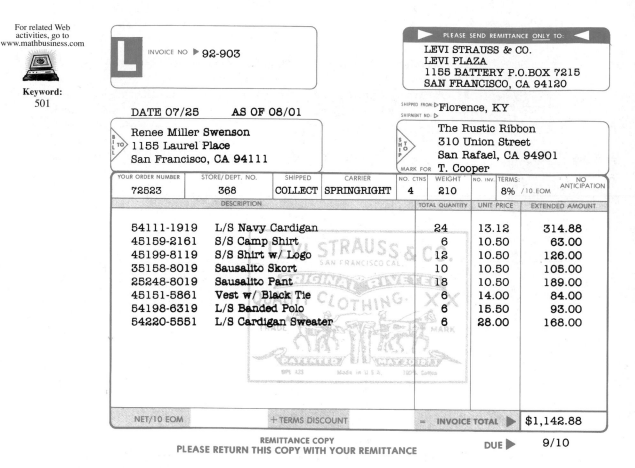

EXAMPLE 3	An invoice for a shipment of Australian glassware is dated October 21 AS OF November 1 with
Using Postdating AS OF with Invoices	terms of 3/15, n/30. Find **(a)** the last date on which the cash discount may be taken and **(b)** the net payment date.

Solution

(a) Beginning with the postdate (AS OF) of November 1, the last date for taking the discount is November 16 (**1 + 15**).

(b) The net payment date is December 1 (29 days remaining in November and 1 day in December).

Business customers as well as consumers will often let a discount help influence their decision to buy. A greater number of discounts taken by a business allow the business to sell their products at a lower price and still operate at a profit. The following newspaper article reminds us of what happens when more discounts are offered.

> **NOTE**   Sometimes a sliding scale of cash discounts is offered. For example, with the cash discount 3/10, 2/20, 1/30, n/60, a discount of 3% is given if payment is made within 10 days, 2% if paid from the 11th through the 20th day, and 1% if paid from the 21st through the 30th day. The entire amount (net) must be paid no later than 60 days from the date of the invoice.

Shoppers Hit Malls for Bargains

The holiday-shopping season got off to an uncertain start as browsers appeared to outnumber buyers over the weekend.

"The crowds were 10-deep in many malls, but there were not many shopping bags," says retail analyst Kurt Barnard. "Consumers are very reluctant to spend a lot of money."

Deep discounts—especially at mass merchandisers Wal-Mart, Target, JCPenney, and Sears—drew droves of shoppers early Friday. Foot traffic at 35 malls owned by the Simon DeBartolo Group was up 5.5% over last year. But by Sunday, with many special sales over, crowds had slacked off.

Visa USA reported the number of transactions Friday and Saturday increased 16% to 38.8 million over last year while dollar volume surged 12% to $2.5 billion. But the average transaction went down from $68 to $66.

TeleCheck Services, which tracks check purchases at 27,000 retailers, says sales at stores open at least a year rose 2.2% Friday over last year.

William Ford, TeleCheck's senior economic adviser, calls the increase moderate and says it is "just a glimpse of what we might expect for the rest of the shopping season." Most experts predict retailers' revenues will increase about 4%.

Thanksgiving weekend generally accounts for 10% of retailers' November and December revenue. And those two months make up a quarter of retailers' annual sales.

But the day after Thanksgiving is no longer the biggest shopping day of the year. "Many shoppers use this weekend to look for gifts and wait to buy until right before Christmas," says John Konarski, of the International Council of Shopping Centers.

Source: *USA Today*, 12/1/97. Reprinted by permission.

Example 4

Determining Cash Discount Due Dates for Sliding Scale

An invoice from Cellular Products is dated May 18 and offers terms of 4/10, 3/25, 1/40, n/60. Find **(a)** the three final dates for cash discounts and **(b)** the net payment date.

Solution

(a) The three final cash discount dates are

4% if paid by May 28	10 days from May 18
3% if paid by June 12	25 days from May 18
1% if paid by June 27	40 days from May 18

(b) The net payment date is July 17.

> **NOTE** Never take more than one of the cash discounts. *With all methods of giving cash discounts, if the net payment period is not given, the net payment due date is assumed to be 20 days beyond the cash discount period.* After that date, the invoice is considered overdue. If either the final discount date or the net payment date is on a Sunday or holiday, the next business day is used. Many companies insist that payment is made when it is received. It is general practice in non-retail transactions, however, to consider payment made when it is mailed.

6.4 | Cash Discounts: Other Dating Methods

Objectives

 Use the end-of-month dating method.
2 Use the receipt-of-goods dating method.
3 Use the extra dating method.
4 Determine credit given for partial payment of an invoice.

Problem Solving in Business

In addition to the ordinary dating method of cash discounts there are several others cash discount methods which are in common use. Dick and Jeanne Hill of Oaks Hardware must be able to understand and use each of these.

Objective 1 **Use the end-of-month dating method.** This section discusses several other methods of finding cash discounts. **End-of-month** and **proximo** dating, abbreviated **EOM** and **prox.**, are treated the same. For example, both

$$\text{3/10 EOM} \qquad \text{and} \qquad \text{3/10 prox.}$$

mean that 3% may be taken as a cash discount if payment is made by the 10th of the month that follows the sale. The 10 days are counted from the *end of the month* in which the invoice is dated. For example, an invoice dated July 14 with terms of 3/10 EOM would have a discount date 10 days from the end of the month, or the 10th of August (August 10).

Since this is a method of increasing the length of time during which a discount may be taken, it has become common business practice to add an extra month when the date of an invoice is the 26th of the month or later. For example, if an invoice is dated March 25 and the discount offered is 3/10 EOM, the last date on which the discount may be taken is April 10. However, if the invoice is dated March 26 (or any later date in March), and the cash discount offered is 3/10 EOM, then the last date on which the discount may be taken is May 10.

For related Web activities, go to www.mathbusiness.com

Keyword:
HOG

> **PROBLEM-SOLVING HINT** The practice of adding an extra month when the invoice is dated the 26th of a month or after is used *only* with the end-of-month (proximo) dating cash discount. It does *not* apply to any of the other cash discount methods.

Example 1
Using End-of-Month Dating

If an invoice from Harley-Davidson is dated June 10 with terms of 3/20 EOM, find **(a)** the final date on which the cash discount may be taken and **(b)** the net payment date.

Solution

(a) The discount date is July 20 (20 days after the end of June).
(b) The net payment date is August 9 (**20 days** after the last discount date (July 20), since the date is not otherwise given).

Example 2
Using Proximo Dating

Find the amount due on an invoice of $782 for some threaded fasteners, dated August 3, if terms are 1/10 prox. and the invoice is paid on September 4.

Solution

The last date on which the discount may be taken is September 10 (**10 days** after the end of August). September 4 is within the discount period, so the discount is earned. The 1% cash discount is computed on $782, the amount of the invoice. Subtract the discount ($782 × .01 = $7.82) from the invoice amount to find the amount due.

$782.00   invoice amount
−   7.82   **cash discount (1%)**
$774.18   amount due

> **NOTE**   With all methods of cash discounts, if the net payment period is not given, the net payment due date is assumed to be 20 days beyond the cash discount date.

ObjECTIVE **2** **Use the receipt-of-goods dating method.** **Receipt-of-goods dating**, abbreviated **ROG**, offers cash discounts determined from the date on which goods are actually received. This method is often used when shipping time is long. The invoice might arrive overnight by mail, but the goods may take several weeks. Under the ROG method of cash discount, the buyer is given the time to receive and inspect the merchandise and then is allowed to benefit from a cash discount. For example, the discount

3/15 ROG

allows a 3% cash discount if the invoice is paid within 15 days from receipt of goods. The date that goods are received is determined by the delivery date. If the invoice was dated March 5 and goods were received on April 7, the last date to take the 3% cash discount would be April 22 (April 7 plus 15 days). The net payment date, since it is not stated, is 20 days after the last discount date, or May 12 (April 22 plus 20 days).

EXAMPLE 3 Using Receipt-of-Goods Dating	Oaks Hardware received an invoice dated December 12, with terms of 2/10 ROG. The goods were received on January 2. Find **(a)** the final date on which the cash discount may be taken and **(b)** the net payment date.

Solution

(a) The discount date is January 12 (**10 days** after receipt of goods, January 2 plus **10 days**).
(b) The net payment date is February 1 (**20 days** after the last discount date).

EXAMPLE 4 Working with ROG Dating	Find the amount due on an invoice of $285 for some printing services, with terms of 3/10 ROG, if the invoice is dated June 8, the goods are received June 18, and the invoice is paid June 30.

Solution

The last date to take the 3% cash discount is June 28, 10 days after June 18. Since the invoice is paid on June 30, 2 days after the last discount date, **no cash discount may be taken.** The entire amount of the invoice must be paid.

$285   invoice amount
−   0   **no cash discount**
$285   amount due

ObjECTIVE **3** **Use the extra dating method.** **Extra dating (extra, ex., or x)** gives the buyer additional time to take advantage of a cash discount. For example, the discount

2/10–50 extra   or   **2/10–50 ex.**   or   **2/10–50 x**

allows a 2% cash discount if the invoice is paid within 10 + 50 = 60 days from the date of the invoice. The discount is expressed 2/10–50 ex. (rather than 2/60) to show that the 50 days are *extra*, or in addition to the normal 10 days offered.

    There are several reasons for using extra dating. A supplier might extend the discount period during a slack season to generate more sales or to gain a competitive advantage. For example, the seller might offer Christmas merchandise with extra dating to allow the buyer to take the cash discount after the holiday selling period.

EXAMPLE 5

Using Extra Dating

An invoice for paint accessories is dated November 23 with terms 2/10–50 ex. Find **(a)** the final date on which the cash discount may be taken and **(b)** the net payment date.

SOLUTION

(a) The discount date is January 22 (**7 days** remaining in November + 31 days in December = 38; thus, **22 more days** are needed in January to total 60).

(b) The net payment is February 11 (**20 days** after the last discount date).

EXAMPLE 6

Understanding Extra Dating

An invoice for some plumbing parts is dated August 5, amounts to $2250, offers terms of 3/10–30 x, and is paid on September 12. Find the net payment.

SOLUTION

1. The last day to take the 3% cash discount is September 14 (**August 5 + 40 days =** **September 14**). Since the invoice is paid on September 12, the **3%** discount may be taken.

2. The **3%** cash discount is computed on $2250, the amount of the invoice. The discount to be taken is $67.50.

3. Subtract the cash discount from the invoice amount to determine the amount of payment.

$$
\begin{array}{ll}
\$2250.00 & \text{invoice amount} \\
-\quad 67.50 & \text{3\% cash discount} \\
\hline
\$2182.50 & \text{amount of payment}
\end{array}
$$

OBJECTIVE 4 Determine credit given for partial payment of an invoice. Occasionally, a customer may pay only a portion of the total amount due on an invoice. If this **partial payment** is made within a discount period, the customer is entitled to a discount on the portion of the invoice that is paid.

If the terms of an invoice are 3%, 10 days, then only 97% (100% − 3%) of the invoice amount must be paid during the first 10 days. So, for each $.97 paid, the customer is entitled to $1.00 of credit. When a partial payment is made, the credit given for the partial payment (base) is found by dividing the partial payment by the complement of the cash discount percent. Then, to find the balance due, subtract the credit given from the invoice amount. The cash discount is found by subtracting the partial payment from the credit given.

EXAMPLE 7

Finding Credit for Partial Payment

Dave's Body and Paint receives an invoice for $1140 dated March 8 that offers terms of 2/10 prox. A partial payment of $450 is made on April 5. Find **(a)** the amount credited for the partial payment, **(b)** the balance due on the invoice, and **(c)** the cash discount earned.

SOLUTION

(a) The cash discount is earned on the $450 partial payment made on April 5 (April 10 was the last discount date). The amount paid ($450) is part of the base (amount for which credit is given).

$$100\% - 2\% = 98\%$$

The rate 98% is used to solve for base using the formula Base $= \dfrac{\text{Part}}{\text{Rate}}$.

$$B = \frac{P}{R}$$

$$B = \frac{450}{98\%} = \frac{450}{.98} = \$450.18$$

The amount credited for partial payment is $459.18.

(b) Balance due = Invoice amount − Credit given
Balance due = $1140 − **$459.18**
Balance due = $680.82

(c) Cash discount = Credit given − Partial payment
Cash discount = **$459.18** − $450
Cash discount = $9.18

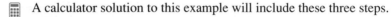 A calculator solution to this example will include these three steps.

(a) First, find the amount of credit given.

450 ÷ .98 = 459.18 (rounded)

(b) Next, store the amount of credit and subtract this amount from the invoice amount to find the balance due.

STO 1140 − RCL = 680.82 (rounded)

(c) Finally, subtract the partial payment from the amount of credit given to find the cash discount.

RCL − 450 = 9.18 (rounded)

Note: All calculator solutions use a scientific calculator. Refer to Appendix B for scientific calculator basics.

> **NOTE**   Cash discounts are important, and a business should make the effort to pay invoices early to earn the cash discounts. In many cases, the money saved through cash discounts has a great effect on the profitability of a business. Often, companies will borrow money to enable them to take advantage of cash discounts. The mathematics of this type of loan is discussed in Section 8.1, Basics of Simple Interest.

The cash discounts discussed here are normally not used when selling to foreign customers or purchasing from foreign suppliers. Instead, other types of discounts may be offered to reduce the price of goods sold to foreign buyers. These discounts may be given as allowances for tariffs paid (import duties) by the customer, reimbursement for shipping and insurance paid by the customer, or in the form of an advertising allowance.

The following newspaper article explains the reasons for closure of Huffy's largest U.S. bicycle factory. Cutthroat competition in the industry and foreign manufacturers concentrating on exporting products to the U.S. at deep discounts are both given as reasons for the factory closing and layoff of 950 employees.

For related Web
activities, go to
www.mathbusiness.com

Keyword:
cycling

Huffy Closes Largest U.S. Plant; 950 Idled

Huffy Corp., moving to combat what it called increasingly "fierce Asian competition" in the bicycle business, said it will close its largest U.S. factory and dismiss 950 workers.

Huffy, the nation's largest bike maker, said it will close its 40-year-old, 850,000-square-foot plant in Celina, Ohio, and move some production to its nonunion plant in Farmington, Mo. Huffy also said it will increase its imports of bicycles from Asia and develop new manufacturing sources in Mexico.

"It was a very difficult decision for us," Don Graber, Huffy's president and chief executive, said in an interview. "But the competition in this industry is continuing to accelerate."

For Huffy, one of the last major bike makers with production in the U.S., the move reflects the realities of the cutthroat bicycle business. Over the past four years, prices of retail bikes have plunged 25%, Huffy said, as Asian manufacturers have driven down prices and eroded profit margins.

Nearly 60% of bicycles purchased in the U.S. last year were produced by foreign makers. That has been a boon for consumers, because foreign-made bikes are almost always less expensive. Huffy estimates a bike produced in Asia costs 10% to 20% less than a comparable model made in the U.S. Huffy's models are generally lower-priced, typically costing less than $200, and are sold at mass retailers like **Wal-Mart Stores** Inc. and **Kmart** Corp.

The Asian fiscal crisis hasn't helped pricing, either. Deflated currencies have forced manufacturers to concentrate on exporting products to the U.S., at deep discounts. "The price pressures have become even more severe," said Mr. Graber. "Their domestic markets are in disarray, and they've put an even higher emphasis on exports."

Huffy also has been hurt as more of its U.S. rivals move production overseas. **Schwin Cycling & Fitness** Inc., for instance, based in Boulder, Colo., now imports all of its products from foreign plants, taking advantage of the industry's excess global capacity.

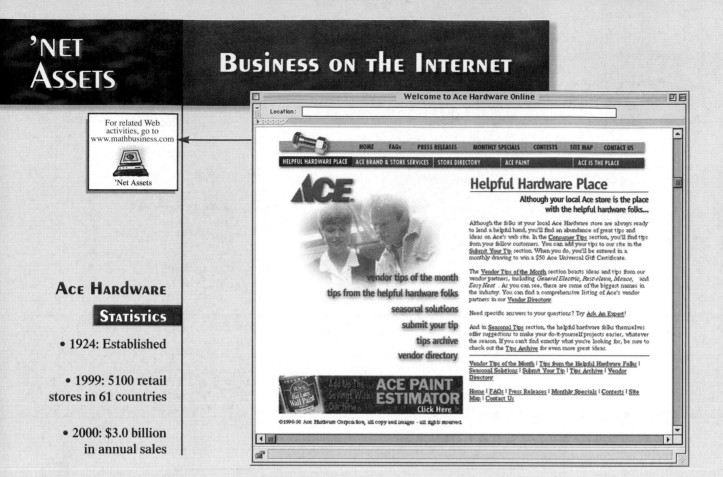

For related Web activities, go to www.mathbusiness.com

'Net Assets

ACE HARDWARE

STATISTICS

- 1924: Established

- 1999: 5100 retail stores in 61 countries

- 2000: $3.0 billion in annual sales

In the entrepreneurial spirit of the 1920s, four Chicago men formed Ace Hardware Stores. Each of the men had operated his own independent hardware businesses, but in 1924 they joined together to improve their buying power, increase their profits, and share common costs. This marked the beginning of Ace Hardware Stores, Inc., a name selected for the determination and outstanding qualities shown by the ace fighter pilots of World War I.

Today, Ace Hardware faces a new breed of competition—large warehouse-type chains. To meet and beat this new challenge head-on, the 5100 independent Ace Hardware Store owners have launched The New Retail Age of Ace, a strategic plan to provide consumers with the best products and service in the marketplace.

1. An Ace Hardware Store owner purchased adjustable shower-curtain rods that were list priced at $8.50. If the supplier offered a trade discount of 20/20, find the cost of one dozen shower-curtain rods.

2. The list price of a high-pressure power washer is $398. The manufacturer gives a 25/10 trade discount and offers a cash discount of 3/15, net/30. Find the cost to the hardware store if both discounts are earned and taken.

3. With over 5000 independently owned Ace Hardware stores, there is most likely one located near you. Ask the owner or manager of an Ace Hardware Store to name five advantages of being part of the Ace Hardware Corporation. How many years of experience in the hardware business would be needed to become a store manager or owner?

4. In recent years, the hardware business has changed greatly due to the entry of large hardware warehouse-type chains. Name four ways that you think independent Ace Hardware store owners will be able to retain their customers and increase their sales.

CHAPTER 6 | Quick Review

CHAPTER TERMS

Review the following terms to test your understanding of the chapter. For each term you do not know, refer to the page number found next to that term.

amount [p. 216]
cash discount [p. 231]
chain discount [p. 218]
COD (cash on delivery) [p. 217]
consumer [p. 215]
end of month (EOM) [p. 239]
extension total [p. 216]
extra dating (extra, ex., x)
  [p. 240]

FAS (free alongside ship)
  [p. 217]
FOB (free on board) [p. 217]
invoices [p. 215]
invoice total [p. 216]
list price [p. 217]
net cost [p. 217]
net cost equivalent [p. 219]
net price [p. 217]

ordinary dating method [p. 231]
partial payment [p. 241]
postdated "AS OF" [p. 233]
prox. [p. 239]
proximo [p. 239]
purchase invoice [p. 216]
receipt-of-goods dating
  [p. 240]
retailer [p. 215]

ROG [p. 240]
sales invoice [p. 216]
series discount [p. 218]
single discount [p. 218]
single discount equivalent
  [p. 227]
total invoice amount [p. 216]
trade discounts [p. 217]
unit price [p. 216]
units shipped [p. 216]
wholesalers [p. 215]

CONCEPTS	EXAMPLES
6.1 Trade discount and net cost First find the amount of the trade discount. Then use the formula: **Net cost = List price − trade discount.**	List price, $28; trade discount, 25%; find the net cost. $28 × .25 = $7 Net cost = $28 − $7 = $21
6.1 Complements with respect to 1 (100%) The complement is the number that must be added to a given discount to get 1 or 100%.	Find the complement with respect to 1 (100%) for each of the following. **(a)** 10% 10% + _____ = 100% 100% − 10% = 90% **(b)** 15% complement = 85% **(c)** 50% complement = 50%
6.1 Complements and series discounts The complement of a discount is the percent paid. Multiply the complements of the series discounts to get the net cost equivalent.	Series discount, 10/20/10; find the net cost equivalent. 10/ 20/ 10 ↓ ↓ ↓ .9 × .8 × .9 = **.648**
6.1 Net cost equivalent (percent paid) and the net cost Multiply the net cost equivalent (percent paid) by the list price to get the net cost.	List price, $280; series discount, 10/30/20; find the net cost. 10/ 30/ 20 ↓ ↓ ↓ .9 × .7 × .8 = **.504** percent paid **.504** × $280 = $141.12
6.2 Single discount equivalent to a series discount Often needed to compare one series discount to another, the single discount equivalent is found by multiplying the complements of the individual discounts to get the net cost equivalent, then subtracting from 1. $1 - \dfrac{\text{Net cost}}{\text{equivalent}} = \dfrac{\text{Single discount}}{\text{equivalent}}$	What single discount is equivalent to a 10/20/20 series discount? 10/ 20/ 20 ↓ ↓ ↓ .9 × .8 × .8 = **.576** 1 − **.576** = .424 = 42.4%

CONCEPTS	EXAMPLES
6.2 Finding net cost, using complements of individual discounts Net cost = List price × complements of individual discounts	List price, $510; series discount, 30/10/5; find the net cost. $$30/ \quad 10/ \quad 5$$ $$\downarrow \quad \downarrow \quad \downarrow$$ $\$510 \times .7 \times .9 \times .95 = \$305.24$ (rounded)
6.2 Finding list price if given the series discount and the net cost First, find the net cost equivalent, percent paid. Then use the standard percent formula to find the list price (base). $$B = \frac{P}{R}$$	Net cost; $224; series discount, 20/20; find list price. $$20/ \quad 20$$ $$\downarrow \quad \downarrow$$ $$.8 \times .8 = .64$$ $$B = \frac{P}{R} = \frac{224}{.64} = \$350 \text{ list price}$$
6.3 Determining number of days and dates | 30-Day Months	31-Day Months
April	All the rest
June	except February with
September	28 days (29 days in leap year)

November			Date, July 24; find 10 days from date.
			July 31 − 24 = 7 remaining in July
			
			    10 total number of days
			  − 7 days remaining in July
			     3 August (future date)

6.3 Ordinary dating and cash discounts With ordinary dating, count days from the date of the invoice. Remember: $$2/ \quad 10, \quad n/ \quad 30$$ $$\downarrow \quad \downarrow \quad \downarrow \quad \downarrow$$ $$\% \quad \text{days} \quad \text{net} \quad \text{days}$$	Invoice amount $182; terms 2/10, n/30; find cash discount and amount due. Cash discount: $182 × .02 = $3.64 Amount due: $182 − **$3.64** = $178.36
6.4 Cash discounts with end-of-month dating (EOM or proximo) The final discount date and the net date are counted from the end of the month. If the invoice is dated the 26th or after, add the entire following month when determining the dates. If not stated, the net date is 20 days beyond the discount date.	Terms, 2/10 EOM; invoice date, Oct. 18; find the final discount date and the net payment date. Final discount date: November 10, which is 10 days from the end of October. Net payment date: November 30, which is 20 days beyond the discount date.
6.4 Receipt-of-goods dating and cash discounts (ROG) Time is counted from the date goods are received to determine the final cash discount date and the net payment date.	Terms 3/10 ROG; invoice date, March 8; goods received, May 10; find the final discount date and the net payment date. Final discount date: May 20 (May 10 + 10 days) Net payment date: June 9 (May 20 + 20 days)

CONCEPTS	EXAMPLES
6.4 Extra dating and cash discounts Extra dating adds extra days to the usual cash discount period, so, 3/10–20 x means 3/30.	Terms, 3/10–20 x, invoice date, January 8; find the final discount date and the net payment date. Final discount date: February 7 (23 days in January + 7 days in February = 30) Net payment date: February 27 (February 7 + 20 days)
6.4 Partial payment credit When only a portion of an invoice amount is paid within the cash discount period, credit will be given for the partial payment. Use the standard percent formula. $$B = \frac{P}{R}$$ Where the credit given is the base, the partial payment is the part, and (100% − the cash discount) is the rate.	Invoice, $400; terms, 2/10, n/30; invoice date, Oct. 10; partial payment of $200 on Oct. 15; find credit given for partial payment and the balance due on the invoice. $$B = \frac{P}{R} = \frac{\$200}{100\% - 2\%} = \frac{\$200}{.98}$$ Credit = $204.08 (rounded) Balance due = $400 − $204.08 = $195.92

CHAPTER 6 | SUMMARY EXERCISE

The Retailer: Invoices, Trade Discounts, and Cash Discounts

Dick and Jeanne Hill of Oaks Hardware order most of their merchandise from Ace Hardware Wholesalers. In early May, they order patio and garden items having a total list price of $2893, and general hardware merchandise having a total list price of $3138. Ace Hardware Wholesalers offers trade discounts of 25/15 on these items and charges for shipping.

The invoice for this order arrives a few days later, is dated May 12, has terms of 3/15 EOM, and shows a shipping charge of $175.14.

Oaks Hardware will need to know all of the following.

(a) The total amount of the invoice excluding shipping.

(a) _____

(b) The final discount date.

(b) _____

(c) The net payment date.

(c) _____

(d) The amount necessary to pay the invoice in full on June 11 including the shipping.

(d) _____

(e) Suppose that on June 11 the invoice is not paid in full, but a partial payment of $2500 is made instead. Find the credit given for the partial payment and the balance due on the invoice including shipping.

(e) _____

_____

Investigate

Talk with an independent business owner or a store manager. Ask what kinds of trade and cash discounts are standard in their particular line of business. Do they take their earned discounts? Are these discounts important to them? Who is responsible for making sure that discounts are taken? Do they do any of their purchasing electronically? How does their electronic purchasing work?

Name	Date	Class

CHAPTER 6 | TEST

To help you review, the numbers in brackets show the section in which the topic was discussed.

Find the net cost (invoice amount) for each of the following. **[6.1]**

1. List price: $172.84 less 20/15/10

1. _____

2. List price: $1308 less 20/25

2. _____

Find (a) *the net cost equivalent and* **(b)** *the single discount equivalent for each of the following series discounts.* **[6.2]**

3. 25/15

(a) _____
(b) _____

4. 20/10/20

(a) _____
(b) _____

Find the final discount date for each of the following. **[6.4]**

Invoice Date	Terms	Date Goods Received	Final Discount Date
5. Feb. 10	4/15 EOM	Feb. 16	_____
6. May 8	2/10 ROG	May 20	_____
7. Dec. 8	4/15 prox.	Jan. 5	_____
8. Oct. 20	2/20–40 extra	Oct. 31	_____

9. The following invoice was paid on November 15. Find **(a)** the invoice total, **(b)** the amount that should be paid after the cash discount, and **(c)** the total amount due, including shipping and insurance. **[6.1–6.4]**

(a) _____
(b) _____
(c) _____

HOLIDAY APPLIANCE REPAIR PARTS

Terms: 2/10, 1/15, n/60   November 6

Quantity	Description	Unit Price	Extension Total
16	M-2 mixers	@ 17.50 ea.	
8	shelf brackets	@ 3.25 ea.	
4	blender, model L	@ 12.65 ea.	
12	bowls, 1 qt. stainless	@ 3.15 ea.	
		Invoice Total	
		Cash Discount	
		Due after Cash Discount	
		Shipping and Insurance	$11.55
		Total Amount Due	

Solve each of the following application problems involving cash and trade discounts.

10. Kelly Melcher Furnishings made purchases at a net cost of $36,458 after a series discount of 20/20/10.   **10.** _____
Find the list price.   **[6.2]**

11. An invoice of $838 from Kara-Dolls has cash terms of 2/15 EOM and is dated March 8. Find **(a)** the   **(a)** _____
final date on which the cash discount may be taken and **(b)** the amount necessary to pay the invoice in   **(b)** _____
full if the cash discount is earned.   **[6.4]**

12. A retailer purchased cellular phones list priced at $195, less series discounts of 10/20/10, with terms of   **12.** _____
3/10–50 extra. If the retailer paid the invoice within 60 days, find the amount paid.   **[6.4]**

13. Fireside Shop offers chimney caps for $120 less 25/10. The same chimney cap is offered by Builders Supply   **(a)** _____
for $111 less 25/5. Find **(a)** the firm that offers the lower price and **(b)** the difference in price.   **[6.1]**   **(b)** _____

14. The amount of an invoice from Cloverdale Creamery is $1780 with terms of 2/10, 1/15, net 30. The   **(a)** _____
invoice is dated March 8. **(a)** What amount should be paid on March 20? **(b)** What amount should be   **(b)** _____
paid on April 3?   **[6.3]**

15. Freitas Pneumatic Service receives an invoice dated April 22 for $1854 with terms of 3/15 EOM. If the   **15.** _____
invoice is paid on May 12, find the amount necessary to pay the invoice in full.   **[6.4]**

16. Matthew Kaminski receives an invoice amounting to $2916 with cash terms of 3/10 prox. and dated   **(a)** _____
June 7. If a partial payment of $1666 is made on July 8, find **(a)** the credit given for the partial payment   **(b)** _____
and **(b)** the balance due on the invoice.   **[6.4]**

CHAPTER 7

MATHEMATICS OF SELLING

Olympic Sports and Leisure carries a full line of sports equipment, sportswear, and athletic shoes for the entire family. The store is best known for its quality and selection of merchandise but is also competitive in its pricing.

The store takes all discounts offered to keep costs of merchandise down and it must adjust the markups on various lines of merchandise to keep prices "in the ballpark," relative to competition. Olympic Sports and Leisure reduces prices on merchandise on a regular basis, using these sale opportunities to clear out existing merchandise and make room for incoming orders.

The success of a business depends on many things. One of the most important is the price it charges for goods and services. Prices must be low enough to attract customers, yet high enough to cover all operating expenses and provide a profit.

The difference between the price a business pays for an item and the price at which the item is sold is called **markup**. For example, if a store buys a package of blank videotapes for $11 and sells it for $15, the markup is $4. This chapter discusses the two standard methods of calculating markup (as a percent of cost and as a percent of selling price), converting markups from one method to the other, markdown, and turnover and valuation of inventory.

7.1 | MARKUP ON COST

Objectives

1. Recognize the terms used in selling.
2. Know the basic formula for markup.
3. Calculate markup based on cost.
4. Apply percent to markup problems.

PROBLEM SOLVING IN BUSINESS	Last week, Olympic Sports and Leisure received a shipment of bicycle helmets. Store manager Cas Shields must determine the selling price of each helmet by using a basic markup formula. She knows what her regular monthly operating expenses are and she knows that she will be sending out an advertising flyer soon. She must price all merchandise with just enough markup so that it is still attractive to customers while at the same time generating enough revenue to attain the store's profit goals.

U.S. POSTAL RATES SINCE 1971

May 16, 1971	8 cents
March 2, 1974	10 cents
Dec. 31, 1975	13 cents
May 29, 1978	15 cents
March 22, 1981	18 cents
Nov. 1, 1981	20 cents
Feb. 17, 1985	22 cents
April 3, 1988	25 cents
Feb. 3, 1991	29 cents
Jan. 1, 1995	32 cents
Jan. 1, 1999	33 cents

Objective 1 Recognize the terms used in selling. The terms used in markup are summarized here.

Cost is the price paid to the manufacturer or supplier after trade and cash discounts have been taken. Shipping and insurance charges are included in cost.

Selling price is the price at which merchandise is offered for sale to the public.

Markup, margin, or **gross profit** is the difference between the cost and the selling price. These three terms are often used interchangeably.

Operating expenses, or **overhead,** include the expenses of operating the business, such as wages and salaries of employees, rent for buildings and equipment, utilities, insurance, and advertising. Even an expense item like postage can add up. Mailing costs average from 6.2% of operating expenses for small companies to as high as 9.2% for the largest companies. Notice in the chart to the side how postal rates have changed during the last thirty years and, in the graphic below, the most recent changes in U.S. postage rates.

For related Web activities, go to www.mathbusiness.com

Keyword: stamps

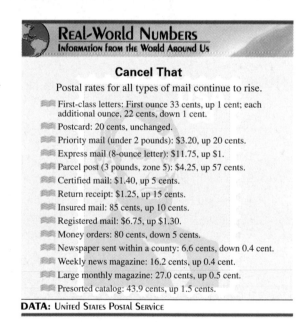

Net profit (net earnings) is the amount (if any) remaining for the business after operating expenses and the cost of goods have been paid. (Income tax is computed on net profit.)

Most manufacturers, many wholesalers, and some retailers calculate markup as a percent of cost (**markup on cost**). Manufacturers usually express inventories in terms of cost, a method most consistent with their operations. Retailers, on the other hand, usually compute **markup on selling price**, since retailers compare most areas of their business operations to sales revenue. Such items of expense as sales commissions, sales taxes, and advertising are expressed as percent of sales. It is reasonable, then, for the retailer to express markup as a percent of sales. Wholesalers, however, use either cost or selling price, so be sure to find out which a wholesaler is using.

Objective 2 Know the basic formula for markup. Whether markup is based on cost or on selling price, the same basic **markup formula** is always used: $C + M = S$, or

The Basic Markup Formula

$$
\begin{array}{c}
\text{Cost} \\
\underline{+ \ \text{Markup}} \\
\text{Selling price}
\end{array}
\qquad \text{or} \qquad
\begin{array}{c}
C \\
\underline{+ \ M} \\
S
\end{array}
$$

This markup formula is shown by the following diagram.

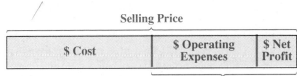

Markup/Margin/Gross Profit

EXAMPLE 1

Using the Basic Markup Formula

Most markup problems give two of the items in the formula and ask for the third. Olympic Sports and Leisure received solid-color polo shirts. Determine the selling price, markup, and cost of the shirts in the following problems.

(a)
$$
\begin{array}{ll}
C & \$10 \\
\underline{+ M} & \underline{\$\ 5} \\
S & \$
\end{array}
$$

(b)
$$
\begin{array}{ll}
C & \$10 \\
\underline{+ M} & \underline{\$} \\
S & \$15
\end{array}
$$

(c)
$$
\begin{array}{ll}
C & \$ \\
\underline{+ M} & \underline{\$\ 5} \\
S & \$15
\end{array}
$$

Solution

(a)
$$
\begin{array}{ll}
C & \$10 \\
\underline{+ M} & \underline{\$\ 5} \\
S & \$15
\end{array}
$$

(b)
$$
\begin{array}{ll}
C & \$10 \\
\underline{+ M} & \underline{\$\ 5} \\
S & \$15
\end{array}
$$

(c)
$$
\begin{array}{ll}
C & \$10 \\
\underline{+ M} & \underline{\$\ 5} \\
S & \$15
\end{array}
$$

Objective ③ **Calculate markup based on cost.** **Markup based on cost** is expressed as a percent of cost. As shown in the discussion of percent in Section 3.5, the base is always 100%. Therefore, cost has a value of 100%. Markup and selling price also have percent values found by comparing their dollar values to the dollar value of the cost. Solve markup problems with the basic formula $C + M = S$, or

$$
\begin{array}{c}
C \\
\underline{+ \ M} \\
S
\end{array}
$$

Write the dollar values of cost, markup, and selling price on the right of the formula, and place the rate or percent value for each of these on the left of the formula.

Suppose an item costs $2 and sells for $3, and that markup is based on cost. To find markup, percent of markup on cost, and percent of selling price on cost, begin as follows.

$$
\begin{array}{lll}
100\% & C & \$2 \\
\underline{\% } & \underline{M} & \underline{\$} \\
\% & S & \$3
\end{array}
$$

The dollar amount of cost and selling price have been written in their corresponding positions to the right of the formula, and **100%** has been written to the left of cost, **since cost is the base.** The dollar amount of markup is the difference between cost and selling price, or

$$
\begin{array}{llll}
100\% & C & \$2 & \text{base} \\
\underline{\% } & \underline{M} & \underline{\$1} & \\
\% & S & \$3 &
\end{array}
$$

Next, find the percent of markup based on cost. Do this by comparing the amount of markup, $1, to the cost, $2. The comparison of 1 to 2 is $\frac{1}{2}$, or **50%**.

> **NOTE**   With markup on cost, the base is cost, and markup is part.

$$
\begin{array}{llll}
 & 100\% & C & \$2 \;\; \text{base} \\
\text{rate} & \underline{50\%} & M & \underline{\$1} \;\; \text{part} \\
 & \% & S & \$3
\end{array}
$$

Finally, add 100% to 50%.

$$
\begin{array}{lllll}
 & & 100\% & C & \$2 \;\; \text{base} \\
\text{Add these} & & \underline{50\%} & M & \underline{\$1} \;\; \text{part} \\
 & & 150\% & S & \$3
\end{array}
$$

> **NOTE**   **Cost plus markup always equals selling price**, both with dollar amounts and rate amounts.

Objective **4** **Apply percent to markup problems.** Knowledge of percent is used to solve markup problems.

EXAMPLE 2
Solving for
Percent of
Markup on Cost

The manager of Roseville Appliance bought a coffee maker manufactured in Spain for $15 and will sell it for $18.75. Find the percent of markup based on cost.

Solution

Set up the problem using the information given.

$$
\begin{array}{llll}
 & 100\% & C & \$15.00 \;\; \text{base} \\
\text{rate} & \underline{\;?\%\;} & M & \$\underline{\quad} \;\;\; \text{part} \\
 & \% & S & \$18.75
\end{array}
$$

The dollar amount of markup is the difference between $18.75 and $15.00, or $3.75.

$$
\begin{array}{lll}
100\% & C & \$15.00 \\
\underline{\;?\%\;} & M & \underline{\$\;3.75} \\
\% & S & \$18.75
\end{array}
$$

The cost, $15.00, is the base (which is identified by the 100%). There are two rates and two corresponding parts. Find percent of markup (a rate) by using the part corresponding to markup, $3.75. Identify the elements in this example as follows.

$$
\begin{array}{llll}
 & 100\% & C & \$15.00 \quad \text{base} \\
\text{rate} & \;?\% & M & \$\;3.75 \quad \text{part} \\
\text{rate} & \% & S & \$18.75 \quad \text{part}
\end{array}
$$

Find the percent of markup based on cost, using the formula for rate.

$$
\text{Rate} = \frac{\text{Part}}{\text{Base}} = \frac{\$3.75}{\$15.00} = .25 = 25\% \text{ markup based on cost}
$$

Complete the problem by adding the rate for cost to the rate for markup and arriving at a rate for selling price.

$$
\begin{array}{llll}
 & 100\% & C & \$15.00 \\
\text{Add} & \underline{25\%} & M & \underline{\$\;3.75} \\
 & 125\% & S & \$18.75
\end{array}
$$

The calculator solution to this example is

(18.75 **−** 15 **)** **÷** 15 **=** .25.

Note: All calculator solutions use a scientific calculator. Refer to Appendix B for scientific calculator basics.

This method can be used for solving all problems involving markup, as shown in the next few examples.

Olympic Sports and Leisure has a markup on a basketball of $14, which is 50% based on cost. Find the cost and the selling price.

EXAMPLE 3
Finding Cost When Cost Is Base

SOLUTION

Set up the problem.

$$
\begin{array}{lll}
100\% & C & \$? \\
50\% & M & \$14 \\
\hline
\% & S & \$ \\
\end{array}
$$

Identify the elements.

$$
\begin{array}{cllll}
& 100\% & C & \$? & \text{base} \\
\text{rate} & 50\% & M & \$14 & \text{part} \\
\text{rate} & 150\% & S & \$ & \text{part} \\
\end{array}
$$

The rate of markup, 50%, and the corresponding part, $14, are used in the formula to find the base. Solve for base.

$$
\text{Base} = \frac{\text{Part}}{\text{Rate}} = \frac{\$14}{.5} = \$28 \text{ cost}
$$

The cost of the basketball is $28.

Now find the selling price by adding the cost and the markup.

$$
\begin{array}{lll}
100\% & C & \$28 \\
50\% & M & \$14 \\
\hline
150\% & S & \$42 \\
\end{array}
$$

The selling price of the basketball is $42.

EXAMPLE 4
Finding the Markup and the Selling Price

Find the markup and the selling price for a Texas Instruments financial calculator (assembled in Italy) if the cost is $23.60 and the markup is 25% of cost.

SOLUTION

Set up the problem.

$$
\begin{array}{lll}
100\% & C & \$23.60 \\
25\% & M & \$? \\
\hline
\% & S & \$ \\
\end{array}
$$

Identify the elements.

$$
\begin{array}{cllll}
& 100\% & C & \$23.60 & \text{base} \\
\text{rate} & 25\% & M & \$? & \text{part} \\
\text{rate} & 125\% & S & \$ & \text{part} \\
\end{array}
$$

If the rate for selling price, 125%, is used in the formula, the resulting part is the selling price. Since markup is to be found, use the rate for markup in the formula. Solve for the markup part.

$$
\text{Part} = \textbf{Base} \times \textbf{Rate} = \textbf{\$23.60} \times .25 = \$5.90 \text{ markup}
$$

The markup is $5.90.

Now solve for selling price by adding cost and markup.

$$
\begin{array}{lll}
100\% & C & \$23.60 \\
25\% & M & \$\ 5.90 \\
\hline
125\% & S & \$29.50
\end{array}
$$

The selling price of the financial calculator is $29.50.

This calculator solution uses the percent add-on feature found on many calculators.

23.6 $\boxed{+}$ 25 $\boxed{\%}$ $\boxed{=}$ 29.5

Note: All calculator solutions use a scientific calculator. Refer to Appendix B for scientific calculator basics.

PROBLEM-SOLVING HINT   Be certain that you use the corresponding rate and part when working with markup problems. If 125% was used as the rate in Example 4, the answer (part) would have been the selling price. This would work but you would have to remember to subtract the cost from the selling price ($29.50 − $23.60) to get the markup of $5.90.

EXAMPLE 5

Finding Cost
When Cost Is
Base

Olympic Sports and Leisure is selling a Wilson baseball glove for $42, which is 140% of the cost. How much did Olympic Sports and Leisure pay for the baseball glove?

SOLUTION

Set up the problem.

$$
\begin{array}{lll}
100\% & C & \$? \\
\% & M & \$ \\
\hline
140\% & S & \$42
\end{array}
$$

Identify the elements.

$$
\begin{array}{llll}
 & 100\% & C & \$? \quad \text{base} \\
\text{rate} & 40\% & M & \$ \\
\hline
\text{rate} & 140\% & S & \$42 \quad \text{part}
\end{array}
$$

The rate for markup, 40%, *cannot* be used in the formula because there is no corresponding part. Solve for base using the *corresponding* rate and part.

$$
\text{Base} = \frac{\text{Part}}{\text{Rate}} = \frac{\$42}{1.4} = \$30 \text{ cost}
$$

The cost of the glove is $30. Check: **.40** × $30 = **$12** (markup); then $30 + **$12** = $42.

EXAMPLE 6

Finding the Cost
and the Markup

The retail (selling) price of an EZC International multimedia computer is $978.75. If the markup is 35% of cost, find the cost and the markup.

SOLUTION

Set up the problem.

$$
\begin{array}{lll}
100\% & C & \$? \\
35\% & M & \$ \\
\hline
 & S & \$978.75
\end{array}
$$

Identify the elements.

$$
\begin{array}{llll}
 & 100\% & C & \$? \quad \text{base} \\
\text{rate} & 35\% & M & \$ \quad\ \text{part} \\
\hline
\text{rate} & 135\% & S & \$978.75 \quad \text{part}
\end{array}
$$

The rate of markup, 35%, *cannot* be used in the formula since there is no corresponding part. Instead, solve for base using the *corresponding* rate and part.

$$\text{Base} = \frac{\text{Part}}{\text{Rate}} = \frac{\$978.75}{1.35} = \$725 \text{ cost}$$

The cost of the computer is $725.

Now solve for the markup by subtracting cost from selling price.

100%	C	$725
35%	M	$
135%	S	$978.75

The markup is $253.75 ($978.75 − $725).

> **NOTE** Remember, when calculating markup on cost, cost is always the base and 100% always goes next to cost.

7.2 | MARKUP ON SELLING PRICE

Objectives

1. Understand the phrase *markup based on selling price.*
2. Solve markup problems when selling price is the base.
3. Use the markup formula to solve variations of markup problems.
4. Determine percent markup on cost and the equivalent percent markup on selling price.
5. Convert markup percent on cost to selling price.
6. Convert markup percent on selling price to cost.
7. Find the selling price for perishables.

PROBLEM SOLVING IN BUSINESS

Olympic Sports and Leisure faces stiff competition. Sportmart has placed a newspaper ad about their baseball equipment particularly aimed at teams, which buy in large quantities. Sportmart offers to pay customers double the difference if the customer finds any item for a lower price at another store. Olympic Sports and Leisure must compete by buying their merchandise at the lowest possible price and keeping markups at a minimum.

For related Web activities, go to www.mathbusiness.com

Keyword: sports

Objective 1 **Understand the phrase** *markup based on selling price.* As mentioned in the previous section, wholesalers sometimes calculate markup based on cost and other times calculate markup based on selling price. In retailing it is common to calculate markup based on selling price. In each problem, markup is given as being "on cost" or "on selling price." If markup is based on selling price, then selling price is the base.

When **markup on selling price** is calculated, the same basic markup formula is used, $C + M = S$, or

%	C	$
% +	M	$
%	S	$

Objective 2 **Solving markup problems when selling price is the base.** The dollar amounts for cost, markup, and selling price are still written to the right of the formula, and the rate amounts for each of these are still written to the left of the formula. However, the base is now the selling price. Since the selling price is the base, and base is always 100%, place 100% next to the selling price on the left-hand side, as follows.

$$
\begin{array}{rcl}
\% & C & \$ \\
\underline{\% } & \underline{M} & \underline{\$} \\
100\% & S & \$ \text{ base}
\end{array}
$$

EXAMPLE 1

Solving for
Markup on Selling
Price

To remain competitive, Olympic Sports and Leisure must sell a 12-pack of Top Flite XL golf balls for $15. They pay $10 for the golf balls and calculate markup on selling price. Find the amount of markup, the percent of markup on selling price, and the percent of cost on selling price.

Solution

Set up the problem.

$$
\begin{array}{rcl}
?\% & C & \$10 \\
?\% & M & \$\,? \\
\hline
100\% & S & \$15
\end{array}
$$

Solve for markup.

$$
\begin{array}{rcl}
?\% & C & \$10 \\
?\% & M & \$\,5 \\
\hline
100\% & S & \$15
\end{array}
$$

Identify the elements.

$$
\begin{array}{llcll}
\text{rate} & ?\% & C & \$10 & \text{part} \\
\text{rate} & ?\% & M & \$\,5 & \text{part} \\
\hline
& 100\% & S & \$15 & \text{base}
\end{array}
$$

Solve for either of the rates, and subtract the result from 100% to find the other. Solve for markup rate.

$$
\text{Rate} = \frac{\text{Part}}{\text{Base}} = \frac{5}{15} = 33\frac{1}{3}\% \text{ markup on selling price}
$$

The rate of markup on selling price is $33\frac{1}{3}\%$, and the rate of cost on selling price is $66\frac{2}{3}\%$ ($100\% - 33\frac{1}{3}\% = 66\frac{2}{3}\%$). In summary:

$$
\begin{array}{rcl}
66\frac{2}{3}\% & C & \$10 \\
33\frac{1}{3}\% & M & \$\,5 \\
\hline
100\% & S & \$15
\end{array}
$$

> **NOTE**   Remember that the part and rate must always correspond. If you use the markup part in the formula, the resulting rate will be the markup rate.

Markups vary widely from industry to industry and from business to business. This variation is a result of different costs of merchandise, operating costs, levels of profit margin, and local competition. The table on the next page shows average markups for different types of retail stores.

Average Markups for Retail Stores (Markup on Selling Price)

Type of Store	Markup	Type of Store	Markup
General merchandise stores	29.97%	Furniture and home furnishings	35.75%
Grocery stores	22.05%	Bars	52.49%
Other food stores	27.31%	Restaurants	56.35%
Motor vehicle dealers (new)	12.83%	Drug and proprietary stores	30.81%
Gasoline service stations	14.47%	Liquor stores	20.19%
Other automotive dealers	29.57%	Sporting goods and bicycle shops	29.72%
Apparel and accessories	37.64%	Gift, novelty, and souvenir shops	41.86%

Source: Sole–proprietorship income tax returns, U.S. Treasury Dept., Internal Revenue Service, Statistics Division.

OBJECTIVE ③ **Use the markup formula to solve variations of markup problems.** As with problems with markup based on cost, this basic formula may be used for all markup problems in which selling price is the base. In each of these examples, the selling price has a percent value of 100%.

EXAMPLE 2
Finding Cost
When Selling
Price Is Base

A bookstore employee knows that the three-ring binders in stock have a markup of $1.72, which is 35% based on selling price. Find the cost of the binders.

SOLUTION

Set up the problem.

$$
\begin{array}{lll}
\% & C & \$? \\
35\% & M & \$1.72 \\
\hline
100\% & S & \$? \\
\end{array}
$$

Identify the elements.

$$
\begin{array}{llll}
\text{rate} & 65\% & C & \$? \\
\text{rate} & 35\% & M & \$1.72 \quad \text{part} \\
\hline
& 100\% & S & \$? \quad \text{base} \\
\end{array}
$$

Now solve for base (selling price), and subtract the markup from selling price to find the cost. Solve for base using the *corresponding* rate and part.

$$
\text{Base} = \frac{\text{Part}}{\text{Rate}} = \frac{1.72}{.35} = \$4.91 \text{ selling price}
$$

Solve for cost.

$$
\begin{array}{ccc}
\text{Selling price} & - \text{Markup} = \text{Cost} \\
\$4.91 & - \quad \$1.72 \quad = \$3.19 \\
\end{array}
$$

The cost is $3.19.

$$
\begin{array}{lll}
65\% & C & \$3.19 \\
35\% & M & \$1.72 \\
\hline
100\% & S & \$4.91 \\
\end{array}
$$

EXAMPLE 3
Finding Markup
When Selling
Price Is Given

Jill Wagon, at Olympic Sports and Leisure, is told to calculate the markup on a pair of athletic socks. The selling price of the socks is $3.95 and the markup is 20% of selling price.

SOLUTION

Set up the problem.

$$
\begin{array}{lll}
\% & C & \$ \\
20\% & M & \$? \\
\hline
100\% & S & \$3.95 \\
\end{array}
$$

Identify the elements.

$$
\text{rate} \quad
\begin{array}{lll}
80\% & C & \$ \\
20\% & M & \$? \quad \text{part} \\
\hline
100\% & S & \$3.95 \quad \text{base}
\end{array}
$$

Solve for part

$$\text{Part} = \text{Base} \times \text{Rate} = \$3.95 \times .2 = \$.79 \text{ markup}$$

The markup is $.79.

PROBLEM-SOLVING HINT If the rate for cost, 80%, had been used in the formula, the result would have been the cost.

EXAMPLE 4

Finding Markup When Cost Is Given

Find the markup on jogging shorts made in Mexico if the cost is $9.15 and the markup is 25% of selling price.

SOLUTION

Set up the problem.

$$
\begin{array}{lll}
\% & C & \$9.15 \\
25\% & M & \$? \\
\hline
100\% & S & \$
\end{array}
$$

Identify the elements.

$$
\begin{array}{llll}
\text{rate} & 75\% & C & \$9.15 \quad \text{part} \\
\text{rate} & 25\% & M & \$? \quad \text{part} \\
\hline
& 100\% & S & \$ \quad\quad \text{base}
\end{array}
$$

Solve for base, using the rate and part that go together. In this example, use the rate and part for cost.

$$\text{Base} = \frac{\text{Part}}{\text{Rate}} = \frac{\$9.15}{.75} = \$12.20 \text{ selling price}$$

$$
\begin{array}{ccc}
\text{Selling price} & - \text{ Cost} & = \text{ Markup} \\
\$12.20 & - \$9.15 = & \$3.05
\end{array}
$$

$$
\begin{array}{lll}
75\% & C & \$\ 9.15 \\
25\% & M & \$\ 3.05 \\
\hline
100\% & S & \$12.20
\end{array}
$$

NOTE Remember, when calculating markup on selling price, selling price is always the base and 100% always goes next to selling price.

OBJECTIVE **4** **Determine percent markup on cost and the equivalent percent markup on selling price.** Sometimes a markup based on cost must be compared to a markup based on selling price. For example, a salesperson who sells to both manufacturers who use markup on cost and to retailers who use markup on selling price might have to make quick conversions from one markup method to the other. Such a conversion might also be necessary for a manufacturer who thinks in terms of cost, and who wants to understand a wholesaler or retail customer. Or perhaps a retailer or wholesaler might convert markup on selling price to markup on cost to better understand the manufacturer.

Make these comparisons by computing first the markup on cost and then the markup on selling price.

EXAMPLE 5

Determining Equivalent Markups

Claire Magersky sells fishing lures to both fishing-equipment wholesalers and sporting-goods stores. If the lure costs her $4.20 and she sells it for $5.25, what is the percent of markup on cost? What is the percent of markup on selling price?

Solution

First compute the rate of markup on cost. Set up the problem.

$$
\begin{array}{rcl}
100\% & C & \$4.20 \\
?\% & M & \$ \\
\hline
\% & S & \$5.25
\end{array}
$$

Identify the elements.

$$
\begin{array}{rrcll}
& 100\% & C & \$4.20 & \textbf{base} \\
\text{rate} & ?\% & M & \$1.05 & \textbf{part} \\
\hline
\text{rate} & \% & S & \$5.25 & \textbf{part}
\end{array}
$$

Solve for rate.

$$
\text{Rate} = \frac{\text{Part}}{\text{Base}} = \frac{\textbf{\$1.05}}{\textbf{\$4.20}} = .25 = 25\% \text{ markup on cost}
$$

The markup on cost is 25%.

Next, compute the rate of markup on selling price. Set up the problem.

$$
\begin{array}{rcl}
\% & C & \$4.20 \\
?\% & M & \$ \\
\hline
100\% & S & \$5.25
\end{array}
$$

Identify the elements.

$$
\begin{array}{rrcll}
\text{rate} & \% & C & \$4.20 & \textbf{part} \\
\text{rate} & ?\% & M & \$1.05 & \textbf{part} \\
\hline
& 100\% & S & \$5.25 & \textbf{base}
\end{array}
$$

Solve for rate.

$$
\text{Rate} = \frac{\text{Part}}{\text{Base}} = \frac{\textbf{\$1.05}}{\textbf{\$5.25}} = .20 = 20\% \text{ markup on selling price}
$$

The markup on selling price is 20%.

The work in this example shows that a 25% markup on cost is equivalent to a 20% markup on selling price.

> **NOTE** In Example 5, the markup on cost was determined first (25%). The problem was then reworked with the same dollar amounts but with the selling price as base. The result was 20%.

Objective ⑤ **Convert markup percent on cost to selling price.** Another method for markup comparisons is to use **conversion formulas**. Convert markup percent on cost to markup percent on selling price with the following formula.

$$
\frac{\% \text{ markup on cost}}{100\% + \% \text{ markup on cost}} = \% \text{ markup on selling price}
$$

EXAMPLE 6

Converting Markup on Cost to Markup on Selling Price

Convert a markup of 25% on cost to its equivalent markup on selling price.

Solution

Use the formula for converting markup on cost to markup on selling price.

$$
\frac{\% \text{ markup on cost}}{100\% + \% \text{ markup on cost}} = \% \text{ markup on selling price}
$$

$$
\frac{25\%}{100\% + 25\%} = \frac{25\%}{125\%} = \frac{.25}{1.25} = .20 = 20\%
$$

As shown, a markup of 25% on cost is equivalent to a markup of 20% on selling price.

The markup on cost (25%) is divided by 100% plus the markup on cost. The parenthesis keys are used here.

$$25 \boxed{\%} \boxed{\div} \boxed{(} \; 100 \boxed{\%} \boxed{+} 25 \boxed{\%} \boxed{)} \boxed{=} 0.2$$

Note: All calculator solutions use a scientific calculator. Refer to Appendix B for scientific calculator basics.

OBJECTIVE $\boxed{6}$ **Convert markup percent on selling price to cost.** Convert markup percent on selling price to markup percent on cost with the following formula.

$$\frac{\% \text{ markup on selling price}}{100\% - \% \text{ markup on selling price}} = \% \text{ markup on cost}$$

EXAMPLE 7

Converting Markup on Selling Price to Markup on Cost

Convert a markup of 20% on selling price to its equivalent markup on cost.

Solution

Use the formula for converting markup on selling price to markup on cost.

$$\frac{\% \text{ markup on selling price}}{100\% - \% \text{ markup on selling price}} = \% \text{ markup on cost}$$

$$\frac{20\%}{100\% - 20\%} = \frac{20\%}{80\%} = \frac{.2}{.8} = .25 = 25\%$$

A markup of 20% on selling price is equivalent to a markup of 25% on cost.

The following table shows common markups expressed as percent on cost and also on selling price.

Markup Equivalents

Markup on Cost	Markup on Selling Price
20%	$16\frac{2}{3}\%$
25%	20%
$33\frac{1}{3}\%$	25%
50%	$33\frac{1}{3}\%$
$66\frac{2}{3}\%$	40%
75%	$42\frac{6}{7}\%$
100%	50%

OBJECTIVE $\boxed{7}$ **Find the selling price for perishables.** When a business sells items that are perishable (such as baked goods, fruits, or vegetables), the fact that some items will spoil and become unsalable must be considered when determining the selling price of each item that is sold.

EXAMPLE 8

Finding Selling Price for Perishables

The Pretzel Bender bakes 60 dozen jumbo pretzels at a cost of $2.16 per dozen. If a markup of 50% on selling price is needed and 5% of the pretzels will not be sold and must be thrown away, find the selling price per dozen pretzels.

Solution

Step 1 First find the cost of the pretzels.

$$\text{Cost} = 60 \text{ dozen} \times \$2.16 = \$129.60$$

Step 2   Next, find the selling price, using a markup of 50% of selling price.

rate				part
50%	C	$129.60	
50%	M	$	
100%	S	$?	base

$$\text{Base} = \frac{\text{Part}}{\text{Rate}} = \frac{\$129.60}{.5} = \$259.20$$

The total selling price is $259.20.

Step 3   Now, find the number of dozen pretzels that will be sold. Since 5% will not be sold, 95% (100% − 5%) will be sold.

$$95\% \times 60 \text{ dozen} = 57 \text{ dozen pretzels sold}$$

The selling price of $259.20 must be received from the sale of 57 dozen pretzels.

Step 4   Find the selling price per dozen pretzels by dividing the total selling price by the number of pretzels sold.

$$\frac{\$259.20}{57} = \$4.55 \text{ selling price per dozen (rounded)}$$

A selling price of $4.55 per dozen gives the desired markup of 50% on selling price while allowing for 5% of the pretzels to be unsold.

7.3 | MARKDOWN

Objectives

1. Define the term *markdown* when applied to selling.
2. Calculate markdown, reduced price, and percent of markdown.
3. Define the terms associated with loss.
4. Determine the break-even point and operating loss.
5. Determine the amount of a gross or absolute loss.

Problem Solving in Business

Cas Shields, the manager of Olympic Sports and Leisure, keeps a close eye on inventory. This January, some of her winter parkas are still on the shelves and she has decided to mark them down in order to sell them. Keeping an eye on inventory is an important management function. Slow-selling and outdated merchandise must be moved out of the store to make room for new, more profitable merchandise.

Markdowns are used to stimulate sales volume when it is low. The following newspaper clipping shows how the personal computer manufacturers must continually battle in the PC pricing war. This price war continues from the manufacturers to the retailers where markdowns and sales are used to attract customers to the latest technology and to closeout equipment of older technology.

Reality Check

Packard Bell Fires $699 Volley in PC Pricing War

Signaling yet another plunge in the price of personal computers, Packard Bell NEC on Thursday unveiled a line of PCs that starts at $699.

While some computers already have hit that price, most are closeouts equipped with older technology. The Packard Bell NEC model is the first from a mainline manufacturer to use newer technology, but industry experts expect other PC makers to quickly follow suit.

"The $699 price establishes a new beachhead for top-tier manufacturers, but I don't expect it to last," said Kevin Hause, an analyst with International Data Corp.

"We'll see (other PC makers) match it and beat it."

Jack Yovanovich, Packard Bell's director of product marketing, said the new machines are aimed at the home user kept out of the market by higher prices and at consumers who may want a second or third PC for the home.

Source: Sacramento Bee, 5/29/98. Reprinted by permission.

For related Web activities, go to www.mathbusiness.com

Keyword: reduced

Objective 1 Define the term *markdown* when applied to selling. When merchandise does not sell at its marked price, the price is often reduced. The difference between the original selling price and the reduced selling price is called the **markdown**, with the selling price after the markdown called the **reduced price**, **sale price**, or **actual selling price**. The basic **formula for markdown** is as follows.

Reduced price = Original price − Markdown

EXAMPLE 1

Finding the Reduced Price

Costco has marked down a Coleman canoe. Find the reduced price if the original price was $960 and the markdown is 25%.

Solution

The markdown is 25% of $960, or .25 × $960 = $240. Find the reduced price as follows.

Objective **2** **Calculate markdown, reduced price, and percent of markdown.**

$$
\begin{array}{ll}
\$960 & \text{original price} \\
\underline{-\ 240} & \text{markdown (.25 × $960)} \\
\$720 & \text{reduced price (70\% of original price)}
\end{array}
$$

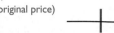 The calculator solution to this example uses the complement, with respect to one, of the discount.

$$960 \;\boxed{\times}\; \boxed{(} \; 1 \; \boxed{-} \; .25 \; \boxed{)} \; \boxed{=} \; 720$$

Note: All calculator solutions use a scientific calculator. Refer to Appendix B for scientific calculator basics.

For related Web activities, go to www.mathbusiness.com

Keyword:
base

The next example shows how to find a **percent of markdown**.

> **NOTE**   The original selling price is always the base or 100% and the percent of markdown is always calculated on the original selling price.

EXAMPLE 2
Calculating the Percent of Markdown

The total inventory of Mother's Day cards at a large gift shop has a retail value of $785. If the cards were sold at reduced prices that totaled $530, what is the percent of markdown on the original price?

Solution

First find the amount of the markdown.

$$
\begin{array}{ll}
\$785 & \text{original price} \\
\underline{-\ 530} & \text{reduced price} \\
\$255 & \text{markdown}
\end{array}
$$

Finding the percent of the original price that is the markdown is a rate problem (see Chapter 3).

$$\text{Rate} = \frac{\text{Part}}{\text{Base}} = \frac{255}{785} = .3248 = 32\% \text{ markdown rounded to the nearest whole percent}$$

The cards were sold at a markdown of 32%.

EXAMPLE 3
Finding the Original Price

Find the original price if a child's raincoat is offered at a reduced price of $18 after a 40% markdown from the original price.

Solution

After the 40% markdown, the reduced price, $18, represents 60% of the original price. The original price, or base, must be found.

$$\text{Base} = \frac{\text{Part}}{\text{Rate}} = \frac{18}{.6} = \$30 \text{ original price}$$

The original price of the coat was $30.

> **PROBLEM-SOLVING HINT**   In Example 3, notice that 60% is used in the formula rather than 40%. The reduced price, $18, is represented by 60%.

Objective **3** **Define the terms associated with loss.**   The amount of a markdown must be large enough to sell the merchandise while providing as much profit as possible. Merchandise that is marked down will result in either a **reduced net profit**, **breaking even**, an **operating loss**, or a **gross** or **absolute loss**.

The following diagram illustrates the meaning of these terms.

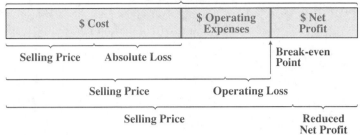

Reduced net profit results when the reduced price is still within the net profit range (is greater than the total cost plus operating expenses).

Objective **4** **Determine the break-even point and operating loss.** The **break-even point** is the point at which the reduced price just covers cost plus overhead (operating expenses).

An **operating loss** occurs when the reduced price is less than the break-even point. The operating loss is the difference between the break-even point and the reduced selling price.

Objective **5** **Determine the amount of a gross or absolute loss.** An **absolute loss** or **gross loss** is the result of a reduced price that is below the cost of the merchandise alone. The absolute or gross loss is the difference between the cost and reduced selling price.

The following formulas are helpful when working with markdowns.

> Break-even point = Cost + Operating expenses
>
> Operating loss = Break-even point − Reduced selling price
>
> Absolute loss = Cost − Reduced selling price

Example 4

Determining a Profit or a Loss

Cordova Appliance Company paid $40 for a garbage disposal. If operating expenses are 30% of cost and the garbage disposal is sold for $50, find the amount of profit or loss.

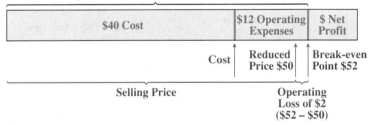

Solution

Operating expenses are 30% of cost, or

$$\text{Operating expenses} = .30 \times \$40 = \$12$$

The break-even point for the garbage disposal is

$$\text{Cost} + \text{Operating expenses} = \text{Break-even point}$$
$$\$40 + (.3 \times \$40) = \$40 + \$12 = \$52 \text{ break-even point}$$

Since the break-even point is $52 and the selling price is $50, there is a loss of

$$\$52 - \$50 = \$2$$

The $2 loss is an operating loss since the selling price is less than the break-even point but greater than the cost.

The calculator solution to this example is

$$40 \boxed{+} \boxed{(} .3 \boxed{\times} 40 \boxed{)} \boxed{-} 50 \boxed{=} 2.$$

Note: All calculator solutions use a scientific calculator. Refer to Appendix B for scientific calculator basics.

EXAMPLE 5
Determining the Operating Loss and the Absolute Loss

A set of graphite golf clubs normally selling for $360 at Olympic Sports and Leisure is marked down 30%. If the cost of the golf clubs is $260 and the operating expenses are 20% of cost, find **(a)** the operating loss and **(b)** the absolute loss.

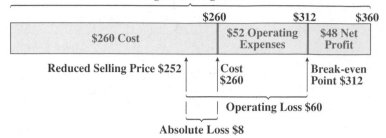

Solution

(a) The break-even point (cost + operating expenses) is $312 ($260 + .2 × $260 = $260 + $52). The reduced price is

$$\$360 - (.3 \times \$360) = \$360 - \$108 = \$252.$$

The operating loss is

$$\$312 \text{ break-even point} - \$252 \text{ reduced price} = \$60 \text{ operating loss.}$$

(b) The absolute or gross loss is the difference between the cost and the reduced price.

$$\$260 \text{ cost} - \$252 \text{ reduced price} = \$8 \text{ absolute loss}$$

The following newspaper article, while humorous, does a lot to explain why stores offer huge markdowns to customers. Stores can't always tell what customers will buy and what they won't buy. Sometimes, their goal becomes minimizing a loss.

Reality Check

Ask Marilyn

It drives me nuts when I see the postholiday season sale prices, especially on clothes. It amazes me that they have that much of a markup the rest of the time, and it makes me feel like such a fool for ever paying the full price! Am I missing something?
—J.W., San Diego, Calif.
Yes! Those sale prices are great bargains. Many people believe that if a tie first sells for $50, then gets reduced to $35 and finally goes down to $20 if it still hasn't sold, the store owners must have paid far less than $20 for it in the first place (or they wouldn't sell it for $20). But what would be their alternative? Even if the store paid $40 for the tie, it would be better to sell it for $20 than to discard it, which would add $0 to their bank account.

Let's say that a store's tie-buyer underestimates the customers' taste and pays $40 each for 50 ties with little smiley faces painted on them, pricing them at $50 each. By the end of the holiday season, 49 ties are left unsold. (One was sold to a woman who couldn't stand her husband.) Dismayed, the store reduces the price to $25 each to get rid of the darned things. (So far, the store has spent $2000 and taken in $50.) At the end of the sale season, 48 ties are left unsold. (Another one was sold to a woman who couldn't stand her son-in-law.)

After transferring the buyer to the children's department, the store reduces the price to $10 each. (It has now spent $2000 and taken in $75.) At this point, someone like you walks in, picks up one of the ties and says, "The *nerve* of these people! They must be making a *fortune* in this place. No *wonder* they've got Newt Gingrich's face painted on all these ties."

Source: "Ask Marilyn" by Marilyn vos Savant, *Parade*, 2/5/95. Copyright © 1995 by *Parade*. Reprinted by permission.

7.4 | TURNOVER AND VALUATION OF INVENTORY

Objectives

1. Determine average inventory.
2. Calculate stock turnover.
3. Use uniform product codes.
4. Use the specific identification method to value inventory.
5. Determine inventory value using the weighted-average method.
6. Use the FIFO method to value inventory.
7. Use the LIFO method to value inventory.
8. Estimate inventory value using the retail method.

PROBLEM SOLVING IN BUSINESS

Many of the items stocked and sold by Olympic Sports and Leisure are ordered year round. One example is the Explorer Internal Frame backpack. Cas Shields, the manager, wants to make sure that her products are turning over (selling) so that the store does not have too much cash tied up in stock that is not selling. She also wants to be sure that the store has enough of the most popular products.

Objective 1 **Determine average inventory.** The average time for merchandise to sell is a common measure of a business's efficiency. The number of times that the merchandise sells during a certain period of time is called the **inventory turnover** or the **stock turnover**. A business such as a florist shop or produce stand has a very fast turnover of merchandise, perhaps just a few days. On the other hand, a furniture store normally has a much slower turnover, perhaps several months.

Find stock turnover by first calculating **average inventory**. Find the average inventory for a certain period by adding the inventories taken during the time period and then dividing the total by the number of times that the inventory was taken.

EXAMPLE 1

Determining Average Inventory

For related Web activities, go to www.mathbusiness.com

Keyword: count

Inventory at Olympic Sports and Leisure was $168,520 on April 1 and $143,240 on April 30. What was the average inventory?

Solution

First add the inventory values.

$$
\begin{array}{ll}
\$168,520 & \text{April 1} \\
+\ 143,240 & \text{April 30} \\
\hline
\$311,760 &
\end{array}
$$

Then divide by the number of times inventory was taken.

$$\frac{\$311,760}{2} = \$155,880$$

The average inventory is $155,880.

> **PROBLEM-SOLVING HINT** In Example 1, the inventory was taken twice to find the average inventory for one month. To find the average inventory for a period of time, an inventory must always be taken at the beginning of the period and one final time at the end of the period. For example, to find average inventory for a full year, businesses commonly find inventory on the first day of each month and on the last day of the last month. They then find the average inventory by adding 13 inventory amounts and dividing by 13, the number of inventories taken.

Keeping a close watch on inventory is an ongoing concern of management. The following newspaper advertisement is promoting a year-end sale with no money to be paid until June of the following year. This sale should have a major impact in reducing the store's inventory.

MONDAY–FRIDAY 10AM–9PM SATURDAY 10AM–8PM & SUNDAY 11AM–6PM. PRICES GOOD 'TIL TUESDAY!

GET HUGE STOREWIDE SAVINGS!

YEAR-END SALE!

**No Money Down, No Interest & No Payment 'til June
...On Every Item ...On Every Room!**

Same As Cash Option. On Approved Credit With No Down Payment, Interest Accrues From Delivery Date if not Paid in Full by June

NO DOWN PAYMENT, NO INTEREST & NO PAYMENTS 'TIL JUNE   ON 8-WAY, HAND-TIED LEATHER

Turnover is the number of times that the value of the merchandise (inventory value) in the store has sold during a period of time.

Objective **2** **Calculate stock turnover.** Although most businesses value inventory at retail, some value it at cost. For this reason, **stock turnover** is found by using either of these formulas.

$$\text{Turnover at retail} = \frac{\text{Retail sales}}{\text{Average inventory at retail}}$$

$$\text{Turnover at cost} = \frac{\text{Cost of goods sold}}{\text{Average inventory at cost}}$$

The turnover ratio may be identical by using either method. The variation that often exists is caused by stolen merchandise (called *inventory shrinkage*) or merchandise that has been marked down or has become unsellable. Normally, turnover at retail is slightly lower than turnover at cost. For this reason, many businesses prefer this more conservative figure.

EXAMPLE 2
Finding Stock Turnover at Retail

During May, Skater's World has retail sales of $32,032 and an average retail inventory of $9856. Find the stock turnover at retail.

Solution

Turnover at retail is

$$\text{Turnover} = \frac{\text{Retail sales}}{\text{Average inventory at retail}} = \frac{\$32,032}{\$9856} = 3.25 \text{ at retail.}$$

On the average, the store turned over its entire inventory 3.25 times during the month.

EXAMPLE 3
Finding Stock Turnover at Cost

If the average inventory value at cost for Skater's World in Example 2 was $5913, and the cost of goods sold was $19,396, find the stock turnover on cost.

Solution

Turnover on cost is

$$\text{Turnover} = \frac{\text{Cost of goods sold}}{\text{Average inventory at cost}} = \frac{\$19,396}{\$5913} = 3.28 \text{ at cost (rounded).}$$

The stock turnover ratio is useful for comparison purposes only. Many trade organizations publish such operating statistics to permit businesses to compare their operation with the industry as a whole. In addition to this, management will compare turnover from period to period and from department to department.

It is not always easy to place a value on each of the items in inventory. Many large companies keep a **perpetual inventory** by using a computer. As new items are received, the quantity, size, and cost of each are entered in the computer. Salesclerks enter product codes into the cash register (or uniform product codes are entered automatically with an optical scanner).

OBJECTIVE **3** **Use uniform product codes.** **Uniform product codes (UPC)** are the vertical stripes, or bar codes, that appear on most items sold in stores. Each product and product size is assigned its own code number. These UPCs are a great help in keeping track of inventory.

A reproduction of a Cracker Jack box showing its product code is shown at the left. The UPC number on the package is 4125723276. The checkout clerk in a retail store passes the coded lines over an optical scanner. The numbers are picked up by a computer, which recognizes the product by its code. The computer then forwards the price of the item to the cash register. At the same time the price is being recorded, the computer is subtracting the item automatically from inventory. After all the items being purchased have passed over the scanner, the customer receives a detailed cash-register receipt that gives a description of each item, the price of each item, and a total purchase price. Since the computer keeps track of stock on hand and is programmed to respond when inventory gets low, it provides more accurate inventory control and lower labor costs for the store.

Most businesses take a **physical inventory** (an actual count of each item in stock at a given time) at regular intervals. For example, inventory may be taken monthly, quarterly, semiannually, or just once a year. An inventory taken at regular intervals is called a **periodic inventory**.

There are four major methods used for inventory valuation. They are: the specific identification method, the weighted-average method, the first-in first-out method, and the last-in first-out method.

OBJECTIVE **4** **Use the specific identification method to value inventory.** The **specific identification method** is useful if items are easily identified and costs do not fluctuate. Each item is cost coded with either numerals or letters. These costs are then added to find ending inventory.

Since the cost of many items changes with time, there may be several of the same item in stock that were purchased at different costs. For this reason, many businesses prefer taking inventory at retail. The retail value of all identical items is the same.

OBJECTIVE **5** **Determine inventory value using the weighted-average method.** The **weighted average (average cost)** of inventory involves finding the average cost of an item and then multiplying the number of items remaining by the average cost per item.

EXAMPLE 4

Using Weighted Average (Average Cost) Inventory Valuation

Suppose Olympic Sports and Leisure made the following purchases of the Explorer Internal Frame backpack during the year.

Beginning inventory	20 backpacks at $70
January	50 backbacks at $80
March	100 backpacks at $90
July	60 backpacks at $85
October	40 backpacks at $75

At the end of the year there are 75 backpacks in inventory. Use the weighted-average method to find the inventory value.

Solution

Find the total cost of all the backpacks.

Beginning inventory	**20**	×	$70	=	$1400
January	**50**	×	$80	=	$4000
March	**100**	×	$90	=	$9000
July	**60**	×	$85	=	$5100
October	**40**	×	$75	=	$3000
Total	**270**				$22,500

Find the average cost per backpack by dividing this total cost by the number purchased. The average cost per backpack is

$$\frac{\$22,500}{270} = \$83.33 \text{ (rounded)}.$$

Since the average cost is \$83.33 and 75 backpacks remain in inventory, the weighted-average method gives the inventory value of the remaining backpacks as \$83.33 × 75 = \$6249.75.

The calculator solution to this example has several steps. First, find the total number of backpacks purchased and place the total in memory.

20 **+** 50 **+** 100 **+** 60 **+** 40 **=** 270 **STO**

Next, find the total cost of all the backpacks purchased and divide by the number stored in memory. This gives the average cost per backpack.

20 **×** 70 **+** 50 **×** 80 **+** 100 **×** 90 **+** 60 **×** 85 **+**

40 **×** 75 **=** **÷** **RCL** **=** 83.3333

Finally, round the average cost to the nearest cent and multiply by the number of backpacks in inventory to get the weighted average inventory value.

83.33 **×** 75 **=** 6249.75

Note: All calculator solutions use a scientific calculator. Refer to Appendix B for scientific calculator basics.

The following graphic shows the average price paid for a tennis racket in various countries around the world. One of the greatest influences on retail price is the cost of items purchased by the retailer. Changing costs of store merchandise makes it more challenging when trying to determine the value of inventory.

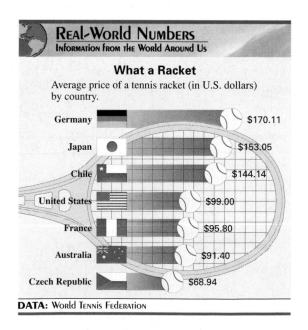

Real-World Numbers
Information from the World Around Us

What a Racket
Average price of a tennis racket (in U.S. dollars) by country.

Germany — \$170.11
Japan — \$153.05
Chile — \$144.14
United States — \$99.00
France — \$95.80
Australia — \$91.40
Czech Republic — \$68.94

DATA: World Tennis Federation

OBJECTIVE 6 Use the FIFO method to value inventory. The **first-in first-out (FIFO) method** of inventory valuation assumes a natural flow of goods through the inventory. The first goods to arrive are the first goods to be sold, so the last items purchased are the items remaining in inventory.

EXAMPLE 5

Using FIFO to Determine Inventory Valuation

Use the FIFO method to find the inventory value of the 75 backpacks from Olympic Sports and Leisure in Example 4.

SOLUTION

With the FIFO method, the 75 remaining backpacks are assumed to consist of the 40 backpacks bought in October and 35 (75 − 40 = 35) backpacks from the previous purchase in July. The value of the inventory is:

October	40 backpacks at $75 =	$3000	value of last 40
July	35 backpacks at $85 =	$2975	value of previous 35
	75 valued at	$5975	

The value of the backpack inventory is $5975 using the FIFO method.

OBJECTIVE **7** **Use the LIFO method to value inventory.** The **last-in, first-out (LIFO) method** of inventory valuation assumes a flow of goods through the inventory that is just the opposite of the FIFO flow. With LIFO, the goods remaining in inventory are those goods that were first purchased.

EXAMPLE 6

Using LIFO to Determine Inventory Valuation

Use the LIFO method to value the 75 backpacks in inventory at Olympic Sports and Leisure (see Example 4).

SOLUTION

The calculation starts with the beginning inventory and moves through the year's purchases, resulting in 75 backpacks. The beginning inventory and January purchases come to 70 backpacks, so the cost of 5 more (75 − 70 = 5) backpacks from the March purchase is needed.

Beginning inventory	20 backpacks at $70 =	$1400	value of first 20
January	50 backpacks at $80 =	$4000	value of next 50
March	5 backpacks at $90 =	$ 450	value of last 5
Total	75 valued at	$5850	

The value of the backpack inventory is $5850 using the LIFO method.

Depending on the method of valuing inventories that is used, Olympic Sports and Leisure may show the inventory value of the 75 backpacks as follows.

Average cost method	$6249.75
FIFO	$5975
LIFO	$5850

The preferred inventory valuation method would be determined by Olympic Sports and Leisure, perhaps on the advice of an accountant.

> **NOTE** While the FIFO method of inventory evaluation is the most commonly used method, accepted accounting practice insists that the method used to evaluate inventory be stated on the company financial statements.

OBJECTIVE **8** **Estimate inventory value using the retail method.** An estimate of the value of inventory may be found using the **retail method of estimating inventory**. With this method, the cost of goods available for sale is found as a percent of the retail value of the goods available for sale during the same time period. This percent is then multiplied by the retail value of inventory at the end of the time period. The result is an estimate of the inventory at cost.

EXAMPLE 7

Estimating Inventory Value Using the Retail Method

The inventory on December 31 at Olympic Sports and Leisure was $129,200 at cost and $171,000 at retail. Purchases during the next three months were $165,400 at cost, $221,800 at retail, and net sales were $168,800. Use the retail method to estimate the value of inventory at cost on March 31.

Solution

Step 1   Find the value of goods available for sale (inventory) at cost and at retail.

	At cost	**At retail**	
	$129,200	$171,000	beginning inventory
	+ 165,400	+ 221,800	purchases
	$294,600	$392,800	goods available for sale
Step 2 Find the retail value of current inventory.		− 168,800	net sales
		$224,000	March 31 inventory at retail

Step 3   Now find the percent of the value of goods available for sale at cost to goods available for sale at retail (cost ratio).

$$\frac{\$294,600}{\$392,800} \quad \frac{\text{goods available for sale at cost}}{\text{goods available for sale at retail}} = .75 = 75\% \text{ (cost ratio)}$$

Step 4   Finally, the estimated inventory value at cost on March 31 is found by multiplying inventory at retail on March 31 by 75% (cost ratio)

Ending inventory at retail × % (cost ratio) = Inventory at cost

$224,000 × **.75** = $168,000 March 31 inventory at cost.

CHAPTER 7 | Quick Review

CHAPTER TERMS

*Review the following terms to test your understanding of the chapter. For
each term you do not know, refer to the page number found next to that term.*

absolute loss [**p. 277**]	gross profit [**p. 256**]	markup on selling price [**p. 256**]	reduced net profit [**p. 277**]
actual selling price [**p. 275**]	inventory turnover [**p. 281**]	net earnings [**p. 256**]	reduced price [**p. 275**]
break-even point [**p. 277**]	last-in, first-out (LIFO) method	net profit [**p. 256**]	retail method of estimating
breaking even [**p. 277**]	[**p. 285**]	operating expenses [**p. 256**]	inventory [**p. 285**]
conversion formulas [**p. 269**]	margin [**p. 256**]	operating loss [**p. 277**]	sale price [**p. 275**]
cost [**p. 256**]	markdown [**p. 275**]	overhead [**p. 256**]	selling price [**p. 256**]
first-in, first-out (FIFO) method	markup [**p. 255**]	percent of markdown [**p. 275**]	specific identification method
[**p. 284**]	markup based on cost [**p. 257**]	periodic inventory [**p. 283**]	[**p. 283**]
formula for markdown [**p. 275**]	markup formula [**p. 257**]	perpetual inventory [**p. 283**]	stock turnover [**p. 281**]
gross loss [**p. 277**]	markup on cost [**p. 256**]	physical inventory [**p. 283**]	uniform product code (UPC)
			[**p. 283**]
			weighted-average (average
			cost) method [**p. 283**]

CONCEPTS   EXAMPLES

7.1 Markup on cost

$$
\begin{array}{l}
100\% \quad \text{Cost} \\
\underline{+ \text{ Markup? (part)}} \\
\text{Selling Price}
\end{array}
$$

Cost is base. Use the basic percent formula.
$$P = B \times R$$

	100%	C	$160	(base)
(rate)	25%	M	?	(part)
		S		

$$P = B \times R$$
$$P = \$160 \times .25$$
$$P = \$40 \text{ markup}$$

7.1 Calculating the percent of markup

$$
\begin{array}{cccc}
 & 100\% & C & \$ \\
(\text{rate}) & ?\% & M & \$ \\
 & \% & S & \$
\end{array}
$$

Solve for rate.

	100%	C	$420	(base)
(rate)	?	M	$	(part)
		S	$546	(part)

$$\$546 - \$420 = \$126 \text{ markup}$$
$$R = \frac{P}{B} = \frac{126}{420}$$
$$R = 30\%$$

7.1 Finding the cost and the selling price

$$
\begin{array}{ccc}
100\% & C & \$? \text{ (base)} \\
 & M & \$ \\
\hline
 & S & \$? \text{ (part)}
\end{array}
$$

Solve for base.

	100%	C	$?	(base)
(rate)	50%	M	$56	
	%	S	$?	(part)

$$R = \frac{P}{B} = \frac{56}{.5}$$
$$B = \$112 \text{ cost}$$
$$\$112 + \$56 = \$168 \text{ selling price}$$

7.2 Markup on selling price

$$
\begin{array}{ccc}
\% & C & \$ \\
\% & M & \$? \text{ (part)} \\
\hline
100\% & S & \$
\end{array}
$$

Solve for part.

	%	C	$	
(rate)	25%	M	$?	(part)
	100%	S	$6.00	(base)

$$P = B \times R$$
$$P = \$6.00 \times .25$$
$$P = \$1.50$$

CONCEPTS	EXAMPLES
7.2 Finding the cost $\begin{array}{lll} \% & C & \$\ ? \text{ (part)} \\ \underline{\% \quad M \quad \$\quad\quad} \\ 100\% & S & \$ \end{array}$	$\begin{array}{llll} & \% & C & \$\ ? \quad \text{(part)} \\ \text{(rate)} & 35\% & M & \$87.50 \text{ (part)} \\ & \overline{100\%} & \overline{S} & \overline{\$\quad\quad} \text{ (base)} \end{array}$ $B = \dfrac{P}{R} = \dfrac{87.5}{.35} = \$250 \text{ selling price}$ $\$250 - \$87.50 = \$162.50 \text{ markup}$
7.2 Calculating the selling price and the markup $\begin{array}{lll} \% & C \\ \underline{\% \quad M \quad \$\ ? \text{ (part)}} \\ 100\% & S & \$\ ? \text{ (base)} \end{array}$	$\begin{array}{llll} \text{(rate)} & 75\% & C & \$150 \text{ (part)} \\ & 25\% & M & \$\ ? \text{ (part)} \\ & \overline{100\%} & \overline{S} & \overline{\$\ ?} \text{ (base)} \end{array}$ $100\% - 25\% = 75\% \text{ cost}$ $B = \dfrac{P}{R} = \dfrac{150}{.75} = \$200$ $\$200 - \$150 = \$50$
7.2 Converting markup on cost to markup on selling price Use the formula $\% \text{ markup on selling price} = \dfrac{\% \text{ markup on cost}}{100\% + \% \text{ markup on cost}}$	Convert 25% markup on cost to markup on selling price. $\dfrac{\% \text{ markup on}}{\text{selling price}} = \dfrac{25\%}{100\% + 25\%}$ $= \dfrac{.25}{1.25}$ $= .2 = 20\%$
7.2 Converting markup on selling price to markup on cost Use the formula $\% \text{markup on cost} = \dfrac{\% \text{ markup on selling price}}{100\% - \% \text{ markup on selling price}}$	Convert 20% markup on selling price to markup on cost. $\dfrac{\% \text{ markup on}}{\text{cost}} = \dfrac{20\%}{100\% - 20\%}$ $= \dfrac{.2}{.8}$ $= .25 = 25\%$
7.2 Finding selling price for perishables 1. Find total cost and selling price. 2. Subtract total sales at reduced prices from total sales. 3. Divide the remaining sales by the number of saleable units to get selling price per unit.	60 doughnuts cost 15¢ each; 10 are not sold; 50% markup on selling price. Find selling price per doughnut. $\text{Cost} = 60 \times \$.15 = \$9$ $\begin{array}{llll} \text{(rate)} & 50\% & C & \$9 \text{ (part)} \\ & \underline{50\% \quad M} \\ & 100\% & S & ? \quad \text{(base)} \end{array}$ $B = \dfrac{P}{R} = \dfrac{9}{.5} = \$18$ $60 - 10 = 50 \text{ doughnuts sold}$ $\$18 \div 50 = \$.36 \text{ per doughnut}$
7.3 Percent of markdown Markdown is always a percent of the original price. Use the formula $R = \dfrac{P}{B}$ $\text{Markdown percent} = \dfrac{\text{Markdown amount}}{\text{Original price}}$	Original price, \$76; markdown, \$19; find the percent of markdown. $R = \dfrac{P}{B} = \dfrac{19}{76} = .25$ $R = 25\% \text{ markdown}$

CONCEPTS	EXAMPLES
7.3 Break-even point The cost plus operating expenses equals the break-even point.	Cost, $54; operating expenses, $16; find the break-even point. $54 cost + **$16 operating expenses** = $70 break-even point
7.3 Operating loss The difference between the break-even point and the reduced price (when below the break-even point) is the operating loss.	Break-even point, $70; reduced price, $58; find the operating loss. $70 break-even point − **$58 reduced price** $12 operating loss
7.3 Absolute loss (gross loss) When the reduced price is below cost, the difference between the cost and reduced price is the absolute loss.	Cost, $54; reduced price, $48; find the absolute loss. $54 cost − **$48 reduced price** = $6 absolute loss
7.4 Average inventory Inventory is taken two or more times. Totals are added together, then divided by the number of inventories to get the average.	Inventories, $22,635, $24,692, and $18,796; find the average inventory. $$\frac{\$22,635 + \$24,692 + \$18,796}{3}$$ $$= \frac{\$66,123}{3}$$ $$= \$22,041 \text{ average inventory}$$
7.4 Turnover at retail Use the formula $$\text{Turnover} = \frac{\text{Retail sales}}{\text{Average inventory at retail}}$$	Retail sales, $78,496; average inventory at retail, $18,076; find turnover at retail. $$\frac{\$78,496}{\$18,076} = 4.34 \text{ at retail} \quad \text{rounded}$$
7.4 Turnover at cost Use the formula $$\text{Turnover} = \frac{\text{Cost of goods sold}}{\text{Average inventory at cost}}$$	Cost of goods sold, $26,542; average inventory at cost, $6592; find turnover at cost. $$\frac{\$26,542}{\$6592} = 4.03 \text{ at cost} \quad \text{rounded}$$
7.4 Specific identification to value inventory Each item is cost coded and the cost of each of the items is added to find total inventory.	Individual cost of each item in inventory is: item 1, $593; item 2, $614; item 3, $498; find total value of inventory. $593 + $614 + $498 = $1705 total value of inventory
7.4 Weighted-average (average cost) method of inventory valuation This method values items in an inventory at the average cost of buying them.	Beginning inventory of 20 at $75; purchases of 15 at $80; 25 at $65; 18 at $70; 22 remain in inventory. Find the inventory value. 20 × $75 = $1500 15 × $80 = $1200 25 × $65 = $1625 18 × $70 = $1260 Total 78 $5585 $$\frac{\$5585}{78} = \$71.60 \text{ average cost} \quad \text{rounded}$$ $71.60 × 22 = $1575.20 weighted average method inventory value

CONCEPTS	EXAMPLES
7.4 First-in, first-out (FIFO) method of inventory valuation First items in are first sold. Inventory is based on cost of last items purchased.	Beginning inventory of 25 items at $40; purchase on Aug. 7, 30 items at $35; 35 remain in inventory. Find the inventory value. $\begin{aligned} 30 \times \$35 &= \$1050 \\ 5 \times \$40 &= \$\ 200 \\ \hline 35 \qquad\quad &\ \ \$1250 \end{aligned}$ value of last 30 value of previous 5 value of inventory FIFO method
7.4 Last-in, first-out (LIFO) method of inventory valuation The items remaining in inventory are those items that were first purchased.	Beginning inventory of 48 items at $20 each; purchase on May 9, 40 items at $25 each; 55 remain in inventory. Find the inventory value. $\begin{aligned} 48 \times \$20 &= \$\ 960 \\ 7 \times \$25 &= \$\ 175 \\ \hline 55 \qquad\quad &\ \ \$1135 \end{aligned}$ value of first 48 value of last 7 value of inventory LIFO method

7.4 Estimating inventory value using the retail method

$$\frac{\text{Goods available for sale at cost}}{\text{Goods available for sale at retail}} = \% \ (\text{cost ratio})$$

$$\begin{array}{c}\text{Ending inventory}\\\text{at retail}\end{array} \times \% \ (\text{cost ratio}) = \begin{array}{c}\text{Inventory}\\\text{at cost}\end{array}$$

	Cost	Retail
beginning inventory	$9000	$15,000
purchases	+ 36,000	+ 60,000
goods available for sale	$45,000	$75,000
net sales		− 54,000
ending inventory		$21,000

$$\frac{\$45,000}{\$75,000} \quad \begin{array}{l}\text{goods available for sale at cost}\\\text{goods available for sale at retail}\end{array}$$

$$= .6 = 60\%$$

$$\$21,000 \times .6 = \$12,600 \text{ inventory value at cost}$$

CHAPTER 7 | SUMMARY EXERCISE

MARKDOWN: REDUCING PRICES TO MOVE MERCHANDISE

Olympic Sports and Leisure purchased two dozen pairs of Roller Derby Baja adult in-line skates at a cost of $1950. Operating expenses for the store are 25% of cost while total markup on this type of product is 35% of selling price. Only 6 pairs of the skates sell at the original price and the manager decides to mark down the remaining skates. The price is reduced 25% and 6 more pairs sell. The remaining 12 pairs of skates are marked down 50% of the original selling price and are finally sold.

(a) _____

(a) Find the original selling price of each pair of skates.

(b) Find the total of the selling prices of all the skates.

(b) _____

(c) Find the operating loss.

(c) _____

(d) Find the absolute loss.

(d) _____

Investigate

Talk with the owner or manager of a retail store. Does the store calculate markup based on cost or retail? Does the store use markdowns to promote the sale or liquidation of merchandise? How does the management decide how much to mark down merchandise? Ask the manager for an example of a product that had to be marked down so much that a gross loss resulted.

For related Web activities, go to www.mathbusiness.com

'Net Assets

REI

STATISTICS

- 1938: Established by a group of 24 moutaineers

- 1998: $567 million in sales

- 1999: 49 stores located in 21 states

- Named in 100 Best Companies to Work For by *Fortune* magazine

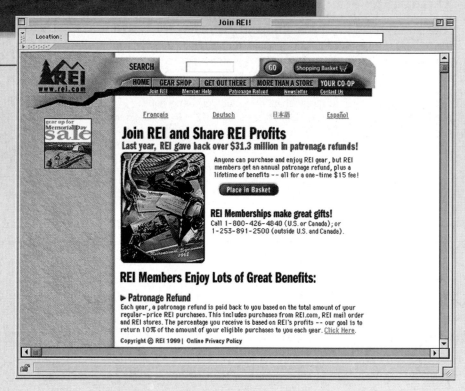

REI was formed in 1938 by a group of 24 mountain climbers from Seattle, Washington. They wanted the finest-quality climbing equipment and formed a buying cooperative, (membership group) in order to find the best prices for their equipment. Today, anyone may shop at REI, but members—those who pay a one-time $15 fee to join—share in the company's profits through an annual patronage refund. In 1998, REI declared a total patronage refund of 10.4 percent to 1.6 million active members for a total of $31.3 million. REI is a privately held company and does not sell stock.

REI's easy-to-navigate Internet store provides access to more than 10,000 outdoor products, and offers a variety of interactive education opportunities for outdoor enthusiasts. In addition to selecting from thousands of products and securely placing on-line orders, customers can use gear checklists, interact with gear experts, and learn basic outdoor skills by accessing educational clinics.

1. REI purchased one dozen Jansport backpacks at a cost of $504. If the company uses a markup of 25% on selling price, find the selling price of each backpack.

2. A two-person dome tent with a full rain fly has a wholesale price of $78. If the store has operating expenses of 24.5% of cost and a net profit of 10.5% of cost, find the selling price.

3. Do you have a special activity, sport, or hobby for which it is sometimes difficult to get the right kind and quality of equipment or supplies? Would you consider buying what you need by mail-order catalog or over the Internet? Why or why not?

4. List five possible advantages and five possible disadvantages of buying through the Internet. How could the disadvantages be eliminated or reduced? Do you see a time when you will be making half or more of your purchases through the Internet?

Name   Date   Class

CHAPTER 7 | TEST

To help you review, the numbers in brackets show the section in which the topic was discussed.

Solve for (a), (b), and (c). **[7.1 AND 7.2]**

1. 100%   *C* $32.00
  (a) %   *M* $ 6.40
  (b) %   *S* $(c)

2. 100%   *C* $(b)
  38%   *M* $(c)
  (a) %   *S* $504.39

3. (a)%   *C* $67.20
  (b)%   *M* $(c)
  100%   *S* $84.00

4. (a)%   *C* $(c)
  (b)%   *M* $ 6.15
  100%   *S* $24.60

Find the equivalent markup on either cost or selling price, using the appropriate formula. Round to the nearest tenth of a percent. **[7.2]**

Markup on Cost	*Markup on Selling Price*	*Markup on Cost*	*Markup on Selling Price*
5. 25%	_____	**6.** $33\frac{1}{3}$%	_____

Complete the following. If there is no operating loss or absolute loss, write "none." **[7.3]**

	Cost	*Operating Expense*	*Break-even Point*	*Reduced Price*	*Operating Loss*	*Absolute Loss*
7.	$160	$40	_____	$186	_____	_____
8.	$75	_____	$99	$66	_____	_____

Find the stock turnover at cost and at retail in the following. Round to the nearest hundredth. **[7.4]**

	Average Inventory at Cost	*Average Inventory at Retail*	*Cost of Goods Sold*	*Retail Sales*	*Turnover at Cost*	*Turnover at Retail*
9.	$7060	$12,786	$40,656	$73,264	_____	_____

Solve the following application problems.

10. Olympic Sports and Leisure buys jogging shorts manufactured in Indonesia for $97.50 per dozen pair. Find the selling price per pair if the retailer maintains a markup of 35% on selling price.   **[7.2]**

10. _____

11. Circuit City sells a dishwasher for $395 while using a markup of 20% on cost. Find the cost. **[7.1]**

11. _____

12. The Computer Service Center sells a DeskJet print cartridge for $18.75. If the print cartridge costs the store $11.25, find the markup as a percent of selling price. **[7.2]**

12. _____

13. Wild Sports offers an inflatable boat for $199.95. If the boats cost $1943.52 per dozen, find **(a)** the markup, **(b)** the percent of markup on selling price, and **(c)** the percent of markup on cost. Round to the nearest tenth of a percent. **[7.1 and 7.2]**

(a) _____
(b) _____
(c) _____

14. A commercial riding lawn mower originally priced at $9250 is marked down to $6660. Find the percent of markdown on the original price. **[7.3]**

14. _____

15. John Cross Pool Supply, a retailer, pays $285 for a diving board. The original selling price was $399, but was marked down 40%. If operating expenses are 30% of cost, find **(a)** the operating loss and **(b)** the absolute loss. **[7.3]**

(a) _____
(b) _____

16. Red Cross Medical Supplies had an inventory of $58,664 on January 1, $73,815 on July 1, and $62,938 on December 31. Find the average inventory. **[7.4]**

16. _____

Round to the nearest dollar amount.

17. Clutch Masters made the following purchases of universal joints during the year: Beginning inventory, 30 at $18.50 each; June, 25 at $21.80 each; September, 20 at $20.50 each; and November, 30 at $21.25 each. An inventory shows that 55 universal joints remain. Find the inventory value using the weighted average method. **[7.4]**

17. _____

18. Find the inventory value listed in Exercise 17 using **(a)** the FIFO method and **(b)** the LIFO method. **[7.4]**

(a) _____
(b) _____

Name   Date   Class

CUMULATIVE REVIEW | CHAPTERS 4–7

The following credit-card transactions were made at Gifts and Such. Answer 1–5 using this information.
[4.2]

	Sales		Credits
$93.50	$315.26	$22.51	$99.84
$117.75	$38.00	$162.15	$72.68
$173.05	$92.18		$35.63

1. Find the total amount of the sales slips.   1. _____

2. What is the total amount of the credit slips?   2. _____

3. Find the total amount of the deposit.   3. _____

4. Assuming that the bank charges the retailer a $2\frac{1}{4}$% discount charge, find the amount of the   4. _____
   discount charge at the statement date.

5. Find the amount of the credit given to the retailer after the fee is subtracted.   5. _____

Solve the following application problems.

6. Angela Perez worked 7 hours on Monday, 10 hours on Tuesday, 8 hours on Wednesday, 9 hours on   6. _____
   Thursday, and 10 hours on Friday. Her regular hourly pay is $12.80. Find her gross earnings for the
   week if Perez is paid overtime for all hours over 8 worked in a day.   **[5.1]**

7. The employees of Feather Farms paid a total of $968.50 in Social Security tax last month, $223.50 in   7. _____
   Medicare tax, and $1975.38 in federal withholding tax. Find the total amount that the employer must
   send to the Internal Revenue Service.   **[5.4]**

Find the net cost (invoice amount) for each of the following.   **[6.1]**

8. List price $280, less 10/20 _____   9. List price $375, less 25/10/5 _____

Find the single discount equivalent for each of the following series discounts.   **[6.2]**

10. 10/20 _____   11. 30/40/10 _____

Find the discount date and the net payment date for each of the following (the net payment date is 20 days after the final discount date). **[6.4]**

	Invoice Date	Terms	Date Goods Received	Final Discount Date	Net Payment Date
12.	Oct. 18	2/10 ROG	Dec. 8	_____	_____
13.	Feb. 5	3/20 EOM		_____	_____
14.	June 24	4/10–30 ex.		_____	_____

Complete the following. If there is no operating loss or absolute loss, write "none." **[7.3]**

	Cost	Operating Expense	Break-even Point	Reduced Price	Operating Loss	Absolute Loss
15.	$312	$88	_____	_____	$120	_____
16.	_____	_____	_____	$220	$112	$32

Solve the following application problems.

17. The list price of a Coleman Sundome 7 tent is $79.98. Find the dealer's cost if given a 25/25 trade discount and a 3/20, n/30 cash discount. Assume that the dealer earns the maximum cash discount. **[6.1 AND 6.3]**

17. _____

18. Computer Towne purchases mouse pads for $43.20 per box of 3 dozen. If the store wants a markup of 52% on the selling price, find the selling price per mouse pad. **[7.2]**

18. _____

19. The Leaded Glass Exchange has an average inventory of $2820 at cost. If the cost of goods sold for the year was $30,375, find the stock turnover at cost. Round to hundredths. **[7.4]**

19. _____

20. Inventory at a local store was taken at retail value four times and was found to be $53,820; $49,510; $60,820; and $56,380. Sales during the same period were $252,077. Find the stock turnover at retail. Round to hundredths. **[7.4]**

20. _____

21. Thunder Manufacturing made the following purchases of rivet drums during the year: 25 at $135 each, 40 at $165 each, 15 at $108.50 each, and 30 at $142 each. An inventory shows that 45 rivet drums remain. Find the inventory value, using the weighted average method. **[7.4]**

21. _____

22. Refer to Exercise 21 above. Find the inventory value, using **(a)** the FIFO method and **(b)** the LIFO method. **[7.4]**

(a) _____

(b) _____

CHAPTER 8

SIMPLE INTEREST

Susan Gilbert is the sole owner of Gilbert Construction Company, a company that builds and sells moderately priced family homes. Gilbert began her company fifteen years ago with herself and an architect as the only employees. She now has twelve employees and builds about thirty homes each year.

Interest rates are a part of housing costs and can influence the number of homes under construction, as you can see from the following graphs.

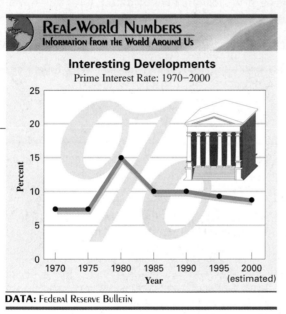

REAL-WORLD NUMBERS
INFORMATION FROM THE WORLD AROUND US

Interesting Developments
Prime Interest Rate: 1970–2000

DATA: Federal Reserve Bulletin

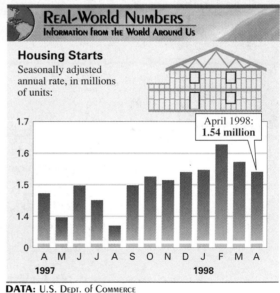

REAL-WORLD NUMBERS
INFORMATION FROM THE WORLD AROUND US

Housing Starts
Seasonally adjusted annual rate, in millions of units:

April 1998: **1.54 million**

DATA: U.S. Dept. of Commerce

For related Web activities, go to www.mathbusiness.com

Keyword: prime

Some of the oldest documents in existence—clay tablets dating back almost 5000 years—show the calculation of interest charges. **Interest**, a fee for borrowing money, is about as old as civilization itself. The largest and financially most secure companies such as IBM and AT&T borrow at the most favorable interest rate known as the **prime rate**. The prime rate is an important factor in determining the rates of interest paid to depositors on savings and the rates of interest charged to borrowers on loans. As you can see in the above left figure, prime rates fluctuate widely although they typically remain between 6% and 15%. It is important to have a good understanding of interest since interest charges can represent a significant cost for a firm.

Two basic types of interest are in common use today: **simple interest** and **compound interest**. Simple interest is interest paid on only the principal. Compound interest is interest paid on both principal and previously earned interest. This chapter discusses simple interest, and Chapter 9 covers compound interest.

8.1 | Basics of Simple Interest

Objectives

1. Solve for simple interest.
2. Calculate maturity value.
3. Determine the number of days from one date to another, using a table.
4. Determine the number of days from one date to another, using the actual number of days in the month.
5. Find exact and ordinary interest.
6. Define the basic terms used with notes.
7. Find the due date of a note.

Problem Solving in Business

Gilbert Construction Company has been hired to build a new 1800-square-foot home. Susan Gilbert must borrow money to pay for building materials and wages. Her firm will not receive any revenue until after the home is sold, which may be months from now. It is very important that she keep construction costs down, because the firm will make a profit only if the income from the sale exceeds the cost of construction, including interest charges on borrowed money.

Objective 1 Solve for simple interest. Simple interest, interest charged on the entire principal for the entire length of the loan, is found with the following formula, a modification of the basic percent formula.

The simple interest *I* on a **principal** or loan amount of *P* dollars at a rate of interest *R* per year for *T* years is given by

$$I = P \cdot R \cdot T = PRT$$

Be careful with the substitution of values for letters in the formula $I = PRT$. Look carefully at the following notes.

> **NOTE** Time is *in years*. This means that a time period given in months or days *must be converted* to a fraction of a year before being substituted into the formula for *T*. For example, convert 3 months to $\frac{3}{12}$ of a year before substituting in for *T*.

> **NOTE** Rate must be changed to a decimal or fraction before substituting into the formula $I = PRT$. For example, change 12% to .12 or $\frac{12}{100}$ before substituting into the formula for rate (*R*).

EXAMPLE 1
Finding Simple Interest

Gilbert Construction Company must borrow $60,000 to build an 1800-square-foot home. The owner, Susan Gilbert, wants to find the cost added to the home for interest if she borrows the funds **(a)** at 8% for 9 months and **(b)** $8\frac{1}{2}$% for $1\frac{1}{2}$ years. Find the simple interest on both loans.

Solution

(a) Use the formula $I = PRT$. Substitute $60,000 for *P*, .08 (the decimal form of 8%) for *R*, and $\frac{9}{12}$ for *T*.

$$I = PRT$$
$$I = \$60,000 \times .08 \times \frac{9}{12}$$
$$I = \$3600 \text{ simple interest}$$

(b) Again use the simple interest formula; however, now use $R = .085$ $(= 8\frac{1}{2}\%)$ and $T = 1.5$ $(= 1\frac{1}{2})$.

$$I = PRT$$

$$I = \$60,000 \times .085 \times 1.5$$

$$I = \$7650 \text{ simple interest}$$

Borrowing money under one of these plans would add either $3600 or $7650 to Gilbert Construction Company's cost of building the home.

The calculator solution for part (b) is

60,000 ⊠ 8.5 % ⊠ 1.5 ⊟ 7650.

Note: All calculator solutions use a scientific calculator. Refer to Appendix B for scientific calculator basics.

Objective **2** **Calculate maturity value.** The amount that must be repaid when the loan is paid off is the **maturity value** of the loan. Find this value by adding principal and interest.

Calculating Loan Maturity Value

Maturity value = Principal + Interest

or: the maturity value M of a loan having a principal P and interest I is given by

$$M = P + I$$

Example 2

Finding Maturity Value

Jim Wilcox would like to remodel his small bookstore so that he can serve customers coffee and allow them to sit and browse. To remodel the store, he borrows $7200 for 21 months at 9.25% interest. Find the interest due on the loan and the maturity value.

Solution

Interest due is found using $I = PRT$, where T is in years (21 months $= \frac{21}{12}$ years).

$$I = PRT$$

$$I = \$7200 \times .0925 \times \frac{21}{12} = \$1165.50$$

Find the maturity value using $M = P + I$ where $P = \$7200$ and $I = \$1165.50$.

$$M = P + I$$

$$M = \$7200 + \$1165.50 = \$8365.50$$

Objective **3** **Determine the number of days from one date to another, using a table.** The preceding examples discussed simple interest for loans of a given number of months or years. In business, it is common for loans to be for a given number of days. For example, the loan may be due in 90 days or in 120 days, or it may be due at some fixed date such as April 17.

One way to find the number of days from one date to another assigns a number to each day of the year. For example, June 11 is day 162 of the year (day 163 of a leap year), and December 25 is day 359 (360 in a leap year). Look at the table on the next page and find the number of days from one date to another, such as the number of days from June 11 to December 25, by subtracting as shown.

December 25 is day	359
June 11 is day	− 162
	197 days from June 11 to December 25

There are **197** days from June 11 to December 25.

The Number of Each of the Days of the Year*

Number of Days	Jan.	Feb.	Mar.	Apr.	May	June	July	Aug.	Sept.	Oct.	Nov.	Dec.	Number of Days
1	1	32	60	91	121	152	182	213	244	274	305	335	1
2	2	33	61	92	122	153	183	214	245	275	306	336	2
3	3	34	62	93	123	154	184	215	246	276	307	337	3
4	4	35	63	94	124	155	185	216	247	277	308	338	4
5	5	36	64	95	125	156	186	217	248	278	309	339	5
6	6	37	65	96	126	157	187	218	249	279	310	340	6
7	7	38	66	97	127	158	188	219	250	280	311	341	7
8	8	39	67	98	128	159	189	220	251	281	312	342	8
9	9	40	68	99	129	160	190	221	252	282	313	343	9
10	10	41	69	100	130	161	191	222	253	283	314	344	10
11	11	42	70	101	131	162	192	223	254	284	315	345	11
12	12	43	71	102	132	163	193	224	255	285	316	346	12
13	13	44	72	103	133	164	194	225	256	286	317	347	13
14	14	45	73	104	134	165	195	226	257	287	318	348	14
15	15	46	74	105	135	166	196	227	258	288	319	349	15
16	16	47	75	106	136	167	197	228	259	289	320	350	16
17	17	48	76	107	137	168	198	229	260	290	321	351	17
18	18	49	77	108	138	169	199	230	261	291	322	352	18
19	19	50	78	109	139	170	200	231	262	292	323	353	19
20	20	51	79	110	140	171	201	232	263	293	324	354	20
21	21	52	80	111	141	172	202	233	264	294	325	355	21
22	22	53	81	112	142	173	203	234	265	295	326	356	22
23	23	54	82	113	143	174	204	235	266	296	327	357	23
24	24	55	83	114	144	175	205	236	267	297	328	358	24
25	25	56	84	115	145	176	206	237	268	298	329	359	25
26	26	57	85	116	146	177	207	238	269	299	330	360	26
27	27	58	86	117	147	178	208	239	270	300	331	361	27
28	28	59	87	118	148	179	209	240	271	301	332	362	28
29	29		88	119	149	180	210	241	272	302	333	363	29
30	30		89	120	150	181	211	242	273	303	334	364	30
31	31		90		151		212	243		304		365	31

Add 1 to each date after February 29 for a leap year

EXAMPLE 3

Finding the Number of Days from One Date to Another, Using a Table

Find the number of days from **(a)** March 24 to July 22 and **(b)** November 8 to February 17 of the next year. Assume that it is not a leap year.

SOLUTION

(a) March 24 is day 83, and July 22 is day 203.

July 22 is day	203
March 24 is day	− 83
	120

There are 120 days from March 24 to July 22.

(b) Since November 8 is in one year and February 17 is in the next year, first find the number of days from November 8 to the end of the year.

Last day of the year is number	365
November 8 is day	− 312
	53

There are 53 days from November 8 to the end of the year.

708-709-3000

Then find the number of days from the beginning of the next year to February 17. According to the preceding table, February 17 is the **48th day** of the year. The total number of days is

November 8 to end of year	53
January 1 to February 17	+ 48
	101

There are 101 days from November 8 to February 17 of the next year.

Objective 4 **Determine the number of days from one date to another, using the actual number of days in the month.** An alternate way of finding the number of days, useful when the table is not available, is to use the actual number of days in each month, as shown here.

Number of Days in Each Month

31 Days		30 Days	28 Days
January	August	April	February
March	October	June	(29 days in
May	December	September	leap year)
July		November	

EXAMPLE 4

Finding the Number of Days from One Date to Another Using Actual Days

Find the number of days from November 4 to February 21.

Solution

Since November has 30 days, there are $30 - 4 = 26$ days left in November, then 31 days in December, 31 days in January, and an additional 21 days in February for a total as follows:

30	26	days remaining in November
31	31	December
31	31	January
22	+ 21	February
114	**109**	

There are 109 days from November 4 to February 21.

> **NOTE** In this method you are *not counting the day that the loan was made,* but you are counting the day that the money was returned as a full day.

Objective 5 **Find exact and ordinary interest.** In the formula for simple interest, time is measured in years or fractions of a year. In previous examples, the period of the loan was in months and was divided by 12 to convert from months to years. Things are not quite as simple when the time period is in days.

First, the number of days in the loan period must be found. Then find T with the following formula before using $I = PRT$.

$$T = \frac{\text{Number of days in the loan period}}{\text{Number of days in a year}}$$

There are two common values used for the number of days in a year.

> **1.** The method known as **exact interest** uses 365 as the number of days in a year.
>
> **2.** The method known as **ordinary interest or banker's interest** uses 360 as the number of days in a year.

The method used to form the time fraction used for T in the formula $I = PRT$ is summarized as follows.

> **For exact interest:**
>
> $$T = \frac{\text{Number of days in a loan period}}{365}$$
>
> **For ordinary or banker's interest:**
>
> $$T = \frac{\text{Number of days in a loan period}}{360}$$

For related Web activities, go to www.mathbusiness.com

Government agencies and the Federal Reserve Bank use exact interest, as do many credit unions. Even with computers, many banks and other financial institutions *still use ordinary interest* for commercial loans because of tradition and because it produces more interest for the financial institution.

EXAMPLE 5

Finding Exact and Ordinary Interest

Tyler Radio borrowed $17,650 on May 12. The loan, at an interest rate of 13.5%, is due on August 27. Find the interest on the loan using **(a)** exact interest and **(b)** ordinary interest.

Solution

Using the table or calculating the number of days in each month, there are 107 days from May 12 to August 27.

(a) The exact interest is found from $I = PRT$ with $P = \$17,650$, $R = .135$, and $T = \frac{107}{365}$. (Remember to use 365 as the denominator with exact interest.)

$$I = PRT$$

$$I = \$17,650 \times .135 \times \frac{107}{365}$$

$$I = \$698.50 \text{ (rounded)}$$

(b) Find ordinary interest with the same formula and values, except that $T = \frac{107}{360}$.

$$I = PRT$$

$$I = \$17,650 \times .135 \times \frac{107}{360}$$

$$I = \$708.21 \text{ (rounded)}$$

In this example, the ordinary interest is $708.21 - \$698.50 = \$9.71$ more than the exact interest.

> **NOTE**   Throughout the balance of the book, assume ordinary or banker's interest (360 days per year) unless stated otherwise.

OBJECTIVE **6** **Define the basic terms used with notes.** A **promissory note** is a *legal document* in which one person or firm agrees to pay a certain amount of money, on a specific day in the future, to another person or firm. An example of a promissory note follows.

PROMISSORY NOTE

Charlotte, North Carolina ___March 6___

__Ninety days__ after date, ___I___ promise to pay to the order of

___Charles D. Miller___ / ___$2500.00___

___Two thousand, five hundred and__ $\frac{00}{100}$_ Dollars with interest at ___12% per year___

_____ , payable at ___Wells Fargo Bank Country Club Center Office___

Due ___June 4___   _Madeline Sullivan_

The person borrowing the money is called the **maker** or **payer** of the note (Madeline Sullivan for this note). The person who loaned the money, and who will receive the payment, is called the **payee** (Charles D. Miller for this note). The length of time until the note is due is called the **term** of the note (90 days for this note). The **face value** or principal of the note ($2500 for this note) is the amount written on the line in front of *dollars*. The interest rate on the note is 12% per year.

The **maturity value** of the loan is the face value plus any interest that is due. Since the interest for this note is found by using formulas for simple interest, this note is a **simple interest note**. When using the formulas for simple interest, the face value of the note is used as the value for the principal, *P*. Find the interest on the loan as follows.

$$\textbf{Interest} = \textbf{Face value} \times \textbf{Rate} \times \textbf{Time}$$
$$\text{Interest} = \$2500 \times .12 \times \frac{90}{360} = \$75$$

The maturity value of the loan is

$$\textbf{Maturity value} = \textbf{Face value} + \textbf{Interest}$$
$$= \$2500 + \$75 = \$2575$$

Madeline Sullivan must pay $2575 to Charles D. Miller at the note's maturity, or June 4, which is 90 days after March 6.

Almost all notes written by banks are secured by **collateral**. That is, the person borrowing the money *must pledge assets* such as cars, stock, or real estate that are of equal or greater value to the amount of the loan. In the event of nonpayment, the bank will take the collateral and sell or liquidate it. The bank then uses the proceeds to pay off the note—any excess is returned to the maker of the note.

Objective **7** **Find the due date of a note.** When a promissory note is given in months, the loan is due on the same day of the month, after the given number of months has passed. For example, a 4-month note made on May 25 would be due 4 months in the future on September 25. Other examples follow.

Date Made	Length of Loan	Date Due
March 12	5 months	August 12
April 24	7 months	November 24
October 7	9 months	July 7
January 31	3 months	April 30

A loan made on January 31 for 3 months would normally be due on April 31. However, there are only 30 days in April, so the loan is due on April 30. Whenever a due date does not exist, such as February 30 or November 31, use the last day of the month (February 28 or November 30 in these examples).

EXAMPLE 6

Finding Due Date, Interest, and Maturity Value

Find the due date, interest, and maturity value for a loan made September 30 for 5 months at 9.5% with a face value of $2380.

Solution

Counting 5 months from September 30 produces February 30. Since February has only 28 days (if not in a leap year), the note would be due on the last day of February, or February 28. Interest for **5 months** is

$$I = \$2380 \times .095 \times \frac{5}{12} = \$94.21 \text{ (rounded)}$$

with maturity value

$$M = \$2380 + \$94.21 = \$2474.21.$$

A total of $2474.21, representing both principal and interest, must be paid on February 28.

> **PROBLEM-SOLVING HINT** When the length of the loan is given in months, do not convert the time to days in order to find the date due.

8.2 | Finding Principal, Rate, and Time

Objectives

1 Find the principal.
2 Find the rate.
3 Find the time.

Principal, rate, and time were given for most of the problems presented so far in this chapter and interest was calculated. In this section, interest is given and one of the following—principal, rate, or time—is calculated.

> **NOTE** For simplicity, *all problems will assume ordinary interest*, although only a slight change would be needed for exact interest.

Objective 1 Find the principal. The principal (P) can be found by rewriting the simple interest formula $I = PRT$ as

Calculating Principal

$$\text{Principal} = \frac{\text{Interest}}{\text{Rate} \times \text{Time}} \quad \text{or} \quad P = \frac{I}{RT}$$

The various formulas related to the equation $I = PRT$ can either be derived as shown at right below, or can be remembered using a sketch shown at left below. In the sketch, the letter I (for interest) goes on top, with P (principal), R (rate), and T (time) on the bottom. The formula for principal is then found from the sketch by covering the letter P and reading the remaining letters. Notice that interest is always on top.

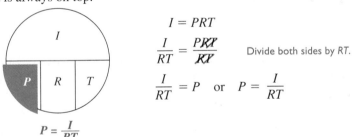

$$I = PRT$$

$$\frac{I}{RT} = \frac{P\cancel{RT}}{\cancel{RT}} \qquad \text{Divide both sides by } RT.$$

$$\frac{I}{RT} = P \quad \text{or} \quad P = \frac{I}{RT}$$

$$P = \frac{I}{RT}$$

See Appendix A for a review of algebra.

> **NOTE** As before, remember that time is measured in years.

EXAMPLE 1
Finding Principal Given Interest in Days

Gilbert Construction Company borrows funds at 10% for 54 days to build a home. Find the principal that results in interest of $780.

Solution
Write the rate as .10, the time as $\frac{54}{360}$, and then use the formula for principal.

$$P = \frac{I}{RT}$$

$$P = \frac{\$780}{.10 \times \dfrac{54}{360}}$$

$$.10 \times \frac{54}{360} = .015 \qquad \text{Simplify the denominator.}$$

$$P = \frac{\$780}{.015} = \$52,000 \qquad \text{Divide.}$$

The principal is $52,000.

Check the answer using the formula for simple interest.

$$I = PRT$$

The interest is $780, the principal is $52,000, the rate is 10%, and the time is 54 days or $\frac{54}{360}$ year.

$$I = \$52,000 \times .10 \times \frac{54}{360} = \$780$$

 The calculator approach to this problem uses parentheses so that the numerator is divided by the entire denominator.

$$780 \boxed{\div} \boxed{(} \ .10 \boxed{\times} \ 54 \boxed{\div} \ 360 \boxed{)} \boxed{=} \ 52{,}000$$

Note: All calculator solutions use a scientific calculator. Refer to Appendix B for scientific calculator basics.

EXAMPLE 2
Finding Principal Given Length of Loan

Frank Thomas took out a loan to pay his college tuition on February 2. The loan was due to be repaid on April 15. The interest on the loan was $37.80 at a rate of 10.5%. Find the principal.

Solution
First find the number of days.

26	days remaining in February
31	March
15	April
72	days from February 2 to April 15

$$T = \frac{72}{360}$$

Now use the following formula.

$$P = \frac{I}{RT}$$

$$P = \frac{\$37.80}{.105 \times \dfrac{72}{360}} \qquad \text{Substitute values into the formula.}$$

$$P = \frac{\$37.80}{.021} = \$1800 \qquad \text{Simplify the denominator.}$$

The principal is $1800. Check the answer using the formula for simple interest.

$$I = \$1800 \times .105 \times \frac{72}{360} = \$37.80$$

OBJECTIVE 2 Find the rate. To find the rate, R, rewrite the formula $I = PRT$ as

$$\text{Rate} = \frac{\text{Interest}}{\text{Principal} \times \text{Time}} \qquad \text{or} \qquad R = \frac{I}{PT}$$

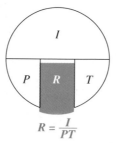

$$R = \frac{I}{PT}$$

$$I = PRT$$

$$\frac{I}{PT} = \frac{\cancel{P}R\cancel{T}}{\cancel{P}\cancel{T}} \qquad \text{Divide both sides by } PT.$$

$$\frac{I}{PT} = R \quad \text{or} \quad R = \frac{I}{PT}$$

See Appendix A for a review of algebra.

EXAMPLE 3

Finding Rate Given Length of Loan

An American living in Brazil invests $2500 in American dollars in a Brazilian bank for 45 days and earns $37.50 interest in American dollars. Find the rate.

SOLUTION

The rate of interest can be found with the following formula.

$$R = \frac{I}{PT}$$

$$R = \frac{\$37.50}{\$2500 \times \dfrac{45}{360}}$$

$$R = \frac{\$37.50}{312.50} \qquad \text{Simplify the denominator.}$$

$$R = .12 \qquad \text{Divide.}$$

Convert .12 to a percent to get the rate of 12%. Then check the answer using the formula for simple interest.

EXAMPLE 4

Finding Rate Given Length of Loan

Jim Rubillo deposits $720 from June 1 to August 16. If he earns $15 interest, what is the rate of interest?

SOLUTION

First, find the number of days, using the table on page 304.

$$
\begin{array}{rr}
\text{August 16 is day} & 228 \\
\text{June 1 is day} & -\ 152 \\
\hline
& \mathbf{76\ days}
\end{array}
$$

There are 76 days from June 1 to August 16

$$T = \frac{76}{360}$$

Now use the formula.

$$R = \frac{I}{PT}$$

$$R = \frac{\$15}{\$720 \times \dfrac{76}{360}} = \frac{15}{152} = .099 \text{ rounded}$$

The rate of interest rounded to the nearest tenth of a percent is 9.9%.

OBJECTIVE **3** **Find the time.** The last letter in the formula $I = PRT$ is T; find T (the time) in years with the following formula.

$$\text{Time (in years)} = \frac{\text{Interest}}{\text{Principal} \times \text{Rate}} \qquad \text{or} \qquad T = \frac{I}{PR}$$

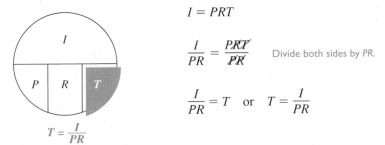

$$I = PRT$$

$$\frac{I}{PR} = \frac{P\!R\!T}{P\!R} \qquad \text{Divide both sides by } PR.$$

$$\frac{I}{PR} = T \quad \text{or} \quad T = \frac{I}{PR}$$

See Appendix A for a review of algebra.

This formula gives the time *in years*. In most problems, however, the time *in days* is needed. Convert time in years to time in days by multiplying the time in years by 360. (For example, $\frac{1}{2}$ year is $\frac{1}{2} \times 360 = 180$ days.) With this change, the formula for time in days is as follows.

$$\text{Time in days} = \frac{I}{PR} \times 360$$

EXAMPLE 5

Finding Time in Days Given Principal and Rate

Suppose $960 is deposited at 8% and earns $64 interest. Find the time in days.

SOLUTION

Find the time in days as follows.

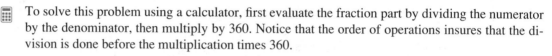

$$\text{Time in days} = \frac{\$64}{\$960 \times .08} \times 360 = \frac{\$64}{960 \times .08} \times \frac{360}{1} = 300$$

The money was deposited for 300 days.

To solve this problem using a calculator, first evaluate the fraction part by dividing the numerator by the denominator, then multiply by 360. Notice that the order of operations insures that the division is done before the multiplication times 360.

$$64 \boxed{\div} \boxed{(} 960 \boxed{\times} .08 \boxed{)} \boxed{\times} 360 \boxed{=} 300$$

Note: All calculator solutions use a scientific calculator. Refer to Appendix B for scientific calculator basics.

SUMMARY

Interest	$I = PRT$	
Principal	$P = \dfrac{I}{RT}$	
Rate	$R = \dfrac{I}{PT}$	All of these are modifications of the formula $I = PRT$.
Time	$T \text{ (in years)} = \dfrac{I}{PR}$	
	$T \text{ (in months)} = \dfrac{I}{PR} \times 12$	
	$T \text{ (in days)} = \dfrac{I}{PR} \times 360$	

8.3 | SIMPLE DISCOUNT NOTES

Objectives

1. Define the basic terms used with simple discount notes.
2. Find the bank discount and proceeds.
3. Find the face value.
4. Find the effective interest rate.

PROBLEM SOLVING IN BUSINESS

Susan Gilbert of Gilbert Construction Company must be familiar with different types of notes because she works with many different lending agencies. Susan Gilbert clearly remembers the first time a banker offered to lend her money using a simple discount note. At the time, she did not understand since she had always used simple interest notes. Now, she commonly uses both types of notes.

Objective 1 Define the basic terms used with simple discount notes. The dollar amount written on the front of a *simple interest note* is called the face value (or principal). The face value of a simple interest note is the amount actually loaned to the borrower. However, face value is *defined differently* in the simple discount notes discussed in this section.

A **simple discount note** has the interest deducted *in advance* from the face value written on the note. In this type of note, the borrower ***never receives*** the face value—rather the borrower receives the face value less interest. These notes are sometimes called **interest-in-advance notes** since the interest is subtracted *before* any money is given to the borrower.

> **NOTE** A simple discount note represents another method for calculating interest.

The face value and the maturity value of a simple discount note are the same. The amount of interest charged is called the **bank discount**, or just the **discount**. The borrower receives a sum of money called the **proceeds**, which equals the face value of the note less the discount.

SIMPLE INTEREST VERSUS SIMPLE DISCOUNT NOTES

Type of Note	Loan Amount		Interest		Repayment Amount
Simple interest	Face value (**Principal**)	+	Interest	=	Maturity value
Simple discount	Proceeds	+	Discount (**Interest**)	=	Face value (**Maturity value**)

As an example of a simple discount note, suppose a borrower signs a note for $2000 with a bank discount of $150. The borrower receives proceeds of

$$\$2000 - \$150 = \$1850.$$

The face value or maturity value of the note is $2000 and the interest charge is $150.

> **NOTE** Simple interest is calculated on the *principal* while simple discount is calculated on the *maturity value*.

Objective 2 Find the bank discount and proceeds. The formula for finding the bank discount is similar to the formula for calculating simple interest. Different letters are used to emphasize that the loan is a discount loan.

Calculating Bank Discount

Bank discount = Face value × Discount rate × Time   or $B = MDT$

where

B = Bank discount

M = Face value (Maturity value)

D = Discount rate

T = Time (in years)

Then, if P is the proceeds:

Proceeds (Loan amount) = Face value − Bank discount   or $P = M - B$

Example 1

Finding Discount and Proceeds

Marie Gostowski borrowed $12,000 for 10 months from Bank of America so that she could buy a new, larger commercial oven for her bakery. The banker discounts the note at 9%. Find the amount of the discount and the proceeds.

Solution

Find the discount with the formula $B = MDT$, with $M = \$12,000$, $D = 9\%$, and $T = \frac{10}{12}$ or $\frac{5}{6}$.

$$B = MDT$$

$$B = \$12,000 \times .09 \times \frac{5}{6} = \textbf{\$900}$$

The discount of $900 is the interest charge on the loan. The proceeds that Gostowski actually receives when making the loan is found using $P = M - B$.

$$P = M - B$$

$$P = \$12,000 - \$900 = \$11,100$$

After signing the note for $12,000, Gostowski will be given $11,100. Then 10 months later, she must make a single payment of $12,000 to the bank.

For related Web activities, go to www.mathbusiness.com

Keyword: repayment

Objective ⬛ **Find the face value.**   Usually, a borrower knows the amount he or she would like to borrow. The following formula can be used to find the face value of a simple discount note so that the proceeds to the borrower will be the amount needed by the borrower. The face value of a simple discount note is the sum of the proceeds to the borrower plus the interest ($M = P + B$).

The face value M of a simple discount note that will give proceeds P, at a discount rate D, and time T in years is

$$M = \frac{P}{1 - DT}$$

The formula derivation is:

$$P = M - B$$
$$P = M - MDT \qquad \text{Substitute } MDT \text{ in place of } B.$$
$$P = M(1 - DT) \qquad \text{Factor } M \text{ out of both terms.}$$
$$M = \frac{P}{(1 - DT)} \qquad \text{Divide both sides by } (1 - DT).$$

EXAMPLE 2

Finding the Face Value

Mike Collins needs $4000 to repair his roof. Find the face value of a note that will provide the $4000 in proceeds if he plans to repay the note in 180 days and the bank charges a 12% discount rate.

SOLUTION

Use the formula.

$$M = \frac{P}{1 - DT}$$

Replace P with $4000, D with .12, and T with $\frac{180}{360}$.

$$M = \frac{\$4000}{1 - \left(.12 \times \frac{180}{360}\right)} = \$4255.32 \text{ (rounded)}$$

Collins must sign a note with a face value of $4255.32 (to the nearest cent) to receive the $4000 needed to repair the roof.

 The expression $\dfrac{\$4000}{1 - \left(.12 \times \frac{180}{360}\right)}$

can be evaluated using a scientific calculator by first thinking of the problem as shown with brackets to set off the denominator:

$$\$4000 \div \left[1 - \left(.12 \times \frac{180}{360}\right) \right].$$

Parentheses are not really needed due to order of operations. The problem is then solved as follows.

4000 $\boxed{\div}$ $\boxed{(}$ 1 $\boxed{-}$ .12 $\boxed{\times}$ 180 $\boxed{\div}$ 360 $\boxed{)}$ $\boxed{=}$ 4255.32 (rounded)

Note: All calculator solutions use a scientific calculator. Refer to Appendix B for scientific calculator basics.

> **PROBLEM-SOLVING HINT**   A discount rate of 12% is not the same as an interest rate of 12% as shown in the next example.

EXAMPLE 3

Comparing Discount Notes and Simple Interest Notes

Susan Gilbert of Gilbert Construction Company is comparing a simple interest note to a simple discount note. Each note has a face value of $7500 and a time of 90 days. One note has a simple interest rate of 12% and the other a discount rate of 12%.

SOLUTION

(a) Find the interest owed on each.

Simple Interest Note	Simple Discount Note
$I = PRT$	$B = MDT$
$I = \$7500 \times .12 \times \frac{90}{360}$	$B = \$7500 \times .12 \times \frac{90}{360}$
$I = \$225$	$B = \$225$

In each case, the interest is $225.

(b) Find the amount actually received by the borrower in each case.

Simple Interest Note	Simple Discount Note
Principal = Face value = $7500	Proceeds = $M - B$ = $7500 - $225 = $7275

With the simple interest note, the borrower has the use of $7500, but only $7275 is available with the simple discount note. In each case, the interest charge is the same, $225, but more money is available with the simple interest note. Thus, 12% simple interest is better for the borrower than is 12% simple discount.

(c) Find the maturity value for each note.

Simple Interest Note	Simple Discount Note
$M = P + I$	Maturity value = Face value
$\quad = \$7500 + \$225$	$= \$7500$
$\quad = \$7725$	

The differences between these two notes can be summarized as follows.

	Simple Interest Note	Simple Discount Note
Face value	$7500.00	$7500.00
Interest	$225.00	$225.00
Amount available to borrower	$7500.00	$7275.00
Maturity value	$7725.00	$7500.00

Objective **4** **Find the effective interest rate.** Because of possible confusion resulting from the different ways of calculating interest charges, the **Federal Truth-in-Lending Act** was passed in 1969. This law requires that all interest rates be given as comparable percents. While this law is discussed in more detail in Chapter 11, the next example shows how to get the simple interest rate corresponding to the given discount rate of Example 3.

EXAMPLE 4

Finding Effective Interest Rate

Find the effective rate of interest for the simple discount note of Example 3.

Solution

The discount (nominal or stated) rate of 12% given in Example 3 is not the effective or true rate of interest, since the 12% applies to the maturity value of $7500 and not to the proceeds of $7275 received by the borrower. Find the effective interest rate using the formula for simple interest, $I = PRT$. Here, $I = \$225$ (the discount), $P = \$7275$ (the proceeds), $T = \frac{90}{360}$ year, and R must be found.

Find the effective rate of interest with the formula for rate, given earlier:

$$R = \frac{I}{PT}$$

Then substitute the given numbers.

$$R = \frac{\$225}{\$7275 \times \dfrac{90}{360}} = 12.37\% \text{ (rounded)}$$

The interest rate 12.37% is called the **effective rate of interest** or **true rate of interest**. Federal regulations require that rates be rounded to the nearest quarter of a percent when communicated to a borrower. 12.37% is closer to 12.25% than to 12.50%. Therefore, an **annual percentage rate (APR)** of 12.25% must be reported to someone signing a discount note with a face value of $7500 for 90 days at a discount rate of 12%.

> **PROBLEM-SOLVING HINT** The discount rate is not an interest rate to be applied to proceeds (loan amount)—rather it is applied to face value.

One common use of discount interest is related to **U.S. Treasury bills** or **T-bills**, as they are also called. The federal government uses T-bills to borrow money. They are currently available with maturities of 13 weeks, 26 weeks, and 52 weeks. An investor buys a T-bill at a price equal to the proceeds *after the discount is subtracted* and receives the full face value from the government at maturity. T-bills are considered a very safe investment since they are loans to the U.S. government.

EXAMPLE 5
Finding Facts
About T-Bills

An Italian bank is worried about devaluation of their currency, so it purchases $1,000,000 in U.S. T-bills in order to place cash in a safe place for a short period of time. The T-bills are at a 4% discount rate for 26 weeks. Find **(a)** the total purchase price, **(b)** the total maturity value, **(c)** the interest earned, and **(d)** the effective rate of interest.

Solution

$M = \$1,000,000; D = .04; T = \frac{26}{52}$

(a) Bank discount = Face value × Discount rate × Time
$$= \$1,000,000 \times .04 \times \tfrac{26}{52} = \$20,000$$

Purchase price = Face value − Bank discount
$$= \$1,000,000 - \$20,000 = \$980,000$$

(b) Maturity value = Face value
$$= \$1,000,000$$

(c) Interest = Bank discount
$$= \$20,000$$

(d) Effective rate $= \dfrac{\text{Interest earned}}{\text{Purchase price (proceeds)} \times \text{Time}}$

$$= \frac{\$20,000}{\$980,000 \times \frac{26}{52}} = .04081 = 4.08\%$$

8.4 | DISCOUNTING A NOTE BEFORE MATURITY

Objectives

1. Find the bank discount.
2. Find the proceeds.

Susan Gilbert of Gilbert Construction Company needed cash. Her first thought was to sell the $100,000 Treasury bill she had bought only 8 weeks earlier, but she didn't know how much she would receive for it. (See Example 3.)

Objective 1 Find the bank discount. A note represents *a legal responsibility* for one party to pay a certain amount of money, on a specific date, to a second party. These notes can readily be sold or transferred.

Businesses often accept either simple interest notes or simple discount notes instead of immediate payment for goods or services. For example, a manufacturer of pleasure boats may deliver goods to retail stores in February *but not collect* from the stores until August, or even later. The manufacturer may request promissory notes from each retail store receiving boats in order to insure payment.

The manufacturer may have a lot of cash tied up in promissory notes that will not be paid until August. The firm can get cash *before the notes mature* in August by selling them to a bank. The bank gives the manufacturer the maturity value of the notes *less a fee* charged by the bank for the service. The fee, which is interest charged for the number of days the bank will hold each note before it is paid, is called the **bank discount** or just **discount**. The process of finding the value for *the* note as of a specific date is called **discounting a note**.

Objective 2 Find the proceeds. The amount of cash actually received by the manufacturer of pleasure boats on the sale of a promissory note to the bank is called the **proceeds**. The bank collects the maturity value from the maker of the note when it becomes due. Normally, such notes are sold with **recourse**. This means that if the maker of the note *does not pay*, the bank collects from the seller of the note, which protects the bank against loss.

Use the following procedure to discount a note.

> 1. Find the **maturity value** of the original note (if necessary).
> 2. Find the **discount period**.
> 3. Find the **discount**, using the formula $B = MDT$.
> 4. The **proceeds** are found by using $P = M - B$.

This method is shown in the next examples.

EXAMPLE 1

Finding Proceed

Blues Recording Studio holds a 200-day simple interest note from a rock music group that agreed to pay them to record an album and produce 1000 copies on compact discs. The note is dated March 24 and has a face value of $4800 with simple interest of 12%. Blues Recording wishes to convert the note to cash on August 15. Given a discount rate of 12.5%, find the proceeds to the Recording Studio.

Solution

Go through the four steps of discounting a note.

Step 1 First find the interest on the simple interest note if held until maturity.

$$\text{Interest} = \$4800 \times .12 \times \frac{200}{360} = \$320$$

The **maturity value** is: $4800 + $320 = $5120.

Step 2   Find the **discount period**, the number of days remaining from August 15 until the note is due. The discount period is often found by using a diagram as shown.

In this example, the date of the note is March 24, the discount date is August 15, and the due date is October 10. August 15 to October 10 is 56 days found as follows.

16	days left in August
30	days in September
10	days until note is due in October
56	days of discount period

Verify 56 days using the number of each of the days of the year table on page 304.

Step 3   Find the bank **discount**, using the formula $B = MDT$, where $M = \$5120$, $D = 12.5\%$, and T is $\frac{56}{360}$.

$$B = \$5120 \times .125 \times \frac{56}{360} = \$99.56 \text{ (rounded)}$$

The bank discount is $99.56.

Step 4   Find the **proceeds** using the formula $P = M - B$

$$P = \$5120 - \$99.56 = \$5020.44$$

The bank purchases the note on August 15 for $5020.44 in cash paid to Blues Recording Studio. Then, on the maturity date of October 10, the bank will collect $5120 from the maker of the note. In summary:

Date	Transaction
March 24	Rock group signs 200-day simple interest note for $4800.
August 15	Blues Recording Studio sells note to bank for $5020.44.
October 10	Bank receives $5120 from payer (rock group).

> **NOTE**   In discounting a note, the business receives less money but it will receive the money sooner.

EXAMPLE 2
Finding Proceeds

On March 27, Andrews Motors received a 150-day note with a face value of $3500, at 11% interest per year. On April 24, the firm discounts the note at the bank. Find the proceeds to Andrews Motors if the bank discount rate is 14%.

SOLUTION

Again, go through the four steps in discounting a note.

Step 1   Find the interest and maturity value.

$$\text{Interest} = \$3500 \times .11 \times \frac{150}{360} = \$160.42$$

The interest on the note is $160.42. The maturity value is

$$M = \$3500 \text{ (face value)} + \$160.42 \text{ (interest)} = \$3660.42$$

Step 2 Find the discount period using the diagram. (Remember, the discount period is calculated from the discount date of the loan, not the date the loan was made.)

Discount Period = 122 Days

Date Loan Was Made — Discount Date — Loan Due Date

March 27 — April 24 — August 24

Length of Loan: 150 Days

The discount period here is 122 days.

Step 3 Find the bank discount, using the discount rate of 14%.

$$\$3660.42 \times .14 \times \frac{122}{360} = \$173.67$$

The bank discount is $173.67.

Step 4 Find the proceeds.

$$P = M - B$$
$$P = \$3660.42 - \$173.67 = \$3486.75$$

Andrews Motors receives $3486.75 from the bank on April 24. The bank then collects $3660.42 from the maker of the note on August 24, the maturity date.

> **PROBLEM-SOLVING HINT** Be sure to use the maturity value and *not the face value* when determining the bank discount.

Not only are notes discounted, it is also common for a business needing cash to sell part of its accounts receivable (money owed to the business) to a financial institution. This process is called **factoring**, and those who buy the accounts receivable are called **factors**. The calculations involved in factoring are the same as those for finding the discount discussed in this section.

EXAMPLE 3
Finding the Proceeds

Gilbert Construction Company used excess cash to purchase a $100,000 Treasury bill with a term of 26 weeks at a 6.5% discount rate. However, the firm needs cash exactly 8 weeks later and sells the T-bill. During the 8 weeks, market interest rates moved up slightly so that the bill was sold at a 7% discount rate. Find **(a)** the initial purchase price of the T-bill, **(b)** the proceeds received by the firm at the subsequent sale of the T-bill, and **(c)** the effective interest rate received by the firm.

SOLUTION

(a) Find the discount and initial cost of the T-bill.

$$B = MDT = \$100,000 \times .065 \times \frac{26}{52} = \$3250$$

Initial purchase price $= M - B = \$100,000 - \$3250 = \$96,750$

(b) Discount the note at 7%.
The T-bill was sold 26 − 8 = **18 weeks before its due date.**

$$B = MDT = \$100,000 \times .07 \times \frac{18}{52} = \$2423.08$$

$$P = M - B = \$100,000 - \$2423.08 = \$97,576.92$$

The proceeds from the sale of the T-bill equal $97,576.92.

(c) Gilbert Construction Company spent $96,750 to buy the T-bill and received $97,576.92 for it 8 weeks later.

$$\text{Interest received} = \$97,576.92 - \$96,750 = \mathbf{\$826.92}$$

$$R = \frac{\$826.92}{\$96,750 \times \frac{8}{52}} = 5.56\% \text{ (rounded)}$$

The construction company would have earned 6.5% on the T-bill had they left it invested until maturity. Instead, they sold it after market interest rates rose but before the T-bill matured. This caused them to end up with an effective interest rate somewhat less than 6.5%.

Name   Date   Class

Supplementary Exercises on Simple Interest and Simple Discount

The **Quick Start** *exercises in each section contain solutions to help you get started.*

There are similarities and differences between simple interest and simple discount calculations. This exercise set compares these two important concepts. First, the key similarities between the two are as follows.

1. Both types of notes involve lump sums repaid with a single payment at the end of a stated period of time.
2. The length of time is generally 1 year or less.

The following table compares simple interest and simple discount notes.

	Simple Interest Note	Simple Discount Note
Variables	I = Interest P = Principal (face value) R = Rate of interest T = Time, in years or fraction of a year M = Maturity value	B = Discount P = Proceeds D = Discount rate T = Time, in years or fraction of a year M = Maturity value
Face value	Stated on note	Same as maturity value
Interest charge	$I = PRT$	$B = MDT$
Maturity value	$M = P + I$	Same as face value
Amount received by borrower	Face value or principal	Proceeds, $P = M - B$
Identifying phrases	Interest at a certain rate Maturity value greater than face value	Discount at a certain rate Proceeds Maturity value equal to face value
Effective interest rate	Same as stated rate, R	Greater than stated rate, D

> **NOTE**   The variable P is used for *principal or face value* in simple interest notes, but P is used for *proceeds* in simple discount notes. P represents the amount received by the borrower.

Solve the following application problems. Round rates to the nearest tenth of a percent, time to the nearest day, and money to the nearest cent.

Quick Start

1. The owner of Ben's Bagel Shop signed a note for $25,000 to expand his store. The note was for 250 days at a discount rate of 12%. Find the proceeds.

   $B = \$25{,}000 \times .12 \times \frac{250}{360} = \$2083.33; \ P = \$25{,}000 - \$2083.33 = \$22{,}916.67$

1. $22,916.67

2. Bill Travis signed a note for $18,500 with his uncle to start an auto repair shop on Commerce Street. The note is due in 300 days and has a discount rate of 14%. Travis hopes that a bank will refinance the note for him at a lower rate after he has been in business for 300 days. Find the proceeds.

$B = \$18,500 \times .14 \times \frac{300}{360} = \$2158.33$; $P = \$18,500 - \$2158.33 = \$16,341.67$

2. $16,341.67

3. A simple interest note has a face value of $9800, a rate of $10\frac{1}{4}\%$, and interest of $669.67. Find the length of the loan in days.

3. _____

4. Jackson Company signed a $45,000 note with a 13.5% discount of $1248.75. What is the length of the the loan in days?

4. _____

5. A loan to a German bank was for $1,290,000 with a maturity value of $1,327,410 and a rate of 6%. Find the time.

5. _____

6. Joanna Walker loaned her twin sister Jessie $1400. Jessie agreed to repay $1500 at 10% interest. Find the term of the loan.

6. _____

7. Gilbert Construction Company signed a 5-month, $145,000 note at a 11.5% discount rate. Find the effective rate of interest.

7. _____

8. First Bank signed an 80-day, $82,000 note at a 12% discount rate. Find the effective rate of interest.

8. _____

9. On October 14, Citibank loaned $10,000,000 to Fleet Mortgage Company for 180 days at a 10.5% discount rate. Find **(a)** the due date and **(b)** the proceeds.

(a) _____
(b) _____

10. On December 24, Junella Martin signed a 100-day note for $80,000 for a new Jaguar. Given a discount rate of 11%, find **(a)** the due date and **(b)** the proceeds.

(a) _____
(b) _____

Name	Date	Class

11. Lupe Galvez has a serious problem—two of her more energetic preschoolers keep getting out of the yard of her child-care center. She signs a note with interest charges of $670.83 to put a new fence around the entire yard and to rebuild the playground at the same time. The simple interest note is for 140 days at 11.5%. Find the principal to the nearest dollar.

11. _____

12. Mr. Thomas signed a simple interest note with an interest rate of 14%, interest charges of $199.99, and a term of 85 days. Find the principal.

12. _____

13. Tom Watson Insurance accepted a 270-day, $8000 note on May 25. The interest rate on the note is 12%. The note was then discounted at 16% on August 7. Find the proceeds.

13. _____

14. On November 19, a firm accepts an $18,000, 150-day note with an interest rate of 9%. The firm discounts the note at 12% on February 2. Find the proceeds.

14. _____

15. Linda Youngman accepted a $16,000, 150-day note from a customer. The note had an interest rate of 11% and was accepted on May 12. The note was then discounted at 13% on July 20. Find the proceeds to Youngman.

15. _____

16. The Florist Wholesale Shop accepted a 210-day, $6420 note on December 12. Find the proceeds if the interest rate on the note is 12% and the note was discounted at 15% on January 19.

16. _____

17. Fine Furniture, Inc. wishes to borrow $65,000 for 150 days to cover a shipment of furniture. One bank agrees to a simple interest note with a loan amount of $65,000 at 13% interest. A second bank agrees to a simple discount note with proceeds of $65,000 and a 14% simple discount rate. Find **(a)** the interest for the simple interest note, **(b)** the maturity value of the discount note, **(c)** the interest for the discount note, and **(d)** the savings in interest charges of the simple interest note over the discount note.

(a) _____
(b) _____
(c) _____
(d) _____

18. Gilbert Construction Company needs to borrow $380,000 for $1\frac{1}{2}$ years to purchase some land to subdivide. One bank offers the firm a simple interest note with a principal of $380,000 and a rate of 12%. A second bank offers them a discount note with proceeds of $380,000 and an 11% discount rate. **(a)** Which note produces the lower interest charges? **(b)** What is the difference in interest?

(a) _____

(b) _____

19. Show with an example that the effective interest rate is greater than the discount rate stated on a note.

20. Explain the difference in meaning of the variable P (principal) in a simple interest note and the variable P (proceeds) in a simple discount note.

CHAPTER TERMS

Review the following terms to test your understanding of the chapter. For each term you do not know, refer to the page number found next to that term.

annual percentage rate [**p. 324**]
bank discount [**p. 321**]
collateral [**p. 307**]
compound interest [**p. 301**]
discount [**p. 321**]
discounting a note [**p. 331**]
discount period [**p. 332**]
discount rate [**p. 322**]

effective rate of interest [**p. 324**]
face value [**p. 307**]
factors [**p. 333**]
factoring [**p. 333**]
Federal Truth-in-Lending Act [**p. 324**]
interest [**p. 301**]
interest-in-advance notes [**p. 321**]

maker of a note [**p. 307**]
maturity value [**p. 303**]
payee of a note [**p. 307**]
payer of a note [**p. 307**]
prime rate [**p. 301**]
principal [**p. 302**]
proceeds of a note [**p. 321**]
promissory note [**p. 306**]
rate [**p. 322**]

recourse [**p. 331**]
simple interest [**p. 301**]
simple discount note [**p. 321**]
simple interest note [**p. 307**]
T-bills [**p. 324**]
term of a note [**p. 307**]
true rate of interest [**p. 324**]
U.S. Treasury bills [**p. 324**]

CONCEPTS	EXAMPLES
8.1 Finding simple interest when time is expressed in years 1. Use formula $I = PRT$. 2. Express R in decimal form. 3. Express time in years. 4. Substitute values for P, R, and T and multiply.	A loan of $5900 is made for $1\frac{3}{4}$ years at 10% per year; find the simple interest. $I = PRT$ $I = \$5900 \times .10 \times 1.75 = \$1032.50$ The simple interest is $1032.50.
8.1 Finding simple interest when time is expressed in months 1. Use formula $I = PRT$. 2. Express R in decimal form. 3. Express time in years by dividing number of months by 12. 4. Substitute values for P, R, and T and multiply.	Find the simple interest on $2400 for 15 months at 10%. $I = PRT$ $I = \$2400 \times .10 \times \dfrac{15}{12} = \$300$ The simple interest is $300.
8.1 Finding the maturity value of a loan 1. Find I, using the formula $I = PRT$. 2. Find the maturity value using the formula $M = P + I$.	A loan of $2500 is made for 2 years at 9%; find the maturity value of the loan. $I = PRT$ $I = \$2500 \times .09 \times 2 = \$450$ $M = P + I$ $M = \$2500 + \$450 = \$2950$ The maturity value is $2950.
8.1 Finding the number of days from one date to another using a table 1. Find the day corresponding to the final date using the table. 2. Find the day corresponding to the initial date. 3. Subtract the smaller number from the larger number.	Find the number of days from February 15 to July 28. 1. July 28 is day 209 2. Feb. 15 is day 46 3. Number of days is $\begin{array}{r} 209 \\ -\ 46 \\ \hline 163 \end{array}$ There are 163 days from February 15 to July 28.

CONCEPTS	EXAMPLES
8.1 Finding the number of days from one date to another using actual number of days in a month Add actual number of days in each month or partial month from initial date to final date.	Find the number of days from April 20 to June 27. April 20–April 30 10 days May 31 days June <u>27 days</u> 68 days
8.1 Finding exact interest Use the formula $$I = PRT$$ with $T = \dfrac{\text{No. of days of loan}}{365}$	Find the exact interest on a \$9000 loan at 8% for 140 days. $$I = PRT$$ $$I = \$9000 \times .08 \times \frac{140}{365} = \$276.16$$ The exact interest is \$276.16.
8.1 Finding ordinary or banker's interest Use the formula $$I = PRT$$ with $T = \dfrac{\text{No. of days of loan}}{360}$	Find the ordinary interest on a loan of \$1200 at 7% for 120 days. $$I = PRT$$ $$I = \$1200 \times .07 \times \frac{120}{360} = \$28$$ The ordinary or banker's interest is \$28.
8.1 Finding the due date, interest, and maturity value of a promissory note when the term of loan is in months Add number of months in term of note to initial date of note. Use formula $I = PRT$ to find interest. Find maturity value as follows. Maturity value = Principal + Interest	Find the due date, the interest, and the maturity value of a loan made on February 15 for 7 months at 8% with a face value of \$1500. September 15 is 7 months from February 15, so note is due on September 15. $$I = PRT$$ $$I = \$1500 \times .08 \times \frac{7}{12} = \$70$$ $$M = \text{Principal} + \text{Interest}$$ $$M = \$1500 + \$70 = \$1570$$
8.1 Finding due date of a promissory note when term of loan is expressed in days Use either a table or the actual number of days.	A loan is made on August 14 and is due in 80 days. Find the due date. August 14–August 31 17 days September 30 days October <u>31 days</u> 78 days The loan is for 80 days, which is 2 days more than 78. Therefore, the loan is due on November 2.
8.1 Finding the time of a note in days given maturity value, face value, and interest rate Use formula $I = M - P$ to find interest (I). Use the formula $$T = \frac{I}{PR} \times 360$$ to find the time in days.	A note has a face value of \$4800, an interest rate of 12%, and a maturity value of \$5200. Find the time of the note in days. $$I = \$5200 - \$4800 = \$400$$ $$T = \frac{\$400}{\$4800 \times .12} \times 360 = 250 \text{ days}$$

CONCEPTS	EXAMPLES
8.2 Finding principal given interest, interest rate, and time Use the formula $$P = \dfrac{I}{RT}$$ 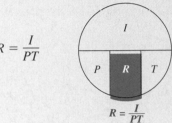 $P = \dfrac{I}{RT}$	Find the principal that gives an interest of $24 at 9% for 60 days. $$P = \dfrac{I}{RT}$$ $$P = \dfrac{\$24}{.09 \times \dfrac{60}{360}} = \$1600$$ The principal is $1600.
8.2 Finding the rate of interest given principal, interest, and time Use the formula $$R = \dfrac{I}{PT}$$ 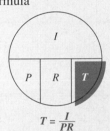 $R = \dfrac{I}{PT}$	A principal of $8000 deposited for 45 days earns interest of $40. Find the rate of interest. $$R = \dfrac{I}{PT}$$ $$R = \dfrac{\$40}{\$8000 \times \dfrac{45}{360}} = .04$$ Rate of interest = 4%.
8.2 Finding the time given principal, rate of interest, and interest To find the time in days use the formula $$T \text{ (in days)} = \dfrac{I}{PR} \times 360$$ $T = \dfrac{I}{PR}$	Tom Jones invested $4000 at 8% and earned an interest of $160. Find the number of days. $$T = \dfrac{I}{PR} \times 360$$ $$T = \dfrac{\$160}{\$4000 \times .08} \times 360 = 180 \text{ days}$$
8.3 Finding the proceeds of a simple discount note Calculate bank discount using the formula $B = MDT$. Then calculate the proceeds or loan amount using the formula $P = M - B$.	Bill Pattern borrows $6000 for 130 days at a discount rate of 12%. Find the proceeds. $$B = MDT$$ $$B = \$6000 \times .12 \times \dfrac{130}{360} = \$260$$ $$P = M - B$$ $$P = \$6000 - \$260 = \$5740$$
8.3 Finding the face value of a simple discount note Use the formula $$M = \dfrac{P}{1 - DT}$$	Sam Spade needs $15,000 to expand his restaurant. Find the face value of a note that will provide the $15,000 in proceeds if he plans to repay the note in 180 days and the bank charges an 11% discount rate. $$M = \dfrac{P}{1 - DT}$$ $$M = \dfrac{\$15,000}{1 - \left(.11 \times \dfrac{180}{360}\right)} = \$15,873.02 \text{ (rounded)}$$

CONCEPTS	EXAMPLES

8.3 Finding the effective interest rate

Find the interest (B) from the formula

$$B = MDT.$$

Find proceeds from the formula

$$P = M - B.$$

Then use the formula

$$R = \frac{I}{PT}.$$

A 150-day, 11% simple discount note has a face value of $12,400. Find the effective rate to the nearest tenth of a percent.

$$I = \$12,400 \times .11 \times \frac{150}{360} = \$568.33$$

$$P = \$12,400 - \$568.33 = \$11,831.67$$

$$R = \frac{\$568.33}{\$11,831.67 \times \frac{150}{360}} = 11.5\% \text{ (rounded)}$$

8.4 Finding the proceeds to an individual or firm that discounts a note

Use the following steps:

1. Find the maturity value.
2. Determine the discount period.
3. Calculate the bank discount.
4. Find the proceeds.

Moe's Ice Cream holds a 150-day note dated March 1 with a face value of $1500 and interest rate of 9%. Moe sells the note at a discount on June 1. Assume a discount rate of 11%. Find the proceeds.

$$\text{Interest} = \$1500 \times .09 \times \frac{150}{360} = \$56.25$$

$$\text{Maturity value} = \$1500 + \$56.25 = \$1556.25$$

The discount period is 58 days.

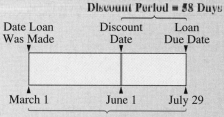

Calculate the bank discount.

$$B = \$1556.25 \times .11 \times \frac{58}{360} = \$27.58$$

Find the proceeds.

$$P = \$1556.25 - \$27.58 = \$1528.67$$

CHAPTER 8 | SUMMARY EXERCISE

BANKING IN A GLOBAL WORLD: HOW DO LARGE BANKS MAKE MONEY?

A bank in California, Bank of America, borrowed $80,000,000 at 9% interest for 180 days from a Japanese investment house. At the same time, the bank made the following loans, each for the exact same 180-day period:

1. An 11% simple interest note for $38,000,000 to a Canadian firm that extracts oil from Canadian tar sands;

2. A 12.8%, simple discount note for $27,500,000 to a French contractor building a factory in South Africa; and

3. A 12%, simple discount note for $14,500,000 to a Louisiana company building minesweepers in New Orleans for the Egyptian government.

For related Web
activities, go to
www.mathbusiness.com

Keyword:
yen

(a) Find the difference between interest received and interest paid by the bank on these funds.

(a) _____

(b) The bank did not loan out all $80,000,000. Find the amount they actually loaned out.

(b) _____

Investigate

Interest rates vary from country to country. In fact, the very idea of interest is not equally accepted in all societies. For example, interest is not allowed in many Islamic countries. Banking still exists in these countries; it just works somewhat differently. Use financial newspapers, magazines, or the World Wide Web and find interest rates in three different countries and compare them to rates in the United States.

For related Web activities, go to www.mathbusiness.com

'Net Assets

U.S. HOME

STATISTICS

• 1954: Established

• 1998: Revenues of $1.5 billion

• Average sale price of homes: $182,600

• Named National Builder of the Year by *Professional Builder* magazine

U.S. Home was established in 1954 with the intention of becoming a nation-wide home-building company that provides unique home design in a variety of locations across the United States. Having achieved this goal, the firm has built nearly 300,000 homes in 12 states. The company builds homes in more than 190 communities and has become one of the nation's largest retirement and active-adult home builders.

With a mortgage company as part of the organization, U.S. Home is also able to provide funding to thousands of home buyers each year. U.S. Home Mortgage Corporation, finances over 80% of the homes that the company builds. The mortgage group helps individuals finance houses using FHA, VA, or conventional loans. The company borrows money to purchase and develop large tracts of acreage. At the end of 1998, long-term debt was $425 million.

1. U.S. Home plans to build 10,000 homes in 2001. If U.S. Home Mortgage Corporation finances 83% of these, how many homes should they prepare to finance in 2001? Assume an average sales price of $185,000 and find the total value of the homes U.S. Home Mortgage Corporation should expect to finance in 2001?

2. Assume U.S. Home borrows $28,000,000 at 8% on a simple interest note from Bank of America for 9 months. Find the interest and maturity value.

3. What do you think would happen to U.S. Home's business if interest rates suddenly went much higher? Why?

4. What type of image do you think U.S. Home wishes to convey to the potential home buyer? Why?

CHAPTER 8 | TEST

To help you review, the numbers in brackets show the section in which the topic was discussed.

Find the simple interest for each of the following. Round to the nearest cent. **[8.1]**

1. $12,500 at $10\frac{1}{2}$% for 280 days

1. _____

2. $8250 at $9\frac{1}{4}$% for 8 months

2. _____

3. A loan of $6000 at 11% made on June 8 and due August 22

3. _____

4. A promissory note for $4500 at 10.3% made on November 13 and due March 8

4. _____

Find the maturity value for the following simple interest note using exact interest. (Round to the nearest cent or to the nearest tenth of a percent, whichever applies.) **[8.1]**

Principal	Rate	Time	Maturity Value
5. $23,400	10.8%	220 days	_____

6. Tom's Toy Shop borrowed $12,500. The loan was repaid in 5 months, with interest at 12%. Find the total amount of the repayment. **[8.1]**

6. _____

7. Glenda Pierce plans to borrow $14,000 for a new hot tub and deck for her home. She has decided on a term of 200 days at 10.5%. However, she has a choice of two lenders. One finds interest using a 360-day year and the other uses a 365-day year. Find the amount of interest Pierce will save by using the lender with the 365-day year. **[8.1]**

7. _____

8. Lupe Gonzalez has $6500 in her retirement account. Find the interest rate required for the fund to grow to $7247.50 in 15 months. **[8.2]**

8. _____

9. Hilda Heinz lends $1200 to her sister Olga at a rate of 9%. Find how long it will take for her investment to earn $100 in interest. (Round to the nearest day.) **[8.2]**

9. _____

10. A woman invested money received from an insurance settlement for 7 months at 5% interest. If she received $1254.17 interest on her investment during this time, find the amount that she invested. (Round to the nearest dollar.) **[8.2]**

10. _____

11. Mike Fagan needs $25,000 to expand his flower shop. Find the face value of a note that will provide the $25,000 in proceeds if he plans to repay the note in 240 days and the bank charges a 9% discount rate. **[8.3]**

11. _____

Find the discount and the proceeds for the following simple discount notes. **[8.3]**

Face Value	Discount Rate	Time (Days)	Discount	Proceeds
12. $9800	11%	120	_____	_____
13. $10,250	9.5%	60	_____	_____

14. Nancy Diggs borrowed $6350 at a 12% discount rate for 120 days. Find the effective rate, rounded to the nearest tenth. **[8.3]**

14. _____

15. A $20,000 T-bill is purchased at a 3.75% discount rate for 13 weeks. Find **(a)** the purchase price of the T-bill, **(b)** the maturity value, **(c)** the interest earned, and **(d)** the effective rate of inerest to the nearest hundredth of a percent. **[8.3]**

(a) _____
(b) _____
(c) _____
(d) _____

Each of the following notes was discounted at 16%. Find the discount period, the discount, and the proceeds. **[8.4]**

Date Loan Was Made	Face Value	Length of Loan	Rate	Date of Discount	Discount Period	Discount	Proceeds
16. Mar. 24	$7000	90 days	12%	Apr. 24	_____	_____	_____
17. Jan. 25	$9200	90 days	10%	Mar. 12	_____	_____	_____

18. Ms. Flower of Flower's Day Care loans $8000 to her uncle for 120 days at 12% interest on October 30. On January 3, Flower sells the note at a discount of 13%. Find **(a)** the discount and **(b)** the proceeds. **[8.4]**

(a) _____
(b) _____

CHAPTER 9

COMPOUND INTEREST

 ank of America is a large bank with branches across the country. Individuals and firms deposit money with the bank through checking ac counts, savings accounts, and certificates of deposit. In turn, the bank lends money to individuals and firms with good credit histories. There are many things Bank of America customers can do *electronically over the Internet*, including balancing their checking accounts, applying for loans and credit cards, and transferring money.

For related Web activities, go to www.mathbusiness.com

Simple interest is interest paid only on the principal—not on any past interest. However, bank deposits commonly earn **compound interest**. Compound interest is calculated on any interest previously credited (paid) to the account in addition to the original principal.

Keyword: interested

9.1 | COMPOUND INTEREST

Objectives

1. Find compound interest, using the formula $I = PRT$.
2. Decide on a period of compounding.
3. Use the formulas and tables to find compound amount and compound interest.

PROBLEM SOLVING IN BUSINESS

Suppose you have $2000 to deposit for 3 years. Should you deposit the money with Bank of America at 7% compounded annually, or would you be better off lending the money to your uncle who has agreed to pay you 7% simple interest? Knowing the difference between the types of interest when saving or borrowing money can save you hundreds of dollars.

Objective **1** **Find compound interest, using the formula** $I = PRT$. **Compound interest** is found by calculating interest on both interest *previously credited* and the original principal. Using the example of a 3 year deposit of $2000 at 7% per year compounded annually, interest at the end of the first year is found using $I = PRT$ and maturity value is found using $M = P + I$.

$$\text{Interest} = \$2000 \times .07 \times 1 = \$140$$
$$\text{Value at end of 1 year} = \$2000 + \$140 = \mathbf{\$2140}$$

Interest and maturity value for the *second* year is similarly calculated except the year 2 beginning principal is $2140, not $2000.

$$\text{Interest} = \mathbf{\$2140} \times .07 \times 1 = \$149.80$$
$$\text{Value at end of 2 years} = \$2140 + \$149.80 = \mathbf{\$2289.80}$$

Interest and maturity value for the *third* year is based on a beginning principal of $2289.80.

$$\text{Interest} = \mathbf{\$2289.80} \times .07 \times 1 = \$160.29$$
$$\text{Maturity value} = \$2289.80 + \$160.29 = \$2450.09$$

This amount, $2450.09, the final amount on deposit at the end of the 3 years, is called the **compound amount**. The interest earned during the 3 years is found as follows.

> **Interest = Compound amount − Original principal**

The total interest paid over the 3 years in this example is

$$\text{Interest} = \$2450.09 - \$2000 = \$450.09.$$

As a comparison, *simple* interest on $2000 for 3 years is

$$\text{Interest} = \$2000 \times .07 \times 3 = \$420.$$

The use of compound interest results in an extra $450.09 − $420 = $30.09 in interest over the 3 years.

Compound interest has a significant effect when applied over long periods of time. For example, assume $1 was invested in an account paying 3% compounded annually in 1492, the year Christopher Columbus arrived in the Americas. The $1 investment *would have grown to over* $3,300,000 by year 2000. If your parents invested $1 for you when you were born, it would grow to $79.06 by your 75th birthday assuming 6% per year compounded annually.

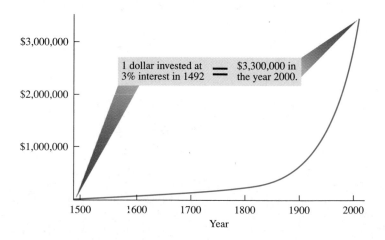

PROBLEM-SOLVING HINT Relatively small differences in interest rates can add up to large differences in compound amount over time.

EXAMPLE 1

Finding Compound Interest

Tom and Gloria Peters hope to have $5000 in 4 years for a down payment on their first home. They invest $3800 in an account that pays 6% interest at the end of each year, on previous interest in addition to principal. **(a)** Find the excess of compound interest over simple interest after 4 years. **(b)** Will they have enough money at the end of 4 years to meet their goal of a down payment?

SOLUTION

(a)

Year	Interest	Compound Amount
1	$3800.00 × .06 × 1 = $228.00	$3800.00 + **$228.00** = $4028.00
2	$4028.00 × .06 × 1 = $241.68	$4028.00 + **$241.68** = $4269.68
3	$4269.68 × .06 × 1 = $256.18	$4269.68 + **$256.18** = $4525.86
4	$4525.86 × .06 × 1 = $271.55	$4525.86 + **$271.55** = $4797.41

Compound interest = $4797.41 − $3800 = $997.41
Simple interest = $3800 × .06 × 4 = $912
Difference = $997.41 − $912 = $85.41

(b) No, they will be short of their goal by $5000 − $4797.41 = $202.59.

OBJECTIVE **2** **Decide on a period of compounding.** Compound interest is often calculated more often than once a year. Banks may calculate compound interest every 6 months (compounded semiannually), every 3 months (compounded quarterly), every month (compounded monthly), or every day (compounded daily).

EXAMPLE 2

Finding the Compounding Period

Find the compounding period for each.

(a) Assume Bank of America pays interest of 8% compounded semiannually. Then semiannually, or twice a year, interest of $\frac{8\%}{2}$ = 4% is added to all money that has been on deposit for 6 months or more.

(b) An interest rate of 12% per year, compounded quarterly, means that every 3 months, interest of $\frac{12\%}{4}$ = 3% is added to all money that has been on deposit for at least 1 quarter.

(c) An interest rate of 9% per year, compounded monthly, means that $\frac{9\%}{12}$ = .75% is added to all money that has been on deposit for one month or more.

SOLUTION

The period of compounding is 6 months in **(a)** above, 3 months in **(b)** above, and 1 month in **(c)** above.

NOTE The interest per compounding period (i) is equal to the annual interest rate (R) times the fraction of a year over which compounding occurs (T). Assuming 10% compounded quarterly, $i = 10\% \times \frac{1}{4} = \frac{10\%}{4} = 2.5\%$.

OBJECTIVE **3** **Use the formulas and tables to find compound amount and compound interest.** The **formula for compound interest** uses **exponents**, a short way of writing repeated products. For example, write the product $2 \times 2 \times 2$ as 2^3, where the 3 tells how many times the 2 is multiplied. Also, $4^2 = 4 \times 4 = 16$, and $3^4 = 3 \times 3 \times 3 \times 3 = 81$.

If P dollars are deposited at a rate of interest i per period for n periods, then the compound amount M, or the final amount on deposit, is

FORMULA FOR COMPOUNDING INTEREST

$$M = P(1 + i)^n$$

The interest earned, I, is

$$I = M - P$$

> **NOTE** It is important to keep in mind that i is the interest rate *per compounding period*, not per year, and that n is the total number of compounding periods.

Compound Interest Table
n = number of compounding periods; i = interest rate per compounding period

i / n	1%	1½%	2%	2½%	3%	4%	5%	6%	8%	10%	12%	n
1	1.01000	1.01500	1.02000	1.02500	1.03000	1.04000	1.05000	1.06000	1.08000	1.10000	1.12000	1
2	1.02010	1.03023	1.04040	1.05063	1.06090	1.08160	1.10250	1.12360	1.16640	1.21000	1.25440	2
3	1.03030	1.04568	1.06121	1.07689	1.09273	1.12486	1.15763	1.19102	1.25971	1.33100	1.40493	3
4	1.04060	1.06136	1.08243	1.10381	1.12551	1.16986	1.21551	1.26248	1.36049	1.46410	1.57352	4
5	1.05101	1.07728	1.10408	1.13141	1.15927	1.21665	1.27628	1.33823	1.46933	1.61051	1.76234	5
6	1.06152	1.09344	1.12616	1.15969	1.19405	1.26532	1.34010	1.41852	1.58687	1.77156	1.97382	6
7	1.07214	1.10984	1.14869	1.18869	1.22987	1.31593	1.40710	1.50363	1.71382	1.94872	2.21068	7
8	1.08286	1.12649	1.17166	1.21840	1.26677	1.36857	1.47746	1.59385	1.85093	2.14359	2.47596	8
9	1.09369	1.14339	1.19509	1.24886	1.30477	1.42331	1.55133	1.68948	1.99900	2.35795	2.77308	9
10	1.10462	1.16054	1.21899	1.28008	1.34392	1.48024	1.62889	1.79085	2.15892	2.59374	3.10585	10
11	1.11567	1.17795	1.24337	1.31209	1.38423	1.53945	1.71034	1.89830	2.33164	2.85312	3.47855	11
12	1.12683	1.19562	1.26824	1.34489	1.42576	1.60103	1.79586	2.01220	2.51817	3.13843	3.89598	12
13	1.13809	1.21355	1.29361	1.37851	1.46853	1.66507	1.88565	2.13293	2.71962	3.45227	4.36349	13
14	1.14947	1.23176	1.31948	1.41297	1.51259	1.73168	1.97993	2.26090	2.93719	3.79750	4.88711	14
15	1.16097	1.25023	1.34587	1.44830	1.55797	1.80094	2.07893	2.39656	3.17217	4.17725	5.47357	15
16	1.17258	1.26899	1.37279	1.48451	1.60471	1.87298	2.18287	2.54035	3.42594	4.59497	6.13039	16
17	1.18430	1.28802	1.40024	1.52162	1.65285	1.94790	2.29202	2.69277	3.70002	5.05447	6.86604	17
18	1.19615	1.30734	1.42825	1.55966	1.70243	2.02582	2.40662	2.85434	3.99602	5.55992	7.68997	18
19	1.20811	1.32695	1.45681	1.59865	1.75351	2.10685	2.52695	3.02560	4.31570	6.11591	8.61276	19
20	1.22019	1.34686	1.48595	1.63862	1.80611	2.19112	2.65330	3.20714	4.66096	6.72750	9.64629	20
21	1.23239	1.36706	1.51567	1.67958	1.86029	2.27877	2.78596	3.39956	5.03383	7.40025	10.80385	21
22	1.24472	1.38756	1.54598	1.72157	1.91610	2.36992	2.92526	3.60354	5.43654	8.14027	12.10031	22
23	1.25716	1.40838	1.57690	1.76461	1.97359	2.46472	3.07152	3.81975	5.87146	8.95430	13.55235	23
24	1.26973	1.42950	1.60844	1.80873	2.03279	2.56330	3.22510	4.04893	6.34118	9.84973	15.17863	24
25	1.28243	1.45095	1.64061	1.85394	2.09378	2.66584	3.38635	4.29187	6.84848	10.83471	17.00006	25
26	1.29526	1.47271	1.67342	1.90029	2.15659	2.77247	3.55567	4.54938	7.39635	11.91818	19.04007	26
27	1.30821	1.49480	1.70689	1.94780	2.22129	2.88337	3.73346	4.82235	7.98806	13.10999	21.32488	27
28	1.32129	1.51722	1.74102	1.99650	2.28793	2.99870	3.92013	5.11169	8.62711	14.42099	23.88387	28
29	1.33450	1.53998	1.77584	2.04641	2.35657	3.11865	4.11614	5.41839	9.31727	15.86309	26.74993	29
30	1.34785	1.56308	1.81136	2.09757	2.42726	3.24340	4.32194	5.74349	10.06266	17.44940	29.95992	30
31	1.36133	1.58653	1.84759	2.15001	2.50008	3.37313	4.53804	6.08810	10.86767	19.19434	33.55511	31
32	1.37494	1.61032	1.88454	2.20376	2.57508	3.50806	4.76494	6.45339	11.73708	21.11378	37.58173	32
33	1.38869	1.63448	1.92223	2.25885	2.65234	3.64838	5.00319	6.84059	12.67605	23.22515	42.09153	33
34	1.40258	1.65900	1.96068	2.31532	2.73191	3.79432	5.25335	7.25103	13.69013	25.54767	47.14252	34
35	1.41660	1.68388	1.99989	2.37321	2.81386	3.94609	5.51602	7.68609	14.78534	28.10244	52.79962	35
36	1.43077	1.70914	2.03989	2.43254	2.89828	4.10393	5.79182	8.14725	15.96817	30.91268	59.13557	36
37	1.44508	1.73478	2.08069	2.49335	2.98523	4.26809	6.08141	8.63609	17.24563	34.00395	66.23184	37
38	1.45953	1.76080	2.12230	2.55568	3.07478	4.43881	6.38548	9.15425	18.62528	37.40434	74.17966	38
39	1.47412	1.78721	2.16474	2.61957	3.16703	4.61637	6.70475	9.70351	20.11530	41.14478	83.08122	39
40	1.48886	1.81402	2.20804	2.68506	3.26204	4.80102	7.03999	10.28572	21.72452	45.25926	93.05097	40
41	1.50375	1.84123	2.25220	2.75219	3.35990	4.99306	7.39199	10.90286	23.46248	49.78518	104.21709	41
42	1.51879	1.86885	2.29724	2.82100	3.46070	5.19278	7.76159	11.55703	25.33948	54.76370	116.72314	42
43	1.53398	1.89688	2.34319	2.89152	3.56452	5.40050	8.14967	12.25045	27.36664	60.24007	130.72991	43
44	1.54932	1.92533	2.39005	2.96381	3.67145	5.61652	8.55715	12.98548	29.55597	66.26408	146.41750	44
45	1.56481	1.95421	2.43785	3.03790	3.78160	5.84118	8.98501	13.76461	31.92045	72.89048	163.98760	45
46	1.58046	1.98353	2.48661	3.11385	3.89504	6.07482	9.43426	14.59049	34.47409	80.17953	183.66612	46
47	1.59626	2.01328	2.53634	3.19170	4.01190	6.31782	9.90597	15.46592	37.23201	88.19749	205.70605	47
48	1.61223	2.04348	2.58707	3.27149	4.13225	6.57053	10.40127	16.39387	40.21057	97.01723	230.39078	48
49	1.62835	2.07413	2.63881	3.35328	4.25622	6.83335	10.92133	17.37750	43.42742	106.71896	258.03767	49
50	1.64463	2.10524	2.69159	3.43711	4.38391	7.10668	11.46740	18.42015	46.90161	117.39085	289.00219	50

EXAMPLE 3

Finding Compound Interest

A savings account at the Royal Bank of Canada pays 7% interest per year compounded semiannually. Given an initial deposit of $2500, **(a)** use the formula to find the compound amount after 2 years, and **(b)** find the compound interest.

Solution

(a) Every 6 months, $\frac{7\%}{2} = 3.5\%$ is added to all funds on deposit for 6 months or more. The number of 6-month periods in 2 years is 4.

$$M = P(1 + i)^n$$
$$= \$2500 \times (1 + .035)^4$$
$$= \$2500 \times (1.035)^4$$
$$= \$2500 \times 1.035 \times 1.035 \times 1.035 \times 1.035$$
$$= 2868.81$$

(b)
$$I = M - P$$
$$= \$2868.81 - \$2500 = \$368.81$$

For related Web activities, go to www.mathbusiness.com

Keyword: calculator

Frequently, it is impractical to calculate values for $(1 + i)^n$ directly. Values for this expression can be obtained from the table. The number in the body of the table represents the compound amount or maturity value on $1. The interest rate i at the top of the table is the rate per compounding period (monthly rate, quarterly rate, etc.). The value of n down the far left and far right columns of the table is the number of compounding periods (number of months, number of quarters, etc.). The compound amount for any principal is found using:

Compound amount = Principal × Number from Compound Interest Table

Alternatively, financial calculators can be used to calculate compound amount directly without having to first find a value for $(1 + i)^n$.

EXAMPLE 4

Finding Compound Interest

In each case, find the interest earned on a $2000 deposit.

(a) for 3 years, compounded annually at 4%
(b) for 6 years, compounded quarterly at 8%
(c) for 4 years, compounded monthly at 12%

Solution

(a) Look across the top of the compound interest table, on page 000, for 4% and down the side for 3 periods to find **1.12486**. The compound amount is as follows

$$M = \$2000 \times 1.12486 = \$2249.72$$
$$I = \$2249.72 - \$2000 = \$249.72$$

(b) Interest compounded quarterly is compounded 4 times a year. In 6 years, there are $4 \times 6 = 24$ quarters, or 24 periods. Interest of 8% per year is $\frac{8\%}{4} = 2\%$ per quarter. In the compound interest table, locate 2% across the top and 24 periods at the left, finding the number **1.60844**. The compound amount is as follows

$$M = \$2000 \times 1.60844 = \$3216.88$$
$$I = \$3216.88 - \$2000 = \$1216.88$$

(c) In 4 years, there are $4 \times 12 = 48$ monthly periods. Interest of 12% per year is $\frac{12\%}{12} = 1\%$ per month. Look in the compound interest table for 1% and 48 periods, finding the number **1.61223**. The compound amount is as follows

$$M = \$2000 \times 1.61223 = \$3224.46$$
$$I = \$3224.46 - \$2000 = \$1224.46$$

> **NOTE** Example 1 in Appendix C shows how a financial calculator can be used to solve this same type of problem.

The more often interest is compounded, the greater the amount of interest earned. Use of a financial calculator, a compound interest table (more complete than the compound interest table included here), or the compound interest formula will give the results shown in the following table. (Leap years were ignored in finding daily interest.)

Interest on $1000 at 8% per Year for 10 Years

Compounded	Interest
Not at all (simple interest)	$ 800.00
Annually	$1158.92
Semiannually	$1191.12
Quarterly	$1208.04
Monthly	$1219.64
Daily	$1225.35

EXAMPLE 5

Finding Compound Interest

John Smith inherits $15,000, which he deposits in a retirement account that pays interest compounded semiannually. How much will he have after 25 years if the funds grow **(a)** at 6%, **(b)** at 8%, and **(c)** at 10%?

Solution

In 25 years, there are $2 \times 25 = 50$ semiannual periods. The semiannual interest rates are **(a)** $\frac{6\%}{2}$ = 3%, **(b)** $\frac{8\%}{2}$ = 4%, and **(c)** $\frac{10\%}{2}$ = 5%. Using factors from the table

(a) $15,000 × **4.38391** = $65,758.65.
(b) $15,000 × **7.10668** = $106,600.20.
(c) $15,000 × **11.46740** = $172,011.00.

> **PROBLEM-SOLVING HINT** Simple interest rate calculations are usually indicated by phrases such as: simple interest, simple interest note, or discount rate. Compound interest rate calculations are usually indicated by phrases such as: compounded annually, 6% per quarter, or compounded daily.

9.2 | SAVINGS ACCOUNTS AND INFLATION

Objectives

1. Define the passbook account.
2. Find interest compounded daily.
3. Define time deposit accounts.
4. Define inflation and the consumer price index.

PROBLEM SOLVING IN BUSINESS

Individuals, businesses, and even countries have money on deposit at Bank of America. These deposits can be in many forms, including checking accounts, savings accounts, and time deposits, such as certificates of deposits.

Banks make money by charging *higher interest on funds they lend out* to customers than on funds they have on deposit at the bank. They also make money from fees for services such as safe deposit boxes, transferring money from one place to another, use of the ATM, and checking accounts with low balances.

Some people think that banks have huge vaults of stored cash. Actually, most bank assets are in loans to customers. You can think of most of these funds, including your checking account balance, as *bits of information* stored on the magnetic disks of computers.

For related Web
activities, go to
www.mathbusiness.com

Keyword:
confidence

Objective 1 **Define the passbook account.** **Savings accounts** or **passbook accounts** meet the daily money needs of a person or business. Money may be deposited in or withdrawn from a passbook account anytime, with no penalty, although you cannot write checks on funds in a savings account. Interest rates on savings accounts can vary from $2\frac{1}{2}$% to 6%. The Truth in Savings Act of 1991 resulted in Regulation DD, which requires that interest on savings accounts be paid based on the *exact number of days*.

A savings account can be *one of the safest places* for money. Savings accounts at most, but not all, institutions are insured by the Federal Deposit Insurance Corporation (FDIC) on deposits up to $100,000. Call your bank to determine that your funds are federally insured.

Objective 2 **Find interest compounded daily.** Interest on savings accounts is found using compound interest. It is common for banks to pay interest **compounded daily** so that interest is credited for every day that the money is on deposit.

The formula for daily compounding is *exactly* the same as that given in the last section. However, because the annual interest rate must be divided by 365 (for daily compounding), the arithmetic is very tedious. To avoid this, use the following special tables that give the necessary numbers for 1 to 90 days, as well as for 1 to 4 ninety-day quarters, assuming $3\frac{1}{2}$% interest compounded daily. The table goes to only 90 days since interest is normally credited to the depositor's account only quarterly, even with daily compounding. The four quarters in a year begin on January 1, April 1, July 1, and October 1.

> **NOTE** See Appendix C for financial calculator solutions that do not require the use of a table.

Thus, if the compounding period is expressed in days or quarters, the formulas to calculate the compound amount and interest follow.

Compound amount = Principal × Number from table

Interest = Compound amount − Principal

Values of $(1 + i)^n$ for $3\frac{1}{2}\%$ Compounded Daily

Number of Days n	Value of $(1 + i)^n$	n	Value of $(1 + i)^n$	n	Value of $(1 + i)^n$	n	Value of $(1 + i)^n$	n	Value of $(1 + i)^n$
1	1.000095890	19	1.001823491	37	1.003554076	55	1.005287650	73	1.007024219
2	1.000191790	20	1.001919556	38	1.003650307	56	1.005384048	74	1.007120783
3	1.000287699	21	1.002015631	39	1.003746548	57	1.005480454	75	1.007217357
4	1.000383617	22	1.002111714	40	1.003842797	58	1.005576870	76	1.007313939
5	1.000479544	23	1.002207807	41	1.003939056	59	1.005673296	77	1.007410531
6	1.000575480	24	1.002303909	42	1.004035324	60	1.005769730	78	1.007507132
7	1.000671426	25	1.002400021	43	1.004131602	61	1.005866174	79	1.007603742
8	1.000767381	26	1.002496141	44	1.004227888	62	1.005962627	80	1.007700362
9	1.000863345	27	1.002592271	45	1.004324184	63	1.006059089	81	1.007796990
10	1.000959318	28	1.002688410	46	1.004420489	64	1.006155560	82	1.007893628
11	1.001055300	29	1.002784558	47	1.004516803	65	1.006252041	83	1.007990276
12	1.001151292	30	1.002880716	48	1.004613127	66	1.006348531	84	1.008086932
13	1.001247293	31	1.002976882	49	1.004709460	67	1.006445030	85	1.008183598
14	1.001343303	32	1.003073058	50	1.004805802	68	1.006541538	86	1.008280273
15	1.001439322	33	1.003169243	51	1.004902153	69	1.006638056	87	1.008376958
16	1.001535350	34	1.003265438	52	1.004998513	70	1.006734583	88	1.008473651
17	1.001631388	35	1.003361641	53	1.005094883	71	1.006831119	89	1.008570354
18	1.001727435	36	1.003457854	54	1.005191262	72	1.006927665	90	1.008667067

Note: The value of $(1 + i)^n$ for $3\frac{1}{2}\%$ compounded daily for a quarter with 91 days is 1.008763788 and for a quarter with 92 days is 1.008860519.

Interest by Quarter for $3\frac{1}{2}\%$ Compounded Daily Assuming 90-Day Quarters

Number of Quarters	Value of $(1 + i)^n$
1	1.008667067
2	1.017409251
3	1.026227205
4	1.035121585

EXAMPLE 1

Finding Daily Interest

Mr. Watson wants his 6-year-old son Billy to learn about savings and interest. He took Billy to a bank on September 12 and opened a savings account with $500 to which Billy added $23.50 he had received from doing chores. Find the amount of interest Billy has earned by his birthday, November 20, if he earns $3\frac{1}{2}\%$ compounded daily.

Solution

There are 18 days remaining in September, 31 days in October, and 20 days in November. The money was on deposit for $18 + 31 + 20 = 69$ days. The table value for 69 days is 1.006638056, so the compound amount is

$$\$523.50 \times 1.006638056 = \$526.98$$

and the interest earned is $526.98 − $523.50 = $3.48. Billy is old enough that he isn't impressed with $3.48. Mr. Watson, thinking of the long term, insists that Billy continue to save part of his earnings.

EXAMPLE 2

Finding Quarterly Interest

Tom Blackmore is a private investigator. On January 10, he deposited $2463 in a savings account paying $3\frac{1}{2}\%$ compounded daily. He deposits an additional $1320 on February 18 and $840 on March 3. Find the interest earned through April 10.

Solution

Treat each of the three amounts separately. The $2463 was in the account for 21 days in January, 28 days in February, 31 days in March, and 10 days in April for a total of 90 days. The compound amount is found using 1.008667067 from the table.

Compound amount = $2463 × 1.008667067 = $2484.35   First deposit plus interest

A deposit of $1320 was made on February 18. This amount was on deposit for 10 days in February, 31 days in March, and 10 days in April for a total of 51 days.

Compound amount = $1320 × 1.004902153 = $1326.47   Second deposit plus interest

The final deposit of $840 was on deposit for 28 days in March and 10 days in April or for a total of 38 days.

Compound amount = $840 × 1.003650307 = $843.07   Final deposit plus interest

The total amount in the account is found by adding the three compound amounts together, and the interest earned is the total amount in the account minus deposits.

Total in account = $2484.35 + $1326.47 + $843.07 = $4653.89
Interest earned = $4653.89 − ($2463 + $1320 + $840) = $30.89

The interest earned is $30.89.

EXAMPLE 3
Finding Quarterly Interest

Beth Gardner owns Blacktop Paving, Inc. She needs a place to keep extra cash, a place that will earn interest but that will allow her to get funds when needed. She opened a savings account on July 20 with a $24,800 deposit. She then withdrew $3800 on August 29 for an unexpected truck repair and she made another withdrawal for $8200 on September 29 for payroll. Find the interest earned through October 1, given interest at $3\frac{1}{2}$% compounded daily.

Solution

Of the original $24,800, a total of $24,800 − $3800 − $8200 = $12,800 earned interest from July 20 to October 1 or for 274 − 201 = 73 days. Find the factor 1.007024219 from the table.

Compound amount = $12,800 × 1.007024219 = $12,889.91
Interest = $12,889.91 − $12,800 = **$89.91**

The withdrawn $3800 earned interest from July 20 to August 29 or for 241 − 201 = 40 days.

Compound amount = $3800 × 1.003842797 = $3814.60
Interest = $3814.60 − $3800 = **$14.60**

Finally, the withdrawn $8200 earned interest from July 20 to September 29 or for 272 − 201 = 71 days.

Compound amount = $8200 × 1.006831119 = $8256.02
Interest = $8256.02 − $8200 = **$56.02**

The total interest earned is ($89.91 + $14.60 + $56.02) = $160.53. The total in the account on October 1 is found as follows.

deposits + interest − withdrawals = balance on October 1
$24,800 + $160.53 − ($3800 + $8200) = $12,960.53

Objective **3** **Define time deposit accounts.** The rest of this section looks at another type of savings account called a **time deposit**. Banks pay more interest for funds left *on deposit for longer time periods.* For example, one local savings and loan pays $3\frac{1}{2}$% on money in a day-in and day-out passbook account but pays $5\frac{1}{2}$% on money left in a time deposit for 2 years. A **certificate of deposit (CD)** requires a minimum amount of money to be on deposit for a minimum period of time.

The higher interest paid by some certificates of deposit can be found with the following table. Incidentally, the table assumes daily compounding and 365 days per year.

Compound Interest for Time Deposit Accounts Compounded Daily

| Number Years | Interest Rate | | | | | | Number of Years |
	5%	6%	7%	8%	9%	10%	
1	1.051267496	1.06183131	1.07250098	1.08327757	1.09416214	1.10515578	1
2	1.105163349	1.12748573	1.15025836	1.17349030	1.19719080	1.22136930	2
3	1.161822307	1.19719965	1.23365322	1.27121572	1.30992085	1.34980334	3
4	1.221386028	1.27122407	1.32309429	1.37707948	1.43326581	1.49174297	4
5	1.284003432	1.34982552	1.41901993	1.49175931	1.56822519	1.64860837	5
10	1.648664814	1.82202895	2.01361755	2.22534585	2.45933025	2.71790955	10

> **PROBLEM-SOLVING HINT** The preceding compound interest table assumes daily compounding; the compound interest table on page 354 of Section 9.1 *does not*.

To calculate the compound amount and interest earned for time deposit accounts, use the following formulas.

> Compound amount = Principal × Number from the table
>
> Interest = Compound amount − Principal

EXAMPLE 4

Finding Interest and Compound Amount for Time Deposits

Toni Sanchez plans to purchase three machines for his auto-repair shop. Bank of America requires $20,000 in collateral before making the loan. Therefore, Toni deposits $20,000 with the bank in a 2-year certificate of deposit yielding 6%. Find the compound amount and interest.

Solution

Look at the table for 6% and 2 years, finding **1.12748573**.

$$\text{Compound amount} = \$20{,}000 \times \mathbf{1.12748573} = \$22{,}549.71$$
$$\text{Interest} = \$22{,}549.71 - \$20{,}000 = \$2549.71$$

Objective [4] **Define inflation and the consumer price index.** Your grandfather and his family would have done well with an income of only $500 per month in 1950. Today, this amount *will not go far* in terms of taking care of a family. Five hundred dollars would not purchase nearly as much in the year 2000 as it did in 1950. Why?

Inflation is the culprit. It results in a continuing rise in the general price level of goods and services. The effect of inflation can be seen by the increasing costs in a grocery store.

Item	1970 Price	2000 Price
Loaf of bread	$0.24	$1.50
1 gal. of milk	$0.66	$2.25
1 lb. of bacon	$0.95	$2.50

For related Web activities, go to www.mathbusiness.com

Keyword: indicators

The **consumer price index (CPI)** is calculated by the government annually in the United States and is often referred to as the *cost of living index*. Other countries calculate similar indexes. The CPI can be used to track inflation—it measures the average change in prices from one year to the next for a common bundle of goods and services bought by the average consumer on a regular basis. The common bundle of goods and services is defined by the government to include food, housing, fuels, utilities, apparel, transportation, insurance, health care, recreation, and even pet care among other items. There is some debate about how the CPI index is calculated. In fact, in 1998 the government updated the weights applied to the different items used to find the CPI index. The following headline shows that inflation is an important issue for business and government.

Inflation Threatens to Rain on USA's Economic Parade

Even the boy who cried wolf was right once.

That's something that Federal Reserve Chairman Alan Greenspan and his fellow policymakers at the inflation-stingy central bank want to include consumer, producer, and asset prices has been increasing at a 6% annual clip. That compares to a 1.4% rise for consumer prices.

"Reports of inflation's demise were clearly exaggerated," says

Source: USA Today, 5/18/98. Reprinted by permission.

Yearly inflation as measured by the CPI index differs substantially from year to year as you can see from the following chart.

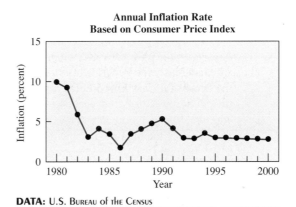

**Annual Inflation Rate
Based on Consumer Price Index**

DATA: U.S. Bureau of the Census

EXAMPLE 5
Estimating the Effects of Inflation

Inflation from one year to the next was 4.8% as measured by the CPI index. **(a)** Find the effect of the increase on a family with an annual income and budget of $19,800 (after taxes). **(b)** What is the overall effect if the family members only receive a 2% (after tax) increase in pay for the year?

Solution

(a) This is a percent problem. The cost of the goods and services that this family buys, if they buy the common bundle of goods and services, went up by 4.8% as measured by the CPI, or by

$$.048 \times \$19,800 = \$950.40.$$

Therefore, these same goods and services will cost the family

$$\$19,800 + \$950.40 = \textbf{\$20,750.40 next year.}$$

(b) The family's income only went up 2% after taxes or by

$$.02 \times \$19,800 = \textbf{\$396}.$$

Thus, their new income is $19,800 + $396 = $20,196. However, the cost of buying the same goods and services as they bought the previous year is $20,750.40. In effect, the family has lost $20,750.40 − $20,196 = $554.40 in purchasing power.

As shown in Example 5, inflation *slowly erodes* fixed income or incomes with a small annual increase built into them. Imagine the effect of losing purchasing power every year for 10 years in a row. Inflation can erode people's purchasing power *even as* their annual salaries are increasing. Retired people are particularly concerned with inflation since they must live off of Social Security and the assets they have accumulated during their lifetime. Some retired people do not have ways of increasing their income to keep pace with inflation and must *lower their standards of living* during their 10 to 30 or more years of retirement. Other retired people have investments such as stocks that help them stay ahead of inflation.

Example 6

Estimating the Effects of Inflation

Joan Jones has $14,650 in a savings account paying $3\frac{1}{2}\%$ interest compounded daily. Ignoring taxes, what is her gain or loss in purchasing power in a year in which the CPI index increases by 4.2%?

Solution

Use the interest by quarter table on page 362 to find the compound amount factor for 4 quarters, that is 1.035121585.

$$\text{Compound amount at end of year} = \$14,650 \times 1.035121585 = \textbf{\$15,164.53}$$

In order to keep up with inflation, Jones needs to earn 4.2% on her investment.

$$\text{Needed to keep up with inflation} = \$14,650 \times 1.042 = \textbf{\$15,265.30}$$

The difference of $15,265.30 − $15,164.53 = $100.77 is the loss in purchasing power. The purchasing power of Jones' savings actually went down, even though she earned interest for the year.

The federal government generally tries to keep inflation at moderate levels *since inflation can be so harmful*. When the economy becomes overheated (grows too quickly) and inflationary pressures increase, the Federal Reserve increases interest rates to reduce borrowing slightly and slow the economy. This action helps reduce inflationary pressures. Conversely, if inflation is low and the economy is growing very slowly or not at all, the Federal Reserve reduces interest rates to stimulate the economy and create more jobs. The Federal Reserve has been assigned the *very difficult task* of maintaining a growing and healthy economy with low levels of inflation.

9.3 | PRESENT VALUE

Objectives

1. Define the terms *future value* and *present value*.
2. Use tables to calculate present value.

Objective **1** **Define the terms *future value* and *present value*.** In Sections 9.1 and 9.2, compound interest calculations were used to find the **future value** (value at some future date) of an investment. The initial deposit, interest rate, and term were given and future value was calculated.

In this section, the problem is reversed—the future value, interest rate, and term are given. The goal is to find the amount that must be deposited today to produce the desired future value at the specified future date. The amount that must be deposited today is called the **present value**.

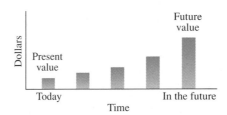

Objective **2** **Use tables to calculate present value.** The numbers in the present-value table represent the amount that must be invested today to end up with $1 in the future. The present value of an amount is found by multiplying the amount (the future value) times the number from the table.

$$\text{Present value } (P) = \text{Future value} \times \text{Table value}$$

Keep in mind that in the table,

n = the number of compound periods, and
i = the interest rate per compounding period.

The interest rate per compounding period is found by dividing the annual interest rate by n, the number of compounding periods per year.

> **NOTE** See Appendix C for financial calculator solutions that do not require use of a table.

EXAMPLE 1
Finding Present Value

Joan Trestrail wishes to purchase a Morgan horse costing $6000 in 5 years. What lump sum deposited today at 8% compounded annually will grow to $6000? How much interest will be earned?

Solution

Look at the table on the next page for 8% and 5 periods to find **.68058**. Now multiply.

$$\text{Present value} = \$6000 \times \mathbf{.68058} = \$4083.48$$

A deposit of $4083.48 today at 8% compounded annually will produce $6000 in 5 years. Of this $6000,

$$\$6000 \quad \$4083.48 = \$1916.52$$

represents interest earned on the initial deposit of $4083.48.

Check this result: go back to the compound interest table in Section 9.1, and look up 8% and 5 periods, finding **1.46933**. Multiply this number and $4083.48.

$$\$4083.48 \times 1.46933 = \$5999.98 \text{ (or } \$6000, \text{ rounded)}$$

This check shows that a deposit of $4083.48 today, at 8% compounded annually for 5 years, does produce the needed $6000.

Present Value of a Dollar Table
n = number of periods; i = interest rate per period

i / n	1%	1½%	2%	2½%	3%	4%	5%	6%	8%	10%	12%	i / n
1	.99010	.98522	.98039	.97561	.97087	.96154	.95238	.94340	.92593	.90909	.89286	1
2	.98030	.97066	.96117	.95181	.94260	.92456	.90703	.89000	.85734	.82645	.79719	2
3	.97059	.95632	.94232	.92860	.91514	.88900	.86384	.83962	.79383	.75131	.71178	3
4	.96098	.94218	.92385	.90595	.88849	.85480	.82270	.79209	.73503	.68301	.63552	4
5	.95147	.92826	.90573	.88385	.86261	.82193	.78353	.74726	.68058	.62092	.56743	5
6	.94205	.91454	.88797	.86230	.83748	.79031	.74622	.70496	.63017	.56447	.50663	6
7	.93272	.90103	.87056	.84127	.81309	.75992	.71068	.66506	.58349	.51316	.45235	7
8	.92348	.88771	.85349	.82075	.78941	.73069	.67684	.62741	.54027	.46651	.40388	8
9	.91434	.87459	.83676	.80073	.76642	.70259	.64461	.59190	.50025	.42410	.36061	9
10	.90529	.86167	.82035	.78120	.74409	.67556	.61391	.55839	.46319	.38554	.32197	10
11	.89632	.84893	.80426	.76214	.72242	.64958	.58468	.52679	.42888	.35049	.28748	11
12	.88745	.83639	.78849	.74356	.70138	.62460	.55684	.49697	.39711	.31863	.25668	12
13	.87866	.82403	.77303	.72542	.68095	.60057	.53032	.46884	.36770	.28966	.22917	13
14	.86996	.81185	.75788	.70773	.66112	.57748	.50507	.44230	.34036	.26333	.20462	14
15	.86135	.79985	.74301	.69047	.64186	.55526	.48102	.41727	.31524	.23939	.18270	15
16	.85282	.78803	.72845	.67362	.62317	.53391	.45811	.39365	.29189	.21763	.16312	16
17	.84438	.77639	.71416	.65720	.60502	.51337	.43630	.37136	.27027	.19784	.14564	17
18	.83602	.76491	.70016	.64117	.58739	.49363	.41552	.35034	.25025	.17986	.13004	18
19	.82774	.75361	.68643	.62553	.57029	.47464	.39573	.33051	.23171	.16351	.11611	19
20	.81954	.74247	.67297	.61027	.55368	.45639	.37689	.31180	.21455	.14864	.10367	20
21	.81143	.73150	.65978	.59539	.53755	.43883	.35894	.29416	.19866	.13513	.09256	21
22	.80340	.72069	.64684	.58086	.52189	.42196	.34185	.27751	.18394	.12285	.08264	22
23	.79544	.71004	.63416	.56670	.50669	.40573	.32557	.26180	.17032	.11168	.07379	23
24	.78757	.69954	.62172	.55288	.49193	.39012	.31007	.24698	.15770	.10153	.06588	24
25	.77977	.68921	.60953	.53939	.47761	.37512	.29530	.23300	.14602	.09230	.05882	25
26	.77205	.67902	.59758	.52623	.46369	.36069	.28124	.21981	.13520	.08391	.05252	26
27	.76440	.66899	.58586	.51340	.45019	.34682	.26785	.20737	.12519	.07628	.04689	27
28	.75684	.65910	.57437	.50088	.43708	.33348	.25509	.19563	.11591	.06934	.04187	28
29	.74934	.64936	.56311	.48866	.42435	.32065	.24295	.18456	.10733	.06304	.03738	29
30	.74192	.63976	.55207	.47674	.41199	.30832	.23138	.17411	.09938	.05731	.03338	30
31	.73458	.63031	.54125	.46511	.39999	.29646	.22036	.16425	.09202	.05210	.02980	31
32	.72730	.62099	.53063	.45377	.38834	.28506	.20987	.15496	.08520	.04736	.02661	32
33	.72010	.61182	.52023	.44270	.37703	.27409	.19987	.14619	.07889	.04306	.02376	33
34	.71297	.60277	.51003	.43191	.36604	.26355	.19035	.13791	.07305	.03914	.02121	34
35	.70591	.59387	.50003	.42137	.35538	.25342	.18129	.13011	.06763	.03558	.01894	35
36	.69892	.58509	.49022	.41109	.34503	.24367	.17266	.12274	.06262	.03235	.01691	36
37	.69200	.57644	.48061	.40107	.33498	.23430	.16444	.11579	.05799	.02941	.01510	37
38	.68515	.56792	.47119	.39128	.32523	.22529	.15661	.10924	.05369	.02673	.01348	38
39	.67837	.55953	.46195	.38174	.31575	.21662	.14915	.10306	.04971	.02430	.01204	39
40	.67165	.55126	.45289	.37243	.30656	.20829	.14205	.09722	.04603	.02209	.01075	40
41	.66500	.54312	.44401	.36335	.29763	.20028	.13528	.09172	.04262	.02009	.00960	41
42	.65842	.53509	.43530	.35448	.28896	.19257	.12884	.08653	.03946	.01826	.00857	42
43	.65190	.52718	.42677	.34584	.28054	.18517	.12270	.08163	.03654	.01660	.00765	43
44	.64545	.51939	.41840	.33740	.27237	.17805	.11686	.07701	.03383	.01509	.00683	44
45	.63905	.51171	.41020	.32917	.26444	.17120	.11130	.07265	.03133	.01372	.00610	45
46	.63273	.50415	.40215	.32115	.25674	.16461	.10600	.06854	.02901	.01247	.00544	46
47	.62646	.49670	.39427	.31331	.24926	.15828	.10095	.06466	.02686	.01134	.00486	47
48	.62026	.48936	.38654	.30567	.24200	.15219	.09614	.06100	.02487	.01031	.00434	48
49	.61412	.48213	.37896	.29822	.23495	.14634	.09156	.05755	.02303	.00937	.00388	49

Expanding Hog Heaven: Small Shop Makes It Big

East Texas, TX—With plans to double the size of their East Texas Harley-Davidson franchise, selling motorcycles has put Orrin and Bennie Latch in hog heaven. Started with minimal capital, the Latches opened a small motorcycle sales-and-service operation specializing in the Harley-Davidson brand, whose cult status amongst motorcycle owners has kept a steady flow of customers both young and old coming through their door.

EXAMPLE 2

Finding Present Value

The local Harley-Davidson shop has seen business grow rapidly. They plan to double the size of their 6000-square-foot shop in one year at a cost of $280,000. Ignoring taxes, how much should be invested in an account paying 6% compounded semiannually in order to have the funds needed?

Solution

There are $1 \times 2 = 2$ semiannual periods in 1 year. A rate of 6% per year is 3% for each semiannual period. Look across the top of the table for 3% and down the side for 2 periods to find **.94260**.

$$\text{Present value} = \$280,000 \times .94260 = \$263,928$$

A deposit of $263,928 today at 6% compounded semiannually will actually provide $280,001.22 in one year—the difference is due to rounding.

EXAMPLE 3

Applying Present Value

Vicki Frederick owns an Italian restaurant worth $125,000. She is confident that its value will increase at the rate of 16% per year, compounded semiannually, for the next 4 years.

(a) Find the future value of the restaurant in 4 years.

(b) If she sells the restaurant today, she will invest the proceeds in an account at Bank of America paying 8% compounded quarterly. What selling price would she have to receive in order to have the same future value in 4 years?

Solution

(a) The restaurant is growing at $\frac{16\%}{2} = 8\%$ per compounding period for $4 \times 2 = 8$ periods. Using the compound interest table in Section 9.1,

$$\text{Future value} = \$125,000 \times \textbf{1.85093} \text{ from the compound interest table}$$

$$\text{Future value} = \$231,366.25$$

(b) Now find the present value of this sum, assuming that money can be invested at 8% compounded quarterly. The interest rate per quarter is $8\% \div 4 = 2\%$, with $4 \times 4 = 16$ periods. Find the number **.72845** in the present value table. The present value is

$$\$231,366.25 \times \textbf{.72845} \text{ from the present value table} = \$168,538.74.$$

Frederick should not sell the restaurant for less than $168,538.74. An investment of this amount at 8% compounded quarterly for 4 years will produce the same future amount as the growth in the value of the business.

EXAMPLE 4

Applying Present Value

Telco Telecommunications wishes to partner with a Korean company in the purchase of a satellite in 3 years. Telco plans to make a cash down payment of 40% of their anticipated $8,000,000 cost and borrow the remaining funds from a bank. Find the amount they should invest today in an account earning 6% compounded annually to have the down payment needed in 3 years.

Solution

First find the down payment to be paid in 3 years.

$$\text{Down payment} = .40 \times \$8,000,000 = \$3,200,000$$

This is the future value needed exactly 3 years from now. Using the present value of a dollar table with 3 periods and 6% per period provides

$$\$3,200,000 \times .83962 = \$2,686,784.$$

Telco must invest $2,686,784 today at 6% interest compounded annually in order to have the required down payment of $3,200,000 in 3 years.

Chapter 9 | Quick Review

CHAPTER TERMS

*Review the following terms to test your understanding of the chapter. For
each term you do not know, refer to the page number found next to that term.*

CD [**p. 363**]
CPI [**p. 364**]
certificate of deposit [**p. 363**]
compound amount [**p. 352**]

compound interest [**p. 364**]
compounded daily [**p. 361**]
consumer price index [**p. 364**]
exponents [**p. 353**]

formula for compound interest
  [**p. 353**]
future value [**p. 371**]
inflation [**p. 364**]

passbook accounts [**p. 361**]
present value [**p. 371**]
savings accounts [**p. 361**]
simple interest [**p. 352**]
time deposit [**p. 363**]

CONCEPTS	EXAMPLES
9.1 Finding compound amount and compound interest Find the number of compounding periods (n) and the interest rate per period (i). Use the compound interest table to find the interest on $1. Multiply table value by the principal to obtain compound amount. Subtract principal from compound amount to obtain interest.	Tom Jones invested $3000 at 6% compounded quarterly for 7 years. There are $7 \times 4 = 28$ quarters or compounding periods in 7 years. Interest of 6% per year $= \frac{6\%}{4} = 1\frac{1}{2}\%$ per period. Find $1\frac{1}{2}\%$ across the top of the compound interest table and 28 down the left side to find 1.51722. Compound amount $= \$3000 \times 1.51722 = \$4551.66$ Interest $= \$4551.66 - \$3000 = \$1551.66$

9.2 Finding the interest earned when the interest is compounded daily
 	
 Find number of days that the deposit earns interest.
 	
 Use the 90-day or 1-quarter table to calculate interest on $1.
 	
 Find compound amount using the formula
   Compound amount $=$ Principal $\times$ Table value.
 	
 Find interest earned using the formula
   Interest $=$ Compound amount $-$ Principal.
	Mary Carver deposits $1000 at $3\frac{1}{2}\%$ compounded daily on May 15. She withdraws the money on July 17. Find the compounded amount and interest earned.
	
	   May 15–May 31 16 days
	   June 30 days
	   July 1–July 17 <u>17 days</u>
	                63 days
	
	 Table value $=$ **1.006059089**
	 Compound amount $= \$1000 \times$ **1.006059089**
	 Interest $= \$1006.06 - \$1000 = \$6.06$

9.2 Finding the interest on time deposits
 	
 Use the compound interest for time deposit accounts table to find the interest on $1.
 	
 Find the compound amount using the formula
   Compound amount $=$ Principal $\times$ Table value.
 	
 Find interest using the formula
   Interest $=$ Compound amount $-$ Principal.
	John Walker invests $12,000 in a certificate of deposit paying 7%. Find the compound amount and interest earned after 5 years.
	
	 Value from table for 7% and 5 years is **1.41901993**.
	
	 Compound amount $= \$12,000 \times$ **1.41901993** $= \$17,028.24$
	 Interest $= \$17,028.24 - \$12,000 = \$5028.24$

9.2 Finding the effect of inflation on a pay raise Find the new salary by multiplying the old salary times 1 + percent increase. Find the salary needed to offset inflation by multiplying old salary times 1 + inflation rate. Find the gain or loss by subtracting.	Leticia Jaramillo earns $45,000 per year as a computer programmer. She gets a raise of 3.5% in a year in which inflation is 5%. Ignoring taxes, find the effect on her purchasing power. New salary $= \$45,000 \times 1.035 =$ **$46,575** Salary needed to offset inflation $= \$45,000 \times 1.05 =$ **$47,250** Loss in purchasing power $= \$47,250 - \$46,575 = \$675$
9.3 Finding the present value of a future amount Determine the number of compounding periods (n). Determine the interest per compounding period (i). Use the values of n and i to determine the table value from the present value table. Find present value from the formula Present value $=$ Future value $\times$ Table value	Sue York must pay a lump sum of $4500 in 6 years. What lump sum deposited today at 6% compounded quarterly will amount to $4500 in 6 years? Number of compounding periods $= 6 \times 4 = 24$ Interest per compounding period $= \frac{6\%}{4} = 1\frac{1}{2}\%$ **per period** Table value $=$ **.69954** Present value $= \$4500 \times$ **.69954** $= \$3147.93$

CHAPTER 9 | SUMMARY EXERCISE

VALUING A CHAIN OF MCDONALD'S RESTAURANTS

James and Mary Watson own a small chain of McDonald's restaurants that is valued at $2,300,000. They believe that the chain will grow in value at 12% per year compounded annually for the next 5 years. If they sell the chain, the funds will be invested at a rate of 6% compounded semiannually. They expect inflation to be 4% per year for the next 5 years. Ignore taxes and answer the following; round answers to the nearest dollar.

(a) Find the future value of the chain after 5 years. Then find the price they should sell the chain for if they wish to have the same future value at the end of 5 years.

(a) _____

(b) Find the future value of the chain if it only grows at 2% per year for 5 years. Then find the price they should ask for the chain given a 2% growth rate per year.

(b) _____

(c) What future value would the chain be worth if it grew at their expected rate of inflation. Find the price they should ask for the chain if it grows at the rate of inflation.

(c) _____

(d) Complete the following table.

Growth Rate	Future Value	Market Value Today
2%	_____	_____
4% (inflation)	_____	_____
12%	_____	_____

> **NOTE** The value of the chain varies by more than one million dollars depending on the rate of growth assumed for the business for the next 5 years.

Investigate

The interest rates that a bank pays depend on whether the money is in a checking account, savings account or time deposit. Go to a bank near you and find the different interest rates that the bank will pay. Identify the conditions such as the minimum amount in an account, minimum deposit, and the length of time the money must be on deposit to earn each interest rate.

CHAPTER 9 | TEST

To help you review, the numbers in brackets show the section in which the topic was discussed.

In each of these problems, round to the nearest cent. Find the compound amount and the interest earned for the following.   [9.1]

	Amount	Rate	Compounded	Time (Years)	Compound Amount	Interest Earned
1.	$8700	10%	annually	8	_____	_____
2.	$7200	12%	semiannually	7	_____	_____
3.	$9800	6%	semiannually	5	_____	_____
4.	$12,500	10%	quarterly	4	_____	_____

Find the interest earned by the following. Assume $3\frac{1}{2}$% interest compounded daily.   [9.2]

5. $6400 deposited September 24 and withdrawn December 15   5. _____

6. $63,340 deposited December 5 and withdrawn March 2   6. _____

7. $37,650 deposited December 12 and withdrawn on February 29 (leap year)   7. _____

Find the present value of the following.   [9.3]

	Amount Needed	Time (Years)	Rate	Compounded	Present Value
8.	$18,000	20	12%	annually	_____
9.	$15,750	7	6%	quarterly	_____
10.	$56,900	10	4%	semiannually	_____

Solve the following application problems.

11. The Train Company deposited $12,500 in a savings account on July 3 and then deposited an additional $3450 in the account on August 5. Find the balance on October 1 assuming an interest rate of $3\frac{1}{2}$% compounded daily.   **[9.2]**

11. _____

12. Discount Auto Insurance deposited $1800 in a savings account paying $3\frac{1}{2}$% compounded daily on January 1 and deposited an additional $2300 in the account on March 12. Find the balance on April 1.   **[9.2]**

12. _____

13. Liz Mulig earns $52,000 per year as an accounting professor. She receives a raise of 2.5% in a year in which the CPI index increases by 3.8%. Ignoring taxes, find the effect of the two on her purchasing power.   **[9.2]**

13. _____

14. Meg Arnosti earned 8% per year, compounded quarterly, by depositing $10,000 with a bank for 4 years. Find **(a)** the compound amount and **(b)** the interest earned.   **[9.1]**

(a) _____
(b) _____

15. A note for $3500 was made at 8% per year compounded annually for 3 years. Find **(a)** the maturity value and **(b)** the present value of the note assuming 5% per year compounded semiannually.   **[9.3]**

(a) _____

(b) _____

16. Computers, Inc. accepted a 2-year note for $12,540 in lieu of immediate payment for computer equipment sold to a local firm. Find **(a)** the maturity value given a 10% rate compounded annually and **(b)** the present value of the note at 6% per year compounded semiannually.   **[9.3]**

(a) _____

(b) _____

17. A business worth $180,000 is expected to grow 12% per year compounded annually for the next 4 years. **(a)** Find the expected future value. **(b)** If funds from the sale of the business today would be placed in an account yielding 8% compounded semiannually, what would be the minimum acceptable price for the business at this time?   **[9.3]**

(a) _____

(b) _____

18. A corporation worth 40 million dollars is expected to grow at 8% per year compounded annually for 5 years. **(a)** Find the future value to the nearest million. **(b)** They then propose to sell the firm and invest the proceeds in a new venture that should grow at 12% for 4 years. Beginning with the future value from part (a) rounded to the nearest million, find the expected future value to the nearest million at the end of 4 additional years.   **[9.1]**

(a) _____

(b) _____

Chapter 10

Annuities, Stocks, and Bonds

Tish Baker just received her nursing degree and began work at her first professional job at Boston Children's Hospital. She was excited about the job, but, *on her first day*, she found that she did not understand retirement planning when she spoke with the hospital's benefits coordinator. In this chapter, we look at some things that will help Tish invest and plan for her retirement.

10.1 | Annuities

Objectives

1. Define the basic terms involved with annuities.
2. Find the amount of an annuity.
3. Find the amount of an annuity due.
4. Find the value of an IRA.

Problem Solving in Business

The benefits coordinator at Children's Hospital asked Tish Baker if she wanted to put her retirement funds in an annuity. He also asked if she preferred an investment paying a guaranteed interest or an investment in a mutual fund with stocks and/or bonds. Baker did not know how to answer, but she knew that she wanted to *plan early* so that her young family would never be poor like her grandfather.

Objective 1 **Define the basic terms involved with annuities.** The ideas of compound interest presented earlier involved lump sums of money. However, many common business problems such as mortgage payments on a home or regular investments into a retirement account involve *a series of equal payments made at regular time intervals*. A sequence of payments such as this is called an **annuity**. Regular, equal payments made to a retired person by a life insurance company is another example of an annuity.

The time between payments is the **payment period** and the time from the beginning of the first payment period through the end of the last payment period is the **term of the annuity**. The sum of the compound amounts of all payments, compounded to the end of the term is called the **amount of the annuity** or **future value of the annuity**.

An example of an ordinary annuity is given by a small firm that is accumulating funds for a new vehicle. The firm makes deposits of $3000 at the end of each year, for 6 years, in an account earning 8% per year compounded annually. The first deposit of $3000 is made at the *end* of year 1 and earns interest *for only 5 years*. Using the compound interest table in Section 9.1 (page 354) for 5 years and 8%, the first payment grows to

$$\$3000 \times 1.46933 = \$4407.99$$

in 5 years. The amount of the annuity is the sum of the compound amounts of all 6 payments.

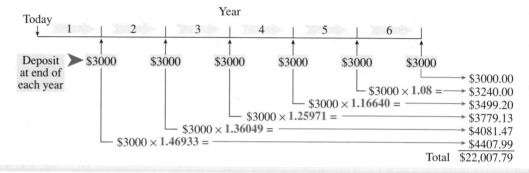

		$3000.00
$3000 × 1.08 =	→	$3240.00
$3000 × 1.16640 =		$3499.20
$3000 × 1.25971 =		$3779.13
$3000 × 1.36049 =		$4081.47
$3000 × 1.46933 =		$4407.99
	Total	$22,007.79

> **NOTE** The annuity ends on the day of the last payment—therefore, the last payment earns no interest.

OBJECTIVE **2** **Find the amount of an annuity.** The amount of an annuity can also be found using the amount of an annuity table. The number from the table is the amount or future value of an annuity with a payment of $1. The formula for obtaining the amount of an annuity follows.

$$\text{Amount} = \text{Payment} \times \text{Number from amount of an annuity table}$$

As a check, go back to the annuity of $3000 at the end of each year for 6 years at 8% compounded annually. Locate 8% at the top of the table and 6 periods in the left column to find **7.33593**.

$$\text{Amount} = \$3000 \times \textbf{7.33593} = \$22,007.79$$

which is identical to the amount calculated above.

> **NOTE** See Appendix C for financial calculator solutions that do not require the use of a table.

EXAMPLE 1
Finding the Value of an Annuity and Interest Earned

Tish Baker decides to save $150 at the end of each quarter, which is the amount paid into her retirement plan by the hospital where she works. If she chooses an investment fund that guarantees 6% per year compounded quarterly, how much will she have in 10 years?

Solution

Interest of $\frac{6\%}{4} = 1\frac{1}{2}\%$ is earned per quarter for $10 \times 4 = 40$ quarters. Look across the top of the table for $1\frac{1}{2}\%$ and down the side for 40 periods to find **54.26789**.

$$\text{Amount} = \$150 \times \textbf{54.26789} = \$8140.18$$

Amount of an Annuity Table
n = number of periods in annuity; i = interest per period

n	1%	1½%	2%	2½%	3%	4%	5%	6%	8%	10%	12%	n
1	1.00000	1.00000	1.00000	1.00000	1.00000	1.00000	1.00000	1.00000	1.00000	1.00000	1.00000	1
2	2.01000	2.01500	2.02000	2.02500	2.03000	2.04000	2.05000	2.06000	2.08000	2.10000	2.12000	2
3	3.03010	3.04522	3.06040	3.07562	3.09090	3.12160	3.15250	3.18360	3.24640	3.31000	3.37440	3
4	4.06040	4.09090	4.12161	4.15252	4.18363	4.24646	4.31013	4.37462	4.50611	4.64100	4.77933	4
5	5.10101	5.15227	5.20404	5.25633	5.30914	5.41632	5.52563	5.63709	5.86660	6.10510	6.35285	5
6	6.15202	6.22955	6.30812	6.38774	6.46841	6.63298	6.80191	6.97532	7.33593	7.71561	8.11519	6
7	7.21354	7.32299	7.43428	7.54743	7.66246	7.89829	8.14201	8.39384	8.92280	9.48717	10.08901	7
8	8.28567	8.43284	8.58297	8.73612	8.89234	9.21423	9.54911	9.89747	10.63663	11.43589	12.29969	8
9	9.36853	9.55933	9.75463	9.95452	10.15911	10.58280	11.02656	11.49132	12.48756	13.57948	14.77566	9
10	10.46221	10.70272	10.94972	11.20338	11.46388	12.00611	12.57789	13.18079	14.48656	15.93742	17.54874	10
11	11.56683	11.86326	12.16872	12.48347	12.80780	13.48635	14.20679	14.97164	16.64549	18.53117	20.65458	11
12	12.68250	13.04121	13.41209	13.79555	14.19203	15.02581	15.91713	16.86994	18.97713	21.38428	24.13313	12
13	13.80933	14.23683	14.68033	15.14044	15.61779	16.62684	17.71298	18.88214	21.49530	24.52271	28.02911	13
14	14.94742	15.45038	15.97394	16.51895	17.08632	18.29191	19.59863	21.01507	24.21492	27.97498	32.39260	14
15	16.09690	16.68214	17.29342	17.93193	18.59891	20.02359	21.57856	23.27597	27.15211	31.77248	37.27971	15
16	17.25786	17.93237	18.63929	19.38022	20.15688	21.82453	23.65749	25.67253	30.32428	35.94973	42.75328	16
17	18.43044	19.20136	20.01207	20.86473	21.76159	23.69751	25.84037	28.21288	33.75023	40.54470	48.88367	17
18	19.61475	20.48938	21.41231	22.38635	23.41444	25.64541	28.13238	30.90565	37.45024	45.59917	55.74971	18
19	20.81090	21.79672	22.84056	23.94601	25.11687	27.67123	30.53900	33.75999	41.44626	51.15909	63.43968	19
20	22.01900	23.12367	24.29737	25.54466	26.87037	29.77808	33.06595	36.78559	45.76196	57.27500	72.05244	20
21	23.23919	24.47052	25.78332	27.18327	28.67649	31.96920	35.71925	39.99273	50.42292	64.00250	81.69874	21
22	24.47159	25.83758	27.29898	28.86286	30.53678	34.24797	38.50521	43.39229	55.45676	71.40275	92.50258	22
23	25.71630	27.22514	28.84496	30.58443	32.45288	36.61789	41.43048	46.99583	60.89330	79.54302	104.60289	23
24	26.97346	28.63352	30.42186	32.34904	34.42647	39.08260	44.50200	50.81558	66.76476	88.49733	118.15524	24
25	28.24320	30.06302	32.03030	34.15776	36.45926	41.64591	47.72710	54.86451	73.10594	98.34706	133.33387	25
26	29.52563	31.51397	33.67091	36.01171	38.55304	44.31174	51.11345	59.15638	79.95442	109.18177	150.33393	26
27	30.82089	32.98668	35.34432	37.91200	40.70963	47.08421	54.66913	63.70577	87.35077	121.09994	169.37401	27
28	32.12910	34.48148	37.05121	39.85980	42.93092	49.96758	58.40258	68.52811	95.33883	134.20994	190.69889	28
29	33.45039	35.99870	38.79223	41.85630	45.21885	52.96629	62.32271	73.63980	103.96594	148.63093	214.58275	29
30	34.78489	37.53868	40.56808	43.90270	47.57542	56.08494	66.43885	79.05819	113.28321	164.49402	241.33268	30
31	36.13274	39.10176	42.37944	46.00027	50.00268	59.32834	70.76079	84.80168	123.34587	181.94342	271.29261	31
32	37.49407	40.68829	44.22703	48.15028	52.50276	62.70147	75.29883	90.88978	134.21354	201.13777	304.84772	32
33	38.86901	42.29861	46.11157	50.35403	55.07784	66.20953	80.06377	97.34316	145.95062	222.25154	342.42945	33
34	40.25770	43.93309	48.03380	52.61289	57.73018	69.85791	85.06696	104.18375	158.62667	245.47670	384.52098	34
35	41.66028	45.59209	49.99448	54.92821	60.46208	73.65222	90.32031	111.43478	172.31680	271.02437	431.66350	35
36	43.07688	47.27597	51.99437	57.30141	63.27594	77.59831	95.83632	119.12087	187.10215	299.12681	484.46312	36
37	44.50765	48.98511	54.03425	59.73395	66.17422	81.70225	101.62814	127.26812	203.07032	330.03949	543.59869	37
38	45.95272	50.71989	56.11494	62.22730	69.15945	85.97034	107.70955	135.90421	220.31595	364.04343	609.83053	38
39	47.41225	52.48068	58.23724	64.78298	72.23423	90.40915	114.09502	145.05846	238.94122	401.44778	684.01020	39
40	48.88637	54.26789	60.40198	67.40255	75.40126	95.02552	120.79977	154.76197	259.05652	442.59256	767.09142	40
41	50.37524	56.08191	62.61002	70.08762	78.66330	99.82654	127.83976	165.04768	280.78104	487.85181	860.14239	41
42	51.87899	57.92314	64.86222	72.83981	82.02320	104.81960	135.23175	175.95054	304.24352	537.63699	964.35948	42
43	53.39778	59.79199	67.15947	75.66080	85.48389	110.01238	142.99334	187.50758	329.58301	592.40069	1081.08262	43
44	54.93176	61.68887	69.50266	78.55232	89.04841	115.41288	151.14301	199.75803	356.94965	652.64076	1211.81253	44
45	56.48107	63.61420	71.89271	81.51613	92.71986	121.02939	159.70016	212.74351	386.50562	718.90484	1358.23003	45
46	58.04589	65.56841	74.33056	84.55403	96.50146	126.87057	168.68516	226.50812	418.42607	791.79532	1522.21764	46
47	59.62634	67.55194	76.81718	87.66789	100.39650	132.94539	178.11942	241.09861	452.90015	871.97485	1705.88375	47
48	61.22261	69.56522	79.35352	90.85958	104.40840	139.26321	188.02539	256.56453	490.13216	960.17234	1911.58980	48
49	62.83483	71.60870	81.94059	94.13107	108.54065	145.83373	198.42666	272.95840	530.34274	1057.18957	2141.98058	49
50	64.46318	73.68283	84.57940	97.48435	112.79687	152.66708	209.34800	290.33590	573.77016	1163.90853	2400.01825	50

Baker will have \$8140.18 at the end of 10 years. The interest earned is the amount of the annuity less 40 payments of \$150 each.

$$\text{Interest} = \$8140.18 - (40 \times \$150) = \$2140.18$$

The calculator solution to finding the interest follows.

$$8140.18 \boxed{-} 40 \boxed{\times} 150 \boxed{=} 2140.18$$

Note: All calculator solutions use a scientific calculator. Refer to Appendix B for scientific calculator basics.

EXAMPLE 2

Finding the Amount of an Annuity and Interest Earned

At the birth of her grandson, Junella Smith commits to help pay for his college education. She decides to make deposits of \$600 at the end of each 6 months into an account for 18 years. Find the amount of the annuity assuming 6% compounded semiannually.

Solution

Interest of $\frac{6\%}{2} = 3\%$ is earned each semiannual period. There are $2 \times 18 = 36$ semiannual periods in 18 years. Find 3% across the top and 36 periods down the side of the table to find **63.27594**.

$$\text{Amount} = \$600 \times \mathbf{63.27594} = \$37{,}965.56$$
$$\text{Interest} = \$37{,}965.56 - (36 \times \$600) = \$16{,}365.56$$

Although Smith knows that a college education will cost a lot more in 18 years than it does today, she feels that \$37,965.56 will be of great help to her grandson when he enters college.

> **NOTE** Example 2 in Appendix C shows how a financial calculator can be used to solve these same types of problems.

OBJECTIVE **3** **Find the amount of an annuity due.** Payments were made at the *end of each period* in the ordinary annuities discussed previously. In contrast, an annuity in which payments are made at the *beginning of each time period* is called **annuity due**. To find the amount of an annuity due, treat each payment as if it were made at *the end of the preceding period*, then

1. add 1 to the number of periods and find the amount using the table, and
2. subtract 1 payment from this amount.

EXAMPLE 3

Find the Amount of an Annuity Due

Mr. and Mrs. Thompson set up an investment program using an *annuity due* with payments of \$500 *at the beginning of each quarter*. Find the amount of the annuity if they make payments for 7 years in an account paying 12% compounded quarterly.

Solution

Interest of $\frac{12\%}{4} = 3\%$ is earned each quarter. There are $4 \times 7 = 28$ periods in 7 years. Since it is an annuity due, add 1 period to 28 making 29 periods. Look across the top of the table for 3% and down the side for 29 periods to find **45.21885**.

$$\text{Amount} = \$500 \times \mathbf{45.21885} = \$22{,}609.43$$

Now, subtract one payment.

$$\$22{,}609.43 - \mathbf{\$500} = \$22{,}109.43$$

The account will contain \$22,109.43 after 7 years.

> **PROBLEM-SOLVING HINT** For an annuity due, be sure to add 1 period to the number of compounding periods and subtract 1 payment from the amount calculated.

Objective **4** **Find the value of an IRA.** One great investment vehicle that working people can use to save for retirement is an **Individual Retirement Account**, also called an **IRA**. There are two types of IRA accounts, regular IRAs and Roth IRAs.

Deposits to a **regular IRA** account are usually excluded from federal income taxes in the current year. Therefore, a contribution to a regular IRA may reduce the amount of income taxes *that you must pay this year*. Interest earned in a regular IRA is not subject to income taxes in the year earned. At retirement, the account holder withdraws funds from the regular IRA and pays taxes at that time. As a result, a regular IRA may allow you to save for retirement *without having to pay taxes* on the savings for years or even decades!

Deposits to a **Roth IRA** are not excluded from federal taxes in the year paid, so they *do not* reduce current income taxes. However, the deposits and interest do grow tax free. In addition, one huge advantage is that the withdrawals from the Roth IRA at retirement are **not** subject to income taxes. This offers you a great opportunity to save money for retirement without having to pay as much in income tax as your retirement funds grow.

Roth IRA

WHICH IRA IS BEST FOR YOU?
If you've been contributing to a non-deductible, traditional IRA, the new Roth IRA where earnings grow tax free, is by far the better option. If you're trying to decide between a deductible IRA and a Roth, here are some facts that may help.

	DEDUCTIBLE IRA	ROTH IRA
Tax deductible?	If you qualify	No
Taxable at withdrawal?	Yes	No
Penalty for early withdrawal?	Yes, prior to age 59.5	Yes*
Mandatory withdrawal age?	70.5	None
Penalty-free withdrawals?	$10,000 for first-time home buyers; unlimited for education	$10,000 for first-time home buyers, after five-year wait; unlimited for education

*Never any penalty for withdrawing your own contributions, but a penalty applies to withdrawal of any gains within five years of opening the account and/or before turning 59.5.

EXAMPLE 4
Finding the Value of an IRA

For related Web activities, go to www.mathbusiness.com

Keyword:
education

At 27, Joann Gretz sets up an IRA with Merrill Lynch where she plans to deposit $2000 at the end of each year until age 60.

Find the amount of the annuity if she invests in **(a)** a treasury bill fund that has historically yielded 6% compounded annually versus **(b)** a stock fund that has historically yielded 10% compounded annually. Assume that future yields equal historical yields.

Solution
Age 60 is $60 - 27 =$ **33 years away**.

Treasury Bill Fund
Look down the left column of the amount of an annuity table on page 385 for 33 years and across the top for 6% to find **97.34316**.

$$\text{Amount} = \$2000 \times \mathbf{97.34316} = \$194,686.32$$

Stock Fund
Look down the left column of the table for 33 years and across the top for 10% to find **222.25154**.

$$\text{Amount} = \$2000 \times \mathbf{222.25154} = \$444,503.08$$

Gretz can see the projected difference in the results of the treasury bill fund and the stock fund using the graph. However, she is worried about the possibility of losing money in the stock fund. See Exercise 20 at the end of this section to find her investment choice.

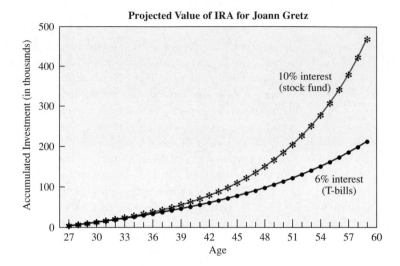

Projected Value of IRA for Joann Gretz

10.2 | PRESENT VALUE OF AN ANNUITY

Objectives

1. Define the present value of an annuity.
2. Use the formula to find the present value of an annuity.
3. Find the equivalent cash price of an annuity.

Objective 1 Define the present value of an annuity. The previous section discussed how to find the amount of an annuity after a series of equal periodic payments. This section considers the present value of such an annuity. There are two ways to think of the **present value of an annuity**.

PRESENT VALUE OF AN ANNUITY

1. The present value of an annuity is a lump sum that can be deposited today that will grow to the same future amount as would *periodic payments* into an annuity (see Example 1), or

2. the present value of an annuity is a lump sum that could be deposited today so that equal *periodic withdrawals* can be made (see Example 2).

Objective 2 Use the formula to find the present value of an annuity. The present value of an annuity with periodic payments at the end of each period is found using values from the table.

CALCULATING PRESENT VALUE OF AN ANNUITY

$$\text{Present value} = \text{Payment} \times \frac{\text{Number from present value}}{\text{of an annuity table}}$$

EXAMPLE 1
Finding the Present Value of an Annuity

Dion Martinez has decided to make annual payments of $1200 at the end of each year for 15 years into an investment that she thinks will yield 8% compounded annually. What lump sum deposited today at 8% compounded annually will result in the same future value?

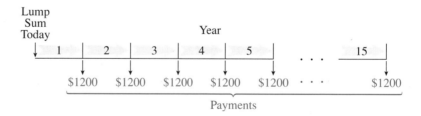

Solution

Look in the present value of an annuity table on the next page for 8% across the top and 15 periods down the side to find **8.55948**.

$$\text{Present value} = \$1200 \times \textbf{8.55948} = \$10{,}271.38$$

A lump sum of $10,271.38 deposited today at 8% compounded annually will result in the same total after 15 years as year-end deposits of $1200 for 15 years at 8% compounded annually. This result can be checked as follows.

From compound interest table in Section 9.1

Future value of lump sum = $10,271.38 × 3.17217 = $32,582.56

Future value of periodic payments = $1200 × 27.15211 = $32,582.53

From amount of an annuity table in Section 10.1

The difference of 3 cents is due to rounding.

Present Value of an Annuity Table
n = number of periods; i = interest rate per period

i / n	1%	1½%	2%	2½%	3%	4%	5%	6%	8%	10%	12%	i / n
1	.99010	.98522	.98039	.97561	.97087	.96154	.95238	.94340	.92593	.90909	.89286	1
2	1.97040	1.95588	1.94156	1.92742	1.91347	1.88609	1.85941	1.83339	1.78326	1.73554	1.69005	2
3	2.94099	2.91220	2.88388	2.85602	2.82861	2.77509	2.72325	2.67301	2.57710	2.48685	2.40183	3
4	3.90197	3.85438	3.80773	3.76197	3.71710	3.62990	3.54595	3.46511	3.31213	3.16987	3.03735	4
5	4.85343	4.78264	4.71346	4.64583	4.57971	4.45182	4.32948	4.21236	3.99271	3.79079	3.60478	5
6	5.79548	5.69719	5.60143	5.50813	5.41719	5.24214	5.07569	4.91732	4.62288	4.35526	4.11141	6
7	6.72819	6.59821	6.47199	6.34939	6.23028	6.00205	5.78637	5.58238	5.20637	4.86842	4.56376	7
8	7.65168	7.48593	7.32548	7.17014	7.01969	6.73274	6.46321	6.20979	5.74664	5.33493	4.96764	8
9	8.56602	8.36052	8.16224	7.97087	7.78611	7.43533	7.10782	6.80169	6.24689	5.75902	5.32825	9
10	9.47130	9.22218	8.98259	8.75206	8.53020	8.11090	7.72173	7.36009	6.71008	6.14457	5.65022	10
11	10.36763	10.07112	9.78685	9.51421	9.25262	8.76048	8.30641	7.88687	7.13896	6.49506	5.93770	11
12	11.25508	10.90751	10.57534	10.25776	9.95400	9.38507	8.86325	8.38384	7.53608	6.81369	6.19437	12
13	12.13374	11.73153	11.34837	10.98318	10.63496	9.98565	9.39357	8.85268	7.90378	7.10336	6.42355	13
14	13.00370	12.54338	12.10625	11.69091	11.29607	10.56312	9.89864	9.29498	8.24424	7.36669	6.62817	14
15	13.86505	13.34323	12.84926	12.38138	11.93794	11.11839	10.37966	9.71225	8.55948	7.60608	6.81086	15
16	14.71787	14.13126	13.57771	13.05500	12.56110	11.65230	10.83777	10.10590	8.85137	7.82371	6.97399	16
17	15.56225	14.90765	14.29187	13.71220	13.16612	12.16567	11.27407	10.47726	9.12164	8.02155	7.11963	17
18	16.39827	15.67256	14.99203	14.35336	13.75351	12.65930	11.68959	10.82760	9.37189	8.20141	7.24967	18
19	17.22601	16.42617	15.67846	14.97889	14.32380	13.13394	12.08532	11.15812	9.60360	8.36492	7.36578	19
20	18.04555	17.16864	16.35143	15.58916	14.87747	13.59033	12.46221	11.46992	9.81815	8.51356	7.46944	20
21	18.85698	17.90014	17.01121	16.18455	15.41502	14.02916	12.82115	11.76408	10.01680	8.64869	7.56200	21
22	19.66038	18.62082	17.65805	16.76541	15.93692	14.45112	13.16300	12.04158	10.20074	8.77154	7.64465	22
23	20.45582	19.33086	18.29220	17.33211	16.44361	14.85684	13.48857	12.30338	10.37106	8.88322	7.71843	23
24	21.24339	20.03041	18.91393	17.88499	16.93554	15.24696	13.79864	12.55036	10.52876	8.98474	7.78432	24
25	22.02316	20.71961	19.52346	18.42438	17.41315	15.62208	14.09394	12.78336	10.67478	9.07704	7.84314	25
26	22.79520	21.39863	20.12104	18.95061	17.87684	15.98277	14.37519	13.00317	10.80998	9.16095	7.89566	26
27	23.55961	22.06762	20.70690	19.46401	18.32703	16.32959	14.64303	13.21053	10.93516	9.23722	7.94255	27
28	24.31644	22.72672	21.28127	19.96489	18.76411	16.66306	14.89813	13.40616	11.05108	9.30657	7.98442	28
29	25.06579	23.37608	21.84438	20.45355	19.18845	16.98371	15.14107	13.59072	11.15841	9.36961	8.02181	29
30	25.80771	24.01584	22.39646	20.93029	19.60044	17.29203	15.37245	13.76483	11.25778	9.42691	8.05518	30
31	26.54229	24.64615	22.93770	21.39541	20.00043	17.58849	15.59281	13.92909	11.34980	9.47901	8.08499	31
32	27.26959	25.26714	23.46833	21.84918	20.38877	17.87355	15.80268	14.08404	11.43500	9.52638	8.11159	32
33	27.98969	25.87895	23.98856	22.29188	20.76579	18.14765	16.00255	14.23023	11.51389	9.56943	8.13535	33
34	28.70267	26.48173	24.49859	22.72379	21.13184	18.41120	16.19290	14.36814	11.58693	9.60857	8.15656	34
35	29.40858	27.07559	24.99862	23.14516	21.48722	18.66461	16.37419	14.49825	11.65457	9.64416	8.17550	35
36	30.10751	27.66068	25.48884	23.55625	21.83225	18.90828	16.54685	14.62099	11.71719	9.67651	8.19241	36
37	30.79951	28.23713	25.96945	23.95732	22.16724	19.14258	16.71129	14.73678	11.77518	9.70592	8.20751	37
38	31.48466	28.80505	26.44064	24.34860	22.49246	19.36786	16.86789	14.84602	11.82887	9.73265	8.22099	38
39	32.16303	29.36458	26.90259	24.73034	22.80822	19.58448	17.01704	14.94907	11.87858	9.75696	8.23303	39
40	32.83469	29.91585	27.35548	25.10278	23.11477	19.79277	17.15909	15.04630	11.92461	9.77905	8.24378	40
41	33.49969	30.45896	27.79949	25.46612	23.41240	19.99305	17.29437	15.13802	11.96723	9.79914	8.25337	41
42	34.15811	30.99405	28.23479	25.82061	23.70136	20.18563	17.42321	15.22454	12.00670	9.81740	8.26194	42
43	34.81001	31.52123	28.66156	26.16645	23.98190	20.37079	17.54591	15.30617	12.04324	9.83400	8.26959	43
44	35.45545	32.04062	29.07996	26.50385	24.25427	20.54884	17.66277	15.38318	12.07707	9.84909	8.27642	44
45	36.09451	32.55234	29.49016	26.83302	24.51871	20.72004	17.77407	15.45583	12.10840	9.86281	8.28252	45
46	36.72724	33.05649	29.89231	27.15417	24.77545	20.88465	17.88007	15.52437	12.13741	9.87528	8.28796	46
47	37.35370	33.55319	30.28658	27.46748	25.02471	21.04294	17.98102	15.58903	12.16427	9.88662	8.29282	47
48	37.97396	34.04255	30.67312	27.77315	25.26671	21.19513	18.07716	15.65003	12.18914	9.89693	8.29716	48
49	38.58808	34.52468	31.05208	28.07137	25.50166	21.34147	18.16872	15.70757	12.21216	9.90630	8.30104	49
50	39.19612	34.99969	31.42361	28.36231	25.72976	21.48218	18.25593	15.76186	12.23348	9.91481	8.30450	50

> **NOTE** There are 2 different methods to produce $32,582.53 in 15 years at 8% compounded annually. One way is a single deposit of $10,271.38 today. The other way is 15 end-of-year payments of $1200 each.

EXAMPLE 2
Finding the
Present Value

Fred and Sara Chou recently divorced. As part of the divorce settlement, Fred must pay Sara $2000 at the end of each year for 10 years. If money can be deposited at 6% compounded annually, find the lump sum he could deposit today to have enough money, with principal and interest, to make the payments. How much interest will be earned?

Solution

Look across the top of the present value of an annuity table for 6% and down the side for 10 periods to find **7.36009**.

$$\text{Present value} = \$2000 \times \textbf{7.36009} = \$14,720.18$$

A deposit of $14,720.18 today at 6% compounded annually is sufficient to make the 10 payments of $2000 each. The difference between the sum of all payments, $10 \times \$2000 = \$20,000$, and the amount deposited today is the interest.

$$\text{Interest} = 10 \times \$2000 - \textbf{\$14,720.18} = \$5279.82$$

> **NOTE** Although the $2000 withdrawals are at the end of each year, the original deposit must be made at the beginning of year 1.

EXAMPLE 3
Finding the
Present Value

An Australian petroleum engineering firm hires a new manager for their North American operations. The contract states that if the new manager works for 5 years, then he will receive a retirement benefit of $15,000 at the end of each semiannual period for 8 years. Find the lump sum the firm could deposit today to satisfy the retirement contract if funds can be invested at 10% compounded semiannually.

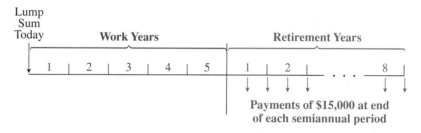

Payments of $15,000 at end of each semiannual period

Solution

First find the present value of an annuity with $2 \times 8 = 16$ periods at $\frac{10\%}{2} = 5\%$ per compounding period. Using the present value of an annuity table,

$$\text{Present value} = \$15,000 \times \textbf{10.83777} = \$162,566.55.$$

The firm needs $162,566.55 at the end of the 5 year work period to satisfy retirement benefits.

They can meet this liability today by depositing the present value of $162,566.55 given 10% compounded semiannually over 5 years. Using the present value of a dollar table in Section 9.3 (page 372) with $5 \times 2 = 10$ periods and $\frac{10\%}{2} = 5\%$ interest results in

$$\text{Present value} = \$162,566.55 \times \textbf{.61391} = \$99,801.23.$$

A lump sum of $99,801.23 deposited today will grow to $162,566.55 in 5 years which, with interest, is enough to make all 16 retirement payments of $15,000 each.

For related Web
activities, go to
www.mathbusiness.com

Keyword:
scheme

EXAMPLE 4
Determining
Retirement Income

Tish Baker plans to retire from nursing at age 65 and hopes to withdraw $25,000 per year until she is 90. **(a)** If money earns 8% per year compounded annually, how much will she need at age 65? **(b)** If she deposits $2000 per year into her retirement plan beginning at age 32, and if the retirement plan earns 8% per year compounded annually, will her retirement account have enough for her to meet her goals?

Solution

(a) The amount needed at age 65 is the present value of an annuity of $25,000 per year for 90 − 65 = 25 years, with interest of 8% compounded annually. Using the present value of an annuity table,

$$\text{Present value} = \$25,000 \times \mathbf{10.67478} = \$266,869.50$$

Baker will need $266,869.50 at age 65; this sum, at 8% compounded annually, will permit withdrawals of $25,000 per year until age 90.

(b) Baker makes payments of $2000 at the end of each year for 65 − 32 = 33 years, at 8% compounded annually. These payments form a regular annuity and using the amount of an annuity table in Section 10.1,

$$\text{Future value} = \$2000 \times \mathbf{145.95062} = \$291,901.24.$$

The value in the retirement account at 65 (**$291,901.24**) exceeds the amount needed to fund 25 yearly withdrawals of $25,000 each (**$266,869.50**). Therefore, Tish Baker will have more than enough money.

> **NOTE** Example 7 in Appendix C shows how a financial calculator can be used to solve a problem similar to Example 4.

Objective $\boxed{3}$ **Find the equivalent cash price of an annuity.** By now, it is clear that two sums of money may differ and yet be equivalent because the sums of money *are available at different periods of time*. As in the next example, the present value of a future sum must be calculated to permit meaningful comparisons.

Example 5

Comparing Methods of Investment

Julia Smithers is an attorney trying to settle an estate. The estate owns a piece of property that is desired by two different developers. Developer A offers $140,000 in cash today for the land. Developer B offers $50,000 now as a down payment, with payments of $8000 at the end of each quarter for 4 years. Money may be invested at 12% compounded quarterly. If Developer B offers a bank guarantee that the payment will be made, making each offer equally safe, which bid should the attorney accept?

Solution

The bids can be compared only if the present value of the offer of Developer B is found. This offer is a down payment and an annuity of $8000 at the end of each quarter for 4 years. The present value of this annuity is found in the present value of an annuity table with 4 × 4 = 16 periods and $\frac{12\%}{4} = 3\%$ interest per period.

$$\text{Present value} = \$8000 \times \mathbf{12.56110} = \$100,488.80$$

The present value of the annuity is $100,488.80. Since Developer B also offers a down payment of $50,000, the **equivalent cash price** offer amounts to

$$\$50,000 + \$100,488.80 = \$150,488.80.$$

Since this amount exceeds the $140,000 offered by Developer A, the attorney should accept the offer of Developer B.

10.3 | Sinking Funds (Finding Annuity Payments)

Objectives

1 Understand the basics of a sinking fund.
2 Set up a sinking fund table.

Problem Solving in Business

Children's Hospital, where Tish Baker works, estimates that they will need a new magnetic resonance imaging (MRI) machine in 3 years. MRI machines use superconductivity, magnetic fields, radio waves, and high-speed computers to form images of the inside of the human body. For example, MRI technology can be used *to locate a tumor in the brain or a bone spur inside a knee*. The hospital has decided to set up a sinking fund that will help them accumulate funds to purchase the MRI machine.

Objective 1 **Understand the basics of a sinking fund.** Individuals and businesses often need to raise a certain amount of money for use *at some fixed time in the future*. For example, Paul Pence needs $28,000 to purchase a truck in 3 years. Using 8% compounded quarterly and the amount of an annuity table in Section 10.1, one can guess the required payment at the end of each quarter needed to accumulate the $28,000:

Estimated quarterly payment	From table	Future value	The guess is
$1500	$1500 × **13.41209** = $20,118.14		too low
$2800	$2800 × **13.41209** = $37,553.85		too high

Clearly this method is awkward. The exact payment in this example can be found by dividing the future value of $28,000 by 13.41209, or by using the table and methods provided in this section.

A fund set up to receive periodic payments is called a **sinking fund**. Sinking funds are used to provide money *to pay off a loan* in one lump sum *or to accumulate money* to build new factories, buy equipment, and so on. Large corporations and some government agencies use a form of debt called a **bond**, which is a promise to pay a fixed amount of money at some stated time in the future. Bonds are discussed in detail in Section 10.5—this section covers only the use of a sinking fund to pay off a bond when it is due.

The amount of the periodic payment needed, at the end of each period, to accumulate a fixed amount at a future date is

Payment = Future value × Number from sinking fund table

Example 1
Finding Periodic Payments

KidsToys, Inc. sold $100,000 worth of bonds that must be paid off in 8 years. They now must set up a sinking fund to accumulate the necessary $100,000 to pay off their debt. Find the amount of each payment into a sinking fund if the payments are made at the end of each year and the fund earns 10% compounded annually. Find the amount of interest earned.

Solution

Look along the top of the sinking fund table for 10% and down the side for 8 periods to find .08744.

Payment = $100,000 × **.08744** = $8744

KidsToys must deposit $8744 at the end of each year for 8 years in an account paying 10% compounded annually to accumulate $100,000. The interest earned is the future value less all payments.

Interest = $100,000 − (8 × **$8744**) = $30,048

Sinking Fund Table
n = number of periods; i = interest rate per period

i n	1%	$1\frac{1}{2}$%	2%	$2\frac{1}{2}$%	3%	4%	5%	6%	8%	10%	12%	i n
1	1.00000	1.00000	1.00000	1.00000	1.00000	1.00000	1.00000	1.00000	1.00000	1.00000	1.00000	1
2	.49751	.49628	.49505	.49383	.49261	.49020	.48780	.48544	.48077	.47619	.47170	2
3	.33002	.32838	.32675	.32514	.32353	.32035	.31721	.31411	.30803	.30211	.29635	3
4	.24628	.24444	.24262	.24082	.23903	.23549	.23201	.22859	.22192	.21547	.20923	4
5	.19604	.19409	.19216	.19025	.18835	.18463	.18097	.17740	.17046	.16380	.15741	5
6	.16255	.16053	.15853	.15655	.15460	.15076	.14702	.14336	.13632	.12961	.12323	6
7	.13863	.13656	.13451	.13250	.13051	.12661	.12282	.11914	.11207	.10541	.09912	7
8	.12069	.11858	.11651	.11447	.11246	.10853	.10472	.10104	.09401	.08744	.08130	8
9	.10674	.10461	.10252	.10046	.09843	.09449	.09069	.08702	.08008	.07364	.06768	9
10	.09558	.09343	.09133	.08926	.08723	.08329	.07950	.07587	.06903	.06275	.05698	10
11	.08645	.08429	.08218	.08011	.07808	.07415	.07039	.06679	.06608	.05396	.04842	11
12	.07885	.07668	.07456	.07249	.07046	.06655	.06283	.05928	.05270	.04676	.04144	12
13	.07241	.07024	.06812	.06605	.06403	.06014	.05646	.05296	.04652	.04078	.03568	13
14	.06690	.06472	.06260	.06054	.05853	.05467	.05102	.04758	.04130	.03575	.03087	14
15	.06212	.05994	.05783	.05577	.05377	.04994	.04634	.04296	.03683	.03147	.02682	15
16	.05794	.05577	.05365	.05160	.04961	.04582	.04227	.03895	.03298	.02782	.02339	16
17	.05426	.05208	.04997	.04793	.04595	.04220	.03870	.03544	.02963	.02466	.02046	17
18	.05098	.04881	.04670	.04467	.04271	.03899	.03555	.03236	.02670	.02193	.01794	18
19	.04805	.04588	.04378	.04176	.03981	.03614	.03275	.02962	.02413	.01955	.01576	19
20	.04542	.04325	.04116	.03915	.03722	.03358	.03024	.02718	.02185	.01746	.01388	20
21	.04303	.04087	.03878	.03679	.03487	.03128	.02800	.02500	.01983	.01562	.01224	21
22	.04086	.03870	.03663	.03465	.03275	.02920	.02597	.02305	.01803	.01401	.01081	22
23	.03889	.03673	.03467	.03270	.03081	.02731	.02414	.02128	.01642	.01257	.00956	23
24	.03707	.03492	.03287	.03091	.02905	.02559	.02247	.01968	.01498	.01130	.00846	24
25	.03541	.03326	.03122	.02928	.02743	.02401	.02095	.01823	.01368	.01017	.00750	25
26	.03387	.03173	.02970	.02777	.02594	.02257	.01956	.01690	.01251	.00916	.00665	26
27	.03245	.03032	.02829	.02638	.02456	.02124	.01829	.01570	.01145	.00826	.00590	27
28	.03112	.02900	.02699	.02509	.02329	.02001	.01712	.01459	.01049	.00745	.00524	28
29	.02990	.02778	.02578	.02389	.02211	.01888	.01605	.01358	.00962	.00673	.00466	29
30	.02875	.02664	.02465	.02278	.02102	.01783	.01505	.01265	.00883	.00608	.00414	30
31	.02768	.02557	.02360	.02174	.02000	.01686	.01413	.01179	.00811	.00550	.00369	31
32	.02667	.02458	.02261	.02077	.01905	.01595	.01328	.01100	.00745	.00497	.00328	32
33	.02573	.02364	.02169	.01986	.01816	.01510	.01249	.01027	.00685	.00450	.00292	33
34	.02484	.02276	.02082	.01901	.01732	.01431	.01176	.00960	.00630	.00407	.00260	34
35	.02400	.02193	.02000	.01821	.01654	.01358	.01107	.00897	.00580	.00369	.00232	35
36	.02321	.02115	.01923	.01745	.01580	.01289	.01043	.00839	.00534	.00334	.00206	36
37	.02247	.02041	.01851	.01674	.01511	.01224	.00984	.00786	.00492	.00303	.00184	37
38	.02176	.01972	.01782	.01607	.01446	.01163	.00928	.00736	.00454	.00275	.00164	38
39	.02109	.01905	.01717	.01544	.01384	.01106	.00876	.00689	.00419	.00249	.00146	39
40	.02046	.01843	.01656	.01484	.01326	.01052	.00828	.00646	.00386	.00226	.00130	40
41	.01985	.01783	.01597	.01427	.01271	.01002	.00782	.00606	.00356	.00205	.00116	41
42	.01928	.01726	.01542	.01373	.01219	.00954	.00739	.00568	.00329	.00186	.00104	42
43	.01873	.01672	.01489	.01322	.01170	.00909	.00699	.00533	.00303	.00169	.00092	43
44	.01820	.01621	.01439	.01273	.01123	.00866	.00662	.00501	.00280	.00153	.00083	44
45	.01771	.01572	.01391	.01227	.01079	.00826	.00626	.00470	.00259	.00139	.00074	45
46	.01723	.01525	.01345	.01183	.01036	.00788	.00593	.00441	.00239	.00126	.00066	46
47	.01677	.01480	.01302	.01141	.00996	.00752	.00561	.00415	.00221	.00115	.00059	47
48	.01633	.01437	.01260	.01101	.00958	.00718	.00532	.00390	.00204	.00104	.00052	48
49	.01591	.01396	.01220	.01062	.00921	.00686	.00504	.00366	.00189	.00095	.00047	49
50	.01551	.01357	.01182	.01026	.00887	.00655	.00478	.00344	.00174	.00086	.00042	50

> **NOTE** The interest rate a company earns on sinking fund investments frequently differs from the interest rate they must pay on debts such as bonds.

OBJECTIVE **2** Set up a sinking fund table. A **sinking fund table** is used to show the interest earned and the accumulated amount of a sinking fund at the end of each period.

EXAMPLE 2
Setting up a
Sinking Fund
Table

KidsToys, Inc., in Example 1, deposited $8744 at the end of each year for 8 years in a sinking fund that earned 10% compounded annually. Set up a sinking fund table for these deposits.

Solution

The sinking fund account contains no money until the end of the first year, when a single deposit of $8744 is made. Since the deposit is made at the end of the year, no interest is earned.

At the end of the second year, the account contains the original $8744, plus the interest earned by this money. This interest is found by the formula for simple interest.

$$I = \$8744 \times .10 \times 1 = \textbf{\$874.40}$$

An additional deposit is also made at the end of the second year, so that the sinking fund then contains a total of

$$\$8744 + \textbf{\$874.40} + \$8744 = \$18,362.40$$

Continue this work to get the following sinking fund table.

	Beginning of Period		End of Period	
Period	**Accumulated Amount**	**Periodic Deposit**	**Interest Earned**	**Accumulated Amount**
1	$0	$8744.00	$0	$8744.00
2	$8744.00	$8744.00	$874.40	$18,362.40
3	$18,362.40	$8744.00	$1836.24	$28,942.64
4	$28,942.64	$8744.00	$2894.26	$40,580.90
5	$40,580.90	$8744.00	$4058.09	$53,382.99
6	$53,382.99	$8744.00	$5338.30	$67,465.29
7	$67,465.29	$8744.00	$6746.53	$82,955.82
8	$82,955.82	$8748.60	$8295.58	$100,000.00

> **NOTE** The last payment differs by $4.60 due to rounding. The accumulated amount must equal $100,000.

In Example 1, a sinking fund was set up to pay off the principal due on some bonds. A sinking fund can be set up to pay off *both principal and interest* on a loan. The following example presents another application for a sinking fund in which funds are accumulated for a large purchase.

EXAMPLE 3
Finding Periodic
Payments and
Interest Earned

Children's Hospital plans to purchase a new MRI machine in 3 years. The machine currently sells for $2,100,000, but the price is expected to increase at 8% per year compounded semiannually. The hospital decides to set up a sinking fund to purchase the machine. Find the amount of each year-end payment into the fund, if annual payments are made and the money is expected to earn 6% compounded annually. Round the payment to the nearest dollar.

Solution

First, find the future price of the MRI machine using $\frac{8\%}{2} = 4\%$ interest for $3 \times 2 = 6$ periods in the compound interest table on page 354.

$$\text{Future price} = \$2,100,000 \times \textbf{1.26532} = \$2,657,172$$

This is the total amount that the sinking fund must accumulate. The required payment is found using the sinking fund table with 3 periods and 6% interest to find **.31411**.

Payment = $2,657,172 × .31411 = $834,644 (rounded)

Payments of $834,644 at the end of each year into a sinking fund paying 6% per year compounded annually will produce enough to pay cash for the MRI machine in 3 years.

Two different interest rates are involved in Example 3. The price is increasing at 8% per year compounded semiannually, but deposits in the sinking fund earn 6% compounded annually. **Interest rate spreads** such as this are common in business. For example, banks use an interest rate spread between what they pay for funds on deposit and what they charge on loans to customers.

Name   Date   Class

10.3 | EXERCISES

The Quick Start exercises in each section contain solutions to help you get started.

Find the amount of each payment needed to accumulate the indicated amount in a sinking fund. Round to the nearest cent. (See Examples 1–3.)

Quick Start

1. $8400, money earns 10% compounded annually, 5 years

   Payment = $8400 × .16380 = $1375.92

   1. <u>$1375.92</u>

2. $3500, money earns 6% compounded annually, 6 years

   Payment = $3500 × .14336 = $501.76

   2. <u>$501.76</u>

3. $8200, money earns 6% compounded semiannually, 5 years

   3. _____

4. $12,000, money earns 10% compounded semiannually, 3 years

   4. _____

5. $50,000, money earns 4% compounded quarterly, 5 years

   5. _____

6. $25,000, money earns 12% compounded quarterly, 4 years

   6. _____

7. $7894, money earns 12% compounded monthly, 3 years

   7. _____

8. $29,804, money earns 12% compounded monthly, 2 years

   8. _____

9. Explain interest rate spread and include actual examples of such a spread. (See Example 3.)

10. Explain the difference between a sinking fund (see Objective 1) and the present value of an annuity discussed in Section 10.2.

Solve each application problem. Round to the nearest cent.

Quick Start

11. **TRUCK PURCHASE** Paul Pence needs $28,000 to purchase a truck in 3 years. **(a)** Find the amount of each payment if payments are made at the end of each quarter with interest at 8% compounded quarterly. **(b)** Find the total amount of interest earned.

    (a) Payment = $28,000 × .07456 = $2087.68
    (b) Interest = $28,000 − (12 × $2087.68) = $2947.84

    (a) <u>$2087.68</u>
    (b) <u>$2947.84</u>

Quick Start

12. ALLIGATOR HUNTING Cajun Jack needs $45,000 in 4 years for a boat used to hunt alligators. **(a)** Find the amount of each payment if payments are made at the end of each quarter with interest at 6% compounded quarterly. **(b)** Find the total amount of interest earned.

(a) $2509.65
(b) $4845.60

    (a) Payment = $45,000 × .05577 = $2509.65
    (b) Interest = $45,000 − (16 × $2509.65) = $4845.60

13. NEW EQUIPMENT PURCHASE A Canadian gold mining company needs $4,000,000 to purchase some new equipment in 2 years. **(a)** Find the amount of each payment if payments are made at the end of each semiannual period with interest at 10% per year compounded semiannually. **(b)** Find the total amount of interest earned.

(a) _____
(b) _____

14. ROBOT PURCHASES A Japanese electronics factory needs $850,000 in 3 years for new robots. **(a)** Find the amount of each payment if payments are made at the end of each semiannual period with interest at 5% per year compounded semiannually. **(b)** Find the total amount of interest earned.

(a) _____
(b) _____

15. NEW MACHINERY Smith Dry Cleaning must buy a new cleaning machine in 7 years for $120,000. The firm sets up a sinking fund for this purpose. Find the payment into the fund at the end of each year if money in the fund earns 10% compounded annually.

15. _____

16. A NEW AUDITORIUM The membership of the Green Acres Baptist Church is large and growing rapidly. The leaders of the church are planning to build a new auditorium, with special features for their televised broadcasts, at a cost of $2,800,000 in 5 years. They have set up a sinking fund with the idea of making a payment at the end of each quarter. Find the payment needed if money earns 8% compounded quarterly.

16. _____

17. A NEW SHOWROOM A Denver Ford dealership wants to build a new showroom costing $2,300,000. They set up a sinking fund with end of the month payments in an account earning 12% compounded monthly. Find the amount that should be deposited in this fund each month if they wish to build the showroom **(a)** in 3 years and **(b)** in 4 years.

(a) _____
(b) _____

18. AIRPORT IMPROVEMENTS A city near Chicago sold $9,000,000 in bonds to pay for improvements to an airport. They set up a sinking fund with end of the quarter payments in an account earning 8% compounded quarterly. Find the amount that should be deposited in this fund each quarter if they wish to pay off the bonds in **(a)** 7 years and **(b)** 12 years.

(a) _____
(b) _____

Name   Date   Class

19. LAND SALE   Helen Spence sells some land in Nevada. She will be paid a lump sum of $60,000 in 4   **(a)** _____
years. Until then, the buyer pays 8% simple interest every quarter. **(a)** Find the amount of each   **(b)** _____
quarterly interest payment. **(b)** The buyer sets up a sinking fund so that enough money will be present
to pay off the $60,000. The buyer wants to make semiannual payments into the sinking fund; the
account pays 8% compounded semiannually. Find the amount of each payment into the fund.
(c) Prepare a table showing the amount in the sinking fund after each deposit.

(c)

Payment Number	Amount of Deposit	Interest Earned	Total in Account

20. RARE STAMPS   Jeff Reschke bought a rare stamp for his collection. He agreed to pay a lump sum of   **(a)** _____
$4000 after 5 years. Until then, he pays 6% simple interest every 6 months. **(a)** Find the amount of   **(b)** _____
each semiannual interest payment. **(b)** Reschke sets up a sinking fund so that money will be present
to pay off the $4000. He wants to make annual payments into the fund. The account pays 8%
compounded annually. Find the amount of each payment into the fund. **(c)** Prepare a table showing
the amount in the sinking fund after each deposit.

(c)

Payment Number	Amount of Deposit	Interest Earned	Total in Account

21. MRI MACHINE   Prepare a sinking fund table for the purchase of the MRI machine by Children's
Hospital in Example 3.

Payment Number	Amount of Deposit	Interest Earned	Total in Account

22. COMMERCIAL BUILDING   Joan Miller plans to make a down payment of $70,000 on a commercial building for her plumbing company in 5 years. Construct a sinking fund table given semiannual payments of $6106.10 at the end of each period and an interest rate of 6% compounded semiannually.

Payment Number	Amount of Deposit	Interest Earned	Total in Account

10.4 | Stocks

Objectives

1. Define the types of stock.
2. Read stock tables.
3. Find the current yield on a stock.
4. Find the stock's PE ratio.
5. Define the Dow Jones Industrial Average.
6. Define a mutual fund.

Problem Solving in Business

Tish Baker has started her first professional job as a nurse. She wonders if investing in stocks or in a mutual fund can help achieve her financial goals. By knowing her investment options and the choices she has, Baker can establish a solid retirement plan.

Almost all large businesses, as well as many smaller ones, are set up as **corporations**, which is a form of business that gives the owners **limited liability**. Limited liability can offer the owners protection from lawsuits—an owner of a corporation can never lose more than he or she has invested in the corporation.

A corporation is set up with money, or **capital**, raised through the sale of shares of **stock**. A share of stock represents partial ownership of a corporation. If one million shares of stock are sold to establish a new firm, the owner of one share will own one-millionth of the corporation. The ownership of stock is shown by **stock certificates**, like the one shown here.

In most states, corporations are required to have an **annual meeting**. At this meeting, open to all **stockholders** (owners of stock), the management of the firm is open to questions from stockholders. The stockholders also elect a **board of directors**—a group of people who represent the stockholders. The board of directors hires the **executive officers** of the corporation, such as the president, vice-presidents, and so on. The board of directors also distributes a portion of any profits in the form of **dividends** that are paid to the stockholders.

> **NOTE** You may wish to go to the Web site of a discount stock broker such as E*TRADE or Ameritrade. These firms allow individuals to buy or sell stocks very cheaply through the use of the World Wide Web. E*TRADE will also let you play a game of buying and selling stocks with imaginary money.

OBJECTIVE **1** **Define the types of stock.** The two types of stock normally issued are **preferred stock** and **common stock**. As the name suggests, preferred stock *has certain rights* over common stock. For example, owners of preferred stock must be paid dividends *before* any dividends can be paid to owners of common stock. Also, corporate debt and preferred shareholders must be paid *before* common shareholders receive anything in the event a corporation declares bankruptcy.

The shares of **publicly held corporations** are typically owned by many different individuals and institutions. Share prices of these firms are determined by supply and demand in public markets called **stock exchanges**. The New York Stock Exchange is the largest of the several exchanges in the United States. This exchange is located on Wall Street in New York City. Most foreign countries including Japan, Taiwan, England, Canada, and Mexico have their own stock exchanges. One of the most widely circulated financial newspapers in the country is the *Wall Street Journal,* which is published daily by Dow Jones & Company, Inc. It provides the reader with stock and bond quotes in addition to presenting general business, marketing, and financial news.

OBJECTIVE **2** **Read stock tables.** Daily stock prices are quoted in numerous sources including many local newspapers. The format of the information differs from one paper to the next. Each paper will explain the information given.

EXAMPLE 1
Working with the Stock Table

Tish Baker's stockbroker recommended that she look at the stock of a company that she knows. She chose to look at the following data on McDonald's taken from the *Wall Street Journal.*

SOLUTION

52 Weeks					Yld		Vol				Net
Hi	Lo	Stock	Sym	Div	%	PE	100s	Hi	Lo	Close	Chg
64⅛	42⅛	McDonald's	MCD	.33	.5	28	35924	66	63½	65⅞	+3 1/16

The numbers 64⅛ and 42⅛ in front of McDonald's are the highest (64⅛ = $64.125) and lowest (42⅛ = $42.125) price that the stock has traded at during the past 52 weeks. Following the stock symbol for the company (MCD) is *the annual dividend* paid to shareholders of $.33 per share. This dividend equals .5% of the current stock price, which is shown as the close (closing price) for the day (65⅞ = $65.875) or .005 × $65.875 = $.33 rounded. The price-to-earnings ratio (PE) is discussed later.

Then comes 35,924, which is the sales for the day in hundreds of shares. On this particular day, the number of shares of McDonald's that traded was

$$35,924 \times 100 = 3,592,400 \text{ shares.}$$

Next are the highest price (66) and the lowest price (63½) that McDonald's stock sold at during this particular day. Following the closing price of 65⅞, the net change of +3 1/16 means that McDonald's stock increased in value by 3 1/16 of a dollar ($3.0625), compared to the previous day.

–M–M–M–

52 Weeks Hi	52 Weeks Lo	Stock	Sym	Div	Yld %	PE	Vol 100s	Hi	Lo	Close	Net Chg
17	10	MaterlSci	MSC		...	24	4179	10 1/4	9 15/16	10	−1/16
12 1/4	6 3/4	MatlackSys	MLK		...	27	3	8 1/4	8 1/4	8 1/4	...
211	135 1/8	MatsuElec	MC	.99e	.6	...	59	168	164 3/8	165	+4 1/2
46 9/16	28 3/8	Mattel	MAT	.32f	.8	23	16700	39 7/16	38 7/16	39 3/16	−1/2
19	11 3/4	Mattel dep pfC		.41	2.6	...	2591	15 7/8	15 1/2	15 7/8	−11/16
4 3/8	3 1/2	MaunaLoa	NUT	.30	7.4	2	432	4 1/16	4	4 1/16	+1/16
10 7/8	3 13/16	Mavesa ADR	MAV	.08e	2.0	...	78	4 1/16	4	4	...
19 3/8	10	MaximGrp	MXG		...	17	285	17 3/16	16 7/8	16 7/8	−1/4
x 26 7/8	25 1/2	MaxusEngy pfA		2.50a	9.7	...	96	25 7/8	25 11/16	25 11/16	...
29	14 1/8	MaxximMed	MAM		...	18	383	25 3/4	25 1/8	25 3/4	+5/8
66 1/2	46 5/8	MayDeptStrs	MAY	1.27	2.0	20	1501	64 11/16	63 13/16	64 5/8	+3/16
55 3/4	24 3/8	Maytag	MYG	.64	1.2	23	7127	53 3/16	52 3/16	52 1/2	+1/4
35 3/16	25 1/8	McClatchy A	MNI	.38	1.3	18	307	30	29 7/8	29 15/16	...
52 1/4	22 1/8	McDermott	JRM		...	dd	1769	45 3/8	44 1/8	44 1/8	−1 3/4
43 15/16	23 5/8	McDermInt	MDR	.20	.5	dd	4487	40 3/4	38 3/4	38 3/8	−2 1/2
43 1/2	30	McDermInt	pfA	2.20	5.6		20	41	39 3/8	39 3/8	−2 1/8
31 3/4	29 3/8	McDermInt	pfB	2.60	8.3	...	334	31 1/2	31 5/16	31 1/2	+1/4
s 31 1/2	17 7/8	McDnldInv	MDD	.25	.8	15	146	29 5/8	29 5/16	29 5/8	+3/16
▲ 64 1/8	42 1/8	McDonalds	MCD	.33	.5	28	35924	66	63 1/2	65 7/8	+3 1/16
26 3/8	24 1/2	McDonalds 2037	MCJ	1.88	7.3	...	37	25 11/16	25 9/16	25 11/16	+1/16
26 5/16	24 1/2	McDonalds sbdt	MCW	1.88	7.4	...	102	25 11/16	25 1/2	25 9/16	−1/16
79 15/16	52 1/8	McGrawH	MHP	1.56	2.1	25	4654	75 7/16	74 1/4	75 7/16	+1 3/16
75 1/4	36 5/8	McKesson	MCK	.50	.7	46	3358	74 7/8	72 15/16	73 15/16	−11/16
28 1/8	21 1/4	McWhorter	MWT		...	18	83	28	27 7/8	27 7/8	−1/8
s 37 11/16	27 1/16	Mead	MEA	.64	1.8	23	1624	35	34 5/8	34 15/16	+3/16
35	21 1/2	♣MdwbrkInsGp	MIG	.08	.3	22	10	31 7/16	31 1/8	31 7/16	+1/4
n 17 1/8	9 3/4	Meadowcrft	MWI		...	...	77	16 9/16	16 5/16	16 5/16	−1/8

–N–N–N–

52 Weeks Hi	52 Weeks Lo	Stock	Sym	Div	Yld %	PE	Vol 100s	Hi	Lo	Close	Net Chg
26 11/16	24 1/4	NB CapTr	TOPRS	1.96	7.6	...	254	25 3/4	25 5/8	25 5/8	...
73	58 15/16	NCH	NCH	1.40	2.2	15	31	64 7/16	63 13/16	64 3/8	+1/16
38 1/2	25 5/8	NCR Cp	NCR		...	cc	2631	37 1/8	36 13/16	36 15/16	+3/8
s 22	12 21/32	♣NFO Wrldwde	NFO		...	32	87	19	18 13/16	19	+1/16
20	13 15/16	NGC Cp	NGL	.05	.3	23	182	14 15/16	14 11/16	14 11/16	−1/8
25 13/16	24 1/8	Nipsco QDCS A	NIC	1.94	7.7	...	25	25 5/16	25 1/4	25 1/4	−1/16
s 28 1/2	20 1/8	NIPSCO	NI	.96	3.6	18	3864	26 1/2	25 7/8	26 7/16	+9/16
23	12 1/8	♣NL Ind	NL	.03e	.1	3	270	20 3/8	19 7/8	20 3/16	+5/16
41 3/8	6	NS Gp	NSS		...	11	2151	13	12 5/8	12 11/16	−3/16
26 3/8	24 1/2	NSP Fin TOPrS		1.97	7.7	...	60	25 3/4	25 5/8	25 3/4	+1/16
29 5/8	19 3/4	NUI	NUI	.98	4.0	15	1336	24 11/16	24 5/16	24 5/8	−1/16
26 1/8	24 3/4	NWPS CapTr pf		2.03	7.9	...	11	25 5/8	25 5/8	25 5/8	−1/8
54 1/4	37 1/2	Nabisco	NA	.70	1.5	30	5376	47 1/16	45 11/16	46 13/16	+1 1/16
177	48 1/2	♣NACCO	NC	.82f	.5	15	343	160	155 15/16	157	−2 15/16
42 7/16	35 3/4	Nalco	NLC	1.00	2.6	18	1441	38 3/16	37 3/4	38 1/16	+3/8
17 1/2	9 1/2	Nashua	NSH			dd	117	16	15 13/16	16	+1/16
81 1/4	63 1/2	NtlAuslBk	NAB	1.70e	2.4	...	163	70 1/8	69 1/4	69 3/4	−7/16
30 3/8	25 7/8	NtlAustBk Ex	NAU	1.97	6.8	...	189	29 1/8	29	29	−1/16
77 1/2	50	♣NtlCity	NCC	1.84	2.6	22	4548	70 3/4	69 1/2	69 7/8	+7/8
46 1/2	32 1/8	♣NtlDataCp	NDC	.30	.8	cc	302	39 1/2	39 1/4	39 1/2	+1/16
18 1/2	10	NtlDiscBrkr	NDB		...	13	80	11 11/16	11 9/16	11 9/16	−1/8
49 1/8	40 1/8	NtlFuelGas	NFG	1.74	4.0	49	513	43 7/16	42 15/16	43 1/4	+1/4
35	28 5/16	♣NtlGolfProp	TEE	1.72	5.8	23	841	29 13/16	29 9/16	29 9/16	−3/8
44 3/4	32 1/8	NtlHlthInv	NHI	2.96	8.6	11	352	34 11/16	34 1/4	34 9/16	−1/16
39 1/4	30 1/2	NtlHlthInv pf		2.13	6.8	...	73	31 1/4	31	31 1/4	+1/2
8 1/4	1 3/8	NtlMedia	NM		...	dd	1011	1 9/16	1 3/8	1 1/2	−1/16
s 44 7/16	22 1/4	NtlOilwell	NOI		...	28	1673	35 3/4	33 1/2	33 3/4	−1 13/16

Source: *Wall Street Journal*, 5/21/98. Reprinted by permission of Dow Jones, Inc. via Copyright Clearance Center, Inc.

The public does not go directly to an exchange to buy and sell stock. Instead, they buy stock through **stockbrokers** who have access to an exchange. The broker charges a commission for executing an order. Commissions today are competitive and vary considerably among brokers. For example, **discount brokers** charge lower commissions. Stocks can also be bought and sold *over the Internet* without speaking to a broker, at even lower commissions.

EXAMPLE 2

Finding the Cost of Stocks

Ignoring commissions, find Tish Baker's cost

(a) of purchasing 100 shares of McDonald's (MCD) at the closing price for the day and

(b) of purchasing 50 shares of NIPSCO (NI) at the low for the day.

Then, find the annual dividend on all 150 shares of stock.

SOLUTION

(a) The total cost of 100 shares of McDonald's is the price per share, **$65\frac{7}{8}$**, times the number of shares.

$$65\tfrac{7}{8} \times 100 = \mathbf{\$65.875} \times 100 = \$6587.50$$

(b) The total cost of 50 shares of NIPSCO at the low price of **$25\frac{7}{8}$** is

$$\mathbf{\$25.875} \times 50 = \$1293.75.$$

(c) The total annual dividend is the sum of the dividends from both companies. The dividend paid by McDonald's is \$.33 per share per year and the dividend paid by NIPSCO is \$.96 per share per year.

$$\text{Total dividend} = (100 \times \$.33) + (50 \times \$.96) = \$81$$

OBJECTIVE 3 **Find the current yield on a stock.** There is no certain way of choosing stocks that will go up in price. However, two **stock ratios** that people commonly look at before buying shares of a company are the **current yield** and the **price-earnings ratio** defined on the next page. The current yield (annual cash return as a percent of current price) on a stock is used to compare the dividends paid by stocks selling at different prices. Find current yield with the following formula.

$$\text{Current yield} = \frac{\text{Annual dividend per share}}{\text{Closing price per share}}$$

This result usually is converted to a percent (rounded to the nearest tenth). The annual dividend rate and the current yield can be found in the stock tables in daily newspapers.

EXAMPLE 3

Finding the Current Yield

Find the current yield for each of the following stocks:

(a) NCH (NCH), dividend $1.40 per year, purchase price 64½
(b) Nalco (NLC), dividend $1.00 per year, purchase price 37¾

Solution

(a) Current yield $= \dfrac{\$1.40}{\$64.50} = .022 = 2.2\%$ (rounded)

(b) Current yield $= \dfrac{\$1.00}{\$38.0625} = .026 = 2.6\%$ (rounded)

> **NOTE**   A stock pays *no dividend* when the company has been going through bad times or is investing in research or new plants that promise a long-term payoff. Sometimes a small, new company *pays no dividends during its early years*, preferring to reinvest the money for long-term growth.

Objective [4] **Find the stock's PE ratio.**   One number that some people use to help decide which stock to buy is the **price-earnings ratio** (abbreviated **PE ratio**). This ratio is found with the following formula.

$$\text{PE ratio} = \frac{\text{Closing price per share}}{\text{Annual net income per share}}$$

EXAMPLE 4

Finding the PE Ratio

You would like to own stock in Exxon or Harley-Davidson, but you do not know if either stock is a good buy. One thing you can do is look at the PE ratio for each.

(a) Exxon, price per share 71¼, annual net income per share $3.24, and
(b) Harley-Davidson, price per share 34¹³⁄₁₆, annual net income per share $1.16.

Solution

Use the formula for PE ratio to get

(a) PE ratio for Exxon $= \dfrac{\$71.25}{\$3.24} = 22$ (rounded)

(b) PE ratio for Harley-Davidson $= \dfrac{\$34.8125}{\$1.16} = 30$ (rounded)

   The PE ratio is not a perfect guide to future market behavior of a particular stock. Sometimes a low PE ratio suggests that a stock may be a "sleeper" and is undervalued in the market—in other words, a good buy. Other times a low PE ratio is an indication that investors see a poor future for the company.

For related Web
activities, go to
www.mathbusiness.com

Keyword:
trivia

OBJECTIVE **5** **Define the Dow Jones Industrial Average.** The **Dow Jones Industrial Average** is frequently used as an indicator of overall trends in stock prices. Actually, Dow Jones & Co. publishes *several different averages*. The one most commonly used refers to an average of 30 large, industrial companies. It is the movement of this average that is typically quoted on the evening television news and in the newspapers.

As you can see from the following chart, the Dow Jones Industrial Average *has increased a great deal* between 1900 and today. You can see the effect of the Great Depression on stock prices in the early 1930s—it took *until the 1950s* before stock prices as measured by the Dow Jones Industrial Average returned to the pre-Depression levels. Nevertheless, you can clearly see that *the general trend of stock prices* has been upwards during the 20th century.

Dow Jones Industrial Average Performance Since 1900

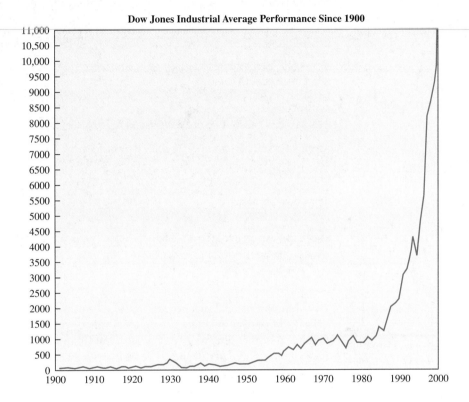

OBJECTIVE **6** **Define a mutual fund.** Ownership of shares in a single company *can be risky*—the company may suffer poor financial results causing the stock price to fall. This risk *can be reduced* by simultaneously investing in the stocks of several different companies. One way of doing this is to invest with a mutual fund that buys stocks. A **mutual fund** that invests in stocks receives investment funds from many different investors and uses the money to purchase stock in several different companies. For example, a $1000 investment in a typical mutual fund owning stock means that you own a very small piece of perhaps 100 different companies or more.

Over periods of many years, *stocks have consistently provided a greater return* on investment than savings accounts, certificates of deposit, or bonds. Most financial planners agree that stocks should be a part of any long-range retirement or investment plan.

The table on the next page shows that some mutual funds *specialize* by investing in the stocks *of different types* of publicly held companies. For example, mutual funds may specialize in large-cap (large companies), small-cap (small companies), overseas (global), or specialty (real estate, oil, banking, etc.). Many financial planners say that *the first fund* one should invest in is an **index fund**. An *index fund* is a fund that is designed to track an index such as the Dow Jones Industrial Average or Standard and Poors.

> **NOTE** Many mutual-fund companies advertise on the World Wide Web, including
> Fidelity and Vanguard. Several of them will also let you track fund balances and make
> exchanges between funds using the World Wide Web.

Fund Performance: A Sampling

LARGE-CAP

FUND NAME	Style[1]	% annualized return				% maximum sales charge	% annual expenses	Minimum initial investment (in dollars)	Net assets (millions of dollars)	Telephone (800)
		One year	Three years	Five years	10 years					
Babson Value	Value	41.0	28.4	22.8	17.3	None	0.97	1,000	1,697.2	422-2766
Clipper	Value	35.3	29.3	20.3	17.5	None	1.08	5,000	973.2	776-5033
Dodge & Cox Stock	Value	37.5	28.0	21.6	17.5	None	0.59	2,500	4,454.1	621-3979
Domini Social Equity	Blend	50.4	32.6	21.3	—	None	0.98	1,000	397.5	762-6814
Dreyfus Appreciation	Growth	42.9	33.2	22.6	17.7	None	0.91	2,500	2,578.5	373-9387
Founders Growth	Growth	43.0	31.0	22.9	19.5	None	1.19	1,000	1,967.6	525-2440

OVERSEAS

FUND NAME	% annualized return				% maximum sales charge	% annual expenses	Minimum initial investment (in dollars)	Net assets (millions of dollars)	Telephone (800)
	One year	Three years	Five years	10 years					
American Century-20th Century Intl. Growth	33.8	23.2	17.7	—	None	1.65	2,500	1,838.6	345-2021
Brinson Global	18.4	17.1	11.9	—	None	1.04	2,500	630.9	448-2430
BT Investment International Equity	34.9	24.5	21.1	—	None	1.50	2,500	922.5	730-1313
Capital World Growth & Income	29.9	24.2	19.4	—	5.75	0.85	1,000	7,978.0	421-4120
EuroPacific Growth	21.0	18.9	16.4	14.2	5.75	0.90	250	20,454.7	421-4120
Fidelity Diversified International	25.7	21.7	17.1	—	None	1.23	2,500	1,909.9	544-8888
GAM International A	40.5	21.5	24.8	18.5	5.00	1.56	5,000	2,082.0	426-4685

SPECIALTY

FUND NAME	% annualized return				% maximum sales charge	% annual expenses	Minimum initial investment (in dollars)	Net assets (millions of dollars)	Telephone (800)
	One year	Three years	Five years	10 years					
CGM Realty	19.4	28.7	—	—	None	1.00	2,500	430.0	345-4048
FBR Financial Services A	62.6	—	—	—	5.50	1.65	1,000	43.6	N/A
Hancock Financial Services A	55.6	—	—	—	5.00	1.20	1,000	790.3	225-5291
Longleaf Partners Realty	23.2	—	—	—	None	1.20	10,000	825.0	445-9469
PBHG Technology & Communications	38.3	—	—	—	None	1.35	2,500	492.0	433-0051
Vanguard Specialized Health Care	44.1	33.1	28.2	22.8	None	0.38	3,000	5,258.9	851-4999

Data: *Money magazine*, 6/98.

EXAMPLE 5

Comparing Investment Alternatives

One thing a financial planner might do for you is to compare a retirement plan that uses certificates of deposit to one that uses mutual funds with stocks (or in the next section we talk about bonds). Assume an annuity payment of $1000 per year for 25 years. Then consider two investment options: 1) a certificate of deposit paying 8% compounded annually and 2) a mutual fund that has paid 12% compounded annually over the past 15 years. Find the amount of an annuity **(a)** that uses certificates of deposit and **(b)** that uses the mutual fund. **(c)** Find the difference in the two amounts.

Solution

(a) Use 8% and 25 years in the table in Section 10.1 to find **73.10594**.

$$\text{Amount} = \$1000 \times \textbf{73.10594} = \$73,105.94$$

(b) Use 12% and 25 years in the table in Section 10.1 to find **133.33387**.

$$\text{Amount} = \$1000 \times \textbf{133.33387} = \$133,333.87$$

(c) Difference = $133,333.87 − $73,105.94 = $60,227.93

If the certificate of deposit yields 8% and the mutual fund yields 12% over the next 25 years, the mutual fund investment will result in an additional $60,227.93.

> **NOTE** Neither the 8% on the certificates of deposit nor the 12% on the mutual fund in the above example *are guaranteed* for 25 years. Certificate of deposit rates are typically guaranteed for 3 to 6 years whereas *yields on mutual funds are not guaranteed* for any length of time. People tend to look at the yields on a fund over the past 5 or 10 years and assume that same yield will continue to apply in the future. Of course, this assumption may or may not be valid.

10.5 | Bonds

Objectives

1. Define the basics of bonds.
2. Read bond tables.
3. Find the commission charge on bonds and the cost of bonds.
4. Understand how mutual funds containing bonds are used for monthly income.

PROBLEM SOLVING IN BUSINESS

Tish Baker has thought about using stocks for her financial plans; now she is wondering about bonds. What are they? How do they work? Who buys and uses bonds? Baker wonders if she can use bonds to help her meet her goal.

Objective 1 **Define the basics of bonds.** A publicly held corporation can raise money either *by borrowing or by selling* shares of stock. They can borrow money from a bank or perhaps an insurance company for short-term money needs. However, companies commonly borrow money for long-term borrowing (5 years or more) using bonds. A **bond** is a promise to repay the borrowed money at some specified time in the future. It is also a promise to pay annual interest to the holder of the bond. Large cities, states, and the U.S. government also issue bonds.

Bonds are a debt; a corporation owes money to its bondholders. As such, bondholders *have first claim*, after bankruptcy lawyers, on the assets of the corporation if it goes into bankruptcy—*stockholders have the last claim* on assets of a bankrupt corporation. Even so, bondholders may only receive a few cents on the dollar in the event of bankruptcy.

The financial world has grown very complex in the modern global society in which we live. The following headline shows that the financial markets watch the actions of the Fed (the U.S. Federal Reserve) in terms of interest rates. Movement of interest rates either up or down affects stock and bond markets around the world. The chart below shows long-term interest rates for different countries.

Fed Probably Won't Touch Rates This Week: Future Changes May Be Down Not Up

Source: Barron's, 5/18/98. Reprinted by permission.

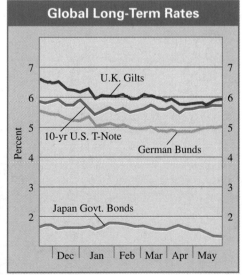

Data: Barron's, 5/18/98.

Objective 2 **Read bond tables.** The **face value** or **par value** of a bond is *the original amount of money* borrowed by a company. Most corporations issue bonds with a par value of $1000. Suppose that a bond's owner needs money before the maturity date of the bond. In that event, the bond can be quickly sold through a bond dealer such as Merrill Lynch. However, the price of the bond is not determined by its initial price, rather *by market conditions at the time of the sale*. Interest rates on bonds and other debt instruments fluctuate as shown in the graph.

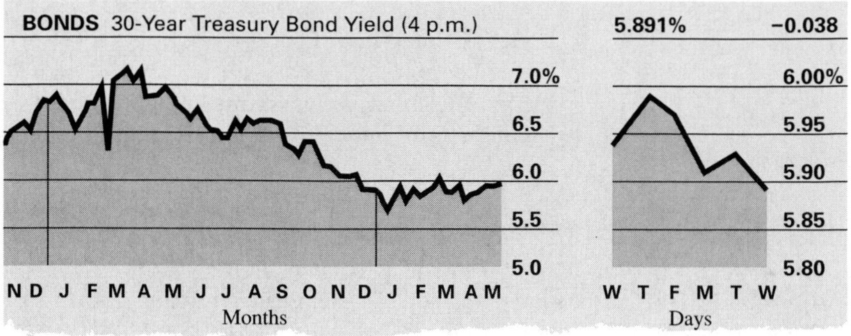

Source: *Wall Street Journal*, 5/21/98. Reprinted by permission of Dow Jones, Inc. via Copyright Clearance Center, Inc. © 1998 Dow Jones & Co., Inc. All rights reserved worldwide.

Example 1

Working with the Bond Table

Jamie Loomis received funds from an insurance settlement related to an auto accident that left her paralyzed. She has $70,000 to invest, but she wants to be very careful not to lose any principal and she needs monthly income. Loomis' broker shows her information from the *Wall Street Journal* on some bonds issued by AT&T (ATT 6¾04). Interpret the data on the bonds.

Solution

Bonds	Cur Yld	Vol	Close	Net Chg
ATT 6¾04	6.5	100	103⅛	+¼

The 6¾ indicates that each of these AT&T bonds pays 6¾% simple interest each year on a face value of $1000 to the holder of the bond.

$$\text{Interest per bond} = \$1000 \times .0675 = \$67.50$$

Find the daily selling price of a bond by looking in the Corporate Bond section of the daily newspaper. A portion of the *Wall Street Journal* corporate bond section is shown below.

CORPORATION BONDS
Volume, $12,486,000

Bonds	Cur Yld.	Vol.	Close	Net Chg.	Bonds	Cur Yld.	Vol.	Close	Net Chg.
AMR 9s16	7.6	10	118	− ¾	IntShip 9s03	8.8	52	102	− ½
ANR 7s25	6.8	32	102¾	+ ¾	JCPL 7½23	7.4	6	102	− 1
ATT 6s00	6.0	1	100	+ ⅛	JumboSp 4½00	cv	24	37½	+ ¼
ATT 5⅛01	5.2	191	98	+ ⅜	KCS En 8⅞08	9.2	245	97	− ⅞
ATT 7⅛02	6.9	202	103⅝	+ ⅛	KaufB 9⅜03	9.1	98	102¾	+ ¼
ATT 6¾04	6.5	100	103⅛	+ ¼	KaufB 7¾04	7.8	145	100	− 1
ATT 7s05	6.7	10	104½	+ ⅛	KentE 4½04	cv	60	82	− ½
ATT 7½06	6.9	45	108	+ ⅜	Kolmrg 8¾09	cv	9	104	+ 1
ATT 7¾07	7.0	25	110½	...	Loews 3⅛07	cv	53	96½	− 2¾
ATT 8⅛22	7.6	26	106⅝	− ⅛	LglsL† 8⅝04	8.5	47	101⅜	− ⅛
ATT 8⅛24	7.7	50	106⅛	...	LglsL† 7½07	7.3	10	103⅜	+ ⅜
ATT 8⅝31	7.8	20	110	− ⅛	LglsL† 9¾21	9.7	15	101	...
Aames 10½02	10.0	29	105⅛	...	LglsL† 8.2s23	8.3	26	109	+ ¼
AlldC zr2000	...	19	87⅛	+ ½	LglsL† 9⅝24	9.6	40	100⅝	...
AlldC zr09	...	55	47⅞	+ ⅝	MacNS 7⅞04	cv	11	103½	− ½
Allwst 7¼14	cv	20	76⅞	− 1⅛	Mascotch 03	cv	132	96	− ½
Alza 5s06	cv	17	140	− 1½	Medtrst 7½01	cv	7	107	+ 1
ARetire 5¾02	cv	100	100	− 3	MerLyStkMk 99	...	2	100⅜	...
Amresco 10s04	9.6	15	104⅜	...	MichB 7s12	6.9	20	101⅜	...
Anhr 8⅝16	8.3	6	103½	− ⅜	MKT 5½33fr	...	40	90⅜	+ 2⅜
AnnTaylr 8¾00	8.6	55	101¼	+ ⅛	MPac 4¾30f	...	10	65	− ⅛
BstBuy 8⅝00	8.5	102	101⅜	− ⅛	MPac 5s45f	...	5	64½	+ ½
					Mobil 8⅜01	7.9	10	106	+ ⅛

Source: *Wall Street Journal*, 5/21/98. Reprinted by permission of Dow Jones, Inc. via Copyright Clearance Center, Inc. © 1998 Dow Jones & Co., Inc. All rights reserved worldwide.

The 04 indicates that the bonds **mature** in the year 2004. Thus, the holder of each bond will receive the par value of $1000 in 2004. The *current yield* on the bonds is 6.5% simple interest based on the market price of the bond (the market price of a bond is usually *different* than the par value of the bond). The 100 indicates that 100 bonds, each with a face value of $1000, were sold that day.

For related Web
activities, go to
www.mathbusiness.com

Keyword:
bonds

The close price is the current price of the bonds in the marketplace. The bond prices in the table represent **percents, not dollar amounts.** Therefore, 103 ⅛ says that the bond is selling at 103.125% of its par value of $1000. An investor who sold these bonds at this price would receive

$$\$1000 \times \mathbf{1.03125} = \$1031.25 \text{ for each bond.}$$

The selling price of $1031.25 is higher than the face value of $1000 since market rates on this particular date are lower than the 6¾% rate paid by this bond. Each AT&T 6¾04 bond increased in value by ¼ of a percent of $1000 or by .0025 × $1000 = $2.50 on this day.

EXAMPLE 2

Working with the Bond Table

Find the sales volume and current selling price of the following bonds.

(a) Amresco, 10% bonds of 2004

(b) Loews, 3⅛ bonds of 2007

(c) Mobil, 8⅜ bonds of 2001

SOLUTION

Company	Sales Volume	Current Selling Price at Close
(a) Amresco	15 bonds	$1000 × 1.04375 = $1043.75
(b) Loews	53 bonds	$1000 × .965 = $965
(c) Mobil	10 bonds	$1000 × 1.06 = $1060

OBJECTIVE **3** **Find the commission charge on bonds and the cost of bonds.** Commissions charged on bond sales vary among brokers. A common charge is $10 per bond, either to buy or to sell.

EXAMPLE 3

Find the Charges for Buying Bonds

(a) Assuming a sales charge of $10 per bond, find the total cost of purchasing 20 bonds of KentE 4½ 2004. **(b)** Find the total annual interest paid on these bonds. **(c)** Find the effective interest rate based on the total cost of a person buying 20 bonds (this would include the cost of commissions).

SOLUTION

(a) From the bond table, the price is seen to be **82**, after having decreased by ½ during the day. The cost to buy one bond of $1000 par value and the cost of twenty of these bonds follow.

$$\text{Price per bond} = \$1000 \times .82 = \$820$$
$$\text{Price for 20 bonds} = \$820 \times 20 = \$16,400$$

The commission is $10 per bond, or 20 × $10 = $200 total commission. The total purchase price of the 20 bonds is $16,400 + $200 = $16,600.

(b) Total annual interest is the interest yield on each bond (4½%) times the par value times the number of bonds owned.

$$\text{Interest} = .045 \times \$1000 \times 20 - \$900 \text{ per year}$$

(c) The effective interest rate is the total interest divided by the total cost, which includes the commission cost.

$$\text{Rate} = \frac{\$900}{\$16,000} = 5.4\% \text{ per year (rounded)}$$

Assuming a sales charge of $10 per bond, find the net amount received from the sale of 30 MichB 7s12 bonds at the close price for the day.

EXAMPLE 4

Find the Net Amount from the Sale of Bonds

SOLUTION

From the table, the close price per bond is **101**$\frac{3}{8}$.

$$\text{Price per bond} = \$1000 \times \mathbf{1.01375} = \$1013.75$$
$$\text{Price for 30 bonds} = \$1013.75 \times 30 = \$30,412.50$$

The net amount received by the seller is the total amount less the commission.

$$\text{Net amount received} = \$30,412.50 - 30 \times \$10 = \$30,112.50$$

OBJECTIVE **4** **Understand how mutual funds containing bonds are used for monthly income.** A mutual fund can invest in stocks, in bonds, or partially in stocks and partially in bonds. Typically, people and companies invest in stocks *when they have a longer time horizon* during which they are accumulating funds. They tend to invest in bonds *when they need the income* from their investments.

Many financial planners suggest that people invest in both stocks and bonds throughout their adult lifetime—perhaps a higher percent of *stocks when young* and a higher percent of *bonds when approaching retirement.*

EXAMPLE 5

Using a Bond
Fund for Income

Jamie Loomis from Example 1 is disabled and needs both safety of principal and income from her $70,000. She places the money in a mutual fund, managed by Merrill Lynch, that owns bonds in many different companies. **(a)** Assuming that the mutual fund continues to generate the 8.1% that it is currently yielding, find her annual income. **(b)** How much would Loomis need to invest in this fund if she needs $12,000 per year in income? Round the answer to the nearest dollar.

SOLUTION

(a) Use the formula for simple interest $I = PRT$.

$$\text{Annual income} = \$70,000 \times .081 = \$5670$$

(b) Again use the formula for simple interest, but now the principal (P) is unknown. Divide both sides of $I = PRT$ by RT to get the following form of the equation.

$$\text{Principal} = P = \frac{I}{RT} = \frac{\$12,000}{.081 \times 1} = \$148,148 \text{ (rounded)}$$

CHAPTER 10 | Quick Review

CHAPTER TERMS

*Review the following terms to test your understanding of the chapter. For
each term you do not know, refer to the page number found next to that term.*

amount of the annuity
  [**p. 384**]
annual meeting [**p. 405**]
annuity [**p. 384**]
annuity due [**p. 386**]
board of directors [**p. 405**]
bond [**p. 415**]
capital [**p. 405**]
common stock [**p. 406**]
corporations [**p. 405**]
current yield [**p. 408**]
discount brokers [**p. 407**]

dividends [**p. 406**]
Dow Jones Industrial Average
  [**p. 409**]
equivalent cash price
  [**p. 394**]
executive officers [**p. 405**]
face value [**p. 415**]
future value of the annuity
  [**p. 384**]
IRA [**p. 387**]
individual retirement account
  [**p. 387**]

index fund [**p. 409**]
interest rate spreads [**p. 400**]
limited liability [**p. 405**]
mature [**p. 416**]
mutual fund [**p. 409**]
par value [**p. 415**]
PE ratio [**p. 408**]
payment period [**p. 384**]
preferred stock [**p. 406**]
present value of an annuity
  [**p. 391**]
price-earnings ratio [**p. 407**]

publicly held corporations
  [**p. 406**]
regular IRA [**p. 387**]
Roth IRA [**p. 387**]
sinking fund [**p. 397**]
sinking fund table [**p. 399**]
stock [**p. 405**]
stock certificates [**p. 405**]
stock exchanges [**p. 406**]
stock ratios [**p. 407**]
stockbrokers [**p. 407**]
stockholders [**p. 405**]
term of the annuity [**p. 384**]

CONCEPTS	EXAMPLES
10.1 Finding the amount of an annuity Determine the number of periods in the annuity (n) and the interest rate per annuity period (i). Use n and i in the annuity table to find the value of $1 at term of annuity. Find the value of annuity using Amount = Payment × Number from table.	Ed Navarro deposits $800 at the end of each quarter for 10 years into an IRA. Given interest of 8% compounded quarterly, find the future value. $$n = 10 \times 4 = 40 \text{ periods}; \quad i = \frac{8\%}{4} = 2\% \text{ per period}$$ Number from table is **60.40198**. Amount = $800 × **60.40198** = $48,321.58
10.1 Finding the amount of an annuity due Determine the number of periods in the annuity. Add 1 to the value and use this as the value of n. Determine the interest rate per annuity period and use the table to find the value of $1 at term of annuity. The value of the annuity is Payment × Number from table − 1 payment.	Find the amount of an annuity due if payments of $700 are made at the beginning of each month for 3 years in an account paying 12% compounded monthly. $$n = 3 \times 12 + 1 = 37; \quad i = \frac{12\%}{1} = 1\%$$ Number from table is **44.50765**. Amount = $700 × **44.50765** − $700 = $30,455.36
10.2 Finding the present value of an annuity Determine the payment per period. Determine the number of periods in the annuity (n). Determine the interest rate per period (i). Use the values of n and i and find the number in the present value of an annuity table. The present value of an annuity is Present value = Payment × Number from table.	What lump sum deposited today at 8% compounded annually will yield the same total as payments of $600 at the end of each year for 10 years? Payment = $600; n = 10 Interest = 8% Number from table is **6.71008**. Present value = $600 × **6.71008** = **$4026.05**
10.2 Finding equivalent cash price Determine the amount of the annuity payment. Determine the number of periods in the annuity (n). Determine the interest rate per annuity period (i). Use n and i in the present value of an annuity table. Add the present value of the annuity to the down payment to obtain today's equivalent cash price.	A buyer offers to purchase a business for $75,000 down and payments of $4000 at the end of each quarter for 5 years. Money is worth 8% compounded quarterly. How much is the buyer actually offering for the business? Payment = $4000; n = 20 Interest = $\frac{8\%}{4}$ = 2% Number from table is **16.35143**. Present value = $4000 × **16.35143** = $65,405.72 Equivalent cash value = $75,000 + $65,405.72 = $140,405.72

CONCEPTS	EXAMPLES

10.3 Determining the payment into a sinking fund

Determine the number of payments (n). Determine the interest rate per period (i). Find the value of the payment needed to accumulate $1 from the sinking fund table.

Calculate the payment using
   Payment = Future value × Number from table.

No-Leak Plumbing plans to accumulate $500,000 in 4 years in a sinking fund for a new building. Find the amount of each semiannual payment if the fund earns 10% compounded semiannually.

$$n = 4 \times 2 = 8 \text{ periods}; \quad i = \frac{10\%}{2} = 5\% \text{ per period}$$

Number from table is **.10472.**
Payment = $500,000 × **.10472** = $52,360

10.3 Setting up a sinking fund table

Determine the required payment into the sinking fund.
Calculate the interest at the end of each period.
Add the previous total, next payment, and interest to determine total.
Repeat these steps for each period.

A company wants to set up a sinking fund to accumulate $10,000 in 4 years. It wishes to make semiannual payments into the account, which pays 8% compounded semiannually. Set up a sinking fund table.
$n = 8; i = 4\%$
Number from table is **.10853**.
Payment = $10,000 × **.10853** = $1085.30

Pay. #	Amount of Deposit	Interest Earned	Total
1	$1085.30	$0	$1085.30
2	$1085.30	$43.41	$2214.01
3	$1085.30	$88.56	$3387.87
4	$1085.30	$135.51	$4608.68
5	$1085.30	$184.35	$5878.33
6	$1085.30	$235.13	$7198.76
7	$1085.30	$287.95	$8572.01
8	$1085.11	$342.88	$10,000.00

10.4 Reading the stock table

Locate the stock involved and determine the various quantities required.

Use the stock table in Section 10.4 to find the following information for Maytag (MYG).

Dividend	Stock sales
High for day	Yearly high
Low for day	Yearly low

Stock table entry is:

55¾ 24⅜ Maytag MYG .64 1.2 23 7127 53³⁄₁₆ 52³⁄₁₆ 52½ +¼

Dividend is $.64
High for the day is $53.1875.
Low for the day is $52.1875.
Stock sales for the day are 712,700 shares.
Yearly high is $55.75.
Yearly low is $24.375.

10.4 Finding the current yield on a stock

To determine the current yield, use the formula

$$\text{Current yield} = \frac{\text{Annual dividend}}{\text{Closing price}}.$$

Find the current yield for a stock if the purchase price is $35 and the annual dividend is $.64.

$$\text{Current yield} = \frac{\$.64}{\$35} = 1.8\% \text{ (rounded)}$$

10.4 Finding the price-earnings (PE) ratio

To find the price-earnings ratio, use the formula

$$\text{PE ratio} = \frac{\text{Price per share}}{\text{Annual net income per share}}.$$

Find the PE ratio for a stock which is priced at 38¹⁄₁₆ and has earnings of $2.11.

$$\text{PE Ratio} = \frac{\$38.0625}{\$2.11} = 18 \text{ (rounded)}$$

CHAPTER 10 QUICK REVIEW   **423**

CONCEPTS	EXAMPLES
10.5 Determining the cost of purchasing bonds First locate the bond in the table. Then determine the price of the bond and multiply this value by $1000 and the number of bonds purchased. Finally add $10 per bond to the total cost of bonds purchased.	Find the cost, including sales charges, of 40 AT&T bonds that are selling for 101⅜. $$40 \times \mathbf{1.01375} \times \$1000 + 40 \times \$10 = \$40{,}950$$
10.5 Determining the amount received from the sale of bonds First locate the bond in the table. Then determine the price of the bond and multiply this value by 1000 and the number of bonds sold. Finally subtract $10 per bond from the total selling price.	Find the amount received from the sale of 30 Eastman Kodak bonds that are selling for 99¼. $$30 \times \mathbf{.9925} \times \$1000 - 30 \times \$10 = \$29{,}475$$

CHAPTER 10 | SUMMARY EXERCISE

PLANNING FOR RETIREMENT

At age 32, Tish Baker has decided to invest $1800 per year for 33 years until she is 65, in her retirement plan. She has also decided to place one-half of the funds in a stock index fund that roughly tracks the return on Standard and Poors. The other half of the funds will be placed in a mutual fund containing bonds.

(a) Find the amount she will have at 65 assuming the stock fund averages 12% per year compounded annually and the bond fund averages 8% per year compounded annually. Using 33 periods find the values in the table corresponding to 12% and 8%.

(a) _____

(b) The amount found in part **(a)** seems like a lot of money. But Baker knows that inflation will increase her cost of living. She wants to see the effect of 3% annual inflation on her financial goals. Find the income she needs at age 65 to have the same purchasing power as an income of $20,000 today. (*Hint:* Look at the section on inflation in Section 9.2 and use the compound interest table in Section 9.1.)

(b) _____

(c) Baker wishes to fund her retirement for 20 years (to age 85). Find the present value of the annual income found in part **(b)** assuming that the funds earn 8% per year compounded annually.

(c) _____

(d) Will her expected savings from part **(a)** fund her retirement at a purchasing power of $20,000 per year in today's dollars?

(d) _____

Reality Check

Social Security Wins 3-Year Reprieve

WASHINGTON—The booming economy is bolstering Social Security and postponing the retirement program's projected insolvency by three years, to 2032, the system's trustees said Tuesday.

The number of workers for each retiree will fall from 3.4 now to two in 2030.

"Although there is no immediate financial crisis, the time to act is now to prevent a crisis," Social Security Commissioner Kenneth Apfel said.

Members of Congress warned against complacency.

"We should not have a false sense of security just because the Social Security program will go bankrupt a few years later than expected," said Sen. Judd Gregg, R-N.H.

This year's report on Social Security comes as both parties are debating ideas for altering the program, including proposals from conservatives and moderates to place some payroll taxes into privately controlled investments.

Source: USA Today, 4/29/98. Reprinted by permission.

Investigate

There is some discussion about the ability of Social Security to pay retirement benefits as you can see from the newspaper clipping. Do you think Social Security will be around to help you during your retirement? What percent of your retirement needs do you think Social Security will pay? Try to support your views with recent articles from newspapers, magazines, or information from the World Wide Web.

Name   Date   Class

CHAPTER 10 | TEST

To help you review, the numbers in brackets show the section in which the topic was discussed.

Find the amounts of the following annuities.   **[10.1]**

Amount of Each Deposit	Deposited	Rate per Year	Number of Years	Type of Annuity	Amount of Annuity
1. $1000	annually	6%	8	ordinary	_____
2. $4500	semiannually	10%	9	ordinary	_____
3. $30,000	quarterly	8%	6	due	_____
4. $2600	semiannually	10%	12	due	_____

5. Bill Smith decides to place $2000 at the end of each year into an IRA beginning at age 30. Assume a return on investment of 10% compounded annually and find the amount he has accumulated in 40 years, by age 70.

5. _____

6. At the end of every 6 months, Bill Phillips puts $1000 into a mutual fund that has been paying 8% compounded semiannually. Find the account balance in 15 years if the mutual fund continues yielding 8% compound semiannually.

6. _____

Find the present value of the following annuities.   **[10.2]**

Amount per Payment	Payment at End of Each	Number of Years	Interest Rate	Compounded	Present Value
7. $1000	year	9	6%	annually	_____
8. $4500	6 months	6	10%	semiannually	_____
9. $708	month	3	12%	monthly	_____
10. $18,000	quarter	10	12%	quarterly	_____

11. Betty Yowski borrows money for a new swimming pool and hot tub. She agrees to repay the note with a payment of $1200 per quarter for 6 years. Find the amount she must set aside today to satisfy this capital requirement in an account earning 10% compounded quarterly.

11. _____

12. Dan and Mary Fisher just divorced. The divorce settlement included $650 a month payment to Mary for the 4 years until their son turns 18. Find the amount Dan must set aside today, in an account earning 12% per year compounded monthly, to satisfy this financial obligation.

12. _____

Find the amount of each payment into a sinking fund for the following.   **[10.3]**

Amount Needed	Years Until Needed	Interest Rate	Interest Compounded	Amount of Payment
13. $100,000	9	6%	annually	_____
14. $250,000	10	8%	semiannually	_____
15. $360,000	11	6%	quarterly	_____
16. $800,000	12	10%	semiannually	_____

Solve the following application problems.

17. The owner of Hickory Bar-B-Que plans to open a new restaurant in 4 years at a cost of $200,000. Find the required monthly payment into a sinking fund if funds are invested in an account earning 12% per year compounded monthly.

17. _____

18. Lupe Rivera owes her retired mother $45,000 on a piece of land. Find the required monthly payment if Lupe pays it off in 4 years and the interest rate is 12% per year compounded monthly.

18. _____

19. George Jones purchases 200 shares of Merck stock at 39½. Find **(a)** the total cost and **(b)** the annual dividend if the dividend per share is $1.20.   **[10.4]**

(a) _____
(b) _____

20. Belinda Johnson purchases 22 IBM 7 ¼ bonds that mature in 2004 for 95. Find **(a)** the total cost if commissions are $10 per bond and **(b)** the annual interest.   **[10.5]**

(a) _____
(b) _____

Name   Date   Class

CUMULATIVE REVIEW | CHAPTERS 8–10

Round money amounts to the nearest cent, time to the nearest day, and rates to the nearest tenth of a percent.

Find the value of the unknown quantity using simple interest. Use banker's interest. **[8.1–8.2]**

	Interest	Principal	Rate	Time		
1.	_____	$4500	8%	5 months	1.	_____
2.	_____	$6200	9.7%	250 days	2.	_____
3.	$46.67	_____	7%	100 days	3.	_____
4.	$302.60	_____	12.5%	70 days	4.	_____
5.	$50.93	$2100	_____	90 days	5.	_____
6.	$306	$6800	_____	120 days	6.	_____
7.	$202.22	$9100	10%	_____	7.	_____
8.	$915	$18,300	12%	_____	8.	_____

Find the discount and the proceeds. **[8.3]**

	Face Value	Discount Rate	Time (Days)	Discount	Proceeds
9.	$9000	12%	90	_____	_____
10.	$875	$6 \frac{1}{2}$%	210	_____	_____

Find the net proceeds when each of the following is discounted. **[8.4]**

Maturity Value	Discount Rate	Discount Period	Net Proceeds
11. $5000	10%	90 days	_____
12. $12,000	12%	150 days	_____

Find the compound amounts for the following. **[9.1]**

13. $1000 at 4% compounded annually for 17 years

13. _____

14. $3520 at 8% compounded annually for 10 years

14. _____

Find the interest earned and compound amounts for each of the following. Assume $3\frac{1}{2}\%$ interest compounded daily. **[9.2]**

Amount	Date Deposited	Date Withdrawn	Interest Earned	Compound Amount
15. $12,600	March 24	June 3	_____	_____
16. $7500	November 20	February 14	_____	_____

Find the present value and the amount of interest earned for the following. Round to the nearest cent. **[9.3]**

Amount Needed	Time (Years)	Interest	Compounded	Present Value	Interest
17. $1000	7	8%	annually	_____	_____
18. $19,000	9	5%	semiannually	_____	_____

Find the amount of each of the following ordinary annuities. **[10.1]**

Amount of Each Deposit	Deposited	Rate	Time (Years)	Amount of Annuity	Interest Earned
19. $1000	annually	4%	8	_____	_____
20. $2000	annually	6%	6	_____	_____

Name   Date   Class

Find the present value of the following annuities.   **[10.2]**

	Amount per Payment	Payment at End of Each	Time (Years)	Rate of Investment	Compounded	Present Value
21.	$925	6 months	11	8%	semiannually	_____
22.	$27,235	quarter	8	8%	quarterly	_____

Find the required payment into a sinking fund.   **[10.3]**

	Future Value	Interest Rate	Compounded	Time (Years)	Payment
23.	$3600	8%	annually	7	_____
24.	$4500	10%	quarterly	7	_____

Solve the following application problems. Use 360-day years where applicable.

25. Walter Bates sets aside $5000 today to help pay his son's college expenses which begin in 9 years. Given a rate of 8% compounded semiannually, find the future value of this investment.   **[9.1]**

25. _____

26. According to the terms of a divorce settlement, one spouse must pay the other a lump sum of $2800 in 17 months. What lump sum can be invested today, at 18% compounded monthly, so that enough will be available for the payment?   **[9.3]**

26. _____

27. Bill Jones borrowed $12,000 on a simple interest note at 8% for 40 days. Find **(a)** the interest and **(b)** the maturity value.   **[8.1]**

(a) _____
(b) _____

28. Sherie Whatly borrowed $15,000 on a simple discount note at 10% for 100 days. Find **(a)** the interest and **(b)** the proceeds.   **[8.3]**

(a) _____
(b) _____

29. Tom Davis owes $7850 to a relative. He has agreed to pay the money in 5 months, at an interest rate of 6%. One month before the loan is due, the relative discounts the loan at the bank. The bank charges a 7.92% discount rate. How much money does the relative receive?   **[8.4]**

29. _____

30. Marja Strutz needs $31,709 to buy new equipment for her business. The bank charges a discount of 15.8%. Find the maturity value of Strutz's loan if she borrows the money for 10 months.   **[8.3]**

30. _____

31. Jerry Walker purchased 50 shares of Microsoft at 120½ for his spouse. Find the cost of the stock.   **[10.4]**

31. _____

32. Martin Wicker buys 8000 Converse 7¼ bonds due in 2010 at 98¾ for the mutual fund that he manages. Find the total cost assuming a cost of $1 for each bond purchased.   **[10.5]**

32. _____

33. Carla Fresquez decides to set up a sinking fund with Merrill Lynch for the purpose of accumulating enough money for a new $85,000 German import automobile that she hopes to buy in 3 years. What quarterly payment must she invest in a fund that earns 8% compounded quarterly, to arrive at her goal?   **[10.3]**

33. _____

34. A public utility needs $60 million in 5 years for a major capital expansion. What annual payment must they place in a sinking fund earning 10% per year in order to accumulate the required funds?   **[10.3]**

34. _____

35. At 58, Thomas Jones knows that he must start saving for his retirement. He decides to invest $300 per quarter in an account paying 10% compounded quarterly. Find the accumulated amount **(a)** at age 65 and **(b)** at age 70.   **[10.1]**

(a) _____
(b) _____

36. Jana Smallwood convinces her daughter Jessica to begin saving for retirement at age 30. Jessica decides to put $1200 per year in an account paying 10% compounded annually. Find the accumulated amount **(a)** at age 65 and **(b)** at age 70   **[10.1]**

(a) _____
(b) _____

37. The owner of Jessica's Cookies has an extra $3200 that he puts into a savings account paying $3\frac{1}{2}$% per year compounded daily. Find the interest if the funds are left there for 65 days.   **[9.2]**

37. _____

38. Jerry Black, age 52, wins a state lottery for $10,000,000 and chooses to receive $4,000,000 in cash. **(a)** Find the amount he receives after paying 30% in taxes. **(b)** Then find the amount remaining after purchasing a new house (with furniture) for $250,000, three new cars with a total cost of $120,000, and vacations and presents for family costing $80,000. Assume that remaining funds are invested in mutual funds which should earn 12% per year compounded annually on average. **(c)** Find the accumulated investment amount at age 65. Round to the nearest dollar.   **[9.1]**

(a) _____
(b) _____
(c) _____

CHAPTER 11

BUSINESS AND CONSUMER LOANS

George Willis works for Teachers Credit Union, which is a cooperative organization, similar to a bank, that provides consumer and mortgage loans to its members. In addition, the credit union offers checking accounts, savings accounts, certificates of deposit, Automated Teller Machines (ATMs), and even a Visa credit card.

Teachers Credit Union differs from a bank in that only teachers of certain local school districts can be members. Other credit unions limit membership to federal employees in a specific region, employees of a large employer, and so on.

It is almost impossible to pay cash for everything. Using the phone, turning on the lights, and using running water are just three examples of using credit. Many people buy on credit at the department store, use a credit card at the gas station, or buy cars or furniture on the installment plan. Occasionally it is necessary to borrow to pay taxes, medical expenses, or educational costs. Almost everyone borrows when buying a home. Recent data on household debt, excluding debt on the home itself, is shown in the chart.

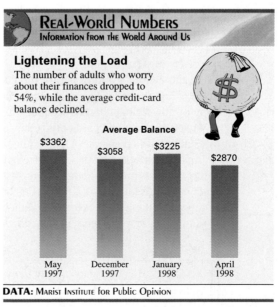

REAL-WORLD NUMBERS
INFORMATION FROM THE WORLD AROUND US

Lightening the Load
The number of adults who worry about their finances dropped to 54%, while the average credit-card balance declined.

Average Balance

May 1997	December 1997	January 1998	April 1998
$3362	$3058	$3225	$2870

DATA: MARIST INSTITUTE FOR PUBLIC OPINION

Credit was originally extended to consumers *as an additional service* to attract customers and increase sales. Today, consumer credit is not merely a service to the customer; the interest or finance charge often represents a large portion of a company's profits. This chapter examines various methods used in determining interest charges on purchases.

11.1 | Open-End Credit and Charge Cards

Objectives

1. Define open-end credit.
2. Define revolving charge accounts.
3. Use the unpaid balance method.
4. Use the average daily balance method.
5. Define loan consolidation.

Problem Solving in Business

In addition to making loans, George Willis of Teachers Credit Union also helps people with budgets. Bill and Cynthia Taylor came to George Willis for help in managing their auto loans, home loan, and credit-card debt. Although the Taylors have been making regular payments, it has been very difficult for them to do so.

For related Web activities, go to www.mathbusiness.com

Keyword: plastic

Objective 1 **Define open-end credit.** A common way of buying on credit, called **open-end credit**, has no fixed payments. The customer continues making payments until no outstanding balance is owed. With open-end credit, additional credit is often extended before the initial amount is paid off. Examples of open-end credit include most department-store charge accounts and charge cards, including MasterCard and Visa. Individuals are given a **credit limit** or a maximum amount that may be charged on these accounts that is based on income and other debts.

Objective 2 **Define revolving charge accounts.** With a typical department store account or bank card, a customer might make several small purchases during a month. Such accounts are often *never paid off*, and new purchases are continually being made, although a minimum amount must be paid each month. Since the account may never be paid off, it is called a **revolving charge account**.

Visa, MasterCard, Discover, and some oil-company charge cards use this method of extending credit. Sometimes there is an annual membership fee or a minimum monthly charge for the use of this service. A sample copy of a receipt signed by a customer using a credit card is shown at the top of the next page.

At the end of a billing period the customer receives a statement of payments and purchases made. This statement typically takes one of two forms: **country club billing** provides a carbon copy of all original charge receipts, while **itemized billing**, more and more common because of its lower cost to credit card companies, provides an itemized listing of all charges, without copies of each individual charge. A typical itemized statement is also shown.

Any charges beyond the cash price of an item are called **finance charges**. Finance charges include interest, credit life insurance, a time payment differential, and carrying charges. Many lenders charge **late fees** for payments that are received after the due date and **over-the-limit fees** in the event the debt exceeds that authorized by the lender. Both late fees and over the limit fees tend to be high; avoid them if you can.

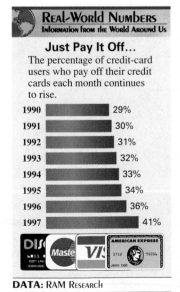

Real-World Numbers
Information from the World Around Us

Just Pay It Off...
The percentage of credit-card users who pay off their credit cards each month continues to rise.

1990	29%
1991	30%
1992	31%
1993	32%
1994	33%
1995	34%
1996	36%
1997	41%

DATA: RAM RESEARCH

NOTE Lenders may simply *deny charges* to an account that cause the debt to exceed previously established credit limits.

Sales Slip

7156 3120 1000 8581   5928772

DO NOT CIRCLE EXPIRATION DATE — USE BOX BELOW

02/9   01/9
Widjan Cadura

6388 312805392
Tower Sports
Phoenix MD

PURCHASER SIGN HERE

X *Widjan Cadura*

Cardholder acknowledges receipt of goods and/or services in the amount of the Total shown hereon and agrees to perform the obligations set forth in the cardholder's agreement with the issuer.

PRESS FIRMLY — USE BALLPOINT PEN

EXPIRATION ☒ DATE / CHECKED

QUAN.	CLASS	DESCRIPTION	PRICE	AMOUNT
1		Pr. Aerobic Shoes		39.95
2		Sweatshirts	20.00	40.00
1		Pr. Socks		2.95

DATE 10/3   AUTHORIZATION   SUB TOTAL 82.90
REFERENCE NO.   REG./DEPT.   TAX 4.15
FOLIO/CHECK NO.   SERVER/CLERK   TIPS MISC.

Society BANK   **SALES SLIP**   TOTAL 87.05

MERCHANT COPY

IMPORTANT: RETAIN THIS COPY FOR YOUR RECORDS

AMERICA'S CHARGE CARD
★ ★ ★ ★ ★ ★ ★ ★

$ ____
WRITE IN THE AMOUNT OF YOUR PAYMENT

IMPORTANT! 1. Return this portion of your statement with your check; please do not fold or bend   2. Write your account number on the face of your check   3. Make checks payable to America's Charge Card

ACCOUNT NUMBER	BILLING DATE	PAYMENT DUE DATE	NEW BALANCE	MINIMUM PAYMENT DUE
5211-1234-5678	10-18	11-12	609.26	30.00

JOHN Q. CARDHOLDER
1000 MAIN STREET
ANYTOWN, USA 00000

52112345678 0060926003000

PLEASE BE SURE OUR MAILING ADDRESS ON THE REVERSE SIDE APPEARS IN THE WINDOW OF THE RETURN ENVELOPE ▶

DO NOT INCLUDE INQUIRIES WITH PAYMENT. SEE REVERSE SIDE

PLEASE PRINT

FOR CHANGE OF ADDRESS	NEW STREET ADDRESS		APT. P.O. BOX NO.
	CITY	STATE	ZIP CODE

- -

RETAIN THIS PORTION FOR YOUR RECORDS

Account Number	Credit Line	Available Credit	Past Due Amount	BILLING DATE
5211-1234-5678	1,000.00	390.74	.00	10-18

TRAN DATE	POSTING DATE	REFERENCE NUMBER	TRANSACTION DESCRIPTION			TRANSACTION AMOUNT
09 06	09 09	12009230	TURNSTYLE 702	CHICAGO	IL	25.17CR
09 07	09 13	55190432	POLK BROS	CHICAGO	IL	150.00
09 13	09 21	86235671	MINNESOTA FABRICS 32	NORRIDGE	IL	39.54
09 14	09 19	21345678	SPIEGELS, INC.	CHICAGO	IL	60.10
09 20	09 20	93703523	PAYMENT THANK YOU			110.00CR
09 21	09 26	86245671	MINNESOTA FABRICS 32	NORRIDGE	IL	42.64
09 25	09 28	12001051	TURNSTYLE 702	CHICAGO	IL	14.49

PREVIOUS BALANCE	AVERAGE DAILY BALANCE	FINANCE CHARGE	NEW BALANCE	Minimum Payment
432.64	501.80	5.02	609.26	30.00

SEE ITEM NUMBER ON REVERSE SIDE FOR YOUR PERIODIC RATE(S). THE RANGE OF AVERAGE DAILY BALANCE(S) TO WHICH IT APPLIES AND THE CORRESPONDING

ANNUAL PERCENTAGE RATE

For Customer Service Call	Charge Transactions	PAYMENTS	CREDITS	PAYMENT DUE DATE
	306.77	110.00	25.17CR	11-12

Additional **FINANCE CHARGE** on purchases may be avoided if total NEW BALANCE is paid in full by PAYMENT DUE DATE

NOTICE: SEE REVERSE SIDE FOR IMPORTANT INFORMATION

YOU MAY AT ANY TIME PAY ALL OR PART OF THE BALANCE OWING ON YOUR ACCOUNT

OBJECTIVE [3] **Use the unpaid balance method.** Finance charges on open-end credit accounts are usually calculated by one of two methods: the **unpaid balance method** or the **average daily balance method**. The explanation of each of these methods follows.

When a store or financial institution uses the unpaid balance method to calculate the finance charge, it is common to use the **unpaid balance** at the *end of the previous month*. Any purchases or returns during the current month are *not* used in calculating the finance charge. The next example shows how the unpaid balance method works.

EXAMPLE 1

Finding Finance Charge Using the Unpaid Balance Method

(a) Peter Brinkman's MasterCard account had an unpaid balance of $870.40 on November 1. During November, he made a payment of $100 and purchased a registered German Shepherd for $150 using the card. Find the finance charge and the unpaid balance on December 1 if the bank charges 1.5% per month on the unpaid balance.

A finance charge of 1.5% per month on the unpaid balance would be

$$\$870.40 \times .015 = \$13.06 \text{ for the month.}$$

Find the unpaid balance on December 1 as follows.

Previous balance		Finance charge		Purchases during month		Payment		New balance
↓		↓		↓		↓		↓
$870.40	+	$13.06	+	$150	−	$100	=	$933.46

(b) During December, Brinkman made a payment of $50, charged $240.56 for Christmas presents, returned $35.45 worth of items, and took his family to dinner several times with charges of $92.45. Find his unpaid balance on January 1.

The finance charge calculated on the unpaid balance is $933.46 × .015 = $14.00. The unpaid balance on January 1 is

$$\$933.46 + \$14.00 + \$240.56 + \$92.45 - \$35.45 - \$50 = \$1195.02.$$

Month	Unpaid Balance at Beginning of Month	Finance Charge	Purchases during Month	Returns	Payment	Unpaid Balance at End of Month
November	$870.40	$13.06	$150.00	—	$100	$ 933.46
December	$933.46	$14.00	$333.01	$35.45	$ 50	$1195.02

The total finance charge during the 2-month period was $13.06 + $14.00 = $27.06.

(c) Brinkman knows that his debt is increasing. He moves the balance to another charge card that charges only .8% per month. Find his savings in finance charges for January.

$$\text{Savings} = \$1195.02 \times .015 - \$1195.02 \times .008 = \$8.37$$

> **PROBLEM-SOLVING HINT** The monthly finance charge was calculated on the unpaid balance at the beginning of the month.

OBJECTIVE [4] **Use the average daily balance method.** Most revolving charge plans now calculate finance charges using the **average daily balance method**. First the balance owed on the account is found at the end of each day during a month or billing period. All of these amounts are added, and the total is divided by the number of days in the month or billing period. The result is the average daily balance of the account, which is used to calculate the finance charge.

EXAMPLE 2

Finding Average Daily Balance

The activity in the MasterCard account of Kay Chamberlin for one billing period is shown in the following table. **(a)** Find the average daily balance on the next billing date of April 3 if the previous balance was \$209.46. Given a finance charge of $1\frac{1}{2}\%$ on the average daily balance, find **(b)** the finance charge and **(c)** the balance owed on April 3.

Transaction Description	Transaction Amount
Previous balance \$209.46	
March 3 Billing date	
March 12 Payment	\$50.00 CR*
March 17 Clothes	\$28.46
March 20 Mail order	\$31.22
April 1 Auto parts	\$59.10

*CR represents credit.

Solution

(a) At the close of business on March 3, the unpaid balance was \$209.46. This balance was the same for 9 days until March 12, when it changed to

$$\$209.46 - \$50 = \$159.46.$$

This balance was the same for 5 days until March 17, when it became

$$\$159.46 + \$28.46 = \$187.92.$$

In 3 days, on March 20, the balance became

$$\$187.92 + \$31.22 = \$219.14$$

which remained unchanged for 12 days, becoming

$$\$219.14 + \$59.10 = \$278.24$$

on April 1 at which time it remained for 2 days, until April 3, which was the new billing date. Find the average daily balance as follows.

Date	Unpaid Balance	Number of Days Until Balance Changes
March 3	\$209.46	9
March 12	\$159.46	5
March 17	\$187.92	3
March 20	\$219.14	12
April 1	\$278.24	2
		31 total number of days in billing period

There are 31 days in the billing period (March has 31 days). Find the average daily balance by multiplying each unpaid balance by the number of days for that balance, total the products, and then divide by 31, for the 31 days of the billing cycle. Do all this with the following procedure.

Unpaid Balance		Days		Total Balance
\$209.46	×	9	=	\$1885.14
\$159.46	×	5	=	797.30
\$187.92	×	3	=	563.76
\$219.14	×	12	=	2629.68
\$278.24	×	2	=	556.48
				\$6432.36

(For example, $209.46 $\times$ 9 = $1885.14 represents the sum of the average daily balances at the end of the day from March 3 through March 11.) Now divide the total by **31**.

$$\frac{\$6432.36}{31} = \$207.50 \text{ average daily balance}$$

Chamberlin will pay a finance charge based on the average daily balance of $207.50.

(b) The finance charge is .015 $\times$ $207.50 = $3.11 (rounded).

(c) The amount owed on April 3 is the beginning unpaid balance less any returns or payments, plus new charges and the finance charge.

Previous balance	Payment	New charges	Finance charge	
↓	↓	↓	↓	
$209.46	− $50	+ ($28.46 + $31.22 + $59.10) +	$3.11	= $281.35

> **PROBLEM-SOLVING HINT**   The billing period in Example 2 is 31 days. Some billing periods are 30 days (or 28 or 29 days in February). Be sure to use the correct number of days for the month of the billing period.

If the finance charges are expressed on a per month basis, find the **annual percentage rate** by multiplying the monthly rate by 12, the number of months in a year. For example, $1\frac{1}{2}\%$ per month is

$$1\tfrac{1}{2}\% \times 12 = 1.5 \times 12 = 18\% \text{ per year}$$

Objective **5** **Define loan consolidation.**   Credit is *easy to get* in our society. Look at the chart that shows the frequency with which college students use credits cards. In fact, credit is so easy to get that people sometimes *get in trouble* by borrowing too much. In that case, individuals sometimes **consolidate their loans** into one, lower interest loan, frequently with a longer term. This allows them to handle their monthly payments *rather than defaulting* on debt, which ruins their credit history. People who consolidate their loans and then borrow even more can get into very serious financial difficulties.

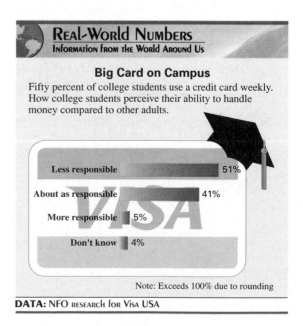

EXAMPLE 3

Loan
Consolidation

Between auto loans, a home loan, and the revolving-account loans shown below, teachers Bill and Cynthia Taylor have more debt than they can handle. They have gone to George Willis at Teachers Credit Union for help.

Revolving Account	Debt	Annual Percentage Rate	Minimum Payment
Sears	$3880.54	18%	$150
Dillards	$1620.13	16%	$ 50
MasterCard	$3140.65	14%	$100
Visa	$4920.98	20%	$135
Totals	$13,562.30		$435

Solution

George Willis (1) put the Taylors on a **strict budget**, (2) consolidated the revolving account debts into one, longer-term low interest loan at the credit union, and (3) decreased the payment on one auto by refinancing it at a lower interest rate.

In all, Willis reduced the Taylors' monthly payments by about $280 per month. The Taylors should be all right as long as they *stay on the budget*, *do not make additional credit purchases*, and *pay off some of the debt* on a regular basis.

11.2 | INSTALLMENT LOANS

Objectives

1. Define installment loan.
2. Find the total installment cost and the finance charge.
3. Use the formula for approximate APR.
4. Find APR, using the table.

| Problem Solving in Business | Most of the loans George Willis makes on behalf of Teachers Credit Union are installment loans that require equal periodic payments. The first example is about a loan that George Willis made to a piano teacher for a new piano. |

Objective 1 Define installment loan. A loan is **amortized** if both principal and interest are paid off by a sequence of periodic payments. An example is the paying of $250 per month for 48 months on a car loan. This type of loan is called an **installment loan**. Installment loans are used for cars, boats, home improvements, and even for consolidating several smaller loans into one affordable payment. The following headline shows that 6-year car loans are returning. The table shows the interest you might have to pay to finance a new automobile with an installment loan. Look on the World Wide Web to find competitive interest rates for car loans. Incidently, you can also check the market value of an automobile on the web.

REAL-WORLD NUMBERS
Information from the World Around Us

All Told

What you'll pay for a $30,000 loan at 8% interest for a well-equipped SUV.

Loan term (years)	Monthly payment	Interest paid
3	$940	$3845
4	$732	$5156
5	$526	$7872

DATA: Microsoft Carpoint

More Car Buyers Drive Away with 6-Year Loans

Six-year car loans—a year or more longer than normal—are making a quiet comeback.

Automakers have revived them to meet cutthroat competition from banks and to lure buyers who can't afford bigger payments on shorter loans.

"Stupid," says industry watcher Art Spinella at CNW Marketing Research. Buyers wind up still making payments on 80,000-mile cars they're also having to repair.

It also could signal worry about a slowdown. "In the second year of a downturn, to attract people with lower payments, I could see it," Brown says. "We forecast the market slowing later this year. Maybe some see it" sooner, or harder.

Ford Motor Credit is offering 72-month loans in Phoenix, Florida, and northwest states, where many buyers are using the loans to lower payments on sport-utility vehicles, often priced more than $30,000.

"There's no initiative at GMAC to promote this as the way to go. But dealers sometimes ask us for it to keep a customer," General Motors Acceptance Corp. spokesman Terry Sullivan says.

Ford "did it because other banks and captive finance companies are out there pushing it. Customers are interested, and we feel we have to offer it to be competitive," says Della DiPietro, spokeswoman for Ford Motor Credit. "It's something that is often not the best choice for customers."

Source: USA Today, 3/30/98. Reprinted by permission.

For related Web activities, go to www.mathbusiness.com

Keyword: installment

The **Federal Truth-in-Lending Act** (Regulation Z) of 1969 requires lenders to report their **finance charge** (the charge for credit) and **annual percentage rate (APR)** on installment loans. The federal government *does not* regulate rates, each individual state sets the maximum allowable rates and charges.

The **nominal**, or **stated**, interest rate can differ from the APR. The APR is the true effective annual interest rate for a loan. For example, a $1000 loan for 1 year with $120 in interest charges has an APR of 12% $\left(R = \dfrac{I}{PT} = \dfrac{\$120}{\$1000 \times 1} \right)$. A loan of $1000 for 9 months with interest charges of $120 has an APR of 16% $\left(R = \dfrac{I}{PT} = \dfrac{\$120}{\$1000 \times \frac{9}{12}} \right)$.

Interest charges *vary significantly* from one loan source to another and can be quite high as you can see from the table. The finance charge for a loan depends on the borrower's past credit record, income, down payment, and other factors. **It pays to shop and make comparisons based on APR figures before borrowing!**

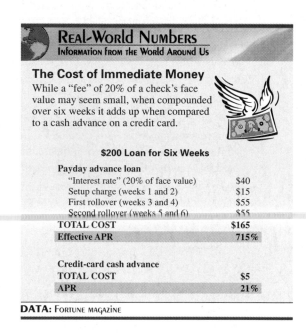

Real-World Numbers
Information from the World Around Us

The Cost of Immediate Money

While a "fee" of 20% of a check's face value may seem small, when compounded over six weeks it adds up when compared to a cash advance on a credit card.

$200 Loan for Six Weeks

Payday advance loan

"Interest rate" (20% of face value)	$40
Setup charge (weeks 1 and 2)	$15
First rollover (weeks 3 and 4)	$55
Second rollover (weeks 5 and 6)	$55
TOTAL COST	**$165**
Effective APR	**715%**

Credit-card cash advance

TOTAL COST	**$5**
APR	**21%**

DATA: Fortune magazine

Objective **2** **Find the total installment cost and the finance charge.** Find the annual percentage rate by first finding the **total installment cost** (or the **deferred payment price**) and the **finance charge** on the loan. Do this with the following steps.

> *Step 1* Find the total installment cost.
>
>   Total installment cost = Down payment + (Amount of each payment × Number of payments)
>
> *Step 2* Find the finance charge.
>
>   Finance charge = Total installment cost − Cash price
>
> *Step 3* Finally, find the amount financed.
>
>   Amount financed = Cash price − Down payment

EXAMPLE 1
Finding Total Installment Cost

Betsy Jones makes her living by teaching piano both at home and at a nearby community college where she is a professor of music. She purchased a new baby grand piano for $8500 with $1500 down and 48 monthly payments of $184.34 each. Find **(a)** the total installment cost, **(b)** the finance charge, and **(c)** the amount financed.

Solution

(a) Find the total installment cost by adding the down payment to the total amount of all her payments.

$$\text{Total installment cost} = \$1500 + 48 \times \$184.34 = \$10{,}348.32$$

(b) The finance charge is the total installment cost less the cash price.

$$\text{Finance charge} = \$10{,}348.32 - \$8500 = \$1848.32$$

(c) The amount financed is $\$8500 - \$1500 = \$7000$.

> **NOTE** In determining the total installment cost, the down payment is added to the total of the monthly payments.

For related Web activities, go to www.mathbusiness.com

Keyword: tuition

Students frequently borrow money using a **Stafford loan**, which is a type of installment loan. The government pays the interest on a *subsidized* Stafford loan while the student borrower is in school on a half-time basis. On the other hand, the student is responsible for interest on *unsubsidized* Stafford Loans. Repayment of a loan begins six months after the borrower ceases at least half-time enrollment. You can find information about Stafford loans at the financial aid office at your college or at a bank.

Objective 3 Use the formula for approximate APR. The **approximate annual percentage rate (APR)** for a loan paid off in monthly payments can be found with the following formula.

$$\text{Approximate APR} = \frac{24 \times \text{Finance charge}}{\text{Amount financed} \times (1 + \text{Total number of payments})}$$

The formula is *only an estimate* of the APR. It is not accurate enough for the purposes of the Federal Truth-in-Lending Act, which requires the use of tables.

EXAMPLE 2

Finding Annual Percentage Rate

Ed Chamski decides to buy a used car for $6400. He makes a down payment of $1200 and monthly payments of $169 for 36 months. Find the approximate annual percentage rate.

Solution

Use the steps outlined above.

$$\begin{aligned}
\text{Total installment cost} &= \$1200 + (\$169 \times 36 \text{ months}) \\
&= \$7284 \text{ total installment cost}
\end{aligned}$$

$$\begin{aligned}
\text{Finance charge} &= \$7284 - \$6400 = \$884 \\
\text{Amount financed} &= \$6400 - \$1200 = \$5200
\end{aligned}$$

Use the formula for approximate APR. Replace the finance charge with $884, the amount financed with $5200, and the number of payments with 36.

$$\begin{aligned}
\text{Approximate APR} &= \frac{24 \times \text{Finance charge}}{\text{Amount financed} \times (1 + \text{Total number of payments})} \\
&= \frac{24 \times \$884}{\$5200 \times (1 + 36)} \\
&= \frac{\$21{,}216}{\$192{,}400} \\
&= .110 \text{ or } 11\% \text{ approximate APR}
\end{aligned}$$

The approximate annual percentage rate on this loan is 11%. Example 3 shows how to find the actual APR for this loan.

> **NOTE** The precise APR can be found using a financial calculator as shown in examples in Appendix C.

Objective **4** **Find APR, using the table.** Annual percentage rate tables, available from the nearest Federal Reserve Bank or the Board of Governors of the Federal Reserve System, Washington, D.C. 20551, are used for APR rates that *are accurate enough* to satisfy federal law. The table on page 447 is a portion of these tables, which incidentally consist of two volumes.

The APR is found using the annual percentage rate table as follows:

ANNUAL PERCENTAGE RATE (APR)

Step 1 Multiply the finance charge by $100, and divide by the amount financed.

$$\frac{\text{Finance charge} \times \$100}{\text{Amount financed}}$$

The result is the finance charge per $100 of the amount financed.

Step 2 Read down the left column of the annual percentage rate table to the proper number of payments. Go across to the number closest to the number found in step 1. Read across the top of the column to find the annual percentage rate.

The annual percentage rate found with this method is accurate to the nearest quarter of a percent, as required by federal law.

EXAMPLE 3
Finding Annual
Percentage Rate

In Example 2, a used car costing $6400 was financed at $169 per month for 36 months after a down payment of $1200. The total finance charge was $884, and the amount financed was $5200. Find the annual percentage rate.

Solution

Use the steps outlined: multiply the finance charge by $100, and divide by the amount financed.

$$\frac{\$884 \times \$100}{\$5200} = \$17.00$$

This gives the finance charge per $100 of amount financed.

Read down the left column of the annual percentage rate table to the line for 36 months (the actual number of monthly payments). Follow across to the right to find the number closest to $17.00. Here, find **$17.01**. Read across the top of this column of figures to find the annual percentage rate, 10.50%.

In this example, 10.50% is the annual percentage rate that must be disclosed to the buyer of the car. In Example 2, the formula for the approximate annual percentage rate gave an answer of 11%, which is not accurate enough to meet the requirements of the law.

> **PROBLEM-SOLVING HINT** The annual percentage rate table contains the finance charge per $100 of amount financed.

Annual Percentage Rate Table for Monthly Payment Plans

Annual Percentage Rate (Finance Charge per $100 of Amount Financed)

Number of Payments	10.00%	10.25%	10.50%	10.75%	11.00%	11.25%	11.50%	11.75%	12.00%	12.25%	12.50%	12.75%	13.00%	13.25%	13.50%	13.75%	Number of Payments
1	0.83	0.85	0.87	0.90	0.92	0.94	0.96	0.98	1.00	1.02	1.04	1.06	1.08	1.10	1.12	1.15	1
2	1.25	1.28	1.31	1.35	1.38	1.41	1.44	1.47	1.50	1.53	1.57	1.60	1.63	1.66	1.69	1.72	2
3	1.67	1.71	1.76	1.80	1.84	1.88	1.92	1.96	2.01	2.05	2.09	2.13	2.17	2.22	2.26	2.30	3
4	2.09	2.14	2.20	2.25	2.30	2.35	2.41	2.46	2.51	2.57	2.62	2.67	2.72	2.78	2.83	2.88	4
5	2.51	2.58	2.64	2.70	2.77	2.83	2.89	2.96	3.02	3.08	3.15	3.21	3.27	3.34	3.40	3.46	5
6	2.94	3.01	3.08	3.16	3.23	3.31	3.38	3.45	3.53	3.60	3.68	3.75	3.83	3.90	3.97	4.05	6
7	3.36	3.45	3.53	3.62	3.70	3.78	3.87	3.95	4.04	4.12	4.21	4.29	4.38	4.47	4.55	4.64	7
8	3.79	3.88	3.98	4.07	4.17	4.26	4.36	4.46	4.55	4.65	4.74	4.84	4.94	5.03	5.13	5.22	8
9	4.21	4.32	4.43	4.53	4.64	4.75	4.85	4.96	5.07	5.17	5.28	5.39	5.49	5.60	5.71	5.82	9
10	4.64	4.76	4.88	4.99	5.11	5.23	5.35	5.46	5.58	5.70	5.82	5.94	6.05	6.17	6.29	6.41	10
11	5.07	5.20	5.33	5.45	5.58	5.71	5.84	5.97	6.10	6.23	6.36	6.49	6.62	6.75	6.88	7.01	11
12	5.50	5.64	5.78	5.92	6.06	6.20	6.34	6.48	6.62	6.76	6.90	7.04	7.18	7.32	7.46	7.60	12
13	5.93	6.08	6.23	6.38	6.53	6.68	6.84	6.99	7.14	7.29	7.44	7.59	7.75	7.90	8.05	8.20	13
14	6.36	6.52	6.69	6.85	7.01	7.17	7.34	7.50	7.66	7.82	7.99	8.15	8.31	8.48	8.64	8.81	14
15	6.80	6.97	7.14	7.32	7.49	7.66	7.84	8.01	8.19	8.36	8.53	8.71	8.88	9.06	9.23	9.41	15
16	7.23	7.41	7.60	7.78	7.97	8.15	8.34	8.53	8.71	8.90	9.08	9.27	9.46	9.64	9.83	10.02	16
17	7.67	7.86	8.06	8.25	8.45	8.65	8.84	9.04	9.24	9.44	9.63	9.83	10.03	10.23	10.43	10.63	17
18	8.10	8.31	8.52	8.73	8.93	9.14	9.35	9.56	9.77	9.98	10.19	10.40	10.61	10.82	11.03	11.24	18
19	8.54	8.76	8.98	9.20	9.42	9.64	9.86	10.08	10.30	10.52	10.74	10.96	11.18	11.41	11.63	11.85	19
20	8.98	9.21	9.44	9.67	9.90	10.13	10.37	10.60	10.83	11.06	11.30	11.53	11.76	12.00	12.23	12.46	20
21	9.42	9.66	9.90	10.15	10.39	10.63	10.88	11.12	11.36	11.61	11.85	12.10	12.34	12.59	12.84	13.08	21
22	9.86	10.12	10.37	10.62	10.88	11.13	11.39	11.64	11.90	12.16	12.41	12.67	12.93	13.19	13.44	13.70	22
23	10.30	10.57	10.84	11.10	11.37	11.63	11.90	12.17	12.44	12.71	12.97	13.24	13.51	13.78	14.05	14.32	23
24	10.75	11.02	11.30	11.58	11.86	12.14	12.42	12.70	12.98	13.26	13.54	13.82	14.10	14.38	14.66	14.95	24
25	11.19	11.48	11.77	12.06	12.35	12.64	12.93	13.22	13.52	13.81	14.10	14.40	14.69	14.98	15.28	15.57	25
26	11.64	11.94	12.24	12.54	12.85	13.15	13.45	13.75	14.06	14.36	14.67	14.97	15.28	15.59	15.89	16.20	26
27	12.09	12.40	12.71	13.03	13.34	13.66	13.97	14.29	14.60	14.92	15.24	15.56	15.87	16.19	16.51	16.83	27
28	12.53	12.86	13.18	13.51	13.84	14.16	14.49	14.82	15.15	15.48	15.81	16.14	16.47	16.80	17.13	17.46	28
29	12.98	13.32	13.66	14.00	14.33	14.67	15.01	15.35	15.70	16.04	16.38	16.72	17.07	17.41	17.75	18.10	29
30	13.43	13.78	14.13	14.48	14.83	15.19	15.54	15.89	16.24	16.60	16.95	17.31	17.66	18.02	18.38	18.74	30
31	13.89	14.25	14.61	14.97	15.33	15.70	16.06	16.43	16.79	17.16	17.53	17.90	18.27	18.63	19.00	19.38	31
32	14.34	14.71	15.09	15.46	15.84	16.21	16.59	16.97	17.35	17.73	18.11	18.49	18.87	19.25	19.63	20.02	32
33	14.79	15.18	15.57	15.95	16.34	16.73	17.12	17.51	17.90	18.29	18.69	19.08	19.47	19.87	20.26	20.66	33
34	15.25	15.65	16.05	16.44	16.85	17.25	17.65	18.05	18.46	18.86	19.27	19.67	20.08	20.49	20.90	21.31	34
35	15.70	16.11	16.53	16.94	17.35	17.77	18.18	18.60	19.01	19.43	19.85	20.27	20.69	21.11	21.53	21.95	35
36	16.16	16.58	17.01	17.43	17.86	18.29	18.71	19.14	19.57	20.00	20.43	20.87	21.30	21.73	22.17	22.60	36
37	16.62	17.06	17.49	17.93	18.37	18.81	19.25	19.69	20.13	20.58	21.02	21.46	21.91	22.36	22.81	23.25	37
38	17.08	17.53	17.98	18.43	18.88	19.33	19.78	20.24	20.69	21.15	21.61	22.07	22.52	22.99	23.45	23.91	38
39	17.54	18.00	18.46	18.93	19.39	19.86	20.32	20.79	21.26	21.73	22.20	22.67	23.14	23.61	24.09	24.56	39
40	18.00	18.48	18.95	19.43	19.90	20.38	20.86	21.34	21.82	22.30	22.79	23.27	23.76	24.25	24.73	25.22	40
41	18.47	18.95	19.44	19.93	20.42	20.91	21.40	21.89	22.39	22.88	23.38	23.88	24.38	24.88	25.38	25.88	41
42	18.93	19.43	19.93	20.43	20.93	21.44	21.94	22.45	22.96	23.47	23.98	24.49	25.00	25.51	26.03	26.55	42
43	19.40	19.91	20.42	20.94	21.45	21.97	22.49	23.01	23.53	24.05	24.57	25.10	25.62	26.15	26.68	27.21	43
44	19.86	20.39	20.91	21.44	21.97	22.50	23.03	23.57	24.10	24.64	25.17	25.71	26.25	26.79	27.33	27.88	44
45	20.33	20.87	21.41	21.95	22.49	23.03	23.58	24.12	24.67	25.22	25.77	26.32	26.88	27.43	27.99	28.55	45
46	20.80	21.35	21.90	22.46	23.01	23.57	24.13	24.69	25.25	25.81	26.37	26.94	27.51	28.08	28.65	29.22	46
47	21.27	21.83	22.40	22.97	23.53	24.10	24.68	25.25	25.82	26.40	26.98	27.56	28.14	28.72	29.31	29.89	47
48	21.74	22.32	22.90	23.48	24.06	24.64	25.23	25.81	26.40	26.99	27.58	28.18	28.77	29.37	29.97	30.57	48
49	22.21	22.80	23.39	23.99	24.58	25.18	25.78	26.38	26.98	27.59	28.19	28.80	29.41	30.02	30.63	31.24	49
50	22.69	23.29	23.89	24.50	25.11	25.72	26.33	26.95	27.56	28.18	28.80	29.42	30.04	30.67	31.29	31.92	50
51	23.16	23.78	24.40	25.02	25.64	26.26	26.89	27.52	28.15	28.78	29.41	30.05	30.68	31.32	31.96	32.60	51
52	23.64	24.27	24.90	25.53	26.17	26.81	27.45	28.09	28.73	29.38	30.02	30.67	31.32	31.98	32.63	33.29	52
53	24.11	24.76	25.40	26.05	26.70	27.35	28.00	28.66	29.32	29.98	30.64	31.30	31.97	32.63	33.30	33.97	53
54	24.59	25.25	25.91	26.57	27.23	27.90	28.56	29.23	29.91	30.58	31.25	31.93	32.61	33.29	33.98	34.66	54
55	25.07	25.74	26.41	27.09	27.77	28.44	29.13	29.81	30.50	31.18	31.87	32.56	33.26	33.95	34.65	35.35	55
56	25.55	26.23	26.92	27.61	28.30	28.99	29.69	30.39	31.09	31.79	32.49	33.20	33.91	34.62	35.33	36.04	56
57	26.03	26.73	27.43	28.13	28.84	29.54	30.25	30.97	31.68	32.39	33.11	33.83	34.56	35.28	36.01	36.74	57
58	26.51	27.23	27.94	28.66	29.37	30.10	30.82	31.55	32.27	33.00	33.74	34.47	35.21	35.95	36.69	37.43	58
59	27.00	27.72	28.45	29.18	29.91	30.65	31.39	32.13	32.87	33.61	34.36	35.11	35.86	36.62	37.37	38.13	59
60	27.48	28.22	28.96	29.71	30.45	31.20	31.96	32.71	33.47	34.23	34.99	35.75	36.52	37.29	38.06	38.83	60

11.3 | Early Payoffs of Loans

Objectives

1. Use the United States Rule when prepaying a loan.
2. Find the amount due on the maturity date using the United States Rule.
3. Use the Rule of 78 when prepaying a loan.

OBJECTIVE 1 Use the United States Rule when prepaying a loan. It is common for a payment to be made on a loan *before it is due*. This may occur when a person receives extra money or when refinancing a debt at a lower interest rate somewhere else. Prepayments of loans are discussed in this section.

The first method for calculating early loan payment is the **United States Rule** and it is used by the U.S. government as well as most states and financial institutions. Under the United States Rule, any payment is first applied to any interest owed. The balance of the payment is then used to reduce the principal amount of the loan.

The United States Rule

Step 1 Find the simple interest due from the date the loan was made until the date the partial payment is made. Use the formula $I = PRT$.

Step 2 Subtract this interest from the amount of the payment.

Step 3 Any difference is used to reduce the principal.

Step 4 Treat additional partial payments in the same way, always finding interest on *only* the unpaid balance after the last partial payment.

Step 5 Remaining principal plus interest on this unpaid principal is then due on the due date of the loan.

OBJECTIVE 2 Find the amount due on the maturity date using the United States Rule. If the partial payment is not large enough to pay the interest due, the payment is simply held until enough money is available to pay the interest due. This means that a partial payment smaller than the interest due offers no advantage to the borrower—the lender just holds the partial payment until enough money is available to pay the interest owed.

> **NOTE**   We will continue to use 360-day years in the calculations of this section.

EXAMPLE 1
Finding the Amount Due

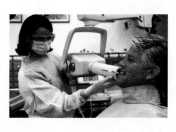

On August 14, Jane Ficker signed a 180-day note for $28,500 for an X-ray machine for her dental office. The note has an interest rate of 10% compounded annually. On October 25, a payment of $8500 is made. **(a)** Find the balance owed on the principal. **(b)** If no additional payments are made, find the amount due at maturity of the loan.

Solution

(a) First find the interest from August 14 to October 25 (298 − 226 = **72 days**) using $I = PRT$.

$$\text{Interest} = \$28{,}500 \times .10 \times \frac{72}{360} = \$570$$

Subtract the interest from the October 25 payment to find the amount of the payment to be applied to principal. Then reduce the original principal by this amount.

$$\text{Applied to principal} = \$8500 - \$570 = \$7930$$
$$\text{New principal} = \$28{,}500 - \$7930 = \$20{,}570$$

(b) The note was originally for 180 days with the partial payment made after 72 days. Thus, interest on the new principal of $20,570 will be charged for $180 - 72 = 108$ days.

$$\text{Interest} = \$20{,}570 \times .10 \times \frac{108}{360} = \mathbf{\$617.10}$$

If no additional partial payments are made, the amount due at the maturity date is the remaining principal plus interest on that remaining principal.

$$\text{Amount due at maturity} = \$20{,}570 + \mathbf{\$617.10} = \$21{,}187.10$$

EXAMPLE 2
Finding the
Interest Paid and
Amount Due

A lawn-furniture manufacturer signs a 140-day note on February 5. The note, for $45,600, is to a supplier of aluminum tubing for the furniture and carries an interest rate of 14%. On March 19, the manufacturer receives an unexpected payment from a customer, and applies $16,000 toward the note. Another early payment permits a second $13,250 partial payment on April 23. Find the interest paid on the note and the amount paid on the due date of the note.

Solution

The first partial payment is made on March 19, which is $23 + 19 = 42$ days after the loan is made. In 42 days, the interest owed on the note is

$$I = PRT = \$45{,}600 \times .14 \times \frac{42}{360} = \$744.80.$$

A partial payment of $16,000 is made on March 19. Of this amount, $744.80 is applied to interest, with

$16,000.00	amount of payment
− 744.80	interest owed
$15,255.20	applied to principal

After March 19, the balance on the loan is

$45,600.00	original amount of loan
− 15,255.20	applied to principal
$30,344.80	new amount owed

After March 19, the balance on the note is $30,344.80. A second partial payment is made on April 23, which is $12 + 23 = 35$ days later. Interest on $30,344.80 for 35 days is

$$I = \$30{,}344.80 \times .14 \times \frac{35}{360} = \$413.03.$$

A payment of $13,250 is made on April 23. Of this, $413.03 applies to interest, leaving

$$\$13{,}250 - \$413.03 = \mathbf{\$12{,}836.97}$$

to reduce the principal. After April 23, the principal is

$30,344.80	previous balance
− 12,836.97	applied to principal
$17,507.83	new principal

The first partial payment is made 42 days after the note was signed, with the second payment made 35 days after that. The second payment is made $42 + 35 = 77$ days after the note is signed. Since the note is for 140 days, the note is due $140 - 77 = 63$ days after the second partial payment. Interest on the new balance of **$17,507.83** for 63 days is

$$I = \mathbf{\$17{,}507.83} \times .14 \times \frac{63}{360} = \$428.94.$$

On the date the loan matures, a total of

$$\$17,507.83 + \$428.94 = \$17,936.77$$

must be paid. The total interest paid over the life of the loan is

$$\$744.80 + \$413.03 + \$428.94 = \$1586.77.$$

All of this work can be summarized in the following table.

Date Payment Made	Amount of Payment	Applied to Interest	Applied to Principal	Remaining Balance
March 19	$16,000	$744.80	$15,255.20	$30,344.80
April 23	$13,250	$413.03	$12,836.97	$17,507.83
Date of maturity (June 25)	$17,936.77	$428.94	$17,507.83	$0
Total		$1586.77	$45,600.00	

Objective 3 Use the Rule of 78 when prepaying a loan. A variation of the United States Rule, called the **Rule of 78**, is still used by many lenders. This rule allows a lender *to earn more of the finance charge during the early months* of the loan compared to the United States Rule. Lenders typically use this rule to protect against early payoffs on small loans. Effectively, the lender will earn a higher rate of interest in the event of an early payoff under the Rule of 78 than under the United States Rule.

The Rule of 78 gets its name based on a loan of 12 months—the sum of the months $1 + 2 + 3 + \cdots + 12 = 78$. The finance charge for the first month is $\frac{12}{78}$ of the total charge, with $\frac{11}{78}$ in the second month, $\frac{10}{78}$ in the third month, and $\frac{1}{78}$ in the final month. The Rule of 78 can be applied to loans *with terms other than 12 months*. For example, the sum of the months in a 6-month contract is $1 + 2 + 3 + 4 + 5 + 6 = 21$. The finance charge for the first month would be $\frac{6}{21}, \frac{5}{21}$ for the second month, and so on. Similarly, the sum of the months in a 15-month contract is $1 + 2 + \cdots + 15 = 120$. The finance charge for the first month of a 15-month contract is $\frac{15}{120}$ or $\frac{1}{8}$, and so on.

The total finance charge on an installment loan is calculated when a loan is first made. Early payoff of a loan results in a lower finance charge. The portion of the finance charge that is NOT EARNED by the lender under the Rule of 78, called **unearned interest** or **refund**, is found using the following formula.

$$U = F \left(\frac{N}{P} \right) \left(\frac{1 + N}{1 + P} \right)$$

where: U = unearned interest, F = finance charge,
N = number of payments remaining, and P = total number of payments

EXAMPLE 3

Finding Unearned Interest and Balance Due

Adrian Ortega borrowed $600, which he is paying back in 24 monthly payments of $29.50 each. With 9 payments remaining, he decides to repay the loan in full. Find **(a)** the amount of unearned interest and **(b)** the amount necessary to repay the loan in full. Use the Rule of 78.

Solution

(a) Ortega makes 24 payments of $29.50 each, for a total repayment of

$$24 \times \$29.50 = \$708.$$

His finance charge is

$$\$708 - \$600 = \$108.$$

Find the amount of unearned interest as follows. The finance charge is $108, the scheduled number of payments is 24, and the loan is paid off with 9 payments left. Solve as follows.

$$\text{Unearned interest} = \$108 \times \frac{9}{24} \times \frac{(1 + 9)}{(1 + 24)} = \$16.20$$

(b) When Ortega decides to pay off the loan, he has 9 payments of $29.50 left. These payments total

$$9 \times \$29.50 = \$265.50.$$

By paying the loan off early, Ortega saves the unearned interest of $16.20, so only

$$\$265.50 - \$16.20 = \$249.30$$

is needed to pay the loan in full.

11.4 | PERSONAL PROPERTY LOANS

Objectives

1. Define personal property and real estate.
2. Use the formula for amortization to find payment.
3. Set up an amortization table.
4. Find monthly payments.

Problem Solving in Business

George Willis at Teachers Credit Union specializes in personal property loans. It is not unusual for him to take five or more loan applications each day. Loan applications require the applicant to supply information on his or her job, income, and any debts. After taking the loan application, George carefully checks the credit worthiness of each applicant. As you can see from the headline, credit reports, which are supplied by national credit bureaus, are not always accurate.

Reality Check

For related Web activities, go to www.mathbusiness.com

Keyword: watchdog

Watchdog Group Finds 29% of Credit Reports Have Errors

If you haven't checked your credit report lately, maybe you should.

Nearly a third of credit reports contained serious mistakes, a recent test by the U.S. Public Interest Research Group (U.S. PIRG), a nonprofit consumer watchdog, found.

PIRG says of 133 credit reports obtained by 88 PIRG staffers, 29% had serious errors, including false delinquencies and closed accounts listed as still open.

Altogether, the study says, 70% of the reports contained mistakes of some kind, including misspelled names or missing accounts—credit, mortgage or loan accounts that would have shown credit worthiness.

These mistakes are often serious enough to cause someone to be denied a mortgage or even a job.

Source: USA Today, 3/13/98. Reprinted by permission.

Objective 1 Define personal property and real estate. Items that can be moved from one location to another such as an automobile, a boat, or a stereo are called **personal property**. In contrast, land and homes cannot be moved and are called **real estate** or **real property**. Personal property loans are discussed in this section and real estate loans are discussed in the next section.

People can end up with more debt than they can afford. In that event, individuals are sometimes forced to return personal property, such as an automobile, to the lender. When this happens, the property is said to be **repossessed** by the lender. Interest rates for personal property loans vary significantly from one lender to another. Use the World Wide Web to find current interest rates for car loans.

For related Web activities, go to www.mathbusiness.com

Keyword: financed

Objective 2 Use the formula for amortization to find payment. The periodic payment needed at the end of each period to amortize a loan with interest i per period, over n periods, is found using the following formula. The number from the table is found using the interest rate from the table (i) and the number of periods.

> Payment = Loan amount × Number from amortization table

EXAMPLE 1
Finding Amortization Information

Pablo Valdez recently received his college degree and accepted a job as a designer of World Wide Web pages. Valdez and his spouse, a teacher and avid water skier, decide to borrow $15,000 to purchase a new ski boat. They go to Teachers Credit Union where George Willis checks their credit and authorizes a 36-month loan at 12% per year. Find **(a)** the monthly payment, **(b)** the portion of the first payment that is interest, **(c)** the balance due after 1 payment, **(d)** the interest owed for the second month, and **(e)** the balance after the second payment.

Solution

(a) Use $\frac{12\%}{12}$ = 1% per period and 36 periods in the amortization table to find **.03321**

> Payment = $15,000 × **.03321** = $498.15 at the end of each month

(b) Interest for the month is found using the simple interest formula

$$I = PRT = \$15,000 \times .12 \times \frac{1}{12} = \$150.$$

The amount of the first payment that is applied to reduce the loan principal is

> $498.15 − $150 = **$348.15**.

(c) The remaining debt after the first payment is

> $15,000 − **$348.15** = $14,651.85.

(d) Interest owed for the second month is found using the loan balance after the first payment.

$$\text{Interest} = \$14,651.85 \times .12 \times \frac{1}{12} = \$146.52$$

A payment of $498.15 is made at the end of period 2 and a total of

> $498.15 − $146.52 = **$351.63 is applied to the debt.**

(e) The balance after the second payment is found as follows.

> $14,651.85 − $351.63 = $14,300.22

OBJECTIVE **3** Set up an amortization table.

EXAMPLE 2
Creating an Amortization Table

Clarence Thomas purchased new commercial-grade washers and dryers for his laundromat at a cost of $22,300. He made a down payment of $5000 and agreed to pay the balance off in quarterly payments over 2 years at 12% compounded quarterly. Find **(a)** the quarterly payment and **(b)** show the first four payments in an **amortization table**.

Solution

(a) The amount financed is $22,300 − $5000 = $17,300. Find the factor from the table using 2 × 4 = 8 periods and $\frac{12\%}{4}$ = 3% per period, then multiply the amount financed times the factor to find the payment.

> Payment = $17,300 × .14246 = $2464.56 (rounded)

(b)   **Amortization Schedule**

Payment Number	Amount of Payment	Interest for Period	Portion to Principal	Principal at End of Period
0	—	—	—	$17,300.00
1	$2464.56	$519.00	$1945.56	$15,354.44
2	$2464.56	$460.63	$2003.93	$13,350.51
3	$2464.56	$400.52	$2064.04	$11,286.47
4	$2464.56	$338.59	$2125.97	$ 9,160.50

Amortization Table n = **number of payments;** i = **interest rate per period**

n	1%	$1\frac{1}{2}$%	2%	$2\frac{1}{2}$%	3%	4%	5%	6%	8%	10%	12%	n
1	1.01000	1.01500	1.02000	1.02500	1.03000	1.04000	1.05000	1.06000	1.08000	1.10000	1.12000	1
2	.50751	.51128	.51505	.51883	.52261	.53020	.53780	.54544	.56077	.57619	.59170	2
3	.34002	.34338	.34675	.35014	.35353	.36035	.36721	.37411	.38803	.40211	.41535	3
4	.25628	.25944	.26262	.26582	.26903	.27549	.28201	.28859	.30192	.31547	.32923	4
5	.20604	.20909	.21216	.21525	.21835	.22463	.23097	.23740	.25046	.26380	.27741	5
6	.17255	.17553	.17853	.18155	.18460	.19076	.19702	.20336	.21632	.22961	.24323	6
7	.14863	.15156	.15451	.15750	.16051	.16661	.17282	.17914	.19207	.20541	.21912	7
8	.13069	.13358	.13651	.13947	.14246	.14853	.15472	.16104	.17401	.18744	.20130	8
9	.11674	.11961	.12252	.12546	.12843	.13449	.14069	.14702	.16008	.17364	.18768	9
10	.10558	.10843	.11133	.11426	.11723	.12329	.12950	.13587	.14903	.16275	.17698	10
11	.09645	.09929	.10218	.10511	.10808	.11415	.12039	.12679	.14008	.15396	.16842	11
12	.08885	.09168	.09456	.09749	.10046	.10655	.11283	.11928	.13270	.14676	.16144	12
13	.08241	.08524	.08812	.09105	.09403	.10014	.10646	.11296	.12652	.14078	.15568	13
14	.07690	.07972	.08260	.08554	.08853	.09467	.10102	.10758	.12130	.13575	.15087	14
15	.07212	.07494	.07783	.08077	.08377	.08994	.09634	.10296	.11683	.13147	.14682	15
16	.06794	.07077	.07365	.07660	.07961	.08582	.09227	.09895	.11298	.12782	.14339	16
17	.06426	.06708	.06997	.07293	.07595	.08220	.08870	.09544	.10963	.12466	.14046	17
18	.06098	.06381	.06670	.06967	.07271	.07899	.08555	.09236	.10670	.12193	.13794	18
19	.05805	.06088	.06378	.06676	.06981	.07614	.08275	.08962	.10413	.11955	.13576	19
20	.05542	.05825	.06116	.06415	.06722	.07358	.08024	.08718	.10185	.11746	.13388	20
21	.05303	.05587	.05878	.06179	.06487	.07128	.07800	.08500	.09983	.11562	.13224	21
22	.05086	.05370	.05663	.05965	.06275	.06920	.07597	.08305	.09803	.11401	.13081	22
23	.04889	.05173	.05467	.05770	.06081	.06731	.07414	.08128	.09642	.11257	.12956	23
24	.04707	.04992	.05287	.05591	.05905	.06559	.07247	.07968	.09498	.11130	.12846	24
25	.04541	.04826	.05122	.05428	.05743	.06401	.07095	.07823	.09368	.11017	.12750	25
26	.04387	.04673	.04970	.05277	.05594	.06257	.06956	.07690	.09251	.10916	.12665	26
27	.04245	.04532	.04829	.05138	.05456	.06124	.06829	.07570	.09145	.10826	.12590	27
28	.04112	.04400	.04699	.05009	.05329	.06001	.06712	.07459	.09049	.10745	.12524	28
29	.03990	.04278	.04578	.04889	.05211	.05888	.06605	.07358	.08962	.10673	.12466	29
30	.03875	.04164	.04465	.04778	.05102	.05783	.06505	.07265	.08883	.10608	.12414	30
31	.03768	.04057	.04360	.04674	.05000	.05686	.06413	.07179	.08811	.10550	.12369	31
32	.03667	.03958	.04261	.04577	.04905	.05595	.06328	.07100	.08745	.10497	.12328	32
33	.03573	.03864	.04169	.04486	.04816	.05510	.06249	.07027	.08685	.10450	.12292	33
34	.03484	.03776	.04082	.04401	.04732	.05431	.06176	.06960	.08630	.10407	.12260	34
35	.03400	.03693	.04000	.04321	.04654	.05358	.06107	.06897	.08580	.10369	.12232	35
36	.03321	.03615	.03923	.04245	.04580	.05289	.06043	.06839	.08534	.10334	.12206	36
37	.03247	.03541	.03851	.04174	.04511	.05224	.05984	.06786	.08492	.10303	.12184	37
38	.03176	.03472	.03782	.04107	.04446	.05163	.05928	.06736	.08454	.10275	.12164	38
39	.03109	.03405	.03717	.04044	.04384	.05106	.05876	.06689	.08419	.10249	.12146	39
40	.03046	.03343	.03656	.03984	.04326	.05052	.05828	.06646	.08386	.10226	.12130	40
41	.02985	.03283	.03597	.03927	.04271	.05002	.05782	.06606	.08356	.10205	.12116	41
42	.02928	.03226	.03542	.03873	.04219	.04954	.05739	.06568	.08329	.10186	.12104	42
43	.02873	.03172	.03489	.03822	.04170	.04909	.05699	.06533	.08303	.10169	.12092	43
44	.02820	.03121	.03439	.03773	.04123	.04866	.05662	.06501	.08280	.10153	.12083	44
45	.02771	.03072	.03391	.03727	.04079	.04826	.05626	.06470	.08259	.10139	.12074	45
46	.02723	.03025	.03345	.03683	.04036	.04788	.05593	.06441	.08239	.10126	.12066	46
47	.02677	.02980	.03302	.03641	.03996	.04752	.05561	.06415	.08221	.10115	.12059	47
48	.02633	.02938	.03260	.03601	.03958	.04718	.05532	.06390	.08204	.10104	.12052	48
49	.02591	.02896	.03220	.03562	.03921	.04686	.05504	.06366	.08189	.10095	.12047	49
50	.02551	.02857	.03182	.03526	.03887	.04655	.05478	.06344	.08174	.10086	.12042	50

> **NOTE**   Notice that the principal, and therefore the interest on the principal, decreases with additional payments. Much of the first few payments *goes to pay interest* and is not used to reduce the loan amount. On the other hand, little of the last few payments goes to pay interest since the principal is small by then.

> **NOTE**   The very last payment will typically vary slightly from the regular monthly payments due to rounding.

Objective **4** **Find monthly payments.**   As an alternative to the amortization table, the loan payoff table can also be used to find the monthly payment. This table has a different format since the APR is *down the left column* and the number of months is *across the top* of this table. The monthly payment is found by multiplying the amount to be financed by the number from the table.

Loan Payoff Table

APR \ Mos.	18	24	30	36	42	48	54	60	Mos. \ APR
8%	.059138	.045229	.036887	.031336	.027376	.024413	.022113	.020277	8%
9%	.0596	.045683	.037347	.0318	.027845	.024885	.022589	.020758	9%
10%	.060056	.046146	.03781	.032267	.028317	.025363	.023072	.021247	10%
11%	.060516	.046608	.038277	.032739	.028793	.025846	.023561	.021742	11%
12%	.060984	.047075	.038747	.033214	.029276	.026333	.024057	.022245	12%
13%	.06145	.047542	.03922	.033694	.029762	.026827	.024557	.022753	13%
14%	.061917	.048013	.0397	.034178	.030252	.027327	.025065	.023268	14%
15%	.062383	.048488	.04018	.034667	.03075	.027831	.025578	.02379	15%
16%	.062855	.048963	.040663	.035159	.03125	.02834	.026096	.024318	16%
17%	.063328	.049442	.04115	.035653	.031755	.028854	.026620	.024853	17%
18%	.063806	.049925	.04164	.036153	.032264	.029369	.027152	.025393	18%
19%	.064283	.050408	.042133	.036656	.032779	.0299	.027687	.02594	19%
20%	.064761	.050896	.04263	.037164	.033298	.030431	.02823	.026493	20%
21%	.065244	.051388	.04313	.037675	.033821	.030967	.028776	.027053	21%

EXAMPLE 3
Finding Amortization Payments

After allowances for a trade-in, Linda Dean owes $8700 on a Honda Civic. She wishes to pay the car off in 60 monthly payments. Find the amount of each payment and the finance charge, if the APR on her loan is 16%.

Solution

Multiply the amount to be financed and the number from the table for 60 months and 16% (**.024318**).

$$\text{Monthly payment} = \$8700 \times .024318 = \$211.57$$

The finance charge is the sum of all payments less the loan amount.

$$\text{Finance charge} = 60 \times \$211.57 - \$8700 = \$3994.20$$

Notice that interest adds $3994.20 to the loan amount.

The calculator solution to this example follows.

$$60 \boxed{\times} \ 211.57 \boxed{-} \ 8700 \boxed{=} \ 3994.20$$

Note: All calculator solutions use a scientific calculator. Refer to Appendix B for scientific calculator basics.

11.5 | REAL ESTATE LOANS

OBJECTIVES

1. Determine monthly payments on a home.
2. Prepare a repayment schedule.
3. Define escrow accounts.
4. Define fixed and variable rate loans.

For related Web
activities, go to
www.mathbusiness.com

Keyword:
property

OBJECTIVE 1 **Determine monthly payments on a home.** A home is *one of the most expensive purchases* that a person will make in his or her lifetime. The monthly payment for a home depends on the amount borrowed, the interest rate, and the term of the loan. As you can see from the chart, interest rates on **mortgages** have varied widely in the past. Use the World Wide Web to find current mortgage rates.

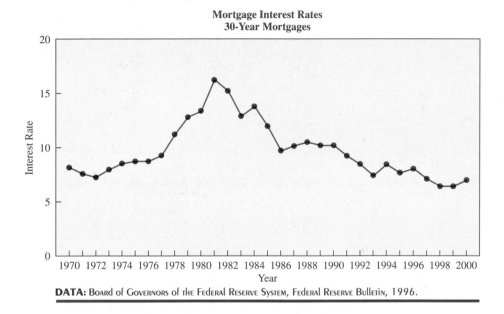

**Mortgage Interest Rates
30-Year Mortgages**

DATA: BOARD OF GOVERNORS OF THE FEDERAL RESERVE SYSTEM, *Federal Reserve Bulletin*, 1996.

For related Web
activities, go to
www.mathbusiness.com

Keyword:
process

The amount of the monthly payment is found by the methods given in the previous section, but special tables are used for real estate loans because of the long repayment periods. The real estate amortization table shows the monthly payment necessary to repay a $1000 loan for differing interest rates and lengths of repayment.

Real-Estate Amortization Table (Principal and Interest per Thousand Dollars Borrowed)

Terms in Years	7%	$7\frac{1}{4}$%	$7\frac{1}{2}$%	$7\frac{3}{4}$%	8%	$8\frac{1}{4}$%	$8\frac{1}{2}$%	$8\frac{3}{4}$%	9%	$9\frac{1}{4}$%	$9\frac{1}{2}$%	$9\frac{3}{4}$%	Terms in Years
10	11.62	11.75	11.88	12.01	12.14	12.27	12.40	12.54	12.67	12.81	12.94	13.08	10
15	8.99	9.13	9.28	9.42	9.56	9.71	9.85	10.00	10.15	10.30	10.45	10.60	15
20	7.76	7.91	8.06	8.21	8.37	8.53	8.68	8.84	9.00	9.16	9.33	9.49	20
25	7.07	7.23	7.39	7.56	7.72	7.89	8.06	8.23	8.40	8.57	8.74	8.92	25
30	6.66	6.83	7.00	7.17	7.34	7.52	7.69	7.87	8.05	8.23	8.41	8.60	30

EXAMPLE 1

Finding Payments
to Amortize a
Loan

Bob and Mary McArthur need to borrow $65,300 to purchase a home and are trying to decide whether they should finance it for 15 years or for 30 years. They are also looking at the effect of interest rates on total costs. **(a)** Find the monthly payment for both 15 years and 30 years at both $7\frac{1}{2}$% and $9\frac{3}{4}$%. **(b)** Then find the total cost of financing the home for each case.

SOLUTION

(a) First, find the amount to be financed in thousands ($65,300 ÷ 1000 = 65.3 thousands). Then, multiply this number times the factor from the table for each loan. For example, to find the payment for a 15-year amortization at $7\frac{1}{2}$%, multiply 65.3 × 9.28 = $605.98, which is rounded to the nearest cent. The monthly payments are as follows.

Monthly Payments

Term of Mortgage	Interest Rate	
	$7\frac{1}{2}$%	$9\frac{3}{4}$%
15 years	$605.98	$692.18
30 years	$457.10	$561.58

The monthly payments can vary from $457.10 to $692.18, or a difference of $235.08 per month, depending on rates and term.

(b) The total cost for a loan is the associated monthly payment times the number of payments. For example, the total cost for a 15-year $7\frac{1}{2}$% mortgage is as follows.

$$\$605.98 \times 12 \text{ months/year} \times 15 \text{ years} = \$109,076.40$$

The total costs for each loan are rounded to the nearest dollar and shown below.

Total Costs

Term of Mortgage	Interest Rate	
	$7\frac{1}{2}$%	$9\frac{3}{4}$%
15 years	$109,076	$124,592
30 years	$164,556	$202,169

Notice that the total costs to finance the $65,300 loan vary from about $109,000 to about $202,000 depending on the option chosen. The monthly payment on a 15-year loan is higher, but the total cost of financing the home *is considerably lower*. Of course, it is always best to get the lowest interest rate that you can when borrowing.

> **PROBLEM-SOLVING HINT**   Be sure to divide the loan amount by $1000 before calculating the monthly payment.

> **NOTE**   The effect of different interest rates on a house payment are calculated with a financial calculator in Example 6 in Appendix C.

Mortgage payoffs of 25 or 30 years have been common in the past. However, **accelerated mortgages**, with payoffs of 15 or 20 years, are becoming more common for the reason pointed out in Example 1—lower total costs.

OBJECTIVE **2** **Prepare a repayment schedule.**   Many lenders supply an **amortization schedule** also called a **repayment schedule** showing the amount of each payment that goes to pay off interest, the amount that is applied to principal, and the principal balance for each month over the entire life of the loan. These calculations can be done by hand as shown in the next example, but they are commonly done on computers.

EXAMPLE 2

Preparing a Repayment Schedule

Prepare a repayment schedule for the first 2 months on a loan of $60,000 at 8% interest for 30 years. The monthly payment on this loan is $440.40.

SOLUTION

Find the interest owed for the first month using the formula for simple interest.

$$\text{Interest} = P \times R \times T$$

$$\text{Interest} = \$60,000 \times .08 \times \frac{1}{12} = \$400.00$$

Subtract to find the amount of the first payment that reduces the debt.

$$\$440.40 - \$400.00 = \mathbf{\$40.40}$$

Find the remaining debt after the first payment by subtracting.

$$\$60,000 - \mathbf{\$40.40} = \$59,959.60$$

Use the simple interest formula with the new loan balance to find the interest for month 2.

$$\text{Interest} = \$59,959.60 \times .08 \times \frac{1}{12} = \$399.73$$

Subtract to find the amount of the second payment that reduces the debt.

$$\$440.40 - \$399.73 = \mathbf{\$40.67}$$

Find the remaining debt after the second payment by subtracting.

$$\$59,959.60 - \mathbf{\$40.67} = \$59,918.93$$

The following repayment schedule shows the first and second months of this loan.

Repayment Schedule

Payment Number	Monthly Payment	Interest Payment	Principal Payment	Remaining Balance
0	—	—	—	$60,000.00
1	$440.40	$400.00	$40.40	$59,959.60
2	$440.40	$399.73	$40.67	$59,918.93

The monthly interest on a real estate loan is based on principal. At first, most of the payment goes to pay interest and *very little goes to reduce principal*. This is easily seen in the loan reduction schedule on the next page for the loan in Example 2. In fact, during the first 12 months a total of $4781.81 is paid to interest and the remaining balance is reduced by *only* $502.97.

The 257th payment is the first payment in which a larger amount goes to principal than to interest. The remaining balance drops below one-half of the original loan of $60,000 only after 269 payments (22 years, 5 months). In other words, it takes almost $22\frac{1}{2}$ years to cut the loan balance in half and then about $7\frac{1}{2}$ years more to pay off the other half of the loan. The final payment is $230.21.

Loan Reduction Schedule*

Payment Number	Interest Payment	Principal Payment	Remaining Balance	Payment Number	Interest Payment	Principal Payment	Remaining Balance
1	400.00	40.40	59,959.60	256	220.50	219.90	32,854.74
2	399.73	40.67	59,918.93	257	219.03	221.37	32,633.37
3	399.46	40.94	59,877.99	258	217.55	222.85	32,410.53
4	399.19	41.21	59,836.78	259	216.07	224.33	32,186.20
5	398.91	41.49	59,795.29	260	214.57	225.83	31,960.37
6	398.64	41.76	59,753.53	261	213.07	227.33	31,733.04
7	398.36	42.04	59,711.49	262	211.55	228.85	31,504.19
8	398.08	42.32	59,669.17	263	210.03	230.37	31,273.82
9	397.79	42.61	59,626.56	264	208.49	231.91	31,041.91
10	397.51	42.89	59,583.67	265	206.95	233.45	30,808.46
11	397.22	43.18	59,540.49	266	205.39	235.01	30,573.45
12	396.94	43.46	59,497.03	267	203.82	236.58	30,336.87
13	396.65	43.75	59,453.28	268	202.24	238.16	30,098.72
14	396.36	44.04	59,409.24	269	200.66	239.74	29,858.98
15	396.06	44.34	59,364.90	270	199.06	241.34	29,617.64
16	395.77	44.63	59,320.27				
17	395.47	44.93	59,275.34				
18	395.17	45.23	59,230.11	355	15.87	424.53	1,955.31
19	394.87	45.53	59,184.58	356	13.04	427.36	1,527.95
20	394.56	45.84	59,138.74	357	10.19	430.21	1,097.74
21	394.26	46.14	59,092.60	358	7.32	433.08	664.66
22	393.95	46.45	59,046.15	359	4.43	435.97	228.69
23	393.64	46.76	58,999.39	360	1.52	228.69	0.00
24	393.33	47.07	58,952.32				
					$98,331.96	$60,000	

*Interest rate 8%, loan amount $60,000, monthly principal and interest $440.40, term in years 30, 360 total payments.

Objective 3 Define escrow accounts. Many lenders require **escrow accounts** (also called **impound accounts**) for people taking out a mortgage. With an escrow account, buyers pay $\frac{1}{12}$ of the total estimated property tax and insurance each month. The lender holds these funds until the taxes and insurance fall due and then *pays the bills for the borrower*. Many consumer groups oppose this practice, since the lender earns interest on the money while waiting for payments to come due. In fact, a few states require that interest be paid on escrow accounts on any homes located in those states.

EXAMPLE 3
Finding Total Monthly Payment

George Willis arranged for a client to receive a $75,000 loan for 25 years at 8% to purchase a summer cabin. Annual insurance and taxes on the property are $654 and $1329, respectively. Find the total monthly payment.

Solution
Use the real estate amortization table to find **$7.72**. Add monthly insurance and taxes to the payment amount.

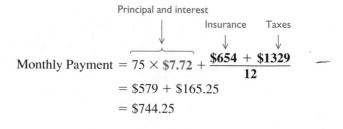

$$\text{Monthly Payment} = 75 \times \$7.72 + \frac{\$654 + \$1329}{12}$$
$$= \$579 + \$165.25$$
$$= \$744.25$$

Objective 4 **Define fixed and variable rate loans.** Home loans with fixed, stated interest rates are called **fixed rate loans**. These loans help borrowers during times of rising interest rates since monthly payments remain fixed. Conversely, fixed rate loans hurt lenders during times of rising interest rates. The lenders may have to pay higher interest rates on deposits than they receive on loans. This can result in large losses to the financial institutions.

As a result, many lenders now use **variable interest rate loans**, also called **adjustable rate mortgages**. The interest rates on these loans *can vary up or down at stated periods* over the life of the loan depending on the movement of interest rates in general. The monthly payments will change as interest rates are changed on the loan. Thus a borrower's monthly payment is not fixed for 15 or 30 years, but may go up or down every few years. In Canada and Britain, variable rate mortgages are the only ones available.

CHAPTER 11 | Quick Review

CHAPTER TERMS

*Review the following terms to test your understanding of the chapter. For
each term you do not know, refer to the page number found next to that term.*

APR [**p.** 443]
accelerated mortgages [**p.** 470]
adjustable rate mortgages
  [**p.** 473]
amortize [**p.** 443]
amortization schedule [**p.** 470]
amortization table [**p.** 462]
annual percentage rate [**p.** 443]
approximate annual percentage
  rate [**p.** 445]
average daily balance method
  [**p.** 434]

consolidate loans [**p.** 436]
country club billing [**p.** 432]
credit limit [**p.** 432]
escrow accounts [**p.** 472]
Federal Truth-in-Lending Act
  [**p.** 443]
finance charges [**p.** 432]
fixed rate loans [**p.** 473]
impound accounts [**p.** 472]
installment loan [**p.** 443]
itemized billing [**p.** 432]

late fees [**p.** 432]
mortgages [**p.** 469]
nominal rate [**p.** 444]
open-end credit [**p.** 432]
over-the-limit fees [**p.** 432]
personal property [**p.** 461]
real estate [**p.** 461]
real property [**p.** 461]
refund of unearned interest
  [**p.** 455]
repayment schedule [**p.** 470]

repossessed [**p.** 461]
revolving charge account
  [**p.** 432]
Rule of 78 [**p.** 455]
Stafford loan [**p.** 445]
stated rate [**p.** 444]
unearned interest [**p.** 455]
United States Rule [**p.** 453]
unpaid balance method [**p.** 434]
variable interest rate loans
  [**p.** 473]

CONCEPTS

**11.1 Finding the finance charge on a revolving charge
account, using the unpaid balance method**

Start with the unpaid balance of the previous month.
Then add the finance charge on the unpaid balance.
Next, add the finance charge and any purchases.
Finally, subtract any payments made.

EXAMPLES

Debbie Mahoney's MasterCard account had an unpaid
balance of $385.65 on March 1. During March, she made a
$100 payment and charged $68.92. Find the finance charge
and the unpaid balance on April 1 if the bank charges 1.25%
per month on the unpaid balance.

$$\text{Finance charge} = \$385.65 \times .0125 = \$4.82$$

Previous Balance	Finance Charge	Purchases	Payment	New Balance
$385.65 +	$4.82 +	$68.92 −	$100 =	$359.39

**11.1 Finding the finance charge on a revolving charge
account, using the average daily balance method**

First find the unpaid balance on each day of the
month. Then add up the daily unpaid balances.

Next divide the total of the daily unpaid balances by
the number of days in the billing period.

Finally, calculate the finance charge by multiplying
the average daily balance by the finance charge.

The following is a summary of a credit-card account.

  Previous balance $115.45
  November 1 Billing date
  November 15 Payment of $35.00
  November 22 Charge of $45.00

Find the average daily balance and the finance charge if
interest is 1% per month on the average daily balance.

Balance on November 1 = $115.45
Nov. 1–15 = 14 days at $115.45

$$14 \times \$115.45 = \$1616.30$$

Payment on Nov. 15 = $35.00
Balance on Nov. 15 = $115.45 − $35 = $80.45

Nov. 15–Nov. 22 = 7 days at $80.45

$$7 \times \$80.45 = \$563.15$$

Charge on Nov. 22 of $45.00
Balance on Nov. 22 = $80.45 + $45 = $125.45

Nov. 22–Dec. 1 = 9 days at $125.45

$$9 \times \$125.45 = \$1129.05$$

Daily Balances

$$\$1616.30 + \$563.15 + \$1129.05 = \$3308.50$$

Average Daily Balance

$$= \frac{\$3308.50}{30} = \$110.28$$

Finance Charge

$$= \$110.28 \times .01 = \$1.10$$

CONCEPTS	EXAMPLES
11.2 Finding the total installment cost, finance charge, and amount financed	Joan Taylor bought a leather coat for $1580. She put $350 down and then made 12 payments of $115 each. Find the total installment cost, the finance charge, and the amount financed.

Total Installment Cost
= Down payment
+ (Amount of each payment × number of payments)

Finance Charge
= Total installment cost − Cash price

Amount Financed
= Cash price − Down payment

Total Installment Cost
= $350 + (12 × $115) = $1730

Finance Charge
= $1730 − $1580 = $150

Amount Financed
= $1580 − $350 = $1230

11.2 Determining the approximate APR using a formula

First determine the finance charge. Then find the amount financed. Next calculate approximate APR using the formula.

Approximate APR =

$$\frac{24 \times \text{Finance charge}}{\text{Amt. fin.} \times \left(\begin{array}{c}1 + \text{Total no.}\\ \text{of payments}\end{array}\right)}$$

Tom Jones buys a motorcycle for $8990. He makes a down payment of $1800 and then makes monthly payments of $240 for 36 months. Find the approximate APR.

Total Installment Cost
= $1800 + ($240 × 36) = $10,440

Finance Charge
= $10,440 − $8990 = $1450

Amount Financed
= $8990 − $1800 = $7190

Approximate APR =

$$\frac{24 \times \$1450}{\$7190 \times (1 + 36)} = 13.1\% \text{ (rounded)}$$

11.2 Finding APR using table

First determine the finance charge per $100 of amount financed, using the formula

$$\frac{\text{Finance charge} \times \$100}{\text{Amount financed}}$$

Then read down the left column of the annual percentage rate table to the proper number of payments. Go across to the number closest to the number found above. Read across the top of the column to find the annual percentage rate.

Lupe Torres buys a used car for $6500. She makes a down payment of $1000 and agrees to make 24 monthly payments of $260.83. Use the table to find the APR.

Finance charge = $1000 + 24 × $260.83 − $6500
= $759.92

Amount financed = $5500

Finance charge per $100

$$\frac{\$759.92 \times \$100}{\$5500} = 13.817$$

Use 24-payment row in the table to find APR = 12.75%

CONCEPTS	EXAMPLES

11.3 Finding amount due on maturity date using the United States Rule

First determine the simple interest due from the date loan was made until the date of the partial payment. Then subtract this interest from the amount of the payment and reduce the principal by the difference. Next find the interest from the date of partial payment to the due date of note, and add the unpaid balance and interest to find the total owed.

Sam Wiley signs a 90-day note on August 1 for $5000 at an interest rate of 12%. On September 15, he makes a payment of $1800. Find the balance owed on the principal. If no additional payments are made, find the amount due on the maturity date of the loan.

From August 1 to September 15, there are $30 + 15 = 45$ days.

$$I = \$5000 \times .12 \times \frac{45}{360} = \$75 \text{ interest due}$$

$$
\begin{array}{rl}
\$1800 & \text{payment} \\
- \quad 75 & \text{interest due} \\
\hline
\$1725 & \text{applied to prinicpal} \\
& \text{reduction}
\end{array}
$$

$$
\begin{array}{rl}
\$5000 & \text{amount owed} \\
- \quad 1725 & \text{principal reduction} \\
\hline
\$3275 & \textbf{balance owed}
\end{array}
$$

Note is for 90 days, a partial payment was made after 45 days. Interest on $3275 will be charged for $90 - 45 = 45$ days.

$$I = \$3275 \times .12 \times \frac{45}{360} = 49.13$$

$$
\begin{array}{rl}
\$3275.00 & \text{principal owed} \\
+ \quad 49.13 & \text{interest} \\
\hline
\$3324.13 & \textbf{total owed}
\end{array}
$$

11.3 Finding the unearned interest using the Rule of 78

First calculate the finance charge. Then find the unearned interest using the formula.

$$U = F\left(\frac{N}{P}\right)\left(\frac{1 + N}{1 + P}\right)$$

where: U = unearned interest, F = finance charge, N = number of payments remaining, and P = total number of payments

Next find the total of the remaining payments. Finally, subtract the unearned interest to find balance remaining.

Tom Fish borrows $1500, which he is paying back in 36 monthly installments of $52.75 each. With 10 payments remaining he decides to pay the loan in full. Find **(a)** the amount of unearned interest and **(b)** the amount necessary to pay the loan in full.

36 payments of $52.75 each for a total repayment of $36 \times \$52.75 = \$1899$.

Finance charge

$$= \$1899 - \$1500$$
$$= \$399 = \$1899 - \$1500 = \$399$$

Unearned interest

$$= \$399 \times \frac{10}{36} \times \frac{(1 + 10)}{(1 + 36)} = \$32.95$$

10 payments of $52.75 are left. These payments total

$$\$52.75 \times 10 = \$527.50$$
$$\$527.50 - \$32.95 = \$494.55.$$

This is the amount needed to pay the loan in full.

CONCEPTS	EXAMPLES

11.4 Finding the periodic payment for amortizing a loan

First determine the number of periods for the loan and the interest rate per period.

The payment is found by multiplying the loan amount by the number from the amortization table.

Bob Smith agrees to pay $12,000 for a car. The amount will be repaid in monthly payments over 3 years at an interest rate of 12%. Find the amount of each payment.

$$12 \times 3 = \textbf{36 periods (payments)};$$
$$\frac{12\%}{12} = \textbf{1\% per period}$$

Number from table is **.03321**.

Payment = $12,000 × .03321 = $398.52

11.4 Setting up an amortization schedule

First find the periodic payment. Then calculate the interest owed in the first period using the formula $I = PRT$. Next subtract the value of I from the periodic payment.

This is the amount applied to the reduction of the principal. Then find the balance after the first periodic payment by subtracting the value of the debt reduction from the original amount. Now repeat the above steps until the original loan is amortized (paid off).

Terri Meyer borrows $1800. She will repay this amount in 2 years with semiannual payments at an interest rate of 10%. Set up an amortization schedule.

4 periods (payments); 5% per period

Number from table is .28201.

Payment = $1800 × .28201 = $507.62

$$I = PRT$$

Interest owed = $1800 × .10 × $\frac{1}{2}$ = $90

Debt reduction = $507.62 − $90 = $417.62

Balance of loan = $1800 − $417.62 = $1382.38

Payment Number	Amount of Payment	Interest for Period	Portion to Principal	Principal at End of Period
0	—	—	—	$1800.00
1	$507.62	$90.00	$417.62	$1382.38
2	$507.62	$69.12	$438.50	$ 943.88
3	$507.62	$47.19	$460.43	$ 483.45
4	$507.62	$24.17	$483.45	$ 0

11.4 Finding monthly payments, total amount paid, and finance charge

First multiply the amount to be financed by the number from the amortization table or the loan payoff table to find the periodic payment. Then find the total amount repaid by multiplying the periodic payment by the number of payments. Finally, subtract the amount financed from the total amount repaid to obtain the finance charge.

Ben Apostolides purchased a new Toyota Camry and owes $16,400 after the trade-in. He decides on a term with 50 monthly payments. Assume an interest rate of 12% compounded monthly and find the amount of each payment and the finance charge.

Monthly payment = $16,400 × .02551 = $418.36
Finance charge = 50 × $418.36 − $16,400 = $4518

CONCEPTS	EXAMPLES
11.5 Finding the amount of monthly home loan payments and total interest charges over the life of a home loan Using the number of years and the interest rate, find the amortization value per thousand dollars from the real estate amortization table. Next multiply the table value by the number of thousands in the principal to obtain monthly payment. Then find total amount of the payments and subtract the original amount owed from the total payments to obtain interest paid.	Lou and Rose Waters buy a house at the beach. After a down payment, they owe $75,000. Find the monthly payment at $9\frac{3}{4}\%$ and the total interest charges over the life of a 25-year loan. $$n = 25 \qquad i = 9\frac{3}{4}\%$$ **Table value $= 8.92$** There are $\dfrac{\$75,000}{1000} = 75$ thousands in $75,000. **Monthly payment $= 75 \times \$8.92 = \$669$** There are $25 \times 12 = 300$ payments. **Total payment $= 300 \times \$669 = \$200,700$** **Interest paid $= \$200,700 - \$75,000 = \$125,700$**

CHAPTER 11 | SUMMARY EXERCISE
CONSOLIDATING LOANS

John and Kathy MacGruder are struggling to make their monthly payments. Kathy works one job and takes care of their two small children. John has had to take on a second job to make the payments.

(a) Find the monthly payments on each of the following purchases and the total monthly payment.

Purchase	Original Loan Amount	Interest Rate	Term of Loan	Monthly Payment
Honda Accord	$18,800	12%	4 years	_____
Ford Truck	$14,300	18%	4 years	_____
Home	$96,500	$8\frac{1}{2}\%$	15 years	_____
2nd Mortgage on Home	$ 4,500	12%	3 years	_____
			Total	_____

(b) These monthly expenses do not include car insurance ($215 per month), health insurance ($120 per month), or taxes on their home ($2530 per year) among other expenses. Find their total monthly outlay for all of these expenses.

Expense	Monthly Outlay
Payments on debt from **(a)**	_____
Car insurance	_____
Health insurance	_____
Taxes on home	_____
Total	_____

(c) After discussing things with George Willis at Teachers Credit Union, the MacGruders have learned that they can (1) refinance the remaining $14,900 amount on the Honda Accord at 12% over 4 years, (2) refinance the remaining $8600 loan amount on the Ford Truck at 12% over 3 years, (3) refinance the remaining $94,800 loan amount on their home at 8% over 30 years, and (4) reduce their car insurance payments by $28 per month. Complete the table below.

Item	New Loan Amount	New Interest Rate	New Term of Loan	New Monthly Payment
Honda Accord				_____
Ford Truck				_____
Home				_____
2nd Mortgage on Home				
Car insurance				_____
Health insurance				_____
Taxes on home				_____
				_____
				_____

(d) Find the reduction in their monthly payments.

(d) _____

NOTE Part of the savings in the monthly payment came from reducing the interest rates; the remainder of the savings came from extending the loans further into the future.

For related Web
activities, go to
www.mathbusiness.com

Keyword:
consolidate

Investigate

The interest rate that you are charged for borrowing money will differ depending on the company you go to for a loan. Find current interest rates for financing a 2-year-old car from at least two banks in the area in which you live. Then go onto the World Wide Web and look for a lower interest rate.

For related Web activities, go to www.mathbusiness.com

'Net Assets

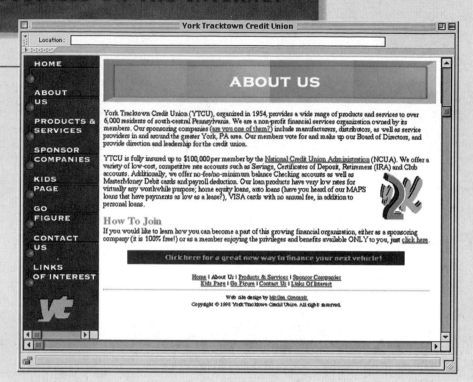

York Tracktown Credit Union

STATISTICS

- 1999: 6000 customers

- Non-profit

- FDIC insured up to $100,000 per member

- Up to 72-month financing of a new automobile

York Tracktown Credit Union (YTCU) provides a wide range of products and services to residents located in south-central Pennsylvania. Only individuals that are employees of companies sponsoring the credit union can be members. The company offers a variety of competitive-rate accounts such as savings, certificates of deposit, and retirement accounts such as IRAs. In addition, the firm offers no-fee, no-minimum-balance checking accounts as well as debit cards and payroll deduction. YTCU will also arrange for you to lease an automobile for those who prefer to lease over purchasing.

Credit unions are similar to banks in that you can have a savings or checking account with them and in turn you can borrow money for virtually any worthwhile purpose such as home-equity loans and auto loans. Interest rates paid on savings are typically higher at a credit union and interest rates paid on loans are typically lower than area banks—check out any credit union that you are eligible to join.

1. Loan officer George Willis loaned Betty Faber $14,000 for a two-year-old Honda Accord. Given that the interest rate was 12% per year compounded monthly and the loan was for four years, find the monthly payment rounded to the nearest dollar.

2. Betty Faber also borrowed $84,000 to purchase a home, from George Willis at the credit union. Find the payment on the 30-year loan at 7% and at 9% interest rates.

3. List three advantages of using a bank over a credit union, and then list three advantages of using a credit union over a bank.

4. Look in your telephone book and find a credit union near you. Call the credit union and find out what it takes to become a member and ask them for three advantages of being a member.

Name   Date   Class

CHAPTER 11 | TEST

To help you review, the numbers in brackets show the section in which the topic was discussed.

Solve each of the following problems.

1. The Big Catch Company purchased a depth finder for locating fish, having a cash price of $785. If the down payment was $100 with 24 monthly payments of $32, find the total finance charge. **[11.1]**

1. _____

2. The balance on John Baker's MasterCard on November 1 is $680.45. In November, he charges an additional $337.32 of purchases, has returns of $45.42, and makes a payment of $50. Given that finance charges are calculated at 1.5% per month on the unpaid balance, find his balance on December 1. **[11.1]**

2. _____

Find the annual percentage rate, using the annual percentage rate table. **[11.2]**

Amount Financed	Finance Charge	Number of Payments	APR
3. $5280	$1010.59	36	_____
4. $1130	$149.84	24	_____

Solve each of the following application problems.

5. Computers Inc. wishes to include financing terms in their advertising. If the price of a personal computer is $2100 and the finance charge with no down payment is $96 over a 9-month period with monthly payments, find the annual percentage rate. **[11.2]**

5. _____

6. A note with a face value of $7000 is made on June 21. The note is for 90 days and carries interest of 13%. A partial payment of $2800 is made on July 17. Find the amount due on the maturity date of the note. **[11.3]**

6. _____

7. Mock Construction Company bought a truck and financed $7400 with 48 monthly payments of $228.14 each. Suppose the firm pays the loan off with 12 payments left. Find **(a)** the amount of unearned interest and **(b)** the amount necessary to pay off the loan. **[11.3]**

(a) _____
(b) _____

Find the amount of each payment necessary to amortize the following loans. **[11.4]**

8. ABC Plumbing borrows $28,100 to buy a new truck. They agree to make quarterly payments for 3 years at 12% per year. Find the amount of the quarterly payment.

8. _____

9. Low Fat Pizza has its building remodeled for $36,000. They pay $6000 down and pay off the balance in payments made at the end of each quarter for 5 years. Interest is 10% compounded quarterly. Find the amount of each payment so that the loan is amortized.

9. _____

Find the monthly payment necessary to amortize the following home mortgages. **[11.5]**

10. $123,500, $7\frac{1}{2}$%, 30 years

10. _____

11. $134,560, 7%, 15 years

11. _____

Work the following application problems. **[11.5]**

12. Mr. and Mrs. Zagorin plan to buy a $90,000 home, paying 20% down and financing the balance at 8% for 30 years. The taxes are $960 per year, with fire insurance costing $252 per year. Find the monthly payment (including taxes and insurance).

12. _____

13. General Business Forms purchases a $145,000 commercial building, pays 25% down and finances the balance at $9\frac{3}{4}$% for 15 years. (a) Find the total monthly payment given taxes of $2300 per year and insurance of $1350 per year. (b) Assume that insurance and taxes do not increase and find the total cost of owning the building for 15 years (including the down payment).

(a) _____

(b) _____

14. Jerome Watson, owner of Watson Welding, purchases a building for his business and makes a $25,000 down payment. He finances the balance of $122,500 for 20 years at 8%. (a) Find the total monthly payment given taxes of $3200 per year and insurance of $1275 per year. (b) Assume that insurance and taxes do not increase and find the total cost of owning the building for 20 years (including the down payment).

(a) _____

(b) _____

CHAPTER 12

TAXES AND INSURANCE

Brian Katavich is the owner of a Round Table Pizza restaurant. The restaurant serves pizzas, salads, assorted beverages, and other foods and also takes telephone orders for delivery directly to the customer's home or business. Two years ago, Katavich purchased the lot and building that he had been renting from the owner.

In addition to operating his own business, he now has all the responsibilities that go with the ownership of commercial real estate.

As a business owner, it's essential for Katavich to keep on top of the constantly changing tax laws as well as knowing the types of insurance coverage that can protect his enterprise.

Taxes and insurance are facts of life. In the early part of this century, Justice Oliver Wendell Holmes, Jr., of the United States Supreme Court said that "taxes are the price we pay to live in a civilized society." Tax dollars provide national defense, education, health services, streets and highways, parks and recreation facilities, police and fire protection, public assistance for the poor, support for libraries, and even pay for streetlights. As government provides more services, taxes go up to pay for these services.

People and businesses buy insurance to protect against risk. Insurance is based on the idea that many pay into a fund while a few draw out of the fund. For example, a business may pay a fire insurance premium of a few hundred dollars for several years without ever having a fire loss. However, should a fire occur, the loss may result in many thousands of dollars being paid to the business.

This chapter first examines the basics of property tax and personal income tax. Next, it discusses fire insurance and motor vehicle insurance and, in the final section, the many types of life insurance policies.

12.1 | PROPERTY TAX

Objectives

1. Define *fair market value* and *assessed valuation*.
2. Use the formula for tax rate.
3. Use the formula for property tax.
4. Express tax rate in percent, in dollars per $100, in dollars per $1000, and in mills.
5. Find taxes given the assessed valuation and the tax rate.

PROBLEM SOLVING IN BUSINESS

The value of the land and building occupied by Round Table Pizza is assessed annually by the tax assessor. Using this assessed value and the local tax rate, the annual property taxes are determined and the property tax bill is then mailed to the owner. Katavich likes to understand how the property taxes are determined so he calculates his own taxes.

For related Web activities, go to www.mathbusiness.com

Keyword: assessment

In virtually every area of the nation, owners of real property (such as buildings and land) must pay a property tax. The money raised by this tax is used to provide services needed by the local community, such as police and fire protection, roads, schools, and other city and county services.

Objective 1 Define *fair market value* and *assessed valuation*. So that the amount of tax can be found, each piece of real property in an area is assessed. In this process, the local tax assessor estimates the **fair market value** of the property—the price at which the property could reasonably be expected to be sold. The assessor then finds the **assessed valuation** of the property by multiplying the fair market value by a certain percent called the assessment rate. The percent used varies widely from state to state, but normally remains constant within a state.

In some states, assessed valuation is 25% of fair market value, while in other states, the assessed valuation is 40% to 60% or even 100% of fair market value. Using an assessed valuation that is a percent of fair market value has become an accepted practice over the years.

EXAMPLE 1
Finding the Assessed Value of Property

Find the assessed valuation for the following pieces of property owned by Lynn Colgin.
(a) Fair market value: $112,000; assessment rate: 25%
(b) Fair market value $1,382,500; assessment rate 60%

SOLUTION

Multiply the fair market value by the assessment rate.
(a) $112,000 × .25 = $28,000 assessed valuation
(b) $1,382,500 × .60 = $829,500 assessed valuation

Objective 2 Use the formula for tax rate. After calculating the assessed valuation of all the taxable property in an area and determining the amount of money needed to provide the necessary services (the budget), the agency responsible for levying the tax announces the annual **property tax rate**.

This tax rate is determined by the formula

$$\text{Tax rate} = \frac{\text{Total tax amount needed (budget)}}{\text{Total assessed value}}$$

EXAMPLE 2
Finding the Tax Rate

Find the tax rate for the following park districts in River County.
(a) Total tax amount needed $368,400, total assessed value $7,368,000
(b) Total tax amount needed $633,750, total assessed value $28,800,000

SOLUTION

Divide the total tax amount needed by the total assessed value.
(a) $368,400 ÷ $7,368,000 = .05 = 5% tax rate
(b) $633,750 ÷ $28,800,000 = .022 = 2.2% tax rate   rounded to the nearest tenth of a percent

Almost all of us agree on one thing. We think our taxes are too high. The graph on the following page shows that Americans work an average of 129 days to pay their federal, state, and local taxes.

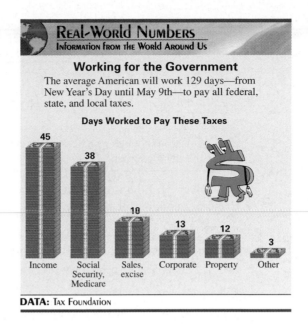

Objective **3** **Use the formula for property tax.** Property tax rates are expressed in different ways in different parts of the country. However, property tax is always found with the formula

$$\text{Tax} = \text{Tax rate} \times \text{Assessed valuation}$$

Objective **4** **Express tax rate in percent, in dollars per \$100, in dollars per \$1000, and in mills.** **PERCENT.** Some areas express tax rates as a percent of assessed valuation. The tax on a piece of property with an assessed valuation of \$74,000 at a tax rate of 9.42% would be

$$\text{Tax} = .0942 \times \textbf{\$74,000} = \$6970.80.$$

Dollars per \$100. In some areas, the rate is expressed as a number of dollars per \$100 of assessed valuation. For example, the rate might be expressed as \$11.42 per \$100 of assessed valuation. Assuming a tax rate of \$11.42 per \$100, find the tax on a piece of land having an assessed valuation of \$42,000 as follows. First divide by 100 by moving the decimal point two places to the left to find the number of hundreds in \$42,000.

$$\$42,000 = \textbf{420 hundreds} \qquad \text{move the decimal 2 places to the left}$$

Then find the tax.

$$\text{Tax} = \text{Tax rate} \times \textbf{Number of hundreds of valuation}$$
$$= \$11.42 \times \textbf{420} = \$4796.40$$

Dollars per \$1000. In other areas, the tax rate is expressed as a number of dollars per \$1000 of assessed valuation. If the tax rate is \$98.12 per \$1000, a piece of property having an assessed valuation of \$197,000 would be taxed as follows.

$$\$197,000 = \textbf{197 thousands} \qquad \text{move the decimal 3 places to the left to divide by 1000}$$

$$\text{Tax} = \$98.12 \times \textbf{197} = \$19,329.64$$

Mills. Other areas express tax rates in mills (a mill is one-tenth of a cent, or one-thousandth of a dollar). For example, a tax rate might be expressed as 46 mills per dollar (or \$.046 per dollar). The tax rate on a property having an assessed valuation of \$81,000, at a tax rate of 46 mills, is

$$\text{Tax} = \textbf{.046} \times \$81,000 \qquad \text{46 mills} = \$.046$$
$$= \$3726.$$

The following chart shows the same tax rates written in the four different systems.

Percent	Per $100	Per $1000	In Mills
12.52%	$12.52	$125.20	125.2
3.2%	$3.20	$32	32
9.87%	$9.87	$98.70	98.7

> **NOTE**   Although expressed differently, the rates in each row of this chart are equivalent tax rates.

Objective [5] **Find taxes given the assessed valuation and the tax rate.**   Property taxes are found by multiplying the tax rate and the assessed valuation as shown in the following example.

EXAMPLE 3

Finding the Property Tax

Find the taxes on each of the following pieces of property. Assessed valuations and tax rates are given.
(a) $58,975; 8.4%   **(b)** $875,400; $7.82 per $100
(c) $129,600; $64.21 per $1000   **(d)** $221,750; 94 mills

Solution
Multiply the tax rate by the assessed valuation.
(a) 8.4% = .084

$$\text{Tax} = \text{Tax rate} \times \text{Assessed valuation}$$
$$\text{Tax} = .084 \times \$58,975 = \$4953.90$$

(b) $875,400 = **8754 hundreds**

$$\text{Tax} = \$7.82 \times \mathbf{8754} = \$68,456.28$$

(c) $129,600 = **129.6 thousands**

$$\text{Tax} = \$64.21 \times \mathbf{129.6} = \$8321.62$$

(d) 94 mills = .094

$$\text{Tax} = .094 \times \$221,750 = \$20,844.50$$

> **NOTE**   Some states offer certain tax exemptions that will reduce the amount of property tax due. One type of exemption is the Homeowner's Tax Exemption, which allows a specific amount of tax exemption to a person who owns and occupies a home or condominium as a personal residence.

The following figure shows the sales tax, state income tax, and the property tax rates in five locations across the United States. These towns were identified by the *Wall Street Journal* as "Five Hometowns for the Future." Notice the variations in the tax rates.

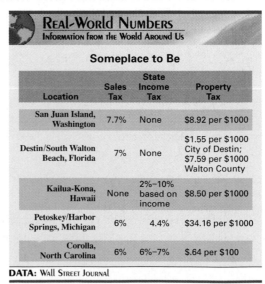

REAL-WORLD NUMBERS
Information from the World Around Us

Someplace to Be

Location	Sales Tax	State Income Tax	Property Tax
San Juan Island, Washington	7.7%	None	$8.92 per $1000
Destin/South Walton Beach, Florida	7%	None	$1.55 per $1000 City of Destin; $7.59 per $1000 Walton County
Kailua-Kona, Hawaii	None	2%–10% based on income	$8.50 per $1000
Petoskey/Harbor Springs, Michigan	6%	4.4%	$34.16 per $1000
Corolla, North Carolina	6%	6%–7%	$.64 per $100

DATA: Wall Street Journal

Name   Date   Class

12.1 | EXERCISES

The Quick Start exercises in each section contain solutions to help you get started.

Find the assessed valuation for each of the following pieces of property. (See Example 1.)

Quick Start

Fair Market Value	Rate of Assessment	Assessed Valuation		Fair Market Value	Rate of Assessment	Assessed Valuation
1. $64,800	30%	$19,440	2. $218,500	70%	
$64,800 × .3 = $19,440						
3. $142,300	50%	_____	4. $98,200	42%	_____
5. $1,300,500	25%	_____	6. $2,450,000	80%	_____

Find the tax rate for the following. Write the tax rate as a percent rounded to the nearest tenth. (See Example 2.)

Quick Start

Total Tax Amount Needed	Total Assessed Value	Tax Rate		Total Tax Amount Needed	Total Assessed Value	Tax Rate
7. $625,000	$5,200,000	12%	8. $322,500	$4,300,000	
$625,000 ÷ $5,200,000 = 12%						
9. $1,580,000	$19,750,000	_____	10. $2,175,000	$54,375,000	_____
11. $1,224,000	$40,800,000	_____	12. $2,941,500	$81,700,000	_____

Complete the following list comparing tax rates. (See Example 3.)

Quick Start

	Percent	Per $100	Per $1000	In Mills
13.	4.84%	(a) $4.84	(b) $48.40	(c) 48.4
14. (a)	_____	$6.75	(b) _____	(c) _____
15. (a)	_____	(b) _____	$70.80	(c) _____
16. (a)	_____	(b) _____	(c) _____	28

17. What is the difference between fair market value and assessed value. How is the assessment rate used when finding the assessed value? (See Objective 1.)

18. Select any tax rate and express it as a percent. Write this tax rate in three additional equivalent forms and explain what each form means. (See Objective 4.)

Find the property tax for the following. (See Example 3.)

Quick Start

	Assessed Valuation	Tax Rate	Tax		Assessed Valuation	Tax Rate	Tax
19.	$86,200	$6.80 per $100	$5861.60	**20.**	$41,300	$46.40 per $1000	
	862 × $6.80 = $5861.60						
21.	$128,200	42 mills		**22.**	$37,250	3.4%	

Solve the following application problems.

Quick Start

23. PIZZA RESTAURANT OWNER Brian Katavich owns the real estate on which he operates his business, Round Table Pizza. The property has a fair market value of $378,000, property in the area is assessed at 30% of market value, and the tax rate is 4.28%. Find the amount of the property tax.

    $378,000 × .3 = $113,400; $113,400 × .0428 = $4853.52

23. $4853.52

24. APARTMENT OWNER Chad LeCompte owns a six unit apartment building with a fair market value of $192,600. Property in the area is assessed at 40% of market value and the tax rate is 5.5%. Find the amount of the property tax.

24. _____

25. COMMERCIAL PROPERTY TAX A new FM radio station broadcasts from a building having a fair market value of $334,400. The building is in an area where property is assessed at 25% of market value and the tax rate is $75.30 per $1000 of assessed value. Find the property tax.

25. _____

26. The Consumer's Cooperative owns property with a fair market value of $785,200. The property is located in a county that assesses at 80% of market value. Find the property tax if the tax rate is $14.30 per $1000 of assessed value.

26. _____

27. Downtown Office Park has a fair market value of $5,700,000. Property is assessed in the area at 25% of market value. The tax rate is $14.10 per $100 of assessed valuation. Find the property tax.

27. _____

28. Harley-Davidson of Lincoln has property with a fair market value of $518,600. The property is located in an area that is assessed at 35% of market value. The tax rate is $7.35 per $100. Find the property tax.

28. _____

29. COMPARING PROPERTY TAX In one parish (county), property is assessed at 40% of market value, with a tax rate of 32.1 mills. In a second parish, property is assessed at 24% of market value, with a tax rate of 50.2 mills. Gerry Baby Products is trying to decide where to place a building with a fair market value of $95,000. **(a)** Which parish would charge the lower property tax? **(b)** Find the annual amount saved.

(a) _____
(b) _____

30. Property taxes vary from one county to the next. In one county, property is assessed at 30% of market value, with a tax rate of 45.6 mills. In a second county, property is assessed at 48% of market value, with a tax rate of 29.3 mills. If Henry Hernandez is trying to decide where to build his $140,000 dream house **(a)** find which county would charge the lower property tax and **(b)** find the annual amount saved.

(a) _____
(b) _____

12.2 | PERSONAL INCOME TAX

Objectives

1. Recall the four steps that determine tax liability.
2. List the facts needed to find adjusted gross income.
3. Find adjusted gross income.
4. Know the standard deduction amounts.
5. Recall the different income tax rates.
6. List possible deductions.
7. Determine a balance due or a refund from the Internal Revenue Service.
8. Prepare a 1040A and a Schedule 1 federal tax form.

The federal government, most states, many local governments, and some cities use income tax as a source of revenue. However, for most people, the federal income tax is the largest tax expense.

Instructions provided with the tax forms have to cover every possible situation for each taxpayer, from students who earn very little money to professional people, such as lawyers and doctors, who often have complicated financial affairs. For this reason, many people take their tax returns to a professional tax preparer. But even tax preparers do not solve all the problems of the taxpayer—the taxpayer still must supply all necessary information. Tax preparers only insert the figures in the correct places on the correct forms and then do the necessary calculations.

The following graph shows how long before the April 15 tax filing deadline small-business owners start their taxes.

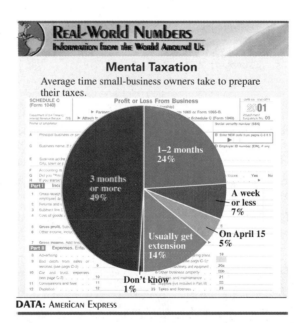

Real-World Numbers
Information from the World Around Us

Mental Taxation
Average time small-business owners take to prepare their taxes.

- 3 months or more 49%
- 1–2 months 24%
- A week or less 7%
- On April 15 5%
- Usually get extension 14%
- Don't know 1%

DATA: American Express

Objective 1 Recall the four steps that determine tax liability. There are four basic steps in finding total tax liability.

STEPS FOR PREPARING YOUR INCOME TAX RETURN

Step 1 Find the adjusted gross income (AGI) for the year.

Step 2 Find the taxable income.

Step 3 Find the tax.

Step 4 Check to see if a refund is due or if more money is owed to the government.

OBJECTIVE **2** **List the facts needed to find adjusted gross income.** These steps are explained in order.

First find the **adjusted gross income** for the year by collecting all the **W-2 forms** that were provided by employers during the year. A sample W-2 form is shown below. The form shows the total amount of money paid to the employee by the employer. It also shows the total amount that was withheld from the employee's paycheck and sent, in his or her name, to the Internal Revenue Service (IRS). Add up all the amounts paid to the employee. Also, collect any **1099 forms** that may have been received. These informational forms, copies of which also go to the IRS, show miscellaneous income received, such as interest on checking or savings accounts or stock dividends. A sample 1099 form is shown at the bottom of this page. Also, include any tips or other employee compensation, and enter the total on the correct line of the income tax form.

a Control number		22222	Void ☐	For Official Use Only ▶ OMB No. 1545-0008		
b Employer identification number 94–1287319				**1** Wages, tips, other compensation $ 24,738.41	**2** Federal income tax withheld $ 3275.60	
c Employer's name, address, and ZIP code Class Printing 1568 Liberty Heights Avenue Baltimore, MD 21230				**3** Social security wages $ 24,738.41	**4** Social security tax withheld $ 1533.78	
				5 Medicare wages and tips $ 24,738.41	**6** Medicare tax withheld $ 358.71	
				7 Social security tips	**8** Allocated tips	
d Employee's social security number 418–23–0152				**9** Advance EIC payment	**10** Dependent care benefits	
e Employee's name (first, middle initial, last)				**11** Nonqualified plans	**12** Benefits included in box 1	
Jennifer Crum 2136 Old Road Towson, MD 21285				**13** See instrs. for box 13	**14** Other	
				15 Statutory employee ☐ Deceased ☐ Pension plan ☐ Legal rep. ☐ Deferred compensation ☐		
f Employee's address and ZIP code						
16 State MD	Employer's state I.D. no. 600–5076	**17** State wages, tips, etc.	**18** State income tax	**19** Locality name	**20** Local wages, tips, etc.	**21** Local income tax

Form **W-2** **Wage and Tax Statement**   Department of the Treasury–Internal Revenue Service

9292 ☐ VOID ☐ CORRECTED			
PAYER'S name, street address, city, state, ZIP code, and telephone no. Employees Credit Union 2572 Brookhaven Drive Dundalk, MD 21222	Payer's RTN (optional)	OMB No. 1545-0112 **200_** Interest Income	
PAYER'S Federal identification number 94–1287319	RECIPIENT'S identification number 418–23–0152	**1** Interest income not included in box 3 $ 427.82	Copy A **For Internal Revenue Service Center** File with Form 1096.
RECIPIENT'S name Jennifer Crum		**2** Early withdrawal penalty $	**3** Interest on U.S. Savings Bonds and Treas. obligations $
Street address (including apt. no.) 2136 Old Road		**4** Federal income tax withheld $	For Paperwork Reduction Act Notice and instructions for completing this form, see the **1998 Instructions for Forms 1099, 1098, 5498, and W-2G.**
City, state, and ZIP code Towson, MD 21285		**5** Foreign tax paid $	**6** Foreign country or U.S. possession $
Account number (optional)	2nd TIN Not. ☐		

Form **1099-INT**   Cat. No. 14410K   Department of the Treasury - Internal Revenue Service

Objective ⬛3 **Find adjusted gross income.** Using the information from the W-2 and 1099 forms, and adding any amounts given for dividends, capital gains, unemployment compensation, tips, or other employee compensation, enter the total on the correct line of the income tax form. Subtract any adjustments to income, such as an **Individual Retirement Account (IRA)**, or alimony payments. The result is the **adjusted gross income**.

EXAMPLE 1

Finding Adjusted Gross Income (AGI)

As an assistant manager at Class Printing, Jennifer Crum earned $24,738.41 last year and $427.82 in interest from her credit union (see her W-2 and 1099 forms). She had $1500 in IRA contributions. Find her adjusted gross income.

Solution

Add the income from her job ($24,738.41) and the interest ($427.82). Then subtract the IRA contribution.

$$\$24{,}738.41 + \$427.82 - \mathbf{\$1500} = \$23{,}666.23$$

> **NOTE** When filing your income tax, a copy of all W-2 forms is sent to the Internal Revenue Service along with the completed tax forms. However, the IRS does not require copies of 1099 forms to be sent to them.

REAL-WORLD NUMBERS
INFORMATION FROM THE WORLD AROUND US

Getting It Back (for Now)

Each allowance claimed on a W-4 form increases annual take-home pay.

Federal income tax bracket	Take-home pay increases by
15%	$405
28%	$756
31%	$837
36%	$972
39.6%	$1069

DATA: INTERNAL REVENUE SERVICE

Objective ⬛4 **Know the standard deduction amounts.** Most people are almost finished at this point. If deductions for medical expenses, interest, and so on are not to be itemized, and if there are no further adjustments, then the **standard deduction** amount must be determined and subtracted from the adjusted gross income. The current standard deduction amounts are shown as follows.

$4150 for single people
$6900 for married people filing jointly and qualifying widow(er)s
$3450 for married people filing separately
$6050 for head of a household

Additional standard deductions are given for taxpayers and dependents who are blind or 65 years of age or older.

Now, only one step remains before the tax owed is found: determine the number of **personal exemptions**. An exemption is taken for the head of the household and for each of his or her dependents, including spouse and children. For example, a married person with a spouse and three children would be allowed to claim five exemptions. The taxpayer is allowed a $2650 reduction in gross income for each exemption. After subtracting $2650 per exemption from the adjusted gross income, the result, **taxable income**, is multiplied by the proper tax rate to determine taxes due. The table at the side shows how much each allowance claimed increases your annual take home pay.

For related Web activities, go to www.mathbusiness.com

Keyword: taxable

Objective ⬛5 **Recall the different income tax rates.** Most recently, individual income tax rates have been either 15%, 28%, 31%, 36%, or 39.6%, depending on the amount of taxable income and the taxpayer's filing status. The tax rate schedule on the following page shows the individual tax rates for each filing status.

> **PROBLEM-SOLVING HINT** When taxable income goes beyond the 15% tax rate amount, do not make the mistake of using the 28% tax rate on the entire amount of taxable income. For example, for a single person having a taxable income greater than $24,650, a tax rate of 15% is used for the first $24,650 and a tax rate of 28% is used only on the amount over $24,650.

EXAMPLE 2

Finding Taxable Income and the Income Tax Amount

Find the taxable income and use the tax rate schedule for each of the following people.

(a) David Shea, single, one exemption, adjusted gross income, $20,346.
(b) The Zagorins, married, filing jointly, five exemptions, adjusted gross income, $64,308.

Tax Rate Schedule

	Single				Married Filing Jointly or Qualifying Widow(er)		
Over—	But Not Over—	Tax Is—	of the Amount Over—	Over—	But Not Over—	Tax Is—	of the Amount Over—
$0	$24,650	.... 15%	$0	$0	$41,200	.... 15%	$0
24,650	59,750	$3,697.50 + 28%	24,650	41,200	99,600	$6,180.00 + 28%	41,200
59,750	124,650	13,525.50 + 31%	59,750	99,600	151,750	22,532.00 + 31%	99,600
124,650	271,050	33,644.50 + 36%	124,650	151,750	271,050	38,698.50 + 36%	151,750
271,050	....	86,348.50 + 39.6%	271,050	271,050	....	81,646.50 + 39.6%	271,050

	Married Filing Separately				Head of Household		
Over—	But Not Over—	Tax Is—	of the Amount Over—	Over—	But Not Over—	Tax Is—	of the Amount Over—
$0	$20,600	.... 15%	$0	$0	$33,050	.... 15%	$0
20,600	49,800	$3,090.00 + 28%	20,600	33,050	85,350	$4,957.50 + 28%	33,050
49,800	75,875	11,266.00 + 31%	49,800	85,350	138,200	19,601.50 + 31%	85,350
75,875	135,525	19,349.25 + 36%	75,875	138,200	271,050	35,985.00 + 36%	138,200
135,525	....	40,823.25 + 39.6%	135,525	271,050	....	83,811.00 + 39.6%	271,050

Solution

(a) Taxable income is $13,546 ($20,346 − $4150 standard deduction − $2650 for one exemption). The tax is calculated as follows:

$$15\% \times \$13,546 = \$2031.90$$

The tax is $2031.90.

(b) Taxable income is $44,158 ($64,308 − $6900 standard deduction − $13,250 for five exemptions). Tax for married filing jointly is:

$$15\% \times \$41,200 = \$6180.00$$
$$28\% \times \$2958 (\$44,158 - \$41,200) = \underline{\$\ 828.24}$$
$$\text{Total } \$7008.24.$$

The tax is $7008.24

Objective **6** **List possible deductions.** A **tax deduction** is any expense that the Internal Revenue Service allows the taxpayer to subtract from adjusted gross income. A reduction in adjusted gross income results in less tax owed.

To be of benefit, itemized deductions *must exceed* the automatic standard deduction allowed by the Internal Revenue Service. Usually, taxpayers benefit from itemized deductions when they purchase a home and are allowed to deduct the interest on the loan.

The 20% of Americans who do itemize deductions must go through one additional step before subtracting exemptions to determine their taxable income: listing all deductions. The most common deductions are listed here.

Medical and dental expenses. Not all such expenses are deductible. In general, only amounts in excess of 7.5% of the adjusted gross income may be deducted. For most people, the restriction limits medical deductions to catastrophic illnesses. Expenses reimbursed by insurance companies may not be deducted.

Taxes. State and local income taxes, real estate taxes, and personal property taxes may be deducted (but not federal income or gasoline taxes).

Interest. Home mortgage interest on the taxpayer's principal residence and a qualified second home is deductible. Other interest charges (including credit-card interest) may *not* be deducted.

Contributions. Contributions to most charities may be deducted.

Miscellaneous deductions. Miscellaneous expenses are only deductible to the extent that the total amount of such deductions exceeds 2 percent of the taxpayer's adjusted gross income. These deductions include income tax-preparation fees, tax-preparation books or computer software, appraisal fees for tax purposes, and legal fees for tax planning or tax litigation.

> **NOTE**   The taxpayer gets to take whichever is higher—the standard deduction *or* the itemized deductions. When itemizing deductions, the gain in deductions is not the total of all itemized deductions but the difference between the standard deduction and the total itemized deductions. The taxpayer must be able to document these deductions with carefully kept records and receipts.

EXAMPLE 3

Using Itemized Deductions to find Taxable Income and Income Tax

For related Web activities, go to www.mathbusiness.com

Keyword: april

Electronic Update   Many more people are filing electronically, which typically means speedier refunds and fewer mistakes. The IRS received 20.6 million returns electronically as of March 27, up 25% from a year earlier. This includes filings by computer or by phone.

Source: Wall Street Journal. Reprinted by permission of Dow Jones, Inc. via Copyright Clearance Center, Inc. © 1999 Dow Jones & Co., Inc. All rights reserved worldwide.

Chris Kelly is single, has no dependents, and had an adjusted gross income of $26,735 last year, with deductions of $1352 for other taxes, $3118 for mortgage interest, and $317 for charity. Find his taxable income and his income tax.

Solution

First find the total of all deductions.

$$\text{Deductions} = \$1352 + \$3118 + \$317 = \$4787$$

Since Kelly is single, and the standard deduction is $4150, the larger itemized deduction amount, $4787, as well as an exception, is taken. Now find taxable income.

$$\text{Taxable income} = \$26{,}735 - \$4787 - \$2650 = \$19{,}298$$

Finally, income tax is determined.

$$15\% \times \$19{,}298 = \$2894.70$$

His tax is $2894.70.

In preparing personal income tax, refer to current Internal Revenue Service publications, and always use the current tax rates.

Objective **7** **Determine a balance due or a refund from the Internal Revenue Service.** After calculating the proper tax, determine whether a refund will be due from the government. Look again at the W-2 forms to find out how much already has been paid toward the tax bill. These forms show the total amount the employer has withheld and sent to the government. (Usually, no money is withheld for amounts on 1099 forms.) If the amount withheld is greater than the tax owed, the taxpayer is entitled to a refund. If the amount withheld is less than the tax owed, then the taxpayer must send the difference along with the tax return. The article to the left discusses how a greater number of taxpayers are choosing to file their tax returns electronically with the Internal Revenue Service.

EXAMPLE 4

Determining Tax Due or a Tax Refund

Lauren Morse had $375.20 per month withheld for federal income tax from her checks last year. She is single and has taxable income of $24,056 for the year. Does she get a refund? If so, how much?

Solution

Morse had $375.20 × 12 = $4502.40 withheld from her checks last year. The tax due on taxable income of $24,056 is $3608.40; therefore, she will receive a refund in the amount of

$$\$4502.40 - \$3608.40 = \$894.$$

> **PROBLEM-SOLVING HINT**   Be certain that the proper income tax form is used when filing your individual income tax. The 1040EZ form is used by many students but you *must be single* to use this form. If you have over $400 in interest or any adjustments to income, a 1040A form is used. In order to itemize deductions, the taxpayer must use a 1040 form. There are additional considerations and restrictions that determine whether the 1040EZ, 1040A, or 1040 forms should be used.

Objective **8** **Prepare a 1040A and a Schedule 1 federal tax form.** The next example shows how to complete an income tax return using **Form 1040A** and **Schedule 1 (Form 1040A)**.

> **NOTE**   When completing income tax forms and calculations, notice that all amounts may be rounded to the nearest dollar.

Reality Check

Example 5

Preparing a 1040A and a Schedule 1

Jennifer Crum is single and claims one exemption. Her income appears on the W-2 and 1099 forms on page 494. Crum contributes $1500 to an IRA. Since she has interest income over $400 but does not itemize her deductions she may use Form 1040A and must also file a Schedule 1 (Form 1040A). Complete her income tax return.

Form
1040A

Department of the Treasury–Internal Revenue Service

U.S. Individual Income Tax Return (H)

IRS Use Only–Do not write or staple in this space.

Label   (See page 14.)   **Use the IRS label.**   Otherwise, please print in **ALL CAPITAL LETTERS**.

OMB No. 1545-0085

Your social security number

4 1 8 2 3 0 1 5 2

L A B E L   H E R E

Your first name Init. Last name	
JENNIFER CRUM	
If a joint return, spouse's first name Init. Last name	
Home address (number and street). If you have a P.O. box, see page 14.	Apt. no.
2136 OLD ROAD	
City, town or post office. If you have a foreign address, see page 14. State ZIP code	
TOWSON MD 21285	

Spouse's social security number

For Privacy Act and Paperwork Reduction Act Notice, see page 42.

Presidential Election Campaign Fund (See page 19.)

	Yes	No
Do you want $3 to go to this fund?		X
If a joint return, does your spouse want $3 to go to this fund?		

Note: *Checking "Yes" will not change your tax or reduce your refund.*

1 ☒ Single

2 ☐ Married filing joint return (even if only one had income)

3 ☐ Married filing separate return. Enter spouse's social security number above and full name here. ▶ _____

4 ☐ Head of household (with qualifying person). (See page 15.) If the qualifying person is a child but not your dependent, enter this child's name here. ▶ _____

5 ☐ Qualifying widow(er) with dependent child (year spouse died ▶ 19____). (See page 16.)

6a ☒ **Yourself.** If your parent (or someone else) can claim you as a dependent on his or her tax return **do not** check box 6a.

b ☐ Spouse

No. of boxes checked on 6a and 6b   **1**

c **Dependents.** If more than six dependents, see page 16.

(1) First name Last name	(2) Dependent's social security number	(3) Dependent's relationship to you	(4) No. of months lived in your home in 1997

No. of your children on 6c who:
• lived with you
• did not live with you due to divorce or separation (see page 17)

Dependents on 6c not entered above

Add numbers entered in boxes above   **1**

d Total number of exemptions claimed. ▶

	Dollars	Cents
7 Wages, salaries, tips, etc. Attach Form(s) W-2.	**7**	24,738	
8a **Taxable** interest income. Attach Schedule 1 if required	**8a**	428	
b **Tax-exempt** interest. DO NOT include on line 8a. **8b**		
9 Dividends. Attach Schedule 1 if required.	**9**	
10a Total IRA distributions. **10a** **10b** Taxable amount (see page 19).	**10b**	
11a Total pensions and annuities. **11a** **11b** Taxable amount (see page 19).	**11b**	
12 Unemployment compensation.	**12**	
13a Social security benefits. **13a** **13b** Taxable amount (see page 21).	**13b**	
14 Add lines 7 through 13b (far right column). This is your **total income.** ▶	**14**	25,166	
15 IRA deduction (see page 21).	**15**	1,500	
16 Subtract line 15 from line 14. This is your **adjusted gross income.** If under $29,290 (under $9,770 if a child did not live with you), see the EIC instructions on page 27. ▶	**16**	23,666	

Attach Copy B of W-2 and 1099-R here.

Cat. No. 11327A

Form 1040A

Form 1040A page 2

17	Enter the amount from line 16.		17	23,666.

18a Check   ☐ **You** were 65 or older   ☐ Blind }   **Enter number of**
if: ☐ **Spouse** was 65 or older   ☐ Blind }   **boxes checked ▶ 18a** ☐

b If you are married filing separately and your spouse itemizes deductions, see page 23 and check here . . . . ▶ 18b ☐

19 Enter the **standard deduction** for your filing status. **But** see page 24 if you checked any box on line 18a or 18b **OR** someone can claim you as a dependent.
- Single–$4,150   • Married filing jointly or Qualifying widow(er)–$6,900
- Head of household–$6,050   • Married filing separately–$3,450   **19**   4,150.

20	Subtract line 19 from line 17. If line 19 is more than line 17, enter 0.	20	19,516.
21	Multiply $2,650 by the total number of exemptions claimed on line 6d.	21	2,650.
22	Subtract line 21 from line 20. If line 21 is more than line 20, enter 0. **This is your taxable income.** **If you want the IRS to figure your tax, see page 24.** ▶	22	16,866.
23	Find the tax on the amount on line 22 (see page 24).	23	2,530.

24a	Credit for child and dependent care expenses. Attach Schedule 2.	24a		
b	Credit for the elderly or the disabled. Attach Schedule 3.	24b		
c	Adoption credit. Attach Form 8839.	24c		
d	Add lines 24a, 24b, and 24c. These are your **total credits**		24d	

25	Subtract line 24d from line 23. If line 24d is more than line 23, enter 0.	25	2,530.
26	Advance earned income credit payments from Form(s) W-2.	26	
27	Household employment taxes. Attach Schedule H.	27	
28	Add lines 25, 26, and 27 This is your **total tax.** ▶	28	2,530.

29a	Total Federal income tax withheld from Forms W-2 and 1099	29a	3,276.
b	1997 estimated tax payments and amount applied from 1996 return.	29b	
c	**Earned income credit.** Attach Schedule EIC if you have a qualifying child.	29c	
d	Nontaxable earned income: amount ▶ [ ] and type ▶		
e	Add lines 29a, 29b, and 29c. These are your **total payments.** ▶	29e	3,276.

30	If line 29e is more than line 28, subtract line 28 from line 29e. This is the amount you **overpaid.**	30	746.

31a Amount of line 30 you want **refunded to you.** If you want it directly deposited, see page 33 and fill in 31b, 31c, and 31d.   **31a**   746.

b Routing number [   ]   **c** Type: ☐ Checking ☐ Savings

d Account number [   ]

32	Amount of line 30 you want **applied to your 1998 estimated tax.**	32	

33	If line 28 is more than line 29e, subtract line 29e from line 28. This is the **amount you owe.** For details on how to pay, see page 34.	33	
34	Estimated tax penalty (see page 34).	34	

Sign here

Under penalties of perjury, I declare that I have examined this return and accompanying schedules and statements, and to the best of my knowledge and belief, they are true, correct, and accurately list all amounts and sources of income I received during the tax year. Declaration of preparer (other than the taxpayer) is based on all information of which the preparer has any knowledge.

Your signature	Date	Your occupation
Jennifer Crum	3/5	Assistant Manager

Keep a copy of this return for your records.

Spouse's signature. If joint return, BOTH must sign.	Date	Spouse's occupation

Paid preparer's use only

Preparer's signature ▶	Date	Check if self-employed ☐	Preparer's SSN
Firm's name (or yours if self-employed) and address ▶		EIN	
		ZIP code	

Schedule 1
(Form 1040A)

Department of the Treasury–Internal Revenue Service

Interest and Ordinary Dividends
for Form 1040A Filers

OMB No. 1545-0085

Name(s) shown on Form 1040A	Your social security number
Jennifer Crum	418 23 0152

Part I

Interest

(See pages 24 and 56.)

Note: *If you received a Form 1099–INT, Form 1099–OID, or substitute statement from a brokerage firm, enter the firm's name and the total interest shown on that form.*

			Amount	
1	List name of payer. If any interest is from a seller-financed mortgage and the buyer used the property as a personal residence, see page 56 and list this interest first. Also, show that buyer's social security number and address.			
	Employee Credit Union	1	428	
2	Add the amounts on line 1.	2	428	
3	Excludable interest on series EE U.S. savings bonds issued after 1989 from Form 8815, line 14. You **must** attach Form 8815 to Form 1040A.	3		
4	Subtract line 3 from line 2. Enter the result here and on Form 1040A, line 8a.	4	428	

Part II

Ordinary dividends

(See pages 24 and 56.)

Note: *If you received a Form 1099–DIV or substitute statement from a brokerage firm, enter the firm's name and the ordinary dividends shown on that form.*

		Amount	
5	List name of payer		
		5	
6	Add the amounts on line 5. Enter the total here and on Form 1040A, line 9.	6	

For Paperwork Reduction Act Notice, see Form 1040A instructions.   Cat. No. 12075R   **Schedule 1 (Form 1040A)**

Name   Date   Class

12.2 Exercises

The Quick Start exercises in each section contain solutions to help you get started.

Find the adjusted gross income for each of the following people. (See Example 1.)

Quick Start

Name	Income from Jobs	Interest	Misc. Income	Dividend Income	Adjustments to Income	Adjusted Gross Income
1. R. Garrett	$18,610	$74	$1936	$115	$135	**$20,600**

$18,610 + $74 + $1936 + $115 − $135 = $20,600

2. C. Manly	$38,156	$285	$73	$542	$317	**$38,739**

$38,156 + $285 + $73 + $542 − $317 = $38,739

3. The Hanks	$21,380	$625	$139	$184	$618	_____
4. The Jazwinskis	$33,650	$722	$375	$218	$473	_____
5. The Brashers	$38,643	$95	$188	$105	$0	_____
6. The Ameens	$41,379	$1174	$536	$186	$2258	_____

Find the amount of taxable income and the tax owed for each of the following people. Use the tax rate schedule. The letter following the names indicates the marital status, and all married people are filing jointly. (See Examples 2 and 3.)

Quick Start

Name	Number of Exemptions	Adjusted Gross Income	Total Deductions	Taxable Income	Tax Owed
7. E. Gragg, S	1	$24,200	$1795	**$17,400**	**$2610**

$24,200 − $4150 − $2650 = $17,400; $17,400 × .15 = $2610

8. E. Biondi, S	1	$15,615	$3182	**$8815**	**$1322.25**

$15,615 − $4150 − $2650 = $8815; $8815 × .15 = $1322.25

9. The Cooks, M	3	$38,751	$5968	_____	_____
10. The Loveridges, M	7	$52,532	$6972	_____	_____

Name	Number of Exemptions	Adjusted Gross Income	Total Deductions	Taxable Income	Tax Owed
11. The Jordans, M	5	$71,800	$4509	_____	_____
12. G. Clarke, S	1	$32,322	$4318	_____	_____
13. D. Collins, S	1	$35,350	$4486	_____	_____
14. A. Crowley, S	1	$32,502	$2365	_____	_____
15. B. Kammerer, S	1	$38,526	$2793	_____	_____
16. The Prentices, M	5	$28,664	$3518	_____	_____
17. The Albers, M	2	$62,613	$7681	_____	_____
18. The Reents, M	8	$78,544	$7053	_____	_____

Find the tax refund or tax due for the following people. The letter following the names indicates the marital status. Assume a 52-week year and that married people are filing jointly. (See Example 4.)

Quick Start

Name	Taxable Income	Federal Income Tax Withheld from Checks	Tax Refund or Tax Due
19. Karecki, S	$13,378	$243.10 monthly	$910.50 tax refund
$2917.20 − $2006.70 = $910.50			
20. Woo, C., S	$27,204	$347.80 monthly	_____
21. Hunziker, S	$23,552	$72.18 weekly	_____
22. The Fungs, M	$38,238	$119.27 weekly	_____
23. The Todds, M	$21,786	$208.52 monthly	_____
24. The Fords, M	$39,436	$128.35 weekly	_____

25. List four sources of income for which an individual might receive W-2 and 1099 forms. (See Objective 3.)

26. List four possible tax deductions, and explain the effect that a tax deduction will have on taxable income and on income tax due. (See Objective 6.)

Name	Date	Class

Find the tax in each of the following application problems.

27. MARRIED—INCOME TAX   The Tobins had an adjusted gross income of $45,378 last year. They had deductions of $482 for state income tax, $187 for city income tax, $472 for property tax, $3208 in mortgage interest, and $324 in contributions. They file a joint return and claim five exemptions.

27. _____

28. SINGLE—INCOME TAX   Diane Bolton had an adjusted gross income of $34,975 last year. She had deductions of $971 for state income tax, $564 for property tax, $2747 in mortgage interest, and $235 in contributions. Bolton claims one exemption and files as a single person.

28. _____

29. SINGLE—INCOME TAX   Susan Winslow, filing as a single person and claiming one exemption, had an adjusted gross income of $31,998. Her deductions amounted to $3255.

29. _____

30. MARRIED—INCOMIE TAX   The Slausons had an adjusted gross income of $36,116 last year. They had deductions of $1078 for state income tax, $253 for city income tax, $879 for property tax, $5218 in mortgage interest, and $386 in contributions. They claim three exemptions and file a joint return.

30. _____

31. ADJUSTED GROSS INCOME (AGI)   The Hamptons had wages of $68,645, dividends of $385, interest of $672, and adjustments to income of $1058 last year. They had deductions of $877 for state income tax, $342 for city income tax, $986 for property tax, $5173 in mortgage interest, and $186 in contributions. They claim five exemptions and file a joint return.

31. _____

32. John Walker had wages of $30,364, other income of $2892, dividends of $240, interest of $315, and an IRA contribution of $750 last year. He had deductions of $1163 for state income tax, $1268 for property tax, $1294 in mortgage interest, and $540 in contributions. Walker claims one exemption and files as a single person.

32. _____

33. John and Vicki Karsten had combined wages and salaries of $45,428, other income of $5283, dividend income of $324, and interest income of $668. They have adjustments to income of $2484. Their itemized deductions are $7615 in mortgage interest, $729 in state income tax, $1185 in real estate taxes, and $1219 in charitable contributions. The Karstens filed a joint return and claimed 6 exemptions.

33. _____

34. Colleen Mannel had wages and salaries of $43,846, other income of $1682, dividend income of $478, and interest income of $986. She has an adjustment to income of $1452. Her itemized deductions are $4615 in mortgage interest, $1136 in state income tax, $856 in real estate taxes, and $835 in charitable contributions. Mannel claims one exemption and is a single person.

34. _____

12.3 | FIRE INSURANCE

Objectives

1. Define the terms *policy*, *face value*, and *premium*.
2. Find the annual premium for fire insurance.
3. Use the coinsurance formula.
4. Understand multiple carrier insurance.
5. List additional types of insurance coverage.

PROblEM SolviNG iN BusiNEss

As the owner of Round Table Pizza, Brian Katavich is well aware of his need for insurance. One type of insurance coverage that he must have would cover losses due to fire. A fire that either partially or totally destroyed his building could leave him in financial ruins. However, with the proper fire-insurance policy, his losses could be recovered and he could rebuild his business.

There is only a slight chance that a particular building will be damaged by fire during a given year. However, if such fire damage did occur, the financial loss could be very large. To protect against this small chance of a large loss, people pay an amount equal to a small percent of the value of their property to a fire-insurance company. The company collects money for a large number of properties and then pays for expenses due to fire damage for those few buildings having such damage.

Objective **1** **Define the terms *policy*, *face value*, and *premium*.** The contract between the owner of a building and a fire-insurance company is called a **policy**. The amount of insurance provided by the company is called the **face value** of the policy. The charge for the policy is called the **premium**.

Objective **2** **Find the annual premium for fire insurance.** The amount of the premium charged by the insurance company depends on several factors. Among them are the type of construction of the building, the contents and use of the building, the location of the building, and the type and location of any fire protection that is available. Wood frame buildings generally are more likely to be damaged by fire than masonry buildings and thus require a larger premium. Categories are assigned to building types by insurance company **underwriters**. These categories are usually designated by letters such as *A*, *B*, and *C*. Underwriters also assign ratings called **territorial ratings** to each area that describe the quality of fire protection in the area. Although fire-insurance rates vary from state to state, the rates in the following table are typical.

Annual Rates for Each $100 of Insurance

	Building Classification					
	A		B		C	
Territorial Rating	Building	Contents	Building	Contents	Building	Contents
1	$.25	$.32	$.36	$.49	$.45	$.60
2	$.30	$.44	$.45	$.55	$.54	$.75
3	$.37	$.46	$.54	$.60	$.63	$.80
4	$.50	$.52	$.75	$.77	$.84	$.90
5	$.62	$.58	$.92	$.99	$1.05	$1.14

EXAMPLE 1

Finding the Annual Fire Insurance Premium

Round Table Pizza is in a building having a rating of class B. The territory is rated 3. Find the annual premium to insure the building that is worth $378,000 and has contents valued at $92,000.

Solution

According to the table, the rates per $100 for a class-B building in area 3 are $.54 for the building and $.60 for the contents. The premium for the building is found as follows.

$$\text{Value of building} = \$378,000 \div 100 = \textbf{3780 hundreds}$$
$$\text{Rate for building (from table)} = \textbf{\$.54}$$
$$\text{Premium for building} = \text{Value (in hundreds)} \times \text{Rate}$$
$$= \textbf{3780} \times \textbf{\$.54}$$
$$= \$2041.20$$

The premium for the contents can be found in the same way.

$$\text{Value of contents} = \$92,000 \div 100 = \textbf{920 hundreds}$$
$$\text{Rate for contents} = \textbf{\$.60} \text{ (from table)}$$
$$\text{Premium for contents} = \text{Value (in hundreds)} \times \text{Rate}$$
$$= \textbf{920} \times \textbf{\$.60} = \$552$$
$$\text{Total premium} = \$2041.20 \text{ (building)} + \$552 \text{ (contents)}$$
$$= \$2593.20 \text{ (building and contents)}$$

OBJECTIVE **3** **Use the coinsurance formula.** Most fires damage only a portion of a building and the contents. Since complete destruction of a building is rare, many owners save money by buying insurance for only a portion of the value of the building and contents. Realizing this, insurance companies place a **coinsurance clause** in almost all fire-insurance policies. With coinsurance, part of the risk of fire, under certain conditions, is assumed by the business firm taking out the insurance. For example, with an 80% coinsurance clause, full protection requires that the amount of insurance taken out be at least 80% of the market value of the building and contents insured.

If the amount of insurance is less than 80% of the market value, the insurance company pays only a portion of any loss. For example, if a business firm took out insurance with a face value of only 40% of the market value of the building insured and then had a loss, the insurance company would pay only half the loss (40% is half of 80%).

Use the following formula to find the portion of a loss that will be paid by the insurance company.

$$\begin{array}{c}\text{Amount insurance company} \\ \text{will pay (assuming 80\% coinsurance)}\end{array} = \text{Amount of loss} \times \frac{\text{Amount of policy}}{80\% \text{ of market value}}$$

> **NOTE**   The company never pays more than the face value of the policy, nor more than the amount of the loss.

EXAMPLE 2
Using the Coinsurance Formula

Barbara Weaks owns a commercial building valued at $760,000. Her fire-insurance policy (with an 80% coinsurance clause) has a face value of $570,000. The building suffers a fire loss of $144,000. Find the amount of the loss that the insurance company will pay.

Solution

The policy should have been for at least **80%** of the value, or

$$.80 \times \$760,000 = \$608,000$$

Since the face value of the policy ($570,000) is less than 80% of the value of the building, the company will pay only a portion of the loss. Use the formula.

$$\text{Amount insurance company pays} = \$144,000 \times \frac{\$570,000}{\$608,000}$$
$$= \$135,000$$

The company will pay $135,000 toward the loss, and Weaks must pay the additional $9000 ($144,000 − $135,000).

The calculator solution to this example uses chain calculations and parentheses to set off the denominator. The result is then subtracted from the fire loss.

$$144000 \; \boxed{\times} \; 570000 \; \boxed{\div} \; \boxed{(} \; 80 \; \boxed{\%} \; \boxed{\times} \; 760000 \; \boxed{)} \; \boxed{=} \; 135000$$

$$144000 \; \boxed{-} \; 135000 \; \boxed{=} \; 9000$$

Note: All calculator solutions use a scientific calculator. Refer to Appendix B for scientific calculator basics.

EXAMPLE 3

Finding the Amount of Loss Paid by the Insurance Company

A Swedish investment group owns a warehouse valued at $3,450,000. The company has a fire-insurance policy with a face value of $3,400,000. The policy has an 80% coinsurance feature. If the firm has a fire loss of $233,500, find the part of the loss paid by the insurance company.

Solution

The value of the warehouse is $3,450,000. Take 80% of this value.

$$.80 \times \$3,450,000 = \$2,760,000$$

The business has a fire-insurance policy with a face value of more than 80% of the value of the store. Therefore, the insurance company will pay the entire $233,500 loss.

Objective **4** **Understand multiple carrier insurance.** A business may have fire-insurance policies with several companies at the same time. Perhaps additional insurance coverage was purchased over a period of time, as new additions were made to a factory or building complex. Or perhaps the building is so large that one insurance company does not want to take the entire risk by itself, so several companies each agree to take a portion of the insurance coverage and thereby share the risk. In either event, the insurance coverage is divided among **multiple carriers**. When an insurance claim is made against multiple carriers, each insurance company pays its fractional portion of the total claim on the property.

EXAMPLE 4

Understanding Multiple Carrier Insurance

World Recycling Conglomerate (WRC) has an insured loss of $1,800,000 while having insurance coverage beyond its coinsurance requirement. The insurance is divided among Company A with $5,900,000 coverage, Company B with $4,425,000 coverage, and Company C with $1,475,000 coverage. Find the amount of the loss paid by each of the insurance companies.

Solution

Start by finding the total face value of all three policies.

$5,900,000 + $4,425,000 + $1,475,000 = $11,800,000 total face value

$5,900,000	Company A pays $\dfrac{\$5,900,000}{\$11,800,000} = \dfrac{1}{2}$ of the loss	
$4,425,000	Company B pays $\dfrac{\$4,425,000}{\$11,800,000} = \dfrac{3}{8}$ of the loss	
+ $1,475,000	Company C pays $\dfrac{\$1,475,000}{\$11,800,000} = \dfrac{1}{8}$ of the loss	
$11,800,000 total face value		

Since the insurance loss is $1,800,000 the amount paid by each of the multiple carriers is

Company A	$\dfrac{1}{2} \times \$1,800,000 =$	$900,000
Company B	$\dfrac{3}{8} \times \$1,800,000 =$	$675,000
Company C	$\dfrac{1}{8} \times \$1,800,000 =$	$225,000
	Total loss =	$1,800,000

> **PROBLEM-SOLVING HINT**   If the coinsurance requirement is not met, the total amount of the loss paid by the insurance coverage is found, and then the amount that each of the carriers pays is found as in Example 4.

The amount of money paid toward insurance premiums by businesses is quite small when compared to other business expenses. Likewise, the average household pays only a small portion of its budget on insurance premiums. The following graph shows the percent of total household spending going to pay for insurance coverage.

Real-World Numbers
Information from the World Around Us

Small Price to Pay

Homeowner's insurance accounts for less than 1% of household spending and is carried by 95% of homeowners.

Percent of Household Budget

- Housing 31%
- Health care 3%
- Entertainment 4.9%
- Clothing 5.2%
- Homeowner's 0.7%
- Life 1.2%
- Auto 2.2%
- Transportation 16.9%
- Health 2.6%
- All Insurance 6.7%
- Food 13.9%
- Other 10.5%
- Retirement 8.1%

DATA: U.S. Bureau of Labor Statistics

Objective **5** **List additional types of insurance coverage.**   There are many types of insurance coverage that are required or desirable for a business. **Worker's compensation** is usually required by law. **Liability coverage** (coverage against lawsuits resulting from injury to another person on your property and against damage caused by windstorms, hail, and so on) is often made a part of a fire-insurance policy. Homeowners usually buy a **homeowner's policy** protecting against these losses and many others, including all credit cards and ATM cards, business property brought home, and medical costs for guests who are injured. Other policies are designed for condominium owners, rental property owners, and apartment dwellers. Similar additional coverage is available to give comprehensive insurance coverage to businesses.

Name | Date | Class

12.3 | Exercises

The Quick Start *exercises in each section contain solutions to help you get started.*

Find the total annual premium for each of the following. Use the table on page 505. (See Example 1.)

Quick Start

	Territorial Rating	Building Classification	Building Value	Contents Value	Total Annual Premium
1.	4	C	$140,000	$75,000	$1851
2.	5	A	$220,500	$105,000	$1976.10
3.	1	C	$285,000	$152,000	_____
4.	2	B	$272,500	$111,500	_____
5.	5	B	$782,600	$212,000	_____
6.	3	A	$596,400	$206,700	_____

Find the amount to be paid by the insurance company in the following problems. Assume each policy includes an 80% coinsurance clause. (See Examples 2 and 3.)

Quick Start

	Value of Building	Face Value of Policy	Amount of Loss	Amount Paid
7.	$287,000	$232,500	$19,850	$19,850

$287,000 \times .8 = $229,600$ (80%); $19,850

8.	$780,000	$585,000	$10,400	$9750

$780,000 \times .8 = $624,000$ (80%); $\frac{585,000}{624,000} \times $10,400 = 9750

9.	$48,000	$36,000	$4500	_____
10.	$78,500	$47,500	$1500	_____
11.	$218,500	$195,000	$36,500	_____
12.	$750,000	$500,000	$56,000	_____

Find the amount paid by each insurance company in the following problems involving multiple carriers. Assume that the coinsurance requirement is met. (See Example 4.)

Quick Start

	Insurance Loss	Companies	Coverage	Amount Paid
13.	$80,000	Company 1	$750,000	**$60,000**
		Company 2	$250,000	**$20,000**

$$\frac{750,000}{1,000,000} \times \$80,000 = \$60,000; \quad \frac{250,000}{1,000,000} \times \$80,000 = \$20,000$$

	Insurance Loss	Companies	Coverage	Amount Paid
14.	$360,000	Company A	$1,200,000	_____
		Company B	$800,000	_____
15.	$650,000	Company 1	$1,350,000	_____
		Company 2	$1,200,000	_____
		Company 3	$450,000	_____
16.	$1,600,000	Company A	$4,800,000	_____
		Company B	$800,000	_____
		Company C	$2,400,000	_____

Find the annual fire-insurance premium in each of the following application problems. Use the table on page 505.

Quick Start

17. FIRE-INSURANCE PREMIUM   Stephanie Wetherbee owns a class-B building worth $165,400. Contents are valued at $128,000. The territorial rating is 3.

17. $1661.16

1654 × $.54 = $893.16; 1280 × $.60 = $768
$893.16 + $768 = $1661.16

18. INDUSTRIAL FIRE INSURANCE   Valley Crop Dusting owns a class-B building worth $107,500. Contents are worth $39,800. The territorial rating is 2.

18. _____

19. RESTAURANT FIRE INSURANCE   The Rocklin Grill owns a building worth $84,000. The contents are worth $18,500. The building is class B, with a territorial rating of 1.

19. _____

20. INDUSTRIAL BUILDING INSURANCE   London's Dredging Equipment is in a C-rated building with a territorial rating of 4. The building is worth $105,000 and the contents are worth $682,000.

20. _____

Name _____   Date _____   Class _____

21. Describe three factors that determine the premium charged for fire insurance. (See Objective 2.)

22. Explain the coinsurance clause and describe how coinsurance works. (See Objective 3.)

In the following application problems, find the amount of the loss paid by (**a**) *the insurance company and* (**b**) *the insured. Assume an 80% coinsurance clause.*

23. GIFT-SHOP FIRE LOSS   Indonesian Wonder gift shop has a value of $395,000. The shop is insured for $280,000. Fire loss is $22,500.

(**a**) _____
(**b**) _____

24. WELDING-FIRE LOSS   Flashpoint Welding Supplies owns a building valued at $540,000 and is insured for $308,000. Fire loss is $34,000.

(**a**) _____
(**b**) _____

25. SALVATION ARMY LOSS   The main office of the Salvation Army suffers a loss from fire of $45,000. The building is valued at $550,000 and is insured for $300,000.

(**a**) _____
(**b**) _____

26. APARTMENT FIRE LOSS   Kathy Stephenson owns rental units valued at $185,000 and they are insured for $111,000. Fire loss is $28,000.

(**a**) _____
(**b**) _____

27. Explain in your own words multiple-carrier insurance. Give two reasons for dividing insurance among multiple carriers. (See Objective 4.)

28. Several types of insurance coverage beyond basic fire coverage are included in a homeowner's policy. List and explain three losses that would be covered. (See Objective 5.)

In the following application problems, find the amount paid by each of the multiple carriers. Assume that the coinsurance requirement has been met.

29. COINSURED FIRE LOSS Camp Curry Stable had an insured fire loss of $548,000. It had insurance coverage as follows: Company A, $600,000; Company B, $400,000; and Company C, $200,000.

A: _____
B: _____
C: _____

30. The Cycle Centre had an insured fire loss of $68,500. They had insurance as follows: Company 1, $60,000; Company 2, $40,000; and Company 3, $30,000.

1: _____
2: _____
3: _____

31. MAJOR FIRE LOSS Golds Gym had fire insurance coverage as follows; Company 1, $360,000; Company 2, $120,000; and Company 3, $240,000. They had an insured fire loss of $250,000.

1: _____
2: _____
3. _____

32. Global Manufacturing Company had an insured fire loss of $2,100,000. They had insurance as follows: Company A, $2,000,000; Company B, $1,750,000; Company C, $1,250,000.

A: _____
B: _____
C: _____

12.4 | MOTOR-VEHICLE INSURANCE

Objectives

1. Describe the factors that affect the cost of motor-vehicle insurance.
2. Define liability insurance.
3. Define property damage insurance.
4. Describe comprehensive and collision insurance.
5. Define no-fault and uninsured motorist insurance.
6. Apply youthful operator factors.
7. Find the amounts paid by the insurance company and the insured.

PROBLEM SOLVING IN BUSINESS

Brian Katavich has a minivan that is used for deliveries. It also serves as a traveling billboard because it is painted with the company name Round Table Pizza. He must be certain that he has proper insurance coverage on this minivan because employees drive this vehicle in addition to himself. Not having insurance will expose Katavich and his business to financial risk and lawsuits that could be avoided with the proper insurance coverage.

Objective 1   Describe the factors that affect the cost of motor-vehicle insurance.   Automobile accidents increase in number and in seriousness every year, and the average cost of repairing a motor vehicle after an accident continues to rise dramatically. Businesses and individuals take out motor-vehicle insurance to protect against the possible large cost of an accident. The cost of this insurance, the **premium**, is determined by people called **actuaries**, who classify accidents according to location, the age and gender of the drivers, and other factors. Insurance companies use these results to determine premiums. For example, there are more accidents in heavily populated cities than in rural areas. Certain makes and models of automobiles are stolen more often than others. Young male drivers (16 to 25 years of age) are involved in many more accidents than they should be, considering their proportion of the population. The more expensive a vehicle and the newer a vehicle, the more it costs to repair. These are several of the factors that determine the cost of motor-vehicle insurance.

Objective 2   Define liability insurance.   Liability or **bodily injury insurance** protects the insured in case he or she injures someone with a car. Many states have minimum amounts of liability insurance coverage set by law. The amount of liability insurance is expressed as a fraction, such as 15/30. The fraction 15/30 means that the insurance company will pay up to $15,000 for injury to one person, and a total of $30,000 for injury to two or more persons in the same accident.

The following graph shows the number of pedestrians who were killed or injured by automobiles in the United States in a one-year period. Liability insurance protects the insured for these types of accidents.

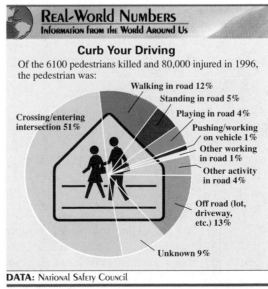

REAL-WORLD NUMBERS
Information from the World Around Us

Curb Your Driving

Of the 6100 pedestrians killed and 80,000 injured in 1996, the pedestrian was:

Crossing/entering intersection 51%

Walking in road 12%
Standing in road 5%
Playing in road 4%
Pushing/working on vehicle 1%
Other working in road 1%
Other activity in road 4%
Off road (lot, driveway, etc.) 13%
Unknown 9%

DATA: National Safety Council

The following table shows typical premium rates for various amounts of liability coverage. Included in the cost of the liability insurance is **medical insurance** provided the driver and passengers in case of injury. For example, the table column 15/30 shows that the insured can also receive reimbursement for up to $1000 of his or her own medical expenses in an accident.

Insurance companies divide the nation into territories based on past claims in all areas. Four territories are shown here. (All tables in this section show annual premiums.)

Liability (Bodily Injury) and Medical Insurance (Per Year)

Territory	Liability (Bodily Injury) Medical Expense				
	15/30 $1000	25/50 $2000	50/100 $3000	100/300 $5000	250/500 $10,000
1	$207	$222	$253	$282	$308
2	148	156	168	196	198
3	310	314	375	398	459
4	216	218	253	284	310

EXAMPLE 1

Finding the Liability and Medical Premium

Brian Katavich, owner of Round Table Pizza, is in territory 2 and wants 100/300 liability coverage. Find the amount of the premium for this coverage and the amount of medical coverage included.

Solution

In the liability and medical insurance table, look up territory 2 and 100/300 coverage to find a premium of $196 including $5000 medical coverage.

Objective **3** Define property damage insurance. **Property damage insurance** pays for damages caused to the property of others. The following table lists the premiums for property damage insurance according to the amount of coverage desired and the territory. The coverage amount is the maximum amount that the insurance company will pay. If a claim for damages exceeds this maximum amount, the insured must pay the excess.

Property Damage Insurance (Per Year)

Territory	Property Damage			
	$10,000	$25,000	$50,000	$100,000
1	$88	$93	$97	$103
2	64	69	76	84
3	129	134	145	158
4	86	101	112	124

EXAMPLE 2

Finding the Premium for Property Damage

Find the premium if Brian Katavich, in territory 2, wants property damage coverage of $50,000.

Solution

Property damage coverage of $50,000 in territory 2 requires a premium of $76.

> **NOTE** Many insurance companies give discounts on insurance premiums. You must be certain that you receive any discounts you are entitled to. The following graph shows the number of states requiring various discounts on insurance premiums.

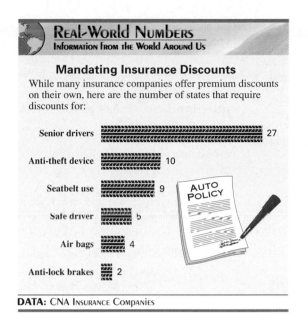

Real-World Numbers
Information from the World Around Us

Mandating Insurance Discounts
While many insurance companies offer premium discounts on their own, here are the number of states that require discounts for:

Senior drivers — 27
Anti-theft device — 10
Seatbelt use — 9
Safe driver — 5
Air bags — 4
Anti-lock brakes — 2

AUTO POLICY

DATA: CNA Insurance Companies

Objective **4** Describe comprehensive and collision insurance. **Comprehensive insurance** pays for damage to a vehicle caused by fire, theft, vandalism, falling trees, and other such events. **Collision insurance** pays for repairs to a vehicle in case of an accident. Collision insurance often includes a **deductible**. The deductible is paid by the insured in the event of a claim, and the insurance company pays the rest. Common deductible amounts are $100, $250, and, in some cases, $500 or $1000. For example, if the cost of repairing damage caused by an accident is $1045 and the deductible amount is $250, the insured pays $250 and the insurance company pays $795 ($1045 − $250 = $795).

> **NOTE** The higher the deductible amount, the lower the cost of the collision coverage. The insured shares a greater portion of the risk as the deductible amount increases.

The following table shows some typical rates for comprehensive and collision insurance. Rates are determined not only by territories, but also by age group and symbol. Here, age group refers to the age of the *vehicle*, not the driver. Age group 1 is a vehicle up to 1 year of age, and age group 6 is a vehicle 6 years of age or older. Symbol is determined by the *cost* of the vehicle.

Comprehensive and Collision Insurance (Per Year)

Territory	Age Group	Comprehensive Symbol			Collision ($250 Deductible) Symbol		
		6	**7**	**8**	**6**	**7**	**8**
1	1	$58	$64	$90	$153	$165	$184
	2, 3	50	56	82	135	147	171
	4, 5	44	52	76	116	128	147
	6	34	44	64	92	110	128
2	1	$26	$28	$40	$89	$95	$104
	2, 3	22	24	36	80	86	98
	4, 5	20	24	34	71	77	86
	6	16	20	28	60	68	77
3	1	$70	$78	$108	$145	$157	$174
	2, 3	60	66	90	128	139	162
	4, 5	52	64	92	111	122	139
	6	42	52	78	88	105	122
43	1	$42	$46	$66	$97	$104	$124
	2, 3	36	40	58	87	94	107
	4, 5	32	38	54	77	84	94
	6	26	32	46	64	74	84

> **NOTE**   A Ford Escort might be a symbol 6, and a Lincoln Continental might be a symbol 8. The collision coverage here is for $250 deductible coverage.

EXAMPLE 3

Finding the Comprehensive and Collision Premium

Brian Katavich, owner of Round Table Pizza, is in territory 2 and has a 2-year-old minivan that has a symbol of 8. Use the comprehensive and collision-insurance table to find the cost for **(a)** comprehensive coverage and **(b)** collision coverage.

Solution

(a) The cost of comprehensive coverage is $36.

(b) The cost of collision coverage is $98.

The following newspaper article shows the results of crash tests at 5 mph. The popular small pickup trucks racked up some large repair bills. The highest repair bill in this 5-mph test was Toyota Tacoma with $4361 in damage. The list at the left shows the top metropolitan areas in the U.S. for vehicle thefts.

Reality Check

Top Metro Areas for Vehicle Thefts

1. Jersey City, NJ
2. Fresno, CA
3. Miami, FL
4. Memphis, TN
5. New York City, NY
6. Phoenix-Mesa, AZ
7. New Orleans, LA
8. Tucson, AZ
9. Pine Bluff, AK
10. Los Angeles-Long Beach, CA
11. Sacramento, CA
12. Detroit, MI
13. Stockton-Lodi, CA
14. Albuquerque, NM
15. Jackson, MS

Source: National Insurance Crime Bureau, 1996.

Truck-Crash Tests

An insurance industry study released Tuesday found that some popular small pickups racked up sizable repair bills in crash tests at just 5 mph. Leading the way was the Toyota Tacoma, which sustained $4,361 in damage over four low-speed tests. Other trucks tested by the Insurance Institute for Highway Safety: the Chevrolet S-10 LS ($2,246 in damage), the Ford Ranger XLT ($2,952), the Dodge Dakota Sport ($3,863) and the Nissan Frontier XE ($3,867). Representatives of the automakers defended the trucks as crashworthy and said the insurance group released the study as part of a campaign to get the government to raise the bumper standard from 2.5 mph to 5 mph.

Source: USA Today, 4/8/98. Reprinted by permission.

Objective **5** **Define no-fault and uninsured motorist insurance.**   With **no-fault insurance**, the insured is reimbursed for medical expenses and all costs associated with an accident by his or her own insurance company no matter who caused the accident, and pain and suffering damages are eliminated except in cases of permanent injury or death. Insurance companies argue that no-fault insurance removes lawyers and the courts and results in easier and less-expensive settlements. On the other hand, trial lawyers and some consumer groups contend that no-fault leaves accident victims unable to recover all of their damages, and unprotected from the abuses of some insurance companies.

In states not having no-fault insurance, a driver must be concerned about an accident with an uninsured driver. For protection, a driver needs **uninsured motorist insurance**, which protects the vehicle owner from financial liability when hit by a vehicle that is not insured. Many states now require motor-vehicle insurance by law. Some insurance companies offer **underinsured motorist insurance**, which provides protection in the event that there is a collision with a vehicle that is underinsured. Typical costs for uninsured motorist insurance are shown in the table on the left.

Uninsured Motorist Insurance (Per Year)	
Territory	Basic Limit
1	$66
2	$44
3	$76
4	$70

EXAMPLE 4

Determining the Premium for Uninsured Motorist Coverage

Brian Katavich, in territory 2, wants uninsured motorist coverage. Find the premium in the uninsured motorist insurance table.

Solution

The premium for the uninsured motorist coverage in territory 2 is $44.

OBJECTIVE **6** **Apply youthful operator factors.** The graph below helps to explain why most insurance companies distinguish between **youthful** and **adult operators.** Although the age at which a youth becomes an adult varies from company to company, drivers of age 25 or less are usually considered youthful drivers, and drivers over 25 are considered adults. Due to the higher proportion of accidents in the 25-and-under bracket, insurance companies add an additional amount to the insurance premium.

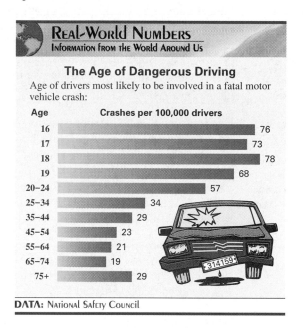

In the following table, there are two categories of youthful drivers, age 20 or less, and age 21–25. Consideration is also given to the youthful operator who has had driver's training. Some companies give discounts to youthful operators who are good students (a B average or better). To use the youthful operator table, first determine the premium for all coverage desired, and then multiply this premium by the appropriate youthful-operator factor to find the total premium.

Youthful-Operator Factor

Age	With Driver's Training	Without Driver's Training
20 or less	1.55	1.75
21–25	1.15	1.40

EXAMPLE 5

Using the Youthful-Operator Factor

Janet Ito lives in territory 4, is 22 years old, has had driver's training, and drives a 5-year-old car with a symbol of 7. She wants a 25/50 liability policy, a $10,000 property damage policy, a comprehensive and collision policy, and uninsured motorist coverage. Find her annual insurance premium using the tables in this section.

Solution

Ito's annual premium for 25/50 liability insurance is $218. Her annual premium for $10,000 property damage coverage is $86. Comprehensive insurance costs $38, and the premium for collision is $84. Uninsured motorist insurance is $70. The youthful-operator factor for a 22-year-old with driver's training is 1.15. First add the premiums from the various tables.

$$\$218 + \$86 + \$38 + \$84 + \$70 = \$496$$

Then multiply by the youthful-operator factor of 1.15 to get

$$\text{Total premium} = \$496 \times 1.15 = \$570.40.$$

The calculator solution to this example uses parentheses and chain calculations.

$$\boxed{(}\ 218\ \boxed{+}\ 86\ \boxed{+}\ 38\ \boxed{+}\ 84\ \boxed{+}\ 70\ \boxed{)}\ \boxed{\times}\ 1.15\ \boxed{=}\ 570.4$$

Note: All calculator solutions use a scientific calculator. Refer to Appendix B for scientific calculator basics.

Objective **7**   **Find the amounts paid by the insurance company and the insured.**   The cost of increasing insurance coverage limits is usually quite small. For example, the additional cost of increasing liability coverage in territory 1 from 50/100 to 100/300 is only $29 per year ($282 − $253). (Medical coverage would also be increased.)

> **NOTE**   Since the insurance company pays only to the maximum amount of insurance coverage with the driver liable for all additional amounts, many people pay an additional premium for increased coverage.

EXAMPLE 6
Finding the Amounts Paid by the Insurance Company and the Insured

Eric Liwanag has 25/50 liability limits, $25,000 property damage limits, and $250 deductible collision insurance. While on vacation, he was at fault in an accident that caused $5800 damage to his car, $3380 in damage to another car, and resulted in severe injuries to the other driver and his passenger. A subsequent lawsuit for injuries resulted in a judgment of $45,000 and $35,000, respectively, to the other parties. Find the amounts that the insurance company will pay for **(a)** repairing Liwanag's car, **(b)** repairing the other car, and **(c)** paying the court judgment resulting from the lawsuit. **(d)** How much will Liwanag have to pay the injured parties?

Solution

(a) The insurance company will pay $5550 ($5800 − $250 deductible) to repair Liwanag's car.

(b) Repairs on the other car will be paid to the property damage limits ($25,000); here, the total repairs of $3380 are paid.

(c) Since more than one person was injured, the insurance company pays the limit of $50,000 ($25,000 to each of the two injured parties).

(d) Liwanag is liable for $30,000 ($80,000 − $50,000), the amount awarded over the insurance limits ($45,000 − $25,000 = $20,000 and $35,000 − $25,000 = $10,000).

Where is the automobile accident death rate the highest? The number of driving deaths per 100,000 male drivers is high in the U.S. The following graph shows that there are some European countries that have much higher death rates than the U.S.

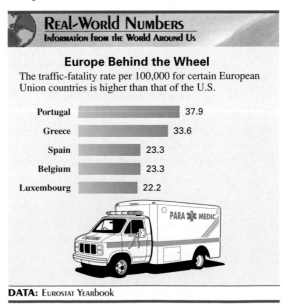

Real-World Numbers
Information from the World Around Us

Europe Behind the Wheel
The traffic-fatality rate per 100,000 for certain European Union countries is higher than that of the U.S.

Portugal	37.9
Greece	33.6
Spain	23.3
Belgium	23.3
Luxembourg	22.2

DATA: Eurostat Yearbook

Name   Date   Class

12.4 | EXERCISES

The Quick Start *exercises in each section contain solutions to help you get started.*

Find the annual premium for the following. (See Examples 1–5.)

Quick Start

	Name	Territory	Age	Driver Training	Liability	Property Damage	Comprehensive Collision Age Group	Symbol	Uninsured Motorist	Annual Premium
1.	Katavich	4	35	—	100/300	$50,000	2	8	Yes	$631

$284 + $112 + $58 + $107 + $70 = $631

2.	Morrissey	1	20	Yes	25/50	$25,000	4	7	No	$767.25

$222 + $93 + $52 + $128 + $0 = $495 × 1.55 = $767.25

3.	Shraim	3	52	—	250/500	$50,000	2	8	Yes	_____
4.	Waldron	2	67	—	50/100	$100,000	1	6	Yes	_____

5. Describe four factors that determine the premium on an automobile insurance policy. (See Objective 1.)

6. Explain in your own words the difference between liability (bodily injury) and property damage. (See Objectives 2 and 3.)

Solve the following application problems.

Quick Start

7. **YOUTHFUL-OPERATOR AUTO INSURANCE** Laura Coaty is 21 years old, has had driver's training, lives in territory 1, and drives a 4-year-old car with a symbol of 6. She wants 50/100 liability limits, $25,000 property damage limits, comprehensive and collision insurance, and uninsured motorist coverage. Find her annual insurance premium.

   $253 + $93 + $44 + $116 + $66 = $572; $572 × 1.15 = $657.80

   7. $657.80

8. **ADULT AUTO INSURANCE** Bill Poole is 47 years old, lives in territory 4, and drives a 2-year-old car with a symbol of 7. He wants 250/500 liability limits, $100,000 property damage limits, comprehensive and collision insurance, and uninsured motorist coverage. Find his annual insurance premium.

   8. _____

9. Sadie Simms lives in territory 3 and drives a new car with a symbol of 7. She wants 250/500 liability limits, $50,000 property damage limits, comprehensive and collision insurance, and uninsured motorist coverage. She is 38 years old. Find her annual insurance premium.

   9. _____

10. **YOUTHFUL OPERATOR—NO DRIVER TRAINING** Michelle Massa is 17 years old, has not had driver's training, lives in territory 2, and purchased a new Jeep Cherokee with a symbol of 6. She wants 50/100 liability limits, $25,000 property damage limits, comprehensive and collision insurance, and uninsured motorist coverage. Find her annual insurance premium.

    10. _____

11. **BODILY INJURY INSURANCE** Suppose your bodily injury policy has limits of 25/50, and you injure a person on a bicycle. The judge awards damages of $36,500 to the cyclist. **(a)** How much will the company pay? **(b)** How much will you pay?

(a) _____
(b) _____

12. Your best friend causes injury to three people and they receive damages of $50,000 each. She has a policy with bodily injury limits of 100/300. **(a)** How much will the company pay to each person? **(b)** How much must your friend pay?

(a) _____
(b) _____

13. **INSURANCE COMPANY PAYMENT** A reckless driver caused Leslie Silva to collide with a car in another lane. Silva had 50/100 liability limits, $25,000 property damage limits, and collision coverage with a $100 deductible. Silva's car had damage of $1878, while the other car suffered $6936 in damages. The resulting lawsuit gave injury awards of $60,000 and $55,000, respectively, in damages for personal injury to the two people in the other car. Find the amount that the insurance company will pay for **(a)** repairing Silva's car, **(b)** repairing the other car, and **(c)** personal injury damages. **(d)** How much must Silva pay beyond her insurance coverage, including the collision deductible?

(a) _____
(b) _____
(c) _____
(d) _____

14. Driving a dangerous vehicle at an excessive speed caused the car driven by Bob Armstrong to crash into another car. Armstrong had 15/30 liability limits, $10,000 property damage limits, and collision coverage with a $100 deductible. Damage to Armstrong's car was $2980, the other car, with a value of $22,800, was totaled. The results of a lawsuit awarded $75,000 and $45,000, respectively, in damages for personal injury to the two people in the other car. Find the amount that the insurance company will pay for **(a)** repairing Armstrong's car, **(b)** repairing the other car, and **(c)** personal injury damages. **(d)** How much must Armstrong pay beyond his insurance coverage?

(a) _____
(b) _____
(c) _____
(d) _____

15. Explain why insurance companies charge a higher premium on auto insurance sold to a youthful operator. Do you think that this higher premium is a good idea or not? (See Objective 6.)

16. Property damage pays for damage caused by you to the property of others. Since the average cost of a new car today is over $20,000, what amount of property damage coverage would you recommend to a friend who owns her own business?

12.5 | Life Insurance

Objectives

1. Define term, decreasing term, and whole life insurance policies.
2. Understand universal life, variable life, limited payment, and endowment policies.
3. Find the annual premium for life insurance.
4. Use premium factors with different modes of premium payment.

Problem Solving in Business

There were some lean years at first, but now Brian Katavich, the owner of Round Table Pizza, is enjoying the success of his business and the resulting income. He realizes that his family depends on his income and that they must have protection in the event that he dies or becomes disabled. A life insurance policy will give him this protection and the first thing he needs to do is learn about the different types of life insurance policies and what they cost.

Individuals buy life insurance for a variety of reasons. Most often the insured wants to provide for the needs of others with life insurance money in the event of early death or disability. Parents may want to guarantee that their children will have enough money for a college education, even if the parents die. Some types of life insurance provide paybacks upon retirement. Paybacks allow a retired person to live better than he or she might otherwise. Insurance money can also be used to pay off mortgages. According to the *World Almanac and Book of Facts*, the average amount of life insurance per household in the United States today is $112,400.

Life insurance is perhaps even more important for a person in business, particularly for an owner or partner in a small business. A business often takes a number of years to grow and may be the owner's main asset. The unexpected death of the owner might leave the business without proper guidance and control, so that the business might suffer drastically before it can be sold. Life insurance on the partners in a business supplies the surviving partner with the necessary money to buy out a deceased partner's interest in the partnership.

Objective **1** **Define term, decreasing term, and whole life insurance policies.** There are several types of life insurance policies available. The most common types are the following.

Term insurance. This insurance provides protection for a fixed term or length of time, such as 1 year, 5 years, or 10 years. At the end of the fixed period of time, the policy can usually be renewed for an additional period of time at a higher premium. Some term policies state that, on the expiration of the term stated in the policy, the insurance can be converted to one of the types described in the following paragraph. Term insurance is the least expensive of the types listed, accounts for 20% of all life policies, and gives the greatest amount of life insurance coverage for the premium dollar. At the expiration of a term insurance policy, however, the insured receives nothing from the insurance company except a request to buy more insurance.

Decreasing term insurance. In this modification of term insurance, the insured pays a fixed premium until age 60 or 65, with the amount of life insurance decreasing periodically. This policy is designed to fit the ages and stages of life as life insurance needs change. For the person just starting out, it gives more protection for less money. A typical policy of this kind, costing $11 per month, is shown in the following table.

Age	Amount of Life Insurance
Under 29	$40,000
30–34	$35,000
35–39	$30,000
40–44	$25,000
45–49	$18,000
50–54	$11,000
55–59	$7000
60–66	$4000
67 and over	$0

Nation's Top Killers

The 10 leading causes of death in the United States, ranked according to the number of lives lost in 1996:

1. Heart disease
2. Cancer
3. Stroke
4. Lung disease
5. Accidents
6. Pneumonia and influenza
7. Diabetes
8. AIDS
9. Suicide
10. Liver disease

Source: National Center for Health Statistics

Decreasing term insurance is commonly available to employees of large companies as a fringe benefit, paid for by either the employee or the employer or both. Most mortgage insurance policies are this type. The amount of life insurance coverage decreases as the amount of the mortgage is reduced.

Whole life insurance (also called **straight life** or **ordinary life insurance**). This type combines life insurance protection with a savings plan. The insured pays a constant premium until death or retirement, whichever occurs sooner. Monthly payments are made by the company to the insured upon retirement, until his or her death.

Whole life insurance builds up **cash value,** or guaranteed money used to pay retirement benefits to the insured. Also, these cash values can be borrowed by the insured at favorable interest rates.

The following graph shows the increase in life expectancy in the U.S. from 1930 to 1996. The nation's leading causes of death are shown to the left.

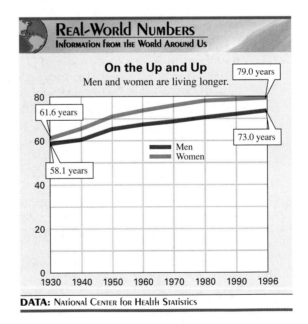

Objective [2] **Understand universal life, variable life, limited payment, and endowment policies.** **Universal life policies** and **variable life policies** provide the life insurance coverage of term insurance (high coverage per premium dollar), plus a tax-deferred way to accumulate assets and earn interest at money market rates. Unlike traditional whole life insurance policies, universal life insurance allows the insured to vary the amount of premium depending on the changing needs of the insured. A younger insured person with limited funds may want maximum insurance protection for the family. At a later date, the insured may want to begin actively building assets and may increase the premium to build cash value for retirement benefits. Universal life insurance is sensitive to interest rate changes. The portion of the premium going into retirement benefits receives money market interest rates and is usually guaranteed a minimum rate of return, regardless of what happens to market rates. The result is that the insured profits from higher interest rates but is also protected if interest rates drop below the guaranteed rate. The idea is that returns will be greater than those given to ordinary life policyholders.

Variable life is the latest attempt to encourage sales of the insurance industry's main product, whole life insurance. It allows you to allocate your premiums among one or more separate investments which offer varying degrees of risk and reward—stocks, bonds, combinations of both, or accounts that provide for guarantees of interest and principal. Typical policies available today allow the policyholder to switch investments from one fund to another twice each year.

> **NOTE** The preceding features, coupled with some tax benefits, have resulted in the variable life policy accounting for 25% and 35%, respectively, of the new policies sold in recent years by two of the largest life insurance companies.

Limited-payment life insurance. Limited-payment life is similar to whole life insurance, except that premiums are paid for only a fixed number of years, such as 20. This type of insurance is thus often called 20-pay life, representing payments of 20 years. The premium for limited-payment life is higher than that for ordinary life policies. Limited payment life is commonly used by athletes, actors, and others whose income is likely to be high for several years and then decline.

Endowment policies are the most expensive type of policy. These policies guarantee payment of a fixed amount of money to a given individual, whether or not the insured lives. Endowment policies might be taken out by parents to guarantee a sum of money for their children's college education. Because of the high premiums, this is one of the least popular types of policies today.

OBJECTIVE **3** **Find the annual premium for life insurance.** Calculation of life insurance rates and premiums uses fairly involved mathematics and is done by actuaries. The results of such calculations are published in tables of premiums. A typical table is shown here.

> **NOTE** Life expectancy for women is greater than for men, so a woman pays a lower life insurance premium than does a man of the same age. Find the insurance premium for a woman by subtracting 5 years from her age before using the table of premiums.

For related Web activities, go to www.mathbusiness.com

Keyword: universal

Annual Premium Rates* Per $1000 of Life Insurance

Age	Renewable Term	Whole Life	Universal Life	20-Pay Life
20	2.28	4.07	3.48	12.30
21	2.33	4.26	3.85	12.95
22	2.39	4.37	4.10	13.72
23	2.43	4.45	4.56	14.28
24	2.52	4.68	4.80	15.95
25	2.58	5.06	5.11	16.60
30	2.97	5.66	6.08	18.78
35	3.41	7.68	7.45	21.60
40	4.15	12.67	10.62	24.26
45	4.92	19.86	15.24	28.16
50		26.23	21.46	32.59
55		31.75	28.38	38.63
60		38.42	36.72	45.74

*For women, subtract 5 years from the actual age. For example, rates for a 30-year-old woman are shown for age 25 in the table.

The premium for a life insurance policy is found with the following formula.

Annual premium = Number of thousands × Rate per $1000

EXAMPLE 1
Finding the Life
Insurance
Premium

Brian Katavich, the owner of Round Table Pizza, is 35 years old and wants to buy a life insurance policy with a face value of $50,000. Use the annual premium rate table to find his annual premium for (a) a renewable term policy, (b) a whole life policy, (c) a universal life policy, and (d) a 20-pay life plan.

SOLUTION
Use the table and the formula. Since the table gives rates per $1000 of face value, first find how many thousands are in $50,000.

$$\$50,000 \div 1000 = \textbf{50 thousands}$$

Now find the rates from the table.

(a) The rate per $1000 for a 35-year-old male for a renewable term plan is **$3.41**. The annual premium is thus

$$\textbf{50} \times \textbf{\$3.41} = \$170.50.$$

(b) For a whole life policy, the rate is **$7.68** per $1000, for an annual premium of

$$\textbf{50} \times \textbf{\$7.68} = \$384.$$

This premium is higher than for renewable term insurance, since this type of insurance builds up cash values, and term insurance does not.

(c) The rate per $1000 for a universal life policy is **$7.45** for an annual premium of

$$\textbf{50} \times \textbf{\$7.45} = \$372.50.$$

(d) For a 20-pay life, the rate per $1000 is **$21.60**, for an annual premium of

$$\textbf{50} \times \textbf{\$21.60} = \$1080.$$

Katavich would pay $1080 annually for 20 years, at which time the plan would be paid up. He then would have insurance protection until retirement, with a retirement income thereafter.

NOTE Remember to subtract 5 years from the age of a female before using the table of premiums.

OBJECTIVE 4 Use premium factors with different modes of premium payment. The annual life insurance premium is not always paid in a single payment. Many companies give the insured the option of paying the premium semiannually, quarterly, or monthly. For this convenience, the policyholder pays an additional amount that is determined by a **premium factor**. The following table shows typical premium factors.

Premium Factors

Mode of Payment	Premium Factor
Semiannually	.51
Quarterly	.26
Monthly	.0908

EXAMPLE 2

Using a Premium Factor

The annual insurance premium on a whole life policy for Brian Katavich is $384. Use the premium factors table to find the amount of the premium and the total annual cost if he pays **(a)** semiannually, **(b)** quarterly, or **(c)** monthly.

Solution

(a) The semiannual premium factor is **.51**, so his premium would be

$$\$384 \times .51 = \$195.84.$$

The total annual cost is $391.68 ($195.84 × 2).

(b) Since the quarterly premium factor is **.26**, his quarterly premium would be

$$\$384 \times .26 = \$99.84.$$

The total annual cost is $399.36 ($99.84 × 4).

(c) The monthly premium factor is **.0908**, so the monthly premium would be

$$\$384 \times .0908 = \$34.87.$$

The total annual cost is $418.44 ($34.87 × 12).

For related Web
activities, go to
www.mathbusiness.com

'Net Assets

Round Table Pizza

STATISTICS

- 1959: First store
opens in Menlo Park,
California

- 1962: Round Table
Pizza is franchised

- 1979: Locations
total 150

- 1999: Over 530
locations

- 2000: 20 Round Table
Pizza locations in
Las Vegas

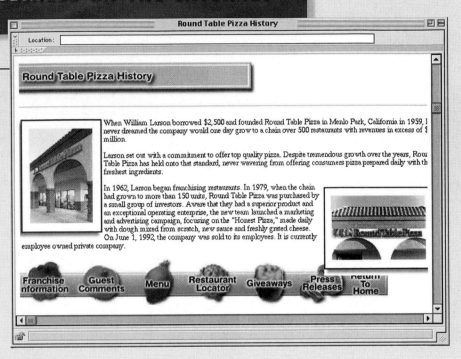

Round Table Pizza History

When William Larson borrowed $2,500 and founded Round Table Pizza in Menlo Park, California in 1959, l never dreamed the company would one day grow to a chain over 500 restaurants with revenues in excess of $ million.

Larson set out with a commitment to offer top quality pizza. Despite tremendous growth over the years, Rour Table Pizza has held onto that standard, never wavering from offering consumers pizza prepared daily with th freshest ingredients.

In 1962, Larson began franchising restaurants. In 1979, when the chain had grown to more than 150 units, Round Table Pizza was purchased by a small group of investors. Aware that they had a superior product and an exceptional operating enterprise, the new team launched a marketing and advertising campaign, focusing on the "Honest Pizza," made daily with dough mixed from scratch, new sauce and freshly grated cheese.
On June 1, 1992, the company was sold to its employees. It is currently employee owned private company.

Franchise Information | Guest Comments | Menu | Restaurant Locator | Giveaways | Press Releases | Return To Home

---

The first Round Table Pizza restaurant was opened in 1959 in Menlo Park, California. Starting with an old English theme and a $2500 loan, the Round Table system was being franchised just three years later. Today, Round Table is one of the nation's largest pizza chains, with more than 530 franchised and company-owned restaurants in the western United States. In addition, they have restaurants in Asia and the Middle East. Most restaurants offer delivery/carry-out service as well as dine-in service.

Round Table Pizza continues to stand out in the pizza marketplace by stressing high-quality, innovative products and ingredients, and by introducing at least two new products per year. Recent additions to their product line have been the Gourmet Sandwiches and Round Table Chicken Wings; however, the company maintains an unswerving commitment to the high quality of their pizza, and advertises itself as the restaurant serving The Last Honest Pizza.

1. A Round Table Pizza restaurant is on property with a fair market value of $476,000. The property is in an area that is assessed at 35% of market value. The property tax rate is $3.10 per $100. Find the property tax.

2. Brian Katavich, owner of a Round Table Pizza restaurant, has annual income of $68,730 from his business, $1586 in interest income, $862 in miscellaneous income, and $315 in dividend income. If Katavich has adjustments to income of $427, find his adjusted gross income.

3. Talk to the owner or manager of any fast-food or restaurant business. Ask which of the two business concerns, taxes or insurance, takes up more of their time as a businessperson.

4. When talking with a restaurant owner or manager, find out what the greatest challenges of their business are. List five major management responsibilities that are part of smoothly operating their business.

Name   Date   Class

12.5 | EXERCISES

The Quick Start exercises in each section contain solutions to help you get started.

Find the annual premium, the semiannual premium, the quarterly premium, and the monthly premium for each of the following. (Note: Subtract 5 years for women.)

Quick Start

	Face Value of Policy	Age of Insured	Sex of Insured	Type of Policy	Annual Premium	Semi-Annual Premium	Quarterly Premium	Monthly Premium
1.	$30,000	60	F	Whole life	$952.50	$485.78	$247.65	$86.49
	\multicolumn{8}{l}{30 × $31.75 = $952.50; $952.50 × .51 = $485.78; $952.50 × .26 = $247.65; $952.50 × .0908 = $86.49}							
2.	$60,000	30	M	Whole life	$339.60	$173.20	$88.30	$30.84
	\multicolumn{8}{l}{60 × $5.66 = $339.60; $339.60 × .51 = $173.20; $339.60 × .26 = $88.30; $339.60 × .0908 = $30.84}							
3.	$35,000	40	M	20-pay life	_____	_____	_____	_____
4.	$60,000	50	F	20-pay life	_____	_____	_____	_____
5.	$85,000	30	M	Universal life	_____	_____	_____	_____
6.	$150,000	45	F	Renewable term	_____	_____	_____	_____
7.	$75,000	21	M	Whole life	_____	_____	_____	_____
8.	$100,000	35	F	Renewable term	_____	_____	_____	_____
9.	$65,000	60	M	20-pay life	_____	_____	_____	_____
10.	$50,000	45	F	Universal life	_____	_____	_____	_____

11. Explain in your own words the advantages and disadvantages of buying renewable term life insurance. Would you buy renewable term life insurance for yourself? Why or why not? (See Objective 1.)

12. Describe premium factors and how they are used. How often do you prefer paying an insurance premium; annually, semiannually, quarterly, or monthly? (See Objective 4.)

Solve the following application problems.

Quick Start

13. WHOLE LIFE PREMIUM Mary Kaye Leonard buys a whole life policy at age 26. The policy has a face value of $70,000. Find the annual premium.

    $70 \times \$4.26 = \$298.20$

    13. $\underline{\$298.20}$

14. RENEWABLE TERM PREMIUM Bill Monroe buys a renewable term policy at age 25. The policy has a face value of $30,000. Find his annual premium.

    14. _____

15. EMPLOYEE LIFE INSURANCE Ozark Steel Foundary feels that it would suffer considerable hardship if the firm's head mold maker died suddenly. Therefore, the firm takes out a $90,000 policy on the mold maker's life. The mold maker is a 45-year-old woman, and the company buys a renewable term policy. Find the semiannual premium.

    15. _____

16. 20-PAY LIFE POLICY Luan Lee buys a $100,000, 20-pay life policy at age 45. Her son Bryan is the beneficiary, and will collect the face value of the policy. (a) Find the annual premium. (b) How much will Bryan get if his mother dies after making payments for 12 years?

    (a) _____
    (b) _____

17. WHOLE LIFE INSURANCE Find the total premium paid over 30 years for a whole life policy with a face value of $20,000. Assume the policy is taken out by a 25-year-old man.

    17. _____

18. UNIVERSAL LIFE INSURANCE Richard Gonsalves takes out a universal life policy with a face value of $50,000. He is 40 years old. Find the monthly premium.

    18. _____

19. PREMIUM FACTORS The annual premium for a whole life policy is $872. Using premium factors, find (a) the semiannual premium, (b) the quarterly premium, and (c) the monthly premium.

    (a) _____
    (b) _____
    (c) _____

20. A universal life policy has an annual premium of $2012. Use premium factors to find (a) the semiannual premium, (b) the quarterly premium, and (c) the monthly premium.

    (a) _____
    (b) _____
    (c) _____

CHAPTER 12 | Quick Review

CHAPTER 12 QUICK REVIEW   **529**

CHAPTER TERMS

Review the following terms to test your understanding of the chapter. For each term you do not know, refer to the page number found next to that term.

1099 forms [**p. 494**]
actuaries [**p. 513**]
adjusted gross income [**p. 494**]
adult operator [**p. 517**]
assessed valuation [**p. 488**]
bodily injury coverage [**p. 513**]
cash value [**p. 522**]
coinsurance clause [**p. 506**]
collision insurance [**p. 515**]
comprehensive insurance [**p. 515**]
contributions [**p. 496**]
decreasing term insurance [**p. 521**]
deductible [**p. 515**]
dollars per $100 [**p. 489**]

dollars per $1000 [**p. 489**]
endowment policies [**p. 523**]
face value [**p. 505**]
fair market value [**p. 488**]
Form 1040A [**p. 497**]
homeowner's policy [**p. 508**]
Individual Retirement Account (IRA) [**p. 495**]
interest [**p. 496**]
liability coverage [**p. 508**]
limited-payment life insurance [**p. 523**]
medical and dental expenses [**p. 496**]
medical insurance [**p. 514**]
mills [**p. 489**]

miscellaneous deductions [**p. 496**]
multiple carriers [**p. 507**]
no-fault insurance [**p. 516**]
ordinary life insurance [**p. 522**]
personal exemptions [**p. 495**]
policy [**p. 505**]
premium [**pp. 505, 513**]
premium factor [**p. 524**]
property damage insurance [**p. 514**]
property tax rate [**p. 489**]
Schedule 1 (Form 1040) [**p. 497**]
standard deduction [**p. 495**]
straight life insurance [**p. 522**]

tax deduction [**p. 496**]
taxable income [**p. 495**]
taxes [**p. 496**]
term insurance [**p. 521**]
territorial ratings [**p. 505**]
underinsured motorist insurance [**p. 516**]
underwriters [**p. 505**]
uninsured motorist insurance [**p. 516**]
universal life policy [**p. 522**]
variable life policy [**p. 522**]
W-2 forms [**p. 494**]
whole life insurance [**p. 522**]
worker's compensation [**p. 508**]
youthful operator [**p. 517**]

CONCEPTS	EXAMPLES
12.1 Fair market value and assessed valuation The value of property is multiplied by a given percent to arrive at the assessed valuation. **Assessment Rate** × Market value = Assessed valuation	The assessment rate is 30%; fair market value is $115,000; find the assessed valuation. $$30\% \times \$115{,}000 = \$34{,}500$$
12.1 Tax rate The tax rate formula is $$\text{Tax rate} = \frac{\text{Total tax amount needed}}{\text{Total assessed value}}$$	Tax amount needed, $81,888; total assessed value, $1,023,600; find the tax rate. $$\frac{81{,}888}{1{,}023{,}600} = .08 = 8\%$$
12.1 Expressing tax rates in different forms and finding tax 1. **Percent**: multiply by assessed valuation. 2. **Dollars per $100**: move decimal 2 places to left in assessed valuation and multiply. 3. **Dollars per $1000**: move decimal 3 places to left in assessed valuation and multiply. 4. **Mills**: move decimal 3 places to the left in rate and multiply by assessed valuation. Use the formula Property tax = Assessed valuation × **Tax rate**	Assessed value, $90,000; tax rate, 2.5% $$\$90{,}000 \times 2.5\% = \$2250$$ Tax rate, **$2.50** per $100 $$900 \times \$2.50 = \$2250$$ Tax rate, **$25** per $1000 $$90 \times \$25 = \$2250$$ Tax rate, 25 mills $$\$90{,}000 \times \$.025 = \$2250$$
12.2 Adjusted gross income Adjusted gross income includes wages, salaries, tips, dividends, and interest. Subtract IRA contributions and alimony.	Salary, $32,540; interest income, $875; dividends, $315; find adjusted gross income. $$\$32{,}540 + \$875 + \$315 = \$33{,}730$$

CONCEPTS	EXAMPLES
12.2 Standard deduction amounts The majority of taxpayers use the standard deduction allowed by the IRS.	**$4150** for single people **$6900** for married people filing jointly **$3450** for married people filing separately **$6050** for head of household
12.2 Taxable income The larger of either the total of itemized deductions or the standard deduction is subtracted from adjusted gross income along with **$2650** for each personal exemption.	Adjusted gross income, $28,200; single taxpayer; itemized deductions total $3440; find taxable income. Standard deduction is $4150; larger than $3440 itemized deduction. Taxable income $= \$28,200 - \$4150 - \$2650$ $= \$21,400$
12.2 Tax rates There are five tax rates, 15%, 28%, 31%, 36%, and 39.6%.	Single 15%; over $24,650, 28%; over $59,750, 31%; over $124,650, 36%; over $271,050, 39.6%. Married filing jointly or qualifying widow(er)s 15%; over $41,200, 28%; over $99,600, 31%; over $151,750, 36%; over $271,050, 39.6%. Married filing separately 15%; over $20,600, 28%; over $49,800, 31%; over $75,875, 36%; over $135,525, 39.6%. Head of household 15%; over $33,050, 28%; over $85,350, 31%; over $138,200, 36%; over $271,050, 39.6%.
12.2 Balance due or a refund from the IRS If the total amount withheld by employers is greater than the tax owed, a refund results. If the tax owed is the greater amount, a balance is due.	Tax owed, $1253; tax withheld, $113 per month for 12 months. Find balance due or refund. $\$113 \text{ withheld} \times 12 = \$1356 \text{ withheld}$ $\$1356 \text{ withheld} - \$1253 \text{ owed} = \$103 \text{ refund}$
12.3 Annual premium for fire insurance The building and territorial ratings are used to find the premiums per $100 for the building and contents. The two are added.	Building value, $80,000; contents, $35,000. Premiums are: building, $.75 per $100; contents, $.77 per $100. Find the annual premium. Building: 800 (hundreds) × $.75 = $600 Contents: 350 (hundreds) × $.77 = $269.50 Total premium: $600 + $269.50 = $869.50
12.3 Coinsurance formula Part of the risk of fire is taken by the insured. An 80% coinsurance clause is common. $\text{Loss paid by insurance company} = \text{Amount of loss} \times \dfrac{\text{Policy amount}}{80\% \text{ of market value}}$	Building value, $125,000; policy amount, $75,000; fire loss, $40,000; 80% coinsurance clause; find the amount of loss paid by insurance company. $\$40,000 \times \dfrac{\$75,000}{\$100,000} = \$30,000$ (amount insurance company pays)

CONCEPTS	EXAMPLES
12.3 Multiple carriers Several companies insuring the same property, which limits the risk of the insurance company, with each paying its fractional portion of any claim.	Insured loss, $500,000 Insurance is Company A with $1,000,000; Company B with $750,000; Company C with $250,000; find the amount of loss paid by each company. Total insurance $= \$1,000,000 + \$750,000 + \$250,000 = \$2,000,000$ Company A $$\frac{1,000,000}{2,000,000} \times \$500,000 = \$250,000$$ Company B $$\frac{750,000}{2,000,000} \times \$500,000 = \$187,500$$ Company C $$\frac{250,000}{2,000,000} \times \$500,000 = \$62,500$$
12.4 Annual auto insurance premium Most drivers are legally required to purchase automobile insurance. The premium is determined by the types of coverage selected, the type of car, geographic territory, past driving record, and other factors.	Determine the premium: territory, 2; liability, 50/100; property damage, $50,000; comprehensive and collision, 3-year-old car with a symbol of 8; uninsured motorist coverage; driver is age 23 with driver's training. $\begin{array}{ll} \$168 & \text{liability} \\ 76 & \text{property damage} \\ 36 & \text{comprehensive} \\ 98 & \text{collision} \\ \underline{44} & \text{uninsured motorist} \\ \$422 \times \mathbf{1.15} & \text{youthful operator factor} \\ = \$485.30 \end{array}$
12.5 Annual life insurance premium There are several types of life policies. Use the table and multiply by the number of $1000s of coverage. Subtract 5 years from the age of females. Premium = Number of thousands × **Rate per $1000**	Find the premiums on a $50,000 policy for a 30-year-old male. **(a)** renewable term $$50 \times \mathbf{\$2.97} = \$148.50$$ **(b)** whole life $$50 \times \mathbf{\$5.66} = \$283$$ **(c)** universal life $$50 \times \mathbf{\$6.08} = \$304$$ **(d)** 20-pay life $$50 \times \mathbf{\$18.78} = \$939$$
12.5 Premium factors Life insurance premiums may be paid semiannually, quarterly, or monthly. The annual premium is multiplied by the premium factor to determine the premium amount.	The annual life insurance premium is $740. Use the table to find the **(a)** semiannual, **(b)** quarterly, and **(c)** monthly premium. **(a)** Semiannual $$\$740 \times \mathbf{.51} = \$377.40$$ **(b)** Quarterly $$\$740 \times \mathbf{.26} = \$192.40$$ **(c)** Monthly $$\$740 \times \mathbf{.0908} = \$67.19$$

CHAPTER 12 | SUMMARY EXERCISE

FINANCIAL PLANNING FOR TAXES AND INSURANCE

Childcare Playground Toys imports parts from Thailand and Malaysia and assembles quality-built playground equipment and riding toys. Planning ahead, the company set aside $53,500 to pay property taxes and fire insurance premiums on the company property and a semiannual life insurance premium for the company president, which are due in the same month. Find each of the following.

(a) The company property has a fair market value of $1,990,000 and is assessed at 75% of this value. If the tax rate is $7.90 per $1000 of assessed value, find the annual property tax.

(a) _____

(b) The building occupied by the company is a class-B building worth $1,730,000. The contents are worth $3,502,000 and the territorial rating is 4. Find the annual fire insurance premium.

(b) _____

(c) The president of Childcare Playground Toys is a 45-year-old woman and the company is buying a $175,000 renewable term life insurance policy on the president's life. Find the semiannual premium.

(c) _____

(d) Find the total amount needed to pay property taxes, the fire insurance premium, and the semiannual life insurance premium.

(d) _____

(e) How much more than the amount needed had the company set aside to pay these expenses?

(e) _____

Investigate

According to a recent article in *Consumer Reports*, there are over 30 World Wide Web sites that offer to help a person shop for term life insurance. The article also lists dial-up services which offer a similar service. Use the World Wide Web to find information and prices for term life insurance to meet your personal life insurance needs.

Name   Date   Class

CHAPTER 12 | TEST

To help you review, the numbers in brackets show the section in which the topic was discussed.

Complete the following chart comparing property tax rates.   **[12.1]**

	Percent	Per $100	Per $1000
1.	5.76%	_____	$57.60
2.	_____	$9.35	$93.50

Find the taxable income and the tax for each of the following people. The letter following the names indicates the marital status.   **[12.2]**

Name	Number of Exemptions	Adjusted Gross Income	Total Deductions	Taxable Income	Tax
3. J. Spalding, S	2	$38,295	$3648	_____	_____
4. The Sparks, M	4	$43,487	$5178	_____	_____

Find the tax owed in the following problems.

5. Bradkin's Toggery owns property with a fair market value of $104,600. Property in the area is assessed at 30% of fair market value with a tax rate of 3.65%. Find the annual tax.   **[12.1]**

5. _____

6. The Todds, married and filing a joint return, have an adjusted gross income of $62,316, five exemptions, and deductions of $4632.   **[12.2]**

6. _____

7. Kari Heen had an adjusted gross income of $35,810 last year. She had deductions of $807 for state income tax, $729 for property tax, $1263 in mortgage interst, and $186 in contributions. Heen claims one exemption and files as a single person.   **[12.2]**

7. _____

Find the annual fire insurance premium for the following. Use the table on page 505.   **[12.3]**

8. Southside Plating owns a class-B building worth $147,000. Contents are valued at $83,500. The territorial rating is 5.

8. _____

9. Foxworthy's warehouse is valued at $220,000. Their fire insurance policy (with an 80% coinsurance clause) has a face value of $150,000. If the building has a fire loss of $50,000, find the amount of the loss that the insurance company will pay.

9. _____

10. Dave's Body and Paint has an insurable loss of $72,000, while having insurance coverage beyond coinsurance requirement. The insurance is divided between Company A with $250,000 coverage, Company B with $150,000 coverage, and Company C with $100,000 coverage. Find the amount of loss paid by each of the insurance companies.

A: _____
B: _____
C: _____

Find the annual motor-vehicle insurance premium for the following people. **[12.4]**

Name	Territory	Age	Driver Training	Liability	Property Damage	Comprehensive Collision Age Group	Symbol	Uninsured Motorist	Annual Premium
11. Ramos	3	18	Yes	15/30	$10,000	5	7	Yes	_____
12. Larik	1	42	—	50/100	100,000	1	8	Yes	_____

Find the annual premium, the semiannual premium, the quarterly premium, and the monthly premium for each of the following life insurance policies. Use the tables in Section 12.5.

	Annual	Semiannual	Quarterly	Monthly
13. Irene Chong, whole life, $28,000 face value, age 35	_____	_____	_____	_____
14. Gil Eckern, 20-pay life, $80,000 face value, age 40	_____	_____	_____	_____

CHAPTER 13

DEPRECIATION

Village Nursery and Landscaping is owned and managed by Julie Maxi. In addition to office equipment and store fixtures, the company owns several trucks and trailers, one forklift, and various other pieces of landscaping machinery.

Business expenses such as salaries, rent, and utilities must be subtracted from company revenues to determine net income. Other expenses including the cost of machinery, buildings, and fixtures are not subtracted all at once. The cost of these purchases, known as assets, must be spread over a number of years using a method called **depreciation**.

Physical assets such as machinery, cars, or computers are **tangible assets**. Assets such as patents and copyrights, franchise fees, or customer lists are **intangible assets**. In general, either type of asset may be depreciated, as long as its useful life can be determined.

The key terms in depreciation are summarized below.

Cost, the basis for determining depreciation, is the total amount paid for the asset.

Useful life is the period of time during which the asset will be used. The Internal Revenue Service has guidelines for estimating the life of an asset used in a particular trade or business. However, useful life depends on the use of the asset, the repair policy, the replacement policy, obsolescence, and other factors.

Salvage value or **scrap value** (sometimes called **residual value**) is the estimated value of an asset when it is retired from service, traded in, disposed of, or exhausted. An asset may have a salvage value of zero, or **no salvage value**.

Accumulated depreciation is the amount of depreciation taken so far, a running balance of depreciation to date.

Book value is the cost of an asset minus the total depreciation to date. The book value at the end of an asset's life is equal to the salvage value. The book value can never be less than the salvage value.

Over the years, several methods of computing depreciation have been used, including **straight-line**, **declining-balance**, **sum-of-the-years'-digits**, and **units-of-production**. These

Department
of the
Treasury

**Internal
Revenue
Service**

Publication 534
Cat. No. 15064O

Depreciation

methods are used in keeping company accounting records and, in many states, preparing state income tax returns. Items purchased after 1981 are depreciated for federal income tax returns with the accelerated cost recovery system or the modified accelerated cost recovery system, discussed later. The use of depreciation for federal income tax purposes is detailed in an Internal Revenue Service publication. The complete title of this publication is shown at the side.

A company need not use the same method of depreciation for all of its various assets. For example, the straight-line method of depreciation might be used on some assets and the declining-balance method on others. Furthermore, the depreciation method used in preparing a company's financial statement may be different from the method used in preparing income tax returns.

13.1 | Depreciation: Straight-Line Method

Objectives

1 Use the straight-line method of depreciation to find the amount of depreciation each year.

2 Use the straight-line method to find the book value of an asset.

3 Use the straight-line method to prepare a depreciation schedule.

**Problem Solving
in Business**

Julie Maxi and her accountant decide on which method of depreciation is to be used for the depreciable assets of Village Nursery and Landscaping. The most commonly used method for both accounting and tax purposes is the straight-line method of depreciation.

Objective 1 Use the straight-line method of depreciation to find the amount of depreciation each year. The simplest method of depreciation, straight-line depreciation, assumes that assets lose an equal amount of value during each year of life. For example, suppose a heavy equipment trailer is purchased by Village Nursery and Landscaping at a cost of $9400. The trailer has an estimated useful life of 8 years, and a salvage value of $1400. Find the amount to be depreciated (**depreciable amount**) using the following formula.

$$\text{Amount to be depreciated} = \text{Cost} - \text{Salvage value}$$

Here, the amount to be depreciated over the 8-year period is:

$$\begin{array}{ll} \$9400 & \text{cost} \\ \underline{-\$1400} & \text{salvage value} \\ \$8000 & \text{amount to be depreciated} \end{array}$$

With the straight-line method, an equal amount of depreciation is taken each year over the 8-year life of the trailer. The annual depreciation for this trailer is

$$\text{Depreciation} = \frac{\text{Amount to be depreciated}}{\text{Years of life}} = \frac{\$8000}{8} = \$1000$$

Each year during the 8-year life of the trailer, the annual depreciation will be $1000, or $\frac{1}{8}$ of the depreciable amount. The annual rate of depreciation is $12\frac{1}{2}\%$ ($\frac{1}{8} = 12\frac{1}{2}\%$).

OBJECTIVE **2** **Use the straight-line method to find the book value of an asset.** The book value, or remaining value, of an asset at the end of a year is the original cost minus the depreciation up to and including that year (accumulated depreciation). With the trailer, the book value at the end of the first year is $8400.

$$\begin{array}{rl}
\$9400 & \text{cost} \\
-\,\$1000 & \text{first year's depreciation} \\
\hline
\$8400 & \text{book value at end of the first year}
\end{array}$$

Book value is found with the following formula.

> Book value = Cost − Accumulated depreciation

EXAMPLE 1

Finding First Year
Depreciation and
Book Value

Dependable Insurance Company purchased a high-end personal computer at a cost of $2650. The estimated life of the computer is 5 years, with a salvage value of $350. Find **(a)** the annual rate of depreciation, **(b)** the annual amount of depreciation, and **(c)** the book value at the end of the first year.

SOLUTION

(a) The annual rate of depreciation is 20% (5-year life = $\frac{1}{5}$ per year = **20%**).

(b)
$$\begin{array}{rl}
\$2650 & \text{cost} \\
-\,\$350 & \textbf{salvage value} \\
\hline
\$2300 & \text{depreciable amount}
\end{array}$$

This $2300 will be depreciated evenly over the 5-year life for an annual depreciation of $460 ($2300 × 20% = $460).

(c) Since the annual depreciation is $460, the book value at the end of the first year will be

$$\begin{array}{rl}
\$2650 & \text{cost} \\
-\,\$460 & \textbf{depreciation in the first year} \\
\hline
\$2190 & \text{book value at the end of the first year}
\end{array}$$

To solve this example using a calculator, first use parentheses to find the depreciable amount. Next, divide to find depreciation. Finally, find the book value.

$$\boxed{(}\ 2650\ \boxed{-}\ 350\ \boxed{)}\ \boxed{\div}\ 5\ \boxed{=}\ 460$$

$$2650\ \boxed{-}\ 460\ \boxed{=}\ 2190$$

Note: All calculator solutions use a scientific calculator. Refer to Appendix B for scientific calculator basics.

If an asset is expected to have **no salvage value** at the end of its expected life, then the entire cost will be depreciated over its life. In Example 1, if the personal computer had been expected to have no salvage value at the end of 5 years, the annual amount of depreciation would have been $530 ($2650 × 20% = $530).

> **NOTE** Find the book value at the end of any year by multiplying the annual amount of straight-line depreciation by the number of years and subtracting this result, the depreciation to date, from the cost.

EXAMPLE 2

Finding the Book Value at the End of Any Year

A lighted display case at Macy's cost $3400 and has an estimated life of 10 years and a salvage value of $800. Find the book value at the end of 6 years.

SOLUTION

The annual rate of depreciation is 10% (10-year life leads to $\frac{1}{10}$ or 10%).

$$\begin{array}{ll} \$3400 & \text{cost} \\ - \ \underline{\$800} & \text{salvage value} \\ \$2600 & \text{depreciable amount} \end{array}$$

Since $2600 is depreciated evenly over the 10-year life of the case, the annual depreciation is $260 (**$2600 × 10% = $260**).

The accumulated depreciation over the 6-year period is

$$\$260 \times \textbf{6 years} = \$1560 \text{ accumulated depreciation (6 years)}$$

Find the book value at the end of 6 years by subtracting the accumulated depreciation from the cost.

$$\begin{array}{ll} \$3400 & \text{cost} \\ - \ \underline{\$1560} & \textbf{accumulated depreciation (6 years)} \\ \$1840 & \text{book value at the end of 6 years} \end{array}$$

For related Web activities, go to www.mathbusiness.com

Keyword: depreciation

After 6 years, this display case would be carried "on the books" with a value of $1840.

NOTE   The book value helps the owner of a business estimate the value of the business, which is important when the owner is borrowing money or trying to sell the business.

OBJECTIVE ③ **Use the straight-line method to prepare a depreciation schedule.** A **depreciation schedule** is often used to show the annual depreciation, accumulated depreciation, and book value over the useful life of an asset. As an aid in comparing three of the methods of depreciation discussed in the text, the depreciation schedule of Example 3 and the schedule shown in the double-declining-balance (see Section 13.2) and sum-of-the-years'-digits methods (see Section 13.3) use the same asset.

EXAMPLE 3

Preparing a Depreciation Schedule

Village Nursery and Landscaping bought a new pickup truck for $18,500. It is estimated that the truck will have a useful life of 5 years, at which time it will have a salvage value (trade-in value) of $3500. Prepare a depreciation schedule using the straight-line method of depreciation.

SOLUTION

The annual rate of depreciation is 20% (5-year life $= \frac{1}{5}$ **per year = 20%**). Find the depreciable amount as follows.

$$\begin{array}{ll} \$18,500 & \text{cost} \\ - \ \underline{\$3,500} & \text{salvage value} \\ \$15,000 & \text{depreciable amount} \end{array}$$

This $15,000 will be depreciated evenly over the 5-year life for an annual depreciation of $3000 ($15,000 × **20% = $3000**).

This depreciation schedule includes a year zero to show the initial purchase of the truck.

Year	Computation	Amount of Depreciation	Accumulated Depreciation	Book Value
0	——	——	——	$18,500
1	(20% × $15,000)	$3000	$3000	$15,500
2	(20% × $15,000)	$3000	$6000	$12,500
3	(20% × $15,000)	$3000	$9000	$9500
4	(20% × $15,000)	$3000	$12,000	$6500
5	(20% × $15,000)	$3000	$15,000	$3500

The depreciation is $3000 each year, the accumulated depreciation at the end of 5 years is equal to the depreciable amount, and the book value at the end of 5 years is equal to the salvage value.

PROBLEM-SOLVING HINT If the rate is a repeating decimal, use the fraction that is equivalent to the decimal. Instead of 33.3%, use the fraction $\frac{1}{3}$; instead of 16.7%, use the fraction $\frac{1}{6}$.

Name   Date   Class

13.1 | EXERCISES

The Quick Start *exercises in each section contain solutions to help you get started.*

Find the annual straight-line rate of depreciation, given the following estimated lives. (See Example 1.)

Quick Start

	Life	Annual Rate		Life	Annual Rate
1.	5 years	**20%**	**2.**	4 years	**25%**
	$\frac{1}{5} = 20\%$			$\frac{1}{4} = 25\%$	
3.	8 years	_____	**4.**	10 years	_____
5.	20 years	_____	**6.**	25 years	_____
7.	15 years	_____	**8.**	30 years	_____
9.	80 years	_____	**10.**	40 years	_____
11.	50 years	_____	**12.**	100 years	_____

Find the annual amount of depreciation for the following, using the straight-line method. (See Examples 1 and 2.)

Quick Start

13.	Cost:	$9000	**14.**	Cost:	$3400
	Estimated life:	20 years		Estimated life:	4 years
	Estimated scrap value:	None		Estimated scrap value:	$800
	Annual depreciation:	**$450**		Annual depreciation:	**$650**

$9000 × 5% = $450

$3400 − $800 = $2600
$2600 × 25% = $650

15.	Cost:	$2700	**16.**	Cost:	$8100
	Estimated life:	3 years		Estimated life:	6 years
	Estimated scrap value:	$300		Estimated scrap value:	$750
	Annual depreciation:	_____		Annual depreciation:	_____

17.	Cost:	$4200	**18.**	Cost:	$12,200
	Estimated life:	5 years		Estimated life:	10 years
	Estimated scrap value:	None		Estimated scrap value:	$3200
	Annual depreciation:	_____		Annual depreciation:	_____

Find the book value at the end of the first year for the following, using the straight-line method. (See Examples 1 and 2.)

Quick Start

19. Cost: $3200
  Estimated life: 8 years
  Estimated scrap value: $400
  Book value: **$2850**

  $3200 − $400 = $2800
  $2800 × 12.5% = $350
  $3200 − $350 = $2850

20. Cost: $35,000
  Estimated life: 10 years
  Estimated scrap value: $2500
  Book value: _____

21. Cost: $5400
  Estimated life: 12 years
  Estimated scrap value: $600
  Book value: _____

22. Cost: $4500
  Estimated life: 5 years
  Estimated scrap value: None
  Book value: _____

Find the book value at the end of 5 years for the following, using the straight-line method. (See Examples 1 and 2.)

Quick Start

23. Cost: $4800
  Estimated life: 10 years
  Estimated scrap value: $750
  Book Value: **$2775**

  $4800 − $750 = $4050
  $4050 × 10% = $405
  $405 × 5 = $2025
  $4800 − $2025 = $2775

24. Cost: $16,000
  Estimated life: 20 years
  Estimated scrap value: $2000
  Book value: _____

25. Cost: $80,000
  Estimated life: 50 years
  Estimated scrap value: $10,000
  Book value: _____

26. Cost: $660
  Estimated life: 8 years
  Estimated scrap value: $100
  Book value: _____

Solve the following application problems.

Quick Start

27. **DEPRECIATING INDUSTRIAL TOOLS** Dallas Tool and Diecasting Company selects the straight-line method of depreciation for a lathe costing $12,000 and having a 3-year life and an expected scrap value of $3000. Prepare a depreciation schedule.

Year	Computation	Amount of Depreciation	Accumulated Depreciation	Book Value
0	—	—	—	$12,000
1	$(33\frac{1}{3}\% \times \$9000)$	$3000	$3000	$9000
2	$(33\frac{1}{3}\% \times \$9000)$	$3000	$6000	$6000
3	$(33\frac{1}{3}\% \times \$9000)$	$3000	$9000	$3000

Name   Date   Class

28. LABORATORY EQUIPMENT Savannah Pipe has purchased a laboratory crusher costing $18,000, having an estimated life of 4 years and a salvage value of $1600. Prepare a depreciation schedule using the straight-line method of depreciation.

Year	Computation	Amount of Depreciation	Accumulated Depreciation	Book Value
0	—	—	—	$18,000
1	25%	4100.00	4100.00	13,900
2	"	4100.00	8200.00	9,800
3	"	4100.00	12300.00	5700
4	"	4100.00	16400.00	1600

29. VEHICLE DEPRECIATION Village Nursery and Landscaping paid $25,600 for a $1\frac{1}{2}$-ton, dual-axle flatbed truck with an estimated life of 6 years and a salvage value of $7000. Prepare a depreciation schedule using the straight-line method of depreciation.

Year	Computation	Amount of Depreciation	Accumulated Depreciation	Book Value
0	—	—	—	$25,600
1	$16\frac{2}{3}\%$			
2	$16\frac{2}{3}\%$			
3	$16\frac{2}{3}\%$			
4	$16\frac{2}{3}\%$			
5	$16\frac{2}{3}\%$			
6	$16\frac{2}{3}\%$			

30. BUSINESS FIXTURES Dorothy Sargent buys fixtures for her shop at a cost of $7800 and estimates the life of the fixtures as 10 years, after which they will have no salvage value. Prepare a depreciation schedule, calculating depreciation by the straight-line method.

Year	Computation	Amount of Depreciation	Accumulated Depreciation	Book Value
0	—	—	—	$7800
1				
2				
3				
4				
5				
6				
7				
8				
9				
10				

31. Develop a single formula that will show how to find annual depreciation using the straight-line method of depreciation. (See Objective 1.)

32. Explain the procedure used to calculate depreciation when there is no salvage value. Why will the book value always be zero at the end of the asset's life?

33. BARGE DEPRECIATION   A Dutch petroleum company purchased a barge for $1,300,000. The estimated life is 20 years, at which time it will have a salvage value of $200,000. Find **(a)** the annual amount of depreciation using the straight-line method and **(b)** the book value at the end of 5 years.

(a) _____

(b) _____

34. DEPRECIATING COMPUTER EQUIPMENT   The new computer equipment at Leisure Travel has a cost of $14,500, an estimated life of 8 years, and scrap value of $2100. Find **(a)** the annual depreciation and **(b)** the book value at the end of 4 years using the straight-line method of depreciation.

(a) _____

(b) _____

35. BOAT-RAMP DEPRECIATION   A freshwater boat ramp has an estimated life of 15 years and no scrap value. If the boat ramp cost $37,900 and the straight-line method is used, find **(a)** the annual depreciation and **(b)** the book value after 7 years. (Round depreciation to the nearest dollar.)

(a) _____

(b) _____

36. BAKERY PACKAGING EQUIPMENT   The packaging equipment line at Rainbow Bakery has a cost of $132,400, an estimated life of 10 years, and a salvage value of $35,000. Find the book value of the packaging equipment line after 8 years using the straight-line method of depreciation.

36. _____

13.2 | DEPRECIATION: DECLINING-BALANCE METHOD

Objectives

1. Describe the declining-balance method of depreciation.
2. Find the double-declining-balance rate.
3. Use the double-declining-balance method to find the amount of depreciation and the book value for each year.
4. Use the double-declining-balance method to prepare a depreciation schedule.

PROBLEM SOLVING IN BUSINESS

Straight-line depreciation assumes that an asset loses an equal amount of value each year of its life. This is not realistic for most of the machinery and equipment owned by Village Nursery and Landscaping. For example, a new tractor loses much more value during its first year of life than during its fifth year of life.

OBJECTIVE 1 Describe the declining-balance method of depreciation. Methods of **accelerated depreciation** are used to more accurately reflect the rate at which assets actually lose value. One of the more common accelerated methods of depreciation is the double-declining-balance method or **200% method**; with this method the **double-declining-balance rate** is first established. This rate is multiplied by last year's book value to get this year's depreciation. Since the book value declines from year to year, the annual depreciation also declines, giving the origin of the name of this method.

OBJECTIVE 2 Find the double-declining-balance rate. Calculate depreciation, using the double-declining-balance method, by first finding the straight-line rate of depreciation. Then adjust the straight-line rate to the desired declining-balance rate of 200% of the straight-line rate.

EXAMPLE 1
Finding the 200% Declining-Balance Rate

Find the straight-line rate and the double-declining-balance (200%) rate for each of the following years of life.

Solution

Years of Life	Straight-Line Rate	Double-Declining-Balance Rate
3	33.33% ($\frac{1}{3}$)	66.67% ($\frac{2}{3}$)
4	25%	50%
5	20%	40%
8	12.5%	25%
10	10%	20%
20	5%	10%
25	4%	8%
50	2%	4%

NOTE Throughout the remainder of this chapter, money amounts will be rounded to the nearest dollar, the common practice with depreciation.

OBJECTIVE 3 Use the double-declining-balance method to find the amount of depreciation and the book value for each year. Use the following formula and multiply the double-declining-balance rate by the declining balance (this is the total cost in the first year and the previous year's book value in following years) to find the amount of depreciation in that year.

Depreciation = Double-declining-balance rate × Declining balance

EXAMPLE 2

Finding Depreciation and Book Value Using Double-Declining-Balance

Village Nursery and Landscaping purchased a portable storage building for $8100. It is expected to have a life of 10 years, at which time it will have no salvage value. Using the double-declining-balance method of depreciation, find the first and second years' depreciation and the book value at the end of the first and second year.

SOLUTION

The straight-line depreciation rate for a 10-year life is 10%. The double-declining-balance rate is 10% times 2, or 20%. The first year's depreciation is 20% of the declining balance or, in the first year, 20% of the cost.

$$20\% \times \$8100 \text{ (cost)} = \$1620 \text{ depreciation in the first year}$$

The book value at the end of the first year is

$$
\begin{array}{ll}
\$8100 & \text{cost} \\
-\,\$1620 & \text{depreciation to date} \\
\hline
\$6480 & \text{book value at the end of the first year}
\end{array}
$$

The second year's depreciation rate is 20% of $6480 (last year's book value or declining balance) or

$$20\% \times \$6480 \text{ (declining balance)} = \$1296 \text{ depreciation in second year.}$$

The book value at the end of the second year is $8100 − **$2916 ($1620 + $1296 = $2916)** = $5184.

For related Web activities, go to www.mathbusiness.com

Keyword: valued

> **NOTE** *Never* subtract the salvage value from the cost when calculating depreciation using the double-declining-balance method.

OBJECTIVE 4 Use the double-declining-balance method to prepare a depreciation schedule. The next example shows a depreciation schedule for the pickup truck discussed in Example 3 of Section 13.1. As this example shows, the same rate is used each year with the declining-balance method, and the rate is multiplied by the declining balance (last year's book value). Also, the amount of depreciation in a given year may have to be adjusted so that book value is never less than salvage value.

EXAMPLE 3

Preparing a Depreciation Schedule

Village Nursery and Landscaping bought a new pickup truck at a cost of $18,500. It is estimated that the truck will have a useful life of 5 years, at which time it will have a salvage value (trade-in value) of $3500. Prepare a depreciation schedule using the double-declining-balance method of depreciation.

SOLUTION

The annual rate of depreciation is 40% (**20% straight-line × 2 = 40%**). Do not subtract salvage value from cost before calculating depreciation. In year 1, the full cost is used to calculate depreciation.

Year	Computation	Amount of Depreciation	Accumulated Depreciation	Book Value
0	—	—	—	$18,500
1	(40% × $18,500)	$7400	$7400	$11,100
2	(40% × $11,100)	$4440	$11,840	$6660
3	(40% × $6660)	$2664	$14,504	$3996
4		$496*	$15,000	$3500
5		$0	$15,000	$3500

> ***NOTE** In year 4 of the preceding table, 40% of $3996 is $1598. If this amount were subtracted from $3996, the book value would drop below the salvage value of $3500. Since book value may never be less than salvage value, depreciation of $496 is taken in year 4, so that book value equals salvage value. No further depreciation remains for year 5. The total amount of depreciation taken over the life of the asset is the same using either the straight-line or the double-declining-balance method of depreciation.

Name   Date   Class

13.2 | Exercises

The Quick Start *exercises in each section contain solutions to help you get started.*

Find the annual double-declining-balance (200% method) rate of depreciation, given the following estimated lives. (See Example 1.)

Quick Start

Life	Annual Rate	Life	Annual Rate
1. 5 years	<u>40%</u>	**2.** 20 years	<u>10%</u>
20% × 2 = 40%		5% × 2 = 10%	
3. 8 years	_____	**4.** 25 years	_____
5. 15 years	_____	**6.** 4 years	_____
7. 10 years	_____	**8.** 30 years	_____
9. 6 years	_____	**10.** 40 years	_____
11. 50 years	_____	**12.** 100 years	_____

Find the first year's depreciation for the following, using the double-declining-balance method of depreciation. (See Example 2.)

Quick Start

13. Cost:	$18,000	**14.** Cost:	$4950
Estimated life:	10 years	Estimated life:	20 years
Estimated scrap value:	$3000	Estimated scrap value:	None
Depreciation (year 1):	<u>**$3600**</u>	Depreciation (year 1):	<u>**$495**</u>
$18,000 × 20% = $3600		$4950 × 10% = $495	

15. Cost:	$10,500	**16.** Cost:	$38,000
Estimated life:	5 years	Estimated life:	40 years
Estimated scrap value:	$500	Estimated scrap value:	$5000
Depreciation (year 1):	_____	Depreciation (year 1):	_____

17. Cost:	$3800	**18.** Cost:	$1140
Estimated life:	4 years	Estimated life:	6 years
Estimated scrap value:	None	Estimated scrap value:	$350
Depreciation (year 1):	_____	Depreciation (year 1):	_____

Find the book value at the end of the first year for the following, using the double-declining-balance method of depreciation. Round to the nearest dollar. (See Examples 1 and 2.)

Quick Start

19. Cost: $4200
   Estimated life: 10 years
   Estimated scrap value: $1000
   Book value: <u>**$3360**</u>

   $4200 × 20% = $840
   $4200 − $840 = $3360 book value

20. Cost: $2500
   Estimated life: 6 years
   Estimated scrap value: $400
   Book value: _____

21. Cost: $1620
   Estimated life: 8 years
   Estimated scrap value: None
   Book value: _____

22. Cost: $5640
   Estimated life: 5 years
   Estimated scrap value: $800
   Book value: _____

Find the book value at the end of 3 years for the following, using the double-declining-balance method of depreciation. Round to the nearest dollar. (See Examples 1 and 2.)

Quick Start

23. Cost: $16,200
   Estimated life: 8 years
   Estimated scrap value: $1500
   Book value: <u>**$6834**</u>

   $16,200 × 25% = $4050 dep. year 1
   $16,200 − $4050 = $12,150
   $12,150 × 25% = $3038 dep. year 2
   $12,150 − $3038 = $9112
   $9112 × 25% = $2278 dep. year 3
   $9112 − $2278 = $6834 book value year 3

24. Cost: $8500
   Estimated life: 10 years
   Estimated scrap value: $1100
   Book value: _____

25. Cost: $6000
   Estimated life: 3 years
   Estimated scrap value: $750
   Book value: _____

26. Cost: $75,000
   Estimated life: 50 years
   Estimated scrap value: None
   Book value: _____

Solve the following application problems.

Quick Start

27. WEIGHT-TRAINING EQUIPMENT Gold's Gym selects the double-declining-balance method of depreciation for some weight training equipment costing $14,400. If the estimated life of the equipment is 4 years and the salvage value is zero, prepare a depreciation schedule.

Year	Computation	Amount of Depreciation	Accumulated Depreciation	Book Value
0	—	—	—	$14,400
1	(50% × $14,400)	$7200	$7200	$7200
2	(50% × $7200)	$3600	$10,800	$3600
3	(50% × $3600)	$1800	$12,600	$1800
4		$1800*	$14,400	$0

*To depreciate to 0 scrap value

Name   Date   Class

28. STUDIO SOUND SYSTEM   A studio sound system costing $11,760 has a 3-year life and a scrap value of $1400. Prepare a depreciation schedule using the double-declining-balance method of depreciation.

Year	Computation	Amount of Depreciation	Accumulated Depreciation	Book Value
0	—	—	—	$11,760
1				
2				
3				$1400

29. COMPUTER SYSTEM   Use the double-declining-balance method of depreciation to prepare a depreciation schedule for a new computer system installed at Camblin Steel. Cost = $14,000; estimated life = 5 years; estimated scrap value = $2500. (Round to the nearest dollar.)

Year	Computation	Amount of Depreciation	Accumulated Depreciation	Book Value
0	—	—	—	$14,000
1	40%	5600	5600	8400
2	40%	3360	8960	5,040
3	"	2016	10 976	3024
4	"	524	11 500	2500
5			—	$2500

30. ELECTRONIC ANALYZER   Neilo Lincoln-Mercury decides to use the double-declining-balance method of depreciation on a Barnes Electronic Analyzer that was acquired at a cost of $25,500. If the estimated life of the analyzer is 8 years and the estimated scrap value is $3500, prepare a depreciation schedule. (Round to the nearest dollar.)

Year	Computation	Amount of Depreciation	Accumulated Depreciation	Book Value
0	—	—	—	$25,500
1				
2				
3				
4				
5				
6				
7				
8				$3500

31. Another name for the double-declining-balance method of depreciation is the 200% method. Explain why the straight-line method of depreciation is often called the 100% method. (See Objective 2.)

32. Explain why the amount of depreciation taken in the last year of an asset's life may be zero when using the double-declining-balance method of depreciation. (See Objective 4.)

33. CARPET-CLEANING EQUIPMENT John Walker, owner of The Carpet Solution, purchased some truck-mounted, carpet-cleaning equipment at a cost of $8200. The estimated life of the equipment is 8 years, and the expected salvage value is $1250. Use the double-declining-balance method of depreciation to find the depreciation in the third year.

33. _____

34. HARBOR BOATS A harbor boat costs $478,000 and has an estimated life of 10 years and a salvage value of $150,000. Find the depreciation in the second year using the double-declining-balance method of depreciation.

34. _____

35. JUICE EXTRACTOR Nature's Products purchased a new juice extractor. The cost of the extractor is $1090, and it has an estimated life of 5 years with no salvage value. Use the double-declining-balance method of depreciation to find the book value at the end of the third year.

35. _____

36. COMMUNICATION EQUIPMENT Laura Rogers purchased some communication equipment for her public-relations firm at a cost of $19,700. She estimates the life of the equipment to be 8 years, at which time the salvage value will be $1000. Use the double-declining-balance method of depreciation to find the book value at the end of 5 years.

36. _____

13.3 | Depreciation: Sum-of-the-Years'-Digits Method

Objectives

[1] Understand the sum-of-the-years'-digits method of depreciation.
[2] Use the sum-of-the-years'-digits method to find the depreciation fraction.
[3] Use the sum-of-the-years'-digits method to find the amount of depreciation for each year.
[4] Use the sum-of-the-years'-digits method to prepare a depreciation schedule.

Objective [1] **Understand the sum-of-the-years'-digits method of depreciation.** The sum-of-the-years'-digits method of depreciation is another accelerated depreciation method. The double-declining-balance method of depreciation produces more depreciation than the straight-line method in the early years of an asset's life and less in the later years. The sum-of-the-years'-digits method, however, produces results in between the straight line and the double-declining-balance method—more than straight line at the beginning and more than double-declining at the end.

Objective [2] **Use the sum-of-the-years'-digits method to find the depreciation fraction.** The use of the sum-of-the-years'-digits method requires a **depreciation fraction** instead of the depreciation rate used earlier. If this depreciation fraction, which decreases annually, is multiplied by the depreciable amount (cost minus salvage value), the result is the annual depreciation.

To find the depreciation fraction, first find the denominator, which remains constant for every year of the life of the asset. The denominator is the sum of all the years of the estimated life of the asset ("sum-of-the-years'-digits"). For example, if the life is 6 years, the denominator is 21 (since $1 + 2 + 3 + 4 + 5 + 6 = 21$). The numerator of the fraction, which changes each year, gives the number of years of life remaining at the beginning of that year.

Example 1

Finding the Depreciation Fraction

Find the depreciation fraction for each year if the sum-of-the-years'-digits method of depreciation is to be used for an asset with a useful life of 6 years.

Solution

First determine the denominator of the depreciation fraction. The denominator is 21 $(1 + 2 + 3 + 4 + 5 + 6 = 21)$. Next determine the numerator for each year. The number of years of life remaining at the beginning of any year is the numerator.

Year	Depreciation Fraction
1	$\frac{6}{21}$
2	$\frac{5}{21}$
3	$\frac{4}{21}$
4	$\frac{3}{21}$
5	$\frac{2}{21}$
6	$\frac{1}{21}$
21 sum of the years' digits	$\frac{21}{21}$

As this table shows, by the sum-of-the-years'-digits method an asset having a life of 6 years is assumed to lose $\frac{6}{21}$ of its value the first year, $\frac{5}{21}$ the second year, and so on. The sum of the six fractions in the table is $\frac{21}{21}$, or 1, so that the entire depreciable amount is used over the 6-year life.

NOTE It is common not to write these fractions in lowest terms, so that the year in question can be seen.

A fast method of finding the sum of the years' digits is by the formula

$$\frac{n(n + 1)}{2}$$

For related Web activities, go to www.mathbusiness.com

Keyword: machinery

where *n* is the estimated life of the asset. For example, if the life is 6 years, **6** is multiplied by **6 + 1**, resulting in **6 × 7**, or 42. Then 42 is divided by 2, giving 21, the same denominator used in the table. This method eliminates adding digits and is especially useful when the life of an asset is long.

Objective **3** Use the sum-of-the-years'-digits method to find the amount of depreciation for each year. Use the following formula and multiply the depreciation fraction in any year by the amount to be depreciated (as in the straight-line method) to calculate the amount of depreciation in that year.

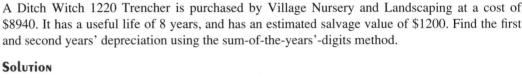

Depreciation = Depreciation fraction × Amount to be depreciated

Example 2

Finding Depreciation Using the Sum-of-the-Year's-Digits Method

A Ditch Witch 1220 Trencher is purchased by Village Nursery and Landscaping at a cost of $8940. It has a useful life of 8 years, and has an estimated salvage value of $1200. Find the first and second years' depreciation using the sum-of-the-years'-digits method.

Solution

The depreciation fraction has a denominator of 36 (or $1 + 2 + 3 + 4 + 5 + 6 + 7 + 8$). The numerator in the first year is 8. The first-year fraction, $\frac{8}{36}$, is then multiplied by the amount to be depreciated, $7740 ($8940 cost − $1200 salvage value).

$$\frac{8}{36} \times \$7740 = \$1720$$

The first year's depreciation is $1720.

The depreciation fraction for the second year, $\frac{7}{36}$, is multiplied by the original depreciable amount, $7740 ($8940 cost − $1200 salvage value). This gives

$$\frac{7}{36} \times \$7740 = \$1505$$

The second year's depreciation is $1505.

Objective **4** Use the sum-of-the-years'-digits method to prepare a depreciation schedule. For comparison, the next example uses the same truck as in Sections 13.1 and 13.2.

Example 3

Preparing a Depreciation Schedule

Village Nursery and Landscaping bought a new pickup truck for $18,500. It is estimated that the truck will have a useful life of 5 years, at which time it will have a salvage value of $3500. Prepare a depreciation schedule using the sum-of-the-years'-digits method of depreciation.

Solution

The depreciation fraction has a denominator of 15 (or $1 + 2 + 3 + 4 + 5$).

Year	Computation	Amount of Depreciation	Accumulated Depreciation	Book Value
0	—	—	—	$18,500
1	($\frac{5}{15}$ × $15,000)	$5000	$5000	$13,500
2	($\frac{4}{15}$ × $15,000)	$4000	$9000	$9500
3	($\frac{3}{15}$ × $15,000)	$3000	$12,000	$6500
4	($\frac{2}{15}$ × $15,000)	$2000	$14,000	$4500
5	($\frac{1}{15}$ × $15,000)	$1000	$15,000	$3500

NOTE The sum-of-the-years'-digits method of depreciation allows rapid depreciation in the early years of the asset's life and yet also provides some depreciation during the last years.

Name   Date   Class

13.3 | EXERCISES

The   Quick Start   exercises in each section contain solutions to help you get started.

Find the sum-of-the-years'-digits depreciation fraction for the first year given the following estimated lives. (See Example 1.)

Quick Start

Life	First-Year Fraction		Life	First-Year Fraction
1. 4 years	$\frac{4}{10}$		**2.** 3 years	$\frac{3}{6}$
$4 + 3 + 2 + 1 = 10; \frac{4}{10}$			$3 + 2 + 1 = 6; \frac{3}{6}$	

3. 6 years $\frac{6}{21}$ **4.** 5 years _____

5. 7 years _____   **6.** 8 years _____

7. 10 years _____   **8.** 20 years _____

Find the first year's depreciation for the following, using the sum-of-the-years'-digits method of depreciation. Round to the nearest dollar. (See Example 2.)

Quick Start

9. Cost:	$4800		**10.** Cost:	$5600	
Estimated life:	4 years		Estimated life:	5 years	
Estimated scrap value:	$700		Estimated scrap value:	$800	
Depreciation (year 1):	**$1640**		Depreciation (year 1):	**$1600**	
$4800 − $700 = $4100			$5600 − $800 = $4800		
$4100 × $\frac{4}{10}$ = $1640			$4800 × $\frac{5}{15}$ = $1600		

11. Cost: $60,000   **12.** Cost: $1440
    Estimated life: 10 years   Estimated life: 8 years
    Estimated scrap value: $5000   Estimated scrap value: None
    Depreciation (year 1): _____   Depreciation (year 1): _____

13. Cost: $1350   **14.** Cost: $9500
    Estimated life: 3 years   Estimated life: 8 years
    Estimated scrap value: $150   Estimated scrap value: $1400
    Depreciation (year 1): _____   Depreciation (year 1): _____

Find the book value at the end of the first year for the following, using the sum-of-the-years'-digits method of depreciation. Round to the nearest dollar. (See Example 3.)

Quick Start

15. Cost: $9500
    Estimated life: 8 years
    Estimated scrap value: $1400
    Book value: **$7700**

    $8100 \times \frac{8}{36} = \$1800$
    $\$9500 - \$1800 = \$7700$

16. Cost: $25,000
    Estimated life: 10 years
    Estimated scrap value: None
    Book value: _____

17. Cost: $3800
    Estimated life: 5 years
    Estimated scrap value: $500
    Book value: _____

18. Cost: $15,650
    Estimated life: 6 years
    Estimated scrap value: $2000
    Book value: _____

Find the book value at the end of 3 years for the following, using the sum-of-the-years'-digits method of depreciation. Round to the nearest dollar. (See Example 3.)

Quick Start

19. Cost: $2240
    Estimated life: 6 years
    Estimated scrap value: $350
    Book value: $890

    $\frac{6}{21} + \frac{5}{21} + \frac{4}{21} = \frac{15}{21}$ dep. in 3 years
    $\$2240 - \$350 = \$1890$
    $\$1890 \times \frac{15}{21} = \$1350$
    $\$2240 - \$1350 = \$890$

20. Cost: $27,500
    Estimated life: 10 years
    Estimated scrap value: None
    Book value: _____

21. Cost: $4500
    Estimated life: 8 years
    Estimated scrap value: $900
    Book value: _____

22. Cost: $6600
    Estimated life: 5 years
    Estimated scrap value: $1500
    Book value: _____

Solve the following application problems.

Quick Start

23. RESTAURANT EQUIPMENT Old South Restaurant has purchased a new steam table for $14,400. The expected life of the unit is 4 years, at which time the salvage value is estimated to be $2400. Complete a depreciation schedule using the sum-of-the-years'-digits method of depreciation.

Year	Computation	Amount of Depreciation	Accumulated Depreciation	Book Value
0	—	—	—	$14,400
1	$(\frac{4}{10} \times \$12,000)$	$4800	$4800	$9600
2	$(\frac{3}{10} \times \$12,000)$	$3600	$8400	$6000
3	$(\frac{2}{10} \times \$12,000)$	$2400	$10,800	$3600
4	$(\frac{1}{10} \times \$12,000)$	$1200	$12,000	$2400

Name   Date   Class

24. DEPRECIATING A COPIER Using the sum-of-the-years'-digits method of depreciation, prepare a depreciation schedule for a copier that costs $3900, has an expected life of 3 years, and has an estimated salvage value of $480.

Year	Computation	Amount of Depreciation	Accumulated Depreciation	Book Value
0	—			$3900
1	3/6	1710	1710	2190
2	2/6	1140	2850	1050
3	1/6	570	3420	480

25. COMMERCIAL FREEZER Big Town Market has purchased a new freezer case at a cost of $10,800. The estimated life of the freezer case is 6 years, at which time the salvage value is estimated to be $2400. Complete a depreciation schedule using the sum-of-the-years'-digits method of depreciation.

Year	Computation	Amount of Depreciation	Accumulated Depreciation	Book Value
0	—	—	—	$10,800
1				
2				
3				
4				
5				
6				

26. FORKLIFT DEPRECIATION Prepare a depreciation schedule for a new forklift using the sum-of-the-years'-digits method of depreciation. Cost = $15,000; estimated life = 10 years; estimated scrap value = $4000.

Year	Computation	Amount of Depreciation	Accumulated Depreciation	Book Value
0	—	—	—	$15,000
1				
2				
3				
4				
5				
6				
7				
8				
9				
10				

27. Write a description of how the depreciation fraction is determined in any year of an asset's life when using the sum-of-the-years'-digits method of depreciation. (See Objective 2.)

28. If you were starting your own business, which of the three depreciation methods, straight-line, double-declining-balance, or sum-of-the-years'-digits, would you decide to use? Why?

29. SOLAR COLLECTOR Find the depreciation in the third year for a solar collector, using the sum-of-the-years'-digits method of depreciation. Cost is $23,000, estimated life is 8 years, and estimated scrap value is $5000.

29. _____

30. LANDSCAPE EQUIPMENT Village Nursery and Landscaping purchased the new Ditch Witch 3500 at a cost of $32,000. The expected life of the unit is 8 years and the salvage value is expected to be $5000. Use the sum-of-the-year's-digits method of depreciation to determine the first year's depreciation.

30. _____

31. HOSPITAL EQUIPMENT Orangevale Rental uses the sum-of-the-years'-digits method of depreciation on all hospital rental equipment. If it purchases new hospital beds at a cost of $12,800 and estimates the life of the beds to be 10 years with no scrap value, find the book value at the end of the fourth year.

31. _____

32. LIGHT-RAIL TOOLING Electro-car, a light-rail manufacturer, purchased a power-wheel and axle jig from a German manufacturer for $31,880. The jig has an expected life of 20 years and an estimated salvage value of $5000. Find the book value at the end of the third year.

32. _____

Name   Date   Class

Supplementary Application Exercises on Depreciation

Round to the nearest dollar if necessary.

1. COPY MACHINES Mail Boxes Etc. purchased a new copy machine at a cost of $9480. Use the straight-line method of depreciation to find the amount of depreciation that should be charged off each year if the equipment has an estimated life of 4 years, and a scrap value of $1500.

1. _____

2. DRY-CLEANING MACHINERY The dry-cleaning machinery at Stopwatch Dry Cleaners cost $52,000, has an estimated life of 40 years, and an estimated scrap value of $8000. Use the straight-line method of depreciation to find the book value of the machinery at the end of 10 years.

2. _____

3. LANDSCAPING EQUIPMENT A landscape contractor purchased a scraper at a cost of $22,000. If the estimated life of the scraper is 10 years, find the book value at the end of 3 years using the double-declining-balance method of depreciation.

3. _____

4. INDUSTRIAL DRILL PRESS Star Bushing Company bought some Belgian-manufactured drill presses at a total cost of $18,500. The estimated life of the drill presses is 5 years, and there is no scrap value. Find the depreciation in the first year using the double-declining-balance method of depreciation.

4. _____

5. CELLULAR PHONES Better Homes Real Estate purchased cellular-phone units and all the accessories for its 6-person sales staff. The equipment has a total cost of $2700, an estimated life of 6 years, and a salvage value of $450. Use the sum-of-the-years'-digits method of depreciation to find the book value of all the cellular-phone equipment at the end of the third year.

5. _____

6. **BUSINESS SIGNAGE** The outdoor sign used by the World of Peace Bookstore cost $7375, has an estimated life of 10 years, and has a salvage value of $500. Use the sum-of-the-years'-digits method of depreciation to find the book value at the end of the third year.

6. _____

7. **CHECKOUT REGISTERS** Consumers Discount Store installed new registers at a cost of $45,600. Using the straight-line method of depreciation, find the amount of depreciation that should be charged off *each year* if the estimated life of the registers is 10 years, and the scrap value is $8000.

7. _____

8. **RECREATION EQUIPMENT** Mountain Recreation purchased some canoes at a cost of $32,000. The estimated life of the canoes is 15 years, and the scrap value is $6500. Find the book value at the end of 10 years using the straight-line method of depreciation.

8. _____

9. **BUSINESS SAFE** Capital Thrift purchased a safe at a cost of $7800. If the estimated life of the safe is 20 years, find the book value at the end of 2 years using the double-declining-balance method of depreciation.

9. _____

10. **HOTEL FURNISHINGS** Holiday Inn Downtown has just installed new furnishings at a total cost of $198,000. The estimated life of the furnishings is 8 years, there is no salvage value, and the double-declining-balance method of depreciation is used. Find the depreciation in the first year.

10. _____

Name	Date	Class

11. MASS-TRANSIT VEHICLE Use the sum-of-the-year's-digits method of depreciation to find the amount of depreciation to be charged off *each year* on a $38,600 mass-transit vehicle that has an estimated life of 4 years and a scrap value of $4400.

11. _____
_____
_____
_____

12. TOUR BUSES Using the sum-of-the-years'-digits method of depreciation, find the amount of depreciation to be charged off each year on a tour bus purchased by Bayside Tours. The bus has a cost of %85,000, an estimated life of 5 years, and a scrap value of $13,000.

12. _____
_____
_____
_____
_____

13. INDUSTRIAL FORKLIFT Lumber and More buys 5 forklifts at a cost of $14,825 each. The life of the forklifts is estimated to be 10 years and the scrap value $3000. Use the sum-of-the-years'-digits method of depreciation to find the total book value of all the forklifts at the end of the fourth year.

13. _____

14. CAR-WASH MACHINERY An automatic car-wash machine that cost $9250 has a scrap value of $1000 and an estimated life of 6 years. Use the sum-of-the-years'-digits method of depreciation to find the book value at the end of the third year.

14. _____

15. **VIDEO EQUIPMENT** Video Productions purchased some studio equipment manufactured in Australia. The total cost of the equipment was $21,600; it has an estimated life of 5 years and a salvage value of $2400. Use the sum-of-the-years'-digits method of depreciation to find the book value of the equipment at the end of the second year.

15. _____

16. **RESTAURANT TABLES** King's Table bought new dining-room tables at a cost of $14,750. If the estimated life of the tables is 8 years, at which time they will be worthless, and the double-declining-balance method of depreciation is used, find the book value at the end of the third year.

16. _____

13.4 | DEPRECIATION: UNITS-OF-PRODUCTION METHOD

Objectives

1. Describe the units-of-production method of depreciation.
2. Use the units-of-production method to find the depreciation per unit.
3. Use the units-of-production method to calculate the annual depreciation.
4. Use the units-of-production method to prepare a depreciation schedule.

Problem Solving in Business

Village Nursery and Landscaping owns a stump chipper that is used to remove tree stumps in established landscapes. Since the machine is not used very often, Julie Maxi's accountant suggests that the stump remover be depreciated based on the number of hours it is used rather than by the number of years it is owned. Using this approach will be more realistic for depreciating the stump chipper and could result in faster or slower depreciation depending on how often the chipper is used.

Objective 1 **Describe the units-of-production method of depreciation.** An asset often has a useful life given in terms of **units of production**, such as hours or miles of service. For example, an airplane or truck may have a useful life given as hours of air time or miles of travel. A steel press or stamping machine may have a life given as the total number of units that it can produce. For these assets, the units-of-production method of depreciation is used. Just as with the straight-line method of depreciation, a constant amount of depreciation is taken with the units-of-production method. With the straight-line method a constant amount of depreciation is taken each year, while the units-of-production method depreciates a constant amount per unit of use or production.

Objective 2 **Use the units-of-production method to find the depreciation per unit.** Find the depreciation per unit with the following formula.

$$\text{Depreciation per unit} = \frac{\text{Depreciable amount}}{\text{Units of life}}$$

For example, suppose the stump chipper owned by Village Nursery and Landscaping costs $15,000, has a salvage value of $3000, and is expected to operate 700 hours. Find the depreciation per hour by dividing the depreciable amount by the number of hours of life.

$$\begin{array}{ll} \$15,000 & \text{cost} \\ -\ \underline{\$3,000} & \text{salvage value} \\ \$12,000 & \text{depreciable amount} \end{array}$$

Objective 3 **Use the units-of-production method to calculate the annual depreciation.**

$$\frac{\$12,000 \text{ depreciable amount}}{700 \text{ hours of life}} = \$17.14 \text{ (rounded) depreciation per hour}$$

Then multiply the depreciation per unit by the number of hours used during the year to find the annual depreciation.

Heavy-Truck Makers Find the Good Times Are Rolling

The newspaper headline above reports that sales of heavy duty trucks, the ones that carry more than 33,000 pounds, are the highest they have been in almost 20 years. These behemoth trucks, also known as Class 8s or 18-wheelers, start at a base price of $70,000 and climb as high as $120,000 and more. To depreciate these trucks, the owners will often give them a life as high as 750,000 miles.

EXAMPLE 1

Using Units-of-Production Depreciation

North American Trucking purchased a new Kenworth truck for $95,000. The truck has a salvage value of $15,000 and an estimated life of 500,000 miles. Find the depreciation for a year in which the truck is driven 128,000 miles.

Solution

First find the depreciable amount.

For related Web activities, go to www.mathbusiness.com

Keyword:
service

$95,000	cost
− $15,000	scrap value
$80,000	depreciable amount

Next find the depreciation per unit.

$$\frac{\$80,000 \text{ depreciable amount}}{500,000 \text{ miles of life}} = \$.16 \text{ depreciation per mile}$$

Multiply to find the depreciation for the year.

$$128,000 \text{ miles} \times \$.16 = \$20,480 \text{ depreciation for the year}$$

EXAMPLE 2

Preparing a Depreciation Schedule

Global Electronics purchaed a shrink-wrapping machine that costs $52,300, has an estimated salvage value of $4000, and has an expected life of 690,000 units. Prepare a depreciation schedule using the units-of-production method of depreciation. Use the following packaging schedule.

Year 1	240,000 units
Year 2	150,000 units
Year 3	90,000 units
Year 4	120,000 units
Year 5	90,000 units

Solution

The depreciable amount is **$48,300 ($52,300 − $4000)**. The depreciation per unit is

$$\frac{\$48,300}{690,000 \text{ units}} = \$.07 \text{ per unit.}$$

The annual depreciation is found by multiplying the number of units packaged each year by the depreciation per unit.

Year 1	240,000 units × **$.07** =	$16,800
Year 2	150,000 units × **$.07** =	$10,500
Year 3	90,000 units × **$.07** =	$6300
Year 4	120,000 units × **$.07** =	$8400
Year 5	90,000 units × **$.07** =	$6300
Total	690,000 units	$48,300 depreciable amount.

OBJECTIVE **4** Use the units-of-production method to prepare a depreciation schedule. These results were used in the preparation of the following depreciation schedule.

Year	Computation	Depreciation	Accumulated Depreciation	Book Value
0	—	—	—	$52,300
1	(240,000 × $.07)	$16,800	$16,800	$35,500
2	(150,000 × $.07)	$10,500	$27,300	$25,000
3	(90,000 × $.07)	$6300	$33,600	$18,700
4	(120,000 × $.07)	$8400	$42,000	$10,300
5	(90,000 × $.07)	$6300	$48,300	$4000

NOTE In Example 2, the book value at the end of year 5 ($4000) is the amount of the salvage value. This is true because the total number of units of life (690,000) has been used up by the machine during the 5 years.

Name   Date   Class

13.4 | Exercises

The Quick Start exercises in each section contain solutions to help you get started.

Find the depreciation per unit in the following. Round to the nearest thousandth of a dollar. (See Example 1.)

Quick Start

	Cost	Salvage Value	Estimated Life	Depreciation per Unit
1.	$22,500	$1500	60,000 units	$.35

$22,500 − $1500 = $21,000; $21,000 ÷ 60,000 = $.35

	Cost	Salvage Value	Estimated Life	Depreciation per Unit
2.	$5000	$400	10,000 units	$.46

$5000 − $400 = $4600; $4600 ÷ 10,000 = $.46

	Cost	Salvage Value	Estimated Life	Depreciation per Unit
3.	$3750	$250	120,000 units	_____
4.	$7500	$500	15,000 miles	_____
5.	$37,500	$7500	125,000 miles	_____
6.	$300,000	$25,000	4000 hours	_____
7.	$175,000	$25,000	5000 hours	_____
8.	$125,000	$20,000	500,000 miles	_____

Find the amount of depreciation in each of the following. (See Example 1.)

Quick Start

	Depreciation per Unit	Units Produced	Amount of Depreciation
9.	$.23	78,000	$17,940

78,000 × $.23 = $17,940

	Depreciation per Unit	Units Produced	Amount of Depreciation
10.	$.15	380,000	$57,000

380,000 × $.15 = $57,000

	Depreciation per Unit	Units Produced	Amount of Depreciation
11.	$.54	32,000	_____
12.	$.73	16,500	_____

	Depreciation per Unit	Units Produced	Amount of Depreciation
13.	$.185	15,000	_____
14.	$.032	73,000	_____
15.	$.40	17,400	_____
16.	$.018	175,000	_____

17. In your own words, describe the conditions under which the units-of-production method of depreciation is most applicable.

18. Use an example of your own to demonstrate how the annual depreciation amount is found using the units-of-production method of depreciation. (See Objective 3.)

Solve the following application problems. (Round to the nearest dollar.)

Quick Start

19. COMMERCIAL DEEP FRYER Dunkin' Donuts purchased a new deep fryer at a cost of $6800. The expected life is 5000 hours of production, at which time it will have a salvage value of $500. Prepare a depreciation schedule, using the units-of-production method, given the following production: year 1: 1350 hours; year 2: 1820 hours; year 3: 730 hours; year 4: 1100 hours.

Year	Computation	Amount of Depreciation	Accumulated Depreciation	Book Value
0	—	—	—	$6800
1	(1350 × $1.26)	$1701	$1701	$5099
2	(1820 × $1.26)	$2293	$3994	$2806
3	(730 × $1.26)	$920	$4914	$1886
4	(1100 × $1.26)	$1386	$6300	$500

20. TRUCKING BUSINESS Jack Armstrong purchased a Kenworth truck at a cost of $87,000. He estimates that it is good for 300,000 miles and will have a salvage value of $15,000. Use the units-of-production method to prepare a depreciation schedule given the following production: year 1: 108,000 miles; year 2: 75,000 miles; year 3: 117,000 miles.

Year	Computation	Amount of Depreciation	Accumulated Depreciation	Book Value
0	—	—	—	$87,000
		25,920	25,920	61,080
		18,000	43,920	43,080
		28,080	72,000	15,000

72,000
300,000
.24 per mile

13.5 | DEPRECIATION: MODIFIED ACCELERATED COST RECOVERY SYSTEM

Objectives

1. Understand the modified accelerated cost recovery system (MACRS).
2. Determine the recovery period of different types of property.
3. Find the depreciation rate given the recovery period and recovery year.
4. Use the MACRS to find the amount of depreciation.
5. Use the MACRS to prepare a depreciation schedule.

PROBLEM SOLVING IN BUSINESS

No matter which methods of depreciation have been used by Village Nursery and Landscaping for their accounting and state-tax purposes, the accountant tells Julie Maxi that the modified accelerated cost recovery system (MACRS) must be used for federal income-tax purposes. This means that every depreciable asset owned by the company must have an MACRS depreciation schedule and that Julie Maxi must also have an understanding of MACRS.

Objective 1 Understand the modified accelerated cost recovery system (MACRS). A depreciation method known as the **accelerated cost recovery system (ACRS)** originated as part of the Economic Recovery Tax Act of 1981. It was later modified by the Tax Equity and Fiscal Responsibility Act of 1982 and again by the Tax Reform Act of 1984. The Tax Reform Act of 1986 brought the most recent and significant overhaul to the accelerated cost recovery system (ACRS), and applies to all property placed in service after 1986. The new method is known as the **modified accelerated cost recovery system (MACRS)**. The result is that there are now three systems for computing depreciation for *federal tax purposes*.

For related Web activities, go to www.mathbusiness.com

Keyword: FAQ

Federal Tax Depreciation Methods

1. The MACRS method of depreciation is used for all property placed in service after 1986.

2. The ACRS method of depreciation will continue to be used for all property placed in service from 1981 through 1986.

3. The straight-line, declining-balance, and sum-of-the-years'-digits methods continue to be used if the property was placed in service before 1981.

NOTE The units-of-production method of depreciation is still allowed under the MACRS.

Keep two things in mind about the MACRS: First, the system is designed, really, for tax purposes (it is sometimes called the **income tax method**), and businesses often use some alternate method of depreciation (in addition to MACRS) for financial accounting purposes. Second, many states do not allow the modified accelerated cost recovery system of depreciation for finding state income tax liability. This means businesses must use the *MACRS* on the *federal tax return* and one of the other methods on the *state tax return*.

Objective 2 Determine the recovery period of different types of property. Under the modified accelerated cost recovery system, assets are placed in one of nine **recovery classes**, depending on whether the law assumes a 3-, 5-, 7-, 10-, 15-, 20-, 27.5-, 31.5-, or 39-year life for the asset. These lives, or **recovery periods**, are determined as follows.

MACRS Recovery Classes

3-year property	Tractor units for use over-the-road, any racehorse that is over 2 years old, or any other horse that is over 12 years old
5-year property	Automobiles, taxis, trucks, buses, computers and peripheral equipment, office machinery (typewriters, calculators), copiers, and research equipment
7-year property	Office furniture and fixtures (desks, files, safes), and any property not designated by law to be in any other class
10-year property	Vessels, barges, tugs, and similar water transportation equipment
15-year property	Improvements made directly to land, such as shrubbery, fences, roads, and bridges
20-year property	Certain farm buildings
27.5-year property	Residential rental real estate such as rental houses and apartments
31.5-year property	Nonresidential rental real estate such as office buildings, stores, and warehouses if placed in service before May 13, 1993
39-year property	Nonresidential property placed in service after May 12, 1993

EXAMPLE 1
Finding the
Recovery Period
for Property

Village Nursery and Landscaping owns the following assets. Determine the recovery period for each of them.

(a)   computer equipment   **(b)**   an industrial warehouse (after May 12, 1993)

(c)   a pickup truck   **(d)**   office furniture   **(e)**   a farm building (storage shed)

SOLUTION

Use the list above.

(a)   5 years   **(b)**   39 years   **(c)**   5 years   **(d)**   7 years   **(e)**   20 years

Modified Accelerated Cost Recovery System (MACRS)

Useful Items
You may want to see:

Publication

☐ **225** Farmer's Tax Guide
☐ **463** Travel, Entertainment, and Gift Expenses
☐ **544** Sales and Other Dispositions of Assets
☐ **581** Basis of Assets
☐ **583** Taxpayers Starting a Business
☐ **587** Business Use of Your Home
☐ **917** Business Use of a Car

Objective ③ **Find the depreciation rate, given the recovery period and recovery year.** With MACRS, salvage value is ignored, so that *depreciation is based on the entire original cost of the asset.* The depreciation rates are determined by applying the double-declining-balance (200%) method to the 3-, 5-, 7-, and 10-year class properties, the 150% declining-balance method to the 15- and 20-year class properties, and the straight-line (100%) method to the 27.5-, 31.5-, and 39-year class properties. Since these calculations are repetitive and require additional knowledge, the Internal Revenue Service provides tables that show the depreciation rates. The rates are shown in the table on the following page. To determine the rate of depreciation for any year of life, find the recovery year in the left-hand column, and then read across to the allowable recovery period.

Notice that the number of recovery years is one greater than the class life of the property. This is because only a half year of depreciation is allowed for the first year the property is placed in service, regardless of when the property is placed in service during the year. This is known as the **half-year convention** and is used by most taxpayers. A complete coverage of depreciation, including all depreciation tables, is included in the **Internal Revenue Service**, **Publication 534**, and may be obtained by contacting the IRS Forms Distribution Center. This publication (534) lists several items that the taxpayer or tax preparer might find useful. This list is shown at the side.

> **PROBLEM-SOLVING HINT**   MACRS is the income tax method of depreciation and several important points should be remembered: **(1)** No salvage value is used; **(2)** The life of the asset is determined by using the recovery periods assigned to different types of property; and **(3)** A depreciation rate is usually found for each year by referring to a MACRS Table of Depreciation Rates.

MACRS Depreciation Rates

Recovery Year	\multicolumn{9}{c}{Applicable Percent for the Class of Property}
	3-Year	5-Year	7-Year	10-Year	15-Year	20-Year	27.5-Year	31.5-Year	39-Year
1	33.33	20.00	14.29	10.00	5.00	3.750	1.818	1.587	2.568
2	44.45	32.00	24.49	18.00	9.50	7.219	3.636	3.175	2.564
3	14.81	19.20	17.49	14.40	8.55	6.677	3.636	3.175	2.564
4	7.41	11.52	12.49	11.52	7.70	6.177	3.636	3.175	2.564
5		11.52	8.93	9.22	6.93	5.713	3.636	3.175	2.564
6		5.76	8.92	7.37	6.23	5.285	3.636	3.175	2.564
7			8.93	6.55	5.90	4.888	3.636	3.175	2.564
8			4.46	6.55	5.90	4.522	3.636	3.175	2.564
9				6.56	5.91	4.462	3.637	3.175	2.564
10				6.55	5.90	4.461	3.636	3.174	2.564
11				3.28	5.91	4.462	3.637	3.175	2.564
12					5.90	4.461	3.636	3.174	2.564
13					5.91	4.462	3.637	3.175	2.564
14					5.90	4.461	3.636	3.174	2.564
15					5.91	4.462	3.637	3.175	2.564
16					2.95	4.461	3.636	3.174	2.564
17						4.462	3.367	3.175	2.564
18						4.461	3.636	3.174	2.564
19						4.462	3.637	3.175	2.564
20						4.461	3.636	3.174	2.564
21						2.231	3.637	3.175	2.564
22							3.636	3.174	2.564
23							3.637	3.175	2.564
24							3.636	3.174	2.564
25							3.637	3.175	2.564
26							3.636	3.174	2.564
27							3.637	3.175	2.564
28							3.636	3.174	2.564
29								3.175	2.564
30								3.174	2.564
31								3.175	2.564
32								3.174	2.564
33–39									2.564

EXAMPLE 2

Finding the Rate of Depreciation with MACRS

Find the rate of depreciation given the following recovery year and recovery period.

	(a)	(b)	(c)	(d)
Recovery Year	4	2	3	9
Recovery Period	5 years	3 years	10 years	27.5 years

Solution

(a) 11.52%   (b) 44.45%   (c) 14.40%   (d) 3.637%

Objective **4** **Use the MACRS to find the amount of depreciation.** No salvage value is subtracted from the cost of property under the MACRS method, and the depreciation rate multiplied by the original cost determines the depreciation amount.

Example 3

Finding the Amount of Depreciation with MACRS

Village Nursery and Landscaping purchased a pickup truck. Find the amount of depreciation in the third year for the pickup truck that had a cost of $18,500.

Solution

A pickup truck has a recovery period of 5 years. From the table, the depreciation rate in the third year of recovery of 5-year property is 19.20%. Multiply this rate by the full cost of the property to determine the amount of depreciation.

$$19.20\% \times \$18,500 = \$3552$$

The amount of depreciation is $3552.

Example 4

Preparing a Depreciation Schedule with MACRS

Omaha Insurance Company has purchased new office furniture at a cost of $24,160. Prepare a depreciation schedule, using the modified accelerated cost recovery system.

Solution

No salvage value is used with MACRS. Office desks and chairs have a 7-year recovery period. The annual depreciation rates for 7-year property are as follows.

Recovery Year	Recovery Percent (Rate)
1	14.29%
2	24.49%
3	17.49%
4	12.49%
5	8.93%
6	8.92%
7	8.93%
8	4.46%

Objective ⑤ **Use the MACRS to prepare a depreciation schedule.** Multiply the appropriate percents by $24,160 to get results shown in the following depreciation schedule.

Year	Computation	Amount of Depreciation	Accumulated Depreciation	Book Value
0	—	—	—	$24,160
1	(14.29% × $24,160)	$3452	$3452	$20,708
2	(24.49% × $24,160)	$5917	$9369	$14,791
3	(17.49% × $24,160)	$4226	$13,595	$10,565
4	(12.49% × $24,160)	$3018	$16,613	$7547
5	(8.93% × $24,160)	$2157	$18,770	$5390
6	(8.92% × $24,160)	$2155	$20,925	$3235
7	(8.93% × $24,160)	$2157	$23,082	$1078
8	(4.46% × $24,160)	$1078	$24,160	$0

The MACRS method of depreciation allows a rapid rate of investment recovery and at the same time results in less complicated computations. By eliminating the necessity for estimating the life of an asset and the need for using a salvage value, the tables provide a more direct method of calculating depreciation.

Name   Date   Class

13.5 | EXERCISES

The Quick Start *exercises in each section contain solutions to help you get started.*

Use the MACRS depreciation rates table to find the recovery percent (rate) given the following recovery year and recovery period. (See Examples 1 and 2.)

Quick Start

	Recovery Year	Recovery Period	Recovery Pecent (Rate)		Recovery Year	Recovery Period	Recovery Percent (Rate)
1.	3	5-year	19.2%	**2.**	2	3-year	44.45%
3.	4	10-year	_____	**4.**	1	7-year	_____
5.	1	5-year	_____	**6.**	2	20-year	_____
7.	14	27.5-year	_____	**8.**	10	31.5-year	_____
9.	6	5-year	_____	**10.**	4	27.5-year	_____
11.	14	39-year	_____	**12.**	4	31.5-year	_____

Find the first year's depreciation for each of the following using the MACRS method of depreciation and the MACRS depreciation rates table. Round to the nearest dollar. (See Example 3.)

Quick Start

13. Cost:	$12,250		**14.** Cost:	$8790	
Recovery period:	7 years		Recovery period:	5 years	
Depreciation (year 1):	**$1751**		Depreciation (year 1):	**$1758**	

14.29% rate
$12,250 × .1429 = $1751 depreciation

20% rate
$8790 × .20 = $1758 depreciation

15. Cost:	$430,500	**16.** Cost:	$72,300
Recovery period:	10 years	Recovery period:	20 years
Depreciation (year 1):	_____	Depreciation (year 1):	_____

17. Cost:	$48,000	**18.** Cost:	$12,340
Recovery period:	10 years	Recovery period:	3 years
Depreciation (year 1):	_____	Depreciation (year 1):	_____

Find the book value at the end of the first year for each of the following using the MACRS method of depreciation and the MACRS depreciation rates table. Round to the nearest dollar. (See Example 4.)

Quick Start

19. Cost:	$9380	**20.** Cost:	$32,750
Recovery period:	3 years	Recovery period:	10 years
Book value:	**$6254**	Book value:	_____

$9380 × .3333 = $3126
$9380 − $3126 = $6254 book value

21. Cost: $18,800   **22.** Cost: $137,000
   Recovery period: 10 years   Recovery period: 27.5 years
   Book value: _____   Book value: _____

Find the book value at the end of 3 years for each of the following using the MACRS method of depreciation and the MACRS depreciation rates table. Round to the nearest dollar. (See Example 4).

Quick Start

23. Cost: $9570   **24.** Cost: $6500
   Recovery period: 5 years   Recovery period: 3 years
   Book value: **$2756**   Book value: _____

   20% + 32% + 19.2% = 71.2% rate 3 years
   $9570 × .712 = $6813.84 = $6814 dep. 3 years
   $9570 − $6814 = $2756 book value year 3

25. Cost: $87,300   **26.** Cost: $390,800
   Recovery period: 27.5 years   Recovery period: 31.5 years
   Book value: _____   Book value: _____

Solve the following application problems. Use the MACRS depreciation rates table. (See Example 4).

Quick Start

27. SMALL TRACTOR Blue Ribbon Septic purchased a tractor for $10,980. Prepare a depreciation schedule using the MACRS method of depreciation. (3-year property.) Round to the nearest dollar.

Year	Computation	Amount of Depreciation	Accumulated Depreciation	Book Value
0	—	—	—	$10,980
1	(33.33% × $10,980)	$3660	$3660	$7320
2	(44.45% × $10,980)	$4881	$8541	$2439
3	(14.81% × $10,980)	$1626	$10,167	$813
4	(7.41% × $10,980)	$813*	$10,980	$0

*due to rounding in prior years

28. COMPANY VEHICLES Village Nursery and Landscaping purchased a pickup truck at a cost of $18,500. Prepare a depreciation schedule using the MACRS method of depreciation. Round to the nearest dollar. (5-year property.)

Year	Computation	Amount of Depreciation	Accumulated Depreciation	Book Value
0	—	—	—	$18,500
1				
2				
3				
4				
5				
6				

Name   Date   Class

29. **OFFSHORE DRILLING**   Gulf Drilling purchased a tugboat for $122,700. Prepare a depreciation schedule using the MACRS method of depreciation. (10-year property.) Round to the nearest dollar.

Year	Computation	Amount of Depreciation	Accumulated Depreciation	Book Value
0	—	—	—	$122,700
1				
2				
3				
4				
5				
6				
7				
8				
9				
10				
11				

30. **RESIDENTIAL RENTAL PROPERTY**   Andy Kirkpatrick purchased some residential rental real estate for $415,000. Find the book value at the end of the tenth year using the MACRS method of depreciation (27.5-year property). (Round to the nearest dollar.)

30. _____

Year	Computation	Amount of Depreciation	Book Value
0	—	—	$415,000
1			
2			
3			
4			
5			
6			
7			
8			
9			
10			

31. The same business asset may be depreciated using two or more different methods. Explain why a business would do this. (See Objective 1.)

32. After learning about MACRS, what three features stand out to you as being unique to this method? (See Objective 3.)

Use the MACRS depreciation rates table in the following application problems.

33. LAPTOP COMPUTERS Susan Carsten purchased a laptop computer for her office for $3700. Find the book value at the end of the third year, using the MACRS method of depreciation.

33. _____

34. OFFICE FURNITURE Smith Chiropractic purchased new furniture for its office at a cost of $13,800. Find the book value at the end of the fifth year, using the MACRS method of depreciation.

34. _____

35. BOOKKEEPING BUSINESS Jim Bralley, owner of Bralley's Bookkeeping, purchased an office building at a cost of $480,000. Find the amount of depreciation for each of the first five years using the MACRS method of depreciation (39-year property).

Year 1: _____
Year 2: _____
Year 3: _____
Year 4: _____
Year 5: _____

36. INDEPENDENT BOOKSTORE OWNERSHIP Maretha Roseborough, owner of the Barnstormer Bookstore, bought a building to use for her business. The cost of the building was $220,000. Find the amount of depreciation for each of the first five years using the MACRS method of depreciation (39-year property).

Year 1: _____
Year 2: _____
Year 3: _____
Year 4: _____
Year 5: _____

CHAPTER 13 | Quick Review

CONCEPTS | EXAMPLES

13.1 Straight-line method of depreciation
The depreciation is the same each year.

$$\text{Depreciation} = \frac{\text{Amount to be depreciated}}{\text{Years of life}}$$

Cost, $500; scrap value, $100; life of 8 years; find the annual amount of depreciation.

$500 cost
−$100 scrap
$400 depreciable amount

$$\frac{\$400}{8} = \$50 \text{ depreciation each year}$$

13.1 Book value
Book value is the remaining value at the end of the year.

$$\text{Book value} = \text{Cost} - \text{Depreciation}$$

Cost, $400; scrap value, $100; life of 3 years; find the book value at the end of the first year.

$400 cost
−$100 scrap value
$300 depreciable amount

$$\frac{\$300}{3} = \$100 \text{ depreciation}$$

$400 cost
−$100 depreciation
$300 book value year 1

13.2 Double-declining-balance rate
First find the straight-line rate, then adjust it. For the 200% method, **multiply by 2.**

Life of an asset is 10 years. Find the double-declining-balance (200%) rate.

$$10 \text{ years} = 10\% \left(\frac{1}{10}\right) \text{ straight-line}$$

$$2 \times 10\% = 20\%$$

13.2 Double-declining-balance depreciation method
First find the double-declining-balance rate and then multiply by the cost in year 1. The rate is then multiplied by the declining book value in the following years.

Cost, $1400; life of 5 years; find the depreciation in years 1 and 2.

$$2 \times 20\% \text{ (straight-line rate)} = 40\%$$

year 1: 40% × $1400 = $560 depreciation year 1

$1400 − $560 = $840 book value year 1

year 2: 40% × $840 = $336 depreciation year 2

CONCEPTS	EXAMPLES
13.3 Sum-of-the-years'-digits depreciation fraction Add the year's digits together to get the denominator. The numerator is the number of years of life remaining. The denominator shortcut is $$\frac{n(n+1)}{2}.$$	Useful life is 4 years; find the depreciation fraction for each year. $$1 + 2 + 3 + 4 = 10$$ | Year	Depreciation Fraction | |---|---| | 1 | $\frac{4}{10}$ | | 2 | $\frac{3}{10}$ | | 3 | $\frac{2}{10}$ | | 4 | $\frac{1}{10}$ |
13.3 Sum-of-the-years'-digits depreciation method First find the depreciation fraction, then multiply by the depreciable amount.	Cost, $2500; salvage value, $400; life of 6 years; find depreciation in year 1. depreciation fraction $= \dfrac{6}{21}$ depreciable amount $= \$2100$ depreciation $= \dfrac{6}{21} \times \$2100 = \$600$
13.4 Units-of-production depreciation amount Use the formula $$\text{Depreciation per unit} = \frac{\text{Depreciable amount}}{\text{Units of life}}.$$	Cost $10,000; salvage value, $2500; useful life of 15,000 units; find depreciation per unit. $$\text{Depreciation per unit} = \frac{\$7500 \text{ depreciable amount}}{15,000 \text{ units of life}} = \$.50$$
13.4 Units-of-production depreciation method Multiply the depreciation per unit (per hour) by the number of units (hours) of production.	Cost, $25,000; salvage value, $2000; useful life, 100,000 units; production in year 1, 22,300 units; find the first year's depreciation. **1.** $25,000 − $2000 = $23,000 depreciable amount **2.** $\dfrac{\$23,000}{100,000} = \$.23$ depreciation per unit **3.** 22,300 × $.23 = $5129 depreciation year 1
13.5 Modified accelerated cost recovery system (MACRS) Established in 1986 for federal tax. No salvage value. Recovery periods are: |		| |---|---|---| | 3-year | 5-year | 7-year | | 10-year | 15-year | 20-year | | 27.5-year | 31.5-year | 39-year | Find the proper rate from the table and then multiply by the cost to find depreciation.	Use the table, finding recovery period column at the top of the table and the recovery year in the left-hand column. Cost: $4850; recovery period 5 years; recovery year, 3; find the depreciation. Rate is **19.20%** from table. $4850 × .192 = $931 depreciation

CHAPTER 13 | SUMMARY EXERCISE

COMPARING DEPRECIATION METHODS: A BUSINESS APPLICATION

Trader Joe's purchased freezer cases at a cost of $285,000. The estimated life of the freezer cases is 5 years, at which time they will have no salvage value. The company would like to compare allowable depreciation methods and decides to prepare depreciation schedules for the fixtures using the straight-line, double-declining-balance, and the sum-of-the-years'-digits methods of depreciation. Using these depreciation schedules, find the answers to these questions for Trader Joe's.

For related Web
activities, go to
www.mathbusiness.com

Keyword:
comprehensive

(a) What is the book value at the end of 3 years using the straight-line depreciation method?

(a) _____

(b) Using the double-declining-balance method of depreciation, what is the book value at the end of the third year?

(b) _____

(c) With the sum-of-the-year's-digits method of depreciation, what is the accumulated depreciation at the end of 3 years?

(c) _____

(d) What amount of depreciation will be taken in year 4 with each of the methods?

(d) _____

_____

_____

Investigate

Identify a store or business with which you are familiar and list six of their depreciable assets. Examples could be such items as buildings, computer equipment, vehicles, and fixtures. Using the information on the MACRS method of depreciation, give the recovery period and the first-year depreciation rate for each of the six depreciable assets listed above.

GMC

STATISTICS

- 1902: First GMC truck built

- 1999: 647,000 employees

- Facilities in 50 countries

- Named Top 100 Products by *Construction Equipment* magazine

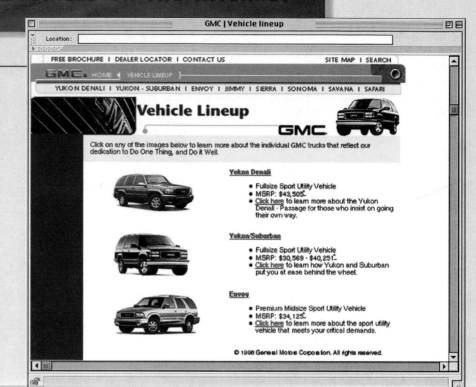

Founded in 1902, General Motors Corporation has grown into the world's largest industrial corporation and full-line vehicle manufacturer. In the late 1990s, the company had partnered with over 30,000 companies worldwide. As the world's largest U.S. exporter of cars and trucks with manufacturing, assembly, or component operations in 50 countries, General Motors has a global presence in over 190 countries.

Village Nursery and Landscaping purchased a new GMC Sierra pickup truck for $22,500. The useful life of the truck is 5 years and the estimated salvage value is $4500.

1. Using the information above, find the book value of the pickup truck after 3 years using the straight-line method of depreciation.

2. If the MACRS depreciation rates for the pickup truck were 20%, 32%, and 19.2% in the first three years of the truck's life, find the book value of the pickup truck at the end of 3 years.

3. List four factors that affect how fast a pickup truck is used up or wears out. Does the book value of an asset necessarily reflect the true value (resale value) of that asset? Explain.

4. Talk to a business owner and list a few of the assets that they are depreciating. If the business had a choice of depreciating gradually over the life an asset (straight-line) or more rapidly using an accelerated depreciation method, what factors would the business owner consider when making their decision?

Name   Date   Class

CHAPTER 13 | TEST

To help you review, the numbers in brackets show the section in which the topic was discussed.

Find the annual straight-line and double-declining rates (percents) of depreciation and the sum-of-the-years'-digits fraction for the first year for each of the following estimated lives.   **[13.1–13.3]**

Life	Straight-Line Rate	Double-Declining Rate	Sum-of-the-Years'-Digits Fraction
1. 4 years	_____	_____	_____
2. 5 years	_____	_____	_____
3. 10 years	_____	_____	_____
4. 20 years	_____	_____	_____

Solve the following application problems.

5. Cloverdale Creamery purchased an ice-cream machine at a cost of $12,400. The machine has an estimated life of 10 years, and a scrap value of $3000. Use the straight-line method of depreciation to find the annual depreciation.   **[13.1]**

5. _____

6. Automated Billing Services purchased some new billing equipment for $38,000. If the estimated life of the billing equipment is 8 years, find the book value at the end of 2 years using the double-declining-balance method of depreciation.   **[13.2]**

6. _____

7. The Feather River Youth Camp has purchased a diesel generator for $8250. Use the sum-of-the-year's-digits method of depreciation to determine the amount of depreciation to be taken during *each of the 4 years* on the diesel generator that has a 4-year life and scrap value of $1500.   **[13.3]**

Year 1: _____
Year 2: _____
Year 3: _____
Year 4: _____

8. A private road costs $56,000 and has a 15-year recovery period. Find the depreciation in the third year using the MACRS method of depreciation. (Round to the nearest dollar.)   **[13.5]**

8. _____

9. The Fashion Express purchased new clothing racks at a cost of $22,400. Using the straight-line method of depreciation, a 5-year life, and a scrap value of $3500, find the accumulated depreciation at the end of the fourth year.   **[13.1]**

9. _____

10. Don Rosa, owner of Southeast Appliance Parts has added paging and intercom features to the communication systems of his 4 stores at a cost of $2800 per store. The estimated life of the systems is 10 years, with no expected salvage value. Using the sum-of-the-years'-digits method of depreciation, find the total book value of all the systems at the end of the third year.   **[13.3]**

10. _____

11. Table Fresh Foods purchased a machine to package their presliced garden salads. The machine costs $20,100 and has an estimated life of 30,000 hours and a salvage value of $1500. Use the units-of-production method of depreciation to find **(a)** the annual amount of depreciation and **(b)** the book value at the end of each year, given the following use information: Year 1: 7800 hours; Year 2: 4300 hours; Year 3: 4850 hours; Year 4: 7600 hours.   **[13.4]**

(a) _____

(b) _____

12. Blue Diamond Almond Growers paid $2,800,000 to build a new warehouse in 1998. The recovery period is 39 years. Use the MACRS method of depreciation to find the book value of the warehouse at the end of the fifth year.   **[13.5]**

12. _____

CHAPTER 14

Financial Statements and Ratios

McDonald's had nearly 14 billion customer visits last year, which is equivalent to serving lunch and dinner *to every person on earth*. Even so, on any given day, McDonald's only serves about 1% of the world's population.

Business owners and managers must keep careful records of the expenses and income of their business. They need these records to help them manage the business, to inform other owners of current operations, to provide required information to lenders from whom they wish to borrow money, and for tax purposes.

Bookkeepers and accountants keep track of *the income and expenses of the firm*. Accountants are concerned with issues such as meeting payroll, paying suppliers on time, estimating and paying taxes, as well as estimating and handling revenues. This chapter covers some of the tools used by managers, accountants, lenders, and investors when looking at the financial health of a firm.

14.1 THE INCOME STATEMENT

Objectives

1. Understand the terms on an income statement.
2. Prepare an income statement.

PROBLEM SOLVING IN BUSINESS

Have you ever been to McDonald's? If so, you aren't alone. The idea behind McDonald's began in 1954 when 52-year-old Ray Kroc saw a very successful restaurant owned by the McDonald brothers in California. Today, McDonald's has grown to over 23,500 restaurants in 109 countries. Would you like to share in their growth? You can by purchasing stock.

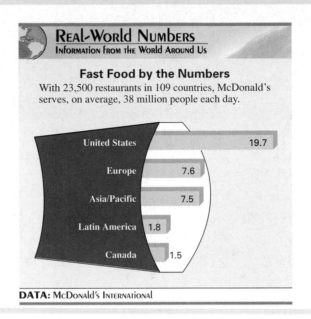

Real-World Numbers
INFORMATION FROM THE WORLD AROUND US

Fast Food by the Numbers
With 23,500 restaurants in 109 countries, McDonald's serves, on average, 38 million people each day.

United States	19.7
Europe	7.6
Asia/Pacific	7.5
Latin America	1.8
Canada	1.5

DATA: McDonald's International

For related Web activities, go to www.mathbusiness.com

Keyword: leftovers

Objective **1** **Understand the terms on an income statement.** An **income statement** is prepared for the management and owners of a business to summarize all income and expenses for a given period of time, such as a month, a quarter, or a year. First, find **gross sales**, which is the total amount of money received from customers for the goods or services sold by the firm. Then subtract the value of any **returns** from customers to arrive at **net sales**, the value of the goods and services bought and kept by customers.

$$\begin{array}{r} \text{Gross sales} \\ - \text{ Returns} \\ \hline \text{Net sales} \end{array}$$

After finding net sales, look at company records to find the **cost of goods sold**, the amount paid by the firm for the items sold to customers during the period of time covered by the income statement. Then, subtract the cost of goods sold from the net sales to find the **gross profit**. Gross profit is often called **gross profit on sales**. The gross profit is the amount of money left over after the business pays for the goods it sells. This money is used to pay the expenses involved in running the business.

$$\begin{array}{r} \text{Net sale} \\ - \text{Cost of goods sold} \\ \hline \text{Gross profit} \end{array}$$

Operating expenses represent the amount paid by the firm in an attempt to sell its goods. Common expenses include rent, salaries and wages, advertising, utilities, losses from uncollectible accounts, and taxes on inventory and payroll. Operating expenses are sometimes called **overhead**. Finally, **net income before taxes** is the actual amount earned by the firm during the given time period. **Net income**, also called **net income after taxes**, is found by subtracting income taxes from net income before taxes.

Gross profit
$-$Operating expenses

Net income before taxes

A portion of McDonald's Corporation 1997 income statement is shown in Example 1. Shares of the company are publicly traded on the New York Stock Exchange under the symbol MCD. Check the New York Stock Exchange page in a newspaper for a current stock price and dividend. The income statement is **consolidated** since it shows the total results of all of the subsidiary companies within McDonald's Corporation.

EXAMPLE 1
Finding Net Income

In 1997, McDonald's Corporation had gross sales of approximately $11,408,800,000. They had no returns to speak of due to the nature of their business, a cost of food and packaging of $2,772,600,000, operating expenses of $6,228,900,000, and income taxes of $764,800,000. Find the net income after taxes for the year.

Solution

Use the formulas in the boxes. For convenience, work with tenths of millions of dollars by dropping the last five digits, i.e., $11,408,800,000 becomes $11,408.8 million.

$$\text{Net sales} = \text{Gross sales} - \text{Returns}$$
$$= \$11,408.8 - 0 = \$11,408.8 \text{ (in millions of dollars)}$$

Gross sales equal net sales since they have no returns. Now find gross profit.

$$\text{Gross profit} = \text{Net sales} - \text{Cost of goods sold}$$
$$= \$11,408.8 - \$2772.6 = \$8636.2 \text{ (in millions of dollars)}$$

The gross profit is used to pay the expenses of running the business. Now find the net income before taxes.

$$\text{Net income before taxes} = \text{Gross profit} - \text{Operating expenses}$$
$$= \$8636.2 - \$6228.9 = \$2407.3 \text{ (in millions of dollars)}$$

Finally, calculate the net income after income taxes.

$$\text{Net income after taxes} = \text{Net income before taxes} - \text{Income taxes}$$
$$= \$2407.3 - \$764.8 = \$1642.5$$

In 1997, McDonald's Corporation paid approximately *$764,800,000 in income taxes* and still had *an after-tax profit of $1,642,500,000*. The results are summarized in the following table.

McDonald's Corporation Consolidated Statements of Income Year Ending December 31, 1997 (in millions of dollars)	
Gross sales	$11,408.8
Returns	$-$ 0
Net Sales	$11,408.8
Cost of Goods Sold	$-$ 2,772.6
Gross Profit	$ 8,636.2
Operating Expenses	$-$ 6,228.9
Net Income Before Taxes	$ 2,407.3
Taxes	$-$ 764.8
Net income After Taxes	$ 1,642.5

Check the results shown on the income statement with the following fundamental formula.

$$\underset{\text{goods sold}}{\text{Cost of}} + \text{Expenses} + \text{Taxes} + \underset{\text{after taxes}}{\text{Net income}} = \text{Net sales}$$
$$\$2772.6 + \$6228.9 + \$764.8 + \$1642.5 = \$11,408.8$$

The income statement checks.

The value of a company's stock is based on *financial results* in addition to *perceived opportunities*. As a publicly held corporation, McDonald's Corporation must publish financial results. The firm's stock price generally rises when profits are rising and generally falls when company profits are falling. You can obtain McDonald's Corporation current financial statements mailed to you *free* by calling their home office in Oak Brook, Illinois. You can also get financial information on the company using the World Wide Web.

Objective **2** **Prepare an income statement.** Example 1 gave the value for the cost of goods sold whereas this amount would normally need to be calculated. The cost of goods sold can be found using the following formula. **Initial inventory** is the value of all goods on hand for sale at the beginning of the period and **ending inventory** is the value of all goods on hand for sale at the end of the period.

> Initial inventory
> + Cost of goods purchased during time period
> + Freight
> <u>‒ Ending inventory</u>
> Cost of goods sold

EXAMPLE 2

Preparing an Income Statement

Josie's Clothing had gross sales of $159,000 during the past year, with returns of $9000. Inventory on January 1 of last year was $47,000. A total of $104,000 worth of goods was purchased last year, with freight on the goods totaling $2000. Inventory on December 31 of last year was $56,000. Wages paid to employees totaled $18,000. Rent was $9000, advertising was $1000, utilities totaled $2000, and taxes on inventory and payroll totaled $4000. Miscellaneous expenses totaled $6000 and income taxes were $500. Complete an income statement for the store using the steps listed below.

PREPARING AN INCOME STATEMENT

Step 1 Enter gross sales and returns. Subtract returns from gross sales to find net sales. Net sales in this example were $150,000.

Step 2 Enter the cost of goods purchased and the freight. Add these two numbers.

Step 3 Add the inventory on January 1 and the total cost of goods purchased.

Step 4 Subtract the inventory on December 31 from the result of step 3. This gives the cost of goods sold.

Step 5 Subtract the cost of goods sold from net sales, which were found in step 1. The result is the gross profit.

Step 6 Enter all expenses and add them to get the total expenses.

Step 7 Subtract the total expenses from the gross profit to find the net income before taxes.

Step 8 Subtract income taxes from net income before taxes to find net income (net income after taxes).

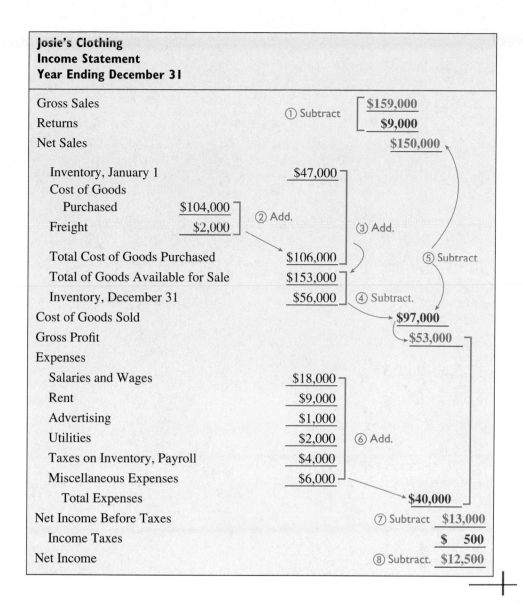

Josie's Clothing
Income Statement
Year Ending December 31

Gross Sales		① Subtract	**$159,000**
Returns			**$9,000**
Net Sales			**$150,000**
Inventory, January 1		$47,000	
Cost of Goods			
Purchased	$104,000	② Add.	
Freight	$2,000		
		③ Add.	
Total Cost of Goods Purchased		$106,000	⑤ Subtract
Total of Goods Available for Sale		$153,000	
Inventory, December 31		$56,000	④ Subtract.
Cost of Goods Sold			**$97,000**
Gross Profit			**$53,000**
Expenses			
Salaries and Wages		$18,000	
Rent		$9,000	
Advertising		$1,000	
Utilities		$2,000	⑥ Add.
Taxes on Inventory, Payroll		$4,000	
Miscellaneous Expenses		$6,000	
Total Expenses			**$40,000**
Net Income Before Taxes		⑦ Subtract	$13,000
Income Taxes			$ 500
Net Income		⑧ Subtract.	**$12,500**

NOTE Be sure to check the results of your income statement by adding the cost of goods sold, expenses, net income, and income taxes. This total should equal net sales.

Name   Date   Class

14.1 | EXERCISES

The Quick Start *exercises in each section contain solutions to help you get started.*

Find (a) the gross profit, (b) the net income before taxes, and (c) the net income after taxes for each firm. (See Example 1.)

Quick Start

1. **CLOTHING STORE** Jerome Buchanan opened a franchise clothing store in the mall three years ago. Last year, the cost of goods sold was $367,200, operating expenses were $228,300, income taxes were $22,700, gross sales were $685,900, and returns were $2350.

   (a) Gross profit = $685,900 − $2350 − $367,200 = $316,350
   (b) Net income before taxes = $316,350 − $228,300 = $88,050
   (c) Net income after taxes = $88,050 − $22,700 = $65,350

   (a) $316,350
   (b) $88,050
   (c) $65,350

2. **CANADIAN BOOKSTORE** A bookstore in Ontario, Canada, had net sales of $376,000, operating expenses of $36,000, a cost of goods sold of $294,000, and paid $6800 in taxes.

   (a) _____
   (b) _____
   (c) _____

3. **AUTO PARTS** Carmichael Auto Parts had gross sales of $284,000 last year, with returns of $6000. The inventory on January 1 was $58,000. A total of $232,000 worth of goods was purchased, with freight of $3000. The inventory on December 31 was $69,000. Wages and salaries were $15,000, rent was $6000, advertising was $2000, utilities were $1000, taxes on inventory and payroll totaled $3000, miscellaneous expenses totaled $4000, and income taxes amounted to $2400. Complete the following income statement. (See Example 2.)

Carmichael Auto Parts Income Statement Year Ending December 31		
Gross Sales		_____
Returns		_____
Net Sales		_____
Inventory, January 1	_____	
Cost of Goods Purchased		
Freight	_____	
Total Cost of Goods Purchased	_____	
Total of Goods Available for Sale	_____	
Inventory, December 31	_____	
Cost of Goods Sold		_____
Gross Profit		_____
Expenses		
Salaries and Wages	_____	
Rent	_____	
Advertising	_____	
Utilities	_____	
Taxes on Inventory, Payroll	_____	
Miscellaneous Expenses	_____	
Total Expenses		_____
Net Income Before Taxes		_____
Income Taxes		_____
Net Income		_____

4. Explain why a lender and an investor would want to look at an income statement before making a loan or an investment. (See Objective 1.)

5. Explain why a banker would look at your personal income statement before approving your loan. (See Objective 1.)

6. DENTAL-SUPPLY COMPANY New England Dental Supply is a regional wholesaler that had gross sales last year of $2,215,000. Returns totaled $26,000. Inventory on January 1 was $215,000. Goods purchased during the year totaled $1,123,000. Freight was $4000. Inventory on December 31 was $265,000. Wages and salaries were $154,000, rent was $59,000, advertising was $11,000, utilities were $12,000, taxes on inventory and payroll totaled $10,000, and miscellaneous expenses were $9000. In addition, income taxes for the year amounted to $287,400. Complete the following income statement for this firm. (See Example 2.)

New England Dental Supply
Income Statement
Year Ending December 31

Gross Sales		_____
Returns		_____
Net Sales		_____
Inventory, January 1	_____	
Cost of Goods		
Purchased	_____	
Freight	_____	
Total Cost of Goods Purchased	_____	
Total of Goods Available for Sale	_____	
Inventory, December 31	_____	
Cost of Goods Sold		_____
Gross Profit		_____
Expenses		
Salaries and Wages	_____	
Rent	_____	
Advertising	_____	
Utilities	_____	
Taxes on Inventory, Payroll	_____	
Miscellaneous Expenses	_____	
Total Expenses		_____
Net Income Before Taxes		_____
Income Taxes		_____
Net Income		_____

14.2 | ANALYZING THE INCOME STATEMENT

Objectives

1. Compare income statements using vertical analysis.
2. Compare income statements to published charts.
3. Compare income statements using horizontal analysis.

PROBLEM SOLVING IN BUSINESS

It is important for you to look carefully at the income statement of McDonald's Corporation, or any other company, before investing in the stock of that company. Invest only if you are convinced the company will be profitable.

OBJECTIVE 1 **Compare income statements using vertical analysis.** A firm can find its net income for a given period of time by going through the steps presented in the previous section. A question that might then be asked is "What happened to each part of the sales dollar?" The first step toward answering this question is to list each of the important items on the income statement as a percent of net sales, in a process called a **vertical analysis** of the income statement.

A vertical analysis of an income statement is another application of the fundamental formula for percent. Since a percent is needed, the formula must be solved for the rate R, as shown.

In a vertical analysis, each item is found as a percent of net sales.

$$R = \frac{P}{B} \quad \text{or} \quad R = \frac{\text{Particular item}}{\text{Net sales}}$$

For example, using data from the 1997 income statement for McDonald's Corporation found on page 583:

$$\text{Percent cost of goods sold} = \frac{\$2772.6}{\$11,408.8} = 24.3\%$$

A **comparative income statement** can be used to compare results from two or more different years.

EXAMPLE 1
Performing a Vertical Analysis

First, perform a vertical analysis of the summary 1996 and 1997 income statements shown below for McDonald's Corporation. Then construct a comparative income statement by showing the results in a table.

For related Web activities, go to
www.mathbusiness.com

Keyword:
SWOT

McDonald's Corporation Consolidated Statements of Income		
	(Millions of Dollars)	
Year Ending December 31,	**1996**	**1997**
Gross Sales	$10,686.5	$11,408.8
Returns	− 0	− 0
Net Sales	$10,686.5	$11,408.8
Cost of Goods Sold	− 2,546.6	− 2,772.6
Gross Profit	$ 8,139.9	$ 8,636.2
Operating Expenses	− 5,888.9	−6,228.9
Net Income Before Taxes	$ 2,251.0	$ 2,407.3

Solution

Calculate each value in the column labeled 1997 as a percent of 1997 net sales. Then do the same using 1996 data.

	Comparative Income Statement	
	1996	**1997**
Percent Cost of Goods Sold	$\dfrac{\$2546.6}{\$10,686.5} = 23.8\%$	$\dfrac{\$2772.6}{\$11,408.8} = 24.3\%$
Percent Gross Profit	$\dfrac{\$8139.9}{\$10,686.5} = 76.2\%$	$\dfrac{\$8636.2}{\$11,408.8} = 75.7\%$
Percent Operating Expenses	$\dfrac{\$5888.9}{\$10,686.5} = 55.1\%$	$\dfrac{\$6228.9}{\$11,408.8} = 54.6\%$
Percent Net Income Before Taxes	$\dfrac{\$2251.0}{\$10,686.5} = 21.1\%$	$\dfrac{\$2407.3}{\$11,408.8} = 21.1\%$

Note that the cost of goods sold **increased** from 23.8% of net sales in 1996 to 24.3% of net sales in 1997. This is *not a good sign* since it suggests that the company may be facing increasing costs. However, they carefully cut their operating expenses from 55.1% of net sales in 1996 to 54.6% of net sales in 1997. As a result, net income before taxes remained constant at 21.1% of net sales. As an investor, you may wish to watch the cost of goods sold to see if it increases over time.

OBJECTIVE **2** **Compare income statements to published charts.** If you own a business or are considering investing in a business, you would be wise to compare the financial figures for that business to industry averages. Published charts of industry averages can be obtained from the Internal Revenue Service.

Type of Business	Cost of Goods	Gross Profit	Total Expenses*	Net Income	Wages	Rent	Advertising
Supermarkets	82.7%	17.3%	13.9%	3.4%	6.5%	.8%	1.0%
Men's and women's apparel	67.0%	33.0%	21.2%	11.8%	8.0%	2.5%	1.9%
Women's apparel	64.8%	35.2%	23.4%	11.7%	7.9%	4.9%	1.8%
Shoes	60.3%	39.7%	24.5%	15.2%	10.3%	4.7%	1.6%
Furniture	68.9%	31.2%	21.7%	9.6%	9.5%	1.8%	2.5%
Appliances	66.9%	33.1%	26.0%	7.2%	11.9%	2.4%	2.5%
Drugs	67.9%	32.1%	23.5%	8.6%	12.3%	2.4%	1.4%
Restaurants	48.4%	51.6%	43.7%	7.9%	26.4%	2.8%	1.4%
Service stations	76.8%	23.2%	16.9%	6.3%	8.5%	2.3%	.5%

*Total Expenses represents the total of all expenses involved in running the firm. These expenses include—but are not limited to—wages, rent, and advertising.

EXAMPLE 2
Compare Business Ratios

Gina Burton wishes to compare the business ratios of her shoe store, Burton's Shoes, to industry averages. Figures from her store and industry averages for shoe stores are shown below.

	Cost of Goods	Gross Profit	Total Expenses	Net Income	Wages	Rent	Advertising
Burton's Shoes	58.2%	41.8%	28.3%	13.5%	11.7%	5.6%	2.8%
Shoes (from chart)	60.3%	39.7%	24.5%	15.2%	10.3%	4.7%	1.6%

Solution

Burton's expenses are higher than the average for other shoe stores and her net income is lower. Wages are higher—perhaps because her store is located in an area with high wages or perhaps the store is not large enough to efficiently utilize its employees. Burton also spends a higher percent than average for advertising. Perhaps she can reduce her advertising expenses without lowering sales.

Objective **3** **Compare income statements using horizontal analysis.** Another way to analyze an income statement is to prepare a **horizontal analysis**. A horizontal analysis finds percents of change (either increases or decreases) between the current time period and a previous time period. This comparison can expose unusual changes such as a rapid increase in expenses or decline in net sales or profits.

A horizontal analysis is done by finding the amount of any change from the previous year to the current year, both in dollars and as a percent. For example, the income statement for McDonald's Corporation on page 589 shows that net sales increased from $10,686.5 (in millions) in 1996 to $11,408.8 (in millions) in 1997, an increase of $11,408.8 − $10,686.5 = $722.3 million. Find the percent of increase by comparing the dollar amount of increase to 1996 sales.

$$\frac{\$722.3}{\$10,686.5} = 6.8\% \text{ (rounded)}$$

For related Web
activities, go to
www.mathbusiness.com

Keyword:
investing

This *relatively slow growth rate in total sales* may be part of the reason that McDonald's stock has been hot and cold as seen in the chart.

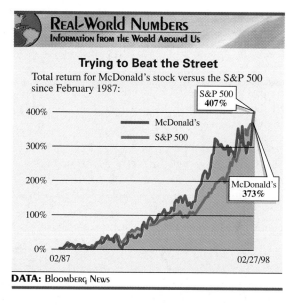

Real-World Numbers
INFORMATION FROM THE WORLD AROUND US

Trying to Beat the Street
Total return for McDonald's stock versus the S&P 500 since February 1987:

S&P 500 **407%**

McDonald's
S&P 500

McDonald's **373%**

DATA: Bloomberg News

To emphasize:

$$\% \text{ of change} = \frac{\text{Change}}{\text{Previous year's amount}}$$

Always use *last year* as the base.

EXAMPLE 3

Performing a
Horizontal
Analysis

Calculate a horizontal analysis for the 1996 and 1997 income statements for McDonald's Corporation using the data shown in Example 1.

Solution

Find the increase by subtracting the 1996 figure from the 1997 figure. Then divide by the 1996 figure to find the percent increase.

McDonald's Corporation Consolidated Statements of Income Year Ending December 31 (in millions of dollars)				
	1996	**1997**	**Increase**	**Percent**
Net Sales	$10,686.5	$11,408.8	$722.3	6.8%
Gross Profit	$ 8,139.9	$ 8,636.2	$496.3	6.1%
Income Before Taxes	$ 2,251.0	$ 2,407.3	$156.3	6.9%

REALITY CHECK

Net sales increased by 6.8% from 1996 to 1997, which is a relatively slow growth rate. A large growth rate probably cannot be maintained and a small growth rate suggests that the company's profits may never increase much above current levels. McDonald's Corporation hopes to maintain a good growth rate by:

1. encouraging existing customers to visit the restaurants more often and

2. finding new customers for their foods in international markets such as China, Russia, and Mexico.

Profits **must also be examined** to determine the financial health of a company. Income before taxes increased 6.9% from 1996 to 1997, which is relatively slow, but it is in line with the growth in net sales. Based on the data from 1996 and 1997, McDonald's Corporation appears to be growing slowly.

McDonald's to Increase Outlets in Central Europe

The fast-food chain will invest more than $400 million in Central Europe to build 400 new restaurants there. That will double the number of McDonald's in the region. An executive with McDonald's International called emerging markets like Central Europe the "cornerstone" of the company's global growth.

Source: Investor's Business Daily, 5/15/98. Reprinted by permission.

Name   Date   Class

14.2 | Exercises

Prepare a vertical analysis for each of the following firms. Round percents to the nearest tenth of a percent. (See Example 1.)

1. GUITAR SHOP In 1999, Classic Guitars had a cost of goods sold (guitars) of $243,570, operating expenses of $140,450, and net sales of $480,300.

1. _____

2. COIN SHOP Traver's Coin Shop, Inc. had net sales of $294,380, operating expenses of $68,650, and a cost of goods sold of $163,890.

2. _____

The following charts show some figures from the income statements of several companies. In each case, prepare a vertical analysis by expressing each item as a percent of net sales. Then write in the appropriate average percent from the table in the book. (See Objective 2.)

3.

Gooden Drugs

	Amount	Percent	Average Percent
Net Sales	$850,000	100%	100%
Cost of Goods Sold	$570,350	_____	_____
Gross Profit	$279,650	_____	_____
Wages	$106,250	_____	_____
Rent	$21,250	_____	_____
Advertising	$12,750	_____	_____
Total Expenses	$209,100	_____	_____
Net Income Before Taxes	$70,550	_____	_____

4.

Ellis Restaurant

	Amount	Percent	Average Percent
Net Sales	$600,000	100%	100%
Cost of Goods Sold	$280,000	_____	_____
Gross Profit	$320,000	_____	_____
Wages	$160,600	_____	_____
Rent	$15,000	_____	_____
Advertising	$8,000	_____	_____
Total Expenses	$255,000	_____	_____
Net Income Before Taxes	$65,000	_____	_____

5. Compare a vertical analysis to a horizontal analysis. (See Objectives 1 and 3.)

6. Why would a lender want to use both vertical and horizontal analyses before making a long-term loan to a firm?

Complete the following comparative income statement. Round to the nearest tenth of a percent.

7.

Hernandez Nursery Comparative Income Statement

	This Year		Last Year	
	Amount	Percent	Amount	Percent
Gross Sales	$1,856,000	_____	$1,692,000	_____
Returns	$6,000	_____	$12,000	_____
Net Sales	_____	100.0%	_____	100.0%
Cost of Goods Sold	$1,202,000	_____	$1,050,000	_____
Gross Profit	$648,000	_____	$630,000	_____
Wages	$152,000	_____	$148,000	_____
Rent	$82,000	_____	$78,000	_____
Advertising	$111,000	_____	$122,000	_____
Utilities	$32,000	_____	$17,000	_____
Taxes on Inv., Payroll	$17,000	_____	$18,000	_____
Miscellaneous Expenses	$62,000	_____	$58,000	_____
Total Expenses	$456,000	_____	$441,000	_____
Net Income Before Taxes	_____	_____	_____	_____

Complete the following horizontal analysis for the Hernandez Nursery comparative income statement given above. Round to the nearest tenth of a percent.

8.

	This Year	Last Year	Increase or (Decrease)	
			Amount	Percent
Gross Sales	$1,856,000	$1,692,000	_____	_____
Returns	$6,000	$12,000	_____	_____
Net Sales	$1,850,000	$1,680,000	_____	_____
Cost of Goods Sold	$1,202,000	$1,050,000	_____	_____
Gross Profit	$648,000	$630,000	_____	_____
Wages	$152,000	$148,000	_____	_____
Rent	$82,000	$78,000	_____	_____
Advertising	$111,000	$122,000	_____	_____
Utilities	$32,000	$17,000	_____	_____
Taxes on Inv., Payroll	$17,000	$18,000	_____	_____
Miscellaneous Expenses	$62,000	$58,000	_____	_____
Net Income Before Taxes	$192,000	$189,000	_____	_____

The following tables give the percents for various items from the income statements of firms in various businesses. Complete these tables by including the appropriate percents from the table on page 590. Identify any areas that might require attention by management.

Type of Store	Cost of Goods	Gross Profit	Total Operating Expenses	Net Income	Wages	Rent	Advertising
9. Women's apparel	66.4%	33.6%	25.3%	8.3%	8.4%	6.5%	1.9%
	____	____	____	____	____	____	____
10. Drug store	71.2%	28.8%	26.5%	2.3%	12.9%	5.3%	2.0%
	____	____	____	____	____	____	____

14.3 | THE BALANCE SHEET

Objectives

1 Understand the terms on a balance sheet.
2 Prepare a balance sheet.

PROBLEM SOLVING IN BUSINESS

Should you look at anything other than the income statement for McDonald's Corporation before buying the stock? The answer is yes, you should also look at the balance sheet, which shows the amount of debt and cash on hand and is not shown in the income statement.

OBJECTIVE 1 **Understand the terms on a balance sheet.** You should also look at the financial ratios in Section 14.4 and you may even wish to visit a few McDonald's restaurants before investing in the stock. An income statement summarizes the financial affairs of a business firm for a given period of time, such as a year. On the other hand, a **balance sheet** describes the financial condition of a firm *at one point in time*, such as the last day of a year. A balance sheet shows the worth of a business at a particular time by listing its **assets**—the things it owns, such as property, equipment, and money owed to the business, as well as its **liabilities**—amounts owed by the business to others. The difference between these two amounts gives the **owner's equity** in the business.

Both assets and liabilities are divided into two categories, **long-term** and **current (short-term)**. Long-term generally applies when the time involved is more than one year whereas short-term applies when the time involved is less than one year. The following items appear as assets on balance sheets.

Assets:

Current assets—cash or items that can be converted into cash within a short period of time such as a year
    Cash—in checking and savings accounts and money-market instruments
    Accounts receivable—funds owed by customers of the firm
    Notes receivable—value of all notes owed to the firm
    Inventory—cost of merchandise that the firm has for sale

Plant and equipment—assets that are expected to be used for more than one year (also called **fixed assets** or **plant assets**)
    Land—book value of any land owned by the firm
    Buildings—book value of any building owned by the firm
    Equipment—book value of equipment, store fixtures, furniture, and similar items owned by the firm

The following items appear as liabilities on balance sheets.

Liabilities:

Current liabilities—items that must be paid by the firm within a short period of time, usually one year
    Accounts payable—amounts that must be paid to other firms
    Notes payable—value of all notes owed by the firm

Long-term liabilities—items that will be paid after one year
    Mortgages payable—total due on all mortgages
    Long-term notes payable—total of all other debts of the firm

The difference between the total of all assets and the total of all liabilities is called the **owner's equity**, which is also referred to as **net worth** or, for a corporation, **stockholder's equity**. The relationship between owner's equity, assets, and liabilities is shown in the fundamental formula below.

$$\text{Owner's equity} = \text{Assets} - \text{Liabilities} \quad \text{or}$$

$$\text{Assets} = \text{Liabilities} + \text{Owner's equity}$$

Objective **2** **Prepare a balance sheet.**

EXAMPLE 1

Preparing a
Balance Sheet

The assets and liabilities of McDonald's Corporation on December 31, 1997, in millions of dollars are: cash and marketable securities, $341.4; accounts receivable, $483.5; inventories, $70.5; other current assets, $246.9; subsidiaries and other assets, $2,137.8; property and equipment, $14,961.4; accounts payable, $650.6; loans and notes payable, $1,293.8; other payables and accrued taxes, $1,040.1; long-term debt $4,834.1; and other liabilities $1,571.3. Complete a balance sheet for the company.

For related Web
activities, go to
www.mathbusiness.com

Keyword:
accounting

SOLUTION

McDonald's Corporation Consolidated Balance Sheet December 31, 1997 (in millions of dollars)		
Current Assets:		
Cash and Equivalents	$ 341.4	
Accounts Receivable	$ 483.5	
Inventories	$ 70.5	
Other Current Assets	$ 246.9	
Total Current Assets	$ 1,142.3	sum of all current assets
Other Assets:		
Subsidiaries and Other Assets	$ 2,137.8	
Property and equipment	$14,961.4	
Total Assets	$18,241.5	sum of current assets plus all other assets
Current Liabilities:		
Accounts Payable	$ 650.6	
Loans and Notes Payable	$ 1,293.8	
Other Payables and Accrued Taxes	$ 1,040.1	
Total Current Liabilities	$ 2,984.5	sum of all current liabilities
Other Liabilities:		
Long-Term Debt	$ 4,834.1	
Other Liabilities	$ 1,571.3	
Total Liabilities	$ 9,389.9	sum of current liabilities plus all other liabilities
Stockholder's Equity	$ 8,851.6	Total Assets − Total Liabilities
Total Liabilities and Equity	$18,241.5	

NOTE   The sum of the liabilities and the stockholder's equity must equal the assets.

A balance sheet shows the position of a company at one point in time—the figures could be very different a month later. For example, McDonald's Corporation had approximately $341,400,000 in cash and equivalents on December 31, 1997. This balance sheet *does not* provide any information about cash and equivalents held on any date other than that specific date.

Name   Date   Class

14.3 | Exercises

Complete the balance sheets for the following business firms. (See Example 1.)

1. CONSTRUCTION OF BRIDGES   Apple Construction (all figures in millions): fixtures, $28; buildings, $290; land, $466; cash, $273; notes receivable, $312; accounts receivable, $264; inventory, $180; notes payable, $312; mortgages payable, $212; accounts payable, $63; long-term notes payable, $55.

Apple Construction Balance Sheet December 31 (in millions)

ASSETS		
Current Assets		
Cash		
Notes Receivable	_____	
Accounts Receivable	_____	
Inventory	_____	
	_____	
Total Current Assets		_____
Plant Assets		
Land		
Buildings	_____	
Fixtures	_____	
	_____	
Total plant Assets		_____
Total Assets		_____

LIABILITIES		
Current Liabilities		
Notes Payable	_____	
Accounts Payable	_____	
	_____	
Total Current Liabilities		_____
Long-Term Liabilities		
Mortgages Payable	_____	
Long-Term Notes Payable	_____	
	_____	
Total Long-Term Liabilities		_____
Total Liabilities		_____

OWNER'S EQUITY		
Owner's Equity		_____
Total Liabilities and Owner's Equity		_____

2. **LOPEZ RENT-ALL** Land is $8750; accounts payable total $49,230; notes receivable are $2600; accounts receivable are $37,820; cash is $14,800; buildings are $21,930; notes payable are $3780; owner's equity is $54,320; long-term notes payable are $18,740; mortgages total $26,330; inventory is $49,680; fixtures are $16,820.

Lopez Rent-All Balance Sheet—December 31

ASSETS

Current Assets
 Cash _____
 Notes Receivable _____
 Accounts Receivable _____
 Inventory _____

   Total Current Assets _____

Plant Assets
 Land _____
 Buildings _____
 Fixtures _____

   Total Plant Assets _____
  Total Assets ══════

LIABILITIES

Current Liabilities
 Notes Payable
 Accounts Payable _____

   Total Current Liabilities _____

Long-Term Liabilities
 Mortgages Payable _____
 Long-Term Notes Payable _____

   Total Long-Term Liabilities _____
  Total Liabilities _____

OWNER'S EQUITY

Owner's Equity _____
   Total Liabilities and Owner's Equity ══════

3. Compare a balance sheet to an income statement.

4. Use the World Wide Web to find the amount of cash and equivalents at the end of the most recent fiscal year for General Motors and the Coca-Cola Company. Which company has more? Why do you suppose they have as much as they do?

14.4 | Analyzing the Balance Sheet

Objectives

1. Compare balance sheets using vertical analysis.
2. Compare balance sheets using horizontal analysis.
3. Find financial ratios.

Objective 1 **Compare balance sheets using vertical analysis.** A balance sheet can be analyzed in much the same way as an income statement. In a **vertical analysis**, each item on the balance sheet is expressed as a percent of total assets. A **comparative balance sheet** shows the vertical analysis for two different years.

Example 1

Comparing Balance Sheets

First, do a vertical analysis for both the 1996 and 1997 balance sheets for McDonald's Corporation by calculating each value as a percent of the total assets for the year. Then compare the percents to identify changes from 1996 to 1997.

Solution

McDonald's Corporation
Consolidated Balance Sheet
December 31, 1997 (in millions of dollars)

	1997		1996	
Assets	**Amount**	**Percent**	**Amount**	**Percent**
Current Assets:				
Cash and Equivalents	$ 341.4	1.9%*	$ 329.9	1.9%
Accounts Receivable	$ 483.5	2.7%	$ 495.4	2.8%
Inventories	$ 70.5	0.4%	$ 69.6	0.4%
Other Current Assets	$ 246.9	1.4%	$ 207.6	1.2%
Total Current Assets	$ 1,142.3	6.4%	$ 1,102.5	6.3%
Other Assets:				
Subsidiaries and Other Assets	$ 2,137.8	11.7%	$ 1,931.4	11.1%
Property and Equipment	$14,961.4	+82.0%	$14,351.1	+82.5%
TOTAL ASSETS	$18,241.5	100.1%	$17,386.0	99.9%
Liabilities	**Amount**	**Percent**	**Amount**	**Percent**
Current Liabilities:				
Accounts Payable	$ 650.6	3.6%	$ 638.0	3.7%
Loans and Notes Payable	$ 1,293.8	7.1%	$ 597.8	3.4%
Other Payables and Accrued Taxes	$ 1,040.1	5.7%	$ 899.5	5.2%
Total Current Liabilities	$ 2,984.5	16.4%	$ 2,135.3	12.3%
Other Liabilities:				
Long-Term Debt	$ 4,834.1	26.5%	$ 4,830.1	27.8%
Other Liabilities	$ 1,571.3	8.6%	$ 1,702.4	9.8%
TOTAL LIABILITIES	$ 9,389.9	51.5%	$ 8,667.8	49.9%
Stockholder's Equity	$ 8,851.6	48.5%	$ 8,718.2	50.1%
Total Liabilities and Owner's Equity	$18,241.5	100.0%	$17,386.0	100.0%

Amounts in the table may not add up due to rounding; percents should add up to total.

*$341.4 ÷ $18,241.5 = 0.18715566 or 1.9%

Notice that current liabilities, which are those expected to be paid in one year, increased from 12.3% of total assets in 1996 to 16.4% of total assets in 1997. This corresponds to a significant increase in short-term debt.

$$\$2,984,500,000 - \$2,135,300,000 = \$849,200,000 \text{ increase}$$

Some of this comes from the fact that the firm is adding more than 2000 new restaurants each year, nevertheless, this is a trend that an investor should watch.

Looking further into their annual report, it is apparent that the strength of the dollar against foreign currencies hurt McDonald's growth in dollar figures. You can see by the following table that McDonald's Corporation works with many different currencies.

McDonald's Corporation: Number of Restaurants

	1997	1996	1995	Ten years ago
U.S.	12,380	12,094	11,368	7,567
Europe	3,886	3,283	2,595	753
Asia/Pacific	4,456	3,633	2,735	951
Latin America	1,091	837	665	99
Other	1,319	1,175	1,017	541
Systemwide Restaurants	23,132	21,022	18,380	9,911

Objective ② **Compare balance sheets using horizontal analysis.** Perform a **horizontal analysis** by finding the change, both in dollars and in percent, for each item on the balance sheet from one year to the next. As before, always use the previous year as a base when finding the percents.

Example 2

Using Horizontal Analysis

According to the balance sheet for McDonald's Corporation, Cash and Equivalents on December 31, 1997, were $341.4 (in millions) compared to $329.9 (in millions) on December 31, 1996. This represents an increase of $341.4 − $329.9 = $11.5 million. The percent increase is

$$\frac{\$11.5}{\$329.9} = 3.5\% \text{ (rounded)}.$$

Similarly, complete a horizontal analysis of the current assets portion of McDonald's Corporation's balance sheet.

Solution

Comparative Analysis of Consolidated Balance Sheets
McDonald's Corporation (in millions of dollars)

			Increase or (Decrease)	
Current Assets—December 31	1997	1996	Amount	Percent
Cash and Equivalents	$341.4	$329.9	$11.5	3.5%
Accounts Receivable	$483.5	$495.4	($11.9)	(2.4%)
Inventories	$ 70.5	$ 69.6	$ .9	1.3%
Other Current Assets	$246.9	$207.6	$39.3	18.9%
TOTAL CURRENT ASSETS	$1,142.3	$1,102.5	$39.8	3.6%

The parentheses around the $11.9 in the Accounts Receivable row of the table is used to indicate a negative number. Accounts receivable actually went down from 1996 to 1997 for a negative increase. The corresponding percent of 2.4% is also shown as a negative number since it represents a decrease.

Objective ③ **Find financial ratios.** After preparing a balance sheet for a business firm, an accountant often calculates several different **financial ratios** for the firm. These ratios can be compared to financial ratios for other firms in the same industry or of the same size. A ratio *that is far out of line when compared to other similar firms or to industry averages* might well indicate coming financial difficulties.

The first two ratios we discuss are designed to measure the **liquidity** of a firm; liquidity refers to a firm's ability to raise cash quickly without being forced to sell assets at a big loss.

Find the **current ratio** by dividing current assets by current liabilities.

$$\text{Current ratio} = \frac{\text{Current assets}}{\text{Current liabilities}}$$

> **NOTE** The current ratio is also known as the **banker's ratio**.

EXAMPLE 3
Finding the Current Ratio

According to the 1997 balance sheet for McDonald's Corporation, current assets were $1142.3 (in millions) and current liabilities were $2984.5 (in millions). Find the current ratio.

Solution
Use the formula for current ratio.

$$\text{Current ratio} = \frac{\$1142.3}{\$2984.5} = .383$$

This ratio is often expressed as .383 to 1 or as .383 : 1. Many lending institutions calculate current ratio in the process of determining if a firm will get a loan. A common rule of thumb, not necessarily applicable to all businesses or at all times, is that the current ratio should be at least 2 : 1. A firm with a current ratio much less than 2 : 1 may have an increased risk of financial difficulty and may have difficulty borrowing money. This rule of thumb probably does not apply to McDonald's Corporation since they are able to turn over their inventory so rapidly during the year.

One disadvantage of the current ratio is that inventory is included in current assets. In a period of financial difficulty a firm might have trouble disposing of the inventory at a reasonable price. Some accountants feel that the **acid test** of a firm's financial health is to consider only **liquid assets:** assets that are either cash or that can be converted to cash quickly, such as securities and accounts and notes receivable.

The **acid-test ratio**, also called the **quick ratio**, is defined as follows.

$$\text{Acid-test ratio} = \frac{\text{Liquid assets}}{\text{Current liabilities}}$$

> **NOTE** As a general rule based on past experience, the acid-test ratio should be at least 1 to 1, so that liquid assets are at least enough to cover current liabilities.

EXAMPLE 4
Finding the Acid-Test Ratio

Find the 1997 acid-test ratio for McDonald's Corporation.

Solution
Liquid assets are made up of cash and equivalents in addition to accounts receivable. Using data from the 1997 balance sheet:

$$\text{Liquid assets} = \$341.4 + \$483.5 = \$824.9.$$

Since current liabilities are $2984.5, the acid-test ratio is

$$\frac{\$824.9}{\$2984.5} = .276$$

Again, the rule of thumb probably does not apply to McDonald's Corporation since they are a large, stable corporation with many customers and a company that can turn their inventory over very quickly.

A company with a large amount of capital invested should have a higher net income than a company with a small amount invested. To check on this, accountants often find the **ratio of net income after taxes to average owner's equity**. The **average owner's equity** is found by adding the owner's equity at the beginning and end of the year and dividing by 2.

$$\frac{\text{Average}}{\text{owner's equity}} = \frac{\text{Owner's equity at beginning} + \text{Owner's equity at end}}{2}$$

Then the ratio of net income after taxes to average owner's equity is found as follows.

$$\frac{\text{Ratio of net income after taxes}}{\text{to average owner's equity}} = \frac{\text{Net income after taxes}}{\text{Average owner's equity}}$$

EXAMPLE 5
Finding the
Return on
Average Equity

Find the 1997 ratio of net income after taxes to average owner's equity for McDonald's Corporation.

Solution

At the end of 1996, which is the same as the beginning of 1997, the firm had a stockholder's equity of $8718.2 (in millions) and at the end of 1997, the stockholder's equity was $8851.6. The average owner's equity was

$$\frac{\$8718.2 + \$8851.6}{2} = \$8784.9.$$

Use of the net income after taxes for 1997 from the income statement in Section 14.1 on page 583 ($1642.5) results in the following ratio of net income after taxes to average owner's equity.

$$\frac{\$1642.5}{\$8784.9} = 18.7\% \text{ (rounded)}.$$

This ratio should be at least as much as the interest paid on savings accounts by banks. Otherwise the capital represented by these assets should be deposited in a bank account. After all, savings accounts should have less risk than an investment in a company. Increased risk should bring a *higher return* to the investor than that of a risk-free savings account. Notice that this ratio is considerably higher than savings account yields!

NOTE The ratio of net income after taxes to average owner's equity is the only ratio of the three we have looked at that requires you to look at both the income statement and the balance sheet.

The financial ratios of this section can be summarized as follows.

SUMMARY OF RATIOS

$$\text{Current ratio} = \frac{\text{Current assets}}{\text{Current liabilities}} \qquad \text{Acid-test ratio} = \frac{\text{Liquid assets}}{\text{Current liabilities}}$$

$$\frac{\text{Ratio of net income after taxes}}{\text{to average owner's equity}} = \frac{\text{Net income after taxes}}{\text{Average owner's equity}}$$

Name   Date   Class

14.4 | EXERCISES

1. **RUBBER SUPPLY COMPANY** Complete this balance sheet using vertical analysis. Round to the nearest tenth of a percent. (See Example 1.)

Interstate Rubber Supply Comparative Balance Sheet

	Amount This Year	Percent This Year	Amount Last Year	Percent Last Year
ASSETS				
Current Assets				
Cash	$52,000	_____	$42,000	_____
Notes Receivable	$8,000	_____	$6,000	_____
Accounts Receivable	$148,000	_____	$120,000	_____
Inventory	$153,000	_____	$120,000	_____
Total Current Assets	_____	_____	_____	_____
Plant Assets				
Land	$10,000	_____	$8,000	_____
Buildings	$14,000	_____	$11,000	_____
Fixtures	$15,000	_____	$13,000	_____
Total Plant Assets	_____	_____	_____	_____
TOTAL ASSETS	_____	100%	_____	100%
LIABILITIES				
Current Liabilities				
Accounts Payable	$3,000	_____	$4,000	_____
Notes Payable	$201,000	_____	$152,000	_____
Total Current Liabilities	_____	_____	_____	_____
Long-Term Liabilities				
Mortgages Payable	$20,000	_____	$16,000	_____
Long-Term Notes Payable	$58,000	_____	$42,000	_____
Total Long-Term Liabilities	_____	_____	_____	_____
TOTAL LIABILITIES	_____	_____	_____	_____
Owner's Equity	$118,000	_____	$106,000	_____
TOTAL LIABILITIES AND OWNER'S EQUITY	_____	_____	_____	_____

2. POOLS AND SPAS Complete the following horizontal analysis for a portion of the balance sheet for Peerless Pools & Spas. Note that figures are shown in thousands of dollars. (Round to tenths of a percent). (See Example 1.)

	This Year	Last Year	Increase or (Decrease) Amount	Increase or (Decrease) Percent
ASSETS				
Current Assets				
Cash	$52,000	$42,000	_____	_____
Notes Receivable	$8,000	$6,000	_____	_____
Accounts Receivable	$148,000	$120,000	_____	_____
Inventory	$153,000	$120,000	_____	_____
Total Current Assets	$361,000	$288,000	_____	_____
Plant Assets				
Land	$10,000	$8,000	_____	_____
Buildings	$14,000	$11,000	_____	_____
Fixtures	$15,000	$13,000	_____	_____
Total Plant Assets	$39,000	$32,000	_____	_____
TOTAL ASSETS	$400,000	$320,000	_____	_____

In Exercises 3–6, find (a) the current ratio and (b) the acid-test ratio. Round each ratio to the nearest hundredth. (c) Do the ratios suggest that the company is financially healthy using the guidelines given in the text? (See Examples 3 and 4.)

3. Peerless Pools & Spas has the balance sheet given above and current liabilities of $204,000. Find the ratios for this year.

(a) _____
(b) _____
(c) _____

4. MUSIC STORE Virginia Music has current assets of $216,750, current liabilities of $213,000, cash of $25,400, notes and accounts receivable of $42,500, and an inventory of mostly electric pianos and various electronic equipment valued at $148,850.

(a) _____
(b) _____
(c) _____

5. CADILLAC DEALER Wagner Cadillac has current assets of $2,210,350, current liabilities of $1,232,500, total cash of $480,500, notes and accounts receivable of $279,050, and an inventory of $1,450,800.

(a) _____
(b) _____
(c) _____

Name _____   Date _____   Class _____

6. OXYGEN SUPPLY BlueTex Oxygen Supply has current assets of $2,234,000, current liabilities of $840,000, total cash of $339,000, notes and accounts receivable of $1,215,000, and an inventory of $680,000.

(a) _____
(b) _____
(c) _____

A portion of a comparative balance sheet is shown below. First complete the chart, and then find the current ratio and the acid-test ratio for the indicated year. Round each ratio to the nearest hundredth.

	Amount This Year	Percent This Year	Amount Last Year	Percent Last Year
Current Assets				
Cash	$12,000	_____	$15,000	_____
Notes Receivable	$4,000	_____	$6,000	_____
Accounts Receivable	$22,000	_____	$18,000	_____
Inventory	$26,000	_____	$24,000	_____
Total Current Assets	$64,000	80%	$63,000	84%
Total Plant Assets	$16,000	_____	$12,000	_____
TOTAL ASSETS	_____	100.0%	_____	100.0%
Total Current Liabilities	$30,000	_____	$25,000	_____

7. This year _____

8. Last year _____

Find the ratio of net income after taxes to average owner's equity in the following. (See Example 5.) Round to the nearest tenth of a percent.

9. INTERNATIONAL AIRLINE The stockholder's equity in TNA Airline, a small international airline that uses small airplanes to move freight to and from Mexico, is $845,000 at the beginning of the year and $928,500 at the end of the year. Net income after taxes for the year was $54,400.

9. _____

10. NATURAL-GAS PIPELINE TransCanada Pipe is an international company that does business both in Canada and in the United States. In thousands of dollars, owner's equity at the beginning of the year was $48,340 and $62,842 at the end of the year. Net income after taxes for the year was $6838.

10. _____

Calculate the current ratio and acid-test ratio for the companies given below. Are the companies healthy based on the guidelines given in the text?

11. Bill's Electronics:

Current assets	$125,000
Current liabilities:	$85,000
Liquid assets:	$12,240

11. _____

12. Lupe's Hair Styles:

Current assets:	$18,250
Current liabilities:	$2,400
Liquid assets:	$8,250

12. _____

13. Explain why the acid-test ratio is a better measure of the financial health of a firm than the current ratio. (See Objective 3.)

14. Explain why increased risk requires a higher return on investment. (See Objective 3.)

CHAPTER TERMS

Review the following terms to test your understanding of the chapter. For each term you do not know, refer to the page number found next to that term.

acid test [**p.** 603]
acid-test ratio [**p.** 603]
average owner's equity [**p.** 604]
assets [**p.** 597]
balance sheet [**p.** 597]
banker's ratio [**p.** 603]
comparative balance sheet [**p.** 601]
comparative income statement [**p.** 589]
consolidated [**p.** 583]

cost of goods sold [**p.** 582]
current assets [**p.** 599]
current liabilities [**p.** 597]
current ratio [**p.** 603]
financial ratios [**p.** 603]
fixed assets [**p.** 597]
gross profit [**p.** 582]
gross profit on sales [**p.** 582]
gross sales [**p.** 582]
horizontal analysis [**p.** 591]

income statement [**p.** 582]
liabilities [**p.** 597]
liquid assets [**p.** 603]
liquidity [**p.** 603]
long-term liabilities [**p.** 597]
net income [**p.** 582]
net income after taxes [**p.** 582]
net income before taxes [**p.** 582]
net sales [**p.** 582]
net worth [**p.** 587]

operating expenses [**p.** 582]
overhead [**p.** 582]
owner's equity [**p.** 587]
plant and equipment [**p.** 597]
plant assets [**p.** 597]
quick ratio [**p.** 603]
ratio of net income after taxes to average owner's equity [**p.** 604]
returns [**p.** 582]
stockholder's equity [**p.** 597]
vertical analysis [**p.** 589]

CONCEPTS

14.1 Finding the gross profit and net income

1. Find the net sales.
2. Determine the cost of goods sold.
3. Find gross profit from the formula

Gross profit = Net sales − Cost of goods sold.

4. Find the operating expenses.
5. Find the net income from the formula.

Net income = Gross profit − Operating expenses.

14.2 Find the percent of net sales of individual items

1. Determine net sales using the formula.

Net sales = Gross sales − Returns

2. Use the formula

$$\textbf{Percent of net sales} = \frac{\textbf{Particular item}}{\textbf{Net sales}}$$

for each item.

EXAMPLES

Candy the Way You Like It had a cost of goods sold of $123,500, operating expenses of $48,950, and gross sales of $206,100. Find the gross profit and net income before taxes.

Gross profit = Gross sales − Returns − Cost of goods sold
= $206,100 − 0 − $123,500
= $82,600

Net income before taxes = Gross profit − Operating expenses
= $82,600 − $48,950
= $33,650

Mr. Bill's appliance store lists the following information.

Gross sales = $340,000   Salaries and wages = $19,000
Returns = $15,000   Rent = $8000
Cost of goods sold = $210,000   Advertising = $12,000

Express each item as a percent of net sales. (Round to the nearest tenth of a percent.)

Net sales = $340,000 − $15,000 = $325,000
Gross profit = $325,000 − $210,000 = $115,000
Total expenses = $19,000 + $8000 + $12,000 = $39,000
Net income = $115,000 − $39,000 = $76,000

Find all the desired percents to the nearest tenth of a percent by dividing each item by net sales.

$$\text{Percent gross sales} = \frac{\$340,000}{\$325,000} = \textbf{104.6\%}$$

$$\text{Percent returns} = \frac{\$15,000}{\$325,000} = \textbf{4.6\%}$$

$$\text{Percent cost of goods sold} = \frac{\$210,000}{\$325,000} = \textbf{64.6\%}$$

$$\text{Percent gross profit} = \frac{\$115,000}{\$325,000} = \textbf{35.4\%}$$

$$\text{Percent expenses} = \frac{\$39,000}{\$325,000} = \textbf{12\%}$$

$$\text{Percent salaries and wages} = \frac{\$19,000}{\$325,000} = \textbf{5.8\%}$$

$$\text{Percent net income} = \frac{\$76,000}{\$325,000} = \textbf{23.4\%}$$

$$\text{Percent rent} = \frac{\$8000}{\$325,000} = \textbf{2.5\%}$$

$$\text{Percent advertising} = \frac{\$12,000}{\$325,000} = \textbf{3.7\%}$$

CONCEPTS	EXAMPLES

14.2 Comparing income statements to published charts

In one chart, list the percent of items from a published chart and the particular company.

In the previous example, prepare a vertical analysis of Mr. Bill's appliance store.

Mr. Bill's Appliances

Cost of Goods	Gross Profit	Total Expenses	Net Income	Wages	Rent	Advertising
64.6%	35.4%	12%	23.4%	5.8%	2.5%	3.7%
66.9%	33.1%	26%	7.2%	11.9%	2.4%	2.5%

14.2 Preparing a horizontal analysis chart

1. List last year's and this year's values for each item.
2. Calculate the amount of the increase or decrease of each item.
3. Calculate the percent increase or decrease by dividing the change by last year's amount.

The results of a horizontal analysis of the portion of a business is given. Calculate the percent increases or decreases in each item.

	This Year	Last Year	Increase or (Decrease) Amount	Percent
Gross Sales	$735,000	$700,000	$35,000	5%
Returns	$5,000	$10,000	($5,000)	(50%)
Net Sales	$730,000	$690,000	$40,000	5.8%
Cost of Goods Sold	$530,000	$540,000	($10,000)	(1.9%)
Gross Profit	$200,000	$150,000	$50,000	33.3%

14.3 Constructing a balance sheet

List all of the current assets, other assets, current liabilities, and other liabilities on one page.

Subtract total liabilities from total assets to find stockholder's equity.

Techno's Telephone and Pager has cash of $28,300, accounts receivable of $49,250, and inventories of $4900. Other assets consist of equipment and a truck with total value of $24,300. Accounts payable are $9300 and loans total $12,200. There is no long-term debt. Other liabilities amount to $12,400.

Techno's Telephone and Pager Balance Sheet

Current Assets:		Current Liabilities:	
Cash and Equivalents	$28,300	Accounts Payable	$9,300
Accounts Receivable	$49,250	Loans and Notes Payable	$12,200
Inventories	$4,900	*Total Current Liabilities*	$21,500
Total Current Assets	$82,450	**Other Liabilities:**	$12,400
Other Assets:		*Total Liabilities*	$33,900
Equipment and Truck	$24,300		
Total Assets	$106,750	Stockholder's Equity	$72,850
		Total Liabilities and Equity	$106,750

14.4 Determining the value of the current ratio

1. Determine the current assets.
2. Find the current liabilities.
3. Divide assets by liabilities.

The Circle Tour Agency has $250,000 in current assets and $110,000 in current liabilities. Find the current ratio.

$$\text{Current ratio} = \frac{\text{Current assets}}{\text{Current liabilities}}$$

$$= \frac{\$250,000}{\$110,000} = 2.27 \text{ (rounded)}$$

CONCEPTS	EXAMPLES
14.4 Finding the value of the acid-test ratio **1.** Determine the liquid assets. **2.** Find the current liabilities. **3.** Divide liquid assets by liabilities.	If the Circle Tour Agency has $125,000 in liquid assets, find the acid-test ratio. $$\text{Acid-test ratio} = \frac{\text{Liquid assets}}{\text{Current liabilities}}$$ $$= \frac{\$250,000}{\$110,000} = 1.14 \text{ (rounded)}$$

14.4 Determine the ratio of net income after taxes to the average owner's equity
1. Find the net income after taxes.
2. Determine the average owner's equity for the year using the formula
    Average owner's equity =
        (Owner's equity at beginning
        + Owner's equity at end)/2
3. Divide the net income by the average owner's equity.
	At the beginning of the year, the Circle Tour Agency had an owner's equity of $140,000. At the end of the year, the owner's equity was $180,000. The net income after taxes for the agency was $25,000. Find the ratio of net income after taxes to average owner's equity.
	Net income after taxes = $25,000
	Average owners equity
	$$= \frac{\$140,000 + \$180,000}{2} = \$160,000$$
	Ratio of net income after taxes to average owner's equity
	$$= \frac{\$25,000}{\$160,000} = 15.6\% \text{ (rounded)}$$

CHAPTER 14 | SUMMARY EXERCISE
OWNING YOUR OWN SMALL BUSINESS

Tom Walker wants to expand his Bicycle Shop and has gone to a bank for a loan. The commercial loan officer asks Walker for his most recent income statement and balance sheets based on the following data.

Gross Sales	$212,000	Salaries and Wages	$37,000
Returns	$12,500	Rent	$12,000
Inventory on January 1	$44,000	Advertising	$2000
Cost of Goods Purchased	$75,000	Utilities	$3000
Freight	$8000	Taxes on Inventory, Payroll	$7000
Inventory on December 31	$26,000	Miscellaneous Expenses	$4500

(a) Prepare an income statement.

Walker Bicycle Shop
Income Statement
Year Ending December 31

Gross Sales		_____
Returns		_____
Net Sales		_____
Inventory, January 1	_____	
Cost of Goods Purchased	_____	
Freight	_____	
Total Cost of Goods Purchased	_____	
Total of Goods Available for Sale	_____	
Inventory, December 31	_____	
Cost of Goods Sold		_____
Gross Profit		_____
Expenses		
Salaries and Wages	_____	
Rent	_____	
Advertising	_____	
Utilities	_____	
Taxes on Inventory, Payroll	_____	
Miscellaneous Expenses	_____	
Total Expenses		_____
NET INCOME BEFORE TAXES		=======

(b) Express the following items as a percent of net sales. (Round to nearest tenths of a percent.)

Gross Sales	_____	Salaries and Wages	_____
Returns	_____	Rent	_____
Cost of Goods Sold	_____	Utilities	_____

(c) After the year is completed, Walker has $62,000 in cash, $2500 in notes receivable, $8200 in accounts receivable, and $26,000 in inventory. He has land worth $7600, buildings valued at $28,000, and fixtures worth $13,500. He also has $4500 in notes payable and $27,000 in accounts payable, mortgages for $15,000, long-term notes payable of $8000, and owner's equity of $93,300. Prepare a balance sheet.

Walker Bicycle Shop
Balance Sheet
December 31

ASSETS

Current Assets

  Cash   ————

  Notes Receivable   ————

  Accounts Receivable   ————

  Inventory   ————

    Total Current Assets   ————

Plant Assets

  Land   ————

  Buildings   ————

  Fixtures   ————

    Total Plant Assets   ————

Total Assets   ═══

LIABILITIES

Current Liabilities

  Notes Payable   ————

  Accounts Payable   ————

    Total Current Liabilities   ————

Long-Term Liabilities

  Mortgages Payable   ————

  Long-Term Notes Payable   ————

    Total Long-Term Liabilities   ————

Total Liabilities   ————

OWNER'S EQUITY

Owner's Equity   ————

TOTAL LIABILITY AND OWNER'S EQUITY   ═══

(d) Find the current ratio and the acid-test ratio for Walker's business. (Round to nearest hundredths.) ————————————

(e) If you were the commercial loan officer, would you approve Walker's requested loan? Why or why not?

Investigate

Publicly held companies must publish their financial statements and make them available to anyone who wishes to look at them. Choose a publicly held company that you are familiar with and obtain their financial statements by either contacting the main offices of the company or by using the World Wide Web. Calculate the financial ratios introduced in the last section of this chapter for the company you choose (current ratio, acid-test ratio, average owner's equity, and ratio of net income after taxes to average owner's equity).

For related Web
activities, go to
www.mathbusiness.com

For related Web
activities, go to
www.mathbusiness.com

'Net Assets

McDonald's

STATISTICS

- 1998: Revenues of $12 billion

- 267,000 employees

- 24,500 restaurants in 115 countries

McDonald's – Corporate

mcdonalds.com   Help | Index

What's New
Corporate
Investor Info
Franchising
Information
Our People
Alliances
Food
Careers
Community
Sports
Merchandise
Collectibles

CORPORATE

McDonald's is a global business that operates in a very decentralized manner, but here we have tried to provide a central source for information about McDonald's business, people and history. Here you can find information about McDonald's as an investment; what we look for in a franchisee; development efforts with our alliance partners; plus the people behind the Golden Arches and our history.

Investor Information
- About McDonald's
- Financial Reports
- Financial Press Releases
- Stock Price
- Shareholder Information

Franchising
- Franchising Introduction
- Franchising Inside the U.S.
- Franchising Outside the U.S.

© 1999 McDonald's Corporation.
All rights reserved.
McDonald's Privacy Policy

In 1954, a 52-year-old salesman named Ray Kroc mortgaged his home and invested his entire life savings to become the exclusive distributor of a five-spindled milk shake maker called the Multimixer. Hearing about a McDonald's hamburger stand in California that was running eight Multimixers at a time, he packed up his car and headed west. Kroc made a deal with the owners of the restaurant in California and opened his first restaurant in 1955.

McDonald's has a global reputation for quick service, quality food at low prices, and cleanliness, as indicated by the 15,000 people who lined up when the first McDonald's opened in Kuwait. Even so, the company serves less than 1% of the world's population. McDonald's is also quite active in helping others, as shown by their aid to families of critically ill children through Ronald McDonald House.

1. Given an annual revenue of $12 billion and 24,500 restaurants around the world, find the average sales per restaurant. Why might this information be important to someone thinking of buying a McDonald's restaurant?

2. Peter Voight owns a McDonald's restaurant with current assets of $124,500, total assets of $289,350, current liabilities of $82,654, and total liabilities of $147,320. Find the current ratio.

3. Assume McDonald's currently feeds 1% of the world's population with a resulting annual revenue of $12 billion. What would McDonald's revenue be if they expanded their market share to the point of serving 1.25% of the world's population? What assumptions did you make to arrive at your answer?

CHAPTER 14 | TEST

To help you review, the numbers in brackets show the section in which the topic was discussed.

1. Jake's Convenience Store had gross sales of $756,300 with returns of $285. The inventory including gasoline on January 1 was $92,370 and the cost of goods purchased during the year was $465,920. Freight costs during the year were $1205. Total inventory on December 31 was $82,350. Salaries and wages totaled $84,900, advertising was $2800, rent was $42,500, utilities were $18,950, taxes on inventory and payroll were $4500, and miscellaneous expenses totaled $18,400. Income taxes were $25,450. Complete the following income statement.   **[14.1]**

Jake's Convenience Store
Income Statement Year
Ending December 31

Gross Sales			_____
Returns			_____
Net Sales			_____
Inventory, January 1		_____	
Cost of Goods Purchased	_____		
Freight	_____		
Total Cost of Goods Purchased		_____	
Total of Goods Available for Sale		_____	
Inventory, December 31		_____	
Cost of Goods Sold			_____
Gross Profit			_____
Expenses			
Salaries and Wages		_____	
Rent		_____	
Advertising		_____	
Utilities		_____	
Taxes on Inventory and Payroll		_____	
Miscellaneous Expenses		_____	
Total Expenses			_____
Net Income Before Taxes			_____
Income Taxes			_____
Net Income After Taxes			_____

2. Complete a horizontal analysis for the following portion of an income statement. Round to the nearest tenth of a percent   **[14.2]**

Marge's Television Shoppe
Comparative Income Statement (Portion)

	This Year	Last Year	Increase or (Decrease) Amount	Increase or (Decrease) Percent
Net Sales	$95,000	$60,000	_____	_____
Cost of Goods Sold	$63,000	$40,000	_____	_____
Gross Profit	$16,000	$12,000	_____	_____

3. Complete the following chart for Franklin's Service Station. Express each item as a percent of net sales, and then write in the appropriate average percent from the chart on page 590. Round to the nearest tenth of a percent.   **[14.2]**

Franklin's Service Station			
	Amount	Percent	Average Percent
Net Sales	$400,000	100%	100%
Cost of Goods Sold	$275,000	_____	_____
Gross Profit	$125,000	_____	_____
Net Income	$37,500	_____	_____
Wages	$37,500	_____	_____
Rent	$8,000	_____	_____
Total Expenses	$87,500	_____	_____

Find **(a)** *the current ratio and* **(b)** *the acid-test ratio for each firm. (Round to the nearest hundredths.)*   **[14.4]**

4. Bell's Dry Goods: Current assets: $1,467,300   **(a)** _____
                       Current liabilities: $670,000   **(b)** _____
                       Cash: $63,000
                       Notes and accounts receivable: $620,400
                       Inventory: $783,900

5. Walter's Rifle Shop: Current assets: $154,000   **(a)** _____
                          Current liabilities: $146,500   **(b)** _____
                          Cash: $22,000
                          Notes and accounts receivable: $32,500
                          Inventory: $99,500

Find the ratio of net income after taxes to average owner's equity for each of the following firms. (Round to the nearest tenth of a percent.)   **[14.4]**

6. Rowe Engineering: Net income after taxes: $120,000   **6.** _____
                       Owner's equity
                          beginning of year: $650,000
                          end of year: $720,000

7. Baker Drilling Co.:   Net income after taxes: $8,465,000   **7.** _____
                         Owner's equity
                            beginning of year: $28,346,000
                            end of year: $36,450,000

CHAPTER 15

BUSINESS STATISTICS

Tina McCartle began working in a fast-food restaurant at age 16 and has managed one for almost 6 years. Recently, she decided to open her own restaurant and call it **Big-n-Juicy Hamburgers**. She used some of her own money, borrowed money from her father, and opened the restaurant in a building owned by her uncle and located on a busy street.

The word *statistics* comes from words that mean *state numbers*, or data gathered by the government such as numbers of births, deaths, etc. Today, the word *statistics* is used in a much broader sense to include data from business, economics, and many other fields. Statistics is a powerful and commonly used tool in business. For example, the Japanese depended on a technique called statistical process control to improve the quality of the production from their factories as they emerged from the ruins of World War II.

Today, many companies use statistics on a regular basis. In this chapter, only a few of the basic ideas of statistics are introduced. We encourage you to take a class in statistics at your college if you wish to know more on this important subject. Statistics is a useful subject for individuals in most career paths.

15.1 | FREQUENCY DISTRIBUTIONS AND GRAPHS

Objectives

1. Construct and analyze a frequency distribution.
2. Make a bar graph.
3. Make a line graph.
4. Draw a circle graph.

Big-n-Juicy Hamburgers sells chicken sandwiches, fries, shakes, and sodas among other items, but they specialize in big, juicy hamburgers made from the best beef with only the freshest lettuce, tomatoes, and onions. The restaurant has only been open for 6 months and Tina McCartle watches sales very carefully. Since many businesses fail within the first 6 months of being open, monitoring sales and being able to interpret and graph sales data is essential.

Objective **1** **Construct and analyze a frequency distribution.** It can be difficult to interpret or find patterns in a large group of numbers. One way of analyzing the numbers is to organize them into a table that shows the frequency of occurrence of the various numbers. This type of table is called a **frequency distribution**.

EXAMPLE 1
Construction of a
Frequency
Distribution

Tina McCartle is analyzing sales activity over the past 24 weeks at Big-n-Juicy Hamburgers. The weekly sales data below is to the nearest thousand dollars. Read down the columns, beginning with the left column, for successive weeks of the year.

$3.9	$4.0	$4.3	$4.6	$5.1	$5.6
$3.2	$4.2	$4.8	$4.9	$4.8	$4.8
$3.3	$4.1	$4.1	$5.2	$5.0	$5.3
$3.5	$3.9	$4.8	$5.0	$5.3	$5.3

Construct a table that shows each value of sales. Then go through the data and place a tally mark (|) next to each corresponding value, thereby creating a frequency distribution table.

Solution

Sales (thousands)	Tally	Frequency	Sales (thousands)	Tally	Frequency	Sales (thousands)	Tally	Frequency
$3.2			1	$4.2			1	$5.1			1
$3.3			1	$4.3			1	$5.2			1
$3.5			1	$4.6			1	$5.3	|||	3
$3.9	||	2	$4.8	||||	4	$5.6			1
$4.0			1	$4.9			1			
$4.1	||	2	$5.0	||	2			

This frequency distribution shows that the most common weekly sales amount was $4800, although there were three weeks with sales of $5300.

The frequency distribution given in the previous example contains a great deal of information, perhaps more than is needed. It can be simplified by combining weekly sales into groups, forming the grouped data shown below.

Grouped Data

Sales (thousands)	Frequency (number of weeks)
$3.1–$3.5	3
$3.6–$4.0	3
$4.1–$4.5	4
$4.6–$5.0	8
$5.1–$5.5	5
$5.6–$6.0	1

15.1 FREQUENCY DISTRIBUTIONS AND GRAPHS **619**

> **PROBLEM-SOLVING HINT** The number of groups in the left column of the
> preceding table is arbitrary and usually varies between 5 and 15.

EXAMPLE 2

Analyzing a
Frequency
Distribution

Based on the data from Big-n-Juicy Hamburgers, answer the following questions.

(a) McCartle can take no salary and the business still loses money when sales are less than or equal to $4000 per week. During how many weeks did this occur?

(b) McCartle can take a small salary out of the company once sales go above $5000 per week. During how many weeks did this occur?

Solution

(a) The first two classes in the grouped data table represent weeks in which sales were equal to or less than $4000. Thus, McCartle took no salary and the restaurant lost money for 6 weeks.

(b) The last two classes in the grouped data table are the number of weeks during which sales were above $5000, or 6 weeks. Therefore, McCartle took a small salary for 6 weeks.

Objective [2] **Make a bar graph.** The next step in analyzing this information is to use it to make a **graph**. In statistics, a graph is a visual presentation of numerical data. One of the most common graphs is a **bar graph**, where the height of a bar represents the frequency of a particular value. A bar graph for the sales data follows.

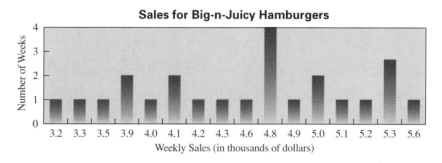

The information from the grouped data is shown in the following bar graph. This graph shows that weekly sales between $4600 and $5000 were the most common. Notice that this graph *does not* show any trend that may be occurring over time.

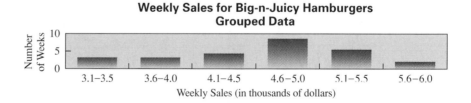

Objective [3] **Make a line graph.** Bar graphs show which numbers occurred and how many times, but do not necessarily show the order in which the numbers occurred. To discover any trends that may have developed, draw a **line graph**.

EXAMPLE 3

Draw a Line
Graph

Show the progression of weekly sales at Big-n-Juicy Hamburgers through the year using a line graph. Do this by totaling the first 4 weeks (the first column) of data in Example 1 for the first data point. Similarly, total the second 4 weeks (second column) of data for the next data point, and so on.

Solution

The total for the first four weeks is $3.9 + $3.2 + $3.3 + $3.5 = $13.9 or $13,900 in sales for the first four weeks. The total for the second four weeks is $4.0 + $4.2 + $4.1 + $3.9 = $16.2 or $16,200 in sales. The six data points of the graph are $13.9, $16.2, $18, $19.7, $20.2, and $21 in thousands of dollars.

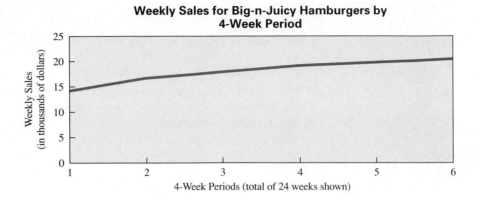

Weekly Sales for Big-n-Juicy Hamburgers by 4-Week Period

It is apparent that weekly sales are growing based on the line graph. Tina McCartle is excited about this trend and she is determined to continue the trend since her livelihood depends on the restaurant. She plans to work very hard in the restaurant over the next few months.

One advantage of line graphs is that two or more sets of data can be shown on the same graph. For example, suppose the managers of a company called Eastside Tire Sales want to compare total sales, profits, and overhead. Assume that they have extracted the following data from their historical records.

Year	Total Sales	Overhead	Profit
1997	$740,000	$205,000	$83,000
1998	$860,000	$251,000	$102,000
1999	$810,000	$247,000	$21,000
2000	$1,040,000	$302,000	$146,000

Separate lines can be made on a line graph for each category so that necessary comparisons can be made. A graph such as this is called a **comparative line graph**.

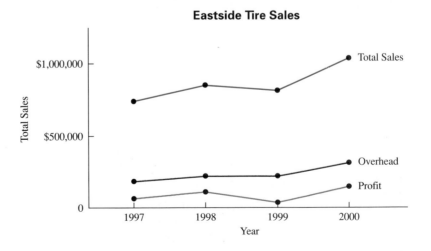

Eastside Tire Sales

OBJECTIVE **4** **Draw a circle graph.**   Suppose a sales manager for Novel Recording Company makes a record of the expenses involved in keeping a sales force on the road. After finding the total expenses, she could convert each expense into a percent of the total, with the following results. Notice that the percents add to 100%.

Item	Percent of Total
Travel	30%
Lodging	25%
Food	15%
Entertainment	10%
Sales meetings	10%
Other	10%

The sales manager can show these percents by using a **circle graph**, sometimes called a pie chart. A circle has 360 degrees (360°). The 360° represents the total expenses. Since entertainment is 10% of the total expenses, she used

$$360° \times 10\% = 360° \times .10 = 36°$$

to represent her entertainment expense. Since lodging is 25% of the total expenses, she used

$$360° \times 25\% = 360° \times .25 = 90°$$

to represent lodging. After she found the degrees that represent each of her expenses, she drew the circle graph shown here.

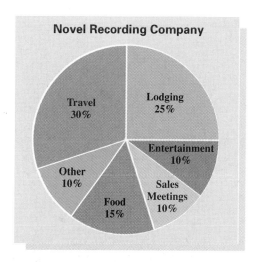

Circle graphs are used to show comparisons *when one item is very small compared to another.* In the circle graph shown here, an item representing 1% of the total could be drawn as a very small but noticeable slice; such a small item would hardly show up in a line graph.

EXAMPLE 4

Interpreting a
Circle Graph

Based on the preceding circle graph of expenses, answer the following questions.
(a) What percent of expenses was spent on travel and entertainment?
(b) What percent of expenses was spent on food and lodging?

For related Web
activities, go to
www.mathbusiness.com

Keyword:
vacation

Solution

(a)

Travel is	30%	(car and plane)
Entertainment is	+ 10%	
Total spent	40%	

(b)

Food is	15%
Lodging is	+ 25%
Total spent	**40%**

Graphs can show information in many interesting ways. The bar graph to the left shows how people cool their mouths after eating hot sauce. The circle graph to the right shows average monthly income of working college students.

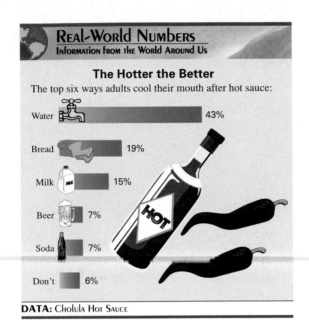

Real-World Numbers
Information from the World Around Us

The Hotter the Better

The top six ways adults cool their mouth after hot sauce:

Water — 43%
Bread — 19%
Milk — 15%
Beer — 7%
Soda — 7%
Don't — 6%

DATA: Cholula Hot Sauce

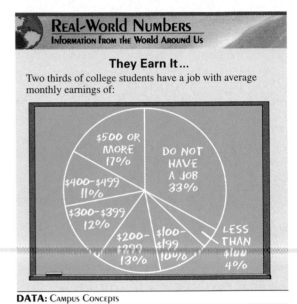

Real-World Numbers
Information from the World Around Us

They Earn It...

Two thirds of college students have a job with average monthly earnings of:

$500 OR MORE 17%
DO NOT HAVE A JOB 33%
$400–$499 11%
$300–$399 12%
$200–$299 13%
$100–$199 10%
LESS THAN $100 4%

DATA: Campus Concepts

Name   Date   Class

15.1 | EXERCISES

The Quick Start *exercises in each section contain solutions to help you get started.*

Answer Exercises 1–3 from the graph Long Distance—Smaller Cost, and answer Exercises 4–6 from the graph Taking a Bite Out of Household Income.

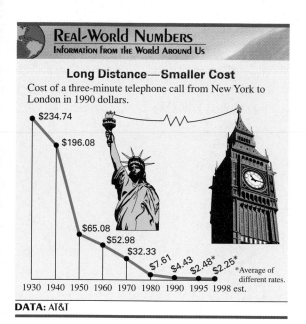

Long Distance—Smaller Cost

Cost of a three-minute telephone call from New York to London in 1990 dollars.

$234.74
$196.08
$65.08
$52.98
$32.33
$7.61
$4.43
$2.48*
$2.25*

*Average of different rates.

1930 1940 1950 1960 1970 1980 1990 1995 1998 est.

DATA: AT&T

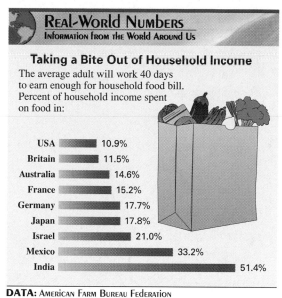

Taking a Bite Out of Household Income

The average adult will work 40 days to earn enough for household food bill. Percent of household income spent on food in:

USA	10.9%
Britain	11.5%
Australia	14.6%
France	15.2%
Germany	17.7%
Japan	17.8%
Israel	21.0%
Mexico	33.2%
India	51.4%

DATA: AMERICAN FARM BUREAU FEDERATION

Quick Start

1. **COST OF LONG DISTANCE** Find the cost of a three-minute telephone call from New York to London in 1950.   1. **$65.08**

2. Estimate the cost of a three-minute telephone call from New York to London in 1985 by finding the average of the cost in 1980 and 1990.   2. **$6.02**

3. By what percent did the cost of a three-minute telephone call from New York to London fall from 1950 to 1998. Round to the nearest percent.   3. _____

4. **FOOD COSTS** Find the share of household income spent for food in the U.S.   4. _____

5. Find the share of household income spent for food in India.   5. _____

6. List all countries in the graph in which less than 15% of household income is spent, on average, for food.   6. _____

The following list shows the number of college credits completed by 30 employees of the Franklin Bank.

74	133	4	127	20	30
103	27	139	118	138	121
149	132	64	141	130	76
42	50	95	56	65	104
4	140	12	88	119	64

Use these numbers to complete the following table. (See Examples 1 and 2.)

Quick Start

Number of Units	Frequency
7. 0–24	4
8. 25–49	_____
9. 50–74	_____
10. 75–99	_____
11. 100–124	_____
12. 125–149	_____

13. Make a line graph using the frequencies that you found.

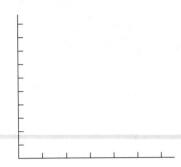

Quick Start

14. How many employees completed less than 25 credits?   14. 4 _____

15. How many employees completed 50 or more credits?   15. _____

16. How many employees completed from 50 to 124 credits?   16. _____

17. How many employees completed from 0 to 49 credits?   17. _____

Six months' data on weekly sales (in thousands of dollars) for Country Grocery follow. The numbers are in chronological order going down the columns. For example, sales for the first and fourth week, respectively, are $302,000 and $304,000.

302	304	318	301	330	337	335	348	339
265	275	279	283	322	349	330	325	334
315	288	299	326	325	342	328	347	

Use the numbers to complete the following table. (See Example 1.)

Quick Start

Sales (in thousands)	Frequency	Sales (in thousands)	Frequency
18. 260–269	1	19. 270–279	2
20. 280–289	2	21. 290–299	1
22. 300–309	3	23. 310–319	2
24. 320–329	5	25. 330–339	6
26. 340–349	4		

Name   Date   Class

27. On the left, make a bar graph using your answers to Exercises 18–26.

28. On the right, make a line graph using the original numbers.

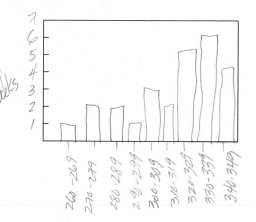

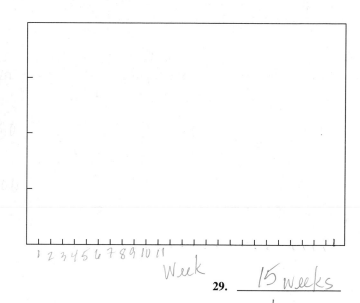

29. How many weeks did sales equal or exceed $300,000?

30. How many weeks did sales fall below $270,000?

29. _15 weeks_

30. _1_

The following numbers show the scores of 80 students on a marketing test.

79	60	74	59	55	98	61	67	83	71
71	46	63	66	69	42	75	62	71	77
78	65	87	57	78	91	82	73	94	48
87	65	62	81	63	66	65	49	45	51
69	56	84	93	63	60	68	51	73	54
50	88	76	93	48	70	39	76	95	57
63	94	82	54	89	64	77	94	72	69
51	56	67	88	81	70	81	54	66	87

Use these numbers to complete the following table. (See Example 1.)

Quick Start

	Score	Frequency		Score	Frequency
31.	30–39	1	**32.**	40–49	6
33.	50–59	____	**34.**	60–69	____
35.	70–79	____	**36.**	80–89	____
37.	90–99	____			

38. Make a bar graph showing your answers to Exercises 31–37.

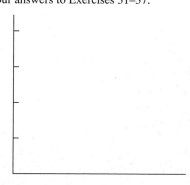

39. How many students passed the marketing test? (passing is 70)   **39.** _____

40. If a grade of B is achieved for a score of 80 or higher, how many students received a B or better?   **40.** _____

41. How many students failed the test? (scored below 70.)   **41.** _____

42. How many students scored from 60 to 79?   **42.** _____

During one recent period Evie Allsot, a student, had $1400 in expenses, as shown in the following table.
Find all numbers missing from the table in Exercises 43–48. (See Objective 4.)

Quick Start

Item	Dollar Amount	Pecent of Total	Degrees of a Circle	Item	Dollar Amount	Percent of Total	Degrees of a Circle
Food	$350	25%	90%				
43. Rent	$280	**20%**	72°	**44.** Clothing	$210	**15%**	**54°**
$\frac{72°}{360°} = .20 = 20\%$				$\frac{\$210}{\$1400} = .15 = 15\%; \ .15 \times 360° = 54°$			
45. Books	$140	10%	_____	**46.** Entertainment	$210	_____	54°
47. Savings	$70	_____	_____	**48.** Other	_____	_____	36°

49. Draw a circle graph using this information. (See Objective 4.)

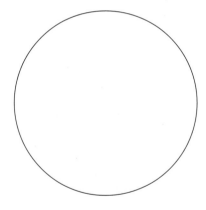

50. What percent did Allsot spend on food and rent?   **50.** _____

51. What pecent did Allsot spend on savings and entertainment?   **51.** _____

Quick Start

52. MANUFACTURING   Stiles Manufacturing has its annual sales divided into five categories as follows.

Item	Annual Sales		
Parts	$25,000	6.25%	22½°
Hand tools	$80,000	20%	72°
Bench tools	$120,000	30%	108°
Brass fittings	$100,000	25%	90°
Cabinet hardware	$75,000	18.75%	67½°

400,000

Name		Date	Class

Make a circle graph showing this distribution. (See Example 4.)

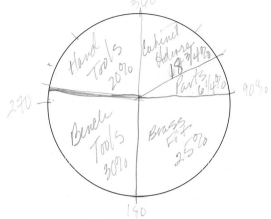

53. BOOK PUBLISHING   Armstrong Publishing Company had 25% of its sales in mysteries, 10% in biographies, 15% in cookbooks, 15% in romance novels, 20% in science, and the rest in business books. Draw a circle graph with this information. (See Example 4.)

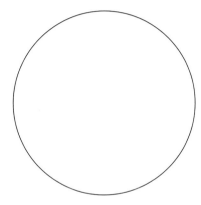

54. SLEEP   According to the Pathfinder Research Group, the positions in which Americans fall asleep are as follows in the graphic to the right. The figures do not add up to 100% due to rounding. Draw a circle graph for this distribution.

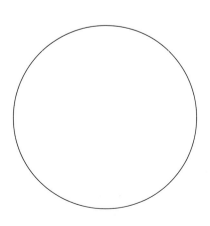

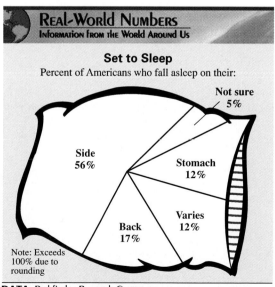

55. **INJURED PEDESTRIANS**   The following circle graph, based on data from the National Safety Council, shows how pedestrians were injured. **(a)** Find the number of pedestrians who were killed or injured when crossing/entering an intersection on foot. **(b)** Find the number of pedestrians who were killed or injured when standing or playing in the road.

(a) _____

(b) _____

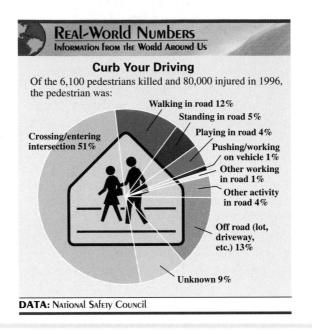

Real-World Numbers
Information from the World Around Us

Curb Your Driving

Of the 6,100 pedestrians killed and 80,000 injured in 1996, the pedestrian was:

Walking in road 12%
Standing in road 5%
Playing in road 4%
Pushing/working on vehicle 1%
Other working in road 1%
Other activity in road 4%

Crossing/entering intersection 51%

Off road (lot, driveway, etc.) 13%

Unknown 9%

DATA: National Safety Council

56. List the advantages of using a graph over a table when looking for trends.

57. Cut out three graphs from newspapers or magazines and tape them to your homework assignment. Be sure to explain the data in each case.

15.2 | MEAN, MEDIAN, AND MODE

Objectives

1. Find the mean of a list of numbers.
2. Find a weighted mean.
3. Find the median.
4. Find the mode.

Objective 1 Find the mean of a list of numbers. Businesses are often faced with the problem of analyzing a mass of raw data. Reports come in from many different branches of a company, or salespeople send in a large number of expense claims, for example. In analyzing all these data, one of the first things to look for is a **measure of central tendency**—a single number that is designed to represent the entire list of numbers. One such measure of central tendency is the **mean**, which is just the **average** of a collection of numbers or data.

$$\text{Mean} = \frac{\text{Sum of all values}}{\text{Number of values}}$$

For example, suppose the sales of carnations at Tom's Flower Shop for each of the days last week were $86, $103, $118, $117, $126, $158, and $149. For Tom's Flower Shop, the mean sales of carnations (rounded to the nearest cent) is

$$\text{Mean} = \frac{86 + 103 + 118 + 117 + 126 + 158 + 149}{7} = \$122.43.$$

One criticism of the mean is that its value *can be distorted* by one very large (or very small) value as shown in the next example. A better measure of central tendency in cases with one abnormally large (or small) value is shown later in this section (Objective 3).

EXAMPLE 1
Finding the Mean

Tina McCartle has promised seven of her employees at Big-n-Juicy Hamburgers that they will all work about the same number of hours. One employee complained that she worked considerably more hours than the other employees last month. The number of hours worked by each of the seven employees during the past month are given. Find the mean to the nearest hour.

75, 63, 76, 82, 70, 81, and 149

Solution
Add the numbers and divide by 7 since there are 7 numbers. Check that the sum of numbers is 596.

$$\text{Mean} = \frac{596}{7} = 85 \text{ (rounded)}$$

The mean of 85 seems a bit large since one employee worked a lot more hours than the other six employees. The mean without this value of 149 is the sum of the remaining 6 hours worked divided by 6.

$$\text{Mean} = \frac{447}{6} = 75 \text{ (rounded)}$$

This value seems more in line with the average number of hours worked. Perhaps there was an unusual reason the one employee worked 149 hours (someone else was sick, etc.).

Averages are used in many different places. For example, the following graph shows that the average total stopping distance on a dry road for a 3000-pound car depends on the speed of the automobile.

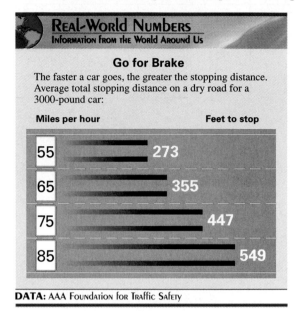

Real-World Numbers
Information from the World Around Us

Go for Brake
The faster a car goes, the greater the stopping distance. Average total stopping distance on a dry road for a 3000-pound car:

Miles per hour	Feet to stop
55	273
65	355
75	447
85	549

DATA: AAA Foundation for Traffic Safety

Objective **2** **Find a weighted mean.** Some of the items in a list might appear more than once. In this case, it is necessary to find a **weighted mean** or **weighted average**, where each value is the product of the number itself and the number of times it occurs.

EXAMPLE 2
Finding the
Weighted Mean

Find the weighted mean of the numbers given in the following table.

Value	Frequency
3	4
5	2
7	1
8	5
9	3
10	2
12	1
13	2

Solution

According to this table, the value 5 occurred 2 times, 8 occurred 5 times, 12 occurred 1 time, and so on. To find the mean, multiply each value by the frequency for that value; then add the products. Also add the Frequency column to find the total number of values.

Value	Frequency	Product
3	4	12
5	2	10
7	1	7
8	5	40
9	3	27
10	2	20
12	1	12
13	2	26
Totals	20	154

The weighted mean is $\dfrac{154}{20} = 7.7$.

A weighted average is used to find a student's grade point average, as shown by the next example.

EXAMPLE 3
Finding the Grade
Point Average

Find the grade point average for the following student to the nearest tenth. Assume A = 4, B = 3, C = 2, D = 1, and F = 0.

Course	Credits	Grade	Grade × Credits
Business Mathematics	3	A (= 4)	4 × 3 = 12
Retailing	4	C (= 2)	2 × 4 = 8
English	3	B (= 3)	3 × 3 = 9
Computer Science	2	A (= 4)	4 × 2 = 8
Computer Science Lab	2	D (= 1)	1 × 2 = 2
Totals	14		39

Solution

The grade point average for this student is $\dfrac{39}{14} = 2.79 = 2.8$

This problem is solved using a scientific calculator as follows.

(4 × 3 + 2 × 4 + 3 × 3 + 4 × 2 + 1 × 2) ÷ (3 + 4 + 3 + 2 + 2) = 2.8
↑
(rounded)

Note: All calculator solutions use a scientific calculator. Refer to Appendix B for scientific calculator basics.

> **NOTE**   It is common to round grade point averages to the nearest tenth as we have done in the previous example.

Objective 3   Find the median.   As we saw in Example 1, the mean is a poor indicator of central tendency in the presence of one very large or one very small number. This effect can be avoided by using another measure of central tendency called the **median**. The median divides a group of numbers in half—half the numbers lie at or above the median, and half lie at or below the median.

Since the median divides a list of numbers in half, the first step in finding a median is to rewrite the list of numbers as an **ordered array**, with the numbers going from smallest to largest. For example, the list of numbers 9, 6, 11, 17, 14, 12, 8 would be written in numerical order as the following ordered array.

6, 8, 9, 11, 12, 14, 17

The median is found from the ordered array as follows. (Notice that the procedure for finding the median depends on whether the number of numbers in the list is *even* or *odd*.)

If the ordered array has an *odd* number of numbers, divide the number of numbers by 2. The next higher whole number in the array gives the location of the median.

If the ordered array has an *even* number of numbers, there is no single middle number. Find the median by first dividing the number of numbers by 2. The median is the average (mean) of the number in this position and the number in the next position in the array.

EXAMPLE 4

Finding the Median

Find the median of the following weights:
(a) 30 lbs, 25 lbs, 28 lbs, 23 lbs, 24 lbs
(b) 14 lbs, 18 lbs, 17 lbs, 10 lbs, 15 lbs, 19 lbs, 18 lbs, 20 lbs

Solution

(a) First place the numbers **in numerical order**, from smallest to largest.

$$23, 24, 25, 28, 30$$

There are 5 numbers, so divide 5 by 2 to get 2.5. The next larger whole number is 3, so the median is the third number, or 25. The numbers 23 and 24 are less than 25 and the numbers 28 and 30 are greater than 25.

(b) Write the numbers **from smallest to largest** as follows.

$$10, 14, 15, 17, 18, 18, 19, 20$$

There are 8 numbers, so divide 8 by 2 to get 4. The median is the mean of the numbers in the 4th and 5th positions.

$$\text{Median} = \frac{17 + 18}{2} = 17.5$$

The following graph refers to a median of 15 hours worked by teenage workers.

Real-World Numbers
Information from the World Around Us

"Kids" on the Clock
Hours per week spent at either full- or part-time jobs by 12 to 17 year olds. (Median is 15 hours.)

30 or more 10%
1–5 20%
21–30 14%
6–10 23%
11–20 33%

DATA: ICR's TeenEXCEL survey for Merril Lynch

Objective 4 **Find the mode.** The last important statistical measure is called the **mode.** The mode is the number that occurs most often. For example, if 10 students earned scores of

$$74, 81, 38, 74, 82, 80, 100, 92, 74, 85$$

on a business law examination, then the mode is 74, since more students obtained this score than any other score.

NOTE   A data set in which every number occurs the same number of times is said to have *no mode.* A data set in which two different numbers occur the same number of times and each occurs more often than any other number in the data set is said to be *bimodal,* referring to two different modes.

Example 5	Professor Miller gave the same test to both his day and evening sections of Business Math at
Finding the Mode	American College. Find the mode of the tests given in each class. Which class has the lower mode?

(a) Day Class: 85, 92, 81, 73, 78, 80, 83, 80, 74, 69, 80, 65, 71, 65, 80, 93, 54, 78, 80, 45, 70, 76, 73, 80, 71, 68

(b) Evening
Class: 68, 73, 59, 76, 79, 73, 85, 90, 73, 69, 73, 75, 93, 73, 76, 70, 73, 68, 82, 84, 77

Solution

(a) The number 80 is the mode for the day class because it occurs more often than any other number.

(b) The number 73 is the mode for the evening class because it occurs more often than any other number.

The evening class has the lower mode.

> **NOTE** It is not necessary to place the numbers in numerical order when looking for the mode, but it helps with a large array of numbers.

Name   Date   Class

15.2 | Exercises

The Quick Start exercises in each section contain solutions to help you get started.

Find the mean for the following lists of numbers. Round to the nearest tenth. (See Example 1.)

Quick Start

1. Inches of rain per month: 3.5, 1.1, 2.8, .8, 4.1   1. **2.5**

$$\frac{3.5 + 1.1 + 2.8 + .8 + 4.1}{5} = 2.5$$

2. Weeks premature: 2, 3, 1, 4, 5, 2   2. **2.8**

$$\frac{2 + 3 + 1 + 4 + 5 + 2}{6} = 2.8$$

3. Math exam scores: 40, 51, 59, 62, 68, 73, 49, 80   3. _____

4. Algebra quiz scores: 32, 26, 30, 19, 51, 46, 38, 39   4. _____

5. Number attending games: 21,900, 22,850, 24,930, 29,710, 28,340, 40,000   5. _____

6. Annual salaries: $38,500, $39,720, $42,183, $21,982, $43,250   6. _____

7. Ounces of gold: 10.6, 12.5, 11.7, 9.6, 10.3, 9.6, 10.9, 6.4, 2.3, 4.1   7. _____

8. Weight of dogs: 30.1, 42.8, 91.6, 51.2, 88.3, 21.9, 43.7, 51.2   8. _____

9. When is it better to use the median, rather than the mean, for a measure of central tendency? Give an example. (See Objective 3.)

10. List some situations where the mode is the best average to use to describe the data. (See Objective 4.)

Find the weighted mean for the following. Round to the nearest tenth. (See Example 2.)

Quick Start

11. | Value | Frequency |
|---|---|
| 9 | 3 |
| 12 | 4 |
| 18 | 2 |

12.3 _____

$9 \times 3 = 27$
$12 \times 4 = 48$
$18 \times 2 = \underline{36}$
         9   111
$\frac{111}{9} = 12.3$

12. | Value | Frequency |
|---|---|
| 9 | 3 |
| 12 | 5 |
| 15 | 1 |
| 18 | 1 |

12 _____

$9 \times 3 = 27$
$12 \times 5 = 60$
$15 \times 1 = 15$
$18 \times 1 = \underline{18}$
          10   120
$\frac{120}{10} = 12$

13. | Value | Frequency |
|---|---|
| 12 | 4 |
| 13 | 2 |
| 15 | 5 |
| 19 | 3 |
| 22 | 1 |
| 23 | 5 |

_____

14. | Value | Frequency |
|---|---|
| 25 | 1 |
| 26 | 2 |
| 29 | 5 |
| 30 | 4 |
| 32 | 3 |
| 33 | 5 |

_____

15. | Value | Frequency |
|---|---|
| 104 | 6 |
| 112 | 14 |
| 115 | 21 |
| 119 | 13 |
| 123 | 22 |
| 127 | 6 |
| 132 | 9 |

_____

16. | Value | Frequency |
|---|---|
| 243 | 1 |
| 247 | 3 |
| 251 | 5 |
| 255 | 7 |
| 263 | 4 |
| 271 | 2 |
| 279 | 2 |

_____

Name   Date   Class

Find the grade point average for the following students. Assume A = 4, B = 3, C = 2, D = 1,
and F = 0. Round to the nearest tenth. (See Example 3.)

17.	Credits	Grade		18.	Credits	Grade
	4	B			3	A
	2	A			3	B
	5	C			4	B
	1	F			2	C
	3	B	_____		4	D	_____

Find the median for the following list of numbers. (See Example 4.)

Quick Start

19. Number of bytes per World Wide Web page (in thousands): 140, 85, 122, 114, 98   **19.** _114_____

85, 98, **114**, 122, 140

↑
Median

20. Cost of new computers: $1400, $1385, $1695, $1150, $1390   **20.** _$1390_____

$1150, $1385, **$1390**, $1400, $1695

↑
Median

21. Number of books loaned: 100, 114, 125, 135, 150, 172   **21.** _____

22. Calories in menu items: 298, 346, 412, 501, 515, 521, 528, 621   **22.** _____

23. Number of students: 37, 63, 92, 26, 44, 32, 75, 50, 41   **23.** _____

24. Number of orders: 1072, 1068, 1093, 1042, 1056, 1005, 1009   **24.** _____

Find the mode or modes for each of the following lists of numbers. (See Example 5.)

> **Quick Start**
>
> **25.** Porosity of soil samples: 21%, 18%, 21%, 28%, 22%, 21%, 25%
>
> If the data are listed according to how many times each number appears.
> 18%, 21%, 22%, 25%, 28%
>   21%
>   21%
>   ↑
>   └── 21% is the mode since 21% is listed more than any other number.
>
> **26.** Low daily temperatures: 21, 32, 46, 32, 49, 32, 49
>
> If the data are listed according to how many times each number appears,
> 21, 32, 46, 49
>   32   49
>   32
>   ↑ 32 is listed most and is the mode.

25. <u>21%</u>

26. <u>32</u>

27. Age of retirees: 80, 72, 64, 64, 72, 53, 64

27. _____

28. Number of pages read: 86, 84, 83, 84, 83, 86, 86

28. _____

29. Number of 5th grade students: 32, 38, 32, 36, 38, 34, 35, 30, 39.

29. _____

30. Number of people on flights from Chicago to Denver:
178, 104, 178, 150, 165, 165, 82

30. _____

A quality-control inspector in a plant that manufactures electric motors measured the following shaft diameters (in thousandths of an inch).

$$35, \quad 33, \quad 32, \quad 34, \quad 35, \quad 34, \quad 35, \quad 35, \quad 34$$

Using these numbers, find each of the following. (Round to the nearest hundredth.)

31. The mean _____

32. The median _____

The quality-control inspector subsequently determined that he had made a mistake when he wrote 32 thousandths of an inch. Eliminate this number from the list and find each of the following.

33. The mean _____

34. The median _____

35. If you want to avoid a single extreme value having a large effect on the average, would you use the mean or the median?

36. Does an employer look at the mean, median, or mode grade on a college transcript when considering hiring a new employee? Which do you think the employer should look at? Explain.

CHAPTER TERMS

Review the following terms to test your understanding of the chapter. For each term you do not know, refer to the page number found next to that term.

average [**p.** 629]	frequency distribution	mean [**p.** 629]	mode [**p.** 632]
bar graph [**p.** 619]	[**p.** 618]	measures of central tendency	ordered array [**p.** 631]
circle graph [**p.** 621]	graph [**p.** 619]	[**p.** 629]	statistics [**p.** 617]
comparative line graph [**p.** 620]	line graph [**p.** 619]	median [**p.** 631]	weighted mean [**p.** 630]

CONCEPTS

EXAMPLES

15.1 Constructing a frequency distribution from raw data

1. Construct a table listing each value and the number of times this value occurs.

2. Combine the pieces of data into groups.

Construct a frequency distribution for weekly sales, in thousands, at a small concrete plant.

$22, $20, $22, $25, $18, $19, $22, $24, $24, $29, $19

Data	Tally	Frequency
$18	|	1
$19	||	2
$20	|	1
$22	|||	3
$24	||	2
$25	|	1
$29	|	1

Classes	Frequency
$18–$20	4
$21–$23	3
$24–$26	3
$27–$29	1

15.1 Constructing a bar graph from a frequency distribution

Draw a bar for each class using the frequency of the class as the height of the bar.

Construct a bar graph from the frequency distribution of the previous example.

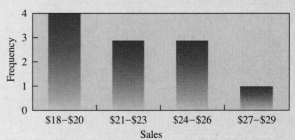

15.1 Constructing a line graph

1. Plot each year on the horizontal axis.

2. For each year, find the value of sales for that year and plot a point at that value.

3. Connect all points with straight lines.

Construct a line graph for the following sales table.

Year	Total Sales
1997	$850,000
1998	$920,000
1999	$875,000
2000	$975,000

CONCEPTS	EXAMPLES

15.1 Constructing a circle graph

1. Determine the percent of the total for each item.
2. Find the number of degrees of a circle that each percent represents.
3. Draw the circle.

Construct a circle graph for the following table, which lists expenses for a business trip.

Item	Amount
Car	$200
Lodging	$300
Food	$250
Entertainment	$150
Other	$100
	$1000

Item	Amount	Percent of Total
Car	$200	$\frac{\$200}{\$1000} = \frac{1}{5} = 20\%$; $360 \times 20\% = 360 \times .20 = 72°$
Lodging	$300	$\frac{\$300}{\$1000} = \frac{3}{10} = 30\%$; $360 \times 30\% = 360 \times .30 = 108°$
Food	$250	$\frac{\$250}{\$1000} = \frac{1}{4} = 25\%$; $360 \times 25\% = 360 \times .25 = 90°$
Entertainment	$150	$\frac{\$150}{\$1000} = \frac{3}{20} = 15\%$; $360 \times 15\% = 360 \times .15 = 54°$
Other	$100	$\frac{\$100}{\$1000} = \frac{1}{10} = 10\%$; $360 \times 10\% = 360 \times .10 = 36°$

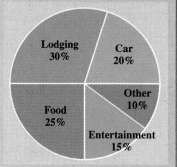

15.2 Finding the mean of a set of numbers

1. Add all numbers to obtain the total.
2. Divide the total by the number of pieces of data.

The quiz scores for Pat Phelan in her business math course were as follows

85 79 93 91
78 82 87 85

Find Pat's quiz average.

$$\text{Mean} = \frac{85 + 79 + 93 + 91 + 78 + 82 + 87 + 85}{8} = 85$$

15.2 Finding the median of a set of numbers

1. Arrange the data in numerical order from lowest to highest.
2. Select the middle value or the average of the two middle values.

Find the median for Pat Phelan's grades from the previous example. The data arranged from the lowest to highest are

78 79 82 85 85 87 91 93

Middle two values are 85 and 85. The average of these two values is

$$\frac{85 + 85}{2} = 85.$$

15.2 Finding the mode of a set of values

Determine the most frequently occurring value.

Find the mode for Phelan's grades in the previous example.

The most frequently occurring score is 85 (it occurs twice), so the mode is 85.

CHAPTER 15 | SUMMARY EXERCISE

WATCHING THE GROWTH OF A SMALL BUSINESS

Pat Gutierrez expanded her company, Christian Books Unlimited, this year by opening stores in different cities. One store was opened in February and the second was opened in June. Sales, in thousands of dollars, for the two stores are given below.

	Feb.	Mar.	Apr.	May	June	July	Aug.	Sep.	Oct.
Store 1	6.5	6.8	7.0	6.9	7.5	7.8	8.0	7.6	8.2
Store 2	—	—	—	—	8.2	6.2	8.2	8.7	9.6

(a) Find the median, mean, and mode sales for each store to the nearest tenth.

(b) Plot sales for both stores on the same line graph with month on the horizontal axis and sales on the vertical axis.

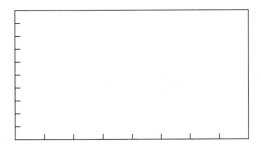

(c) What trends are apparent from the line graph above?

Investigate

Cut at least three graphs and charts out of recent newspapers or magazines. Then explain each of them in writing. Graphs and charts can be great tools for communicating with customers, fellow workers, or even your boss. How can you make sure that a graph or chart clearly communicates the message that you wish it to convey?

For related Web
activities, go to
www.mathbusiness.com

'Net Assets

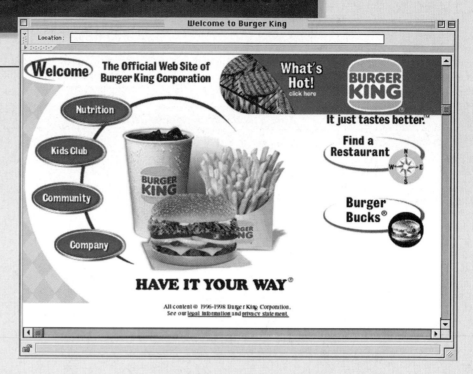

BURGER KING

STATISTICS

- 1998: Revenues of
  $10.3 billion

- 300,000 employees

- 10,188 restaurants

- 14,000,000
  customers served
  daily

Burger King Corporation was founded in 1954 in Miami, Florida. The company introduced the Whopper sandwich in 1957. In 1975, the firm began using drive-through service to satisfy customers who were on-the-go. The drive-through now accounts for about 60% of Burger King's business. In 1985, average restaurant sales passed the $1 million mark and a European training center opened in London to service overseas company and franchise employees. Burger King serves approximately 1404 customers per restaurant per day and the company notes with pride that a customer can order a Whopper in 1024 different possible ways.

1. Sales on consecutive days at a Burger King restaurant rounded to the nearest dollar were: Monday, $1475; Tuesday, $1456; Wednesday, $1278; Thursday, $1503; Friday, $1895; Saturday, $1753; and Sunday, $1298. Find the average daily sales (mean) and also the median.

2. What annual profit do you think a Burger King restaurant with $1 million in sales revenue will make for an owner who also manages her restaurant? Explain how you arrived at your figures.

3. Visit a McDonald's and a Burger King restaurant in your area. Write down five similarities and five differences between the two restaurants.

Name   Date   Class

CHAPTER 15 | TEST

To help you review, the numbers in brackets show the section in which the topic was discussed.

1. The following numbers are the number of gallons of gasoline sold at a convenience store by week for the past 20 weeks.

12,450	11,300	12,800	10,850	14,100
14,900	12,300	11,600	12,400	12,900
13,300	12,500	13,390	12,800	12,500
15,100	13,700	12,200	11,800	12,600

Use these numbers to complete the following table.   **[15.1]**

Gallons of Gasoline	Number of Weeks
10,000–10,999	____
11,000–11,999	____
12,000–12,999	____
13,000–13,999	____
14,000–14,999	____
15,000–15,999	____

2. How many weeks had sales of 13,000 gallons or more?   **[15.1]**

2. _____

3. Use the numbers in the table above to draw a bar graph. Be sure to put a heading and labels on the graph.   **[15.1]**

4. During a 1-year period, the campus newspaper at Comfort Community College had the following expenses. Find all numbers missing from the table.   **[15.1]**

Item	Dollar Amount	Percent of Total	Degrees of a Circle
Newsprint	$12,000	20%	____
Ink	$6000	____	36°
Wire Service	$18,000	30%	____
Salaries	$18,000	30%	____
Other	$6000	10%	____

5. Draw a circle graph using the information in test question 4.   **[15.1]**

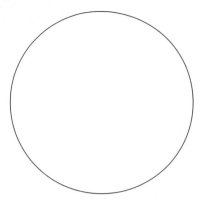

6. What percent of the expenses were for Newsprint, Ink, and Wire Service?   **[15.1]**

6. _____

Find the mean for the following. Round to the nearest tenth if necessary.   **[15.2]**

7. Weight of participants in a diet program: 220, 275, 198, 212, 233, 246

7. _____

8. Length of boards (centimeters): 12, 18, 14, 17, 19, 22, 23, 25

8. _____

9. Weekly commission ($): 458, 432, 496, 491, 500, 508, 512, 396, 492, 504

9. _____

10.

Volume (Quarts)	Frequency
6	7
10	3
11	4
14	2
19	3
24	1
	_____

11.

Sales ($)	Frequency
150	15
160	17
170	21
180	28
190	19
200	7
	_____

Find the median for the following lists of numbers.   **[15.2]**

12. Number of actors trying for a part: 22, 18, 15, 25, 20, 19, 7

12. _____

13. Deliveries per driver: 41, 39, 45, 47, 38, 42, 51, 38

13. _____

Name _____ Date _____ Class _____

14. Hours worked per day: 7.6, 9.3, 21.8, 10.4, 4.2, 5.3, 7.1, 9.0, 8.3   **14.** _____

15. Trees planted: 58, 76, 91, 83, 29, 34, 51, 92, 38, 41   **15.** _____

Find the mode or modes for the following lists of numbers. **[15.2]**

16. Contestant's ages: 51, 47, 48, 32, 47, 71, 82, 47   **16.** _____

17. Customers served: 32, 51, 74, 19, 25, 43, 75, 82, 98, 100   **17.** _____

18. Number of nails: 96, 104, 103, 104, 103, 104, 91, 74, 103   **18.** _____

Solve the following application problems.

19. Big Sandy Concrete Company had the following sales (in thousands of dollars).

Year	Sales
1996	$754
1997	$782
1998	$853
1999	$592
2000	$680

The area in which Big Sandy operates had a business recession (slow down in business) during 1999 and 2000. Do you think the business recession may have affected Big Sandy Concrete Company's business? Support your view by drawing a line graph.

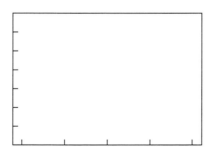

20. Ted Smith sells stocks and bonds at Merrill Lynch. His wife developed a serious illness at the beginning of 2000 and her condition slowly improved through the balance of the year. Do you think his personal problems may have influenced his work performance?

Year	Quarterly Commissions			
1998	$14,250,	$12,375,	$15,750,	$13,682
1999	$13,435,	$14,230,	$11,540,	$15,782
2000	$8207,	$7350,	$10,366,	$11,470

Support your view by drawing a line graph. Be sure and label the quarter in which Mrs. Smith became ill.

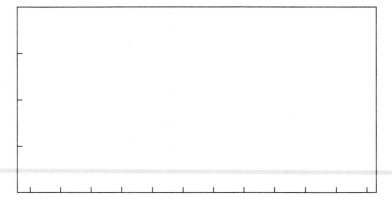

Appendix A

Equations and Formula Review

A.1 | Equations

Objectives

1. Learn the basic terminology of equations.
2. Use basic rules to solve equations.
3. Combine similar terms in equations.
4. Use the distributive property to simplify equations.

Objective 1 Learn the basic terminology of equations. An equation is a statement that says two expressions are equal. For example, in the equation

$$x + 5 = 9$$

the expression $x + 5$ and the number 9 are equal. In dealing with equations certain terminology is used:

EQUATION TERMINOLOGY

The letter x is called a **variable**—a letter that represents a number.

The variable x, as well as the numbers 5 and 9, are called **terms**. A term is a single letter, a single number, or the product of a number and a letter.

Different terms are separated from one another by $+$ or $-$ signs.

The expression $x + 5$ is called the **left side** of the equation; 9 is the **right side**.

A **solution** to the equation is any number that can replace the variable and result in a true statement. The solution for this equation is the number 4, since the replacement of the variable x with the number 4 results in a true statement.

$$x + 5 = 9$$
$$4 + 5 = 9 \quad \text{Let } x = 4.$$
$$9 = 9 \quad \text{True}$$

The check shows an example of **substitution**; the number 4 was substituted for the variable x.

> **NOTE** In the expression $x + 5$, x is the same thing as $+1x$.

Objective 2 Use basic rules to solve equations. In solving equations, the object is to find numbers that can be used to replace the variable so that the equation is a true statement. This is done by changing the equation so that all the terms containing a variable are on one side of the equation and all the numbers are on the other side. Since an equation states that two expressions are equal, as long as both sides of the equation are changed in the same way the resulting expressions remain equal. The rules for solving equations follow.

Rules for Solving Equations

Addition Rule. The same number may be added or subtracted on both sides of an equation.

Multiplication Rule. Both sides of an equation may be multiplied or divided by the same nonzero number.

Remember these two things when solving equations:

1. **What you do to one side of an equation, you must also do to the other side.**
2. **Solve equations using the opposite math operation.**

Example 1

Solving a Linear Equation Using Addition

Solve $x - 9 = 15$.

Solution

To solve this equation, x must be alone on one side of the equal sign, and all numbers collected on the other side. To change the $x - 9$ to x, perform the opposite operation to "undo" what was done. The opposite of subtraction is addition, so add 9 to both sides.

$$x - 9 = 15$$
$$x - 9 + 9 = 15 + 9 \quad \text{Add 9 to both sides.}$$
$$x + 0 = 24$$
$$x = 24$$

To check this answer, substitute 24 for x in the original equation.

$$x - 9 = 15 \quad \text{Original equation.}$$
$$24 - 9 = 15 \quad \text{Let } x = 24.$$
$$15 = 15 \quad \text{True.}$$

The answer, of $x = 24$, checks.

Example 2

Solving a Linear Equation Using Subtraction

Solve $k + 7 = 18$.

Solution

To isolate k on the left side, do the opposite of adding 7, which is *subtracting 7*.

$$k + 7 = 18$$
$$k + 7 - 7 = 18 - 7 \quad \text{Subtract 7.}$$
$$k = 11$$

Example 3

Solving a Linear Equation Using Division

Solve $5p = 60$.

Solution

The term $5p$ indicates the multiplication of 5 and p. Since the opposite of multiplication is division, solve the equation by *dividing* both sides by 5.

$$5p = 60$$
$$\frac{5p}{5} = \frac{60}{5} \quad \text{Divide by 5.}$$
$$p = 12$$

Check by substituting 12 for p in the original equation.

Sometimes we put slash marks through the numbers used to divide both sides; slash marks would be used in Example 3, as follows.

$$5p = 60$$

$$\frac{\cancel{5}p}{\cancel{5}} = \frac{60}{5}$$

$$p = 12$$

EXAMPLE 4

Solving a Linear
Equation Using
Multiplication

Solve $\frac{y}{3} = 9$.

Solution

The bar in $\frac{y}{3}$ means to divide, so solve the equation by multiplying both sides by 3. (The opposite of division is multiplication.) As in the following solution, it is common to use a dot to indicate multiplication.

$$\frac{y}{3} = 9$$

$$3 \cdot \frac{y}{3} = 3 \cdot 9 \quad \text{Multiply by 3.}$$

$$y = 27$$

Example 5 shows how to solve an equation using a reciprocal. To get the **reciprocal** of a nonzero fraction, exchange the numerator and the denominator. For example, the reciprocal of $\frac{7}{9}$ is $\frac{9}{7}$. The product of two reciprocals is 1:

$$\frac{\cancel{7}^{1}}{\cancel{9}_{1}} \cdot \frac{\cancel{9}^{1}}{\cancel{7}_{1}} = 1$$

EXAMPLE 5

Solving a Linear
Equation Using
Reciprocals

Solve $\frac{3}{4}z = 9$.

Solution

Solve this equation by multiplying both sides by $\frac{4}{3}$, the reciprocal of $\frac{3}{4}$. This process will give just $1z$, or z, on the left.

$$\frac{3}{4}z = 9$$

$$\frac{4}{3} \cdot \frac{3}{4}z = \frac{4}{3} \cdot 9 \quad \text{Multiply both sides by } \frac{4}{3}.$$

$$z = 12$$

The equation in Example 6 requires two steps to solve.

EXAMPLE 6

Solving a Linear
Equation Using
Several Steps

Solve $2m + 5 = 17$.

Solution

To solve equations that require more than one step, first isolate the terms involving the unknown (or variable) on one side of the equation and constants (or numbers) on the other side by using addition and subtraction.

$$2m + 5 = 17$$

$$2m + 5 - 5 = 17 - 5 \quad \text{Subtract 5 from both sides.}$$

$$2m = 12$$

Now divide both sides by 2.

$$\frac{2m}{2} = \frac{12}{2} \qquad \text{Divide by 2.}$$
$$m = 6$$

As before, check by substituting 6 for m in the original equation.

> **NOTE**   The unknown can be on either side of the equal sign. $6 = m$ is the same as $m = 6$. The number is the solution when the equation has the variable on the left *or* the right.

OBJECTIVE **3** **Combine similar terms in equations.**   Some equations have more than one term with the same variable. Terms with the same variables can be *combined* by adding or subtracting the coefficients, as shown.

$$5y + 2y = (5 + 2)y = 7y$$
$$11k - 8k = (11 - 8)k = 3k$$
$$12p - 5p + 2p = (12 - 5 + 2)p = 9p$$
$$2z + z = 2z + 1z = (2 + 1)z = 3z$$

EXAMPLE 7

Solving a Linear Equation Using Several Steps

Solve $8y - 6y + 4y = 24$.

Solution

Start by combining terms on the left: $8y - 6y + 4y = 2y + 4y = 6y$. This gives the simplified equation $6y = 24$.

$$6y = 24$$
$$\frac{6y}{6} = \frac{24}{6} \qquad \text{Divide by 6.}$$
$$y = 4$$

OBJECTIVE **4** **Use the distributive property to simplify equations.**   Some of the more advanced formulas used in this book involve a number in front of terms in parentheses. These formulas often require use of the *distributive property*. According to the **distributive property**, a number on the outside of the parentheses can be multiplied by each term inside the parentheses, as shown here.

$$a(b + c) = ab + ac$$

The following diagram may help in remembering the distributive property.

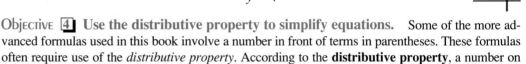

The a is *distributed* over the b and the c, as in the following examples.

$$2(m + 7) = 2m + 2 \cdot 7 = 2m + 14$$
$$8(k - 5) = 8k - 8 \cdot 5 = 8k - 40$$

EXAMPLE 8

Solving a Linear Equation Using the Distributive Property

Solve $8(t - 5) = 16$.

Solution

First use the distributive property on the left to remove the parentheses.

$$8(t - 5) = 16$$
$$8t - 40 = 16$$
$$8t - 40 + 40 = 16 + 40 \qquad \text{Add 40 to both sides.}$$
$$8t = 56$$
$$\frac{8t}{8} = \frac{56}{8} \qquad \text{Divide by 8.}$$
$$t = 7$$

Use the following steps to solve an equation.

Solving an Equation

Step 1. Remove all parentheses on both sides of the equation using the distributive property.

Step 2. Combine all similar terms on both sides of the equation.

Step 3. Add to or subtract from both sides whatever is needed to produce a term with the variable on one side and a number on the other side.

Step 4. Multiply or divide the variable term by whatever is needed to produce a term with a coefficient of 1. Multiply or divide the number term on the other side by the same quantity.

EXAMPLE 9

Solving a Linear Equation Using the Distributive Property

Solve $5r - 2 = 2(r + 5)$.

Solution

$$5r - 2 = 2(r + 5)$$

Use the distributive property on the right side.

$$5r - 2 = 2r + 10$$

$$5r - 2 + 2 = 2r + 10 + 2$$

Add 2 to both sides to get all numbers on the right side.

$$5r = 2r + 12$$

$$5r - 2r = 2r + 12 - 2r$$

Subtract $2r$ from both sides to get all variables on the left side.

$$5r - 2r = 12$$

Combine similar terms on the left side.

$$3r = 12$$

$$\frac{3r}{3} = \frac{12}{3}$$

Divide both sides by 3.

$$r = 4$$

Check by substituting 4 for r in the original equation.

PROBLEM-SOLVING HINT Be sure to check the answer in the *original* equation and not in any other step.

A.2 | BUSINESS APPLICATIONS OF EQUATIONS

Objectives

1 Translate phrases into mathematical expressions.
2 Write equations from given information.
3 Solve applied problems.

Objective 1 **Translate phrases into mathematical expressions.** Most problems in business are expressed in words. Before these problems can be solved, they must be converted into mathematical language.

Word problems tend to have certain phrases that occur again and again. The key to solving word problems is to correctly translate these expressions into mathematical expressions. The next few examples illustrate this process.

EXAMPLE 1

Translating Verbal Expressions Involving Addition

Write the following verbal expressions as mathematical expressions. Use x to represent the unknown. (Other letters could be used to represent this unknown quantity.)

Solution

Verbal Expression	Mathematical Expression	Comments
(a) 5 plus a number	$5 + x$	x represents the number and *plus* indicates **addition**
(b) Add 20 to a number	$x + 20$	x represents the number and *add* indicates **addition**
(c) The sum of a number and 12	$x + 12$	x represents the number and *sum* indicates **addition**
(d) 6 more than a number	$x + 6$	x represents the number and *more than* indicates **addition**

EXAMPLE 2

Translating Verbal Expressions Involving Subtraction

Write each of the following verbal expressions as a mathematical expression. Use p as the variable.

Solution

Verbal Expression	Mathematical Expression	Comments
(a) 3 less than a number	$p - 3$	p represents the number and *less than* indicates **subtraction**
(b) A number decreased by 14	$p - 14$	p represents the number and *decreased by* indicates **subtraction**
(c) 10 fewer than p	$p - 10$	p represents the number and *fewer than* indicates **subtraction**

EXAMPLE 3

Translating Verbal Expressions Involving Multiplication and Division

Write the following verbal expressions as mathematical expressions. Use y as the variable.

Solution

Verbal Expression	Mathematical Expression	Comments
(a) The product of a number and 3	$3y$	y represents the number and *product* indicates **multiplication**
(b) Four times a number	$4y$	y represents the number and *times* indicates **multiplication**
(c) Two thirds of a number	$\frac{2}{3}y$	y represents the number and *of* indicates **multiplication**
(d) The quotient of a number and 2	$\frac{y}{2}$	y represents the number and *quotient* indicates **division**
(e) The sum of 3 and a number is multiplied by 5	$5(3 + y)$ or $5(y + 3)$	This requires **parentheses**

NOTE   When adding or multiplying, the order of the variable and the number doesn't matter. For example:

$$3 + x = x + 3 \quad \text{and} \quad 5 \cdot y = y \cdot 5$$

Now that statements have been translated into mathematical expressions, you can use this knowledge to solve problems. The following steps represent a systematic approach to solving applied problems.

Solving Applied Problems: A Systematic Approach

Step 1. Read the problem very carefully. Reread the problem to make sure that its meaning is clear.

Step 2. Decide on the unknown. Choose a variable to represent the unknown number.

Step 3. Identify the knowns. Use the given information to write an equation describing the relationship given in the problem.

Step 4. Solve the equation.

Step 5. Answer the question asked in the problem.

Step 6. Check the solution by using the original words of the problem.

Step 3 is often the hardest. To write an equation from the information given in the problem, convert the facts stated in words into mathematical expressions. This converted mathematical expression, or equation, is called the *mathematical model* of the situation described in the original words.

Objective **2** **Write equations from given information.** Since equal mathematical expressions represent the same number, any words that mean *equals* or *same* translate into an $=$. The $=$ sign produces an equation which can be solved.

EXAMPLE 4
Writing an Equation from Words

Translate "the product of 5 and a number decreased by 8 is 100" into an equation. Use y as the variable. Solve the equation.

Solution
Translate as follows.

the product of 5		and a number	decreased by	8	is	100
↓	↓	↓	↓	↓	↓	↓
5	·	(y	−	8	=	100

Simplify and complete the solution of the equation.

$$5 \cdot (y - 8) = 100$$
$$5y - 40 = 100 \quad \text{Apply the distributive property.}$$
$$5y = 140 \quad \text{Add 40 to both sides.}$$
$$y = 28 \quad \text{Divide by 5.}$$

Objective **3** **Solve applied problems.**

EXAMPLE 5
Solving a Business Problem

A restaurant manager found that she has 18 more females than males scheduled to work next week. The total number scheduled to work next week is 64. Find the number of females.

Solution
Let m represent the number of males, then $(m + 18)$ is the number of females. The number of males plus the number of females is equal to 64 or the total number scheduled to work. Write this using an equation.

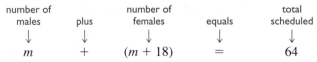

number of males	plus	number of females	equals	total scheduled
↓	↓	↓	↓	↓
m	+	$(m + 18)$	=	64

Solve the equation for the number of males.

$$2m + 18 = 64$$
$$2m + 18 - 18 = 64 - 18 \quad \text{Subtract 18 from each side.}$$
$$2m = 46$$
$$\frac{2m}{2} = \frac{46}{2} \quad \text{Divide by 2.}$$
$$m = 23 \quad \text{There are 23 males scheduled.}$$

Now find the number of females using $(m + 18) = (23 + 18) = 41$ females.

EXAMPLE 6

Applying Equation Solving

A mattress is on sale for $200, which is $\frac{4}{5}$ of its original price. Find the original price.

SOLUTION

Let p represent the original price, $200 is the sale price, and the sale price is $\frac{4}{5}$ of the original price. Use all this information to write the equation.

sale price	**is**	$\frac{4}{5}$	**of**	**original price**
↓	↓	↓	↓	↓
$200	=	$\frac{4}{5}$	×	p

Solve the equation.

$$200 = \frac{4}{5} \cdot p$$
$$\frac{5}{4} \cdot 200 = \frac{5}{4} \cdot \frac{4}{5} \cdot p \quad \text{Multiply by reciprocal.}$$
$$\frac{1000}{4} = 1 \cdot p$$
$$250 = p$$

The original price is $250.

EXAMPLE 7

Solving a Business Problem

The Eastside Nursery ordered 27 trees. Some of the trees were elms, costing $17 each; the rest of the trees were maples at $11 each. The total cost of the trees was $375. Find the number of elms and the number of maples.

SOLUTION

Let x represent the number of elm trees in the shipment. Since the shipment contained 27 trees, the number of maples is found by subtracting the number of elms from 27.

$$27 - x = \text{number of maples}$$

If each elm tree costs $17, then x elm trees will cost $17x$ dollars. Also, the cost of $27 - x$ maple trees at $11 each is $11(27 - x)$. The total cost of the shipment was $375.

A table can be very helpful in identifying the knowns and unknowns.

	Number of Trees	**Cost per Tree**	**Total Cost**
Elms	x	$17	$17x$
Maples	$(27 - x)$	$11	$11(27 - x)$
Totals	27		375

The information in the table is used to develop the following equation.

$$\text{cost of elms} + \text{cost of maples} = \text{total cost}$$
$$17x + 11(27 - x) = 375$$

Now solve this equation. First use the distributive property.

$$17x + 297 - 11x = 375 \quad \text{Combine terms.}$$
$$6x + 297 = 375 \quad \text{Subtract 297 from each side.}$$
$$6x = 78 \quad \text{Divide each side by 6.}$$
$$x = 13$$

There were $x = 13$ elm trees and $27 - 13 = 14$ maple trees.

EXAMPLE 8

Solving Investment Problems

Laurie Zimms has $15,000 to invest. She places a portion of the funds in a passbook account and $3000 more than twice this amount in a retirement account. How much is put into the passbook account? How much is placed in the retirement account?

Solution

Let z represent the amount invested in the passbook account. To find the amount invested in the retirement account, translate as follows.

3000	**more than**	**2 times the amount**
↓	↓	↓
3000	+	$2z$

Since the sum of the two investments must be $15,000, an equation can be formed as follows.

Amount invested in passbook		**Amount invested in retirement account**		**Total amount invested**
z	+	$(3000 + 2z)$	=	$15,000

Now solve the equation.

$$z + (3000 + 2z) = 15,000$$
$$3z + 3000 = 15,000$$
$$3z = 12,000 \quad \text{Subtract 3000.}$$
$$z = 4000 \quad \text{Divide by 3.}$$

The amount invested in the passbook account is z, or $4000. The amount invested in the retirement account is $3000 + 2z$ or $3000 + 2(4000) = \$11,000$.

A.3 | BUSINESS FORMULAS

Objectives

1. Evaluate formulas for given values of the variables.
2. Solve formulas for a specific variable.
3. Use standard business formulas to solve word problems.
4. Evaluate formulas containing exponents.

Objective 1 Evaluate formulas for given values of the variables. Many of the most useful rules and procedures in business are given as **formulas**: equations showing how one number is found from other numbers. One of the single most useful formulas in business is the one for simple interest.

$$\text{Interest} = \text{Principal} \times \text{Rate} \times \text{Time}$$

When written out in words, as shown, a formula can take up too much space and be hard to remember. For this reason, it is common to *use letters as variables for the words* in a formula. Many times the first letter in each word of a formula is used, to make it easier to remember the formula. By this method, the formula for simple interest is written as follows.

$$I = PRT$$

By using letters to express the relationship between interest, principal, rate, and time we have generalized the relationship so that any value can be substituted into the formula. Once three values are substituted into the formula, we can then find the value of the remaining variable.

Example 1

Evaluating a Formula

Use the formula $I = PRT$ and find I if $P = 7000$, $R = .09$, and $T = 2$.

Solution

Substitute 7000 for P, .09 for R, and 2 for T in the formula $I = PRT$. (Remember that writing P, R, and T together as PRT indicates the product of the three letters.)

$$I = PRT$$
$$I = 7000(.09)(2)$$

Multiply on the right to get the solution.

$$I = 1260$$

Example 2

Evaluating a Formula

Use the formula $I = PRT$ and find P if $I = 5760$, $R = .16$, and $T = 3$.

Solution

Substitute the given numbers for the letters of the formula.

$$I = PRT$$
$$5760 = P(.16)(3)$$

On the right, $(.16)(3) = .48$.

$$5760 = .48P$$

To find P, divide both sides of this equation by .48.

$$\frac{5760}{.48} = \frac{.48P}{.48}$$
$$12,000 = P$$

Objective 2 **Solve formulas for a specific variable.** In Example 2 we found the value of P when given the values of I, R, and T. If several problems of this type must be solved, it may be better to rewrite the formula $I = PRT$ so that P is alone on one side of the equation. Do this with the rules of equations given earlier. Since P is multiplied by RT, get P alone by dividing both sides of the equation by RT.

$$I = PRT$$
$$\frac{I}{RT} = \frac{PRT}{RT} \qquad \text{Divide by } RT.$$
$$\frac{I}{RT} = P$$

This process of rearranging a formula is sometimes called *solving a formula for a specific variable.*

Example 3

Solving a Formula for a Specific Variable

Solve for T in the formula $M = P(1 + RT)$.

This formula gives the maturity value (M) of an initial amount of money (P) invested at a specific rate (R) for a certain period of time (T).

Solution

Start by using the distributive property on the right side.

$$M = P(1 + RT)$$
$$M = P + PRT$$

Now subtract P from both sides.

$$M - P = P + PRT - P$$
$$M - P = PRT$$

Divide each side by PR.

$$\frac{M - P}{PR} = \frac{PRT}{PR}$$
$$\frac{M - P}{PR} = T$$

The original formula is now solved for T.

EXAMPLE 4

Solving a Formula for a Specific Variable

Solve for T in the formula $D = \dfrac{B}{MT}$.

Solution

This formula gives the discount rate (D) of a note in terms of the face value (B), the time of a note (T), and the maturity value (M). Solve for T.

$$D = \frac{B}{MT}$$

$$DMT = \frac{B}{MT} MT \qquad \text{Multiply by } MT.$$

$$DMT = B$$

$$\frac{DMT}{DM} = \frac{B}{DM} \qquad \text{Divide by } DM.$$

$$T = \frac{B}{DM}$$

Objective ③ **Use standard business formulas to solve word problems.** In the following examples, application problems that use some common business formulas are solved.

EXAMPLE 5

Finding Gross Sales

Find the gross sales amount from selling 481 fishing lures at $2.65 each.

Solution

The formula for gross sales is $G = NP$. N is the number of items sold and P is the price per item. To find the gross sales from selling 481 fishing lures at $2.65 each, use the formula as shown.

$$G = NP$$
$$G = 481(\$2.65)$$
$$G = \$1274.65$$

The gross sales will be $1274.65.

EXAMPLE 6

Finding Selling Price

A retailer purchased a personal computer with a microphone to digitize voice at a cost of $1265. He then adds a markup of $150 before placing it on the shelf to sell. Find the selling price.

Solution

The selling price is found by adding the cost of the item and the markup.

$$S = C + M$$

The variable C is the cost and M is the markup, which is the amount added to the cost to cover expenses and profit. The selling price is found as shown.

$$S = \$1265 + \$150$$
$$S = \$1415$$

The selling price is $1415.

OBJECTIVE ☐4 **Evaluate formulas containing exponents.** Exponents are used to show repeated multiplication of some quantity. For example:

$$x \cdot x = x^2$$

Exponent: Number of times quantity is multiplied

Base: Quantity being multiplied

Similarly,

$$z \cdot z \cdot z = z^3 \quad \text{and} \quad 5 \cdot 5 \cdot 5 \cdot 5 = 5^4,$$

which is 625.

EXAMPLE 7

Finding Monthly Sales

Trinity Sporting Goods has found that monthly sales can be approximated using

$$\text{Sales} = 40 + 1.6 \times (\text{advertising})^2$$

as long as advertising is less than \$4000. All of the figures in the equation above are in thousands. Estimate sales for a month with \$3500 in advertising.

Solution

Place 3.5 in the equation for the number of thousands of dollars of advertising and find sales.

$$\text{Sales} = 40 + 1.6(3.5)^2$$
$$\text{Sales} = 40 + 1.6(12.25)$$
$$\text{Sales} = 40 + 19.6$$
$$\text{Sales} = 59.6$$

Sales are projected to be \$59,600 for the month.

A.4 | RATIO AND PROPORTION

Objectives

☐1 Define a ratio.
☐2 Set up a proportion.
☐3 Solve a proportion for unknown values.
☐4 Use proportions to solve problems.

OBJECTIVE ☐1 **Define a ratio.** A **ratio** is a quotient of two quantities that can be used to *compare* the quantities. The ratio of the number a to the number b is written in any of the following ways.

$$a \text{ to } b \qquad a : b \qquad \text{or} \qquad \frac{a}{b}$$

This last way of writing a ratio is most common in mathematics, while $a : b$ is perhaps most common in business.

EXAMPLE 1

Writing Ratios

Write a ratio in the form $\frac{a}{b}$ for each word phrase. (Notice in each example that the number mentioned first always gives the numerator.)

Solution

(a) The ratio of 5 hours to 3 hours is $\frac{5}{3}$.

(b) To find the ratio of 5 hours to 3 days, *first convert* 3 days to hours. Since there are 24 hours in 1 day, 3 days = $3 \cdot 24 = 72$ hours. Then the ratio of 5 hours to 3 days is the quotient of 5 and 72.

$$\frac{5}{72}$$

(c) The ratio of $700,000 in sales to $950,000 in sales is written this way.

$$\frac{\$700,000}{\$950,000}$$

Write this ratio in lowest terms.

$$\frac{\$700,000}{\$950,000} = \frac{14}{19}$$

EXAMPLE 2
Writing Ratios

Burger King sold the following items in a one-hour period last Friday afternoon.

70 bacon cheeseburgers
15 plain hamburgers
30 salad combos
45 chicken sandwiches
40 fish sandwiches

Write ratios for the following items sold:

(a) bacon cheeseburgers to fish sandwiches
(b) salad combos to chicken sandwiches
(c) plain hamburgers to salad combos
(d) fish sandwiches to total items sold

Solution

(a) $\dfrac{\text{bacon cheeseburgers}}{\text{fish sandwiches}} = \dfrac{70}{40} = \dfrac{7}{4}$

(b) $\dfrac{\text{salad combos}}{\text{chicken sandwiches}} = \dfrac{30}{45} = \dfrac{2}{3}$

(c) $\dfrac{\text{plain hamburgers}}{\text{salad combos}} = \dfrac{15}{30} = \dfrac{1}{2}$

(d) $\dfrac{\text{fish sandwiches}}{\text{total items sold}} = \dfrac{40}{200} = \dfrac{1}{5}$

OBJECTIVE **2** **Set up a proportion.**   A ratio is used to compare two numbers or amounts. A **proportion** says that two ratios are equal, as in the following example.

$$\frac{3}{4} = \frac{15}{20}$$

This proportion says that the ratios $\frac{3}{4}$ and $\frac{15}{20}$ are equal.
To see whether a proportion is true, use the method of **cross-products**.

Method of Cross-Products

The proportion

$$\frac{a}{b} = \frac{c}{d}$$

is true if the cross-products $a \cdot d$ and $b \cdot c$ are equal (i.e., $ad = bc$).

EXAMPLE 3
Determining if a
Proportion Is True

Decide whether the following proportions are true.

(a) $\dfrac{3}{5} = \dfrac{12}{20}$ **(b)** $\dfrac{2}{3} = \dfrac{9}{16}$

Solution

(a) Find each cross-product.

$$\frac{3}{5} = \frac{12}{20}$$

$$3 \times 20 = 5 \times 12$$

$$60 = 60$$

Since the cross-products are equal, the proportion is true.

(b) Find the cross-products.

$$\frac{2}{3} = \frac{9}{16}$$

$$2 \times 16 = 3 \times 9$$

$$32 \neq 27$$

This proportion is false.

Objective **3** **Solve a proportion for unknown values.** The method of cross-products is just a shortcut version of solving an equation. To see how, start with the proportion

$$\frac{a}{b} = \frac{c}{d}$$

and multiply both sides by the product of the two denominators, bd,

$$bd \cdot \frac{a}{b} = bd \cdot \frac{c}{d}$$

or

$$ad = bc$$

The expressions ad and bc are the cross-products, and this solution shows that they are equal.

Four numbers are used in a proportion. If any three of these numbers are known, the fourth can be found.

EXAMPLE 4

Solving a
Proportion

(a) Find x in this proportion.

$$\frac{3}{5} = \frac{x}{40}$$

Solution

In a proportion, the cross-products are equal. The cross-products in this proportion are $3 \cdot 40$ and $5 \cdot x$. Setting these equal gives the following equation.

$$3 \cdot 40 = 5 \cdot x$$

$$120 = 5x$$

Divide both sides by 5 to find the solution.

$$24 = x$$

(b) Solve this proportion to find k.

$$\frac{3}{10} = \frac{5}{k}$$

Solution

Find the two cross-products and set them equal.

$$3k = 10 \cdot 5$$
$$3k = 50$$
$$k = \frac{50}{3}$$

Write the answer as the mixed number $16\frac{2}{3}$ if desired.

Example 5
Solving
Proportions

A food wholesaler charges a restaurant chain $83 for 3 crates of fresh produce. How much should it charge for 5 crates of produce?

Solution

Let x be the cost of 5 crates of produce. Set up a proportion with one ratio the number of crates and the other ratio the costs. Use this pattern.

$$\frac{\text{crates}}{\text{crates}} = \frac{\text{cost}}{\text{cost}}$$

Now substitute the given information.

$$\frac{3}{5} = \frac{83}{x}$$

Use the cross-products to solve the proportion.

$$3x = 5(83)$$
$$3x = \$415$$
$$x = \$138.33 \quad \text{(rounded to the nearest cent)}$$

The 5 crates should cost $138.33.

Objective ▨4▨ **Use proportions to solve problems.** Proportions are used in many practical applications as shown in the next two examples.

Example 6
Solving
Applications

A firm in Hong Kong and one in Thailand agree to jointly develop an engine-control microchip to be sold to North American auto manufacturers. They agree to split the development costs in a ratio of 8:3 (Hong Kong firm to Thailand firm), resulting in a cost of $9,400,000 to the Hong Kong firm. Find the cost to the Thailand firm.

Solution

Let x represent the cost to the Thailand firm, then

$$\frac{8}{3} = \frac{9,400,000}{x}$$
$$8x = 3 \cdot 9,400,000 \qquad \text{Cross multiply.}$$
$$8x = 28,200,000$$
$$x = 3,525,000 \qquad \text{Divide by 8.}$$

The Thailand firm's share of the costs is $3,525,000.

Example 7
Solving
Applications

Bill Thomas wishes to estimate the amount of timber on some forested land that he owns. One value he needs to estimate is the average height of the trees. One morning, Thomas notices that his own 6-foot body casts an 8-foot shadow at the same time that a typical tree casts a 34-foot shadow. Find the height of the tree.

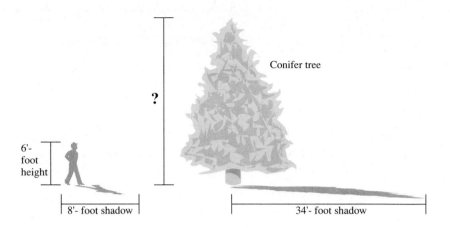

Solution

Set up a proportion in which the height of the tree is given the variable name x.

$$\frac{6}{8} = \frac{x}{34}$$

$$6 \cdot 34 = 8 \cdot x \quad \text{Cross multiply.}$$

$$\frac{204}{8} = \frac{8 \cdot x}{8} \quad \text{Divide by 8.}$$

$$x = 25.5 \text{ feet}$$

The height of the tree is 25.5 feet.

Name   Date   Class

Appendix A | Exercises

In Exercises 1–25, solve each equation for the variable.   **[A.1]**

1. $s + 12 = 15$ _____

2. $k + 15 = 22$ _____

3. $b - 7 = 24$ _____

4. $P - 13 = 52$ _____

5. $12 = b + 9$ _____

6. $7 = m - 3$ _____

7. $8k = 56$ _____

8. $3q = 120$ _____

9. $60 = 30m$ _____

10. $94 = 2z$ _____

11. $\dfrac{m}{5} = 6$ _____

12. $\dfrac{r}{7} = 1$ _____

13. $\dfrac{2}{3}a = 5$ _____

14. $\dfrac{3}{4}m = 18$ _____

15. $\dfrac{9}{5}r = 18$ _____

16. $2x = \dfrac{5}{3}$ _____

17. $3m + 5 = 17$ _____

18. $2y - 5 = 39$ _____

19. $4r + 3 = 9$ _____

20. $2p + \dfrac{1}{2} = \dfrac{3}{2}$ _____

21. $11r - 5r + 6r = 84$ _____

22. $5m + 6m - 2m = 72$ _____

23. $3x + 12 = 3(2x + 3)$ _____

24. $4z + 2 = 2(z + 2)$ _____

25. $2(3x + 9) = 8(2 + x)$ _____

In Exercises 26–35, a formula is given, along with the values of all but one of the variables in the formula. Find the value of the variable that is not given.   **[A.1]**

Quick Start

26. $I = PRT$; $P = 2800, R = .09, T = 2$ **I = 504** _____

27. $S = C + M$; $C = 275, M = 49$ **S = 324** _____

28. $G = NP$; $N = 840, P = 3.79$ _____

29. $M = P(1 + RT)$; $P = 420, R = .07, T = 2\dfrac{1}{2}$ _____

30. $R = \dfrac{D}{1 - DT}$; $D = .04, T = 5$ _____

31. $A = \dfrac{S}{1 + RT}$; $S = 12{,}600, R = .12,$

$T = \dfrac{5}{12}$ _____

32. $T = \dfrac{D}{S}$; $T = 100, S = 2$ _____

33. $\dfrac{I}{PR} = T$; $P = 100, R = .02, T = 500$ _____

34. $d = rt$; $r = .07, t = 12$ _____

35. $I = PRT$; $P = 500, R = .08, T = 3$ _____

In Exercises 36–40, solve for the indicated variables.   **[A.3]**

36. $A = LW$; for W _____

37. $d = rt$; for r _____

38. $I = PRT$; for T _____

39. $P = 1 + RT$; for R _____

40. $A = P + PRT$; for T _____

In Exercises 41–45, write the ratio in lowest terms.   **[A.4]**

41. 250 pesos to 1250 pesos _____

42. 45 women to 110 men _____

43. $1.20 to 75¢ _____

44. 20 hours to 5 days _____

45. 35 dimes to 6 dollars _____

In Exercises 46–50, decide whether the proportions are true or false.   **[A.4]**

46. $\dfrac{2}{3} = \dfrac{42}{63}$ _____

47. $\dfrac{6}{9} = \dfrac{36}{52}$ _____

48. $\dfrac{18}{20} = \dfrac{56}{60}$ _____

49. $\dfrac{12}{18} = \dfrac{8}{12}$ _____

50. $\dfrac{420}{600} = \dfrac{14}{20}$ _____

In Exercises 51–60, solve the proportions.   **[A.4]**

51. $\dfrac{y}{35} = \dfrac{25}{5}$ _____

52. $\dfrac{15}{s} = \dfrac{45}{117}$ _____

53. $\dfrac{a}{25} = \dfrac{4}{20}$ _____

54. $\dfrac{6}{x} = \dfrac{4}{18}$ _____

55. $\dfrac{z}{20} = \dfrac{80}{200}$ _____

56. $\dfrac{25}{100} = \dfrac{8}{m}$ _____

57. $\dfrac{1}{2} = \dfrac{t}{7}$ _____

58. $\dfrac{2}{3} = \dfrac{5}{s}$ _____

59. $\dfrac{2}{9} = \dfrac{p}{12}$ _____

60. $\dfrac{2}{y} = \dfrac{9}{7}$ _____

Solve the following application problems.

61. Cajun Boatin' Inc. bought 5 small boats and 3 large boats for $14,878. A small boat costs $1742. Find the cost of a large boat.   **[A.1]**

61. _____

62. Mike paid $172,000 for a 5-unit apartment house. Find the cost for a 12-unit apartment house.   **[A.4]**

62. _____

63. The tax on a $40 item is $3. Find the tax on a $160 item.   **[A.4]**

63. _____

64. Sam bought 17 table-model television sets for $1942.25. Find the cost of one set.   **[A.4]**

64. _____

Name   Date   Class

65. The bookstore at Steeltrap Community College has a markup that is $\frac{1}{4}$ its cost on a book.   **65.** _____
Find the cost to the bookstore of a book selling for $20.   **[A.2]**

66. An unknown principal (P) invested at 8% for $1\frac{3}{4}$ years yields a maturity value (M) of $1368.   **66.** _____
Use $M = P(1 + RT)$ to find the principal.   **[A.3]**

67. Explain why all terms with a variable should be placed on one side of the equation, and all terms
without a variable should be placed on the opposite side, when solving an equation.   **[A.1]**

68. In your own words, explain formula, ratio, and proportion.   **[A.3 AND A.4]**

Appendix B

Scientific Calculators

Objectives

☐ 1 Learn the basic calculator keys.

☐ 2 Understand the $\boxed{C}$, $\boxed{CE}$, and $\boxed{ON/C}$ keys.

☐ 3 Understand the floating decimal point.

☐ 4 Use the $\boxed{\%}$ and $\boxed{1/x}$ keys.

☐ 5 Use the $\boxed{y^x}$ and $\boxed{\sqrt{\ }}$ keys.

☐ 6 Use the $\boxed{a\,b\,c}$ key.

☐ 7 Solve problems with negative numbers.

☐ 8 Use the calculator memory function.

☐ 9 Solve chain calculations using order of operations.

☐ 10 Use the parentheses keys.

☐ 11 Use the calculator for problem solution.

Calculators are among the more popular inventions of the last three decades. Each year better calculators are developed and costs drop. The first all-transistor desktop calculator was introduced to the market in 1966; it weighed 55 pounds, cost $2500, and was slow. Today, these same calculations are performed quite well on a calculator costing less than $10. And today's $200 pocket calculators have more ability to solve problems than some of the early computers.

Many colleges allow students to use calculators in business mathematics courses. Some courses require calculator use. Many types of calculators are available, from the inexpensive basic calculator to the more complex **scientific, financial**, and **graphing** calculators.

In Appendix B we discuss the common scientific calculator including percent key, reciprocal key, exponent keys, square root key, memory function, order of operations, and parentheses keys. In Appendix C, the financial calculator with its associated financial keys is discussed.

> **NOTE** The various calculator models differ significantly—*use the booklet that came with your calculator* for specifics about that calculator if your answers differ from those in this section.

Objective 1 **Learn the basic calculator keys.** Most calculators use **algebraic logic**. Some problems can be solved by entering number and function keys in the same order as you would solve a problem by hand; others require a knowledge of the order of operations when entering the problem.

EXAMPLE 1

Using the Basic Keys

(a)   12 + 25   **(b)**   456 ÷ 24

Solution

(a) The problem 12 + 25 would be entered as

$$12 \boxed{+} 25 \boxed{=}$$

and 37 would appear as the answer.

(b) Enter 456 ÷ 24 as

$$456 \boxed{÷} 24 \boxed{=}$$

and 19 appears as the answer.

OBJECTIVE **2** Understand the $\boxed{C}$, $\boxed{CE}$, and $\boxed{ON/C}$ keys. All calculators have a $\boxed{C}$ key. Pressing this key erases everything in most calculators and prepares them for a new problem. Some calculators have a $\boxed{CE}$ key. Pressing this key erases only the number displayed, thus allowing for correction of a mistake without having to start the problem over. Many calculators combine the $\boxed{C}$ key and $\boxed{CE}$ key and use an $\boxed{ON/C}$ key. This key turns the calculator on and is also used to erase the calculator display. If the $\boxed{ON/C}$ is pressed after the $\boxed{=}$, or after one of the operations keys ($\boxed{+}$, $\boxed{-}$, $\boxed{×}$, $\boxed{÷}$), everything in the calculator is erased. If the wrong operation key is pressed, simply press the correct key and the error is corrected. For example, in 7 $\boxed{+}$ $\boxed{-}$ 3 $\boxed{=}$ 4, pressing the $\boxed{-}$ key cancels out the previous $\boxed{+}$ key entry.

OBJECTIVE **3** Understand the floating decimal point. Most calculators have a **floating decimal** which locates the decimal point in the final result.

EXAMPLE 2

Calculating with Decimal Numbers

Jennifer Videtto purchased 55.75 square yards of vinyl floor covering, at $18.99 per square yard. Find her total cost.

Solution

Proceed as follows.

$$55.75 \boxed{×} 18.99 \boxed{=} 1058.6925$$

The decimal point is automatically placed in the answer. Since money answers are usually rounded to the nearest cent, the answer is $1058.69.

In using a machine with a floating decimal, enter the decimal point as needed. For example, enter $47 as

$$47$$

with no decimal point, but enter $.95 as follows.

$$\boxed{.} 95$$

One problem utilizing a floating decimal is shown by the following example.

EXAMPLE 3

Placing the Decimal Point in Money Answers

Add $21.38 and $1.22.

Solution

$$21.38 \boxed{+} 1.22 \boxed{=} 22.6$$

The final 0 is left off. Remember that the problem deals with dollars and cents, and write the answer as $22.60.

Objective [4] **Use the** [%] **and** [1/x] **keys.** The [%] key moves the decimal point two places to the left when used following multiplication or division.

EXAMPLE 4

Using the [%] Key

Find 8% of $4205.

Solution

$$4205 \;\boxed{\times}\; 8 \;\boxed{\%}\; \boxed{=}\; 336.4 = \$336.40$$

The [1/x] key replaces a number with the reciprocal of that number.

EXAMPLE 5

Using the [1/x] Key

Find the inverse or reciprocal of 40.

Solution

$$40 \;\boxed{1/x}\; 0.025$$

Objective [5] **Use the** [yˣ] **and** [√] **keys.** The product of 3×3 can be written as:

$$3^2.$$

with labels: Exponent (pointing to the 2) and Base (pointing to the 3)

The exponent (2 in this case) shows how many times the base is multiplied by itself (multiply 3 times itself). The [yˣ] key raises a base to a power; be sure to enter the base first, followed by the exponent.

EXAMPLE 6

Using the [yˣ] Key

Find 5^3.

Solution

$$5 \;\boxed{y^x}\; 3 \;\boxed{=}\; 125$$

Since $3^2 = 9$, the number 3 is called the **square root** of 9. Square roots of numbers are written with the symbol $\sqrt{}$.

$$\sqrt{9} = 3$$

EXAMPLE 7

Using the [√] Key

Find each square root.

(a) $\sqrt{144}$ **(b)** $\sqrt{20}$

Solution

(a) Using the calculator, enter

$$144 \;\boxed{\sqrt{x}}$$

and 12 appears in the display. The square root of 144 is 12.

(b) The square root of 20 is

$$20 \;\boxed{\sqrt{x}}\; 4.472136$$

which may be rounded to the desired position.

Objective [6] **Use the** [a b c] **key.** Many calculators have an [a b c] key that can be used for problems containing fractions and mixed numbers. A mixed number is a number with both a whole number and a fraction such as $7\frac{3}{4}$ which equals $7 + \frac{3}{4}$. The rules for adding, subtracting, multiplying, and dividing both fractions and mixed numbers are given in Chapter 2. Here, we simply show how these operations are done on a calculator.

EXAMPLE 8

Using the [a%] Key with Fractions

Solve the following.

(a) $\dfrac{6}{11} + \dfrac{3}{4}$

(b) $\dfrac{3}{8} \div \dfrac{5}{6}$

Solution

(a) 6 [a%] 11 [+] 3 [a%] 4 [=] $1\dfrac{13}{44}$

(b) 3 [a%] 8 [÷] 5 [a%] 6 [=] $\dfrac{9}{20}$

NOTE   The calculator automatically reduces fractions for you.

EXAMPLE 9

Using the [a%] Key

Solve the following.

(a) $4\dfrac{7}{8} \div 3\dfrac{4}{7}$ (b) $\dfrac{5}{3} \div 27.5$ (c) $65.3 \times 6\dfrac{3}{4}$

Solution

(a) 4 [a%] 7 [a%] 8 [÷] 3 [a%] 4 [a%] 7 [=] $1\dfrac{73}{200}$

(b) 5 [a%] 3 [÷] 27.5 [=] 0.060606061

(c) 65.3 [×] 6 [a%] 3 [a%] 4 [=] 440.775

OBJECTIVE 7   Solve problems with negative numbers. There are several calculations in business that result in a **negative number** or **deficit amount**.

EXAMPLE 10

Working with Negative Numbers

The amount in the advertising account last month was $4800 while $5200 was actually spent. Find the balance remaining in the advertising account.

Solution

Enter the numbers in the calculator.

$$4800 \;[-]\; 5200 \;[=]\; -400$$

The minus sign in front of the 400 indicates that there is a deficit or negative amount. This value can be written as −$400 or sometimes as ($400), which indicates a negative amount. Some calculators place the minus after the number, or as 400−.

Negative numbers may be entered into the calculator by using the [−] before entering the number. For example, if $3000 is now added to the advertising account in Example 10, the new balance is calculated as follows.

$$[-]\; 400 \;[+]\; 3000 \;[=]\; 2600$$

The new account balance is $2600.

The [+/−] key can be used to change the sign of a number that has already been entered. For example, 520 [+/−] changes +520 to −520.

OBJECTIVE 8   Use the calculator memory function. Many calculators feature memory keys, which are a sort of electronic scratch paper. These **memory keys** are used to store intermediate steps in a calculation. On some calculators, a key labeled [M] or [STO] is used to store the numbers in the display, with [MR] or [RCL] used to recall the numbers from memory.

Other calculators have $\boxed{\textbf{M+}}$ and $\boxed{\textbf{M−}}$ keys. The $\boxed{\textbf{M+}}$ key adds the number displayed to the number already in memory. For example, if the memory contains the number 0 at the beginning of a problem, and the calculator display contains the number 29.4, then pushing $\boxed{\textbf{M+}}$ will cause 29.4 to be stored in the memory (the result of adding 0 and 29.4). If 57.8 is then entered into the display, pushing $\boxed{\textbf{M+}}$ will cause

$$29.4 + 57.8 = 87.2$$

to be stored. If 11.9 is then entered into the display, with $\boxed{\textbf{M−}}$ pushed, the memory will contain

$$87.2 - 11.9 = 75.3.$$

The $\boxed{\textbf{MR}}$ key is used to recall the number in memory as needed, with $\boxed{\textbf{MC}}$ used to clear the memory.

> **PROBLEM-SOLVING HINT**   Always clear the memory before starting a problem—not doing so is a common error.

Scientific calculators typically have one or more storage registers in which to store numbers. These memory keys are usually labeled as $\boxed{\textbf{STO}}$ for store and $\boxed{\textbf{RCL}}$ for recall. For example, 32.5 can be stored in register 1 by

$$32.5 \; \boxed{\textbf{STO}} \; 1$$

or it can be stored in memory register 2 by 32.5 $\boxed{\textbf{STO}}$ 2 and so forth. Values are retrieved from a particular memory register by using the $\boxed{\textbf{RCL}}$ key followed by the number of the register. For example, $\boxed{\textbf{RCL}}$ 2 recalls the contents of memory register 2.

With a scientific calculator, a number stays in memory until it is replaced by another number or until the memory is cleared. The contents of the memory are saved even when the calculator is turned off.

EXAMPLE 11
Using the Memory Registers

An elevator repairperson counted the number of people entering an elevator and also measured the weight of each group of people. Find the average weight per person.

Number of People	Total Weight
6	839 pounds
8	1184 pounds
4	640 pounds

Solution

First find the weight of all three groups and store in memory register 1.

$$839 \; \boxed{+} \; 1184 \; \boxed{+} \; 640 \; \boxed{=} \; 2663 \; \boxed{\textbf{STO}} \; 1$$

Then find the total number of people.

$$6 \; \boxed{+} \; 8 \; \boxed{+} \; 4 \; \boxed{=} \; 18$$

Finally, divide the contents of memory register 1 by the 18 people.

$$\boxed{\textbf{RCL}} \; 1 \; \boxed{÷} \; 18 \; \boxed{=} \; 147.94444 \text{ pounds}$$

This value can be rounded as needed.

OBJECTIVE **9** **Solve chain calculations using order of operations.** Long calculations involving several operations (adding, subtracting, multiplying, and dividing) must be done in a specific sequence called the **order of operations** and are called **chain calculations**. The logic of the following order of operations is built into most scientific calculators and can help us work problems without having to store a lot of intermediate values.

> ### Order of Operations
>
> 1. Do all operations inside parentheses first.
> 2. Simplify any expressions with exponents (squares) and find any square roots.
> 3. Multiply and divide from left to right.
> 4. Add and subtract from left to right.

EXAMPLE 12
Using the Order of Operations

Solve the following.

(a) $3 + 7 \times 9\frac{3}{4}$ **(b)** $42.1 \times 5 - 90 \div 4$

Solution

The calculator automatically keeps track of the order of operations for us.

(a) 3 $+$ 7 $\times$ 9 abc 3 abc 4 $=$ $71\frac{1}{4}$

(b) 42.1 $\times$ 5 $-$ 90 $\div$ 4 $=$ 188

OBJECTIVE **10** **Use the parentheses keys.** The parentheses keys can be used to help establish the order of operations in a more complex chain calculation. For example, $\frac{4}{5+7}$ can be written as $\frac{4}{(5+7)}$, which can be solved as follows.

Left-parenthesis key

4 $\div$ $($ 5 $+$ 7 $)$ $=$ 0.3333333

Right-parenthesis key

EXAMPLE 13
Using Parentheses

Solve the following problem.

$$\frac{16 \div 2.5}{39.2 - 29.8 \times .6}$$

Solution

Think of this problem as follows.

$$\frac{(16 \div 2.5)}{(39.2 - 29.8 \times .6)}$$

Using parentheses to set off the numerator and denominator will help you minimize errors.

$($ 16 $\div$ 2.5 $)$ $\div$ $($ 39.2 $-$ 29.8 $\times$ .6 $)$ $=$ 0.3001876

OBJECTIVE **11** **Use the calculator for problem solution.** Scientific calculators are great tools to help you solve problems.

EXAMPLE 14
Finding Sale Price

A compact disc player with an original price of $560 is on sale at 10% off. Find the sale price.

Solution

If the discount from the original price is 10%, then the sale price is 100% − 10% of the original price.

560 $\times$ $($ 100 $-$ 10 $)$ $\%$ $=$ 504

On some calculators the following key strokes will also work:

560 $-$ 10 $\%$ $=$ 504.

Example 15

Applying
Calculator Use to
Problem Solving

A home buyer borrows $86,400 at 10% for 30 years. The monthly payment on the loan is $8.78 per $1000 borrowed. Annual taxes are $780, and fire insurance is $453 a year. Find the total monthly payment including taxes and insurance.

Solution

The monthly payment is the *sum* of the monthly payment on the loan *plus* monthly taxes *plus* monthly fire insurance costs. The monthly payment on the loan is the number of thousands in the loan (86.4) times the monthly payment per $1000 borrowed (8.78).

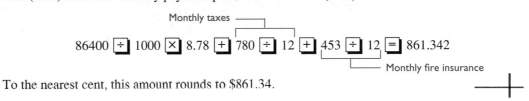

To the nearest cent, this amount rounds to $861.34.

Name _____ Date _____ Class _____

Appendix B | Exercises

Solve each of the following problems on a calculator. Round each answer to the nearest hundredth.

1.
$$\begin{array}{r} 384.92 \\ 407.61 \\ 351.14 \\ +\ \ 27.93 \end{array}$$

2.
$$\begin{array}{r} 85.76 \\ 21.94 \\ +\ 39.89 \end{array}$$

3.
$$\begin{array}{r} 6850 \\ 321 \\ +\ 4207 \end{array}$$

4.
$$\begin{array}{r} 781.42 \\ 304.59 \\ +\ 261.35 \end{array}$$

5.
$$\begin{array}{r} 4270.41 \\ -\ 365.09 \end{array}$$

6.
$$\begin{array}{r} 3000.07 \\ -\ \ \ 48.12 \end{array}$$

7.
$$\begin{array}{r} 384.96 \\ -\ 129.72 \end{array}$$

8. $36.84 - 12.17$

9.
$$\begin{array}{r} 365 \\ \times\ \ \ 43 \end{array}$$

10.
$$\begin{array}{r} 27.51 \\ \times\ \ 1.18 \end{array}$$

11. 3.7×8.4

12. 62.5×81

13. $\dfrac{375.4}{10.6}$

14. $\dfrac{9625}{400}$

15. $96.7 \div 3.5$

16. $103.7 \div .35$

Solve each of the following chain calculations. Round each answer to the nearest hundredth.

17. $\dfrac{9 \times 9}{2 \times 5}$

18. $\dfrac{15 \times 8 \times 3}{11 \times 7 \times 4}$

19. $\dfrac{87 \times 24 \times 47.2}{13.6 \times 12.8}$

20. $\dfrac{2 \times (3 + 4)}{6 + 10}$

21. $\dfrac{2 \times 3 + 4}{6 + 10}$

22. $\dfrac{4200 \times .12 \times 90}{365}$

23. $\dfrac{640 - .6 \times 12}{17.5 + 3.2}$

24. $\dfrac{16 \times 18 \div .42}{95.4 \times 3 - .8}$

25. $\dfrac{14^2 - 3.6 \times 6}{95.2 \div .5}$

26. $\dfrac{9^2 + 3.8 \div 2}{14 + 7.5}$

Solve each of the following problems. Reduce any fractions to lowest terms or round to the nearest hundredth.

27. $7\frac{5}{8} \div \left(1 + \frac{3}{8}\right)$

28. $\left(5\frac{1}{4}\right)^2 \times 3.65$

29. $\left(\frac{3}{4} \div \frac{5}{8}\right)^3 \div 3\frac{1}{2}$

30. $\sqrt{6} \times \dfrac{3^2 + 2\frac{1}{2}}{7 \times \frac{5}{6}}$

31. Describe in your own words the order of operations to be used when solving chain calculations. (See Objective 9.)

32. Explain how the parentheses keys are used when solving chain calculations. (See Objective 9.)

Solve each of the following application problems on a calculator. Round each answer to the nearest cent.

33. Bucks County Community College Bookstore bought 397 used copies of a computer science book at a net cost of $23.86 each; 125 used copies of an accounting book at $28.74 each; and 740 used copies of a real estate text at $21.76 each. Find the total paid by the bookstore.

34. To find the monthly interest due on a certain home mortgage, multiply the mortgage balance by .007292. Find the monthly interest on a mortgage having a balance of $95,830.

35. Find the monthly interest on a mortgage having a balance of $113,720. (See Exercise 34.)

36. Judy Martinez needs to file her expense account claims. She spent 5 nights at the Macon Holiday Inn at $47.46 per night, 4 nights at the Charlotte Sheraton at $51.62 per night, and rented a car for 8 days at $29.95 per day. She drove the car 916 miles with a charge of $.24 per mile. Find her total expenses.

37. In Virginia City, the sales tax is 6.5%. Find the tax on each of the following items: **(a)** a new car costing $17,908.43 and **(b)** an office word processor costing $1463.58.

38. Marja Strutz bought a new commercial fishing boat equipped for sardine fishing at a cost of $78,250. Additional safety equipment was needed at a cost of $4820 and sales tax of $7\frac{1}{4}$% was due on the boat and safety equipment. In addition she was charged a licensing fee of $1135 and a Coast Guard registration fee of $428. Strutz will pay $\frac{1}{3}$ of the total cost as a down payment and will borrow the balance. How much will she borrow?

39. Ben Fick bought a home for $80,000. He paid $8000 down and agreed to make payments of $528.31 each month for 30 years. By how much does the down payment and the sum of the monthly payments exceed the purchase price?

Name	Date	Class

40. Linda Smelt purchased a 32-unit apartment house for $620,000. She made a down payment of $150,000 which she had inherited from her parents and agreed to make monthly payments of $5050 for 15 years. By how much does the sum of her down payment and all monthly payments exceed the original purchase price?

41. Ben Hurd wishes to open a small repair shop but only has $32,400 in cash. He estimates that he will need $15,000 for equipment, $2800 for the first month's rent on a building, and about $28,000 operating expenses until the business is profitable. How much additional funding does he need?

42. Koplan Kitchens wishes to expand their retail store. In order to do so, they must first purchase the $26,000 lot next door to them. They then anticipate $120,000 construction costs plus an additional $28,500 for additional inventory. They have $50,000 in cash and must borrow the balance from a bank. How much must they borrow?

Appendix C

Financial Calculators

Objectives

1. Learn the basic conventions used with cash flows.
2. Learn the basic financial keys.
3. Understand which keys to use for a particular problem.
4. Use the calculator to solve financial problems.

Calculators are among the more popular inventions of recent times. The power and capability of calculators has increased significantly even as their cost has continued to fall. Today, programmable calculators costing less than $100 have more ability to solve problems than some of the early computers.

Objective 1 **Learn the basic conventions used with cash flows.** There is a need to logically separate inflows of cash (cash received) from outflows of cash (cash paid out). The following convention is commonly used for this purpose, and will be used throughout this appendix.

1. Inflows of cash (cash received) are positive.
2. Outflows of cash (cash paid out) are negative.

For example, assume you are making regular investments into an account. Your payments are outflows of cash and should be considered negative numbers. The future value of your savings will eventually be returned to you as an inflow of cash, thereby as a positive number.

Objective 2 **Learn the basic financial keys.** **Financial calculators** have special functions that allow the user to solve financial problems involving time, interest rates, and money. Many of the compound interest problems presented in this text can be solved using a financial calculator. Most financial calculators have financial keys similar to those shown below.

These keys represent the following functions:

> **n**—The number of compounding periods
> **i**—The interest rate *per compounding period*
> **PV**—Present value—the value in *today's* dollars
> **PMT**—The amount of a level payment (e.g., $625 per month); this is used for annuity type problems.
> **FV**—Future value—the value at *some future date*

NOTE Different financial calculators look and work somewhat differently from one another. You *must look at the instruction book* that came with your calculator to determine how the keys are used with that particular calculator.

> **PROBLEM-SOLVING HINT**   You will find that different financial calculators will sometimes give slightly different answers to the same problems due to rounding.

Objective **3**   **Understand which keys to use for a particular problem.**   Most simple financial problems require only four of the five financial keys described on the previous page. Both the number of compounding periods **n** and the interest rate per compounding period **i** *are needed for each financial problem*—these two keys will always be used. Which two of the remaining three financial keys (**PV**, **PMT**, and **FV**) are used depends on the particular problem. Using the convention described under Objective 1, one of these values will be negative and one will be positive. The process of solving a financial problem is to enter values for the three variables that are known, *then press the key for the unknown*, fourth variable.

For example, if you wish to know the future value of a series of known, equal payments, enter the specific values for **n**, **i**, and **PMT**. Then press **FV** for the result. Or, if you wish to know how long it will take for an investment to grow to some specific value at a given interest rate, enter values for **PV**, **i**, and **FV**. Then press **n** to find the required number of compounding periods.

> **PROBLEM-SOLVING HINT**   Be sure to enter a cash inflow as a positive number or a cash outflow as a negative number. Also be sure to clear all values from the memory of your calculator before working a problem.

Objective **4**   **Use the calculator to solve financial problems.**

Example 1	Barbara and Ivan Cushing invest $2500 that they received from the sale of the family car in a stock mutual fund that has historically paid 12% compounded quarterly. Find the future value in 5 years if the fund continues to do as well.
Given n, i, and PV Find FV	

Solution

The present value of $2500 (a cash outflow entered as a negative number) is compounded at 3% per quarter (12% ÷ 4 = 3%) for 20 quarters (4 × 5 = 20). Enter values for **PV**, **i**, and **n**.

$$-2500 \;\; \boxed{PV} \;\; 3 \;\; \boxed{i} \;\; 20 \;\; \boxed{n}$$

Then press **FV** to find the compound amount at the end of 5 years.

$$\boxed{FV} \;\; \$4515.28, \text{ which is the future value.}$$

Example 2	Joan Jones plans to invest $100 at the end of each month in a mutual fund that she believes will grow at 12% per year compounded monthly. Find the future value at her retirement in 20 years.
Given n, i, and PMT Find FV	

Solution

Two hundred forty payments (12 × 20 = 240) of $100 each (cash outflows entered as a negative number) are made into an account earning 1% per month (12% ÷ 12 = 1%). Enter values for **n**, **PMT**, and **i**.

$$240 \;\; \boxed{n} \;\; -100 \;\; \boxed{PMT} \;\; 1 \;\; \boxed{i}$$

Press **FV** for the result.

$$\boxed{FV} \;\; \$98,925.54, \text{ which is the future value.}$$

> **PROBLEM-SOLVING HINT**   The order in which data is entered into the calculator does not matter—just remember to press the financial key for the unknown value last.

Any one of the four values used to solve a particular financial problem *can be unknown*. Look at the next three examples in which the number of compounding periods $\boxed{\text{n}}$, the payment amount $\boxed{\text{PMT}}$, and the interest rate per compounding period $\boxed{\text{i}}$, respectively, are unknown.

EXAMPLE 3
Given *i, PMT,* and *FV* Find *n*

Mr. Trebor needs $140,000 for a new farm tractor. He can invest $8000 at the end of each month in an account paying 6% per year compounded monthly. How many monthly payments are needed?

Solution

The $8000 monthly payment (cash outflow) will grow at .5% per compounding period (6% ÷ 12 = .5%) until a future value of $140,000 (cash inflow at a future date) is accumulated. Enter values for $\boxed{\text{PMT}}$, $\boxed{\text{i}}$, and $\boxed{\text{FV}}$.

$$-8000\ \boxed{\text{PMT}}\ .5\ \boxed{\text{i}}\ 140000\ \boxed{\text{FV}}$$

Press $\boxed{\text{n}}$ to determine the number of payments.

$$\boxed{\text{n}}\ 17 \text{ monthly payments of \$8000 each are needed.}$$

Actually, 17 payments of $8000 each in an account earning .5% per month will grow to slightly more than $140,000:

$$-8000\ \boxed{\text{PMT}}\ .5\ \boxed{\text{i}}\ 17\ \boxed{\text{n}}$$

Press $\boxed{\text{FV}}$ to determine the future value.

$$\boxed{\text{FV}}\ \$141,578.41, \text{ which is the future value.}$$

The seventeenth payment would only need to be

$$\$8000 - (\$141,578.41 - \$140,000) = \$6421.59$$

in order to accumulate exactly $140,000.

EXAMPLE 4
Given *n, i,* and *FV* Find *PMT*

Jane Abel wishes to have $1,000,000 at her retirement in 40 years. Find the payment she must make at the end of each quarter into an account earning 10% compounded quarterly to attain her goal.

Solution

One hundred sixty payments (40 × 4 = 160) are made into an account earning 2.5% per quarter (10% ÷ 4 = 2.5%) until a future value of $1,000,000 (cash inflow at a future date) is accumulated. Enter values for $\boxed{\text{n}}$, $\boxed{\text{i}}$, and $\boxed{\text{FV}}$.

$$160\ \boxed{\text{n}}\ 2.5\ \boxed{\text{i}}\ +1000000\ \boxed{\text{FV}}$$

Press $\boxed{\text{PMT}}$ for the quarterly payment.

$$\boxed{\text{PMT}}\ -\$490.41, \text{ which is the required quarterly payment of cash.}$$

One hundred sixty payments of $490.41 at the end of each quarter in an account earning 10% compounded quarterly will grow to $1,000,000.

EXAMPLE 5
Given *n, PV,* and *FV* Find *i*

Tom Fernandez bought 200 shares of stock in an oil company at $33\frac{1}{2}$ per share. Exactly three years later he sold the stock at $41\frac{1}{4}$ per share. Find the annual interest rate, rounded to the nearest tenth of a percent, that Mr. Fernandez earned on this investment.

Solution

In 3 years, the per share price increased from a present value of $33.50 ($33\frac{1}{2}$) to a future value of $41.25 ($41\frac{1}{4}$). The purchase of the stock is a cash outflow and the eventual sale of the stock is a cash inflow. It is not necessary to multiply the stock price times the number of shares—the interest rate indicating the return on the investment is the same whether 1 share or 200 shares are used. Enter values for $\boxed{\text{n}}$, $\boxed{\text{PV}}$, and $\boxed{\text{FV}}$.

$$3 \boxed{\text{n}} \ -33.50 \ \boxed{\text{PV}} \ 41.25 \ \boxed{\text{FV}}$$

Press $\boxed{\text{i}}$ for the annual interest rate.

$$\boxed{\text{i}} \ 7.18\%, \text{ or about } 7.2\% \text{ per year.}$$

Mr. Fernandez's return on his original investment compounded at 7.2% per year.

Interest rates can have a **great influence** on both individuals and businesses. Individuals borrow for homes, cars, and other personal items whereas firms borrow to buy real estate, expand operations, or cover operating expenses. A small difference in interest rates can make *a large difference* in costs over time as shown in the next example.

Example 6
Compare Monthly House Payments

John and Leticia Adams wish to borrow $62,000 on a 30-year home loan. Find the monthly payment at interest rates of **(a)** 8% and **(b)** 9%. Show **(c)** the monthly savings at the lower rate and **(d)** the total savings in monthly payments over the 30 years.

Solution

(a) Enter a present value of $62,000 (cash inflow) with 360 compounding periods (30 × 12 = 360) and a rate of .666667% per month (8% ÷ 12 = .666667, rounded) and press $\boxed{\text{PMT}}$ to find the monthly payment.

$$62000 \ \boxed{\text{PV}} \ 360 \ \boxed{\text{n}} \ .666667 \ \boxed{\text{i}}$$

$\boxed{\text{PMT}}$ $-$454.93 is the monthly payment at 8% per year, rounded.

(b) Enter the values again using the new interest rate of .75% (9% ÷ 12 = .75%).

$$62000 \ \boxed{\text{PV}} \ 360 \ \boxed{\text{n}} \ .75 \ \boxed{\text{i}}$$

$\boxed{\text{PMT}}$ $-$498.87 is the monthly payment at 9% per year, again, rounded.

(c) The difference in the monthly payment is

$$\$498.87 - \$454.93 = \$43.94.$$

(d) The total difference saved over 30 years (30 × 12 = 360 payments) is

$$\$43.94 \times 360 \text{ payments} = \$15,818.40.$$

The lower interest rate will reduce the Adams' mortgage payments by a total of $15,818.40 over 30 years.

Example 7
Retirement Planning

Courtney and Nathan Wright plan to retire in 25 years and need $3500 per month for 20 years.

(a) Find the amount needed at retirement to fund the monthly retirement payments assuming the funds earn 9% compounded monthly while payments are being made.

(b) Find the amount of the quarterly payment they must make for the next 25 years to accumulate the necessary funds, assuming earnings of 12% compounded quarterly during the accumulation period.

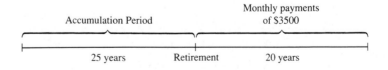

Solution

(a) The accumulated funds at the end of 25 years is, at their retirement, a present value that must generate a cash inflow to the Wrights of $3500 per month for 240 months (20 × 12 = 240) assuming earnings of .75% per month (9% ÷ 12 = .75%). Enter values for ⌷n⌷, ⌷i⌷, and ⌷PMT⌷.

240 ⌷n⌷ .75 ⌷i⌷ 3500 ⌷PMT⌷

Press ⌷PV⌷ to find the amount needed at the end of 25 years.

⌷PV⌷ $389,007.34 is the amount they must accumulate.

(b) The Wrights have 25 years of quarterly payments (100 payments that are cash outflows) in an account earning 3% per quarter (12% ÷ 4 = 3%) to accumulate a future value of $389,007.34. The question is one of what quarterly payment is required. Enter values for ⌷n⌷, ⌷i⌷, and ⌷FV⌷.

100 ⌷n⌷ 3 ⌷i⌷ 389007.34 ⌷FV⌷

Press ⌷PMT⌷ to find the quarterly payment needed.

⌷PMT⌷ −$640.57 is the required quarterly payment.

Thus, the Wrights must make 100 end-of-quarter deposits of $640.57 each into an account earning 3% per quarter in order to subsequently receive 20 years of payments of $3500 per month, assuming 9% per year during the time that payments are made.

Name   Date   Class

Appendix C | Exercises

Using a financial calculator, solve the following problems for the missing quantity. Round dollar answers to the nearest hundredth, interest rates to the nearest hundredth of a percent, and number of compounding periods to the nearest whole number. Assume that any payments are made at the end of the period.

	n	*i*	*PV*	*PMT*	*FV*
1.	20	10%	$5800	—	$39,019.50

20 [n] 10 [i] −5800 [PV] [FV] $39,019.50

2.	7	8%	$8900	—	$15,253.04

7 [n] 8 [i] −8900 [PV] [FV] $15,253.04

3.	10	3%	<u>$8929.13</u>	—	$12,000

10 [n] 3 [i] 12000 [FV] [PV] −8929.13

4.	16	4%	<u>$4378.05</u>	—	$8200

16 [n] 4 [i] 8200 [FV] [PV] −4378.05

5.	7	8%	—	$300	<u>$2676.84</u>

7 [n] 8 [i] −300 [PMT] [FV] 2676.84

6.	25	2%	—	$1000	<u>$32,030.30</u>

25 [n] 2 [i] −1000 [PMT] [FV] 32030.30

7.	30	<u>1.5%</u>	—	$319.67	$12,000

30 [n] 12000 [FV] −319.67 [PMT] [i] 1.5

8.	50	<u>.75%</u>	—	$4718.99	$285,000

50 [n] 285000 [FV] −4718.99 [PMT] [i] .75

9.	360	1%	$83,500	<u>$858.89</u>	—

360 [n] 1 [i] −83500 [PV] [PMT] 858.89

10.	180	.5%	$125,000	<u>$1054.82</u>	—

180 [n] .5 [i] −125000 [PV] [PMT] 1054.82

11.	<u>24</u>	4%	$85,383	$5600	—

4 [i] −85383 [PV] 5600 [PMT] [n] 24

12.	<u>73</u>	2%	$3822	$100	—

2 [i] −3822 [PV] 100 [PMT] [n] 73

Solve each of the following application problems.

13. Juanipa Manglimont inherited $23,500 from her father when he died. She placed the money in a 5-year certificate of deposit earning 6% compounded quarterly. Find the future value at the end of 5 years.

    5 × 4 = 20 quarters; 6% ÷ 4 = 1.5% per quarter
    20 [n] 1.5 [i] −23,500 [PV] [FV] $31,651.09

13. <u>FV = 31,651.09</u>

14. At the end of each month, Tina Ramirez has $50 per month taken out of her paycheck and invested in an account paying .5% per month. Find the future value at the end of 14 years.

14. $\underline{FV = \$13,115.24}$

$14 \times 12 = 168$ payments

168 **n** $.5$ **i** -50 **PMT** **FV** 13115.24

15. Mr. and Mrs. Thrash borrowed $86,500 on a 30-year home loan at 9% per year. Find the monthly payment.

15. $\underline{PMT = \$696}$

$30 \times 12 = 360$ payments; $9\% \div 12 = .75\%$ interest per month

86500 **PV** $.75$ **i** 360 **n** **PMT** -696

16. Terrance Walker wishes to have $20,000 in 10 years when his son begins college. What payment must he make at the end of each quarter in an investment earning 10% compounded quarterly?

16. $\underline{PMT = \$296.72}$

$10 \times 4 = 40$ payments; $10\% \div 4 = 2.5\%$ interest per quarter

40 **n** 2.5 **i** 20000 **FV** **PMT** -296.72

17. The *Daily Gazette* needs $340,000 for new printing presses. They can invest $12,000 per month in an account paying .8% per month. Find the number of payments that must be paid before reaching their goal. Round to the nearest whole number.

17. $\underline{n = 26}$

$.8$ **i** 12000 **PMT** 340000 **FV** **n** 26

18. Mr. and Mrs. Peters wish to build their dream home and must borrow $110,000 on a 30-year mortgage to do so. Find the highest acceptable annual interest rate, to the nearest tenth of a percent, if they cannot afford a monthly payment above $845.

18. $\underline{i = 8.5\%}$

$30 \times 12 = 360$ payments

360 **n** 110000 **PV** -845 **PMT** **i** $.70747\%$ per month

$.70747\% \times 12 = 8.48967\% = 8.5\%$ per year (rounded)

ANSWERS TO SELECTED EXERCISES

Some of the exercises require you to write an answer. Since those answers will vary, we do not give answers for them in this section.

PRETEST

1. 9.9 **3.** $549 **5.** 315.2 **7.** $1\frac{11}{32}$ **9.** $1\frac{7}{8}$ **11.** $\frac{5}{12}$ **13.** $\frac{9}{40}$
15. $\frac{7}{8}$ **17.** 518.477 **19.** 258
21. $4973.52 **23.** $161.84 **25.** 90 days **27.** 30% **29.** $1500

CHAPTER 1

SECTION 1.1 EXERCISES (PAGE 9)

1. three thousand, twenty **3.** thirty-seven thousand, nine hundred one **5.** seven hundred twenty-five thousand, nine **7.** 6090; 6100; 6000 **9.** 46,230; 46,200; 46,000 **11.** 106,050; 106,100; 106,000 **15.** 210 **17.** 2186 **19.** 2946 **21.** 1,383,493 **23.** 668 **25.** 2877 **27.** 21,546 **29.** 6,088,899 **31.** Totals vertically: $293,267; $387,795; $426,869; $373,100; Totals horizontally: $269,761; $267,502; $206,932; $246,587; $244,616; $245,633; $1,481,031 **33.** 9374 **35.** 117,552 **37.** 1,696,876 **39.** 8,107,899 **41.** Estimate: 12,760; Exact: 12,605 **43.** Estimate: 600; Exact: 545 **45.** Estimate: 30,000; Exact: 29,986 **47.** $37 \times 18 = 666$; 66,600 **49.** $376 \times 6 = 2256$; 22,560,000 **51.** $1241\frac{1}{4}$ **53.** $458\frac{21}{43}$ **57.** $2,385\frac{5}{18}$ **59.** $58\frac{4}{13}$ **61.** two hundred eighty million, four hundred eighty-nine thousand **63.** eighteen billion, six hundred thirty million, six hundred four thousand, seven hundred thirty-three **65.** $1905

SECTION 1.2 EXERCISES (PAGE 19)

1. 382 miles **3.** 130 more crimes **5.** 1200 miles **7.** 2477 pounds **9.** 23,993,000 small and midsize businesses **11.** $382,325,000 **13.** $125 **15.** $20,961 **17.** 20 seats

SECTION 1.3 EXERCISES (PAGE 23)

1. thirty-six hundredths **3.** five and sixty-one hundredths **5.** seven and four hundred eight thousandths **7.** thirty-seven and five hundred ninety-three thousandths **9.** four and sixty-two ten-thousandths **13.** 562.4 **15.** 97.62 **17.** 1.0573 **19.** 3.5827 **21.** $1.22 **23.** $.58 **25.** $1.17 **27.** 3.5; 3.52; 3.522 **29.** 2.5; 2.55; 2.548 **31.** 27.3; 27.32; 27.325 **33.** 36.5; 36.47; 36.472 **35.** .1; .06; .056 **37.** $5.06 **39.** $32.49 **41.** $382.01 **43.** $42.14 **45.** $.00 **47.** $1.50 **49.** $2.00 **51.** $752.80 **53.** $26 **55.** $0 **57.** $12,836 **59.** $395 **61.** $4700 **63.** $379 **65.** $722

SECTION 1.4 EXERCISES (PAGE 27)

1. $40 + 20 + 8 = 68$; 63.65 **3.** $6 + 4 + 5 + 7 + 2 = 24$; 23.82 **5.** $2000 + 5 + 3 + 7 = 2015$; 2171.414 **7.** $6000 + 500 + 20 + 8 = 6528$; 6666.061 **9.** $2000 + 70 + 500 + 600 + 400 = 3570$; 3451.446 **11.** 173.273 **13.** 59.3268 **17.** $51.36 **19.** $11,135.15

21. $40 - 8 = 32$; 27.95 **23.** $30 - 20 = 10$; 8.671 **25.** $4000 - 900 = 3100$; 3082.02 **27.** $30 - 10 = 20$; 14.218 **29.** $63,731.53 **31.** $25,297.84

SECTION 1.5 EXERCISES (PAGE 33)

1. $50 \times 4 = 200$; 185.06 **3.** $30 \times 7 = 210$; 231.88 **5.** $40 \times 2 = 80$; 89.352 **7.** 1.9152 **9.** 9.3527; 231.88 **11.** .002448 **13.** $207.35 **15.** $372.07 **17.** 6.543 **19.** 27.442 **21.** 5.507 **23.** 57.977 **25.** 223.448 **29.** $32,199.86 **31.** 64.6 million shares **33.** 35 dosages **35.** $22.098 million or $22,098,000 **37.** 8.2 meters **39.** (a) 159.1 hours (b) $14.86

SUMMARY EXERCISE (PAGE 40)

(a) $12,803 (b) $2197; $7197 (c) 218 guests; $24 left over (d) $46.67 (e) 148 guests; $4 left over (f) 66 guests; $10 left over (g) $644.25

CHAPTER 1 TEST (PAGE 41)

1. 850 **2.** 19,000 **3.** 264,000 **4.** 40,000 **5.** 700,000 **6.** $606 **7.** $8399 **8.** $5.04 **9.** $715.26 **10.** $3528 **11.** 181.535 **12.** 498.795 **13.** 133.6 **14.** 3.7947 **15.** 15.8256 **16.** 8.0882 **17.** 11.56 **18.** 23.8 **19.** 4.25 **20.** $505.31 **21.** $2470.10 **22.** 14,454 gallons saved **23.** $3.93 **24.** 3.6 million shares **25.** 253 seedlings

CHAPTER 2

SECTION 2.1 EXERCISES (PAGE 49)

1. $\frac{11}{8}$ **3.** $\frac{17}{4}$ **5.** $\frac{38}{3}$ **7.** $\frac{183}{8}$ **9.** $\frac{55}{7}$ **11.** $\frac{364}{23}$ **13.** $3\frac{1}{2}$ **15.** $2\frac{2}{3}$ **17.** $3\frac{4}{5}$ **19.** $3\frac{7}{11}$ **21.** $1\frac{62}{63}$ **23.** $7\frac{8}{25}$ **27.** $\frac{1}{2}$ **29.** $\frac{2}{3}$ **31.** $\frac{6}{7}$ **33.** $\frac{5}{9}$ **35.** $\frac{7}{8}$ **37.** $\frac{1}{50}$ **41.** ✓X✓XX✓XX **43.** ✓✓✓✓XX✓ **45.** ✓✓X✓✓X✓✓ **47.** ✓X✓XXXX

SECTION 2.2 EXERCISES (PAGE 55)

1. 9 **3.** 36 **5.** 48 **7.** 42 **9.** 24 **11.** 180 **13.** 480 **15.** 2100 **17.** 360 **21.** $\frac{2}{3}$ **23.** $\frac{1}{2}$ **25.** $\frac{17}{48}$ **27.** $1\frac{23}{36}$ **29.** $\frac{13}{14}$ **31.** $2\frac{1}{15}$ **33.** $2\frac{11}{36}$ **35.** $1\frac{13}{30}$ **37.** $\frac{9}{20}$ **39.** $\frac{7}{24}$ **43.** $\frac{31}{40}$ inch **45.** $\frac{7}{24}$ capacity **47.** $\frac{19}{24}$ of thedebt **49.** $\frac{3}{16}$ inch **51.** $\frac{1}{4}$ **53.** work and travel; 8 hours **55.** $\frac{1}{12}$ mile

SECTION 2.3 EXERCISES (PAGE 61)

1. $97\frac{4}{5}$ **3.** $80\frac{3}{4}$ **5.** $97\frac{7}{40}$ **7.** $53\frac{17}{24}$ **9.** $105\frac{107}{120}$ **11.** $7\frac{1}{8}$ **13.** $162\frac{1}{6}$ **15.** $9\frac{1}{24}$ **17.** $46\frac{23}{30}$ **21.** 30 inches **23.** 130 feet **25.** $1\frac{23}{24}$ cubic yards **27.** $14\frac{23}{24}$ tons

Section 2.4 Exercises (Page 67)
1. $\frac{5}{12}$ **3.** $\frac{99}{160}$ **5.** $\frac{9}{32}$ **7.** $4\frac{3}{8}$ **9.** $9\frac{1}{3}$ **11.** $\frac{1}{3}$ **13.** $4\frac{7}{12}$ **15.** $1\frac{7}{9}$ **17.** $3\frac{1}{3}$ **19.** $\frac{5}{8}$ **21.** $\frac{2}{3}$ **23.** $4\frac{4}{5}$ **25.** $\frac{3}{20}$ **27.** $8\frac{2}{5}$ **31.** $14,375 **33.** $12 **35.** $18.75 **39.** 36 yards **41.** 12 homes **43.** $21\frac{7}{8}$ ounces **45.** 600 shares **47.** 471 rolls **49.** 88 dispensers **51.** 60 trips

Section 2.5 Exercises (Page 75)
1. $\frac{4}{5}$ **3.** $\frac{6}{25}$ **5.** $\frac{73}{100}$ **7.** $\frac{5}{8}$ **9.** $\frac{161}{200}$ **11.** $\frac{12}{125}$ **13.** $\frac{3}{80}$ **15.** $\frac{3}{16}$ **17.** $\frac{1}{625}$ **21.** .75 **23.** .375 **25.** .667 (rounded) **27.** .778 (rounded) **29.** .636 (rounded) **31.** .88 **33.** .883 (rounded) **35.** .993 (rounded)

Summary Exercise (Page 80)
(a) $.375; $.1875; $.875; $.8125 **(b)** $12.69 **(c)** $15.63 **(d)** AT&T; $35.50 **(e)** $7030 **(f)** $5431.25 **(g)** 61 shares **(h)** Coca-Cola, $728.13; Reynolds Metals, −$478.13; $250 gain

Chapter 2 Test (Page 83)
1. $\frac{3}{5}$ **2.** $\frac{3}{8}$ **3.** $\frac{7}{11}$ **4.** $8\frac{1}{8}$ **5.** $4\frac{2}{3}$ **6.** $2\frac{2}{3}$ **7.** $\frac{31}{4}$ **8.** $\frac{94}{5}$ **9.** $\frac{147}{8}$ **10.** 30 **11.** 120 **12.** 72 **13.** $\frac{7}{8}$ **14.** $15\frac{1}{16}$ **15.** $36\frac{5}{16}$ **16.** 36 **17.** $1\frac{1}{2}$ **18.** $24\frac{1}{8}$ pounds **19.** $405.38 **20.** $35\frac{7}{8}$ gallons **21.** 36 pull cords **22.** $\frac{5}{8}$ **23.** $\frac{77}{100}$ **24.** .75 **25.** .889 (rounded)

Chapter 3

Section 3.1 Exercises (Page 89)
1. 20% **3.** 72% **5.** 203.4% **7.** 362.5% **9.** 87.5% **11.** .05% **13.** 345% **15.** 3.08% **17.** .625 **19.** .65 **21.** .125 **23.** .125 **25.** .0025 **27.** .8475 **29.** 1.75 **31.** $\frac{1}{2}$; .5; 50% **33.** $\frac{7}{8}$; .875; 87.5% **35.** $\frac{1}{125}$; .008; .8% **37.** $10\frac{1}{2}$; 10.5; 1050% **39.** $\frac{13}{20}$; .65; 65% **41.** $\frac{1}{200}$; .005; .5% **43.** $\frac{1}{3}$; .3333; $33\frac{1}{3}$% **45.** $2\frac{1}{2}$; 2.5; 250% **47.** $\frac{17}{400}$; .0425; $4\frac{1}{4}$% **49.** $\frac{3}{200}$; .015; 1.5% **51.** $10\frac{3}{8}$; 10.375; 1037.5% **53.** $\frac{1}{400}$; .0025; .25% **55.** $\frac{3}{8}$; .375; $37\frac{1}{2}$%

Section 3.2 Exercises (Page 97)
1. 16 guests **3.** $244.35 **5.** 4.8 feet **7.** 10,185 miles **9.** 182 homes **11.** 148.44 yards **13.** $5366.65 **17.** $52.80 **19.** $645 **21.** 2024 shoppers **23.** $92.06 million **25.** (a) 39% female (b) 2.318 million or 2,318,000 workers **27.** 234 executives **29.** 2156 products **31.** $135 million **33.** $51,844.20 **35.** $510,390 **37.** $6296.40

Section 3.3 Exercises (Page 103)
1. 1060 **3.** 187.5 **5.** 1000 **7.** 4800 **9.** 22,000 **11.** 20,000 **13.** $90,320 **15.** 1750 **17.** 312,500 **19.** 65,400 **21.** 40,000 **25.** 30,000 total workforce **27.** 7761 students **29.** $2800 **31.** 20 million or 20,000,000 adolescents **33.** $23,124.43 **35.** $185,500

Supplementary Exercises on Base and Part (Page 105)
1. $20,200 million or $20,200,000,000 **3.** $288,150 **5.** 478,175 Mustangs **7.** $93.9 million or $93,900,000 **9.** $39,000 **11.** 836 drivers **13.** $23

Section 3.4 Exercises (Page 111)
1. 10% **3.** 125% **5.** 28.3% **7.** 9.3% **9.** 4.1% **11.** 5.9% **13.** 102.5% **15.** 17.6% **17.** 27.8% **21.** 6.2% **23.** 2% **25.** 8.7% **27.** 10.7% **29.** 56.5%

Supplementary Exercises on Base, Rate, and Part (Page 113)
1. .6 million or 600,000 patients **3.** 14.1% **5.** 16,910 economy hotels and motels **7.** 41,771 traffic deaths **9.** $396.05 **11.** (a) 30% (b) 70% **13.** 470,844 workers **15.** 24.4% **17.** 12.5% **19.** 5.5% **21.** 960 candy bars **23.** $8823 **25.** 23.6% **27.** 5742 deaths **29.** 36%

Section 3.5 Exercises (Page 123)
1. $375 **3.** $27.91 **5.** $25 **7.** $854.50 **11.** $165,500 **13.** $86.2 million or $86,200,000 **15.** 160 feet **17.** $15,161.90 **19.** $118,080 **21.** $58.9 billion **23.** $3864 **25.** $1.078 billion **27.** 51.2 million **29.** 20,000 students **31.** 69.4 million **33.** 6564 homes

Summary Exercises (Page 129)
Chipper Jones, $40; Cal Ripken, Jr., −7%; Nomar Garciaparra, $4; Nolan Ryan, $900; Ken Griffey, Jr., $75; Frank Thomas, −11%; Will Clark, $5; Mark McGwire, $20; Sammy Sosa, 4900%; Alex Rodriquez, −25%

Chapter 3 Test (Page 131)
1. 150 members **2.** 24 vans **3.** 1100 shippers **4.** 2.5% **5.** $3.75 **6.** $\frac{6}{25}$ **7.** 960 loads **8.** $\frac{7}{8}$ **9.** 8.5% **10.** $\frac{1}{200}$ **11.** $.91 **12.** 224,000 **13.** 2.71 million vehicles **14.** 21.43 million people **15.** (a) 11% (b) $4488 per year **16.** 68% **17.** $850 **18.** 1200 backpacks **19.** 2.8% **20.** 1.2 million or 1,200,000 permits

Cumulative Review: Chapters 1–3 (Page 133)
1. 78,600 **3.** 62.7 **5.** 3609 **7.** 24,092 **9.** 85 **11.** 35.174 **13.** 12.218 **15.** $193 **17.** $31,658.27 **19.** $\frac{8}{9}$ **21.** $7\frac{2}{15}$ **23.** $13\frac{13}{24}$ **25.** 3 **27.** $42\frac{1}{2}$ acres **29.** 130 feet **31.** $\frac{7}{20}$ **33.** 62.5% **35.** 450 prospects **37.** 25% **39.** 48.7% **41.** 97,757 copies

Chapter 4

Section 4.1 Exercises (Page 145)
1. $14.20 **3.** $20.00 **5.** $17.10 **7.** $21.90 **9.** Mar. 8; $380.71; Patty Demko; Tutoring; 3971.28; 79.26; 4050.54; 380.71; 3669.83 **11.** Dec. 4; $37.52; Paul's Pools; Chemicals; $1126.73; 1126.73; 37.52; 1089.21 **17.** Oct. 10; $39.12; County Clerk; License; $5972.89; 752.18; 23.32; 6748.39; 39.12; 6709.27 **19.** 1379.41; 1230.41; 1348.14; 1278.34; 1608.20; 2026.50; 1916.74; 1302.62; 1270.44; 1791.39 **21.** 3709.32; 3590.92; 3877.24; 3797.24; 2811.02; 2435.52; 3637.34; 2901.66; 2677.72; 3175.73; 3097.49

Section 4.2 Exercises (Page 151)
1. $2419.76 **3.** $2215.90 **5.** $2149.42 **7.** $189.39 **9.** $69.85 **11.** $1064.72 **13.** $991.89 **15.** $962.13 **17.** $60.21 **19.** $59.25

Section 4.3 Exercises (Page 161)
1. $5095.47 **3.** $7690.62 **5.** $18,314.72 **11.** 112, $84.76; 115, 109.38; 117, 42.03; 119, 1429.12; $1665.29; $14,928.42; 54.21, 394.76, 1002.04, 16,379.43, 1665.29, $14,714.14; $14,698.28, 7.00, 14,691.28, 22.86, $14,714.14 **13.** 668, $100.50; 670, 315.62; 671, 67.29; $483.41; $6380.86, 830.75, 7211.61, 483.41, $6728.20; $6800.57, 94.85, 6705.72, 22.48, $6728.20

Summary Exercise (Page 166)
(a) $6101.69 gross deposit **(b)** $5888.13 credit **(c)** $9810.36 total of checks outstanding **(d)** $4882.58 deposits not recorded **(e)** $5188.69 balance

Chapter 4 Test (Page 167)

1. $15.90 **2.** $19 **3.** $10.20 **4.** Aug. 6; $6892.12; Fuel Depot; Fuel; $16,409.82; 16,409.82; 6892.12; 9517.70 **5.** Aug. 8; $1258.36; First Bank; Payment; 9517.70; 1572.00; 11,089.70; 1258.36; 9831.34 **6.** Aug. 14; $416.14; Security Service; Guard dogs; 9831.34; 10,000.00; 19,831.34; 416.14; 19,415.20
7. $1064.72 **8.** $72.83 **9.** $991.89 **10.** $39.68 **11.** $952.21
12. 3221, $82.74; 3229, 69.08; 3230, 124.73; 3232, 51.20; $327.75; $4721.30, 758.06, 32.51, 298.06; 5809.93, 327.75, 5482.18; $5474.60, 2.00, 5472.60, 9.58, $5482.18

Chapter 5

Section 5.1 Exercises (Page 179)

1. 40; 0; $12.15 **3.** 38.75; 0; $11.70 **5.** 40; 5.25; $17.22
7. $329.60; $92.70; $422.30 **9.** $380; $160.31; $540.31
11. $13.20; $347.60; $0; $347.60 **13.** $10.80; $288.00; $48.60; $336.60 **15.** $13.77; $367.20; $58.52; $425.72 **17.** 50.5; 10.5; $4.75; $479.75; $49.88; $529.63 **19.** 53.5; 13.5; $3.75; $401.25; $50.63; $451.88 **21.** 35; 6; $10.05; $234.50; $60.30; $294.80
23. 39.5; 3.75; $10.05; $264.65; $37.69; $302.34 **25.** 39.75; 3.5; $15.30; $405.45; $53.55; $459.00 **29.** $221.54; $443.08; $960; $11,520 **31.** $265.38; $530.77; $575; $13,800 **33.** $830; $899.17; $1798.33; $21,580 **35.** $387 **37.** $467.25 **39.** $832 **41.** $551
43. $556.32 **45.** (a) $1260 biweekly (b) $1365 semimonthly
(c) $2730 monthly (d) $32,760 annually

Section 5.2 Exercises (Page 189)

1. $84.48 **3.** $90.24 **5.** $38.65 **7.** $52.68 **11.** $260.19
13. $284.65 **15.** $401.76 **17.** $471.50 **19.** $208.16
21. $421.65 **23.** $1405 **25.** $688.40 **27.** $478.10 **29.** $628.61

Section 5.3 Exercises (Page 195)

1. $20.13; $4.71 **3.** $28.72; $6.72 **5.** $52.99; $12.39 **7.** $131.98
9. $265.26 **11.** $11.18 **13.** $368.80; $76.07; $444.87; $27.58; $6.45; $4.45 **15.** $263.20; $49.35; $312.55; $19.38; $4.53; $3.13
17. $467.20; $122.64; $589.84; $36.57; $8.55; $5.90
19. (a) $24.07 (b) $5.63 **21.** (a) $95.67 (b) $22.38
(c) $15.43 **23.** $4569.75; $1068.73 **25.** $4317.33; $1009.70
27. $3328.61; $778.46

Section 5.4 Exercises (Page 205)

1. $241 **3.** $54 **5.** $172 **7.** $74 **9.** $69 **11.** $97 **13.** $8.30
15. $8.89 **17.** $88.58 **19.** $25.89; $6.05; $12.89; $372.75
21. $95.00; $22.22; $162.93; $1252.03 **23.** $120.20; $28.11; $199.84; $1590.61 **25.** $122.21; $28.58; $154.06; $1666.21
27. $44.05; $10.30; $44.55; $611.66 **29.** $44.35; $10.37; $110.90; $549.72 **35.** $8748.05 **37.** $53,332.52 **39.** $44,323.10
41. $505.45 **43.** $520.63 **45.** $3616.86

Summary Exercise (Page 212)

(a) $620 (b) $279 (c) $899 (d) $55.74 (e) $13.04
(f) $162.32 (g) $8.99 (h) $39.56 (i) $392.35

Chapter 5 Test (Page 213)

1. 40; 8.5; $482.14 **2.** 38.25; 0; $283.05 **3.** (a) $655 weekly
(b) $1310 biweekly (c) $1419.17 semimonthly (d) $2838.33
monthly **4.** $134 **5.** $1725 **6.** (a) $372.93 (b) $87.22
7. (a) $237.77 (b) $87.22 **8.** $18 **9.** $72 **10.** $151
11. $93 **12.** $104 **13.** $1443.68 **14.** $405.55 **15.** $531.74
16. (a) $31.90 (b) $7.46 (c) $5.14 **17.** (a) $73.79 (b) $26.87

18. (a) $2903.73 (b) $679.10 **19.** (a) $4282.84 (b) $1001.63
20. $2246.54

Chapter 6

Section 6.1 Exercises (Page 223)

1. $54.00 **3.** $64.80 **5.** $297.00 **7.** $524.95 **9.** $37.80
11. $848.96 **13.** $4850.28; $37.45 **15.** foot **17.** pair **19.** kilogram
21. case **23.** drum **25.** liter **27.** gallon **29.** cash on delivery
33. $.9 \times .8 = .72$ **35.** $.8 \times .8 \times .8 = .512$ **37.** $.75 \times .95 = .7125$
39. $.6 \times .7 \times .8 = .336$ **41.** $.5 \times .9 \times .8 \times .95 = .342$ **43.** $267.52
45. $7.01 **47.** $361.46 **49.** $449.28 **51.** $16.83 **53.** $714.42
55. $972 **57.** $640 **63.** $242.99 **65.** (a) 20/15 (b) $1.02
67. $204.12 **69.** $326.40

Section 6.2 Exercises (Page 229)

1. .72; 28% **3.** .6; 40% **5.** .504; 49.6% **7.** .5184; 48.16%
11. $720 **13.** $1920 **15.** (a) $58.29 (b) $64.76 (c) $6.47
17. (a) Turning Point (b) $125.10 **19.** $740 **21.** 25.0%

Section 6.3 Exercises (Page 237)

1. Oct. 18; Nov. 7 **3.** July 25; Sep. 8 **5.** Oct. 1; Oct. 11 **7.** $3.03; $160.90 **9.** $0; $81.25 **11.** $12.70; $675.48 **15.** $3244.19
17. $674.42 **19.** (a) Jan. 28; Feb. 7; Feb. 17 (b) Mar. 9
21. (a) Apr. 25 (b) May 5

Section 6.4 Exercises (Page 245)

1. Mar. 10; Mar. 30 **3.** Dec. 22; Jan. 11 **5.** June 16; July 6
7. $20.47; $661.81 **9.** $0; $785.64 **11.** $168.80; $4051.20
13. $.72; $23.23 **17.** (a) Dec. 13 (b) $951.27 **19.** $4271.33
21. $1495.58 **23.** (a) $244.57 (b) $143.63 **25.** (a) July 10
(b) July 30 **27.** $1509.75 due **29.** (a) $597.94 (b) $522.21

Summary Exercise (Page 252)

(a) $3844.76 (b) June 15 (c) July 5 (d) $3904.56
(e) $2577.32; $1442.58

Chapter 6 Test (Page 253)

1. $105.78 **2.** $784.80 **3.** (a) .6375 (b) 36.25% **4.** (a) .576
(b) 42.4% **5.** Mar. 15 **6.** May 30 **7.** Jan. 15 **8.** Dec. 19
9. (a) $394.40 invoice total (b) $386.51 after discount
(c) $398.06 total amount due **10.** $63,295.14 **11.** (a) Apr. 15
(b) $821.24 **12.** $122.57 **13.** (a) Builders Supply (b) $1.91
14. (a) $1762.20 (b) $1780 full amount **15.** $1798.38 due
16. (a) $1717.53 (b) $1198.47

Chapter 7

Section 7.1 Exercises (Page 263)

1. $4.96; 140%; $17.36 **3.** 100%; $27.17; 20%; $5.43 **5.** 100%; $168.00; 130%; $218.40 **7.** $2.70; $11.70 **9.** 60%; $19.20
11. $61.44; 40% **13.** $33.80; 25% **17.** $39.65 markup
19. $14.95 selling price **21.** $344.40 selling price **23.** 30% **25.**
(a) 126% (b) $5.67 selling price (c) $1.17 markup

Section 7.2 Exercises (Page 273)

1. 75%; $21.00; $28.00 **3.** 58%; $145.00; $105.00 **5.** $19.20; $2400 **7.** $8.46; $22.26; 61.3% **9.** $750; $1050; 28.6% **11.** 50%
13. 15.3% **17.** $2289.30 **19.** (a) $4.50 selling price (b) $2.88
cost (c) 64% **21.** (a) $4990 total received (b) $2710 markup
(c) 54.3% (d) 118.9% **23.** $.60

Section 7.3 Exercises (Page 279)

1. 25%; $645 **3.** 45%; $13.86 **5.** 20%; $5.20 **7.** $60; $10; none
9. $16; $22; $6 **11.** $385; $250; $60 **15.** 41% **17.** $298
operating loss **19.** **(a)** $77.15 operating loss **(b)** $18.77
absolute loss

Section 7.4 Exercises (Page 287)

1. $22,673 **3.** $60,568 **5.** 2.83 at cost; 2.81 at retail
7. 7.98 at cost; 7.94 at retail **9.** 4.69 at cost; 4.66 at retail
11. $182; $195; $170 **13.** $2351.64; $2385; $2312.50
17. 5.43 turnover at cost **19.** **(a)** $506.79 weighted average
method **(b)** $562.50 FIFO **(c)** $520 LIFO **21.** **(a)** $1252.04
weighted average method **(b)** $1430 FIFO **(c)** $1040 LIFO
23. $30,660

Summary Exercise (Page 295)

(a) $125 original selling price **(b)** $2062.50 total selling price
(c) $375 operating loss **(d)** none

Chapter 7 Test (Page 297)

1. **(a)** 20 **(b)** 120 **(c)** 38.40 **2.** **(a)** 138 **(b)** 365.50
(c) 138.89 **3.** **(a)** 80 **(b)** 20 **(c)** 16.80 **4.** **(a)** 75 **(b)** 25
(c) 18.45 **5.** 20% **6.** 25% **7.** $200; $14; None **8.** $24; $33; $9
9. 5.76; 5.73; **10.** $12.50 selling price per pair **11.** $329.17
12. 40% **13.** **(a)** $37.99 **(b)** 19.0% **(c)** 23.5% **14.** 28%
15. **(a)** $131.10 operating loss **(b)** $45.60 absolute loss
16. $65,139 average inventory **17.** $1125 weighted average
method **18.** **(a)** $1157 FIFO **(b)** $1100 LIFO

Cumulative Review: Chapters 4–7 (Page 299)

1. $1014.40 **3.** $806.25 **5.** $788.11 **7.** $4359.38 **9.** $240.47
11. 62.2% **13.** Mar. 20; Apr. 9 **15.** $400; $280; $32 **17.** $43.64
cost **19.** 10.77 turnover at cost **21.** $6489.20 weighted average
method

Chapter 8

Section 8.1 Exercises (Page 309)

1. $209; $4009 **3.** $440; $5940 **5.** 68 **7.** 99 **9.** **(a)** $2493.15
(b) $2527.78 **(c)** $34.63 **11.** **(a)** $1672.71 **(b)** $1695.94
(c) $23.23 **13.** Helen Spence **15.** Donna Sharp **17.** 90 days
19. Jan. 25 **21.** Oct. 18; $5064 **23.** May 9; $6591.38
25. $16,800 **27.** **(a)** Oct. 3 **(b)** $7008.41 **29.** **(a)** Jan. 9
(b) $985.63 **31.** $215,333.33 **33.** $17.23 **35.** **(a)** June 23 of the
following year **(b)** $5424

Section 8.2 Exercises (Page 317)

1. $2916.67 **3.** $504 **5.** $10,800 **7.** 9.5% **9.** 11% **11.** 7.5%
13. 160 days **15.** 62 days **17.** 144 days **19.** 9.5% **21.** 11.5%
23. $14,000 **25.** **(a)** $7200 **(b)** $7650 **27.** 76 days **29.** 8.2%
31. **(a)** $12,000 **(b)** $1200 **33.** 208 days **35.** **(a)** 12.5%
(b) $11.4% (rounded)

Section 8.3 Exercises (Page 327)

1. $785.33; $11,614.67 **3.** $45.07; $904.93 **5.** $304.95;
$11,405.05 **7.** Jun. 20; $4398.75 **9.** Dec. 9; $957.29 **11.** Feb. 8;
$23,600 **13.** **(a)** $220 **(b)** $5780 **15.** 120 days **17.** 10.5%
19. $7891.30 **21.** **(a)** $3780 **(b)** 13.3% **23.** 70 days
25. **(a)** $167,088.61 **(b)** 15.2% **27.** **(a)** $24,625,000
(b) $25,000,000 **(c)** $375,000 **(d)** 6.09%

Section 8.4 Exercises (Page 335)

1. 107 days **3.** 53 days **5.** $5715.62 **7.** $2481.25 **9.** $6362.75;
37 days; $78.47; $6284.28 **11.** $2044; 49 days; $33.39; $2010.61
13. **(a)** $279.67 **(b)** $8669.71 **15.** **(a)** $81,900 **(b)** $79,688.70

Supplementary Exercises on Simple Interest and Simple Discount (Page 339)

1. $22,916.67 **3.** 240 days **5.** 174 days **7.** 12.1% (rounded)
9. **(a)** Apr. 12 **(b)** $9,475,000 **11.** $15,000 **13.** $7960.39
15. $16,243.88 **17.** **(a)** $3520.83 **(b)** $69,026.55 **(c)** $4026.55
(d) $505.72

Summary Exercise (Page 347)

(a) $1,120,000 **(b)** $77,370,000

Chapter 8 Test (Page 349)

1. $1020.83 **2.** $508.75 **3.** $137.50 **4.** $148.06 **5.** $24,923.24
6. $13,125 **7.** $11.19 **8.** 9.2% **9.** 333 days **10.** $43,000
11. $26,595.74 **12.** $359.33; $9440.67 **13.** $162.29; $10,087.71
14. 12.5% **15.** **(a)** $19,812.50 **(b)** $20,000 **(c)** $187.50
(d) 3.79% **16.** 59 days; $189.06; $7020.94 **17.** 44 days; $184.41;
$9245.59 **18.** **(a)** $165.24 **(b)** $8154.76

Chapter 9

Section 9.1 Exercises (Page 357)

1. $7864.78, $1864.78 **3.** $17,910.78, $2910.78 **5.** $2272.46
7. $1285.43 **9.** $18,574.38 **11.** $8491.23 **13.** $4299
15. $2975.04 **17.** $1296; $1417.39; $121.39 **19.** $1440; $2606.60;
$1166.60 **21.** $11,431.57 **23.** 31,669.25 yen **25.** $439.25

Section 9.2 Exercises (Page 367)

1. $38.16 **3.** $35.62 **5.** $101.88 **7.** $4763.41 **9.** $19,171.85
13. **(a)** $3284.75 **(b)** $24.75 **15.** **(a)** $11,638.49 **(b)** $118.49
17. **(a)** $901,988.58 **(b)** $101,988.58 **19.** Loss of $397.50
21. Loss of $2745.07

Section 9.3 Exercises (Page 375)

1. $3564.41; $935.59 **3.** $7674.01; $1675.99 **5.** $8377.18;
$3122.82 **7.** $9792.06; $9060.94 **11.** **(a)** $3175.32 **(b)** $824.68
13. $3503.40 **15.** **(a)** $793,053 **(b)** $492,422.47
17. **(a)** $25,142.04 **(b)** $17,587.86 **19.** **(a)** $26,620 **(b)** $20,989.60

Summary Exercise (Page 380)

(a) $4,053,382; $3,016,081 **(b)** $2,539,384; $1,889,530
(c) $2,798,295; $2,082,183 **(d)** See table.

Growth Rate	Future Value	Market Value Today
2%	$2,539,384	$1,889,530
4% (inflation)	$2,798,295	$2,082,183
12%	$4,053,382	$3,016,081

Chapter 9 Test (Page 381)

1. $18,649.23; $9949.23 **2.** $16,278.48; $9078.48 **3.** $13,170.42;
$3370.42 **4.** $18,556.38; $6056.38 **5.** $50.52 **6.** $530.60
7. $286.28 **8.** $1866.06 **9.** $10,380.83 **10.** $38,291.99
11. $16,077.25 **12.** $4120.01 **13.** Loss of $676 **14.** **(a)** $13,727.90
(b) $3727.90 **15.** **(a)** $4408.99 **(b)** $3801.87 **16.** **(a)** $15,173.40

(b) $13,481.41   **17. (a)** $283,233.60   **(b)** $206,955.96   **18. (a)** $59 million   **(b)** $93 million

Chapter 10

Section 10.1 Exercises (Page 389)
1. $14,866.66; $4466.66   **3.** $201,527.78; $51,527.78
5. $139,509.30; $41,509.30   **7.** $7603.12; $1603.12
9. $207,485.32; $36,485.32   **11.** $51,985.25; $6385.25
15. (a) $18,366.78   **(b)** $3966.78   **17. (a)** $13,412.09
(b) $1412.09   **19.** $24,786.86

Section 10.2 Exercises (Page 395)
1. $14,762.54   **3.** $30,493.92   **5.** $18,991.59   **9.** $839,255.46
11. $8383.84   **13. (a)** $8450.50   **(b)** $2749.50   **15. (a)** $48,879.76
(b) No   **17. (a)** First offer   **(b)** $2769.99   **19.** $208,893.30

Section 10.3 Exercises (Page 401)
1. $1375.92   **3.** $715.29   **5.** $2271   **7.** $183.22   **11. (a)** $2087.68
(b) $2947.84   **13. (a)** $928,040   **(b)** $287,840   **15.** $12,649.20
17. (a) $53,383   **(b)** $37,559   **19. (a)** $1200   **(b)** $6511.80
21.

Payment Number	Amount of Deposit	Interest Earned	Total in Account
1	$834,644.00	$0	$834,644.00
2	$834,644.00	$50,078.64	$1,719,366.64
3	$834,643.36	$103,162.00	$2,657,172.00

Section 10.4 Exercises (Page 411)
1. $39^7/_{16} = $39.4375   **3.** $+^3/_8 = $.375   **5.** $17 = $17
7. No dividend   **9.** $63^{13}/_{16} = $63.8125   **11.** 176,900 shares
13. $73^{15}/_{16} = $73.9375   **15.** .6%   **17.** $50 = $50   **19.** $1600
21. $6925   **23.** $69,750   **25.** $1,270,000   **29.** .8%   **31.** .8%
33. 2.3%   **35.** 14   **37.** 65   **39.** 32   **41.** $23,337.50   **43.**
(a) $47,512.76   **(b)** $77,380.99   **(c)** $29,868.23

Section 10.5 Exercises (Page 419)
1. $1105   **3.** 2007   **5.** No change   **7.** $51,187.50   **9.** $32,400
11. $15,675   **15. (a)** $20,200   **(b)** $1550   **(c)** 7.7%
17. (a) $15,150   **(b)** $862.50   **(c)** 5.7%   **19. (a)** $3600
(b) $97,151.40

Summary Exercise (Page 424)
(a) $439,542.07   **(b)** $53,046.80   **(c)** $520,821.44   **(d)** No, short by $81,279.37

Chapter 10 Test (Page 425)
1. $9897.47   **2.** $126,595.71   **3.** $930,909   **4.** $121,490.46
5. $885,185.12   **6.** $56,084.94   **7.** $6801.60   **8.** $39,884.63
9. $21,316.12   **10.** $416,065.86   **11.** $21,461.99   **12.** $24,683.07
13. $8702   **14.** $8395   **15.** $5835.60   **16.** $17,976   **17.** $3266
18. $734.85   **19. (a)** $7900   **(b)** $240   **20. (a)** $21,120   **(b)** $1595

Cumulative Review: Chapters 8–10 (Page 427)
1. $150   **3.** $2400.17   **5.** 9.7%   **7.** 80 days   **9.** $270; $8730
11. $4875   **13.** $1947.90   **15.** $86.07; $12,686.07   **17.** $583.49;
$416.51   **19.** $9214.23; $1214.23   **21.** $13,367.29   **23.** $403.45
25. $10,129.10   **27. (a)** $106.67   **(b)** $12,106.67   **29.** $7993.14
31. $6025   **33.** $6337.60   **35. (a)** $11,957.94   **(b)** $27,257.87
37. $20.01

Chapter 11

Section 11.1 Exercises (Page 439)
1. $144.92   **3.** $15.02   **5.** $6.12; $419.17; $419.17; $5.87; $541.68;
$541.68; $7.58; $529.22; $529.22; $7.41; $211.71   **9.** $20.42
11. $4.87   **13.** $17.30   **15. (a)** $72.76   **(b)** $38.80   **(c)** $33.96
17. (a) $132.64   **(b)** $1.99   **(c)** $133.80   **19. (a)** $312.91
(b) $4.69   **(c)** $285.94   **21. (a)** $139.71   **(b)** $2.10   **(c)** $74.32

Section 11.2 Exercises (Page 449)
1. $3047.12; $247.12   **3.** $180; $30   **5.** $3543; $643   **7.** 13.5%
9. 11.6%   **11.** 15.4%   **13.** 12.25%   **15.** 10.25%   **17.** 11.25%
21. 11%   **23. (a)** 732,212.32 pesos   **(b)** 13.75%

Section 11.3 Exercises (Page 457)
1. $3643.65; $143.65   **3.** $5752.17; $502.17   **5.** $9862.15; $507.15
7. $59.46   **9.** $103.18   **11.** $28.38   **15. (a)** $6569.44
(b) $131,569.44   **17. (a)** $69,936.02   **(b)** $2286.02
19. (a) $41,176.11   **(b)** $1876.11   **21. (a)** $122.40   **(b)** $818.85

Section 11.4 Exercises (Page 465)
1. $1033.25   **3.** $404.73   **5.** $4185.60   **7.** $161.93   **9.** $124.41;
$678.76   **11.** $321.92; $3452.16   **13.** $255.47; $3578.20
17. (a) $15,987   **(b)** $147,636
19. Payment No. 0, —, —, —, $4000.00;
Payment No. 1, $1207.68, $320.00, $887.68, $3112.32;
Payment No. 2, $1207.68, $248.99, $958.69, $2153.63;
Payment No. 3, $1207.68, $172.29, $1035.39, $1118.24;
Payment No. 4, $1207.70, $89.46, $1118.24, $0
21. Payment No. 0, —, —, —, $14,500.00;
Payment No. 1, $374.77, $132.92, $241.85, $14,258.15;
Payment No. 2, $374.77, $130.70, $244.07, $14,014.08;
Payment No. 3, $374.77, $128.46, $246.31, $13,767.77;
Payment No. 4, $374.77, $126.20, $248.57, $13,519.20;
Payment No. 5, $374.77, $123.93, $250.84, $13,268.36

Section 11.5 Exercises (Page 475)
1. $730.55   **3.** $1111.08   **5.** $1022.90   **9.** $1024.43   **11.** $523.87
13. $873.82   **15.** Yes, they are qualified
17. Payment No. 0, —, —, —, $122,500.00;
Payment No. 1, $1136.80, $765.63, $371.17, $122,128.83;
Payment No. 2, $1136.80, $763.31, $373.49, $121,755.34

Summary Exercise (Page 482)
(a) $495.00, $420.13, $950.53, $149.45; Total: $2015.11
(b) $2015.11, $215.00, $120.00, $210.83; Total: $2560.94   **(c)**

Item	New Loan Amount	New Interest Rate	New Term of Loan	New Monthly Payment
Honda Accord	$14,900	12%	4 years	$ 392.32
Ford Truck	$ 8,600	12%	3 years	$ 285.61
Home	$94,800	8%	30 years	$ 695.83
2nd Mortgage on Home	$ 4,500	12%	3 years	$ 149.45
Car insurance				$ 187.00
Health insurance				$ 120.00
Taxes on home				$ 210.83
			Total	$2041.04

(d) $519.90 per month

Chapter 11 Test (Page 485)

1. $83 **2.** $932.56 **3.** 11.75% **4.** 12.25% **5.** 10.75%
6. $4364.31   **(a)** $235.51 **(b)** $2502.17 **8.** $2822.93
9. $1924.50 **10.** $864.50 **11.** $1209.69 **12.** $629.48
13. (a) $1456.92 **(b)** $298,495.60 **14. (a)** $1398.25
(b) $360,580

Chapter 12.1

Section 12.1 Exercises (Page 491)

1. $19,440 **3.** $71,150 **5.** $325,125 **7.** 12% **9.** 8% **11.** 3%
13. (a) $4.84 **(b)** $48.40 **(c)** 48.4 **15. (a)** 7.08% **(b)** $7.08
(c) 70.8 **19.** $5861.60 **21.** $5384.40 **23.** $4853.52
25. $6295.08 **27.** $200,925 **29. (a)** The second parish
(b) $75.24

Section 12.2 Exercises (Page 501)

1. $20,600 **3.** $21,710 **5.** $39,031 **7.** $17,400; $2610
9. $23,901; $3585.15 **11.** $51,650; $9106 **13.** $28,214; $4695.42
15. $31,726; $5678.78 **17.** $49,632; $8540.96 **19.** $910.50 tax
refund **21.** $220.56 tax refund **23.** $765.66 tax due
27. $3784.20 **29.** $3850.94 **31.** $8036.40 **33.** $3385.65

Section 12.3 Exercises (Page 509)

1. $1851 **3.** $2194.50 **5.** $9298.72 **7.** $19,850 **9.** $4218.75
11. $36,500 **13.** $60,000; $20,000 **15.** $292,500; $260,000;
$97,500 **17.** $1661.16 **19.** $393.05 **23. (a)** $19,936.71
(b) $2563.29 **25. (a)** $30,681.82 **(b)** $14,318.18
29. A: $274,000 B: $182,666.67 C: $91,333.33
31. 1. $125,000 **2.** $41,666.67 **3.** $83,333.33

Section 12.4 Exercises (Page 519)

1. $631 **3.** $932 **7.** $657.80 **9.** $915 **11. (a)** $25,000
(b) $11,500 **13. (a)** $1778 **(b)** $6936 **(c)** $100,000
(d) $15,100

Section 12.5 Exercises (Page 527)

1. $952.50; $485.78; $247.65; $86.49 **3.** $849.10; $433.04;
$220.77; $77.10 **5.** $516.80; $263.57; $134.37; $46.93
7. $319.50; $162.95; $83.07; $29.01 **9.** $2973.10; $1516.28;
$773.01; $269.96 **13.** $298.20 **15.** $190.49 **17.** $3036
19. (a) $444.72 **(b)** $226.72 **(c)** $79.18

Summary Exercise (Page 532)

(a) $11,790.75 **(b)** $39,940.40 **(c)** $370.39 **(d)** $52,101.54
(e) $1398.46

Chapter 12 Test (Page 533)

1. $5.76 **2.** 9.35% **3.** $28,845; $4872.10 **4.** $25,987; $3898.05
5. $1145.37 **6.** $6450.48 **7.** $4918.30 **8.** $2179.05
9. $42,613.64 **10.** A: $36,000 B: $21,600 C: $14,400
11. $1086.55 **12.** $696 **13.** $158.48; $80.82; $41.20; $14.39
14. $1940.80; $989.81; $504.61; $176.22

Chapter 13

Section 13.1 Exercises (Page 541)

1. 20% **3.** 12.5% **5.** 5% **7.** $6\frac{2}{3}$% **9.** 1.25% **11.** 2% **13.** $450
15. $800 **17.** $840 **19.** $2850 **21.** $5000 **23.** $2775
25. $73,000

27. Year 1: ($33\frac{1}{3}$% × $9000); $3000; $3000; $9000;
Year 2: ($33\frac{1}{3}$% × $9000); $3000; $6000; $6000;
Year 3: ($33\frac{1}{3}$% × $9000); $3000; $9000; $3000
29. Year 1: ($16\frac{2}{3}$% × $18,600); $3100; $3100; $22,500;
Year 2: ($16\frac{2}{3}$% × $18,600); $3100; $6200; $19,400;
Year 3: ($16\frac{2}{3}$% × $18,600); $3100; $9300; $16,300;
Year 4: ($16\frac{2}{3}$% × $18,600); $3100; $12,400; $13,200;
Year 5: ($16\frac{2}{3}$% × $18,600); $3100; $15,500; $10,100;
Year 6: ($16\frac{2}{3}$% × $18,600); $3100; $18,600; $7000
33. (a) $55,000 depreciation **(b)** $1,025,000 book value
35. (a) $2527 depreciation **(b)** $20,211 book value

Section 13.2 Exercises (Page 547)

1. 40% **3.** 25% **5.** $13\frac{1}{3}$% **7.** 20% **9.** $33\frac{1}{3}$% **11.** 4%
13. $3600 **15.** $4200 **17.** $1900 **19.** $3360 **21.** $1215
23. $6834 **25.** $750
27. Year 1: (50% × $14,400), $7200; $7200; $7200;
Year 2: (50% × $7200); $3600; $10,800; $3600;
Year 3: (50% × $3600); $1800, $12,600; $1800;
Year 4: —; $1800*, $14,400; $0 (*To depreciate to 0 scrap
value)
29. Year 1: (40% × $14,000); $5600; $5600; $8400;
Year 2: (40% × $8400); $3360; $8960; $5040;
Year 3: (40% × $5040); $2016; $10,976; $3024;
Year 4: —; $524*, $11,500; $2500;
Year 5: —; $0; $11,500 (*To depreciate to $2500 scrap value)
33. $1153 **35.** $235

Section 13.3 Exercises (Page 553)

1. $\frac{4}{10}$ **3.** $\frac{6}{21}$ **5.** $\frac{7}{28}$ **7.** $\frac{10}{55}$ **9.** $1640 **11.** $10,000 **13.** $600
15. $7700 **17.** $2700 **19.** $890 **21.** $2400
23. Year 1: ($\frac{4}{10}$ × $12,000); $4800; $4800; $9600;
Year 2: ($\frac{3}{10}$ × $12,000); $3600; $8400; $6000;
Year 3: ($\frac{2}{10}$ × $12,000); $2400; $10,800, $3600;
Year 4: ($\frac{1}{10}$ × $12,000); $1200; $12,000; $2400
25. Year 1: ($\frac{6}{21}$ × $8400); $2400; $2400; $8400;
Year 2: ($\frac{5}{21}$ × $8400); $2000; $4400; $6400;
Year 3: ($\frac{4}{21}$ × $8400); $1600; $6000; $4800;
Year 4: ($\frac{3}{21}$ × $8400); $1200; $7200; $3600;
Year 5: ($\frac{2}{21}$ × $8400); $800; $8000; $2800;
Year 6: ($\frac{1}{21}$ × $8400); $400; $8400; $2400
29. $3000 depreciation **31.** $4887

Supplementary Application Exercises on Depreciation (Page 557)

1. $1995 **3.** $11,264 **5.** $1092 **7.** $3760 **9.** $6318
11. $13,680; $10,260; $6840; $3420 **13.** $37,575 **15.** $10,080

Section 13.4 Exercises (Page 565)

1. $.35 **3.** $.029 **5.** $.24 **7.** $30 **9.** $17,940 **11.** $17,280
13. $2775 **15.** $6960
19. Year 1: (1350 × $1.26); $1701; $1701; $5099;
Year 2: (1820 × $1.26); $2293; $3994; $2806;
Year 3: (730 × $1.26); $920; $4914; $1886;
Year 4: (1100 × $1.26); $1386; $6300; $500

Section 13.5 Exercises (Page 571)

1. 19.2% **3.** 11.52% **5.** 20% **7.** 3.636% **9.** 5.76%
11. 2.564% **13.** $1751 **15.** $43,050 **17.** $4800 **19.** $6254
21. $16,920 **23.** $2756 **25.** $79,364

27. Year 1: (33.33% × \$10,980); \$3660; \$3660; \$7320;
Year 2: (44.45% × \$10,980); \$4881; \$8541; \$2439;
Year 3: (14.81% × \$10,980); \$1626; \$10,167; \$813;
Year 4: (7.41% × \$10,980); \$813*; \$10,980; \$0 (*due to rounding in prior years)
29. Year 1: (10% × \$122,700); \$12,270; \$12,270; \$110,430;
Year 2: (18% × \$122,700); \$22,086; \$34,356; \$88,344;
Year 3: (14.4% × \$122,700); \$17,669; \$52,025; \$70.675;
Year 4: (11.52% × \$122,700); \$14,135; \$66,160; \$56,540;
Year 5: (9.22% × \$122,700); \$11,313; \$77,473; \$45,227;
Year 6: (7.37% × \$122,700); \$9043; \$86,516; \$36,184;
Year 7: (6.55% × \$122,700); \$8037; \$94,553; \$28,147;
Year 8: (6.55% × \$122,700); \$8037; \$102,590; \$20,110;
Year 9: (6.56% × \$122,700); \$8049; \$110,639; \$12,061;
Year 10: (6.55% × \$122,700); \$8037; \$118,676; \$4024;
Year 11: (3.28% × \$122,700); \$4024*; \$122,700; \$0 (due to rounding in prior years)
33. \$1066   **35. Year 1:** \$12,326; **Year 2:** \$12,307;
Year 3: \$12,307; **Year 4:** \$12,307; **Year 5:** \$12,307

SUMMARY EXERCISE (PAGE 577)

(a) \$114,000   **(b)** \$61,560   **(c)** \$228,000   **(d)** \$57,000 straight-line; \$24,624 double-declining balance; \$38,000 sum-of-the-years'-digits

CHAPTER 13 TEST (PAGE 579)

1. 25%; 50%; $\frac{4}{10}$ **2.** 20%; 40%; $\frac{5}{15}$ **3.** 10%; 20%; $\frac{10}{55}$ **4.** 5%; 10%; $\frac{20}{210}$ **5.** \$940   **6.** \$21,375   **7. Year 1:** \$2700; **Year 2:** \$2025;
Year 3: \$1350; **Year 4:** \$675   **8.** \$4788 dep. year 3
9. \$15,120 dep. 4 years   **10.** \$5702 book value 3 years
11. **(a) Year 1:** \$4836; **Year 2:** \$2666; **Year 3:** \$3007;
Year 4: \$4712   **(b) Year 1:** \$15,264; **Year 2:** \$12,598;
Year 3: \$9591; **Year 4:** \$4879   **12.** \$2,440,928

CHAPTER 14

SECTION 14.1 EXERCISES (PAGE 587)

1. **(a)** \$316,350   **(b)** \$88,050   **(c)** \$65,350   **3.** Gross sales, \$284,000; Returns, \$6,000; Net sales, \$278,000; Inventory, 1/1, \$58,000; Cost of goods purchased, \$232,000; Freight, \$3,000; Total cost of goods purchased, \$235,000; Total of goods available for sale, \$293,000; Inventory, 12/31, \$69,000; Cost of goods sold, \$224,000; Gross profit, \$54,000; Salaries and wages, \$15,000; Rent, \$6,000; Advertising, \$2,000; Utilities, \$1,000; Taxes on inventory, payroll, \$3,000; Miscellaneous expenses, \$4,000; Total expenses, \$31,000; Net income before taxes, \$23,000; Income taxes, \$2400; Net income after taxes, \$20,600

SECTION 14.2 EXERCISES (PAGE 593)

1. 50.7%; 29.2%   **3.** Cost of goods sold, 67.1%, 67.9%; Gross profit, 32.9%, 32.1%; Wages, 12.5%, 12.3%; Rent, 2.5%, 2.4%; Advertising, 1.5%, 1.4%; Total expenses, 24.6%, 23.5%; Net income before taxes, 8.3%, 8.6%   **7.** Gross sales, 100.3%, 100.7%; Returns, .3%, .7%; Net sales, \$1,850,000, \$1,680,000; Cost of goods sold, 65.0%, 62.5%; Gross profit, 35.0%, 37.5%; Wages, 8.2%, 8.8%; Rent, 4.4%, 4.6%; Advertising, 6.0%, 7.3%; Utilities, 1.7%, 1.0%; Taxes on inv., payroll, .9%, 1.1%; Miscellaneous expenses, 3.4%, 3.5%; Total expenses, 24.6%, 26.3%; Net income before taxes, \$192,000, 10.4%, \$189,000, 11.3%   **9.** 64.8%; 35.2%; 23.4%; 11.7%; 7.9%; 4.9%; 1.8%

SECTION 14.3 EXERCISES (PAGE 599)

1. Cash, \$273; Notes receivable, \$312; Accounts receivable, \$264; Inventory, \$180; Total current assets, \$1,029; Land, \$466; Buildings, \$290; Fixtures, \$28; Total plant assets, \$784; Total assets, \$1,813; Notes payable, \$312; Accounts payable, \$63; Total current liabilities, \$375; Mortgages payable, \$212; Long-term notes payable, \$55; Total long-term liabilities, \$267; Total liabilities, \$642; Owner's equity, \$1,171; Total liabilities and owner's equity, \$1,813

SECTION 14.4 EXERCISES (PAGE 605)

1. Cash, 13%, 13.1%; Notes receivable, 2%, 1.9%; Accounts receivable, 37%, 37.5%; Inventory, 38.3%, 37.5%; Total current assets, \$361,000, 90.3%, \$288,000, 90%; Land, 2.5%, 2.5%; Buildings, 3.5%, 3.4%; Fixtures, 3.8%, 4.1%; Total plant assets, \$39,000, 9.8%, \$32,000, 10%; Total assets, \$400,000, 100%, \$320,000, 100%; Accounts payable, .8%, 1.3%; Notes payable, 50.3%, 47.5%; Total current liabilities, \$204,000, 51%, \$156,000, 48.8%; Mortgages payable, 5%, 5%; Long-term notes payable, 14.5%, 13.1%; Total long-term liabilities, \$78,000, 19.5%, \$58,000, 18.1%; Total liabilities, \$282,000, 70.5%, \$214,000, 66.9%; Owner's equity, 29.5%, 33.1%; Total liabilities and owner's equity, \$400,000, 100%, \$320,000, 100%   **3.** **(a)** 1.77   **(b)** 1.02   **(c)** No, current ratio is low   **5.** **(a)** 1.79   **(b)** .62   **(c)** No, both ratios are low   **7.** 2.13; 1.27   **9.** 6.1%   **11.** 1.47; .14; Not healthy; very low liquidity

SUMMARY EXERCISE (PAGE 612)

(a) Gross sales, \$212,000; Returns, \$12,500; Net sales, \$199,500; Inventory, 1/1, \$44,000; Cost of goods purchased, \$75,000; Freight, \$8,000; Total cost of goods purchased, \$83,000; Total of goods available for sale, \$127,000; Inventory, 12/31, \$26,000; Cost of goods sold, \$101,000; Gross profit, \$98,500; Salaries and wages, \$37,000; Rent, \$12,000; Advertising, \$2,000; Utilities, \$3,000; Taxes on inventory, payroll, \$7,000; Miscellaneous expenses, \$4,500; Total expenses, \$65,500; Net income before taxes, \$33,000   **(b)** Gross sales, 106.3%; Returns, 6.3%; Cost of goods sold, 50.6%; Salaries and wages, 18.5%; Rent, 6%; Utilities, 1.5%   **(c)** Cash, \$62,000; Notes receivable, \$2,500; Accounts receivable, \$8,200; Inventory, \$26,000; Total current assets, \$98,700; Land, \$7,600; Buildings, \$28,000; Fixtures, \$13,500; Total plant assets, \$49,100; Total assets, \$147,800; Notes payable, \$4,500; Accounts payable, \$27,000; Total current liabilities, \$31,500; Mortgages payable, \$15,000; Long-term notes payable, \$8,000; Total long-term liabilities, \$23,000; Total liabilities, \$54,500; Owner's equity, \$93,300; Total liability and owner's equity, \$147,800   **(d)** 3.13; 2.31

CHAPTER 14 TEST (PAGE 615)

1. Gross sales, \$756,300; Returns, \$285; Net sales, \$756,015; Inventory, 1/1, \$92,370; Cost of goods purchased, \$465,920; Freight, \$1,205; Total cost of goods purchased, \$467,125; Total of goods available for sale, \$559,495; Inventory, 12/31, \$82,350; Cost of goods sold, \$477,145; Gross profit, \$278,870; Salaries and wages, \$84,900; Rent, \$42,500; Advertising, \$2,800; Utilities, \$18,950; Taxes on inventory and payroll, \$4,500; Miscellaneous expenses, \$18,400; Total expenses, \$172,050; Net income before taxes, \$106,820; Income taxes, \$25,450; Net income after taxes, \$81,370
2. Net sales, \$35,000, 58.3%; Cost of goods sold, \$23,000, 57.5%; Gross profit, \$4000, 33.3%   **3.** Cost of goods sold, 68.8%; 76.8% Gross profit, 31.3%, 23.2%; Net income, 9.4%, 6.3%; Wages, 9.4%, 8.5%; Rent, 2%, 2.3%; Total expenses, 21.9%, 16.9%   **4.** **(a)** 2.19   **(b)** 1.02   **5.** **(a)** 1.05   **(b)** .37   **6.** 17.5%   **7.** 26.1%

CHAPTER 15

SECTION 15.1 EXERCISES (PAGE 623)

1. $65.08   **3.** 97%   **5.** 51.4%   **7.** 4   **9.** 6   **11.** 5
13.

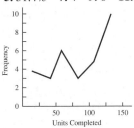

15. 23   **17.** 7   **19.** 2   **21.** 1   **23.** 2   **25.** 6
27.

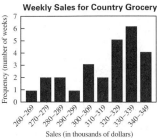

29. 20   **31.** 1   **33.** 13   **35.** 17   **37.** 8   **39.** 38   **41.** 42   **43.** 20%
45. 36°   **47.** 5%; 18°
49.

51. 20%
53.

55. (a) 43,911   (b) 7749

SECTION 15.2 EXERCISES (PAGE 635)

1. 2.5   **3.** 60.3   **5.** 27,955   **7.** 8.8   **11.** 12.3   **13.** 17.2   **15.** 118.8
17. 2.6   **19.** 114   **21.** 130   **23.** 44   **25.** 21%   **27.** 64
29. Bimodal with modes 32 and 38   **31.** 34.11   **33.** 34.38

SUMMARY EXERCISE (PAGE 641)

(a) Store 1 mean = $7.4; Store 2 mean = $8.2; Store 1 median = $7.5; Store 2 median = $8.2; Store 1 has no mode; Store 2 mode = $8.2

(b)

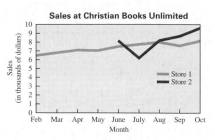

(c) Sales at Store 2 seem to be growing faster than at Store 1.

CHAPTER 15 TEST (PAGE 643)

1. 1, 3, 10, 3, 2, 1   **2.** 6
3.

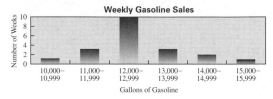

4. Newsprint, 72°; Ink, 10%; Wire service, 108°; Salaries, 108°; Other, 36°
5.

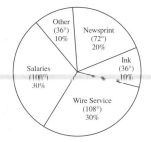

6. 60%   **7.** 230.7   **8.** 18.8 centimeters   **9.** $478.90   **10.** 11.3
11. 173.7   **12.** 19   **13.** 41.5   **14.** 8.3   **15.** 54.5   **16.** 47   **17.** No mode   **18.** Bimodal, 103 and 104
19. It would appear as if the recession had an effect on their business.

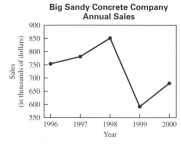

20. It would appear that Mrs. Smith's illness affected Mr. Smith's work.

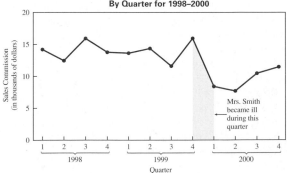

Appendix A

Appendix A Exercises (Page A-17)

1. 3   **3.** 31   **5.** 3   **7.** 7   **9.** 2   **11.** 30   **13.** 7.5   **15.** 10   **17.** 4
19. $\frac{3}{2}$ **21.** 7   **23.** 1   **25.** 1   **27.** $S = 324$ **29.** $M = 493.50$
31. $A = 12,000$ **33.** $I = 1000$ **35.** $I = 120$ **37.** $\frac{d}{t}$ **39.** $\frac{P-1}{T}$
41. $\frac{1}{5}$ **43.** $\frac{8}{5}$ **45.** $\frac{7}{12}$ **47.** false   **49.** true   **51.** 175   **53.** 5   **55.** 8
57. $\frac{7}{2}$ **59.** $\frac{8}{3}$ **61.** $2056   **63.** $12   **65.** $16

Appendix B

Appendix B Exercises (Page B-9)

1. 1171.60   **3.** 11,378   **5.** 3905.32   **7.** 255.24   **9.** 15,695   **11.** 31.08
13. 35.42   **15.** 27.63   **17.** 8.1   **19.** 566.14 rounded   **21.** .63 rounded
23. 30.57 rounded   **25.** .92 rounded   **27.** $5\frac{6}{11}$ **29.** .49 rounded
33. $29,167.32   **35.** $829.25 rounded   **37. (a)** $1164.05 rounded
(b) $95.13 rounded   **39.** $118,191.60   **41.** $13,400

Appendix C

Appendix C Exercises (Page C-7)

1. $39,019.50   **3.** $8929.13   **5.** $2676.84   **7.** 1.5%   **9.** $858.89
11. 24   **13.** FV = $31,651.09   **15.** PMT = $696   **17.** n = 26

Glossary

A

Absolute or gross loss: The loss resulting when the selling price is less than the cost.

Accelerated depreciation: A technique to increase the depreciation taken during the early years of an asset's useful life.

Accelerated mortgages: Mortgages with payoffs of 15 or 18 years.

Accounts payable: Amounts that must be paid to other firms.

Accumulated depreciation: A running balance or total of the depreciation to date on an asset.

Acid-test ratio: The sum of cash, notes receivable, and accounts receivable, divided by current liabilities.

ACRS (Accelerated cost recovery system): A depreciation method introduced as part of the Economic Recovery Tax Act of 1981.

Actual rate of interest: The true annual percentage rate (used as a common denominator for comparing interest rates).

Actuary: A person who determines insurance premiums.

Addends: The numbers added in an addition problem.

Addition rule: The same number may be added or subtracted on both sides of an equation.

Adjustable rate mortgage: Home loans in which the interest rate can vary upwards or downwards.

Adjusted bank balance: The actual current balance of a checking account after reconciliation.

Adjusted gross income: An individual's or family's income for a year, including all sources of income, and after subtracting certain expenses, such as moving expenses and sick pay.

Algebraic logic: Rules used by most calculators for entering and evaluating arithmetic expressions.

Allowances: The number of allowances claimed by a taxpayer affects the amount withheld for income taxes.

American Express: A credit-card plan requiring an annual membership fee.

Amortization table: A table showing the level (unchanging) payment necessary to pay in full a loan for a specific amount of money including interest over a specific length of time.

Amortize: The process of paying off a loan with a sequence of periodic payments over a period of time.

Amount of an annuity: The future value of the annuity.

Amount of depreciation: The dollar amount of depreciation taken. This is usually an annual figure.

Annual meeting: Corporations have annual meetings for stockholders.

Annual percentage rate (APR): A common denominator for comparing interest rates. This is the annual rate of interest.

Annual percentage rate table: A table used to find the annual percentage rate (APR) on a loan or installment purchase.

Annual rate of depreciation: The percent or fraction of the depreciable amount or declining balance to be depreciated each individual year of an asset's useful life.

Annuity: Periodic payments of a given, fixed amount of money.

Annuity due: An annuity whose payments are made at the beginning of a time period.

APR (Annual percentage rate): The cost of credit expressed as a percent per year required by the Truth-in-Lending Act.

"AS OF": A later date that appears on an invoice. The given sales terms may start at this time.

Assessed value: The value of a piece of property. Set by the county assessor, assessed value is used in figuring property taxes.

Asset: An item of value owned by a firm.

ATM (Automated teller machine): A machine that allows bank customers to make deposits, withdrawals, and fund transfers.

Automatic savings transfer account: A bank account that automatically transfers funds from one account to another.

Average: *See* mean.

Average cost method: An inventory valuation method whereby the cost of all purchases during a time period is divided by the number of units purchased.

Average daily balance method: A method used to calculate interest on open-end credit accounts.

Average inventory: The sum of all inventories taken divided by the number of times inventory was taken.

Average owner's equity: Sum of owner's equity at the beginning and end of the year divided by 2.

B

Bad checks: A check that is not honored because there are insufficient funds in the checking account.

Balance brought forward (Current balance): The amount left in a checking account after previous checks written have been subtracted.

Balanced: In agreement. When the bank statement amount and the depositor's checkbook balance agree, they are balanced.

Balance sheet: A summary of the financial condition of a firm at one point in time.

Bank discount: A bank fee charged on a note and subtracted from the amount of a note.

Banker's ratio: *See* current ratio.

Bank statement: Usually sent out monthly by the bank, a list of all charges and deposits made against and to a checking account.

Banker's rule: A formula used to calculate interest by dividing exact days by 360.

Bar graph: A graph using bars to compare various numbers.

Base: The starting point or reference point or that to which something is being compared.

bbl.: Abbreviation for *barrel*.

Blank endorsement: A signature on the back of a check by the person to whom the check is made.

Board of directors: A group of people who represent the stockholders of a corporation.

Bodily injury insurance: A type of automobile insurance that protects a driver in case he or she injures someone with a car.

Bond: A promise by a corporation to repay borrowed money at some specified time.

Book value: The cost of an asset minus depreciation to date.

Break-even point: The cost of an item plus the operating expenses associated with the item. Above this amount a profit is made; below it, a loss is incurred.

Broker: A person who sells stocks, bonds, and other investments owned by others.

Business account: The type of checking account used by businesses.

bx.: Abbreviation for *box*.

C

C: Roman numeral for 100.

Canceled check: A check is canceled after the amount of the check has been transferred from the payer's bank account into the account of the receiver of the check.

Cancellation: A process used to simplify multiplication and division of fractions.

Capital: The amount of money originally invested in a firm. The difference between the total of all the assets and the total of all the liabilities is called the capital or net worth.

Capital gains: Profits made on investments such as stocks or real estate.

cart.: Abbreviation for *carton*.

Cash discount: A discount offered by the seller allowing the buyer to take a discount if payment is made within a specified period of time.

Cashier's check: A check written by the financial institution itself. It has the full faith and backing of the institution.

Cash value: Money that has built up in an ordinary life insurance policy.

Centi-: A prefix used in the metric system meaning hundredth. (For example, a centiliter is one one-hundredth of a liter.)

Centimeter: One one-hundredth of a meter. There are 2.54 centimeters to an inch.

Central tendency: The middle of a set of data.

Certificate of deposit (CD): A savings account in which a minimum amount of money must be deposited and left for a minimum period of time.

Chain calculations: Long calculations done on a calculator.

Chain discount: Two or more discounts that are combined into one discount.

Check register: A table usually found in a check book that is used by the check writer to list all checks written, deposits and withdrawals made, and ATM transactions.

Checks outstanding: Checks written that have not reached and cleared the bank as of the statement date.

Check stub: A stub attached to the check and retained as a record of checks written.

Circle graph: A circle broken into parts based on percentages of 360°.

COD: Cash on delivery.

Coinsurance: A type of insurance in which part of the risk of fire is assumed by the business firm taking out the insurance.

Collateral: Assets foreclosed on by a lender should the borrower default on payments.

Collision insurance: A form of automobile insurance that pays for car repairs in case of an accident.

Commission: A fee charged by a broker for buying and selling stocks and bonds.

Commissions: Payments to an employee that represent a certain percent of the total sales produced by the employee's efforts.

Common denominator: Two or more fractions with the same denominator are said to have common denominators.

Common stock: Ownership of a corporation, held in portions called shares.

Comparative balance sheet: An analysis for two or more periods of time that compares asset categories such as cash.

Comparative income statement: A vertical analysis for two or more years that compares incomes or balance sheet items for each year analyzed.

Comparison graph (Comparative line graph): One graph that shows how several things relate.

Compensatory time (Comp time): Time off given to an employee to compensate for previously worked overtime.

Compound interest: Interest charged or received on both principal and interest.

Comprehensive insurance: A form of automobile insurance that pays for damage to a car caused by fire, theft, vandalism, and weather.

Consolidated statement: A financial statement showing the combined results of all subsidiaries of a firm.

Consumer price index (CPI):   The CPI is a measure of the cost of living.

Conventional loan: A loan made by a bank, savings and loan, or other lending agency that is not guaranteed or insured by the federal government.

Corporation: A form of business that gives the owners limited liability.

Cost: The total cost of an item, including shipping, insurance, and other charges. Most often, the cost is the basis for calculating depreciation of an asset.

Cost (Cost price):   The price paid to the manufacturer or supplier after trade and cash discounts have been taken. This price includes transportation and insurance charges.

Cost of goods sold: The amount paid by a firm for the goods it sold during the time period covered by an income statement.

Country club billing method: A billing method that provides copies of original charge receipts to the customer.

cpm.:   Abbreviation for *cost per thousand*.

Credit union: An organization established to provide its members with savings and loan services.

Credit union share draft account: A credit union account that may be used as a checking account.

Cross-products: The equal products obtained when each numerator of a proportion is multiplied by the opposite denominator.

cs.:   Abbreviation for *case*.

ct.:   Abbreviation for *crate*.

ctn.   Abbreviation for *carton*.

Current assets: Cash or items that can be converted into cash within a given period of time, such as a year.

Current liability: Debts that must be paid by a firm within a given period of time, such as a year.

Current ratio: The quotient of current assets and current liabilities.

Current yield: The annual dividend per share of stock divided by the current price per share.

cwt.:   Abbreviation for *per hundredweight* or *per one hundred pounds*.

D

Daily interest charge: The amount of interest charged per day on a loan.

Daily overtime: The amount of overtime worked in a day.

Debit card: A card that results in a debit to a bank account when the card is used for a purchase.

Decimal: A number written with a decimal point, such as 4.3 or 7.22.

Decimal equivalent: A decimal that has the same value as a fraction.

Decimal point: The starting point in the decimal system (.).

Decimal system: The numbering system based on powers of 10 and using the 10 one place numbers 0, 1, 2, 3, 4, 5, 6, 7, 8, and 9, which are called *digits*.

Declining-balance depreciation: An accelerated depreciation method.

(200%) Declining-balance method: An accelerated method of depreciation using twice, or 200% of, the straight-line rate.

Decrease problem (Difference problem):   A percentage problem in which something is taken away from the base. Usually the base must be found.

Decreasing term insurance: A form of life insurance in which the insured pays a fixed premium until age 60 or 65, with the amount of life insurance decreasing periodically.

Deductible: An amount paid by the insured, with the balance of the loss paid by the insurance company.

Deductions: Amounts that are subtracted from the gross earnings of an employee to arrive at the amount of money the employee actually receives.

Deposit slip: A slip for listing all currency and checks that are part of a deposit into a bank account.

Denominator: The number below the line in a fraction. For example, in the fraction $\frac{7}{9}$, 9 is the denominator.

Depreciation: The decrease in value of an asset caused by normal use, aging, or obsolescence.

Depreciable amount: The amount of an asset's value that can be depreciated.

Depreciation schedule: A schedule or table showing the depreciation rate, amount of depreciation, book value, and accumulated depreciation for each year of an asset's life.

Difference (Remainder):   The answer in a subtraction problem.

Differential piece rate: A rate paid per item that depends on the number of items produced.

Digits: One-place numbers in the decimal system. They are 0, 1, 2, 3, 4, 5, 6, 7, 8, and 9.

Discount: A reduction: the removal or lowering of price or charges.

Discount broker: A stockbroker who charges a reduced fee to customers (and, generally, reduced services).

Discount date: The last date on which a cash discount may be taken.

Discounting a note: Cashing or selling a note at a bank before the note is due from the maker.

Discount method of interest: A method of calculating interest on a loan by subtracting the interest from the amount of the loan. The borrower receives the amount borrowed less the discounted interest.

Discount period: The discount period is the period from the time of sale of a note to the note's due date.

Discount rate: The discount rate is a percent that is multiplied by the face value and time to find bank discount.

Discover: A credit-card plan owned by Sears, Roebuck and Company.

Distributive property: The property that states the product of the sum of two numbers equals the sum of the individual products; that is $a(b + c) = ab + ac$.

Dividend: (1) The number being divided by another number in a division problem. (2) A return on an investment; money paid by a company to the holders of stock.

Divisor: The number doing the dividing in a division problem.

Double-declining balance: A method of accelerated depreciation that doubles depreciation in the early years compared to straight-line depreciation.

Double time: Twice the regular hourly rate. A premium often paid for working holidays and Sunday.

Dow Jones Industrial Average: A frequently quoted average price of the stocks of 30 large industrial companies.

doz.: Abbreviation for *dozen*.

Draw: A draw is an advance on future earnings.

Drawing account: An account from which a salesperson can receive payment against future commissions.

drm.: Abbreviation for *drum*.

E

ea.: Abbreviation for *each*.

Effective rate: The true rate of interest.

Electronic banking: Banking activities that take place over a network, such as the World Wide Web.

Electronic commerce: Purchases that take place over a network, such as the World Wide Web.

Electronic funds transfer: Moving money electronically over a network, such as the World Wide Web.

End-of-month dating (EOM): A system of cash discounts in which the time period begins at the end of the month the invoice is dated. *Proximo* and *prox.* have the same meaning.

Endowment policy: A life insurance policy guaranteeing the payment of a fixed amount of money to a given individual whether or not the insured person lives.

Equation: A statement that two expressions are equal.

Escrow account into which monies are paid: *See* impound account.

Exact interest: A method of calculating interest based on 365 days per year.

Executive officers: The top few officers in a corporation.

Expenses: The amount paid by the firm in an attempt to sell its goods.

Extension total: The number of items purchased times the price per unit.

Extra dating (ex., x): Extra time allowed in determining the net payment date of a cash discount.

F

Face value: The amount shown on the face of a note.

Face value of a bond (Par value of a bond): The amount the company has promised to repay.

Face value of a policy: The amount of insurance provided by the insurance company.

Factors: Companies that buy accounts receivable.

Factoring: The process of selling accounts receivable for cash.

Fair Labor Standards Act: A federal law that sets the minimum wage and also a 40-hour workweek.

Fair market value: The price for which a piece of property could reasonably be expected to be sold in the market.

FAS (Free alongside ship): Free alongside the ship on the loading dock.

Federal Insurance Contributions Act (FICA): An emergency measure passed by Congress in the 1930s that established the so-called Social Security tax. *See* FICA tax.

Federal Reserve Bank: Today, all banks are part of the Federal Reserve system. The Federal Reserve is our national bank.

Federal Truth-in-Lending Act: An act passed in 1969 that requires all interest rates to be given as comparable percents.

Federal Unemployment Tax Act (FUTA): An unemployment insurance tax paid entirely by employers to the federal government for administrative costs of federal and state unemployment programs.

FHA loan: A real estate loan that is insured by the Federal Housing Administration, an agency of the federal government.

FICA tax (Social Security tax): The amount of money deducted from the paychecks of almost all employees, used by the federal government to pay pensions to retired people, survivors' benefits, and disability.

FIFO: An inventory valuation method following the flow of goods: first-in, first-out.

Finance charge: The difference between the cost of something paid for in installments and the cash price.

Financial ratio: A number that can be compared with commonly accepted numbers in industry.

Fixed assets: Items owned by a firm that will not be converted to cash within a year.

Fixed liabilities: Items that will not be paid off within a year.

Fixed-rate loan: A loan made at a fixed, stated rate of interest.

Flat-fee checking account: Bank supplies checking account, check printing, a bank charge card, and other services for a fixed charge per month.

Floating decimal: A feature on most calculators that positions the decimal point where it should be in the final answer.

FOB (Free on board): A notation sometimes used on an invoice. "Free on board shipping point" means the buyer pays for shipping. "Free on board destination" means the seller pays for shipping.

Form 1040A: The form used by most federal income tax payers.

Form 1040EZ: A simplified version of the 1040A federal income tax form.

Fraction: An indication of a part of a whole. (For example, $\frac{3}{4}$ means that the whole is divided into 4 parts, of which 3 are being considered.)

Frequency distribution table: A table showing the number of times one or more events occur.

Fringe benefits: Benefits offered by an employer, not including salary, that can include medical, dental, life insurance, and day care for employee's children.

Front-end rounding: Rounding so that all digits are changed to zero except the first digit.

Future value: The value, at some future date, of an investment.

G

GI (VA) loan: A loan guaranteed by the Veterans Administration and available only to qualified veterans.

Gram: The unit of weight in the metric system. (A nickel weighs about 5 grams.)

Graph: A visual presentation of numerical data.

Gr. gro. (Great gross): Abbreviation for 12 gross (144 × 12 = 1728).

Gro.: Abbreviation for *gross*.

gross: A dozen dozen, or 144 items.

Gross earnings: The total amount of money earned by an employee before any deductions are taken.

Gross loss: *See* absolute loss.

Gross profit: The difference between the amount received from customers for goods and what the firm paid for the goods.

Gross profit on sales: *See* gross profit.

Gross sales: The total amount of money received from customers for the goods or services sold by the firm.

H

Half-year convention: Method of depreciation used for the first year the property is placed in service.

High: The highest price reached by a stock during the day.

Homeowner's policy: An insurance policy that covers a home against fire, theft, and liability.

Horizontal analysis: An analysis that shows the amount of any change from last year to the current year, both in dollars and as a percent.

I

Impound account (Escrow account): An account at a lending institution into which taxes and insurance are paid on a monthly basis by a borrower on real estate. The lender then pays the tax and insurance bills from this account when they become due.

Improper fraction: A fraction with a numerator larger than the denominator. (For example, $\frac{7}{5}$ is an improper fraction; $\frac{1}{9}$ is not.)

Incentive rate: A payment system based on the amount of work completed.

Income statement: A summary of all the income and expenses involved in running a business for a given period of time.

Income tax withholding: Federal income tax that the employer withholds from gross earnings.

Income-to-monthly-payment ratio: A ratio used to determine from an income standpoint whether a prospective borrower meets the lender's qualifications.

Increase problem (Amount problem): A percentage problem in which something has been added to the base. Usually the base must be found.

Index fund: A mutual fund that holds the stocks that are in a particular market index such as the Dow Jones Industrial Average.

Indicator words: Key words that help indicate whether to add, subtract, multiply, or divide.

Individual retirement account (IRA): An account designed to help people prepare for future retirement.

Inflation: Inflation results in a continuing rise in the cost of goods and services. *See* CPI.

Installment loan: A loan that is paid off with a sequence of periodic payments.

Insured: A person or business that has purchased insurance.

Insurer: The insurance company.

Intangible assets: Assets such as patents, copyrights, or customer lists that have a value that cannot be immediately converted to cash, unlike jewelry or stocks.

Interest-in-advance notes: *See* simple discount notes.

Interest: A charge paid for borrowing money or a fee received for lending money.

Interest rate spread: The difference between the interest rate paid to depositors and the rates charged to borrowers by the same lender.

Internal Revenue Service: The branch of the U.S. federal government responsible for collecting taxes.

Inventory: The value of the merchandise that a firm has for sale on the date of balance sheet.

Inventory-to-net-working-capital ratio: Inventory divided by working capital, where working capital is current assets minus current liabilities.

Inventory turnover: The number of times during a certain time period that the average inventory is sold.

Invoice: A printed record of a purchase and sales transaction.

Invoice amount: List price minus trade discounts.

Invoice date: The date an invoice is printed.

Itemized billing method: A billing method that provides an itemization of the customer's charge purchases, but not copies of the original charge receipts.

Itemized deductions: Tax deductions, such as interest, taxes, and medical expenses, that are listed individually on a tax return in order to affect the total amount of taxes payable at the end of the year.

J

Joint return: An income tax return filed by both husband and wife.

K

Kilo-:   A prefix used in the metric system to represent 1000.

Kilogram: A unit of weight in the metric system meaning 1000 grams. One kilogram is about 2.2 pounds.

Kilometer: One thousand meters. A kilometer is about .6 mile.

L

Late fees: Fees required because payments were made after a specific due date.

Least common denominator: The smallest whole number that all the denominators of two or more fractions evenly divide into. (For example, the least common denominator of $\frac{3}{4}$ and $\frac{5}{6}$ is 12.)

Liability: An expense that must be paid by a firm.

LIFO: An inventory valuation method following the flow of goods: last-in, first-out.

Like fractions: Fractions with the same denominator.

Limited liability: A form of protection that shields a company and its shareholders from having to pay large sums of money in the event that the company loses a lawsuit.

Limited-pay life insurance: Life insurance for which premiums are paid for only a fixed number of years.

Line graph: A graph that uses lines to compare numbers.

Liquidity: The ability of a firm or individual to raise cash quickly without being forced to sell assets at a loss.

Liquid assets: Cash or items that can be converted to cash quickly.

List price: The suggested retail price or final consumer price given by the manufacturer or supplier.

Liter: A measure of volume in the metric system. One liter is a little more than 1 quart.

Loan reduction schedule: *See* repayment schedule.

Long-term liabilities: Items that will be paid after one year.

Long-term notes payable: The total of all debts of a firm, other than mortgages, that will not be paid within a year.

Low: The lowest price reached by a stock during the day.

Lowest terms: The form of a fraction if no number except the number 1 divides evenly into both the numerator and denominator.

M

M: Roman numeral for 1000.

MACRS (modified accelerated cost recovery system):   A depreciation method introduced as part of the Tax Reform Act of 1986.

Maintenance charge per month: The charge to maintain a checking account (usually determined by the minimum balance in the account).

Maker of a note: A person borrowing money from another person.

Margin: The difference between cost and selling price.

Marital status: An individual can claim married, single or head of household when filing income taxes.

Markdown: A reduction from the original selling price. It may be expressed as a dollar amount or as a percent of the original selling price.

Marketing channels: The path of products and services beginning with the manufacturer and ending with the consumer.

Markup (Margin, Gross profit):   The difference between the cost and the selling price.

Markup on cost: Markup that is calculated as a percent of cost.

Markup on selling price: Markup that is calculated as a percent of selling price.

Markup with spoilage: The calculation of markup including deduction for spoiled or unsaleable merchandise.

MasterCard: A credit-card plan (formerly known as Master-Charge).

Maturity value: The amount that must be repaid by the maker of a note when the note is due. It equals face value plus interest.

Mean: The sum of all the numbers divided by the number of numbers.

Median: A number that represents the middle of a group of numbers.

Medical insurance: Insurance providing medical protection in the event of accident or injury.

Medicare tax: The amount of money deducted from the paychecks of almost all employees, used by the federal government to pay for Medicare.

Memory function: A feature on some calculators that stores results internally in the machine for retrieval and future use.

Merchant batch header ticket: The bank form used to deposit credit-card transactions.

Meter: A unit of length in the metric system that is slightly longer than 1 yard.

Metric system: A system of weights and measures based on decimals, used throughout most of the world. It is gradually being adopted in the United States.

Milli-:   A prefix used in the metric system meaning thousandth. (For example, a milligram is one one-thousandth of a gram.)

Millimeter: One one-thousandth of a meter. There are 25.4 millimeters to an inch.

Mills: A way of expressing a real estate tax rate that is based on thousandths of a dollar.

Minuend: The number from which another number (the subtrahend) is subtracted.

Mixed number: A number written as a whole number and a fraction. (For example $1\frac{1}{5}$ and $2\frac{5}{9}$ are mixed numbers.)

Mode: The number that occurs most often in a group of numbers.

Modified accelerated cost recovery system: *See* MACRS.

Money order: An instrument that is purchased and is often used in place of cash.

Mortgage: A loan on a home.

Mortgages payable: The balance due on all mortgages owed by a firm.

Multiple carrier insurance: The sharing of risk by several insurance companies.

Multiplicand: A number being multiplied.

Multiplication rule: The same nonzero number may be multiplied or divided on both sides of an equation.

Multiplier: A number doing the multiplying.

Mutual fund: An individual can invest in the stocks and/or bonds of many companies using mutual funds.

N

Negative numbers: Numbers that are the opposite of positive numbers.

Net cost: The cost or price after allowable discounts have been taken. *See* net price.

Net cost equivalent: The decimal number derived from the complement of the single trade discount. This number multiplied by the list price gives the net cost.

Net earnings: The difference between gross margin and expenses. After the cost of goods and operating expenses are subtracted from total sales, the remainder is net profit.

Net income: The difference between gross margin and expenses.

Net pay: The amount of money actually received by an employee after deductions are taken from gross pay.

Net payment date: The date by which an invoice must be paid.

Net price: The list price less any discounts. *See* net cost.

Net proceeds: The amount received from the bank for a discounted note.

Net profit: *See* net earnings.

Net sales: The value of goods bought by customers after the value of goods returned is subtracted.

Net worth (Capital, Stockholder's equity, Owner's equity): The difference between assets and liabilities.

No-fault insurance: A guarantee of reimbursement (provided by the insured's own insurance company) for medical expenses and costs associated with an accident no matter who is at fault.

Nominal rate: The stated interest rate.

No scrap value: A value of zero at the end of an asset's useful life.

Nonsufficient funds (NSF): When a check is written on an account for which there is an insufficient balance, the check is returned to the depositor for nonsufficient funds.

Notes payable: The value of all notes owed by a firm.

Notes receivable: The value of all notes owed to a firm.

NOW account (Negotiable order or withdrawal): Technically a savings account with special withdrawal privileges. It looks the same and is used the same as a checking account.

Numerator: The number above the line in a fraction. (For example, in the fraction $\frac{5}{8}$, 5 is the numerator.)

O

Odd lot: Fewer than 100 shares of stock.

Open-end-credit: Credit with no fixed number of payments. The consumer continues making payments until no outstanding balance is owed.

Operating expenses (Overhead): Expenses of operating a business. Wages, salaries, rent, utilities, and advertising are examples.

Operating loss: The loss resulting when the selling price is less than the break-even point.

Ordered array: A list of numbers arranged from smallest to largest.

Order of operations: The rules that are used when evaluating long arithmetic expressions.

Ordinary annuity: An annuity whose payments are made at the end of a given period of time.

Ordinary dating: A method for calculating the discount date and the net payment date. Days are counted from the date of the invoice.

Ordinary interest: A method of calculating interest, assuming 360 days per year. *See* banker's rule.

Ordinary life insurance (Whole life insurance, Straight life insurance): A form of life insurance whereby the insured pays a constant premium until death or retirement, whichever occurs sooner. Upon retirement, monthly payments are made by the company to the insured until the death of the insured.

Overhead: Expenses involved in running a firm. *See* operating expenses.

Over-the-limit fees: Fees charged when the balance on a credit-card account exceeds the account's credit limit.

Overdraft: An event that results when there is not enough money in a bank account to cover a check that is written from that account.

Overtime: The number of hours worked by an employee in excess of 40 hours per week.

Owner's equity: *See* net worth.

P

Part: The result of multiplying the base times the rate.

Partial payment: A payment made on an invoice that is less than the full amount of the invoice.

Partial product: Part of the process of getting the answer in a multiplication problem.

Par value of a bond: *See* face value of a bond.

Passbook account: A type of savings account for day-in and day-out savings.

Payee: The person who lends money and will receive repayment on a note.

Payer of a note: A person borrowing money from another person. *See* maker of a note.

Payroll: A record of the hours each employee of a firm worked and the amount of money due each employee for a given pay period.

Payroll card: A card maintained by employers showing the name of employee, dates of pay period, days, times, and hours worked.

Payroll ledger: A chart showing all payroll information.

Percent (Rate): Some parts of a whole: hundredths, or parts of a hundred. (For example, a percent is one one-hundredth. Two percent means two parts of a hundred, or $\frac{2}{100}$.)

Percentage method: A method of calculating income tax withholding that is based on percentages.

Per debit charge: A charge per check. Usually continues regardless of the number of checks written.

Periodic inventory: A physical inventory taken at regular intervals.

Perpetual inventory: A continuous inventory system normally involving a computer.

Personal account: The type of checking account used by individuals.

Personal exemption (Exemption):   A deduction allowed each taxpayer for each dependent and the taxpayer himself or herself.

Personal property: Property such as a boat, a car, or a stereo.

Piecework: A method of pay by which an employee receives so much money per item produced or completed.

Plant assets: *See* fixed assets.

Policy: A contract outlining the insurance agreement between an insured and an insurance company.

Postdating: Dating in the future; on an invoice, "AS OF" dating.

pr.:   Abbreviation for *pair*.

Preferred stock: A type of stock that offers investors certain rights over holders of common stock.

Premium: The amount of money charged for insurance policy coverage.

Premium factor: A factor used to adjust an annual insurance premium to semiannually, quarterly, or monthly.

Premium payment: An additional payment for extra service.

Present value: An amount that can be deposited today to yield a given sum in the future.

Price-earnings (PE) ratio: The price per share divided by the annual net income per share of stock.

Prime interest rate: The interest rate banks charge their largest and most financially secure borrowers.

Prime number: A number divisible only by itself or 1 (such as 7 or 13).

Principal: The amount of money either borrowed or deposited.

Proceeds: The amount of money a borrower receives after subtracting the discount from the face value of a note.

Product: The answer in a multiplication problem.

Promissory note: A business document in which one person agrees to repay money to another person within a specified amount of time and at a specified rate of interest in exchange for money borrowed.

Proper fraction: A fraction in which the numerator is smaller than the denominator. (For example, $\frac{2}{3}$ is a proper fraction; $\frac{9}{5}$ is not.)

Property damage insurance: A type of automobile insurance that pays for damages that the insured causes to the property of others.

Proportion: A mathematical statement that two ratios are equal.

Proprietorship: Stockholder's equity.

Proximo (Prox.):   *See* end-of-month dating.

Publicly held corporations: Corporations that are owned by the public and have stock that trades freely.

Purchase invoice: A list of items purchased, prices charged for the items, and payment terms.

Q

Qualifying for a loan: The passing of the test by a buyer when a lender examines the buyer from the standpoint of earnings, past credit ratings, and down payment to determine whether the borrower is a good risk.

Quick ratio: The quotient of liquid assets and current liabilities.

Quota: An expected level of production. A premium may be paid for surpassing quota.

Quotient: The answer in a division problem.

R

Rate: Parts of a hundred. *See* percent.

Rate of interest: The percent of interest charged on a loan for a certain time period.

Ratio: A comparison of two (or more) numbers, frequently indicated by a common fraction.

Real estate: Real property such as a home or a lot.

Receipt-of-goods dating (ROG):   A method of determining cash discounts in which time is counted from the date that goods are received.

Reciprocal: A fraction formed from a given fraction by interchanging the numerator and denominator.

Reconciliation: The process of checking a bank statement against the depositor's own personal records.

Recourse: Should the maker of a note not pay, the bank may have recourse to collect from the seller of the note.

Recovery classes: Classes used to determine depreciation under the modified accelerated cost recovery system.

Recovery period: The life of property depreciated under the accelerated cost recovery system.

Recovery year: The year of life of an asset when using the MACRS method of depreciation.

Reduced net profit: The situation that occurs when a markdown decreases the selling price to a point that is still above the break-even point.

Regulation DD: A Federal Reserve System document that specifies how interest paid to savers is to be calculated.

Regulation Z: A Federal Reserve System document that implements the Truth-in-Lending Act.

Repayment schedule: A schedule showing the amount of payment going toward interest and principal and the balance of principal remaining after each payment is made.

Repeating decimals: Decimal numbers that do not terminate, but that contain numbers that repeat themselves.

Repossess: The taking back of property by a lender when payments have not been made to the lender.

Residual value: *See* scrap value.

Restricted endorsement: A signature or imprint on the back of a check that limits the ability to cash the check.

Retailer: A business that buys from the wholesaler and sells to the consumer.

Retail method: A method used to estimate inventory value at cost that utilizes both cost and retail amounts.

Returned check: A check that was deposited and then returned due to lack of funds in the payer's account.

Return on average total assets: Net income divided by average total assets.

Returns: The total value of all goods returned by customers.

Revolving charge account: A charge account that never has to be paid off.

Roth IRA: A retirement savings account in which deposits to the account are not exempt from state or federal taxes. Funds in the account grow tax free and remain tax free when withdrawn after the account holder reaches a certain age.

Round lot: A multiple of 100 shares of stock.

Rounding off: The reduction of a number with more decimals to a number with fewer decimals.

Rule of 78:   A method of calculating a partial refund of interest that has already been added to the amount of a loan. This calculation is done when the loan is paid off early.

S

Salary: A fixed amount of money per pay period.

Salary plus commission: Earnings based on a fixed salary plus a percent of all sales.

Sale price: The price of an item after markdown.

Sales invoice: *See* purchase invoice.

Sales tax: A tax placed on sales to the final consumer. The tax is collected by the state, county, or local government.

Salvage value: *See* scrap value.

Savings account: An interest paying account that allows day-to-day savings and withdrawals.

Schedule 1:   The part of the 1040A federal tax form that is used to list all interest and dividends.

Scrap value (Salvage value):   The value of an asset at the end of its useful life. For depreciation purposes, this is often an estimate.

Self-employed people: People who work for themselves instead of for the government or for a private company.

Series discount: *See* chain discount.

Shift differential: A premium paid for working a less desirable shift, such as the swing shift or the graveyard shift.

Simple interest note: A note in which interest equals principal times interest rate times time in years.

Simple discount note: A note in which the interest is deducted from the face value in advance.

Simple interest: Interest received on only the principal.

Single discount equivalent: A series, or chain, discount expressed as a single discount.

Single return: An income tax return filed by a single person.

Sinking fund: A fund set up to receive periodic payments in order to pay off a debt at some time in the future.

sk.:   Abbreviation for *sack*.

Sliding scale: Commissions that are paid at increasing levels as sales increase.

Social Security tax: *See* FICA tax.

Special endorsement: A signature on the back of a check that passes the ownership of the check to someone else.

Specific identification method: An inventory valuation method that identifies the cost of each item.

Split-shift premium: A premium paid for working a split shift, for example, for an employee who is on 4 hours, off 4 hours, and then on 4 hours.

Square root: One of two equal positive factors of a number.

Stafford loan: A loan taken out by college students to help pay tuition.

Standard deduction: The average amount that an individual or family is expected to incur in deductible expenses during a year.

State income tax: An income tax that is paid to a state government on income earned in that state.

Statement: Usually sent out monthly by the bank, a list of all charges and deposits made against and to a checking account.

Statistics: Refers both to data and to the techniques used in analyzing data.

Stock: A form of ownership in a corporation that is measured in units called *shares*.

Stockbroker: A person who buys and sells stock at the stock exchange.

Stock exchange: An institution where stock shares are bought and sold.

Stockholders: Individuals who own stock in a particular company.

Stockholder's equity: *See* net worth.

Stock ratios: Ratios calculated from the financial statements of a company—used to determine the financial health of the firm.

Stock turnover: *See* inventory turnover.

Stop payment: A request from a depositor that the bank not honor a check that the depositor has written.

Straight commission: A salary that is a fixed percent of sales.

Straight life insurance: *See* ordinary life insurance.

Straight-line depreciation: A depreciation method in which depreciation is spread evenly over the life of the asset.

Substitution: Method for checking the solution to an equation.

Subtrahend: The number being subtracted or taken away in a subtraction problem.

Sum: The total amount; the answer in addition.

Sum-of-the-years'-digits method: An accelerated depreciation method that results in larger amounts of depreciation taken in earlier years of an asset's life.

T

T-bill: A short-term note issued by the federal government that pays interest to the note holder. Issuing T-bills allows the federal government to raise cash without having to borrow the money from a bank and pay interest.

Tangible assets: Assets such as a car, machinery, or computers.

Taxable income: Adjusted income subject to taxation.

Tax deduction: Any expense that the Internal Revenue Service allows the taxpayers to subtract from adjusted gross income.

Taxes: A sum of money that is paid by an individual based on the individual's yearly income. Many states also require payment of income taxes. Money raised by taxes helps pay for a variety of programs offered by the federal or state government.

Telephone transfer account: An interest bearing checking account into which funds may be transferred by the customer over the telephone.

Term insurance: A form of life insurance providing protection for a fixed length of time.

Term of an annuity: The length of time that an annuity is in effect.

Term of a note: The length of time between the date a note is written and the date the note is due.

Terms: The area of an invoice where cash discounts are indicated if any are offered. The words "terms discount" are often used in place of "cash discount."

Territorial ratings: Ratings used by insurance companies that describe the quality of fire protection in a specific area.

Time-and-a-half rate: One and one-half times the normal rate of pay for any hours worked in excess of 40 per week.

Time card: A card filled out by an employee that shows the number of hours worked by that employee.

Time deposit account: A savings account in which the depositor agrees to leave money on deposit for a certain period of time.

Time rate: Earnings based on hours worked, not for work accomplished.

Total installment cost: Includes the down payment plus the sum of all payments.

Trade discount: A discount offered to businesses. This discount is expressed either as a single discount (like 25%) or a series discount (like 20/10) and is subtracted from the list price.

True rate of interest: *See* effective rate of interest.

Turnover at cost: The cost of goods sold, divided by the average inventory at cost.

Turnover at retail: Sales, divided by the average inventory at retail.

U

Underinsured motorist: A motorist who does not carry enough insurance to cover the costs of an accident.

Underwriters: Term applied to any insurer. Usually associated with an insurance company.

Unearned interest: Interest that a company has received but has not yet earned so that it is not shown in revenues.

Uniform product code (UPC):   The series of black vertical stripes seen on products in stores that cashiers scan. Also called *bar codes.*

Uninsured motorist insurance: Insurance coverage that covers the insured when involved in an accident with a driver who is not insured.

United States Rule: The rule by which a loan payment is first applied to the interest owed, with the balance used to reduce the principal amount of the loan.

Unit price: The cost of one item.

Units-of-production: A depreciation method by which the number of units produced determines the depreciation allowance.

Universal life policy: A policy whose premiums flow into a general account from which the insurance company makes investments.

Unlike fractions: Fractions with different denominators.

Unpaid-balance method: A method used to calculate interest on open-end credit accounts.

Useful life: The estimated life of an asset. The Internal Revenue Service gives guidelines of useful life for depreciation purposes.

V

Valuation of inventory: Determining the value of merchandise in stock. Four common methods are specific-identification, average cost, FIFO, and LIFO.

Variable: A letter that stands for a number.

Variable commission: A commission whose rate depends on the total amount of the sales.

Variable interest rate loan: A loan on which the interest rate can go up or down.

Variable life policy: A policy most of whose premiums the insured may earmark for one or more separate investment funds.

Verbal form: Word form (the form of numbers expressed in words).

Vertical analysis: The listing of each important item on an income statement as a percent of total net sales or each item on a balance sheet as a percent of total assets.

Visa: A credit-card plan (formerly known as Bank Americard).

W

Wage: A rate of pay expressed as a certain amount of dollars per hour.

Wage bracket method: A method of calculating income tax withholding that is based on tables that list income ranges.

Weighted average method: A method for calculating the arithmetic mean for data where each value is weighted (or multiplied) according to its importance.

Whole life insurance: *See* ordinary life insurance.

Whole number: A number made up of digits to the left of the decimal point.

Wholesaler: A business that buys directly from the manufacturer or other wholesalers and sells to the retailer.

Withholding allowance: An allowance for the employee, spouse, and dependents that determines the amount of withholding tax taken from gross earnings.

Withholding tax: The money withheld from an employee's paycheck and deposited to the account of the employee with the federal or state government to cover the amount of income tax owed by the employee.

With recourse: An understanding that the seller of a note is responsible for payment of the note if the original maker of the note does not make payment. The note is sold with recourse.

Worker's compensation: Insurance purchased by companies to cover employees against work-related injuries.

W-2 form: The wage and tax statement given to the employee each year by the employer.

W-4 form: A form usually completed at the time of employment, on which an employee states the number of withholding allowances being claimed.

Y

Youthful operator: A driver of a motor vehicle who is under a certain age, usually 25.

Index of Applications

Index